Interviewing and Interrogation: A Review of Research and Practice Since World War II

Gavin E. Oxburgh, Trond Myklebust,
Mark Fallon and Maria Hartwig
(editors)

2023
Torkel Opsahl Academic EPublisher
Brussels

Editors of this volume:

Dr. **Gavin E. Oxburgh** is Professor of Police Science and Head of Department for Social Sciences at Northumbria University. Dr. **Trond Myklebust** is Assistant Chief of Police and Programme Leader at the Norwegian Police University College and Visiting Professor at Northumbria University. **Mark Fallon**, a counter-terrorism expert, was the Special Agent-in-Charge of the Criminal Investigation Task Force at the US Military's Guantánamo detention camp, and a member of the Steering Committee that developed the Méndez Principles. Dr. **Maria Hartwig** is Professor of Psychology at John Jay College of Criminal Justice.

Front cover: The painting 'Galileo Galilei Before the Inquisitors' by Cristiano Banti (1824-1904) reminds us that interrogation, interviewing and questioning are not only ancient societal practices, but they frequently entail an imbalance of power which bears on the process of establishing facts. This anthology shows the significant strides in our knowledge about interrogation and interviewing since World War II, and it discusses in detail why coercion should not be used. The picture of the Banti painting above the title banner is used courtesy the Marri Collection, Palazzo Foresti, Carpi (near Modena). TOAEP thanks Dr. Alberto Marri for sharing his knowledge about the painting and the beautiful Marri Collection. Below the title banner is a photograph of an imagined extension of Banti's painting, made by Mr. Stefano Ticci, Florence, for the purposes of this dust-jacket.

Back cover: Detail of eroded stone in the terrace at the entrance of Basilica San Miniato al Monte in Florence. Just as water and changing temperature erode the locally-quarried stone, so, by metaphor, the use of coercion in interviewing and interrogation erodes the quality and integrity of criminal justice. The back covers of books in this Publication Series show publicly accessible ground, frequently in Florence where TOAEP has an office.

ISBNs: 978-82-8348-200-3 (print) and 978-82-8348-201-0 (e-book).

PREFACE BY THE CO-EDITORS

This volume brings together a wealth of information around the area of interviewing and interrogation since World War II. There have been so many interviewing and interrogation methods developed since the 1940s which the co-editors believe should be shared *openly* with professionals from policing, law enforcement, military, security and intelligence agencies. All too often have the editors received (or heard) comments from practitioners in the field (from across the world) to the effect of, 'Why didn't we know this?', or, 'How long has that technique been used for?'. Another favourite is, 'Why do academics just write articles and books for themselves without sharing with practitioners?'.

This type of dialogue has sometimes been dubbed 'The dialogue of the deaf':

> The Academic: Why do the police ignore research findings?
>
> *The Police Officer:* Why don't researchers produce useable knowledge?
>
> The Academic: Why do the police always reject any study that is critical of what they do?
>
> *The Police Officer:* Why do researchers always show the police in a bad light?
>
> The Academic: Why don't police officers even read research reports?
>
> *The Police Officer:* Why can't researchers write in plain English?
>
> The Academic: Why are the police so bloody defensive?
>
> *The Police Officer:* Why are academic researchers so bloody virtuous?
>
> The Academic: Why are the police unwilling to examine their own organizational performance?
>
> *The Police Officer:* Why are researchers unwilling to produce information that a practical person exercising power can use to change a limited aspect of the organization instead of theoretical and explanatory structures of no use to us?
>
> The Academic: Why do the police insist that they know better, when the researchers are the experts in knowledge construction?
>
> *The Police Officer:* Why do researchers write recipes when they can't even cook?

Whilst this may be a little 'tongue in cheek', it is very often what practitioners and academics think. However, we know from our own extensive backgrounds and experiences in both academia and law-enforcement practice that academic researchers genuinely want to help change practice for the better but are often restricted by copyright rules and regulations of academic journals and publishing companies. This volume will go some way to change that and will ensure that all relevant interview models and techniques are openly available to all.

But how do we do this in reality – how can we do better in the future? The biggest factor is to ensure that all practitioners involved in the process of non-coercive interviewing have access to the latest scientific research to ensure best practice. The second aspect is to ensure that we all understand the terminologies used. For example, 'interrogation' versus 'interview' versus 'investigative interview': is there a difference in meaning or are they just words? In many jurisdictions, the term 'interrogation' is outlawed given its many perceived negative connotations, yet, in many other countries around the world, this term is widely used. This topic was also a discussion that two of the editors (Gavin Oxburgh and Mark Fallon) had whilst serving on the international Steering Committee that developed the Méndez Principles.[1] It was decided that due to different jurisdictions using differing terminology to describe the neutral process of interviewing during criminal investigations or intelligence gathering, it was relevant to recognize those professionals who use the term 'interrogation' as a non-coercive method to gather accurate and reliable information.

Thus, in the Méndez Principles, an 'interview' has been defined as:

> a structured conversation where one person (the 'interviewer') seeks to gather information from another (the 'interviewee') as part of any investigation or intelligence operation. The objective is to obtain accurate and reliable information while respecting human rights; eliciting facts is the aim, not a confession.[2]

There is no doubt that since World War II, interviewing to elicit information has changed and evolved to ensure scientifically-proven best practice continues. However, although there are international normative legal frameworks that prohibit torture and the ill-treatment of people who are detained, such practices have not been eradicated during questioning by various state agents. Nor has there been effective or consistent application of legal and procedural safeguards to protect detained people. Furthermore, despite decades of empirical and field research to develop effective and ethical interviewing techniques based

---

[1] Anti-Torture Initiative, Association for the Prevention of Torture and the Norwegian Centre for Human Rights, *Principles on Effective Interviewing for Investigations and Information Gathering*, 2021 ('Méndez Principles') (https://www.legal-tools.org/doc/wbfiw1/).

[2] *Ibid.*, p. 2.

on psychological science, the global uptake of such approaches has been inadequate, largely due to scarce resources and the absence of effective knowledge exchange between academics and practitioners (dialogue of the deaf?).

Against this background, the present volume brings together academics and practitioners from across the world, all of whom are experts in their chosen domains. The volume has four inter-linked Parts which bring together the different areas of interviewing.

Part I provides an introduction and background to interviewing. It includes the science of interviewing, working with vulnerable persons, the use of rapport, empathy and relationship-building, the neuropsychology of why torture and coercive techniques do not work, forensic linguistics in interviewing, culture, and false and recovered memories.

Part II deals with models used with interviewing suspects of crime (the Scharff Technique, the Federal Law Enforcement Training Centers ('FLETC') model, structured models (such as PEACE and PRICE), the Cylinder Model, Strategic Use of Evidence ('SUE'), and Observing Rapport-Based Interpersonal Techniques ('ORBIT')).

Part III discusses models used with interviewing victims and witnesses of crime: the cognitive and enhanced cognitive interview, the National Institute of Child Health and Human Development ('NICHD') protocol, Achieving Best Evidence ('ABE'), Self-Administered Interview ('SAI') and SAW-IT, and the Timeline Technique.

Part IV concerns organizations that have been formed to advance scientific knowledge in the area of interviewing: the International Investigative Interviewing Research Group ('iIIRG'), the High-Value Detainee Interrogation Group ('HIG'), the Centre for Research and Evidence on Security Threats ('CREST'), Project Aletheia and ETICA (Global) (both of which are relatively new and commenced in 2021 and 2022, respectively).

The volume follows a timeline of all the different models used in relation to information-retrieval since the 1940s. This is shown in Figure 1 below.

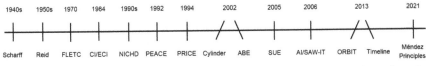

Figure 1: Timeline of dates when specific interview models were introduced.

As editors of this anthology we are committed to ensuring scientifically-proven, best-practice techniques are available to all practitioners around the world regardless of location, jurisdiction or area of professional expertise or experience.

We would like to thank all the contributing authors for taking their valuable time to write about their area of specialization or model, knowing no payment would be made. This really highlights the point made at the start of this preface, namely that academic researchers genuinely want to help change practice for the better.

Heartfelt thanks also go to Chief Constable Winton Keenen QPM, DL (Northumbria Police, United Kingdom) and Kristin Ottesen Kvigne (Director General and Head of the National Criminal Intelligence Service of Norway) for their insightful forewords. We are also grateful to Professor Juan Méndez and Mark Thomson CMG OBE for their excellent and thought-provoking prologue. Finally, we would like to express our sincere gratitude to Morten Bergsmo, Antonio Angotti and Rohit Gupta of the Torkel Opsahl Academic EPublisher for helping make this anthology a reality.

Gavin E. Oxburgh
Trond Myklebust
Mark Fallon
Maria Hartwig
Co-Editors

FOREWORD BY WINTON L. KEENEN

As an active advocate for the need to demonstrate integrity, objectivity and transparency in every element of policing, I was delighted by the publication of *Interviewing and Interrogation: A Review of Research and Practice Since World War II*. As a book dedicated to promoting effective, non-coercive practice across the widest remit of interviewing and interrogation, this area of academic and practitioner study is a vital resource for anyone seeking to further their knowledge and practical abilities in ethically-based interview techniques.

My personal and very particular interest towards fair, equitable and non-coercive interviewing arises from being a serving police officer for 38 years of public service. In addition to my extensive work within the United Kingdom ('UK'), I have also had the privilege to work abroad in several other countries; most notably during a period of deployment to Iraq in 2003–2004 as the first Contingent Commander for UK police officers and Military Police. Whilst in Iraq, I was responsible for the training and development of Iraqi Police Officers and wider law-enforcement staff within a Transitional Integration Programme focused on human rights and ethical behaviour. During that time, I was exposed to a very different approach to interviewing and interrogation from which I developed an even greater determination to strive for equality and ethical behaviour within law enforcement and society more widely. In consequence of the totality of my experience across a wide range and extensive reach of law-enforcement approaches, I can chart much of the reasoning and requirement for the introduction of non-coercive interview methods. Indeed, I am completely aligned with the many tangible benefits to be achieved by such approaches being developed even further.

By way of additional context, I have been able to consider the wider practices of interviewing from my position as the Chief Constable of Northumbria Police, a busy metropolitan force with many varied and complex challenges. Positioned as the sixth largest force in England and Wales, it delivers policing services within extensive geographic boundaries, encompassing over 2,000 square miles of urbanization and rural living. Northumbria is the largest police force in the north-east of England, serving a population in excess of 1.46 million people, spread across the metropolitan boroughs of Newcastle-upon-Tyne, Gateshead, North Tyneside, South Tyneside and the City of Sunderland, as well as the county of Northumberland. As of March 2023, the force is served by a workforce comprising approximately 3,579 police officers, 1,880 police staff, 131 Special Constables, 194 Police Community Support Officers, and a large number of volunteers who provide value-adding contributions across a variety of specialist domains. Of particular importance is the fact that Northumbria Police are credited with the highest levels of public confidence and satisfaction (as determined by the independent survey findings arising from the internationally-renowned Crime Survey of England and Wales), a position long held and greatly valued by the force and our communities alike.

In consequence of the varied career postings and opportunities presented to me throughout my service, I have had the privilege to witness, first-hand, the benefits arising from ethical interview techniques, practised in an objective manner. Conversely, I have had the misfortune to witness the devastating human, organizational and societal costs arising from inappropriate, ill-considered and, ultimately, ineffective approaches to interviewing and interrogation; arising from unintended, unwitting and occasionally deliberate disregard for appropriate practice. Indeed, in consequence of my involvement in international policing matters, I am able to draw comparisons that serve as an all too stark, ever-present reminder of the ineffective and entirely unreliable outcomes generated by oppressive approaches. It is the combination of these and other experiences that allow me to set in context the value to be gained from practitioners being exposed to academic commentary such as that contained in this anthology, as an active supplement to their practical experience and development.

My interest in interview techniques took hold in the early 1990s when I was appointed to the dedicated team of interview skills trainers responsible for the introduction of the PEACE model of interviewing to the policing environment across England and Wales. Since then, my interest in the subject has grown to become a passion and I have had the privilege to become involved in many high-profile investigations as lead interviewer, interview advisor and Senior Investigating Officer. Such circumstances have presented a wide variety of different and often challenging settings, both at home and abroad with foreign police forces and wider investigative bodies. These circumstances serve to highlight the benefits arising from an academic understanding of good, and arguably, the best practice of contemporary interviewing.

Given the majority of my career has been spent as a criminal investigator specializing in areas of major, complex and covert investigations, I have invested a great deal of time working with and surrounded by skilled, enthusiastic investigators. Indeed, having occupied every available rank within the Criminal Investigation Department, from Detective Constable to Detective Chief Superintendent (appointment to positions including those of dedicated Senior Investigating Officer in homicide and major investigations and as senior regional investigative lead for Kidnap and Extortion), I have had the privilege to work with people I consider to be some of the most committed and proficient interviewers in the world. Consequently, I have been exposed to a broad array of interview techniques, strategies and tactics, encompassing simple and complex plans, multi-suspect, strategies, psychological profiling and enhanced question-sets over almost four decades. From this experience, I have witnessed many practitioners who, when asked how they would describe their approach, refer to investigative interviewing as an art rather than a science. In some ways this is understandable, as many of the best interviewers I have witnessed appear to have a natural and innate ability to do the right thing in the right way, and seemingly engage with others in effortless conversation in such a way that elicits the truth, whilst adhering slavishly to very obvious ethical standards and human rights. However, having had the benefit of being the person in overall command of individual major incidents as well as the far wider workings of an entire organization, I am in no doubt that the skills of even the best interviewers can be enhanced significantly by wider awareness of and exposure to academic research such as that set out in this anthology. I would further support this assertion based on the understanding I gained from my own academic research whilst a trainer of interview techniques that provided significant added value to the practical experience I achieved during active personal involvement as an investigative interviewer.

In my experience, the often-interchangeable terms of 'interviewing' and 'interrogation' are all too often confined to association with circumstances involving the questioning of a person already believed by the 'questioner' to hold the status of 'suspect'. In reality, the various stages of any investigation seeking to obtain factual and reliable information in a fair and transparent manner, involve any number of interactions requiring the effective management of the resulting conversations. What better way to ensure the approaches taken in such circumstances are actively compliant with relevant legislation and informed by best practice, than to ensure they are founded on principles that have been academically proven. Additionally, to truly understand why a particular approach is determined most relevant in a given circumstance (when other variations of approach may well have been the default setting of the operating practitioner for many years), recourse must be had to what has gone before, as well as towards what the current, academically-proven, options are – what has worked, what has not? What is legally compliant, what is not? What best suits the given circumstances, what does not? The list of questions can seem long. Furthermore, for the information to be suitably effective, it must be accurate, comprehensive and ultimately reliable. This, in my opinion, is what is now enabled by this anthology – providing an invaluable source of information for any serious practitioner seeking to develop skills as an interviewer.

In consequence of ever-changing approaches to law enforcement and the perceived vagaries of the wider criminal justice systems, I am of the belief that interviews can, on occasion, be considered by some to be of lesser importance than other elements of the investigative process. Indeed, interviewing approaches conforming strictly to any particular model or formally recognized process can, on occasion, be considered a burden rather than an opportunity. By charting and outlining the major milestones in the historic development of interview and interrogation methods on a global scale, this anthology provides the context necessary to assess the worth and efficacy of the varying approaches taken. As such, it provides an invaluable resource to both willing and sceptical interviewing practitioners across the world; setting out the academically-proven benefits of operating in accordance with ethical principles inside repeatable, widely transferable, industry-respected interview frameworks. Additionally, ensuring that ethical and legal standards are maintained consistently in every individual case generates a collective weight of influence which is more able to secure and retain much-needed public confidence in any criminal justice system – the very system so many rely upon for safety, peace of mind, and as an active component of community cohesion and public confidence.

It should also be remembered that interviewing is a highly complex and challenging business. It requires learning and practice to become and remain proficient. Therefore, wider access to contemporary literature on the subject, to ensure that rightly expected high standards are achieved and maintained, is essential. I feel it worthy of note at this point to highlight my contention that those lacking any detailed understanding or working knowledge of investigative interviewing, or those without responsibility or accountability arising from the practice or outcomes of it, can perceive it to be an all too simple, straightforward process. I maintain that this is not the case, reasserting my belief that it is both complex and challenging. Additionally, given the pressures and ever-growing demands placed upon those involved in current, modern-day law enforcement, it must surely be a widely accepted reality that they simply do not have the time or resources to dedicate sufficient effort and research into comparing and contrasting the different models of interviewing currently being practised around the world. As such, the academic reference and practical insight arising from works such as the present anthology are, in my opinion, invaluable sources of information and guidance.

By way of closing, I would like to set out brief details of one particular case that has become well known within the context of learning and development towards investigative interviewing in England and Wales.

In October 1992, I was performing duties as a relatively young Detective Sergeant, leading a team of officers aligned to a homicide inquiry relating to the tragic, needless death of a 7-year-old girl in Sunderland. The brief circumstances of this tragedy involve the reported missing of a young girl by the name of Nikki Allan, following her failure to return home after visiting her grandparents in the Wear Garth area of Sunderland. Tragically, Nikki's body was found in an abandoned building a short distance away from her home. Nikki had been brutally murdered and had been stabbed at least 37 times. During the course of ensuing investigations, a young man was arrested and interviewed – he went on to fully admit to Nikki's murder, offering detailed confessions to his interviewers. Understandably, the tragic death of such a young girl led to the case becoming high-profile, especially in the tight-knit community of Sunderland where Nikki was well-known. At the point of trial, the interviews with the accused were subjected to particularly stringent scrutiny by the 'court', with counsel for the defence alleging the questioning style and manner in which the interview had been conducted rendered all admissions to be unsafe and unreliable. The judge in the case agreed with the submissions made by the defence and refused to allow the jury to listen to, or be provided with, any information arising from the tape-recorded interviews, thereby preventing the contents from being used in evidence. As well as rendering the interviews inadmissible, the judge went on to directly and publicly criticize the police for what he described as 'oppressive questioning' and the misrepresentation of evidence. Ultimately, despite his admissions, the man arrested and charged with Nikki's murder was fully acquitted and thereby exonerated of any guilt in the matter. Since the original court case, a number of other persons have been interviewed, and in May 2022, a 54-year-old man was charged with her murder, scheduled to stand trial at the time of writing.

Having been directly and intimately involved in the investigation of Nikki's murder, I feel suitably well placed to offer a commentary, in further support of the benefit of bringing academics and practitioners closer together. It is clearly the case that the terrible tragedy of Nikki's death led to a further tragedy of an innocent man being put to trial and the undermining of public confidence at the local, regional and national levels. Given my knowledge of the police practice operating at the time, as well as some understanding of the professional standing of the officers involved, I feel at liberty to hypothesize as to the circumstances leading to the outcomes of this case. Policing at that time (late 1980s and early 1990s) commonly saw senior-ranked officers take responsibility for high-profile interviews. Officers of such seniority were very unlikely to be conducting more 'mainstream' interviews on a regular basis. As such, they were the officers least likely to maintain current, up-to-date information on contemporary developments in interview practice or on related expectations from the wider criminal justice process. As such, it is entirely unlikely that the officers involved in the interviews deliberately set out to undermine the investigation. Rather, their approach to the interview process was more likely based on previous experience, devoid of any meaningful, contemporary understanding of what had come to constitute effective, acceptable interview practice.

When taken in their totality, the circumstances of the acquittal of the man originally charged with Nikki's death exemplify the need to maintain both academic and practical knowledge of current interview techniques. This will reduce the likelihood of inadvertent activity that could lead to miscarriages of justice. This highlights the need for, and benefits to be derived from, bringing academic research and practical application far closer together. This, I contend, is what this anthology seeks to do. I commend it to all those involved in interviewing, whether such involvement emanates from the perspective of a practitioner or an academic.

Winton L. Keenen QPM, DL
Chief Constable, Northumbria Police (2018–2023)

FOREWORD BY KRISTIN OTTESEN KVIGNE

Real change, enduring change, happens one step at a time.
Ruth Bader Ginsburg[1]

I was pleased to accept the co-editors' invitation to write a foreword to the important volume *Interviewing and Interrogation: A Review of Research and Practice Since World War II*. In my work, both with the Norwegian Police and Prosecution Service for more than 25 years, as well as during my tenure as Assistant Director at INTERPOL's General Secretariat in Lyon, the development of police non-coercive interview and investigative methodologies has been at the heart of my work.

Investigations are about looking into events of the past with the knowledge of today, whether 'the past' is years or only minutes ago. The range of investigative tools available to police and law-enforcement agencies around the world is ever-expanding. For example, forensic investigations have fundamentally changed over the decades with the knowledge of DNA and digital evidence from mobile devices and computers, giving investigators and their agencies valuable information. Indeed, investigations into crypto currencies are rapidly evolving, as are investigative tools taking advantage of nano-technology.

But at the core of all investigations remains our ability to obtain information. Despite scientific progress, technical evidence may be inconclusive or not available. Thus, the interview is still a core requirement to establish the facts or events in question.

But there are more profound reasons why the interview remains vital. Victims and witnesses of crime have both a right and a need to be heard, and to have the crimes committed acknowledged and fully investigated. Interviews with suspects of crime can, in many cases, provide the motive and explanations needed to determine culpability, but also to provide closure to victims and their families.

Although we all agree on non-coercive and scientifically-proven methodologies for forensic investigations, there are many differences between countries with regards to interviews and interrogations – even between law-enforcement agencies within a single country. This can be attributed to differences in legislation, culture, training and personal preference. However, the fact that

---

[1] Ruth Bader Ginsburg, interviewed in Betsy West and Julie Cohen, "RBG", documentary, 4 March 2018.

international police and law-enforcement agencies approach interviews and interrogations so differently gives cause for reflection and concern in light of the emphasis that is placed on these in all our judicial systems.

Unfortunately, there are many examples of grave miscarriage of justice related to false and forced confessions, sometimes using torture, inhumane or degrading treatment. This is a tragedy for all directly involved – the defendants and victims – but also for justice. We are deeply dependant on the confidence of the public to come forward and provide valuable information to help solve a crime. Our ability to conduct objective investigations is the foundation of criminal justice systems around the world. In the aftermath of wrongful convictions, police and law-enforcement responses have varied, but there is no doubt that important changes in interviewing and investigation methodology have emerged through specific cases. For example, the historic development of the PEACE model of interviewing in England and Wales[2] is a testament to this. The evidence-based research foundation of that model inspired the development of interview techniques in several countries, including the Nordic, and is an impactful example of successful and fruitful collaboration between academia and practitioners.

Bringing together practitioners and academia is not always straightforward. The co-editors of this volume deserve acclaim for doing so in an effort to give police, law-enforcement, military, security and intelligence agencies deeper knowledge of the subject of interviews and interrogation. This book provides a compass for practitioners that is based on scientifically-researched and -proven methods rather than pseudo-science or training 'passed down' as anecdotal knowledge.

For me, starting with its title – *Interviewing and Interrogation: A Review of Research and Practice Since World War II* – this volume is thought-provoking. The title points to the differences between non-coercive and accusatory (or coercive) approaches of investigators. Here, I find the co-editors' generic use of the term 'non-coercive information gathering' helpful in developing such methods rather than arguments about the semantics of 'interviewing' and 'interrogation'.

The chapters looking at the historic evolution of techniques in victim-, witness- and suspect-interviewing provides an in-depth understanding that is useful for all concerned (including practitioners, academic researchers and students). If one does not know the past, it is hard (if not impossible) to shape the future. The Norwegian Police has always been at the forefront of developing techniques in interviewing *per se*, but also specifically involving children and

---

[2]　See Chapter 12 of this book.

other vulnerable persons. We have gained important knowledge through this process; knowledge that has been shared with our partners internationally.

For example, the Norwegian structured model for interviewing is based on the PEACE model of interviewing and, as described in Chapter 12 of this book, the following overarching values and principles are required when implementing PEACE structured interviews in Norway: (i) Communication; (ii) Rule of Law; (iii) Ethics and empathy; (iv) Active consciousness; (v) Trust through openness, and; (vi) Information verified through science. There is a decisively active academic environment at the Norwegian Police University College ('NPUC') which ensures that students and practicing police officers are kept up-to-date on new methodologies and scientific research. With the Norwegian Police reform in 2015, we implemented not only structural changes to the police in general, but also significant changes related to the overall quality of investigations. The aim has been to ensure a knowledge-based, uniform and managed development in the field of investigations.

This book discusses several requirements for non-coercive interviewing skills to be effective. Among them is the notion that investigative techniques need to be thoroughly tested by scientific studies. This is implemented across the Norwegian Police together with NPUC. In order for this to function at its best, we should strive to continually develop international co-operation and collaboration between academics and practitioners. Training programmes need to be ongoing which requires dedication as well as resources. In the Norwegian Police, we have put in place expertise stewardship in defined areas, interviewing being one of them. 'Stewardship' entails the authority to adopt and introduce national procedures and standards to ensure their follow-up and development. Our NPUC ensures that national guidelines, procedures and supporting documentation are prepared in line with adopted process descriptions, supported by both national and international research, as well as ensuring that relevant training is given to dedicated personnel. The process is also aimed at identifying the need for research and subsequent communication of such needs to colleagues at NPUC and other relevant institutions. The idea is always to maintain a focus on systematic application of lessons learned in order to uncover what changes are necessary.

As a police leader with senior management responsibility, I truly value that the presentation of the different models of methods and techniques in this volume also includes reference to the resources needed to enable practitioners to apply them. However, as highlighted in various chapters by the international experts, there is a need for continuous training and evaluation which must be prioritized in order to have the desired positive effect.

With global inter-connectivity, international police co-operation is evolving all the time to the extent where, nowadays, almost every major case has some kind of international link. This can challenge practitioners in different ways, none more than in the field of interviewing. Given the diverse policies, procedures and methodologies used by agencies across the globe, can we base national investigations and prosecutions on interviews conducted in other jurisdictions? This is a big question. It would be easier to provide an answer if non-coercive information elicitation (according to knowledge-based scientific methods) was the standard everywhere. We all know that this is not the case. We are far from having reached our potential. Not only does this book attempt to bridge the gap of standardized methodologies, but Chapter 6 on the Méndez Principles (2021)[3] concerns an important step forward in making this a reality. These Principles essentially acknowledge that the successful outcome of a non-coercive interview is interconnected with the full enjoyment of human rights by a person at every stage of contact with state authorities (regardless of whether such encounters are labelled as 'conversations', 'interrogations', 'interviews' or 'questioning'). The Méndez Principles present an alternative to the risks of coerced statements and the brutality of torture, and a recognition that these tactics lead to false confessions, unfair trials, and undermine the delivery of justice. The continued promotion and dissemination of these principles globally will enhance international co-operation as well as secure the fundamental rights of individuals.

To conclude, I fully endorse this insightful and thought-provoking volume which also highlights the organizations that are actively helping others promote and practice non-coercive interviewing and interrogation. One such organization is the International Investigative Interviewing Research Group ('iIIRG'), founded in 2007 by two of the co-editors of this volume – Gavin Oxburgh and Trond Myklebust. I had the great pleasure of opening its 2010 annual conference in Stavern, Norway. The iIIRG is dedicated to improving interview practice worldwide in order to achieve research-based practice and practice-based research.[4]

As domestic law-enforcement agencies, we are thankful for such organizations. We also thank the co-editors and authors for their inspiring work in this book. We hope that they will continue to use their outstanding abilities to influence standards of ethical and non-coercive interviewing globally, across police, law-enforcement, military, security and intelligence organizations.

An immense amount of work has been carried out by practitioners and academics over the years to change the way interviews and interrogations are conducted. This volume gives their work credit. But there is still room for

---

[3] Anti-Torture Initiative, Association for the Prevention of Torture and the Norwegian Centre for Human Rights, *Principles on Effective Interviewing for Investigations and Information Gathering*, 2021 ('Méndez Principles') (https://www.legal-tools.org/doc/wbfiw1/).

[4] See Chapter 21 of this book.

improvement. This high-quality open-access anthology allows for such improvement to take place. As a consequence, the practice of non-coercive interviewing can only be enhanced.

Kristin Ottesen Kvigne
Director General and Head,
National Criminal Investigation Service, Norway

PROLOGUE BY
JUAN MÉNDEZ AND MARK THOMSON

Gathering information is an essential task in the proper functioning of all systems of justice as well as military and security operations. The reliability of the information collected is of paramount importance in instructing what actions are taken in investigations and military and security operations.

On this we can assume universal agreement. Where we see divergence is in the methods of obtaining information. Some interrogation techniques are clearly designed to coerce confessions, yet they are frequently counter-productive in obtaining accurate and reliable information to enable justice to be administered correctly or military and security operations to achieve their objectives. From our joint perspective of documenting and preventing torture, we have observed that the moment of highest risk of torture and other ill-treatment is during questioning by State authorities in the early hours after deprivation of liberty and while investigation of the facts is ongoing. However, just re-stating that torture and other ill-treatment are illegal has proven insufficient to change these unlawful practices of interrogation. The methods of questioning and the integrity of the whole process of contact between the State and suspects, witnesses and victims of crime, plus other detainees, needed serious revision.

To be sure, torture and interrogation under coercive conditions has been prohibited by international law since the end of World War II, when human rights were firmly incorporated as obligations that States have *vis-à-vis* all persons under their jurisdiction. In fact, as a matter of domestic law in most countries, torture has been banned for two-three centuries. The development of modern criminal law – and subsequently of fundamental international standards of due process and humane treatment – is so well-entrenched that even countries that practice torture deny that they do or resort to euphemisms to pretend that they do not cross that line into barbarity. And yet it takes more than legal and moral arguments to persuade our societies that it is simply untrue that 'torture works'.

As this edited volume reveals, much research and reform have been conducted on information-gathering techniques over the last seventy years. Rapport-based interviewing faithfully respects the prohibition of ill-treatment and also challenges the efficacy of traditional interrogation techniques grounded in various forms of coercion. Interest in this research increased in the context of the repercussions to the terrorist attacks of 11 September 2001, when attempts were made to justify the use of torture and other ill-treatment in the interrogation of persons suspected of association with terrorists. The human rights movement did its best to respond to these spurious attempts to justify torture, invoking its illegality and immorality but also pointing out its ineffectiveness in fighting crime. Yet, in the aftermath of tragic events the gulf between like-minded human rights advocates and researchers, on one side, and interrogators and their superiors in policy-making institutions, on the other, was not conducive to convincing many governments or much of the public.

What has changed since then is that – thanks to efforts such as this edited volume – the knowledge and expertise of scientists, researchers, interrogators and interviewers together with human rights advocates has been shared better in a joint quest to review the effectiveness, legality and integrity of methods of information gathering. The effort has been assisted by the evident failure of 'enhanced interrogation techniques' in providing reliable evidence that can stand in court, and even in dismantling terrorist and organized crime networks.

We have recently co-chaired a multidisciplinary initiative to draw up a set of "Principles on Effective Interviewing for Investigation and Information Gathering" ('The Méndez Principles')[1] which is the focus of Chapter 6 of this book. Because these principles (published in May of 2021) integrate the science and practice of non-coercive interviewing with associated legal safeguards, we believe that they provide a sound framework for policy and practice that is in the mutual interests of State authorities and individuals who are questioned by those authorities. The Méndez Principles have received multiple expressions of support from States at the United Nations ('UN') General Assembly, the UN human rights bodies and mechanisms, the UN Congress on Crime Prevention and Criminal Justice, the Organization of American States, the African Commission on Human and Peoples' Rights, the Council of Europe, the European Union, the Organization for Security and Co-operation in Europe (OSCE) Office for Democratic Institutions and Human Rights, and chiefs of police (for example, in Indonesia, Thailand and Madagascar). We believe that the Méndez Principles are becoming a source of reference for international standards to be adopted in national jurisdictions and practice.

This edited volume is a very welcome addition to that initiative as it provides further detail on the developments in questioning and interviewing techniques and related research. We are now convinced that any solution-oriented approach to interviewing and interrogation must find and encourage this sort of meaningful exchange of information, experience and proposals between a broad

---

[1] Anti-Torture Initiative, Association for the Prevention of Torture and the Norwegian Centre for Human Rights, *Principles on Effective Interviewing for Investigations and Information Gathering*, 2021 (https://www.legal-tools.org/doc/wbfiw1/). For developments on the Méndez Principles, please see the web site of the Association for the Prevention of Torture.

variety of researchers, human rights advocates and officials responsible for gathering information.

Juan E. Méndez

Professor of Human Rights Law in Residence, Washington College of Law;
Former UN Special Rapporteur on Torture (2010–2016)

Mark C.A. Thomson CMG OBE

Former Secretary General, Association for the Prevention of Torture

TABLE OF CONTENTS

Part I:
General

By Rebecca Shaeffer, Veronica Hinestroza and Sean Tait

Part II:
Suspects

Part III:
Victims and Witnesses

By Ronald P. Fisher and Tzachi Ashkenazi

By Trond Myklebust, David J. La Rooy and Carlos E. Peixoto

PART I: GENERAL

1

The Science of Interviewing: How Do We Know What We Know?

Christopher E. Kelly and Melissa B. Russano[*]

1.1. Introduction and Overview

Data-driven decision-making and science-based policies are critical to ensuring that the most effective tools and methods are being used to address real-world issues, such as the challenge of how to effectively elicit information from people during an interview.[1] Academics and practitioners alike have been calling for investigators to transition away from customary, experience-based approaches to interviewing and detecting deception, and toward adoption of science-based approaches in their stead. Increasingly, there are hopeful signs this transition is welcomed by many members of the practitioner community, and a growing number of organizations are seeking out science-based interview and interrogation training.[2]

A fundamental premise of this volume is that science-based methods of interviewing – skills and techniques that have been validated through an objective process of systematic empiricism – are the most effective means of eliciting reliable information from interviewees, and the current volume provides the

---

[*]   **Christopher E. Kelly**, Ph.D., is Professor of Sociology and Criminal Justice at Saint Joseph's University in Philadelphia, Pennsylvania. **Melissa B. Russano**, Ph.D., is a Professor of Criminal Justice at Roger Williams University in Bristol, Rhode Island.

[1]   With a few exceptions in this chapter, we will use the term 'interviewing' to broadly refer to the phenomenon of an agent of the state or government seeking information or intelligence from suspects, witnesses, victims or sources in the course of an investigation. Thus, the term 'interviewing' subsumes other terms such as 'interrogation', 'investigative interviewing', 'information-gathering' or 'intelligence collection'. Although most of the research on interviewing is done in a police or law-enforcement context, this term extends to other settings such as military or intelligence interviews.

[2]   Susan E. Brandon, "Towards a Science of Interrogation", in *Applied Cognitive Psychology*, 2014, vol. 28, no. 6, pp. 945–946; Susan E. Brandon *et al.*, "The High-Value Detainee Interrogation Group (HIG): Inception, Evolution, and Impact", in Mark A. Staal and Sally C. Harvey (eds.), *Operational Psychology: A New Field to Support National Security and Public Safety*, Praeger/ABC-CLIO, Santa Barbara, 2019, pp. 263–285; Christian A. Meissner, Frances Surmon-Böhr, Simon Oleszkiewicz and Laurence J. Alison, "Developing an Evidence-Based Perspective on Interrogation: A Review of the U.S. Government's High-Value Detainee Interrogation Group Research Program", in *Psychology, Public Policy, and Law*, 2017, vol. 23, no. 4, pp. 438–457.

practitioner community with a comprehensive summary of the state of the science of interviewing (with the irony being that, at some point after this volume is published, the science will have advanced). Each chapter in this volume is written by leading scholars in the field or practitioners who have become versed in the science of interviewing and have key insights to share about their use of science-based approaches in the field. The findings and conclusions are based on hundreds, if not thousands, of studies using a wide variety of complex research methodologies and statistical analyses, none of which is particularly easy to understand for people without advanced scientific training. Just as it is foolhardy for academics to assume they understand the challenges and realities of interviewing in the 'real world' without critical insights from and partnerships with experienced practitioners, it is not realistic to expect practitioners to become scientists in their own right, able to consume and put the science into practice without assistance. That said, it is imperative that practitioners are armed with enough knowledge of scientific methods to become *critical consumers* of purported scientific information.

The reason for this is twofold. First, whilst it is certainly reasonable to rely on knowledgeable experts in the field to summarize and assist in translating the science to practitioners, many practitioners will wish to take a deep dive into the science themselves. To do this, a basic understanding of research methodology will be useful. Second, we believe that practitioners will increasingly need to be able to separate the wheat from the chaff – any person or organization wishing to market a profitable interview training programme can label their training 'science-based'. It will be incumbent on knowledgeable practitioners to be able to identify programmes and methods that are actually grounded in solid science as opposed to those who masquerade as scientific while teaching non-validated approaches. So, what does it mean to be a critical consumer of purported scientific information and how does one become one? Key to this ability is understanding the answers to such questions as: How do scientists acquire knowledge? How do they know what they know? How do you know that you can trust something that is labelled scientific? How do you evaluate the quality of a particular study or whether it is relevant to operational settings?

The purpose of the current chapter is to help practitioners (and other interested persons) become critical consumers of information by providing a primer on the research methodologies commonly used to study interviewing.[3] We hope this will serve as a foundation for processing, understanding and applying

---

[3] While we reference specific studies for the purpose of providing examples of various methodological approaches, this chapter is not intended to serve as a review of the content-specific findings from the interviewing literature, as that is the purpose of the other chapters in this volume.

the research findings shared not only in this volume, but also in other sources the practitioner community will encounter as they vet and adopt science-based methods. The introduction begins with a brief explanation of the scientific method and key research concepts, including introducing the main methodological approaches in interviewing science and a description of the peer review and publication process. For those who wish to take a deeper dive into the logic of hypothesis testing and related concepts, we have included these more advanced topics in Appendix A. The heart of the chapter is a review of how we know what we know by each methodology, specifically laboratory experiments, self-report studies and field research. Before continuing, let us strongly endorse a bedrock principle of science that, regardless of methodology, no single study should be considered authoritative or held up as definitive 'proof' of some phenomena. Instead, each study should be evaluated in the context of the larger body of accumulating science on a particular topic, and it is our goal to help readers of this chapter evaluate such scientific evidence.

1.2. The Scientific Method

The nineteenth century philosopher and scientist Charles Peirce proposed four ways that people acquire knowledge or beliefs: tenacity, authority, reason and science.[4] Passer[5] added what he called empiricism to the list, but it might be better conceptualized as personal experience. Tenacity refers to believing something because we have always believed it, with little to no scrutiny of the validity of that belief. Authority is when we rely on others as a source of information, and reason refers to relying on our own logic, intuition and reasoning. Personal experience is when we acquire beliefs and knowledge via direct personal experience or our informal observations. Although tenacity, authority, reason and personal experience can be useful (for example, they are often a catalyst for an important step in the scientific research process, namely developing the *research question*), these methods can also leave one vulnerable to developing knowledge and beliefs that are distorted or inaccurate. Children raised by parents who believe the Earth is flat mistakenly place too much weight in tenacity and authority when adopting that belief themselves, while reasoning, intuition and personal experience can lead us astray when we fall prey to a host of cognitive biases that affect our perception, memory and decision-making.[6]

---

[4]   Charles S. Peirce, "Illustrations of the Logic of Science: The Fixation of Belief", in *Popular Science Monthly*, 1877, vol. 12, pp. 1–15.

[5]   Michael M. Passer, *Research Methods Concepts and Connections*, Worth Publishers, New York, 2017.

[6]   Rüdiger F. Pohl, "What Are Cognitive Illusions?", in Rüdiger F. Phol (ed.), *Cognitive Illusions: Intriguing Phenomena in Thinking, Judgment, and Memory*, Routledge, Abingdon, 2022;

For example, humans tend to focus their attention to certain aspects or features of an event at the expense of others (attentional bias); we tend to think that others agree with us more strongly or often than they do (false consensus effect); we underestimate situational forces on others' behaviour and tend to make internal attributions for their behaviour (fundamental attribution error); we tend to pay more attention and assign more weight to information that is consistent with our pre-existing beliefs while dismissing or downplaying the importance of information that is inconsistent (confirmation bias), to name just a few. Taken together, cognitive biases make it difficult for us to objectively analyse information or a situation via reasoning, intuition, or informal personal observations or experiences.

What is science then, and what makes it different than the other methods for acquiring information? Systematic empiricism, or what is more commonly referred to simply as 'science', is the acquisition of information through systematic observation, which means the observations are made in deliberate and controlled ways, with the method of observation determined in advance. To go about testing, or answering, the research question, researchers develop a *hypothesis*, or the specific prediction the researcher is seeking to test. Generally, researchers are trying to determine whether there is a relationship between two or more variables (that is, anything that varies) grounded in broader scientific theory (that is, a proposed explanation of some phenomena). A scientist must determine what methodology they will use to test that hypothesis, design a study that manipulates or measures the variables of interest, determine what population they will draw their sample participants from, collect and analyse the data, compare the results to their hypothesis, and draw objective conclusions while acknowledging the limitations of the study.

For example, a researcher might be interested in whether certain interview techniques are related to the amount of information an interviewee discloses, or whether age of an interviewee is related to suggestibility. In addition to wanting to know whether a relationship between two or more variables *exists*, researchers often seek to understand the *nature* of that relationship (that is, are the variables simply associated, or does one variable cause the other)? The research methodology chosen determines what kind of conclusions can be drawn about the nature of the relationship (see methodologies section for discussion of this issue); however, regardless of the specific nature of the hypothesis, researchers seek to test whether the data do or do not provide support for the hypothesis. Should the analysis reach *statistical significance*, we can conclude that that there

---

Amos Tversky and Daniel Kahneman, "Judgment under Uncertainty: Heuristics and Biases", in *Science*, 1974, vol. 185, no. 4157, pp. 1124–1131.

is a minuscule chance that the pattern we observed in the data happened purely by chance, and we can conclude that there is a relationship between the variables.

Just because a result is statistically significant, however, does not necessarily mean it has *practical significance*; practical significance has to do with whether the statistically significant relationship between variables is meaningful in the real world. For example, if one finds that a spacious, 'soft' interview room that is designed to prime warmth and openness leads to a statistically significant increase in interviewee disclosure compared to a traditional interview room (for example, there is an average increase of 10 words spoken by interviewees in the 'soft' room), but that difference is either so small or the content of the increased volume of words spoken is irrelevant from an investigatory standpoint, it would be statistically significant but perhaps not practically significant. While designing their study, researchers must also consider the validity of it, which can be thought of very broadly as the quality of the work, and all researchers strive to maximize validity. However, there are multiple types of validity, and internal validity, external validity and ecological validity are three types that are particularly relevant for those seeking to understand interviewing research.

1.2.1. Internal Validity

This term refers to the extent to which a researcher can draw cause and effect conclusions from their research study (in other words, that one variable caused another). To be able to draw causal conclusions, a researcher needs to have high *experimental control*; this means the ability to control all factors in their research study, so that if a relationship between variables is observed, the researcher can be highly confident that the only explanation is that one variable caused another.

1.2.2. External Validity

This refers to the extent to which the results of a study can be extrapolated beyond the specific confines of the research study – in other words, to what extent can the results be generalized to other populations and settings?

1.2.3. Ecological Validity

This is related to the concept of external validity and is the extent to which the results of a study can be generalized to the 'real-world' situation one is trying to understand. Ecological validity is often evaluated in terms of the *mundane realism* of the study, or the extent to which the experience in or the materials used in a study mirror what one would see or experience in a natural setting. Imagine, for example, a study regarding juror perceptions of interrogations. A study that used a live trial reenactment would have higher mundane realism than one that asked participants to read a trial transcript. Arguably more important than mundane realism, however, is *psychological realism* – the extent to which the research adequately engages participants in the underlying psychological processes that the researcher wishes to understand and generalize.[7] Certainly the goal for any applied researcher is for their work to have impact beyond an individual study; however, any single study may have higher or lower external and/or ecological validity. Researchers must ask themselves, and acknowledge, to whom and under what circumstances the results of a particular study can be generalized.

1.2.4. Peer-Review and Publication Process

One of the hallmark features of the development of scientific knowledge is the vetting process research undergoes to ensure that the work is of high quality. Generally speaking, once a researcher completes data collection and analysis on a particular study, the researcher then writes up that work and submits it for publication in an academic journal. The gold-standard for publishing one's work is in a double-blind, peer-reviewed journal. When a manuscript is submitted to this type of journal, the document is stripped of any information that might reveal the identity of the authors. An editor then asks qualified experts (typically two to three) to read the manuscript, and anonymously provide a detailed critique and a recommendation with respect to whether and under what conditions it should be published. The double-blind review process is critical for ensuring that reviewers can provide honest feedback without concern of personal or professional repercussions and helps to mitigate any unconscious bias that might occur if a reviewer was aware of the author's identity. The importance of the peer-review and publication process cannot be overestimated because it functions as a gatekeeper to distinguish between quality and junk science. Another outlet for reliable science is high-quality edited volumes (such as the one you are reading) in which recognized experts in the field serve as authors who summarize and synthesize the literature on a particular topic area.[8]

Original research articles (or some chapters in high-quality edited volumes) that report the detailed results of a study are considered *primary sources*; *secondary sources* are outlets that review the literature in a particular area (usually by summarizing and synthesizing primary source articles). Generally speaking, practitioners will likely find it most useful to rely on secondary sources, but primary source literature should be made available to those who are interested. The current volume is an example of a secondary source, and in the remainder

---

[7]   Elliot Aronson, Timothy D. Wilson and Robin M. Akert, *Social Psychology: The Heart and the Mind*, HarperCollins College Publishers, New York, 1994.

[8]   On the opposite end of the spectrum there exist predatory journals and publishers, the worst of which allow people to simply pay a fee to publish their work and have no meaningful review process.

of this chapter, we will be citing examples of primary source material across the three main methodologies to highlight the process of studying interviewing.

1.3. Common Research Methodologies

There are three common methodologies used in the scientific study of interviewing, and each has its unique strengths and weaknesses in terms of validity, described above, and approach, answering one or more research questions with hypotheses, original data collection and analyses. Which methodology a researcher chooses depends on a number of factors, including the question being asked, the researcher's discipline and training and deeper epistemological matters (for example, 'How do we know what we know?'). It is important to recognize and be honest about the limitations of social science research design, and it is equally important to not give undue weight to one method over another. To this end, in this chapter we will apply the concept of *triangulation* to the research on interrogation and interviewing.

Triangulation for our purposes will consist of examining the three most common methodologies that have been used to study interrogation: controlled experiments, typically conducted in laboratories; self-reports from experienced practitioners, principally in the form of surveys or interviews; and observational or field studies such as systematic content analyses of interview recordings or transcripts. Lab experiments tend to suffer from more external or ecological validity concerns; self-reported data are potentially biased in numerous ways in addition to not being 'objective' 'truth'; and sampling issues abound in field studies and causality is questionable at best. That said, experimenters have unmatched control over their manipulations and can isolate causes of behaviour; who better to learn from than individuals who are practiced in the phenomenon in ways that few researchers are; and systematically observing the actual phenomenon of interest in the field is the very definition of empirical. No one study – regardless of methodology – should be considered authoritative on a topic. If there is one message to take away from this chapter, it is that we seek to find convergence of findings across the various methodologies, which are explored in more detail below. When we find such convergence or agreement, our confidence in the research findings and conclusions increases. Taken together, the studies employing these various methodologies paint a near-complete picture of interviewing research.

1.3.1. Laboratory Studies

The most common methodology utilized by researchers studying interviewing has been laboratory studies or experiments. One of the hallmark features of a laboratory experiment is that the researcher systematically controls and manipulates what occurs during the study. In a basic experimental design, there are two types of variables studied: independent and dependent variables. An independent variable is a variable that the researcher manipulates ('X'), whereas the dependent variable ('Y') is the outcome or behaviour the researcher believes will be affected by the independent variable. The major strength of laboratory research is the ability of researchers to examine *causality*, as opposed to being able to simply determine whether two variables are associated (or *correlated*); in other words, in a well-designed experiment, the researcher can determine not only that X and Y are related, but whether X causes Y. To be able to draw such causal conclusions, the experimenters must exert a high degree of *experimental control* over everything that happens during the experiment. This means that when studying different factors in an experiment, the experimental conditions should be exactly the same except for the manipulation of the independent variable.

Participants in an experiment should be *randomly assigned* to a condition, which means that each participant has an equal chance of being assigned to any condition of the study. This is a critical part of experimental design because it ensures that the two groups of participants are on average *equivalent* on any number of variables that might influence a person's pre-existing likelihood of differing on the dependent variable. In other words, if participants are randomly assigned to a condition, any pre-existing differences people have (for example, gender, age, suggestibility, life experiences, political orientation, *et cetera*) that might be related to what you are interested in measuring will be spread out across the study conditions equally, assuming you have a sufficiently large sample size. Spreading out these pre-existing differences, coupled with the conditions created by the experimenter being identical except for the difference intentionally created by the manipulation of the independent variable, allows us to draw causal conclusions. Since the only difference between groups on average is the difference between the independent variable conditions, any change on the dependent variable *must* be caused by the independent variable.

Frenda and colleagues conducted a study using a basic experimental design.[9] They were interested in whether sleep deprivation (the independent variable) affects false confession rates (the dependent variable). In a laboratory setting, participants were falsely accused of wrongdoing, and the research team created two interview conditions: one in which participants were interrogated while sleep deprived (*experimental* condition), and the other in which participants were not (*control* condition). Importantly, everything the participants experienced was identical except for the amount of sleep they had prior to being

---

[9] Steven J. Frenda, Shari R. Berkowitz, Elizabeth F. Loftus and Kimberly M. Fenn, "Sleep Deprivation and False Confessions", in *PNAS Proceedings of the National Academy of Sciences of the United States of America*, 2016, vol. 113, no. 8, pp. 2047–2050.

interrogated, and participants were randomly assigned to condition. Sleep-deprived participants falsely confessed at a significantly higher rate than the well-rested participants.

Most experimental studies are more complex than the basic design described above, in that there may be multiple independent variables (with more than two conditions for each one) as well as multiple dependent variables. In addition, the example above is illustrative of a *between-participants* research design (in which different people participate in each condition of the experiment) whereas others use a *within-participants* design (where the same people experience all conditions of the experiment)[10] or there is some combination of both across the independent variables (*mixed-participants* design). Regardless of the nuances of the methodology, the common thread and strength of well-designed experiments is the ability to isolate the effects of a single or a few variables and draw cause-and-effect conclusions.

Such higher internal validity, however, tends to come with a trade-off of lower external and ecological validity. Laboratory experiments by definition do not occur in the naturally occurring environment of the phenomena under investigation, and therefore, they tend to oversimplify complex phenomena and interactions. The real-world is messy, and interviewing research almost exclusively focuses on studying human behaviour which, by its nature, is complex. Multiple variables have an impact on human behaviour, and variables interact to affect human behaviour in unique ways, but most laboratory experiments only examine a small number of variables at a time. Moreover, laboratory experiments often cannot fully replicate all components of a phenomenon. For example, although researchers have used creative and highly engaging paradigms to study the elicitation of true and false confession in the laboratory, for ethical and practical reasons, researchers will never be able to accuse participants of committing a serious violent crime in an experimental study and have them believe that they are truly under investigation for that crime and being interviewed by actual law enforcement officers. That does not mean that the underlying psychological processes being studied cannot be generalized beyond the laboratory, but it is always important to consider whether and to what extent limited mundane realism lessens the ecological validity of the work.

A discussion of two commonly used paradigms to study interrogation and confession in the laboratory can be used to understand the balance researchers seek between internal validity and ecological validity concerns. Kassin and

---

[10] In a within-participants design in which all people experience all experiment conditions, random assignment to condition is not applicable; rather, participants will typically be randomly assigned to the order that they experience the experiment conditions (a process called 'counterbalancing').

Kiechel developed the first paradigm to study false confessions in the laboratory. Innocent people are accused of inadvertently pressing the forbidden alt-key during a typing task, which caused the computer to crash and data to be lost. In their first demonstration of the paradigm, the independent variables the researchers manipulated were whether participants were confronted with false evidence (in the form of false witness testimony) and the vulnerability of participants' memories (in the form of the speed of the typing task, with those typing fast being less confident in their memories). Two of the primary dependent variables of interest were whether participants would sign a confession statement (compliance) and whether they would come to believe they were guilty (internalization). Participants confronted with false evidence of their guilt were more likely to sign the confession statement and internalize their guilt, and because of the random assignment of participants to the experimental versus control conditions, we can have a great deal of confidence in the causal connection between false evidence and false confessions.[11]

This groundbreaking study demonstrated for the first time that false confessions could be elicited in the laboratory and provided a way to study a host of interrogation factors (including interrogation approaches and individual risk factors, such as youth and suggestibility).[12] The 'alt-key' paradigm, however, has been criticized on ecological validity grounds, with a specific concern about its lack of mundane realism (that is, the disparity between the experimental situation and what 'real-world' interrogations look like). Specifically, the act wrongdoing participants are accused of in this paradigm is non-criminal in nature, unintentionally committed, of low severity, and there are relatively low-stakes consequences of confessing.

In part to address ecological validity concerns, Russano and colleagues created a new paradigm which involved accusing students of cheating during an

---

[11] Saul M. Kassin and Katherine L. Kiechel, "The Social Psychology of False Confessions: Compliance, Internalization, and Confabulation", in *Psychological Science*, 1996, vol. 7, no. 3, pp. 125–128.

[12] For example, Robert Horselenberg, Harald Merckelbach and Sarah Josephs, "Individual Differences and False Confessions: A Conceptual Replication of Kassin and Kiechel (1996)", in *Psychology, Crime & Law*, 2003, vol. 9, no. 1, pp. 1–8; Kirk A.B. Newring and William O'Donohue, "False Confessions and Influenced Witnesses", in *Applied Psychology in Criminal Justice*, 2008, vol. 4, no. 1, pp. 81–107; Jennifer T. Perillo and Saul M. Kassin, "Inside Interrogation: The Lie, the Bluff, and False Confessions", in *Law and Human Behavior*, 2011, vol. 35, no. 4, pp. 327–337; Allison D. Redlich and Gail S. Goodman, "Taking Responsibility For an Act Not Committed: The Influence of Age and Suggestibility", in *Law and Human Behavior*, 2003, vol. 27, no. 2, pp. 141–156.

experiment.[13] This act and potential consequences are more serious in nature (especially in a university setting), it is an intentionally committed act (that is, participants are certain of their innocence or guilt when accused), and this paradigm allows for the study of both true and false confessions (that is, innocent and guilty participants can be accused). Russano and colleagues found that both explicit and implicit offers of leniency (in the form of minimization tactics) increased both true *and* false confessions. It is important to keep in mind that ecological validity is not an all-or-nothing concept, but rather it lies on a continuum. Although the 'cheating' paradigm arguably has greater ecological validity than other experimental paradigms, it can still be criticized for not approximating actual interrogations. Critics whose focus is purely on the issue of mundane realism (as opposed to psychological realism), however, do not appreciate that the underlying psychological processes can still be generalized beyond the confines of the study even if the study does not fully capture all real-world conditions.[14]

---

[13] Melissa B. Russano, Christian A. Meissner, Fadia M. Narchet and Saul M. Kassin, "Investigating True and False Confessions within a Novel Experimental Paradigm", in *Psychological Science*, 2005, vol. 16, no. 6, pp. 481–486.

[14] The 'alt-key' and 'cheating' paradigms are just two of the many laboratory paradigms used in the interviewing literature, and researchers continually seek to create novel paradigms and modify existing ones to improve ecological validity.

For just a few examples of innovating and interesting laboratory paradigms in various areas of investigating interviewing research, see for instance: R. Edward Geiselman *et al.*, "Enhancement of Eyewitness Memory: An Empirical Evaluation of the Cognitive Interview", in *Journal of Police Science and Administration*, 1984, vol. 12, no. 1, pp. 74–80; Jillian R. Rivard, Ronald P. Fisher, Belinda Robertson and Dana H. Mueller, "Testing the Cognitive Interview With Professional Interviewers: Enhancing Recall of Specific Details of Recurring Events", in *Applied Cognitive Psychology*, 2014, vol. 28, no. 6, pp. 917–925.

In the Cognitive Interview domain, see for example: Maria Hartwig, Pär Anders Granhag, Leif A. Strömwall and Ola Kronkvist, "Strategic Use of Evidence During Police Interviews: When Training to Detect Deception Works", in *Law and Human Behavior*, 2006, vol. 30, no. 5, pp. 603–619; Pär Anders Granhag, Simon Oleszkiewicz, Marthe L. Sakrisvold and Steven M. Kleinman, "The Scharff Technique: Training Military Intelligence Officers to Elicit Information from Small Cells of Sources", in *Psychology, Crime & Law*, 2020, vol. 26, no. 5, pp. 438–460; see also Chapters 10 and 16 of this book.

In the evidence presentation domain, see for example: Drew A. Leins, Ronald P. Fisher and Aldert Vrij, "Drawing on Liars' Lack of Cognitive Flexibility: Detecting Deception Through Varying Report Modes", in *Applied Cognitive Psychology*, 2012, vol. 26, no. 4, pp. 601–607; Aldert Vrij, Sharon Leal, Samantha Mann and Pär Anders Granhag, "A Comparison Between Lying About Intentions and Past Activities: Verbal Cues and Detection Accuracy", in *Applied Cognitive Psychology*, 2011, vol. 25, no. 2, pp. 212–218.

In the credibility assessment domain, see for example: Jacqueline R. Evans *et al.*, "Obtaining Guilty Knowledge in Human Intelligence Interrogations: Comparing Accusatorial and Information-Gathering Approaches With a Novel Experimental Paradigm", in *Journal of*

1.3.2. Self-Report Studies

If you are a practitioner reading this chapter, you may have been approached by a researcher to participate in a study about your professional experiences conducting interviews. After laboratory studies, self-report studies (in the form of surveys, in-depth interviews and focus groups) about interviewing and interrogation are the next most common way we understand the practices. The major benefit of self-report studies is that researchers are able to learn about the practices directly from experts in the field. Generally speaking, self-report studies ask practitioners how often they employ a set of techniques, how they approach different types of interviewees, or their attitudes regarding various aspects of conducting interviews (we note here that surveys and research interviews with people who have been interviewed also exist, though are rarer).[15] Furthermore, self-report studies offer insight into the decision-making process of interviewers (and interviewees) that is otherwise unknowable while simply observing an interview (see Section 1.3.3. below). When researchers understand the perspective of those who have experienced the interview process first-hand, this insight can be used to formulate research questions to be explored in other self-report studies or, ideally, through the other methodologies covered in this chapter.

Of the types of these studies, self-administered surveys (or questionnaires) are, by far, the most common because they are the most straightforward to conduct, assisted in large part due to online survey platforms. Also, the 'self-administered' part of surveys requires little or no effort on the part of the researcher in collecting the data, whereas in-depth interviews and focus groups require the active participation of one or more researchers. While designing a survey, the researcher needs to develop clearly worded questions that leave little-to-no room for ambiguity so that every survey participant understands the question in the same manner. Further, the questions must also actually measure what the researchers think they are measuring (an issue known as *construct validity*).

Applied Research in Memory and Cognition, 2013, vol. 2, no. 2, pp. 83–88; Aldert Vrij *et al.*, "Detection of Concealment in an Information-Gathering Interview", in *Applied Cognitive Psychology*, 2014, vol. 28, no. 6, pp. 860–866.

In the intelligence interview domain, see for example: Saul M. Kassin, Christian A. Meissner and Rebecca J. Norwick, "'I'd Know a False Confession if I Saw One': A Comparative Study of College Students and Police Investigators", in *Law and Human Behavior*, 2005, vol. 29 no. 2, pp. 211–227; Max Guyll *et al.*, "Innocence and Resisting Confession During Interrogation: Effects on Physiologic Activity", in *Law and Human Behavior*, 2013, vol. 37, no. 5, pp. 366–375; Rachel E. Dianiska, Jessica K. Swanner, Laure Brimbal and Christian A. Meissner, "Conceptual Priming and Context Reinstatement: A Test of Direct and Indirect Interview Techniques", in *Law and Human Behavior*, 2019, vol. 43, no. 2, pp. 131–143.

[15] See, for example, Hayley M.D. Cleary and Ray Bull, "Jail Inmates' Perspectives on Police Interrogation", in *Psychology, Crime & Law*, 2019, vol. 25, no. 2, pp. 157–170.

A typical survey about interviewing asks participants to report their use of a number of specific techniques on a specific scale such as from one (never) to five (always), and the average scores are reported from the most frequently used technique to the least. Which techniques and how many are included are left up to the researchers designing the survey, and those decisions can influence the results. For instance, in what was perhaps the first large-scale survey of its kind, Kassin et al.[16] found that the most commonly reported technique out of their list of 16 was "Isolating suspect from family and friends". Subsequent surveys examined up to 67 specific techniques and found that those related to rapport-building were the most commonly employed interview methods.[17]

In addition to the frequency of use, most survey research attempts to draw connections between the rate at which practitioners report using techniques and other elements of interviewing. First, in each of the three published self-report surveys referenced in the previous paragraph, the numerous specific techniques were reduced into a fewer number of categories. This is accomplished in one of two ways: either after-the-fact statistical procedures using the self-reported data that uncover groupings of related techniques[18] or before-the-fact conceptual groupings of related techniques.[19] These categories were then analysed in relation to other self-reported aspects of the interview process or the interviewers themselves. For example, Kassin et al. analysed five attributes of the participants in relation to their four technique groupings – years of experience, if they had received formal training, how confident they were at lie detection, number of interrogations they had conducted and the average length of their interrogations. They found that more experienced participants and those who had received formal training were significantly more likely to employ techniques related to their *presentation of evidence* factor that included showing photographs to the suspect and telling the suspect they failed a polygraph test than those with less experience and those without formal training.

The next type of self-report study is in-depth interviews. Whereas the purpose of surveys is to cover a wide range of topics at a fairly superficial level in order to make broad conclusions about interviewing techniques, in-depth

---

[16] Saul M. Kassin *et al.*, "Police Interviewing and Interrogation: A Self-Report Survey of Police Practices and Beliefs", in *Law and Human Behavior*, 2007, vol. 31, no. 4, pp. 381–400.

[17] Allison D. Redlich, Christopher E. Kelly and Jeaneé C. Miller, "The Who, What, and Why of Human Intelligence Gathering: Self-reported Measures of Interrogation Methods", in *Applied Cognitive Psychology*, 2014, vol. 28, no. 6, pp. 817–828; Wachi Taeko *et al.*, "Police Interviewing Styles and Confessions in Japan", in *Psychology, Crime & Law*, 2014, vol. 20, no. 7, pp. 673–694.

[18] Kassin *et al.*, 2007, see *supra* note 16; Wachi *et al.*, 2014, see *supra* note 17.

[19] Redlich, Kelly and Miller, 2014, see *supra* note 17.

interviews can tap into the richness of practices in ways that surveys cannot. Most studies that utilize an in-depth interview approach use a semi-structured protocol in which all interviewees are asked the same set of questions, but it also allows for spontaneous follow-up questions either at the end of the structured questioning process or in response to a particular answer. Asking all study participants the same set of questions allows researchers to more easily analyse and synthesize (that is, systematically observe) the responses across the entire sample, while the unstructured, spontaneous follow-up questions allow the researchers to explore topics they might not previously have thought of or to get clarification about something the interviewee said.

Researchers conducting in-depth interviews typically must rely on some combination of *purposive convenience* sampling and *snowball* sampling. Purposive convenience sampling is when researchers use their own judgement to identify and reach out to people who fit into the population they wish to study and invite them to participate in the study; researchers often call upon their own network of professional and personal contacts to obtain a sample in this way. Snowball sampling is when people who have participated in the study are asked to identify other prospective participants from the population of interest, and those potential participants are approached and asked to participate. Both of these types of non-probability sampling strategies are typical to the method, but it almost always leads to non-representative samples that may be difficult to generalize beyond the confines of the particular study.

Sampling challenges aside, in-depth interviews are excellent for getting a grasp on what is actually happening in the field and a 'boots-on-the-ground' perspective. Like with survey research, some researchers have used in-depth interview data not just to capture what is happening in the interrogation room from the perspective of the interviewer or interviewee, but also to examine whether the reported interview strategies are related to key outcomes such as interviewee co-operation and disclosure. For example, Goodman-Delahunty, Martschuk and Dhami[20] interviewed an international sample of 34 law enforcement practitioners and 30 individuals who had been questioned about alleged terrorist activities, and they found that rapport-building and other non-coercive strategies facilitated more complete and meaningful disclosures.

Resources can pose a significant challenge for researchers utilizing an in-depth interview approach, in that it tends to be time-consuming and may require significant financial resources. A study by Russano, Narchet, Meissner and Kleinman can be used to illustrate the intensive nature of this type of work. They

[20]   Jane Goodman-Delahunty, Natalie Martschuk and Mandeep K. Dhami, "Interviewing High Value Detainees: Securing Cooperation and Disclosures", in *Applied Cognitive Psychology*, 2014, vol. 28, no. 6, pp. 883–897.

interviewed 42 military, intelligence and law enforcement interrogators, a subset of which had experience interrogating high-value targets.[21] A combination of purposive convenience sampling and snowball sampling was used to identify participants from various federal law enforcement agencies and military branches who were considered 'highly experienced' by themselves and by their professional counterparts. It took great effort to identify, obtain contact information for, and in some cases, gain consent to participate.[22] The interviews lasted two to three hours, and the researcher conducting the interview travelled to the location where the interrogator was located to conduct the interview in person,[23] which required significant financial resources to cover travel costs (for example, flights, hotels, *et cetera*). The goal of Russano *et al.*'s study was to gain an understanding of not only what was occurring during interrogations we typically do not have access to (due to lack of recordings and systematic observations), but to understand highly experienced practitioners' perceptions of what interrogation practices are least and most effective. The audio-recorded interviews were then transcribed by a professional transcription service (also costly), and then two coders needed to develop a coding scheme (see Section 1.3.3., 'Field Studies', for a description of this process) and systematically code what was a very dense and lengthy data set (time intensive) that was primarily qualitative in nature (that is, the focus was not on reducing the data to numerical analysis, but rather to identify common themes in the participant responses). Some of the highlights from the results of this study are that the sample of highly experienced interrogators believed that rapport-building approaches are most effective (and confrontational approaches least effective) at eliciting reliable information and that more advanced training on interviewing and interrogation is needed, including on how to effectively incorporate interpreters into the interview room.

Lastly, a third type of self-report approach is the use of focus groups, which typically consist of a small number of participants (for example, five to ten) with shared experiences who are brought together for a similar, but distinct,

---

[21] Melissa B. Russano, Fadia M. Narchet, Steven M. Kleinman and Christian A. Meissner, "Structured Interviews of Experienced HUMINT Interrogators", in *Applied Cognitive Psychology*, 2014, vol. 28, no. 6, pp. 847–859.

[22] Although most investigators approached were willing to participate, scheduling occasionally prevented participation. In addition, because some participants were active investigators, careful steps were taken to reassure participants that their participation and responses would remain confidential.

[23] This study was conducted before video-conferencing (for example, Zoom) became commonplace. As people have become more comfortable with a virtual platform, these types of interviews could likely be conducted in a remote format, without much compromise in quality of the interviews.

purpose from interviews. Whereas interviews have the benefit of going deep into a topic and allow for the researcher to probe more in-depth where necessary, focus groups can also do this but with the added benefit of having the participants engage with one another. The researcher crafts the prompts, or questions, in fairly broad terms, giving each participant the opportunity to respond. Ideally, the participants will not simply reiterate what the previous ones said but instead build upon and further illuminate the topic, as focus groups are especially suited toward exploring new or understudied topics.

For example, Meehan, Kelly and McClary conducted two focus groups with investigators whose role in a correctional facility is to investigate gang affiliations and activity and rule infractions more broadly.[24] One of the biggest discoveries from the focus groups are what Meehan and colleagues referred to as 'short- versus long-term rapport'. During criminal investigations, the interactions between law enforcement and interviewees are generally confined by the needs of the investigation (short-term), but in a correctional facility where the average stay is eight months, the investigators are conscious of the need to maintain rapport with interviewees over longer periods of time that may also crisscross several different investigations. It is unlikely that such a distinction would be uncovered in a survey, and perhaps researchers would have found this in an interview, but the dynamic of multiple participants weighing in and building upon a single topic can lead to a new discovery.

Although learning directly from experts constitutes the primary strength of self-report methodologies, like every social science method, surveys, interviews and focus groups come with weaknesses as well. First, sampling and generalizability problems abound in self-report studies. This is a specific problem in survey research, as interviews and focus groups are not designed to produce generalizable findings (a limitation in its own right). Recruiting sufficiently large survey samples for appropriate analysis is an ongoing challenge, to say nothing of the near-herculean task of drawing samples that are representative of the population of practitioners or interviewees.

Next, all three self-report methodologies involve the subjective perceptions of the participants involved in the study. This problem has two related components. First, perceptions are not to be considered accurate, objective fact and may be influenced by cognitive biases and the fragility of human memory. It is important to know what practitioners think for the reasons described above, but this is different than treating those thoughts as the unvarnished truth. Simply

---

[24] Nathan Meehan, Christopher E. Kelly and Michael McClary, "The Snitching Hour: Investigations and Interviewing in a County Jail", in *Security Journal*, 2019, vol. 32, no. 2, pp. 198–217. This study is noteworthy because it is an example of a study exploring the non-criminal interviews, which is a relative rarity in the interviewing world.

put, our perceptions are not always accurate for many reasons, not the least of which is that we do not always understand what influences our own behaviour. Finally, all self-report studies potentially suffer from what is known as *social desirability* bias. This is the situation where the participants' answers are influenced – even if on an unconscious level – by what they think they should say or what they think the researcher wants to hear. This occurs because people typically want to be viewed in a positive light and co-operate with the researcher, and this can affect the responses they give. As the level of potential controversy in the topic increases, the risk of social desirability does as well. With contemporary interviewing research being spurred on by rising public awareness of false confessions and coercive tactics, participants of studies in this research area may be motivated to withhold their true feelings or prior practices for fear of experiencing stigma by the researcher.

1.3.3. Field Studies

Arguably the least common methodology employed to study interviewing is known as field studies, or the systematic observation of the actual phenomenon in its naturally occurring environment. In this area, nearly all observations have been conducted using an official record of an interview, primarily transcripts, but researchers are increasingly receiving access to audio and video recordings that allow for a more naturalistic way to observe the interaction between interviewer and interviewee. An additional way to observe an interview is to view it live and in person, though for obvious reasons this is a difficult proposition at best, and the only large-scale study to have actually done it (in combination with having access to video recordings) was Leo's seminal study that essentially established the modern era of interrogation field research.[25]

Because live observation is so rare in the published literature, the remainder of this section will focus on the field studies of transcribed and/or recorded interviews, and it is worth taking a moment to explore the mechanisms of conducting such a study, often known as a 'content analysis'. First, getting access to either medium is a challenge, and it is likely the primary reason for the relative rarity of field research on interviewing. This is changing, as partnerships between the practitioner and academic communities develop and flourish, and the number of studies examining actual interviews is increasing as a result.[26]

---

[25] Richard A. Leo, "Inside the Interrogation Room", in *The Journal of Criminal Law and Criminology*, 1996, vol. 86, no. 2, pp. 266–303.

[26] Melissa B. Russano, Christopher E. Kelly and Christian A. Meissner, "From the Ivory Tower to the Interrogation Room: Training and Field Evaluation Research on Suspect Interviewing", in Ray Bull and Iris Blandon-Gitlin (eds.), *The Routledge International Handbook of Legal and Investigative Psychology*, Routledge, Abingdon, 2019, pp. 287–310.

The typical approach to studying interviewing from official records is a deductive one,[27] meaning that the researcher develops a 'coding scheme' which is a set of definitions of interview methods and interviewee responses. The scheme is applied to the sample of interviews, with researchers (often called 'coders' in this procedure) documenting what they observe in each interview from the coding scheme. Each method and response in the coding scheme is assigned a numerical value and is considered a variable for later analysis. The interview method is considered the predictor variable, the interviewee response is the outcome variable, and the analyses conducted are generally correlational in nature (that is, analysing an association between variables). For a straightforward example, Oxburgh, Ost, Morris and Cherryman found that open-ended questions are associated with more information gain from suspects than closed-ended questions.[28]

In his seminal study, Leo observed whether 25 interrogation techniques (the predictor variables) were used by detectives, and he also counted how many different techniques were used in each interrogation (an additional predictor variable). He observed four informational responses that suspects could have made – no incriminating statement, incriminating statement, partial admission and full confession – which is the outcome variable of increasing success (at least from the perspective of the police). Leo reported a significant relationship between the number of interrogation techniques used and the likelihood of getting an admission or confession: the more techniques used, the more likely the suspect would confess.[29]

Another example is that Kelly, Miller and Redlich measured how investigators emphasized one of four interrogation domains: *rapport and relationship building, emotion provocation, confrontation-competition* and *presentation of evidence*.[30] These predictor variables were analysed by the researchers on their associations with the outcome variable of suspect co-operation, measured on a five-point scale ranging from strong resistance to strong co-operation. They

---

[27] The alternative is an inductive approach in which researchers do not impose such a coding scheme onto the interview; instead, they allow the findings to emerge from observing the interviews. Inductive research is often qualitative, and there is a dearth of such studies examining interviewing. One notable exception is Katz (1999) in which he conducted case studies – itself a rare form of field research – on two interrogations. Jack Katz, *How Emotions Work*, University of Chicago Press, 1999, pp. 274–308.

[28] Gavin E. Oxburgh, James Ost, Paul Morris and Julie Cherryman, "The Impact of Question Type and Empathy on Police Interviews With Suspects of Homicide, Filicide and Child Sexual Abuse", in *Psychiatry, Psychology and Law*, 2014, vol. 21, no. 6, pp. 903–917.

[29] Leo, 1996, see *supra* note 25.

[30] Christopher E. Kelly, Jeaneé C. Miller and Allison D. Redlich, "The Dynamic Nature of Interrogation", in *Law and Human Behavior*, 2016, vol. 40, no. 3, pp. 295–309.

found that *rapport and relationship-building* significantly predicted greater co-operation and that the other three were significantly associated with less co-operation. Using a statistical procedure known as 'lag analysis', they also found that the most accusatorial approach, the *confrontation-competition* domain, suppressed co-operation for up to 15 minutes after it was used by the police investigators.

There are strengths and weaknesses of content analyses depending upon a number of issues, including the medium one has access to. One of the largest benefits of working with electronic recordings, especially video, is that the researcher is able to hear intonation in a speaker's voice or see their physical posture that may influence which code to select. Consider the imperative, 'Tell me where you were on the night of the murder'. When reading this in a transcript, it might be interpreted as a relatively straightforward open-ended question with a neutral tone. What if, however, it was delivered by a frustrated interviewer while standing over a seated suspect? This would certainly be different, taking on a confrontational style and thus coded differently. Working with transcripts, it is very difficult to infer tone or attitude.

On the contrary, having access to only electronic recordings presents its own challenges. First, technology is not perfect or universally of a quality that produces clear audio and video, nor are the ambient conditions in which an interview takes place always pristine. Next, human dialogue is rather fast, and our brains do not pick up every word spoken to one another, especially in our native language, and we rely on context to understand what is being said. This presents an opportunity for potentially missing critical details that are far easier to 'catch' or code when reading word-for-word on a transcript. Thus, having access to both media while conducting such field research may be ideal.

Regardless of medium, contrasted with lab-based research especially, a major strength of field studies is their high levels of external and ecological validity, or the capacity for the research to explain complex, real-life phenomena.[31]

---

[31] See Chapter 15 of this book. For further details, see Alison *et al.*'s ORBIT studies of suspected terrorists and the various papers of Walsh and Bull on benefit fraud interviews for examples of other field studies: Laurence J. Alison *et al.*, "Why Tough Tactics Fail and Rapport Gets Results: Observing Rapport-Based Interpersonal Techniques (ORBIT) to Generate Useful Information from Terrorists", in *Psychology, Public Policy, and Law*, 2013, vol. 19, no. 4, pp. 411–431; Laurence J. Alison *et al.*, "The Efficacy of Rapport-Based Techniques for Minimizing Counter-Interrogation Tactics Amongst a Field Sample of Terrorists", in *Psychology, Public Policy, and Law*, 2014, vol. 20, no. 4, pp. 421–430; Frances Surmon-Böhr, Laurence J. Alison, Paul Christiansen and Emily Alison, "The Right to Silence and the Permission to Talk: Motivational Interviewing and High-Value Detainees", in *American Psychologist*, 2020, vol. 75, no. 7, pp. 1011–1021; Dave Walsh and Ray Bull, "Examining Rapport in Investigative Interviews With Suspects: Does its Building and Maintenance Work?", in *Journal of Police*

As laboratory experiments are otherwise artificial settings by design, field research involves observing interviewing in its natural (if documented) setting. As described above, the challenge is for researchers to develop the language to accurately describe and understand interview methods and interviewee responses, translate those ideas into specific definitions for coding, and then use those variables in analyses which allow us to observe relationships between the predictor and outcome variables.

There are important caveats about field research, namely sampling limitations and questions of causality. As noted earlier in this section, access to a sample of any interviews is a challenge under the best of conditions, but the level of access to an organization's records needed to randomly select a range of interviews from the entire population of them presents a nearly impossible task. The Kelly *et al.* study referred to above analysed a relatively small ($N = 29$) sample of interview recordings provided by the Los Angeles Police Department ('LAPD'), selected by the detectives themselves with the only guidance being that the suspects presented at least a minimum level of resistance at the beginning of the interview. Otherwise, the researchers had no control over the interviews that would be in the final sample, which is ordinarily a source of potential bias in the findings. The adequacy of a sample (both in terms of size and representativeness) directly affects the ability to generalize the study findings to operational settings not included in the study itself.[32]

Causality is also affected by sampling limitations, and without the random assignment and experimental controls of laboratory studies described earlier in this chapter, no one field study can truly be used to draw causal conclusions (that is, to conclude that X caused Y and will likely do so in any future replication of the research). As such, published field studies ought to include a common caveat regarding this limitation. For example, Kelly *et al.* noted that the findings from that one study were not necessarily applicable to interviews of suspects accused of anything other than murder, sexual assault or robbery, to other units within LAPD, or to other police departments in the United States or beyond.

1.4. Integrated Methods

The previous sections constitute the three most common methodologies researchers employ to study interviewing, and they are the foundation for how we know what we know about the phenomenon. That said, there are a variety of

---

and *Criminal Psychology*, 2012, vol. 27, no. 1, pp. 73–84; Dave Walsh and Ray Bull, "Interviewing Suspects: Examining the Association Between Skills, Questioning, Evidence Disclosure, and Interview Outcomes", in *Psychology, Crime & Law*, 2015, vol. 21, no. 7, pp. 661–680.

[32] Kelly, Miller and Redlich, 2016, see *supra* note 30.

additional research designs that seek to integrate otherwise discrete findings into a single analysis, or to integrate different methodologies into a single study. Whereas convergence of findings should be sought within and between laboratory, self-report and field studies, this section will examine the formal integration of methodological approaches or the application of advanced statistical procedures that are intended to strengthen the existing state of the science. These methodologies are not simply summaries of what we know from previous laboratory, self-report and field studies, but rather they use the principles of the scientific method to produce new knowledge.

First, a meta-analysis is a methodological approach that merges the findings from a series of related individual studies into a single one. It is arguably one of the best ways we have to make solid conclusions about any topic, as the synthesizing of results of a large number of studies in a systematic fashion can assist us in hearing the signal amongst the noise of research. Findings of a meta-analysis are generally given significant weight and are considered a more authoritative source than any single study. An excellent example of a meta-analysis was conducted by Meissner and colleagues who sought to integrate the findings about confession research.[33] Their paper actually consisted of two meta-analyses, as the researchers conducted one for field studies (incorporating five studies) and one for experimental studies (12 studies). Meissner *et al.* concluded that information-gathering approaches that align with the PEACE model of interviewing increase true confessions and reduce the incidence of false confessions when compared with accusatorial style of interrogation. Other meta-analyses have been conducted on the Strategic Use of Evidence ('SUE'), the Scharff technique, the Cognitive Interview ('CI'), and cues to deception.[34] As the rate of

---

[33] Christian A. Meissner *et al.*, "Accusatorial and Information-Gathering Interrogation Methods and their Effects on True and False Confessions: A Meta-Analytic Review", in *Journal of Experimental Criminology*, 2014, vol. 10, no. 4, pp. 459–486.

[34] Bella M. DePaulo *et al.*, "Cues to Deception", in *Psychological Bulletin*, 2020, vol. 129, no. 1, pp. 74–118; Maria Hartwig, Pär Anders Granhag and Timothy J. Luke, "Strategic Use of Evidence During Investigative Interviews: The State of the Science", in David C. Raskin, Charles R. Honts and John C. Kircher (eds.), *Credibility Assessment: Scientific Research and Applications*, Academic Press, San Diego, 2014, pp. 1–36; Timothy J. Luke, "A Meta-Analytic Review of Experimental Tests of the Interrogation Technique of Hanns Joachim Scharff", in *Applied Cognitive Psychology*, 2020, vol. 35, no. 2, pp. 360–373; Amina Memon, Christian A. Meissner and Joanne Fraser, "The Cognitive Interview: A Meta-Analytic Review and Study Space Analysis of the Last 25 Years", in *Psychology, Public Policy, and Law*, 2020, vol. 16, no. 4, pp. 340–372; Simon Oleszkiewicz and Steven J. Watson, "A Meta-Analytic Review of the Timing for Disclosing Evidence when Interviewing Suspects", in *Applied Cognitive Psychology*, 2021, vol. 35, no. 2, pp. 342–359.

interviewing research increases[35] so, too, should the rate of meta-analytic approaches to the study of it.

Next, we do not want to neglect studies that do not fit neatly into any of the methodologies we have covered in this chapter, namely those conducted with practitioners in either laboratory or field settings. As partnerships between researchers and practitioners become more common, practitioners are being exposed to science-based methods of interviewing and are being brought more fully into the research being conducted. Luke and colleagues, for example, trained a sample of experienced law enforcement investigators in the SUE method and had them interview mock suspects about cues to deception. They compared these interviews with those conducted by untrained investigators and found that those trained in the SUE approach were able to detect deceit at a significantly higher rate.[36] Examining a train-the-trainer model, Molinaro and colleagues instructed a small group of experienced trainers on the CI who then successfully trained students on the CI who gained more information in mock interviews than did untrained interviewers.[37] Russano and colleagues conducted a series of training evaluation and field validation studies in which a week-long science-based interviewing and interrogation programme delivered to federal and local law enforcement practitioners was evaluated. The investigators who participated in the training submitted recordings of suspect interrogations pre- and post-training.[38] Those transcripts were analysed for evidence that: (i) training increased the use of science-based interviewing methods; and (ii) the science-based methods predicted suspect behaviour as would be expected from laboratory and self-report data. Russano *et al.* found that investigators increased their use of the science-based approaches post-training and that use of the science-based techniques predicted co-operation and information disclosure.[39]

---

[35] Christian A. Meissner *et al.*, "Investigative Interviewing: A Review of the Literature and a Model of Science-Based Practice", in David De Matteo and Kyle C. Scherr (eds.), *The Oxford Handbook of Psychology and Law*, Oxford University Press, 2021.

[36] Timothy J. Luke *et al.*, "Training in the Strategic Use of Evidence Technique: Improving Deception Detection Accuracy of American Law Enforcement Officers", in *Journal of Police and Criminal Psychology*, 2016, vol. 31, no. 4, pp. 270–278.

[37] Peter F. Molinaro, Ronald P. Fisher, Alexandra E. Mosser and Geri E. Satin, "Train-the-Trainer: Methodology to Learn the Cognitive Interview", in *Journal of Investigative Psychology and Offender Profiling*, 2019, vol. 16, no. 1, pp. 32–43.

[38] A pre-post design is an example of a within-participants design, in which the same people experienced both experimental conditions (pre-training and post-training), albeit in a necessarily fixed order.

[39] Melissa B. Russano and Christian A. Meissner, "Training Science-Based Methods of Interrogation With Federal, State, and Local Law Enforcement Officers", in *Final Report Submitted to the High-Value Detainee Interrogation Group*, 2020; see also Chapter 22 in this book.

Rarer still are examples of field experiments which are designed to produce the randomization of conditions just as would be done in the laboratory but conducted on real-world interviews. One such field experiment sought to test whether the physical context in which interviewers were conducted subtly influenced interviewee behaviour, as has been found in the laboratory.[40] Conducted in collaboration with the Philadelphia Police Department, Kelly and colleagues manipulated one of two interview rooms used by an investigations unit to make it more comfortable by adding softer chairs and lighting, area rugs and decoration. The control room was what one might think of as a typical interrogation room with bright overhead lighting and hard plastic chairs. The researchers devised a system whereby witnesses to armed robbery and non-lethal shootings were randomly assigned to one of the two rooms. After the interview was complete, the detectives completed a short survey, and the witnesses were invited (via recorded video) to complete a short survey about their experiences being interviewed. Contrary to their hypotheses, the researchers reported few significant differences between the room conditions.[41]

Another example of a field experiment involved the issue of whether informing suspects that they were being recorded during their interrogation would inhibit suspects from making incriminating statements. Kassin and colleagues[42] partnered with a small metropolitan police department in the northeastern United States who by policy recorded all custodial interrogations in cases where the charge being investigated carries the potential of life imprisonment. Actual criminal suspects were randomly assigned to be informed or not informed that their interrogation was being recorded. Receiving information that they were being recorded did not inhibit suspects; informed suspects were just as likely to waive their *Miranda* rights and make incriminating statements as uniformed suspects. In addition, there was no difference in ultimate case disposition by informed status. Ideally, more field experiments will be conducted in the future, but from an access and resource perspective, these types of studies are some of the most difficult to conduct.

---

[40]   Evan Dawson, Maria Hartwig, Laure Brimbal and Philipp Denisenkov, "A Room With a View: Setting Influences Information Disclosure in Investigative Interviews", in *Law and Human Behavior*, 2017, vol. 41, no. 4, pp. 333–343.

[41]   Christopher E. Kelly, Evan Dawson and Maria Hartwig, "Context Manipulation in Police Interviews: A Field Experiment", in *Journal of Experimental Criminology*, 2021, vol. 17, no. 1, pp. 67–86.

[42]   Saul M. Kassin *et al.*, "Does Video Recording Inhibit Crime Suspects? Evidence From a Fully Randomized Field Experiment", in *Law and Human Behavior*, 2019, vol. 43, no. 1, pp. 45–55.

1.5. Conclusion

Beginning in 2020, the Covid-19 pandemic thrusted discussion of 'science' into the public discourse in both refreshing and frightening ways. Refreshing in terms of calls for public health policies that are evidence-based and that 'follow the science', and frightening as non-scientists who lack the methodological training and skills to evaluate the science promulgated misinformation via social media and beyond. The world watched as the scientific process unfolded in real-time, with all its imperfections, nuances and contradictions. For laypersons, frustration sometimes built as what we thought we collectively knew about Covid-19 changed – and then changed again. Watching the scientific process in action can lead to distrust of scientists by those who do not understand that the ever-changing nature of scientific knowledge is not a fatal flaw, but rather its fundamental strength. Scientific knowledge in any area, whether about Covid-19 or interviewing, evolves incrementally – a real-world problem or research question presents itself, theories are posited, hypotheses are made, studies are designed, data are collected – and based on those data, scientists learn whether their hypotheses were right or wrong, and the process begins anew.

Drawing upon the lessons of the Covid-19 science, practitioners who seek to move toward a science-based approach to investigative interviewing should be applauded for their commitment to best-practices grounded in evidence and data. We hope that this chapter provides insight into how we as researchers know what we know. We urge practitioners and others to look for convergence of findings both within and across the methodologies described in this chapter, understanding the results of a specific study in the context of the wider literature. Moving forward, we believe practitioners will be faced with a difficult challenge, namely, to identify interview practices and training programs truly grounded in science. As practitioners are introduced to use new procedures, we encourage them to ask important critical questions: What scientific research supports these techniques? Can you provide peer-reviewed, published research that supports the efficacy of the approaches? If the answers are some variations of 'I don't know of any' or 'years of personal experience' or 'here are some web pages referencing unpublished, peer-reviewed studies' – we suggest proceeding with extreme caution. The job and task of an interviewer are too important to rely on outdated practices that may or may not be scientifically supported. Fortunately, there is no need to. The science is available to guide your way.

Appendix A
The Logic of Hypothesis Testing:
A Methodological Primer

This appendix is for those readers who wish to learn more about the logic of hypothesis testing and key related concepts. As discussed in the chapter, researchers conduct statistical analyses to determine whether the data support the research hypothesis. Counterintuitively, we do not seek to 'prove' or 'accept' the research hypothesis; rather, we seek to *reject* what is known as the 'null hypothesis'. While the research hypothesis typically posits that there *is* a relationship between variables, the null hypothesis typically predicts that there is *no* relationship. When we perform statistical analyses, we determine whether the results allow us to reject the null hypothesis – in other words, we look to see if we can reject the idea that there is no relationship, and we therefore conclude that there *is* a relationship. We can reject the null hypothesis if the pattern of data we found is highly unlikely to have occurred by chance. Specifically, we examine what is referred to as a 'p-value' (probability value) . The p-value tells us the likelihood that the pattern of data we observed would have occurred just by chance (that is, there is no actual relationship between variables). We compare the p-value associated with our statistical test against a significance level standard (known as 'alpha') that we set in advance. The generally accepted alpha level in most situations is .05, which means that there is a 5 per cent chance that you will conclude there is a relationship or an effect when there is not actually one. If our calculated p-value is less than our alpha, we reject the null hypothesis (and conclude there is a relationship).

Whenever a researcher draws a conclusion based on data, there are four possible decision outcomes. Let us assume that a researcher examines the data, and based on what they see, they reject the null hypothesis, thereby concluding that there is a relationship between variables. Hopefully, that decision is the correct one – if we had a crystal ball and we could know for sure that there actually *is* a relationship between variables (that is, the null hypothesis is actually false), then the researcher has made a correct decision when they conclude there is relationship between variables. However, it is also possible that the decision is incorrect – if there is actually *no* relationship between variables (that is, the null hypothesis is true), but the researcher concludes there is a relationship, this would be an incorrect decision; this type of error is called a 'Type 1 error' (the probability of making a Type 1 error is equal to alpha). Now let us assume that the researcher looked at the data and based on the data they must *fail* to reject the null hypothesis (that is, they conclude that there is no relationship between variables). If there is truly no relationship between the variables, then the researcher has made a correct decision. However, if there actually *is* a relationship between variables, then failing to reject the null hypothesis (that is, concluding there is no relationship when there really is one) is an incorrect decision ('Type 2 error').

Our Covid-19 experiences provides us with a handy analogy here. Imagine a man who suspects he may have contracted the virus, and he takes a rapid home test. In this case, the null hypothesis is that the man does *not* have Covid-19; the research hypothesis is that the man *does* have Covid-19. If the test reveals two lines (that is, the data), he will reject the null hypothesis (that is, he will reject the idea that he does not have Covid-19), and he will conclude that he does in fact have Covid-19. If the man actually is infected, and the test indicates he has Covid-19, then the test is accurate, and the man has reached the correct conclusion. However, if the man does *not* have the virus, he has drawn an incorrect conclusion (that is, that he has Covid-19 when he really does not). This is a Type 1 error, sometimes known as a false positive. Now let us assume that test did not reveal two lines; the man will fail to reject the null hypothesis, and he will conclude that he does not have Covid-19 (that is, he fails to reject the idea that he does not have Covid, therefore he concludes he does not have Covid-19). If, in fact, he does not have Covid-19, this is a correct decision. However, if he is infected with the virus, but the test indicates he is not, he will fail to reject the null hypothesis when it is actually false (that is, he will conclude he does not have Covid-19 when he actually does). This is a Type 2 error, sometimes known as a false negative.

Researchers can never know for sure if they have made a correct decision or an error when drawing a conclusion (since they sadly do not actually have a magic crystal ball), and importantly, making a Type 1 or Type 2 error does not necessarily mean that the researcher did something wrong during the research process. The likelihood of making a correct decision or an error is affected by many factors. For example, if there actually is a relationship between variables, 'power' refers to the ability of your statistical test to detect the relationship. The power of your test is affected by a whole host of factors. Researchers can exert control over some of these factors, such as the sample size used in the study (the greater the sample size – or number of the participants – the greater the power) but not others, such as the inherent magnitude of the relationship between the variables (a concept researchers refer to as 'effect size' – the larger the relationship, the easier it is to detect). These concepts are important to understand because they help us appreciate the possibilities of various conclusions that are drawn in a given study. When researchers observe a statistically significant effect, and conclude there is a relationship between variables, there is always a (typically) very small possibility that they are wrong and that the pattern of the data happened purely by chance. Likewise, when researchers observe a 'null effect' – that is, they fail to reject the null hypothesis and conclude there is no relationship between variables – it could be that there truly is no relationship between the variables of interest in the real-world, but it could also mean that the researchers simply were not able to detect a relationship (oftentimes due to low power) that actually does exist.

2

Do Jurors Understand the Causes of False Confession, and Do They Adjust Their Perceptions of Suspects' Confessions Appropriately?

Deborah Davis and Richard A. Leo[*]

2.1. Case Study

On 26 September 1983, 11-year-old Sabrina Buie's body was found in a soybean field in Red Springs, North Carolina, where she had been raped and murdered. Based solely on 17-year-old high school student Ethel Furmage's report of a rumour, the Red Springs Police suspected 19-year-old Henry McCollum of the murder and interrogated him overnight on 28–29 September 1983 for approximately five hours. During that time, according to McCollum, three police interrogators repeatedly accused him of the rape and murder and yelled at him, with one detective calling McCollum, who is African American, by use of the 'N-word'. The detectives repeatedly and falsely told McCollum that they had a witness who had seen him rape and murder Buie; they threatened McCollum with the death penalty if he did not confess to the rape-murder; and the detectives told McCollum, who had an intelligence quotient ('IQ') of 51, that they could make him a witness and promised he could go home if he signed a police-written confession to the crime. The detectives also suspected Leon Brown, McCollum's 15-year-old brother who was also mentally challenged (with an IQ of 49), as a co-participant in the rape and murder. According to Brown, the detectives repeatedly yelled and pressured him to confess; they also called him by the 'N-word'; and they threatened him with the death penalty by gas chamber if he did not confess in their overnight interrogation on 28–29 September 1983. As with their interrogation of McCollum, the detectives told Brown that if he signed the police-written confession statement (both McCollum and Brown were illiterate and could not read or write), they would let him go home.

Based on their police-written confessions alone (no other evidence linked McCollum or Brown to the crime), McCollum and Brown were convicted of capital murder and sentenced to death. Though both convictions would be

---

[*] **Deborah Davis**, Ph.D., is Professor of Psychology at the University of Nevada. **Richard A. Leo**, Ph.D., J.D., is the Hamill Family Professor of Law and Psychology at the University of San Francisco.

vacated by an appellate court, both McCollum and Brown were convicted a second time of the rape and murder, with McCollum again receiving a death sentence, but Brown being sentenced to life in prison. McCollum and Brown each spent nearly 31 years in prison, many of them on death row, before they would be exonerated by DNA evidence, have their convictions formally vacated, and be pardoned by North Carolina Governor Patrick McCrory in 2015.[1]

2.2. Introductory Remarks

As illustrated by the cases of Henry McCollum and Leon Brown, those in the legal system who must judge the veracity of a confession commonly lack the requisite knowledge to recognize when a confession is false. Studies of proven false confessors have shown that when their cases go to trial, between 73 and 81 per cent are convicted.[2] Neither law enforcement, prosecutors nor jurors were able to correctly judge the validity of their confessions. Such errors are not surprising given the very large range of perceiver knowledge and contextual information necessary to evaluate the potential for false confession. These include chronic and acute vulnerabilities of the suspect, the nature of the accusations and of the interrogation, the reasons why suspects falsely confess, how interrogation tactics persuade and more.[3] Interrogation scholars have accumulated a wealth of data testing the impact of personal and situational factors affecting the likelihood of a false confession.

Yet, when judges have excluded expert testimony on interrogation and confessions, a common justification has been that the information an expert could provide is not beyond common knowledge and therefore not helpful to the

---

[1]   See the National Registry of Exonerations' web site; Richard A. Leo, "Report in the Raymond Tarlton, as guardian ad litem for Henry Lee M. Collum, and J. Duane Gilliam, as guardian of the estate of Leon Brown, *et al.* v. Kenneth Sealey *et al.*", Civil Action No. 5:15-CV-451-BO, 2020 (on file with authors).

[2]   Steven A. Drizin and Richard A. Leo, "The Problem of False Confessions in the Post-DNA World", in *North Carolina Law Review*, 2004, vol. 82, pp. 891–1007; Richard A. Leo and Richard J. Ofshe, "The Consequences of False Confessions: Deprivations of Liberty and Miscarriages of Justice in the Age of Psychological Interrogation", in *Criminal Law and Criminology*, 1998, vol. 88, no. 2, pp. 429–496.

[3]   For further discussions, see, for example, Deborah Davis and Richard A. Leo, "To Walk In Their Shoes: The Problem of Missing, Misrepresented and Misunderstood Context in Judging Criminal Confessions", in *New England Law Review*, 2012, vol. 46, no. 4, pp. 737–767 ('Davis and Leo, 2012a'); *id.*, "Interrogation-Related Regulatory Decline: Ego Depletion, Failures of Self-Regulation, and the Decision to Confess", in *Psychology, Public Policy, and Law*, 2012, vol. 18, no. 4, pp. 673–704 ('Davis and Leo, 2012b'); *id.*, "Acute Suggestibility in Police Interrogation: Self-Regulation Failure as a Primary Mechanism of Vulnerability", in Anne M. Ridley, Fiona Gabbert and David J. La Rooy (eds.), *Suggestibility in Legal Contexts: Psychological Research and Forensic Implications*, Wiley Blackwell, Chichester, 2012, pp. 171–195 ('Davis and Leo, 2012c').

jury. This chapter addresses this claim through a review of scientific studies assessing lay beliefs concerning police interrogation and confession, and a comparison of the content of these lay beliefs to the findings of relevant interrogation science. We first provide a brief description of methods used to assess lay knowledge and then turn to specific findings.

2.3. Methods of Studying Lay Beliefs

Two predominant methods have been used to study lay understanding of interrogations and confession: (i) surveys of beliefs regarding interrogation and confession; and (ii) mock jury studies. Each of these methods have both strengths and weaknesses which will now be discussed.

2.3.1. Surveys: Strengths and Weaknesses

Survey participants are asked about beliefs regarding how interrogations are conducted, the appropriateness of these methods, the reality of false confessions, circumstances in which these are likely to occur, and who is vulnerable to give a false confession and why. These responses are evaluated in light of the findings of scientific research addressing these questions, and in some studies lay responses are compared to those of surveys of expert researchers in the field. Lay responses refer to those of populations that are not interrogation researchers or scholars, but may be professionals of other sorts (for example, those in law enforcement).

The surveys primarily assess core beliefs about interrogation and confession, largely free of the context of case facts, the broader context of interrogation or the combined impact of multiple tactics and vulnerabilities. These beliefs can be regarded as the expectations with which observers might approach judgment of interrogations and confessions in case contexts. Arguably then, in the absence of studies designed to address the question, the beliefs identified in the surveys may not affect judgment in case context or might have different effects in different case contexts.

Another difficulty in interpreting survey findings arises from the way questions are asked. Sometimes questions are categorical *yes–no* questions, and for other questions rating scales are used whereby participants either indicate the likelihood that a particular class of suspect would falsely confess or that a particular tactic might lead to a false confession or rate their agreement that it would or would not do so. If only means are reported for such scales, it is arguable at which point the average response should be denoted as a misconception. Moreover, the means do not give a clear picture of the percentage of population responding at the level that would be designated as a misconception. Some surveys report the percentage of participants that respond above or below the midpoint of the scale, which again raises the question of whether this is the appropriate point to demarcate correct population responses from misconceptions (or whether alternate representations of the degree of misconception present in the population should be devised). This is mostly a problem when such scales are continuous likelihood scales. It is less of a problem when a clear neutral point is identified and responses above or below clearly indicate degree of agreement or disagreement. This is easier to interpret in terms of the percentage of population endorsing a misconception. Overall, in many cases, the results are subject to varying interpretations regarding the issue of appropriate cut-off points. Generally, the variation in the specific questions asked and the way in which these are asked and reported makes comparisons between studies difficult.

It is important to note that the lack of contextualization for the questions of the bulk of surveys regarding false confessions is a serious limitation. One Canadian study[4] is an exception, but it investigated only perceptions of appropriateness, not perceptions of the likelihood that the tactics might elicit a false confession. Yet, there is every reason to believe that expectations regarding the likelihood, and perhaps causes, of a false confession will be different depending upon the nature of the crime. Do we expect that a person will be as likely to falsely confess to burglary as to raping and murdering his own mother or child? Do we expect minimization to have equivalent impact when the charge is murder versus petty theft? As things currently stand, we have no idea about what kinds of crimes participants were contemplating when they responded to the bulk of surveys and how their answers might vary across crime types.

2.3.2. Mock Jury Studies: Strengths and Weaknesses

For the mock jury studies, participants are presented with case summaries in which characteristics of the defendant or the interrogation are varied and the mock juror's reactions are assessed. The intent is to assess whether the mock jurors react to the variations in the way interrogation science suggests that they should. That is, for example, do mock jurors adjust their judgments of the coerciveness of an interrogation or the voluntariness or validity of a confession according to the nature of interrogation tactics during the interrogation or any vulnerabilities of the suspect?

The mock jury studies generally entail confinement to one (or few) case scenario(s). As a result, the mock jury studies have a problem similar to that of the surveys. That is, it can be unclear whether, in another case context, the variables of interest would exert similar effects. Some mock jury studies have revealed such interactions between case characteristics (for example, evidence

---

[4] Victoria Hall, Joseph Eastwood and Kimberley A. Clow, "An Exploration of Laypeople's Perceptions of Confession Evidence and Interrogation Tactics", in *Canadian Journal of Behavioural Science*, 2020, vol. 52, no. 4, pp. 299–313.

strength) and the impact of interrogation or suspect characteristics on relevant judgments. Additionally, some mock jury studies include arguments or information concerning the impact of some of the variables studied, such as when an attorney's argument or an expert testimony is included (sometimes across all conditions). Therefore, the results cannot be taken as indicating how jurors will adjust their judgments based on the manipulated variable alone.

Nevertheless, together, these two classes of studies provide a picture of how jurors' beliefs might affect them as they judge confessions and the interrogations that elicited them. As we shortly review, at least three general classes of mistaken assumptions or missing knowledge appear to underlie many mistaken beliefs identified by these studies. First, understanding of the nature of interrogation tactics, the degree of manipulation and deception involved and their persuasive impact is poor. Second, observers tend to evaluate the decision to confess in rational terms, and therefore find it implausible that a person would decide to confess when it seems so clearly against their self-interest. They fail to understand that the very point (and stated goal) of interrogations in many countries like the United States of America ('US') is to convince a suspect that a confession will actually be in their self-interest.[5] Third, observers cannot imagine circumstances in which they would themselves falsely confess, and therefore cannot readily imagine that others would do so either. This belief that, 'I would never falsely confess' is both widespread and predictive of verdicts.[6]

Keeping these issues in mind, below we review what is known about juror understanding of the existence and risk factors for false confessions. Regarding

---

[5] See also Chapters 6 and 12 of this book regarding the Méndez Principles and non-coercive interview techniques.

[6] John W. Clark, Marcus T. Boccaccini and Darrel Turner, "Attitudes Toward Coerced Confessions: Psychometric Properties of New and Existing Measures in Jury Pool Samples", in *Southwest Journal of Criminal Justice*, 2010, vol. 6, no. 3, pp. 185–203; Mark Costanzo, Netta Shaked-Schroer and Katherine Vinson, "Juror Beliefs About Police Interrogations, False Confessions, and Expert Testimony", in *Journal of Empirical Legal Studies*, 2010, vol. 7, no. 2, pp. 231–247; Linda A. Henkel, Kimberly A.J. Coffman and Elizabeth M. Dailey, "A Survey of People's Attitudes and Beliefs About False Confessions", in *Behavioral Sciences & the Law*, 2008, vol. 26, no. 5, pp. 555–584; Allyson J. Horgan, Melissa B. Russano, Christian A. Meissner and Jacqueline R. Evans, "Minimization and Maximization Techniques: Assessing the Perceived Consequences of Confessing and Confession Diagnosticity", in *Psychology, Crime & Law*, 2012, vol. 18, no. 1, pp. 65–78; Angela M. Jones and Steven Penrod, "Can Expert Testimony Sensitize Jurors to Coercive Interrogation Tactics?", in *Journal of Forensic Psychology Practice*, 2016, vol. 16, no. 5, pp. 393–409; William D. Woody and Krista D. Forrest, "Effects of False-Evidence Ploys and Expert Testimony on Jurors' Verdicts, Recommended Sentences, and Perceptions of Confession Evidence", in *Behavioral Sciences & the Law*, 2009, vol. 27, no. 3, pp. 333–360.

each issue, we discuss findings from both survey and mock jury research. In this context, we address some remaining questions for future research.

The bulk of research on this topic has been conducted with participants from the US. Studies that are conducted in other countries are clearly identified below, and all others should be assumed as from the US.

2.4. Survey Studies

2.4.1. What Interrogation Tactics Are Used, and Are These Permissible, Appropriate or Coercive?

Surveys have addressed four issues regarding police tactics *other than* their tendency to elicit true and false confessions: (i) what tactics the police use in interrogation; (ii) what tactics are legally permissible; (iii) the appropriateness of those tactics; and (iv) their coerciveness.

2.4.2. What Tactics Do Interrogators Use?

Surveys have generally asked participants to rate the likelihood that police would use various tactics. This method is, of course, reactive in the sense that participants may have had no thoughts about these tactics until these are presented in the survey and the participants must provide a response. Therefore, we cannot know from these surveys whether there is general awareness of the use of various tactics. However, the surveys do, at a minimum, indicate what laypersons view as the most likely used among the tactics presented.

For example, Henkel and colleagues[7] asked participants to indicate the likelihood that police would use various tactics. Indicating a mostly correct understanding of what interrogation tactics are used, tactics with mean ratings around 6–7 on a 7-point scale included subjecting the suspect to lengthy interrogations of several hours or more; promising more lenient treatment contingent on a confession; pretending to befriend the suspect; threatening with more severe consequences in the absence of a confession; repeated statements of confidence in the suspect's guilt; depriving suspects of social contact and support; and falsely claiming evidence against the suspect. Deprivation of food, water or sleep were rated close to the midpoint of the scale. When asked specifically about whether the police lie about evidence, most agreed that they do (mean rating of roughly 5 on a 7-point scale) though most viewed this as unacceptable (2 on a 7-point scale).

Similarly, Mindthoff and colleagues had participants rate the likelihood that police would use seven interrogation tactics.[8] All tactics were rated above

---

[7]   Henkel, Coffman and Dailey, 2008, pp. 555–584, see *supra* note 6.

[8]   Amelia Mindthoff *et al.*, "A Survey of Potential Jurors' Perceptions of Interrogations and Confessions", in *Psychology, Public Policy, and Law*, 2018, vol. 24, no. 4, pp. 430–448.

the midpoint of the scale except threats or use of physical harm. Categorizing participants based on those that rated the tactics as 4–5 on a 5-point scale, the authors found that few participants believed that the police use threats or actual physical harm (14 per cent) and relatively few believed the police use rapport-building (56 per cent) or false evidence (42 per cent). The most commonly believed tactics were confrontation with evidence of guilt (83 per cent), bluffs about evidence (78 per cent), promises of leniency (74 per cent), and rejecting suspect denials (64 per cent). The authors also found that participants believed interrogations generally last more than eight hours, which is needed to elicit the confession. In 2009, Leo and Liu[9] found the estimated length to be 4.09 hours and on average that 7.63 hours should be permitted. This is concerning in that these numbers exceed the maximum four hours recommended by interrogation scholars[10] (and now even by Reid & Associates).[11] The police report that the average interrogation lasts about 1.6 hours and the average longest reported interrogation was 4.95 hours.[12]

2.4.3. Perceptions of Permissibility

Only a few studies have addressed lay understanding of the legality of various interrogation tactics. Among the most important of the issues addressed is that of perceptions of the permissibility and use of lying. Studies have indicated that roughly 60 per cent or more of participants believe that the police are *not* allowed to lie to suspects.[13] Yet, despite this, courts in the US have upheld police

---

[9] Richard A. Leo and Brittany Liu, "What Do Potential Jurors Know about Police Interrogation Techniques and False Confessions?", in *Behavioral Sciences & the Law*, 2009, vol. 27, no. 3, pp. 381–399.

[10] Saul M. Kassin *et al.*, "Police Interviewing and Interrogation: A Self-Report Survey of Police Practices and Beliefs", in *Law and Human Behavior*, 2007, vol. 31, no. 4, pp. 381–400.

[11] Reid & Associates is the largest and leading police interrogation training firm in the US. The Reid interrogation training manual is considered the bible of American police interrogation training (see Richard A. Leo, *Police Interrogation and American Justice*, Harvard University Press, Cambridge, 2008).

[12] Kassin *et al.*, 2007, pp. 381–400, see *supra* note 10.

[13] Danielle E. Chojnacki, Michael D. Cicchini and Lawrence T. White, "An Empirical Basis for the Admission of Expert Testimony on False Confessions", in *Arizona State Law Journal*, 2008, vol. 40, no. 1, pp. 1–45; Henkel, Coffman and Dailey, 2008, pp. 555–584, see *supra* note 6; Richard Rogers, "Getting It Wrong About Miranda Rights: False Beliefs, Impaired Reasoning, and Professional Neglect", in *American Psychologist*, 2011, vol. 66, no. 8, pp. 728–736; Hayley M.D. Cleary and Todd C. Warner, "Parents' Knowledge and Attitudes About Youths' Interrogation Rights", in *Psychology, Crime & Law*, 2017, vol. 23, no. 8, pp. 777–793; Jennifer L. Woolard, Hayley M.D. Cleary, Samantha A.S. Harvell and Rusan Chen, "Examining Adolescents' and Their Parents' Conceptual and Practical Knowledge of Police Interrogation: A Family Dyad Approach", in *Journal of Youth and Adolescence*, 2008, vol. 37, no. 6, pp. 685–698.

tactics involving lying or deception, including about evidence.[14] Some interrogation manuals[15] used in the US and some other countries encourage police to misrepresent evidence as an effective way to elicit confessions, and 92 per cent of the police report[16] that they sometimes lie about evidence. Moreover, such lies have been shown to increase the risk of false confessions in laboratory studies and have played a prominent role in interrogations of proven false confessors. As we shortly show, lay respondents consider such tactics to risk false confessions and to be inappropriate. But if they also believe that these are not permitted or used, this may contribute to failure to recognize false confessions in practice.

The perceived permissibility of other individual tactics has been less widely addressed. However, Chojnacki, Cicchini and White did study other misconceptions concerning the permissibility of interrogation tactics.[17] In their study, 56 per cent believed that the police cannot cut off suspect denials, 45 per cent believed that the police cannot downplay the significance of a crime, 59 per cent believed that the police cannot use rude or insulting remarks and 43 per cent believed that it is permissible to threaten harsher punishment if the suspect does not confess. Otherwise, participants were generally informed concerning the permissibility of such tactics as deprivation of food, water or sleep, minimization, implications of leniency and others. Highly educated and white respondents were more likely to be correct regarding these issues of legality. Eighty per cent agreed that expert testimony would be helpful in cases involving disputed confessions.

2.4.4. Perceived Appropriateness

Costanzo and colleagues[18] asked American participants across a number of jurisdictions to rate their agreement that the police *should be* allowed to use various tactics. They found all tactics were rated below the midpoint of the scale, including various forms of lying about evidence and promises and threats regarding consequences of confession (though promises of leniency were viewed as most acceptable at 4.3 on a 10-point scale).

As noted earlier, the majority of surveys addressing interrogation and confession were conducted with American participants. However, in an early

---

[14] For a review, see Laurie Magid, "Deceptive Police Interrogation Practices: How Far is Too Far?", in *Michigan Law Review*, 2001, vol. 99, no. 5, pp. 1168–1210.

[15] See, for example, Fred E. Inbau, John E. Reid, Joseph P. Buckley and Brian C. Jayne, *Criminal Interrogations and Confessions*, 5th ed., Jones & Bartlett Learning, Burlington, 2013.

[16] Saul M. Kassin *et al.*, 2007, pp. 381–400, see *supra* note 10.

[17] Chojnacki, Cicchini and White, 2008, pp. 1–45, see *supra* note 13.

[18] Costanzo, Shaked-Schroer and Vinson, 2010, pp. 231–247, see *supra* note 6.

study, Moston and Fisher[19] questioned Australian students regarding the coerciveness and acceptability of 13 interrogation tactics. For this purpose, the students read a case summary involving a sexual abuse suspect that included a full interrogation transcript incorporating the common tactics. The interrogation resulted either in no confession, invocation of the right to silence, partial admissions or a full confession, though this manipulation had no effect on the ratings. Tactics rated as acceptable by 80 per cent or more participants included non-accusatory questioning, rapport-building or sympathy, interrogator silence and pointing out contradictions in the suspect's story and the advantages of confession. Among the participants, 60 to 72 per cent found directly challenging the suspect, emphasizing the futility of denial and pointing to social advantages of confession acceptable. Claiming to know the suspect was deceptive, minimization and claiming certainty of suspect guilt were viewed as acceptable by only 39–44 per cent of participants.

A second non-US study conducted in Canada[20] inquired about the perceived appropriateness of 18 police tactics on 7-point scales with the midpoint marked as neutral. Only a few tactics were rated above the midpoint (appeal to pride, offers to help and pointing out consequences). The remaining tactics did not fully overlap with those of the other studies reviewed here. However, those most commonly rated as 'very *in*appropriate' were physical abuse, excessive force and denigrating the suspect (such as leaving him naked: 59–68 per cent). Others were rated as inappropriate by a substantial minority, including depriving the suspect, interrogating suspects in an altered (for example, drunk) or vulnerable state (for example, sleep deprived) and lying about evidence (31–41 per cent). Other tactics shown to be associated with the risk of false confessions were not commonly viewed as inappropriate, such as lengthy interrogation (12.5 per cent), exaggerating seriousness (13.2 per cent), normalizing the crime or minimizing suspect guilt (7 per cent and 6 percent respectively), offering help (2.5 per cent) or pointing out consequences (3.1 per cent).

The authors followed up with a study[21] in which the type of interrogation tactic (physical versus psychological), severity of the crime and the strength of evidence were varied, and the perceived appropriateness of interrogation tactics was assessed. Severe crimes included sexual assault and murder and less severe crimes ranged from breaking and entering to vandalism. Severe tactics included repeated punching or excessive force (such as the repeated use of tasers).

---

[19] Stephen Moston and Megan Fisher, "Perceptions of Coercion in the Questioning of Criminal Suspects", in *Journal of Investigative Psychology and Offender Profiling*, 2007, vol. 4, no. 2, pp. 85–95.

[20] Hall, Eastwood and Clow, 2020, see *supra* note 4.

[21] *Ibid.*

Psychological tactics included 'normalization' and 'minimization'. [22] As expected, physical tactics were rated as less appropriate than psychological tactics, and tactics were rated as more appropriate when evidence was weak than when strong. But there was no main effect of crime severity. There was, however, an interaction of tactics and crime severity: such that severe tactics were rated as more appropriate for severe crimes, but crime severity did not affect the perceived appropriateness of psychological tactics. Further, the tactics also interacted with evidence strength. When evidence was weak, physical tactics were rated as less appropriate than when evidence was strong. The opposite was found for psychological tactics.

In a third study, [23] the authors added a fourth variable to those of their second study, varying the outcome of the interrogation – that is, whether a confession was obtained or not. Overall, as expected, tactics were rated as more appropriate if a confession was obtained. Again, severe tactics were rated as more appropriate when crimes were severe, but this time the opposite was true for psychological tactics. The tactics did not interact as expected with evidence strength. Another study illustrated that varied evidence strength, high-pressure interrogations were, however, viewed as less coercive when evidence corroborated the confession. [24]

These latter studies are largely unique among those designed to assess basic attitudes and beliefs about false confessions in that these did situate the ratings in case contexts. As one might expect, these pointed to the variability in attitudes and beliefs one might expect between case contexts and the limited applicability of the numbers obtained in most surveys.

2.4.5. Perceived Coerciveness

Several studies asked participants to rate interrogations according to their coerciveness and separately according to the likelihood that these would elicit true and false confessions. These judgments are related, though here we report them separately. Participants in the aforementioned recent study by Mindthoff and colleagues[25] were asked to rate the degree of coerciveness of seven interrogation tactics, as well as the likelihood that the use of each tactic would result in a true

---

[22] 'Normalization' refers to statements made to the suspect to the effect that what he or she has done is normal or is also done by others to make it seem less reprehensible. 'Minimization' refers to suggesting scenarios as to how or why the crime was committed so as to minimize its psychological, moral or legal seriousness.

[23] Hall, Eastwood and Clow, 2020, see *supra* note 4.

[24] Netta Shaked-Schroer, Mark Costanzo and Dale E. Berger, "Overlooking Coerciveness: The Impact of Interrogation Techniques and Guilt Corroboration on Jurors' Judgments of Coerciveness", in *Legal and Criminological Psychology*, 2015, vol. 20, no. 1, pp. 68–80.

[25] Mindthoff *et al.*, 2018, pp. 430–448, see *supra* note 8.

or false confession. Notably, the authors did not include threats of harsher punishment, length of interrogation, specific methods of implied leniency (such as minimization) and other common tactics. Coerciveness was defined for participants as: "tend[ing] to remove an individual's perception of their freedom to make a meaningful choice [...] the less a suspect feels s/he has a choice as to whether or not to do what is being asked the more coercive and interrogation method is".[26]

Mean ratings of all tactics except rapport-building (2.84 on a 5-point scale) were above the midpoint of the scale, ranging from 3.08 to 3.91 on a 5-point scale (though only the endpoints were labeled as: 'not at all' versus 'extremely coercive'). Authors also reported the percentage of respondents who rated the tactic as a 4 or 5 on a 5-point scale. Tactics rated by the fewest participants as highly coercive were rapport-building (34 per cent), confronting suspects with true evidence of guilt (47 per cent) and rejecting suspect denials (53 per cent). All others were rated as highly coercive by 64–69 per cent of participants. These included bluffs about evidence, use of false evidence, promises of leniency and threats and use of physical harm. Participants familiar with false confession cases rated only two tactics as more coercive than unfamiliar participants – promises of leniency and threatening or using physical harm.

Leo and Liu[27] and Blandón-Gitlin and colleagues[28] asked participants to rate a larger set of tactics on degree of coerciveness. All tactics were rated about the midpoint of the scale except asking the suspect to take a lie detector test or informing him or her truthfully of the results. Those receiving the highest ratings involved implicit or explicit threats of physical harm or actual physical harm (4.0–4.4 on a 5-point scale and 4.2–4.6 on a 5-point scale in the two studies respectively) and confronting the suspect with false DNA, camera or fingerprint evidence (4.0–4.2 on a 5-point scale and 4.0–4.4 on a 5-point scale respectively), followed by repeated accusations, claims that the suspects' alibi is false and cutting off claims of innocence (3.3–3.4 on a 5-point scale and 3.1–3.2 on a 5-point scale respectively) and explicit and implicit promises of lesser charges or sentences for confession (3.4–3.6 on a 5-point scale and 3.2–3.5 respectively). Strangely, these authors did not address threats of harsher charges or punishment.

---

[26] *Ibid.*, Supplemental Materials, p. 4.

[27] Leo and Liu, 2009, see *supra* note 9.

[28] Iris Blandón-Gitlin, Katheryn Sperry and Richard A. Leo, "Jurors Believe Interrogation Tactics Are Not Likely to Elicit False Confessions: Will Expert Witness Testimony Inform Them Otherwise?", in *Psychology, Crime & Law*, 2011, vol. 17, no. 3, pp. 239–260.

Finally, a study by Kaplan and colleagues[29] compared views of the coerciveness of interrogation tactics between a sample of jury-eligible Canadian adults and expert scholars on interrogation and confession. Overall, the laypersons gave lower ratings to the coerciveness of interrogation techniques and to the vulnerabilities posed by various suspect risk factors than the social science experts. The authors further grouped interrogation tactics into groups of 14 prohibited tactics, 11 maximization techniques and 9 minimization techniques.

Prohibited tactics included failure to inform the suspect of (or grant) his or her rights, physical harm, various forms of explicit threats and promises regarding legal consequences, other forms of exchange of benefits for confession, refusal to let suspects leave without rendering a confession, denial of necessities such as food or water and threats to third parties.

Maximization and minimization tactics were defined, as in Kassin and McNall,[30] as:

> a technique in which the interrogator exaggerates the strength of the evidence and the magnitude of the charges, and minimization tactics as those in which the interrogator mitigates the crime and plays down the seriousness of the offense.

Maximization tactics included lying or bluffing about evidence, claiming a failed polygraph test, overstating the reliability of incriminating evidence, the seriousness of the crime, likely conviction or the likely severity of sentencing, and using graphic photos. On the other hand, minimization tactics included expressing sympathy and misrepresenting the interrogators' role as an advocate for the suspect, implying that more favorable legal outcomes can be negotiated, 'theme development', suggesting the suspect can 'help himself out' by confessing and so on.[31] Experts rated all categories as more coercive than laypersons, and both laypersons and experts viewed prohibited and maximization tactics as more coercive than minimization tactics.

2.4.6. Do False Confessions Occur, and If So, Why?

Chief among the beliefs that impede understanding of the potential for false confessions is the conviction that false confessions simply do not occur. Though this is not a belief among the majority of laypersons, Henkel, Coffman and

---

[29] Jeffrey Kaplan *et al.*, "Perceptions of Coercion in Interrogation: Comparing Expert and Lay Opinions", in *Psychology, Crime & Law*, 2020, vol. 26, no. 4, pp. 384–401.

[30] Saul M. Kassin and Karlyn McNall, "Police Interrogations and Confessions: Communicating Promises and Threats by Pragmatic Implication", in *Law and Human Behavior*, 1991, vol. 15, no. 3, p. 233.

[31] Inbau, Reid, Buckley and Jayne, 2013, see *supra* note 15.

Daily[32] found that a substantial minority of 32 per cent held this belief, and further found that 46 per cent believed physical torture was the most likely path to false confession, followed by confession to receive a lesser charge (18 per cent), confession to cover for someone else (18 per cent), confusion and a belief that he or she might actually be guilty (9 per cent), overall stress of the interrogation (7 per cent), and need for notoriety (1 per cent). In contrast, Chojnacki, Cicchini and White[33] found that only 6 per cent believed that innocent suspects would never confess, whereas most believed they would do so only after strenuous pressure. Notably, in the Henkel *et al.* study, participants rated the likelihood that they personally would falsely confess in various circumstances as 2.4 or less on a 5-point scale, except when subjected to physical torture.

In another study, researchers[34] presented participants with a case example and then asked both general and case-specific questions. They also varied the outcome of the case. Participants were asked the extent to which they agreed with the statement 'No one would ever confess to a crime s/he did not commit'. Rated agreement was approximately at the midpoint of the scale across outcome conditions. The authors did not report the percentage of persons who responded at the extremes of the 6-point scales, yet it is clear from the mean rating that many persons believe that suspects do not falsely confess. Participants also responded to the statements 'Some suspects may be too stressed to offer a reliable confession' and 'A suspect might confess to a crime just to end the police interrogation'. These ratings were all approximately 4.5 on a 6-point scale, indicating greater agreement that false confessions can occur than that they cannot.

Almost no attention has been given in surveys to the issue of how the perceived likelihood of false confessions might vary for different crimes, with the exception of the study by Costanzo and colleagues.[35] The authors asked what percentage of confessions were false for four crime categories, finding little difference between them – the highest mean was for theft (24 per cent), followed by rape and murder (22–23 per cent) and child molestation (20 per cent).

Though surveys of lay beliefs about false confessions have spanned only a period of approximately 10 years, there is reason to expect that beliefs regarding false confessions might have changed over time, as the result of increasingly widespread media coverage of false confessions and of the increasing tide of exonerations involving false confessions. Reflecting this concern, a recent large-

---

[32] Henkel, Coffman and Dailey, 2008, pp. 555–584, see *supra* note 6.

[33] Chojnacki, Cicchini and White, 2008, pp. 1–45, see *supra* note 13.

[34] David T. Wasieleski, Mark A. Whatley and Shannon Murphy, "The Hindsight Bias and Attitudes Toward Police Deception in Eliciting Confessions", in *North American Journal of Psychology*, 2009, vol. 11, no. 2, pp. 285–296.

[35] Costanzo, Shaked-Schroer and Vinson, 2010, pp. 231–247, see *supra* note 6.

scale survey was conducted by Mindthoff et al.,[36] including 768 students from 11 universities and 200 'MTurk'[37] participants. The survey included an extensive set of questions regarding false confessions and their causes, as well as an index of exposure to media accounts of false confession cases. Most questions were asked using either likelihood or degree of agreement rating scales.

Because for many issues most participants endorsed correct answers, the authors interpreted their results as indicating widespread understanding of issues relating to false confessions. However, it is important to note that on many issues large minorities did endorse misconceptions. For example, only 63 per cent agreed that suspects might confess to crimes they did not commit; 27 per cent agreed that the only reasons for false confessions were mental illness and torture; and participants estimated that 30 per cent of interrogated innocent suspects will falsely confess. These findings are not much different from those of Henkel and colleagues roughly ten years earlier.[38]

On the other hand, the sample estimated the percentage of all interrogated innocent persons who falsely confess to be 30.25 per cent – a rather large endorsement of the idea that false confessions do occur. Moreover, 63 per cent agreed that others might falsely confess, but only 14 per cent stated that they themselves might do so. More than half of the respondents indicated that others might falsely confess to protect others (86 per cent) or because of pressure or manipulation by the police (61 per cent), but less than half as many indicated that they might do so themselves for such reasons. Regarding changes in perceptions of these issues due to exposure to media accounts of false confessions, participants who recounted more exposure to media accounts were more likely to agree that suspects might falsely confess, and that they might do so for each reason listed – though these differences were very small in magnitude.

2.4.7. What Does a Confession Indicate About Guilt?

As a related way to understand perceptions of the potential that a confession can be false, several surveys asked questions assessing respondents' perceptions of the strength with which a confession indicates guilt. Not surprisingly most respondents felt confessions were highly indicative of guilt. Henkel and colleagues,[39] for example, found that 64 per cent of participants agreed that a confession was a strong indicator of guilt, and that 50 per cent of them agreed that

---

[36] Mindthoff et al., 2018, pp. 430–448, see *supra* note 8.
[37] 'MTurk' is a platform hosted by Amazon for researchers to recruit participants and use online surveys to collect data. See, for example, Michael Buhrmester, Tracy Kwang and Samuel D. Gosling, "Amazon's Mechanical Turk: A New Source of Inexpensive, Yet High-Quality Data?", in *Perspectives on Psychological Science*, 2016, vol. 6, no. 1, pp. 3–5.
[38] Henkel, Coffman and Dailey, 2008, pp. 555–584, see *supra* note 6.
[39] *Ibid.*

if a person confesses they are probably guilty (whereas in the Mindthoff *et al.* survey, 58 per cent of participants agreed). Interestingly, only 7 per cent indicated that a person who signed a written confession in interrogation is definitely guilty (and 59 per cent believed that he is probably guilty).

2.4.8. What Interrogation Tactics Lead to False Confessions?

Most directly related to the issue of lay understanding of how interrogations might induce false confessions, several surveys asked respondents to rate the likelihood that specific tactics would elicit a false confession *if the suspect were innocent.*

Using such a rating scale, both Leo and Liu[40] and Blandón-Gitlin *et al.*[41] reported means below the midpoint of the 5-point scale for all tactics except those involving threats or actual physical harm, and these ranged from 2.9–3.7 and 2.8–3.4, respectively. Among the remaining tactics, lying about DNA, lie detector results, camera evidence and fingerprints received the highest ratings (2.7–2.9). Ratings of tactics involving repetition and implied or explicit promises of leniency ranged from 2.3–2.4.

The authors also reported the percentage of respondents who rated the risk posed by these factors above the scale midpoint. Only actual physical assault rose at or above 50 per cent for this index (61 per cent and 50 per cent for the two studies respectively). Other tactics rated as most likely to elicit a false confession included the various forms of false evidence (25–34 per cent and 20–29 per cent respectively, except for false fingerprint evidence (9.5 per cent)) and explicit and implicit promises of leniency in charges or sentencing (17–19 per cent and 15–19 per cent respectively).

For the risk of false confessions, Mindthoff and colleagues[42] also reported the percentage of participants who rated the tactic as above the midpoint as those who agreed the tactic was likely to induce a false confession. Tactics rated as likely to result in a false confession by the most participants were threatening or using physical harm (68 per cent), confronting suspects with false evidence (63 per cent), bluffing about evidence (58 per cent), promises of leniency (54 per cent), and rejecting suspect denials (53 per cent): and mean ratings of likelihood were above the midpoint for all of these. Confrontation with true evidence of guilt (21 per cent) and rapport-building (23 per cent) were viewed as likely cause false confession only by a minority, and mean ratings of likelihood for these were below the midpoint. Repeated accusations and cutting off denials were least commonly considered likely to result in a false confession (16–19 per cent).

---

[40]   Leo and Liu, 2009, see *supra* note 9.

[41]   Blandón-Gitlin, Sperry and Leo, 2011, pp. 239–260, see *supra* note 28.

[42]   Mindthoff *et al.*, 2018, pp. 430–448, see *supra* note 8.

Only use of false evidence, evidence bluffs and threatening or using harm were rated as more likely to cause false confessions by participants familiar with false confession cases than those who were unfamiliar. Thus, again, there was only mixed support for the impact of media depictions of false confessions.

False evidence ploys ('FEPs') were the focus of a study by Forrest and colleagues.[43] The authors of this study investigated the extent to which demeanor (claims that the suspect's behaviour indicated deception), testimonial (false claims of witnesses against the suspect) and scientific (claims of forensic evidence such as DNA) FEPs were regarded as deceptive and coercive. Participants were also told either that these ploys contribute to true confessions or that they contribute to false confessions. Across all ploys, participants rated them as moderately deceptive (5.2 on a 10-point scale) and moderately coercive (5.63 on a 10-point scale). All types of ploys were rated as coercive, but testimonial ploys were rated as more coercive than demeanor ploys. Unexpectedly, scientific ploys were not viewed as the most deceptive or coercive. Those who had read that FEPs contribute to false confessions viewed these as more deceptive, but not as coercive. There were also a number of significant differences between specific ploys within each type.

Finally, Horgan *et al.*[44] situated minimization or maximization tactics in the case context of the cheating paradigm for laboratory studies of false confessions[45] and manipulated whether the techniques used in the scenario did or did not imply consequences resulting from confession versus denial. Both minimization (for example, face-saving excuses versus appeals to conscience) and maximization techniques (for example, exaggerating consequences versus unfriendly demeanor) were included in each consequence condition. After reading the case scenarios, participants were asked to indicate the likelihood that they would personally confess and that the student in the scenario would do so. The participants believed that other innocent suspects were more likely to falsely confess in response to techniques implying consequences than those not implying consequences, but this was not true for themselves. Moreover, the overall perceived likelihood that others would falsely confess was much greater than participants' reported likelihood that they would do so themselves. Nevertheless,

---

[43] Krista D. Forrest *et al.*, "False-Evidence Ploys and Interrogations: Mock Jurors' Perceptions of False-Evidence Ploy Type, Deception, Coercion, and Justification", in *Behavioral Sciences & the Law*, 2012, vol. 30, no. 3, pp. 342–364.

[44] Horgan, Russano, Meissner and Evans, 2012, pp. 65–78, see *supra* note 6.

[45] Melissa B. Russano, Christian A. Meissner, Fadia M. Narchet and Saul M. Kassin, "Investigating True and False Confessions Within a Novel Experimental Paradigm", in *Psychological Science*, 2005, vol. 16, no. 6, pp. 481–486.

when subjected to an actual interrogation themselves (in Study 2)[46] innocent subjects were twice as likely to confess when interrogation techniques implied consequences than when they did not (42 per cent versus 21 per cent).

2.4.9. When Should a Confession Be Suppressed?

An indirect way to assess whether respondents recognize that a tactic might cause a false confession is to ask if they think a confession should be allowed into trial evidence when such a tactic was used to elicit it. Taking this approach, Mindthoff et al.[47] asked participants about circumstances in which a recanted confession should or should not be allowed as evidence for the jury. They did not, however, put this in any context of explaining criteria for admissibility. Only failure to read *Miranda* rights, denial of a request for an attorney, denial of food or water, and physical assault were viewed as grounds for suppression by 64–65 per cent of participants. Threatening and intimidation were viewed as such by a small majority (54 per cent). But none of the other previously studied seven tactics (see above) was viewed as grounds for suppression by a majority (implied and explicit promises of leniency were viewed as such by roughly only a third of participants).

Asking similar questions, Henkel et al.[48] found that 60 per cent or more agreed that a confession should be suppressed if obtained through torture, if the person was not read his or her rights, if food or water were denied or if interrogators lied about physical evidence. Additionally, 52 per cent agreed that it should be suppressed if the police threatened or intimidated but did not harm the suspect, and 45 per cent believed that it should be suppressed if the suspect is questioned for more than 10 hours.

While it is encouraging that jurors suggest that coercive techniques should lead the confession to be suppressed, mock jury research indicates that this does not always translate into judgment of the confession itself. Even judges tend to find confessors guilty despite recognizing that the interrogation methods were coercive.[49]

2.4.10. Vulnerability to False Confessions

Some of the most well-established findings among interrogation studies concern the enhanced susceptibility of several vulnerable populations to false

---

46 *Ibid.*
47 Mindthoff et al., 2018, pp. 430–448, see *supra* note 8.
48 Henkel, Coffman and Dailey, 2008, pp. 555–584, see *supra* note 6.
49 D. Brian Wallace and Saul M. Kassin, "Harmless Error Analysis: How Do Judges Respond to Confession Errors?", in *Law and Human Behavior*, 2012, vol. 36, no. 2, pp. 151–157.

confessions, including the young,[50] those with low IQ or a mental disability or mental illness, and many others.[51] Other research has identified acute vulnerabilities posed by the physical or mental state of the suspect at the time of interrogation.[52] Still others have pointed to the importance of minority status[53] or type of accusation.[54] Accordingly, many surveys have assessed lay awareness of these vulnerabilities, though the latter two remain unaddressed in surveys.

One study[55] surveyed law enforcement officers regarding developmental issues and interrogation practices with children aged under 14 years, children aged 14–17 years, and adults aged 18 years and older. The authors concluded that while some officers do recognize some relevant developmental differences between children and adults (such as immaturity of judgment, less competent decision-making, suggestibility, lack of an awareness of long-term consequences, temporal discounting and impulsivity), they did not apply this knowledge to the interrogation situation. They generally believed that children can be treated similarly to adults in interrogations and reported that they used similar interrogation tactics for both. Interestingly, more highly ranked or experienced officers tended to believe more strongly that suspects understand their rights and the intent of interrogation, and less strongly believe that interrogation tactics can lead to false memories or false confessions. Overall, the police believed that they elicited false confessions from about 10 per cent of suspects.

[50] Drizin and Leo, 2004, pp. 891–1007, see *supra* note 2; Jessica Owen-Kostelnik, Nicholas D. Reppucci and Jessica Meyer, "Testimony and Interrogation of Minors: Assumptions About Maturity and Morality", in *American Psychologist*, 2006, vol. 61, no. 4, pp. 286–304.

[51] For a review, see Gisli H. Gudjonsson, *The Psychology of False Confessions: Forty Years of Science and Practice*, John Wiley and Sons, Chichester, 2018; Saul M. Kassin *et al.*, "Police-Induced Confessions, Risk Factors, and Recommendations: Looking Ahead", in *Law and Human Behavior*, 2010, vol. 34, no. 1, pp. 49–52; see also Chapter 3 of this book.

[52] For a review, see Davis and Leo, 2012a, see *supra* note 3; Davis and Leo, 2012b, see *supra* note 3; Davis and Leo, 2012c, see *supra* note 3.

[53] Davis and Leo, 2012b, see *supra* note 3; Cynthia J. Najdowski and Bette L. Bottoms, "Understanding Jurors' Judgments un Cases Involving Juvenile Defendants: Effects of Confession Evidence and Intellectual Disability", in *Psychology, Public Policy, and Law*, 2012, vol. 18, no. 2, pp. 297–337; J. Guillermo Villalobos and Deborah Davis, "Interrogation and the Minority Suspect: Pathways to True and False Confession", in Monica K. Miller and Brian H. Bornstein (eds.), *Advances in psychology and law*, vol. 1, Springer International Publishing, Bern, 2016, pp. 1–41.

[54] Deborah Davis and Richard A. Leo, "When Exoneration Seems Hopeless: The Special Vulnerability of Sexual Abuse Suspects to False Confession", in Ros Burnett (ed.), *Wrongful Allegations of Sexual and Child Abuse*, Oxford University Press, 2016, pp. 175–190.

[55] Jessica R. Meyer and Nicholas D. Reppucci, "Police Practices and Perceptions Regarding Juvenile Interrogation and Interrogative Suggestibility", in *Behavioral Sciences & the Law*, 2007, vol. 25, no. 6, pp. 757–780.

Cleary and Warner and Woolard *et al.*[56] surveyed samples of parents regarding issues of interrogation with adolescents. Both studies revealed significant misunderstanding. Cleary and Warner, for example, found that parents answered less than half of the questions regarding interrogation practices correctly. Almost 80 per cent believed that the police cannot lie to suspects. Results of both studies also revealed significant misconceptions regarding the rights of adolescents, including rights to support and the notification and involvement of parents during questioning, among other issues.

Many authors have found that a substantial portion of laypersons do not understand the sources of individual vulnerability to false confessions. Chojnacki *et al.* found that many respondents were either uncertain or denied that children (57 per cent), the mentally impaired (46 per cent) or those who believe that they have faulty memories (74 per cent) are more vulnerable to interrogation-induced false confessions.[57] These authors had participants rate most questions on a 7-point likelihood scale and then combined 1 and 2 as 'Disagree', 3–5 as 'Somewhat Uncertain' and 6–7 as 'Agree'. The authors calculated an overall score for participants based on the agreement of their answers with the scientific findings on the topics. Younger persons who were highly educated and watched relatively little television obtained significantly higher scores.

Henkel and colleagues had participants rate the extent to which various vulnerabilities would contribute to a person falsely confessing, and found that mental illness was viewed as most likely to do so (5.5 on a 7-point scale), followed by being under 10 years of age (4.6), being suggestible or overly trusting (4.5), possessing a low IQ (4.5), being a teenager (4.0), and having a poor memory (3.5).[58] Mindthoff and colleagues asked participants to rate the extent to which various sources of vulnerability would contribute to a person falsely confessing to a crime.[59] As in the Henkel *et al.* study, participants most strongly endorsed mental illness (4.4 on a 5-point scale) as a source of vulnerability. This was followed by impairment due to illegal drugs, alcohol or powerful prescription drugs (4.2), poor memory of the time of the crime (3.8), sleep deprivation or low IQ (3.6), age under 18 years (3.5) or the influence of marijuana (3.4). Also as in the Henkel *et al.* study, two of the most well-documented vulnerabilities (low IQ and youth) were viewed as among the least likely to contribute to false confessions, though all contributing factors were rated fairly high.

[56] Cleary and Warner, 2017, pp. 777–793, see *supra* note 13; Woolard, Cleary, Harvell and Chen, 2008, pp. 685–698, see *supra* note 13.
[57] Chojnacki, Cicchini and White, 2008, pp. 1–45, see *supra* note 13.
[58] Henkel, Coffman and Dailey, 2008, pp. 555–584, see *supra* note 6.
[59] Mindthoff *et al.*, 2018, pp. 430–448, see *supra* note 8.

The previously mentioned study by Kaplan and colleagues, comparing Canadian laypersons to experts also addressed the issue of sources of personal vulnerability.[60] Laypersons gave generally high ratings (above the scale mid-point) for all sources, including youth, diagnosed or apparent mental illness, diagnosed or apparent intellectual disability, low IQ, sleep deprivation, injury, drug withdrawal, intoxication, poor understanding of English, previous interrogation for the same offense and being in custody. Overall, experts rated these vulnerabilities as posing more risk than did laypersons. This difference was significant for most individual items, with the exceptions of the appearance of mental illness, injury, intoxication, poor understanding of English, and being in custody or interrogated previously. Notably, for laypersons, youth was the lowest-rated source of vulnerability, other than previous interrogation and being in custody. For experts, youth ranked only behind intellectual disability. Also of importance, this study is the only one we encountered that inquired about the importance of language abilities (and by implication minority status). Yet, this is an important source of vulnerability in interrogation.[61]

One study specifically addressed perceptions of interrogations of intoxicated suspects.[62] The authors reported the percentage of respondents who agreed that it is permissible to obtain *Miranda* waivers from intoxicated suspects (26 per cent), to interrogate them (26 per cent), and to use confessions elicited from them in court (33 per cent). Many others did not know (33 per cent, 40 per cent and 51 per cent respectively). Thus, a strong majority possessed incorrect or incomplete knowledge regarding what is permitted with intoxicated suspects. When informed that these practices are permitted, participants were then asked if they should be. Most agreed that they should not (61 per cent, 67 per cent and 58 per cent respectively).

After being told that the above are indeed permissible, participants were asked to indicate what per cent of suspects who are interrogated are intoxicated (35 per cent), how much they would rely on a confession from an intoxicated suspect compared to sober suspects as evidence of guilt (72 per cent would rely more on a sober suspect), and whether intoxicated versus sober guilty and innocent suspects are more likely to confess (80 per cent intoxicated for guilty suspects; 69 per cent for innocent suspects). Participants also estimated less likelihood that they themselves would falsely confess than that others would do so.

---

[60] Kaplan *et al.*, 2020, pp. 384–401, see *supra* note 29.

[61] Susan Berk-Seligson, *Coerced Confessions: The Discourse of Bilingual Police Interrogations*, vol. 25, Walter de Gruyter, Berlin, 2009; Villalobos and Davis, 2016, pp. 1–41, see *supra* note 53.

[62] Amelia Mindthoff *et al.*, "Juror Perceptions of Intoxicated Suspects' Interrogation-Related Behaviors", in *Criminal Justice and Behavior*, 2020, vol. 47, no. 2, pp. 222–246.

Finally, participants also read a hypothetical case in which the suspect was described as having an intoxication level of 0.13 milliliters per 100 milliliters of blood and that this was above the legal intoxication limit of 0.08 milliliters per 100 milliliters of blood. They indicated whether the suspect could appropriately waive his rights (72 per cent stated that they could not do so) and rated the truthfulness of his confession (2.8 on a 5-point scale) and the degree to which the interrogation was more coercive for the intoxicated suspect compared to a sober suspect (3.6 on a 5-point scale).

Overall, then, survey participants were aware that some populations are more vulnerable to false confessions, though their views of which sources of vulnerability pose the most risk do not fully comport with the research literature or the views of experts. In particular, the vulnerability posed by youth (particularly teenagers as opposed to young children) tends to be underestimated.

2.4.11. Survey Studies: Limitations and Conclusions

Although the survey studies offer valuable information, there have been some important omissions. First is the issue of the lack of contextualization of the questions for almost all studies, as discussed earlier. This can be particularly important both because participants may have strong views concerning what suspects will and will not confess to, and because the nature of a case can contribute to vulnerability through a sense of hopelessness (or low self-efficacy for defense).[63]

Second, important sources of vulnerability are not addressed. For example, though it is clear that minority suspects can suffer disadvantage in interrogation,[64] suspects' race or ethnicity have not been addressed in survey studies, though they have been examined in some mock jury studies.

Third, the range of tactics addressed in the surveys has been quite limited in comparison to those incorporated into interrogation. Indeed, this is a limitation for mock jury studies as well. Moreover, the questions often refer to broad categories of tactics, as opposed to the different specific ways they are executed. The two Canadian surveys that investigated the broadest range of tactics concerned perceptions of appropriateness and coerciveness, and not potential to elicit false confessions.

Fourth, almost all surveys have addressed single tactics in isolation, and have not examined perceptions of the way in which they might combine to become more coercive, even exponentially more coercive. Those that have

---

63 Davis and Leo, 2016, pp. 175–190, see *supra* note 54.
64 For a review, see Villalobos and Davis, 2016, pp. 1–41, see *supra* note 53.

employed combined tactics have not compared the combination to individual tactics alone.

Fifth, several important issues related to jurors' ability to judge the validity of confessions have remained essentially unaddressed. For example, though a few studies asked participants whether they felt they could distinguish between true and false confessions, we found none that inquired as to what criteria laypersons believe distinguish between true and false confessions. Research has established that false confessions are more likely to be contradicted by case evidence.[65] However, survey questions did not address this or other criteria for distinguishing, including potentially erroneous criteria often caused by the interrogator that might be endorsed by laypersons (such as the inclusion of crime details, expressions of apology or remorse and others).

Finally, it is worth pointing out that, based on the surveys reviewed earlier, there is evidence that jurors do understand some things relevant to interrogation and confession and not others. This duality was reinforced in a recent survey by Alceste and colleagues[66] comparing opinions of laypersons to those of experts (as identified in a previous survey by Kassin and colleagues).[67] The authors asked participants to agree or disagree with 30 statements relevant to interrogation, false confessions and their causes. There were significant differences between experts and laypersons in the percentage of agreement for all but 10 of the 30 statements. The most agreement was found regarding vulnerable populations such as young children, the mentally ill and those with compliant personalities, and regarding lay and professional difficulties with accurate detection of deception. Participants also generally acknowledged the potential that confessions can be false and understood risks associated with harsh techniques such as torture or explicit threats of harm. However, there was much greater disagreement with experts regarding more subtle tactics such as use of false evidence or explicit and implicit promises of leniency (or minimization). Laypersons were also less aware of the vulnerability of juveniles and over-believed in the ability of *Miranda* rights to protect against false confessions. They also expressed considerable faith in the ability of training to improve lie detection abilities and in the diagnosticity of cues to deception soundly contraindicated by research. As a final note, it is important to recognize that this study is the only study dealing

---

[65] See for example: Leo and Ofshe, 1998, pp. 429–496, see *supra* note 2.

[66] Fabiana Alceste *et al.*, "The Psychology of Confessions: A Comparison of Expert and Lay Opinions", in *Applied Cognitive Psychology*, 2020, vol. 35, no. 1, pp. 39–51.

[67] Saul M. Kassin, Allison D. Redlich, Fabiana Alceste and Timothy J. Luke, "On the General Acceptance of Confessions Research: Opinions of the Scientific Community", in *American Psychologist*, 2018, vol. 73, no. 1, pp. 63–80.

with a variety of issues regarding false confessions that compared expert and lay opinions using the same questions and rating scales.

2.5. Mock Jury Studies

2.5.1. Effects of Interrogation Tactics

Mock jury research has yielded a mix of findings regarding the correspondence between research findings on tactics that increase the risk of false confessions and the degree to which the use of these tactics causes mock jurors to moderate their views of defendants and their confessions. Moreover, a number of such studies have shown that even when jurors rate interrogation procedures as coercive they do not always adjust verdicts accordingly; sometimes even adjusting them in the opposite direction than warranted. Others have found appropriate adjustment for some variables and not others within the same experiment.

2.5.2. Lengthy Interrogation

Interrogation scholars have identified distress and the need to escape as a primary motivator for false confessions, and length of interrogation as a primary contributor to that distress and to false confessions.[68] Several studies have addressed the impact of interrogation length, though not always in isolation.

Some of these have varied interrogation length in the context of a comparison of a *set* of coercive tactics. We include those here, though they might just as well be included under other tactics. For example, Shaked-Schroer, Costanzo and Berger manipulated the coerciveness of an interrogation and the degree to which evidence corroborated the confession.[69] High coercion included lengthy interrogation, false blood evidence and falsely claiming the suspect failed a polygraph. The low coercion condition included a two-hour interrogation and no false claims.

When the confession was corroborated by evidence, the interrogation was rated as less coercive (the end justifies the means, as other studies reviewed here have also indicated). This effect was confined, however, to the high-pressure interrogation condition. When participants were asked to indicate what things most affected their judgments of voluntariness, they listed lying about evidence as most influential, followed by the length of the interrogation, the time the suspect was held prior to interrogation and the number of interrogators present (some of these where held constant across interrogation conditions). However, for verdicts, only the effect of corroboration was significant. There was no effect of the coerciveness of the interrogation.

---

[68]   Kassin *et al.*, 2010, pp. 49–52, see *supra* note 51.
[69]   Shaked-Schroer, Costanzo and Berger, 2015, pp. 68–80, see *supra* note 24.

Bernhard and Miller investigated the effects of crime severity (murder versus property theft) and interrogation coercion on judgment of a recanted confession.[70] High coercion consisted of a 10-hour interrogation including isolation, deprivation and threats of consequences. Low coercion consisted of a two-hour interrogation but no police pressure. Defendants were judged as more guilty when coercion was absent if the crime was of high severity, perhaps reflecting jurors' assumptions that a person would not have originally falsely confessed to a serious crime without coercion. But, unexpectedly, if coercion was used, defendants were judged as more guilty for crimes of less severity.

Woestehoff and Meissner presented mock jurors with three levels of interrogative pressures.[71] The low-pressure condition consisted of encouraging the defendant to tell the truth. The medium-pressure condition added telling the defendant that the interrogator would put in his report if the defendant apologized, minimization ('the crime was unplanned' and blaming the victims, 'the crime could have been worse', 'anyone would have reacted the same way'), and false evidence. The high-pressure condition included telling the defendant that he would receive the death penalty if he did not confess; the interrogator also waived his gun around, interrogated the defendant all night and denied breaks on multiple occasions. Unfortunately, this manipulation was confounded by the use of different information on defendant statements and reactions during the interrogation.

The authors found that convictions were more likely when the defendant confessed and less likely in the medium- and high-pressure conditions than the low-pressure condition, but the medium- and high-pressure conditions did not differ. The same pattern held for ratings of likelihood of guilt. A similar pattern was found in a second and third study.[72] Thus, jurors did adjust their guilt perceptions based on the nature of the interrogation. However, interrogation length (along with the other high-pressure techniques) did not cause jurors to further adjust perceptions of guilt beyond the use of the medium-pressure tactics.

[70] Paula A. Bernhard and Rowland S. Miller, "Juror Perceptions of False Confessions versus Witness Recantations", in *Psychiatry, Psychology and Law*, 2018, vol. 25, no. 4, pp. 539–549.

[71] Skye A. Woestehoff and Christian A. Meissner, "Juror Sensitivity to False Confession Risk Factors: Dispositional vs Situational Attributions for a Confession", in *Law and Human Behavior*, 2016, vol. 40, no. 5, pp. 564–579.

[72] Jeremy J. Shifton, "How Interrogation Length, Age, and Crime Impact Perceptions of Evidence in Criminal Trials", in *American Journal of Criminal Justice*, 2022, vol. 47, pp. 266–286; Jeremy J. Shifton, "How Confession Characteristics Impact Juror Perceptions of Evidence in Criminal Trials", in *Behavioral Sciences & the Law*, 2019, vol. 37, no. 1, pp. 90–108.

Jones and Penrod also used an omnibus manipulation of interrogation pressures in their 2018 study.[73] The high-pressure interrogation included false evidence, minimization, maximization, evidence bluffing, and a 10-hour interrogation. The low-pressure interrogation included none of these. The defendant confessed to shooting a victim three times, but not with intent to kill, then immediately recanted or did not confess in the control condition. In the absence of judicial instructions regarding the potential of a false confession, verdicts were not affected by the degree of pressure of the interrogation. However, with such instructions, there was a significant reduction of guilty verdicts in the high-pressure condition.

In a subsequent study interrogation pressure was again varied in omnibus fashion.[74] The high-pressure condition included a 10-hour interrogation, false evidence, evidence bluff, minimization, and maximization. For the low-pressure condition the detective was accusatorial, but during only a 2-hour interrogation and without the other tactics. Guilty verdicts were reduced in the high-pressure condition. Moreover, ratings of likely guilt, evidence strength, detective credibility and voluntariness were likewise reduced in the high-pressure condition.

Shifton varied interrogation length independently of other interrogation factors, finding in both experiments that it led to reduced judgments of guilt, the strength of the confession and voluntariness.[75] Similarly, Kukucka and Evelo[76] studied the length of interrogation as it impacted judgments of wrongfully convicted exonerees seeking damages. In the non-coercive condition, the defendant wrote a full confession after 30 minutes of interrogation. In the coercive condition, he did so after a 9-hour interrogation. Participants rated the police as more responsible and the defendant as less responsible for the confession in the lengthy interrogation condition, recommended greater compensatory and punitive damages and perceived the defendant as less likely to be guilty.

Thus far, then, results of available research are generally consistent with the idea that jurors will adjust verdicts based on interrogation length. More

---

[73] Angela M. Jones and Steven Penrod, "Research-Based Instructions Induce Sensitivity to Confession Evidence", in *Psychiatry, Psychology and Law*, 2018, vol. 25, no. 2, pp. 257–272.

[74] Angela M. Jones, Ashley M. Blinkhorn and Alexis M. Hawley, "Sensitivity to Psychologically Coercive Interrogations: A Comparison of Instructions and Expert Testimony to Improve Juror Decision-Making", in *Journal of Forensic Psychology Research and Practice*, 2021, vol. 21, no. 4, pp. 373–394.

[75] Shifton, 2022 and Shifton, 2019, see *supra* note 72.

[76] Jeff Kukucka and Andrew J. Evelo, "Stigma Against False Confessors Impacts Post-Exoneration Financial Compensation", in *Behavioral Sciences & the Law*, 2019, vol. 37, no. 4, pp. 372–387.

research is needed, however, as most studies confounded length with other interrogation tactics, and one of the two that did not, did not examine verdicts.

2.5.3. Threats and Promises

As the section above illustrates (as well as others to come), many mock jury studies have varied the presence of threats or promises and their effects on perceptions of the confession. However, relatively few of them have tested these variables in isolation. Those that have, very often show differential effects on measures of coercion or voluntariness than on verdicts.

For example, in one of the earliest studies of the effects of threats by researchers,[77] Kassin and Sukel had mock jurors read a case summary in which (i) a confession was elicited in a high-pressure interrogation (defendant was uncomfortable in handcuffs and the detective waived his gun around and yelled at the defendant); (ii) a confession was elicited in a low-pressure interrogation (defendant was described as confessing immediately without any of the high-pressure tactics); or (iii) there was no confession. In a second variation, the interrogation had been ruled as either admissible or inadmissible by a judge. Although the jurors viewed the confession elicited in the high-pressure interrogation as less voluntary and reported that it had less influence on their decisions, it nevertheless did affect their verdicts: defendants who confessed were regarded as more guilty regardless of interrogation pressure.

Despite a clearly documented role of explicit or implied promises of leniency in increasing the risk of false confessions,[78] and consistent with the survey results showing that minimization techniques are rated as less coercive and less likely to induce false confessions than threats and other maximization techniques, several mock jury studies have shown that jurors are less likely to vote 'not guilty' when confessions are obtained through explicit or implied promises of leniency than when obtained through use of maximization or threat, even though in both cases the confessions are viewed as less voluntary than those offered with no incentives.[79]

---

[77] Saul M. Kassin and Holly Sukel, "Coerced Confessions and the Jury: An Experimental Test of the 'Harmless Error' Rule", in *Law and Human Behavior*, 1997, vol. 21, no. 1, pp. 27–46.

[78] For a review, see Richard A. Leo, *Police Interrogation and American Justice*, Harvard University Press, Cambridge, 2008; Kassin *et al.*, 2010, pp. 49–52, see *supra* note 51.

[79] Saul M. Kassin and Lawrence S. Wrightsman, "Coerced Confessions, Judicial Instruction, and Mock Juror Verdicts", in *Journal of Applied Social Psychology*, 1981, vol. 11, no. 6, pp. 489–506; *id.*, "Prior Confessions and Mock Juror Verdicts", in *Journal of Applied Social Psychology*, 1980, vol. 10, no. 2, pp. 133–146; Saul M. Kassin and Karlyn McNall, "Police Interrogations and Confessions: Communicating Promises and Threats by Pragmatic Implication", in *Law and Human Behavior*, 1991, vol. 15, no. 3, pp. 233–251.

Likewise, Moffa and Platania[80] presented participants with a case summary for a murder trial. The defendant had confessed in response to either maximization (strong claims of incriminating evidence) or minimization (blaming the heat of passion and moral justification). Maximization resulted in greater perceptions of pressure on the defendant to confess, but not in lesser perceptions of guilt or greater perceptions of coercion. In another study, the same researchers[81] also examined the effects of minimization (offering sympathy, blaming the victim and downplaying crime seriousness) and maximization (telling the suspect about an eyewitness and recovery of the murder weapon and suggesting that the confession was in his best interests). In a third condition, the interrogation was depicted as lasting 10 hours without interruption. Maximization and length were viewed as entailing more pressure on the defendant than minimization, but maximization resulted in the highest views of coercion compared to the other conditions. Verdicts did not differ across conditions, however.

2.5.4. False Evidence Ploys

FEPs can be viewed as a type of maximization or scare tactic. And, as with the effects of maximization generally, FEPs have been incorporated widely into mock jury studies, but again, often not in isolation (see those in the previous section on interrogation length, for example). In this section, we discuss studies where FEPs are studied individually.

Woody and colleagues[82] examined the effects of implicit ('What if I told you that we have') versus explicit ('We have') FEPs on perceptions of defendant guilt, coerciveness and deceptiveness of the interrogation in the context of a murder trial. In both conditions, participants heard expert testimony concerning false confessions. Both forms of FEPs resulted in higher ratings of deception than the control condition, and explicit FEPs resulted in higher ratings of coercion. However, neither form affected guilt ratings or verdicts.

These results stand somewhat in contrast to an earlier study,[83] finding that explicit FEPs did lead to fewer convictions and shorter sentences, as well as greater perceptions of coercion and deception for the interrogation. This

---

[80] Morgan S. Moffa and Judith Platania, "Effects of Expert Testimony and Interrogation Tactics on Perceptions of Confessions", in *Psychological Reports*, 2007, vol. 100, no. 2, pp. 563–570.

[81] See Morgan S. Moffa and Judith Platania, "The Differential Importance of the Evidence and the Expert on Perceptions of Confessions", in *Journal of Forensic Psychology Practice*, 2009, vol. 9, no. 4, pp. 280–298.

[82] William D. Woody, Krista D. Forrest and Sarah Yendra, "Comparing the Effects of Explicit and Implicit False-Evidence Ploys on Mock Jurors' Verdicts, Sentencing Recommendations, and Perceptions of Police Interrogation", in *Psychology, Crime & Law*, 2014, vol. 20, no. 6, pp. 603–617.

[83] Woody and Forrest, 2009, pp. 333–360, see *supra* note 6.

inconsistency with which ratings are affected by FEPs was also observed by other researchers[84] who found that although mock jurors did recognize that lying about evidence increases pressure to confess, their verdicts were not affected.

A final study by Forrest and colleagues[85] varied the type of FEPs (demeanor, testimonial, scientific (as in their previously described survey study)) incorporated into an interrogation transcript ending in a suspect confession. They also included a description of FEPs that stated either that FEPs tend to lead to true or false confessions (the point of this is not clear). Verdicts were not studied, but rather ratings of deceptiveness, coerciveness and justification. Testimonial FEPs were viewed as more deceptive and coercive than demeanor FEPs. No other differences were significant. However, participants who had been told that FEPs lead to true confessions viewed them as more justified.

2.5.5. The Role of 'Snitches' or Informants

A recent study[86] found discounting of suspect confessions due to an informant incentivized to report an alleged defendant confession, though several prior studies[87] had not found this effect.

2.5.6. Vulnerability to False Confessions

2.5.6.1. Youth

Much evidence exists to document the greater vulnerability of young suspects to false confessions.[88] Lay beliefs do not reliably reflect this vulnerability, either among law enforcement or the general citizenry. Mock jury research has also shown mixed results regarding effects of age on verdicts. Redlich and colleagues[89] provided participants with scenarios involving the interrogation and

---

[84] See *supra* note 79; Moffa and Platania, 2007, pp. 563–570, see *supra* note 80.

[85] Forrest *et al.*, 2012, pp. 342–364, see *supra* note 43.

[86] Evelyn M. Maeder and Emily Pica, "Secondary Confessions: The Influence (or Lack Thereof) of Incentive Size and Scientific Expert Testimony on Jurors' Perceptions of Informant Testimony", in *Law and Human Behavior*, 2014, vol. 38, no. 6, pp. 560–568.

[87] Jeffrey S. Neuschatz *et al.*, "The Effects of Accomplice Witnesses and Jailhouse Informants on Jury Decision Making", in *Law and Human Behavior*, 2008, vol. 32, no. 2, pp. 137–149; Jeffrey S. Neuschatz *et al.*, "Secondary Confessions, Expert Testimony, and Unreliable Testimony", in *Journal of Police and Criminal Psychology*, 2012, vol. 27, no. 2, pp. 179–192.

[88] For reviews, see Hayley M.D. Cleary, "Applying the Lessons of Developmental Psychology to the Study of Juvenile Interrogations: New Directions for Research, Policy, and Practice", in *Psychology, Public Policy, and Law*, vol. 23, no.1, pp. 118–130; Barry C. Feld, "Real Interrogation: What Actually Happens When Cops Question Kids", in *Law & Society Review*, 2013, vol. 47, no. 1, pp. 1–36; Kassin *et al.*, 2010, pp. 49–52, see *supra* note 51.

[89] Allison D. Redlich, Jodi A. Quas and Simona Ghetti, "Perceptions of Children During a Police Interrogation: Guilt, Confessions, and Interview Fairness", in *Psychology, Crime & Law*, 2008, vol. 14, no. 3, pp. 201–223.

confessions of 7-, 11- and 14-year-olds accused of bringing guns to school. Suspect age had no impact on verdicts. Suspects who confessed were judged more guilty than those who did not, but confessors were judged as equally guilty regardless of age. Likewise, the researchers found no effect of an interrogated suspect's age (11 versus 14 years) on ratings of guilt (though a ceiling effect is possible in that 76 per cent judged the suspect guilty overall). Molinaro and Malloy[90] also found that over 80 per cent of students found a juvenile confessor guilty, whether 10- or 16-years-old, and regardless of the consistency of his statement over time. In contrast, Shifton[91] found that juvenile confessions were seen as less indicative of guilt, but age did not predict verdict and did not interact with interrogation length. However, Grove and Kukucka[92] found that young confessors (aged 14 years) were judged as less likely guilty than adult confessors (aged 32 years), but no interaction was found between age and the manipulation of the depicted pressures of the interrogation (and no main effect of the latter).

Finally, the question of how the presence of a parent or attorney would affect perceptions of juvenile confessions was examined by Mindthoff and colleagues.[93] Participants read a case in which type of confession (voluntary, coerced or none) and the presence of an adult (parent, attorney or none) were varied. The coercive interrogation consisted of a 7-hour interrogation, no food, minimization and false evidence. In the voluntary condition, the suspect confessed in response to a question about what happened. In a second study, type of confession and the nature of adult advice (to speak versus to keep quiet) were varied. Across studies, conviction rates were higher in the voluntary condition than in the coerced and no-confession conditions. In the second study, the nature of the adult advice had no effect. However, in the first study, the presence of an adult increased conviction rates. This finding might seem to indicate that the suspect was seen as less vulnerable to coercion when the adult was present, and accordingly that the confession was seen as more voluntary. However, though

---

[90] Peter F. Molinaro and Lindsay C. Malloy, "Statements from Youth in Legal Contexts: Effects of Consistency, Legal Role, and Age", in *Behavioral Sciences & the Law*, 2016, vol. 34, no. 1, pp. 139–159.

[91] Shifton, 2022, see *supra* note 75.

[92] Lauren J. Grove and Jeff Kukucka, "Do Laypeople Recognize Youth as a Risk Factor for False Confession? A Test of the 'Common Sense' Hypothesis", in *Psychiatry, Psychology and Law*, 2021, vol. 28, no. 2, pp. 185–205.

[93] Amelia Mindthoff, Lindsay C. Malloy and Johanna M. Höhs, "Mock Jurors' Perceptions and Case Decisions Following a Juvenile Interrogation: Investigating the Roles of Interested Adults and Confession Type", in *Law and Human Behavior*, 2020, vol. 44, no. 3, pp. 209–222.

voluntariness was not measured, the authors found that defendants were rated as *more* vulnerable with the adult present.

2.5.6.2. Mental Illness

Whereas mental illness has been shown to play a role in vulnerability to false confessions,[94] little research has addressed the extent to which jurors adjust perceptions of the confessions of the mentally ill or how this might differ for different specific forms of mental illness. However, one study[95] looked at two sources of vulnerability. In all conditions, the defendant was described as very emotional, crying, trembling, with a racing heart and profuse sweating. In one condition, he claimed to confess because the police would not let him take his heart medication and he was afraid. In a second condition, he attributed his symptoms to an anxiety disorder for which he was in therapy, and claimed that he confessed due to fears of a panic attack. A third condition offered no attribution for his symptoms other than the stress of the interrogation. In the high-pressure condition, the defendant claimed that he was handcuffed, that the police officer waived his gun around such that the defendant feared that he would be struck, that the police officer repeatedly asserted that the defendant was guilty and should confess and generally intimidated him. In the low-pressure condition, the interrogation was not described. The authors found that that jurors discounted the confession if the suspect confessed due to concerns about a medical disorder, but not if he did so due to the pressures of the interrogation or owing to a mental disorder.

2.5.6.3. Intellectual Disability

Only a few studies have addressed the vulnerability posed by intellectual disability and jurors' ability to adjust perceptions of confessions accordingly – most were conducted depicting juvenile defendants, and therefore posing double vulnerabilities. One study[96] presented a case history describing a 16-year-old Caucasian girl without major psychological problems accused of one of four crimes: shoplifting, a drug offense, assault of a classmate or murder of her father. She either confessed voluntarily (immediately confessed) or under coercion (the interrogator used false evidence, minimization and expressions of sympathy

---

[94] Gisli H. Gudjonsson, *The Psychology of False Confessions. Forty Years of Science and Practice*, John Wiley and Sons, Chichester, 2018; see also Chapter 3 of this book.

[95] Linda A. Henkel, "Jurors' Reactions to Recanted Confessions: Do the Defendant's Personal and Dispositional Characteristics Play a Role?", in *Psychology, Crime & Law*, 2008, vol. 14, no. 6, pp. 565–578.

[96] Cynthia J. Najdowski, Bette L. Bottoms and Maria C. Vargas, "Jurors' Perceptions of Juvenile Defendants: The Influence of Intellectual Disability, Abuse History, and Confession Evidence", in *Behavioral Sciences & the Law*, 2009, vol. 27, no. 3, pp. 401–430.

during a lengthy interrogation) or did not confess. In a second variation, she was described as either mildly mentally retarded or of average intelligence. For the intellectually disabled defendant, ratings of degree of guilt were lower (but not dichotomous verdicts), the confession was viewed as less voluntary and the police were perceived as more coercive. Jurors felt they were less influenced by the disabled defendant's confession, but yet did not rate the truthfulness of that confession any less. Also for the intellectually disabled defendant, she was viewed as equally guilty and responsible regardless of whether she did not confess or confessed under coercion, though the normal defendant was viewed as more guilty if she confessed under coercion. Both types of defendants were viewed as more guilty if they confessed voluntarily than if they did not confess.

Najdowski and Bottoms[97] examined the effects of intellectual disability on judgments of a juvenile accused of murdering her father. The suspects either did not confess or provided confessions that were either voluntary or coerced. Participants saw a video of a juvenile stating that she confessed because she "didn't know what to do". In the coerced condition, she added that she was upset and scared. In the voluntary condition, she confessed immediately and the detective testified that she just blurted it out. In the coerced condition, she confessed after seven hours during which the detective used minimization and lied about evidence.

The percentage of guilty verdicts was less for the coerced condition (51 per cent) than for the voluntary condition (61 per cent), but greater than the no-confession control condition (43 per cent). Only the difference between the coerced and no confession conditions was significant. Thus, participants did appear to discount the confession obtained though coercion. Additionally, fewer jurors believed the confession was true when coerced than when voluntary, but the difference was not significant. Unexpectedly, there was no main effect of disability status on verdicts or on perceived truthfulness of the confession. In contrast, Gibbons and colleagues found people more likely to believe that a suspect described as mentally retarded was coerced into confessing than a normal suspect.[98]

---

[97] Najdowski and Bottoms, 2012, pp. 297–337, see *supra* note 53.

[98] Frederick X. Gibbons, B.N. Gibbons and Saul M. Kassin, "Reactions to the Criminal Behavior of Mentally Retarded and Nonretarded Offenders", in *American Journal of Mental Deficiency*, 1981, vol. 86, no. 3, pp. 235–242.

2.5.6.4. Temporary Incapacities: Intoxication and Sleep Deprivation

Though temporary incapacities such as physical and emotional distress, intoxication and so on can also affect vulnerability to false confessions,[99] little research has addressed juror reactions to such variables.

Mindthoff and colleagues presented an elaborate case summary for a defendant accused of severely injuring another during a bar fight.[100] They varied the intoxication of the suspect and whether or not he confessed. Participants perceived the defendant as more impaired when intoxicated. Overall, the interrogation was rated as more inappropriate for intoxicated defendants, regardless of whether he confessed. But for sober defendants, when the defendant confessed, the interrogation was rated as more appropriate than when he did not.

These judgments did not translate into verdicts. Confession increased rates of convictions. However, sober and intoxicated defendants who confessed were convicted at equal rates (47.6–47.9 per cent). Without a confession, intoxicated defendants were more likely to be convicted (44 per cent versus 34 per cent). Once again, although survey responses and the responses of mock jurors indicated that laypersons are aware of the impairment caused by intoxication, their verdicts did not reflect any adjustment for intoxication. It is important to note, however, that the findings in this study may reflect the combined influence of the recognition of greater impairment among intoxicated suspects (and potential adjustment of perceptions of the confession), but greater tendency to assume guilt for intoxicated suspects. Since the study did not vary interrogation tactics, it does not speak to the issue of whether there would be greater adjustment in guilt ratings for intoxicated suspects subjected to coercive tactics.

2.5.7. Sleep Deprivation

Though sleep deprivation is linked to impairments in cognition, self-regulation and impulse control,[101] almost no studies have addressed the issue of how jurors might adjust perceptions of confessions elicited from sleep deprived suspects. In the only exception we could locate,[102] Shifton conducted two studies varying the sleep deprivation of the suspect. The second study found that recent sleep

---

[99] See, for example, Davis and Leo, 2012a, see *supra* note 3; Davis and Leo, 2012b, see *supra* note 3; Davis and Leo, 2012c, see *supra* note 3.

[100] Berk-Seligson, 2009, see *supra* note 61; Villalobos and Davis, 2016, pp. 1–41, see *supra* note 53.

[101] All posing vulnerability in the interrogation. For a review, see: Davis and Leo, 2012a, see *supra* note 3; Davis and Leo, 2012b, see *supra* note 3; Davis and Leo, 2012c, see *supra* note 3.

[102] Shifton, 2019, see *supra* note 75.

deprivation was linked to perceptions of the evidence strength of the confession and its likely validity and voluntariness (but see weaker results in the first study).

2.5.8. Race

Race is amongst the most commonly studied variables in jury research generally and minorities have been over-represented among proven false confessors.[103] Yet, surveys of juror beliefs about false confessions have not addressed this variable and few mock jury studies of jury reactions to confessions have done so.

In an initial demonstration of the effects of race on perceived voluntariness of a confession, Ratcliff and colleagues conducted three experiments contrasting judgments for white versus minority suspects (black, Chinese).[104] Arguing that race is more salient cognitively when seen visually, they first demonstrated that the confession of a Chinese defendant was viewed as more voluntary if seen on video than if read in a transcript. In the second study, they showed that the confessions of both black and Chinese suspects were seen as more voluntary than those of white suspects. The minority suspects were also seen as more likely guilty. In a third study, the interrogator was either white or Chinese and the suspect was Chinese. Here, the suspect was viewed as more guilty when the interrogator was white, which the authors interpreted as indicating that the suspect's race was more salient when seen in contrast to the white interrogator.

Pickel and colleagues[105] conducted two experiments varying perceived defendant race. Participants watched an interrogation embedded within a 25-minute murder trial. The defendant's appearance remained constant, but the defendant was depicted as white or Arab. The interrogation was mild, involving the accusation of guilt and the advice that the defendant should help himself through confession. If Arab, the defendant's confession was viewed as more voluntary, true and incriminating than if white; and his guilt more likely. Participants also devoted more visual attention to the suspect when he was depicted as Arab.

In a second experiment, the authors manipulated the sexual orientation of the defendant and whether an FEP was used in the interrogation, again within a

---

[103] Margaret B. Kovera, "Racial Disparities in the Criminal Justice System: Prevalence, Causes, and a Search for Solutions", in *Journal of Social Issues*, 2019, vol. 75, no. 4, pp. 1139–1164; Saul M. Kassin, *Duped: Why Innocent People Confess – and Why We Believe Their Confessions*, Prometheus Books, Guilford, 2022.

[104] Jennifer J. Ratcliff *et al.*, "The Hidden Consequences of Racial Salience in Videotaped Interrogations and Confessions", in *Psychology, Public Policy, and Law*, 2010, vol. 16, no. 2, pp. 200–218.

[105] Kerri L. Pickel, Todd Warner, Tarah J. Miller and Zachary Barnes, "Conceptualizing Defendants as Minorities Leads Mock Jurors to Make Biased Evaluations in Retracted Confession Cases", in *Psychology, Public Policy, and Law*, 2013, vol. 19, no. 1, pp. 56–69.

murder trial. The confession of a homosexual defendant was viewed as more voluntary, whereas use of the FEP decreased perceptions of voluntariness. A similar effect of sexual orientation was obtained for judgments of the truth of the confession, likelihood of guilt and guilty verdicts. A main effect of false evidence was obtained only for authenticity and judgments of likelihood of guilt, not for verdicts. As with the Arab defendant, participants devoted more visual attention to the homosexual defendant.

Interactive effects of race and intellectual disability on perceptions of the voluntariness and validity of a confession were examined by Tang and colleagues.[106] Participants rated the confessions of disabled defendants as less voluntary than those of the non-disabled. However, this was only true for white defendants. Also unexpectedly, for black defendants, the confessions of non-disabled defendants were seen as more likely false than of the disabled defendants; the reverse was true for white defendants.

Finally, Smalarz and colleagues examined the effects of ethnicity, the stereotypical fit of the crime to ethnicity (Arab versus black and terrorist attack versus drive-by shooting) and the pressure of interrogation tactics.[107] The high-pressure condition included multiple pressures: handcuffing, berating, threatening with a gun, and harsh treatment by the interrogator. In the low-pressure condition, the defendant said he confessed because he was nervous and no interrogation behaviours were included. The presence of a confession increased the perception of guilt only when the crime was stereotypic for the defendant's ethnicity; and did so regardless of the level of interrogation pressure. Even with a low-pressure interrogation, a confession did not increase perceived guilt if the crime was counter-stereotypic.

2.5.9. Characteristics of the Confession

In his 2010 examination of cases of known false confessions, Brandon Garrett found that 74 per cent contained discrepancies between case facts and the content of the confessions.[108] After all, a false confessor should not know what actually happened and should not be able to recount details correctly. But Garrett also found that 71 per cent contained non-public details and 26 per cent contained information consistent with crime facts. The inclusion of details that

[106] Connie M. Tang, Narina Nunez and Victoria Estrada-Reynolds, "Intellectual Disability Affects Case Judgment Differently Depending on Juvenile Race", in *Journal of Police and Criminal Psychology*, 2020, vol. 35, no. 2, pp. 228–239.

[107] Laura Smalarz, Stephanie Madon and Anna Turosak, "Defendant Stereotypicality Moderates the Effect of Confession Evidence on Judgments of Guilt", in *Law and Human Behavior*, 2018, vol. 42, no. 4, pp. 355–368.

[108] Brandon L. Garrett, "The Substance of False Confessions", in *Stanford Law Review*, 2010, vol. 62, no. 4, pp. 1051–1119.

should only be known to the perpetrator (termed "misleading specialized knowledge")[109] is perceived as particularly incriminating. But for innocent suspects, this typically happens when details are conveyed by the interrogator to the suspect during the course of interrogation (called the "contamination error").[110] Some mock jury studies have addressed the issue of whether participants adjust their perceptions of the validity of a confession based on the content of the confession or the potential that it was fed to them by the interrogator. A number of these have found that verdicts, perceived likelihood of guilt or the reliability of the confession are greater when the confession is consistent rather than inconsistent with case facts.[111]

Several have asked the additional question of whether the fact that the consistent facts were disclosed by the interrogator or volunteered by the suspect would affect verdicts. Henderson and Levett found mixed results.[112] In their first study, they varied whether crucial case facts had or had not been disclosed by the interrogator during the interrogation as well as whether the confession was consistent with the crime facts. The interrogator's disclosure of evidence did result in lower ratings of the interrogation and probability of guilt (but not strength of evidence). The manipulation of consistency did not affect verdicts but did affect perceived probability of guilt, reliability of the confession and strength of evidence; but this was not moderated by whether the interrogator had disclosed case facts.

---

[109] Richard A. Leo, *Police Interrogation and American Justice*, Harvard University Press, Cambridge, 2008.

[110] Richard A. Leo and Steven A. Drizin, "The Three Errors: Pathways to False Confession and Wrongful Conviction", in G. Daniel Lassiter and Christian A. Meissner (eds.), *Police Interrogations and False Confessions: Current Research, Practice and Policy Recommendations*, American Psychological Association, 2010, pp. 9–30.

[111] Fabiana Alceste, William E. Crozier and Deryn Strange, "Contaminated Confessions: How Source and Consistency of Confession Details Influence Memory and Attributions", in *Journal of Applied Research in Memory and Cognition*, 2019, vol. 8, no. 1, pp. 78–91; Kelsey S. Henderson and Lora M. Levett, "Can Expert Testimony Sensitize Jurors to Variations in Confession Evidence?", in *Law and Human Behavior*, 2016, vol. 40, no. 6, pp. 638–649; *id.*, "The Effects of Variations in Confession Evidence and Need for Cognition on Jurors' Decisions", in *Psychology, Public Policy, and Law*, 2020, vol. 26, no. 3, pp. 245–260; Glenys A. Holt and Matthew A. Palmer, "The Variable Influence of Confession Inconsistencies: How Factual Errors (But Not Contradictions) Reduce Belief in Suspect Guilt", in *Applied Cognitive Psychology*, 2020, vol. 35, no. 1, pp. 232–242; Matthew A. Palmer, Lizzie Button, Emily Barnett and Neil Brewer, "Inconsistencies Undermine the Credibility of Confession Evidence", in *Legal and Criminological Psychology*, 2016, vol. 21, no. 1, pp. 161–173.

[112] Kelsey S. Henderson and Lora M. Levett, "The Effects of Variations in Confession Evidence and Need for Cognition on Jurors' Decisions", *Psychology, Public Policy, and Law*, 2020, vol. 26, no. 3, pp. 245–260.

In a second study, the authors did find main effects of both consistency and evidence disclosure by the detective on verdicts and probability of guilt (but no interaction). The expected interaction was found for ratings of the interrogation, the strength of evidence and the reliability of the confession. The authors also found that the need for cognition was associated with less perception of guilt.

On the other hand, Alceste and colleagues found that when the interrogator was the initial source of consistent case facts, participants were less likely to render guilty verdicts and less confident in the defendant's guilt than if the suspect was the source.[113] When case facts were inconsistent, the majority found the defendant not guilty; but when they were consistent, the source mattered. Defendants were also perceived as less guilty when the detective was the source of consistent facts. Notably, half of participants had been instructed to attend to the match between confession and case facts and the source of those facts, while the other half were not. This variation did not affect verdicts.

In a second study, these authors obtained only an unexpected main effect of the source of details on verdicts, such that when details came from the interrogator, the suspect was more likely to be found guilty. In contrast, as in the first study, participants did express greater confidence in guilt when the confession was consistent with crime details and when those details came from the suspect. Consistency again had little effect if the source of the details was the interrogator, but inconsistent suspects were seen as less guilty if they were the source.

The question of whether the effect of inconsistency may depend upon whether the inconsistency appears self-serving was examined by Holt and Palmer.[114] That is, the researchers varied whether the inconsistency made the crime appear more or less severe than if the confession and evidence were consistent. Though the actual variation of consistency did not affect ratings, *perceived* consistency did matter. Perceptions of guilt were reduced regardless of the direction of inconsistency.

Together, the results of studies examining effects of the inconsistency between the content of a confession and the actual case facts indicate that laypersons are indeed sensitive to this issue. They also appear to adjust verdicts according to whether case facts were first raised by the interrogator or suspect. These latter findings are particularly encouraging given that consistency has such a consistent effect on verdicts. To the extent that jurors can be made sufficiently aware of who first introduced case facts, it appears they will be willing to adjust their perceptions of the import of the content of the confession

---

[113] Alceste, Crozier and Strange, 2019, pp. 78–91, see *supra* note 111.
[114] Holt and Palmer, 2021, pp. 232–242, see *supra* note 111.

accordingly. This issue is not always addressed in trials involving recanted confessions at present, but experts should take care to advise their clients on how to identify and address it in the future.

2.5.10. Mock Jury Studies: Limitations and Conclusions

Mock jury studies have offered some insight into how jurors might react to confession evidence. Overall, the results of these studies show, as one would expect, that the presence of a confession increases perceived guilt. Likewise, overall, they show that one or more judgments of the interrogation or confession are commonly affected by the nature of the interrogation tactics or of suspect vulnerabilities.

On the other hand, the degree to which specific tactics or personal characteristics known to increase the likelihood of false confessions also affect judgments of the interrogation or suspect culpability is often unreliable between studies and between measures. Results are plagued by inconsistencies. Some tactics consistently result in under-adjustment for one or more relevant judgments: that is, judgments are not adjusted according to the presence of the tactic or are minimally affected (for example, implied promises of leniency). Others more often have appropriate effects (for example, FEPs). Many studies have gotten null results for some expected effects within their studies and not others, and other studies have indicated that jurors tend to convict confessors regardless of interrogation techniques.[115] Indeed, Jones and Penrod found[116] that although none of the four interrogation tactics affected verdicts, ratings of voluntariness or detective credibility, self-reported likelihood of falsely confessing oneself did do so, adding to similar findings associating self-reported likelihood with ratings of likelihood for others (see earlier discussion).

Recently, a few studies have shown mock jurors to adjust verdicts appropriately in response to physical threats and deprivations, minimizing the seriousness of the crime or lying about evidence.[117] As did Mindthoff et al.[118] regarding surveys, other research by Woestehof and Meissner[119] suggested that knowledge concerning false confessions might be increasing over time in response to media exposure regarding false confessions. Specific false confessions have been increasingly portrayed in documentaries such as The

---

[115] Jones and Penrod, 2016, pp. 393–409, see *supra* note 6; Woody, Forrest and Yendra, 2014, pp. 603–617, see *supra* note 82.

[116] Jones and Penrod, 2016, pp. 393–409, see *supra* note 6.

[117] Bernhard and Miller, 2018, pp. 539–549, see *supra* note 70.

[118] Mindthoff *et al.*, 2018, pp. 430–448, see *supra* note 8.

[119] Woestehoff and Meissner, 2016, pp. 564–579, see *supra* note 71.

Confessions,[120] *The Central Park Five*,[121] *Making a Murderer*,[122] *The Innocent Man*[123] and others.

Despite the reality of these increasing portrayals of false confessions in the media, findings showing jurors to adjust appropriately according to police interrogation tactics do not comport with the bulk of research on the subject (even relatively recent studies), and more research is needed to verify the purported trend toward greater juror sensitivity to coercive tactics.

2.5.11. Conclusions and Directions for Future Research

At this point, the survey studies indicate lay appreciation of the potential for interrogations to be coercive and to elicit false confessions. Though these outcomes may be underestimated for some issues and overestimated for others, overall, laypersons recognize the potential impact for many specific interrogation factors and personal vulnerabilities. Moreover, mock jury studies reflect this knowledge in part. Nevertheless, it seems that research addressing juror knowledge or use of knowledge regarding interrogation and false confessions is at a somewhat unsatisfying point. The reasons for this are somewhat complex and are both overlapping and distinct between survey and mock jury studies.

First is the issue of specificity and breadth. This first issue of this type concerns contextualization. That is, in surveys, the questions are almost never contextualized either in general categories of cases or in a specific instance of a case category. There is every reason to believe, at least with respect to the potential for false confessions, that responses will differ across case categories, case severity and potentially other variations of circumstances. This renders it difficult to know what implications the survey results have for the likely state of relevant knowledge and opinions among jurors for a case involving a specific crime type. Arguably as well, the lack of contextualization may make it more difficult for respondents to know how to answer, rendering their responses less meaningful. Even though the number of specific types of cases is large and the full range of cases cannot easily be addressed (particularly within a single study), it would be helpful to more thoroughly address some of the major categories frequently encountered in court.

A second issue of specificity and breadth concerns the range of tactics addressed. As noted earlier, both survey and mock jury studies have tended to focus on a narrow range of tactics compared to the variety of those deployed by

---

[120] Ofra Bikel, "Frontline: The Confessions", Documentary, 9 November 2010.

[121] Ken Burns, Sarah Burns and David McMahon, "The Central Park 5", Documentary, 23 November 2012.

[122] Laura Ricciardi and Moira Demos, "Making a Murderer", Documentary, 18 December 2015.

[123] Ross M. Dinerstein and Clay Tweel, "The Innocent Man", Documentary, 14 December 2018.

interrogators; and both types of studies have often used either *categories* of tactics or omnibus manipulations including a *set* of tactics. Nor have mock jury studies often manipulated each specific tactic independently to examine their independent *and synergistic* contributions. Given the failure of jurors to adjust verdicts in response to many of the more obviously coercive tactics, there is every reason to believe that they will not do so for more subtle tactics that nevertheless impact the rates of true and false confessions.[124]

Third, there is both agreement and substantial disagreement between studies regarding perceived impact of personal, situational and interrogational factors increasing the risk of false confessions, the overall existence and likelihood of false confessions, and other issues. For example, among the surveys, there are rather large discrepancies in reported beliefs regarding the impact of promises of leniency, the percentage of people who deny that false confessions happen and other crucial issues. In some cases, such discrepancies may reflect method differences. Relatedly, they may reflect the context in which specific questions are asked. For example, ratings of a specific tactic may reflect in part the relative status of that tactic in participants' minds. Therefore, their rating might be greater or less depending upon the other tactics included in the survey and the one most immediately preceding the one in question. Most surveys do not report randomizing the order of questions.

Fourth, some of the numbers obtained in surveys are at the least very surprising and potentially of questionable credibility. For example, Mindthoff and colleagues found the average estimate of the percentage of interrogated innocent suspects who confess to be approximately 30 per cent.[125] This mean seems strangely high, particularly in light of other numbers indicating that only 63 per cent agreed that suspects might confess to crimes they did not commit and 27 per cent agreed that the only reasons for false confessions were mental illness and torture. It raises the question of whether participants correctly understood the questions or whether the overall content of the questions might have made

---

[124] For detailed discussion of the vast array of tactics that remain under-investigated in laboratory studies, please see Deborah Davis, "Lies, Damned Lies, and the Path from Police Interrogation to Wrongful Conviction", in Marti H. Gonzales, Carol Tavris and Joshua Aronson (eds.), *The Scientist and the Humanist: A Festschrift in Honor of Elliot Aronson*, Psychology Press, 2010, pp. 211–247; Deborah Davis and William T. O'Donohue, "The Road to Perdition: Extreme Influence Tactics in the Interrogation Room", in William T. O'Donohue and Eric R. Levensky (eds.), *Handbook of Forensic Psychology: Resource for Mental Health and Legal Professionals*, Elsevier Science, 2004, pp. 897–996; Deborah Davis and Richard A. Leo, "The Problem of Police-Induced False Confession: Sources of Failure in Prevention and Detection", in Stephen J. Morewitz and Mark L. Goldstein (eds.), *Handbook of Forensic Sociology and Psychology*, Springer, New York, 2014, pp. 47–75.

[125] Mindthoff *et al.*, 2018, pp. 430–448, see *supra* note 8.

false confessions so salient as to alter their estimates. This question of reactivity in measurement is potentially important for interpretation of all surveys. The very length and intensity of questions on the single topic cannot help but have some reactive effects due to priming at the least.

Fifth, regarding the surveys, there is the previously mentioned issue, for some questions, regarding what responses (for example, what cut-off points) should be regarded as misconceptions. This is a particularly important issue when presenting evidence of juror misconceptions to the courts to support efforts to introduce expert testimony.

Finally, overall, mock jury research indicates that jurors unreliably adjust verdicts, even sometimes based on the most obviously coercive interrogation tactics. But what explains this? Indeed, among the mock jury studies, verdicts were the least often impacted by the nature of interrogation tactics. In many studies, even as jurors might rate the interrogation as more coercive or inappropriate or the confession as less indicative of guilt, and indicate that they relied less on the confession in response to many tactics, their verdicts remain unaffected. An important question thus far unaddressed is *why* there is so often such a discrepancy. It is not enough to simply repeat the truism that confessions are so powerful a piece of evidence that they overwhelm all other evidence, including the interrogation that produced them. It is also unsatisfying to simply fall back on explanations such as the fundamental attribution error and the tendency to underweight situational causes of behaviour (particular for others: the actor–observer difference). Future research could pursue more nuanced explanations. For example, confessions have been shown to affect interpretation of other evidence to make it seem more valid and incriminating.[126] This may play a role in the failure of mock jurors to adjust verdicts according to the tactics of the interrogation. In other words, does the degree of coercion with which a confession is elicited affect the manner in which it impacts the interpretation of other evidence (a question our laboratory is currently addressing). If not, this may in part explain why the coercion may affect many ratings of the interrogation and confession without similarly affecting verdicts. It might also explain why expert testimony or confession-related jury instructions might not result in greater discounting of coercive interrogations.

Clearly much more research is needed to increase the specificity and breadth of interrogation tactics explored in both surveys and mock juries to

---

[126] Saul M. Kassin, Itiel E. Dror and Jeff Kukucka, "The Forensic Confirmation Bias: Problems, Perspectives, and Proposed Solutions", in *Journal of Applied Research in Memory and Cognition*, 2013, vol. 2, no. 1, pp. 42–52; Stéphanie B. Marion *et al.*, "Lost Proof of Innocence: The Impact of Confessions on Alibi Witnesses", in *Law and Human Behavior*, 2016, vol. 40, no. 1, pp. 65–71.

address some of the methodological issues raised by existing research and to explore possible explanations for the often-found lack of adjustment for interrogation tactics reflected in verdicts among mock jurors in more depth.

3

Background to Interviewing Vulnerable Persons

Gisli H. Gudjonsson[*]

3.1. Introduction

The focus of this chapter is on the investigative interviewing of 'vulnerable' persons, whether victims, witnesses or suspects of crime (or other persons of interest). Vulnerabilities will be defined, categorized and described within the context of investigative interviewing with a primary focus on the vulnerabilities of suspects of crime.

There has been a gradual international shift away from the traditional practice of accusatory techniques to extract confessions (guilt-presumptive), which tends to be coercive and increases risk of unreliable confessions, to a science-based information-gathering (open-minded) approach during investigative interviewing.[1] This change in approach to interviewing has been mainly driven by innovative developments across the United Kingdom ('UK') over the past 40 years, including research, legal changes, formal police-interview training and greater understanding of vulnerabilities and their impact during interviewing.[2] Recently, following four years of consultation and drafting, the Méndez Principles on Effective Interviewing for Investigations and Information Gathering (2021)[3] were published and provide a comprehensive international framework for professional, practice-based interviewing and propose a concrete

---

[*] **Gisli H. Gudjonsson**, Ph.D., is an Emeritus Professor of Forensic Psychology at King's College, London.

[1] Ivar A. Fahsing, Kristina K. Jakobsen and John H. Öhrn, "Investigative Interviewing of Suspects in Scandinavia", in David Walsh, Gavin E. Oxburgh, Allison D. Redlich and Trond Myklebust (eds.), *International Developments and Practices in Investigative Interviewing and Interrogation: Volume 2: Suspects*, Routledge, London, 2016, pp. 180–192; David Walsh and Paulo B. Marques, "Is Confession Really Necessary? The Use of Effective Techniques to Maximize Disclosure from Suspects", in Paulo B. Marques and Mauro Paulino (eds.), *Police Psychology: Trends in Forensic Psychology Science*, Elsevier Science, 2022; Kai L. Chung and Ray Bull, "From interrogation to conversation", *The Psychologist*, February 2022, pp. 48–51.

[2] Gisli H. Gudjonsson, *The Psychology of False Confessions: Forty Years of Science and Practice*, Wiley Blackwell, Chichester, 2018.

[3] Anti-Torture Initiative, Association for the Prevention of Torture and the Norwegian Centre for Human Rights, *Principles on Effective Interviewing for Investigations and Information Gathering*, 2021 ('Méndez Principles') (https://www.legal-tools.org/doc/wbfiw1/); see also Chapter 6 of this book for more details.

alternative to coercive interrogation practices. Principle 2 ('On Vulnerability') specifically focuses on the needs and requirements of 'interviews in situations of vulnerability'.

As a framework for encompassing the function, principles, nature and scope of investigative interviewing within which vulnerabilities sit, the authorized professional practice recommended by the College of Policing (for England and Wales) will be used,[4] as well as Code C of the Police and Criminal Evidence Act ('PACE') of 1984,[5] the Advocate's Gateway Tool Kits for vulnerable victims, witnesses and suspects,[6] the Equal Treatment Bench Book,[7] and the Criminal Procedure Rules and Practice Directions.[8]

The primary objective of this chapter is to provide practitioners, researchers and academics with informed and up-to-date knowledge about vulnerabilities, guided by available legal and practice framework and rigorous empirically-based science and practice.[9]

The chapter provides the reader with a discussion and summary of the key areas relevant to understanding vulnerabilities within the investigative interview process and practices. The current empirically based knowledge is presented in a historical context so that the development of science and practice since the late 1970s is appropriately highlighted and cited.

The chapter will conclude with real-life case examples of false statements that show the dynamic and interactive nature of investigative interviews and provides a conceptual framework for evaluating the vulnerabilities, processes and mechanisms that lead vulnerable witnesses and suspects to give false incriminating statements against others and themselves.

---

[4]   College of Policing (England and Wales), "Investigative Interviewing", 23 October 2013, updated on 26 October 2022 (available on the College of Policing's web site).

[5]   UK, Police and Criminal Evidence Act, 31 October 1984 (https://www.legal-tools.org/doc/b52ec0/); UK Home Office, *Police and Criminal Evidence Act 1984 (PACE): CODE C Revised Code of Practice for the Detention, Treatment and Questioning of Persons by Police Officers*, The Stationery Office, London, August 2019, Section 3.1, p. 14 (used within England and Wales) ('CODE C') (https://www.legal-tools.org/doc/1ld1rc/).

[6]   "The Advocate's Gateway Toolkits" (available on its web site).

[7]   Judicial College, "Equal Treatment Bench Book", February 2021.

[8]   UK, Criminal Procedure Rule Committee and Ministry of Justice, "Criminal Procedure Rules and Practice Directions 2020", 5 October 2020 (see the repository of practice available at https://www.gov.uk/guidance/rules-and-practice-directions-2020).

[9]   Gudjonsson, 2018, see *supra* note 2; Gisli H. Gudjonsson, "The Science-Based Pathways to Understanding False Confessions and Wrongful Convictions", in *Frontiers in Psychology*, 2021, vol. 12, pp. 1–15; Gisli H. Gudjonsson *et al.*, "The Impact of Confabulation on Testimonial Reliability", in *Criminal Law Review*, 2021, vol. 10, pp. 828–850.

3.2. Investigative Interviewing

Gudjonsson[10] outlines the four key pillars of fairness and justice regarding investigative interviewing: *professionalism* (including *integrity*), *humanity, transparency* and *accountability*. These are consistent with the guidance of the College of Policing (England and Wales) to police officers about investigative interviewing. The focus is on professionalism and integrity within the application of the PEACE interviewing model framework for suspects.

The PEACE model and its application to investigative interviews is outlined and described in the College of Policing Website document.[11] A more detailed description and application of the PEACE model is provided online by the Home Office.[12] It comprises five basic steps, using each of the PEACE letters to identify the different step-names of the interview life cycle:

1. **Plan and Prepare** (prepare an interview plan).
2. **Engage and Explain** (introduce yourself and explain reason for interview).
3. **Account, clarify and challenge** (ask the suspect for their account of events)
4. **Closure** (confirmation of what was said and allow suspect clarification).
5. **Evaluation** (reflect on information obtained and identify subsequent actions).

The emphasis is on obtaining all relevant information legally required, transparency, fairness and effective communication. For the background development and interviewer training in the PEACE model, please refer to Chapter 12. For a comparison between the PEACE model and the United States' Reid Technique, see Gudjonsson and Pearse,[13] Snook, Luther and Barron,[14] Vrij, Hope and Fisher,[15] and Meissner *et al.*[16]

---

[10] Gudjonsson, 2018, see *supra* note 2.

[11] College of Policing, 23 October 2013, see *supra* note 4.

[12] See also UK Home Office, "Interviewing Suspects: Version 7.0", 10 February 2020 (available on its web site).

[13] Gisli H. Gudjonsson and John Pearse, "Suspect Interviews and False Confessions", in *Current Directions in Psychological Science*, 2011, vol. 20, pp. 33–37.

[14] Brent Snook, Kirk Luther and Todd Barron, "Interviewing Suspects in Canada", in Walsh, Oxburgh, Redlich and Myklebust (eds.), 2016, pp. 229–239, see *supra* note 1.

[15] Aldert Vrij, Lorraine Hope and Ronald P. Fisher, "Eliciting Reliable Information in Investigative Interviews", in *Policy Insights from Behavioral and Brain Sciences*, 2014, vol. 1, pp. 129–136.

[16] Christian A. Meissner *et al.*, "Accusatorial and Information-Gathering Interrogation Methods and Their Effects on True and False Confessions: A Meta-Analytic Review", in *Journal of Experimental Criminology*, 2014, vol. 10, pp. 459–486.

3.2.1. The Seven Key Interviewing Principles Outlined by the College of Policing

The basic principles behind an investigative interviewing model and compliance with these principles in practice are essential for effective and ethical interviewing. It is helpful when these are clearly articulated and presented. Dr. Tom Williamson, senior British police officer, was a powerful driving force within the police and academia in the 1990s for the development of formal interviewing training and improved professionalism within the police service of England and Wales.[17] The seven key interviewing principles outlined in the College of Policing 2020 guidance document are as follows.

Principle 1: The principal aim of investigative interviewing is "to obtain accurate and reliable accounts from victims, witnesses or suspects about matters under investigation". It is advised that *accurate* information should be as complete as possible and without omissions or distortion. Regarding *reliability*, the information obtained "must have been given truthfully and able to withstand further scrutiny" (for example, in court). "Accurate and reliable accounts ensure that the investigation can be taken further by opening up other lines of enquiry as a basis for questioning others."

Principle 2: The emphasis here is on *fairness* when questioning victims, witnesses or suspects. Interviewers "must ensure that they comply with all the provisions and duties under the Equality Act 2010 and the Human Rights Act 1998". It is pointed out that in the interest of fairness, "the investigator must not approach any interview with prejudice" and "should be prepared to believe the account that they are being given, but use common sense and judgement rather than personal beliefs to assess the accuracy of what is being said".

Principle 3: The focus here is an *investigative mindset*. This includes "further[ing] the [police] enquiry by establishing facts" (the emphasis is on effecting planning of the interview), testing the account given against what is already known or what can be "reasonably established", "set[ting] objectives which will help to corroborate or disprove information already known" and testing and corroborating "the information by other means where possible".

---

[17] Colin Clarke and Rebecca Milne, "Interviewing Suspects in England and Wales", in Walsh, Oxburgh, Redlich and Myklebust (eds.), 2016, pp. 101–118, see *supra* note 1; Tom M. Williamson, "Reflection on Current Practice", in David Morgan and Geoffrey M. Stephenson (eds.), *Suspicion and Silence: The Right to Silence in Criminal Investigation*, Blackstone Press, London, 1994, pp. 107–116; Tom M. Williamson, "Towards Greater Professionalism: Minimizing Miscarriages of Justice", in Tom M. Williamson (ed.), *Investigative Interviewing: Rights, Research, Regulation*, Willan Publishing, Cullompton, 2006, pp. 147–166. David Rose, "Tom Williamson", *The Guardian*, 14 March 2007.

Principle 4: Whilst the interviewer is entitled to ask a range of questions to assist the "investigation and provide sufficient evidence or information", "the interviewing style must not be *unfair* or *oppressive*. The interviewer should act in accordance with the PACE and the PACE codes of practice".[18]

Principle 5: Here the focus is on the *benefits* ('positive impact') of "an early admission in the context of the criminal justice system". Five areas of potential benefits are: the *Victim, Court, Defendant, Police, Prosecution* and *Resources*. A cautionary note: by its nature, this Principle is potentially open to misinterpretation and should be used with caution to inform suspect's decision making rather than coercing a confession.

Principle 6: Here the focus is the interviewer's entitlement to be *persistent* in the questioning. Two examples are given where the interviewer may need to be persistent in their questioning: (i) "they may have reasonable belief that the interviewee is not telling the truth", or (ii) "they may believe further information could be provided". Persistence is said to be "acceptable" provided the interviewer is "careful and consistent but not unfair or oppressive".

Principle 7: The focus here is on the interviewer's *entitlement to continue to ask questions*, "[e]ven when a suspect exercises the right to silence". "This principle extends the right of an investigator to put questions to those they believe can help them to establish the truth of a matter under investigation." Good interview preparation is seen as the key avenue to deal with 'no comment' replies in an "effective and acceptable way". The emphasis is on giving the suspect the opportunity to respond to any relevant questions, and all planned questions must be asked. "Failure to ask all relevant questions in the first place may preclude inference being drawn in court."

3.2.2. The Legal Principle of the Presumption of Innocence

An important legal principle addressed in the College of Policing guidance document is that a "person is innocent until proven guilty. It is the duty of the prosecution to prove their case against a person suspected of committing an offence".

The seven principles and the legal principle provide the mind-set and guidance framework from which the PEACE model should be applied.

---

[18] The recommended definition of the term 'oppression' is provided from that in England and Wales Court of Appeal, Criminal Division, *Regina v. Fulling*, Judgment, 17 February 1987, [1987] 2 WLR 923 (https://www.legal-tools.org/doc/yxexix/): "the exercise of authority or power in a burdensome, harsh, or wrongful manner, or unjust or cruel treatment of suspects or inferiors, or the imposition of unreasonable or unjust burdens in circumstances which would always entail some impropriety on the part of the [interviewer]" (Lord Chief Justice Taylor, quoting the "third definition of the word" from the Oxford English Dictionary).

3.3. Interviewing Vulnerable Suspects

3.3.1. Definition and Description of Vulnerability

Vulnerability during investigative interviewing is best construed as any factor that impairs the *functional capacity* of the suspect (in broad terms this also applies to victims and witnesses)[19] to:

- understand their legal rights (for example, entitlement to free legal advice, their right to have someone informed of their arrest, their right to consult the Codes of Practice,[20] and the right to remain silent – police caution in the UK and the Miranda rights in the United States).[21] For broad international standards, please see the Méndez Principles for investigative interviews;[22]

- understand the purpose of the interview (that is, why they have been arrested, confined and are being interviewed);

- understand the respective role of the people present in the interview;[23]

- understand the questions asked and the implications of their answers;

- make rational decisions;[24]

- communicate appropriately, reliably and effectively.[25]

---

[19] See Brendan M. O'Mahony, Ruth Marchant and Lorna Fadden, "Vulnerable Individuals, Intermediaries and Justice", in Gavin Oxburgh, Trond Myklebust, Tim Grant and Rebecca Milne (eds.), *Communication in Investigative and Legal Contexts*, John Wiley & Sons, Chichester, 2016, pp. 287–313; Coral J. Dando, Edward R. Geiselman, Nicci MacLeod and Andy Griffiths, "Interviewing Adult Witnesses and Victims", in *ibid.*, pp. 79–106.

[20] CODE C, 2019, Section 3.1, p. 14, see *supra* note 5.

[21] For a broader context about functional capacity regarding investigative interviewing, see Gisli H. Gudjonsson and Thomas Grisso, "Legal Competencies in Relation to Confession Evidence", in Alan R. Felthous and Henning Sass (eds.), *International Handbook on Psychopathic Disorders and the Law: Volume 2*, John Wiley & Sons, Chichester, 2008, pp. 177–187; Jodi L. Viljoen, Jessica Klaver and Ronald Roesch, "Legal Decisions of Preadolescent and Adolescent Defendants: Predictors of Confessions, Pleas, Communication With Attorneys, and Appeals", in *Law and Human Behavior*, 2005, vol. 29, pp. 253–277.

[22] Méndez Principles, 2021, see *supra* note 3.

[23] For an early case where this was an issue, see Gisli H. Gudjonsson, "'Fitness for Interview' During Police Detention: A Conceptual Framework for Forensic Assessment", in *Journal of Forensic Psychiatry*, 1995, vol. 6, pp. 185–197.

[24] Richard J. Ofshe and Richard A. Leo, "The Decision to Confess Falsely: Rational Choice and Irrational Action", in *Denver University Law Review*, 1997, vol. 74, pp. 979–1122.

[25] See The Advocate's Gateway Toolkits, Toolkit 5, see *supra* note 6; Judicial College, 2021, see *supra* note 7.

3.3.2. The Background to the Development of PACE

Real life cases have been the key to changes in the legal landscape regarding investigative interviewing and confession evidence within the UK.[26] There was one leading case in London that was of crucial importance in highlighting the risk of false confessions in vulnerable young persons, which led to the introduction of PACE legislation: the Confait case.[27]

In April 1972, three boys, Ahmet Salih (aged 14 years), Ronald Leighton (aged 15 years) and Colin Lattimore (aged 18 years), were manipulated by the police into confessing to arson at Doggett Road, and Leighton and Lattimore also confessed to the murder of Maxwell Confait (aged 26 years) who lived at the premises. Salih confessed to being present when Confait was murdered. Based on their confessions, in November 1972, they were all convicted of arson, and Leighton and Lattimore were also convicted of murder and manslaughter (based on diminished responsibility) respectively. In October 1975, after considerable public pressure following a failed appeal in July 1973, the case was again referred to the Court of Appeal and the convictions were quashed on the basis that their conditions were unsafe.

The acquittal was a game-changer in the UK in highlighting the importance of psychological vulnerabilities (for example, intellectual disability and suggestibility), in addition to low chronological age, leading to a public inquiry headed by Sir Fisher, followed by the setting up and reporting of the Royal Commission on Criminal Procedure (1977–1981) and the creation of the PACE (1984), its Codes of Practice, and subsequent electronic recording of suspect interviews.

3.3.3. The Fisher Inquiry Report and Its Failure to Accept that Suspects Can and Do Sometimes Falsely Confess to Serious Crimes

Whilst accepting that all three boys, for different reasons, had been vulnerable to unreliable testimony during the police interviews, Lord Fisher concluded that on the balance of probability all three boys were guilty of arson, and that both Leighton and Salih had been involved in the killing of Confait, but had

---

[26] Gisli H. Gudjonsson, *The Psychology of Interrogations, Confessions, and Testimony*, John Wiley & Sons, Chichester, 1992; Gisli H. Gudjonsson, *The Psychology of Interrogations and Confessions: A Handbook*, John Wiley & Sons, Chichester, 2003; Gudjonsson, 2018, see *supra* note 2.

[27] Christopher Price and Jonathan Caplan, *The Confait Confessions*, Marion Moyars, London, 1977; Barrie L. Irving and Ian K. McKenzie, *Police Interrogation: The Effects of the Police and Criminal Evidence Act 1984*, The Police Foundation, London, 1989; Tom M. Williamson, "Psychology and Criminal Investigation", in Tim Newburn, Tom M. Williamson and Alan Wright (eds.), *Handbook of Criminal Investigation*, Willan Publishing, Devon, 2007, pp. 68–91; Gudjonsson, 2018, see *supra* note 2.

persuaded Lattimore to falsely confess to having taken part in the killing (Lattimore had a credible alibi for the murder).[28]

Lord Fisher's findings were apparently based on his general belief that it is unlikely that suspects would falsely confess to a serious crime, except in very unusual circumstances like in the case of Lattimore (non-police pressured false confession), his 'blind' faith in the integrity of the police evidence, and his reluctance to accept that the boy's 'special knowledge' may have been caused by contamination. These attitudes were commonly held by judges in the 1980s.[29]

The 292-pages long Fisher Report describes in detail the written and oral evidence that laid the foundation for the inquiry's findings. Barrie Irving, a social psychologist, was allowed to listen to the three boys' evidence before the inquiry (along with his colleague Linden Hilgendorf), submitted a written report, and then gave oral evidence about the boys' confessions.

According to the Fisher Report, Irving's methodology and evidence "sought to derive, from his experience as a psychologist and his knowledge of the psychological literature, possible explanations for the confessions consistent with the assumption (which he made for the purpose of his evidence) of the innocence of the boys".[30]

Irving raised concerns about possible inaccuracies in the police interview transcripts, including possible selective recording of the questions and answers. He raised concerns about the boys' mental functioning, including confusion, disorientation and acquiescence, and, in the case of Lattimore, low intelligence quotient and suggestibility. He also suggested possible contamination of the boys' apparent 'special knowledge' of the crime scene.

Whilst accepting that some of the factors identified by Irving might have been present, Lord Fisher "found it difficult to apply them to the facts of this case".[31] Here Lord Fisher appears to have been influenced by his complete faith in the integrity of the police evidence and went to extreme lengths not to criticize their work in the case.[32]

Following their involvement in the Confait case, Irving and Hilgendorf concluded:

---

[28] Fisher Inquiry, *Report of an Inquiry by the Hon. Sir Henry Fisher into the Circumstances Leading to the Trial of the Three Persons on Charges Arising Out of the Death of Maxwell Confait and the Fire at 27 Doggett Road, London SE6*, His Majesty's Stationery Office ('HMSO'), London, 1977, pp. 8–9 ('Fisher Report') (https://www.legal-tools.org/doc/j80u5c/).

[29] Gudjonsson, 2018, see *supra* note 2.

[30] Fisher Report, pp. 128–129, see *supra* note 28.

[31] *Ibid.*, p. 134.

[32] Irving and McKenzie, 1989, see *supra* note 27. Williamson, 2007, see *supra* note 27.

At present it is not even possible to be certain about how a confession which is known to be false came to be made. The complexity of attempting such post hoc explanations was demonstrated by the Fisher Inquiry.[33]

The main reasons for this lack of knowledge about false confessions in the early 1980s were due to:[34]

1. poor theoretical understanding of the phenomenon of false confession;

2. general reluctance to accept that innocent suspects could, and do on occasions, confess to a serious crime despite having no history of intellectual disability or mental illness (that is, a 'closed' mindset of the police, public and members of the judiciary);

3. lack of systematic and empirical research into false confessions (for example, absence of a solid evidence base about the situational and personal risk factors involved in producing false confessions);

4. lack of knowledge of the potentially powerful impact of context (for example, political and media pressure on police to solve a case, nature of the crime or the strength of the evidence) and individual circumstances (for example, bereavement or relationship with the co-accused);

5. failure to fully understand the dynamic and interactive nature of the custodial and interview processes;

6. lack of electronic recording of investigative interviews;

7. lack of knowledge and understanding about what happened behind the 'closed' door of the interview room;

8. the establishment's 'blind faith' in the integrity of the police and the interview process;

9. poor understanding of vulnerabilities as 'risk factors';

10. the fallacy that the retractions of the defendants are inevitably self-serving and not credible (that is, the judiciary viewing retracted and disputed confessions with great scepticism and lack of open-mindedness and fairness).

3.3.4. PACE Code C on Vulnerability

"Anyone who appears to be under 18, shall, in the absence of clear evidence that they are older, be treated as a juvenile for the purposes of this Code and any other Code"; and "requires the presence of an 'appropriate adult'", whose role

---

[33] Barrie L. Irving and Linden Hilgendorf, "Police Interrogation: The Psychological Approach", in *Royal Commission on Criminal Procedure: Research Study No. 1*, HMSO, London, p. 26.

[34] Gudjonsson, 2018, see *supra* note 2.

is "to safeguard the rights, entitlements and welfare of juveniles and vulnerable persons".[35]

Regarding 'adults' (that is, 18 years or older), the term 'vulnerable' "applies to any person who, because of a mental health condition or mental disorder":[36]

1. may have difficulty understanding or communicating effectively about the full implications for them of any procedures and processes connected with:
   - their arrest and detention; or (as the case may be)
   - their voluntary attendance at a police station or their presence elsewhere (see paragraph 3.21), for the purpose of a voluntary interview; and
   - the exercise of their rights and entitlements.
2. does not appear to understand the significance of what they are told, of questions they are asked or of their replies.
3. appears to be particularly prone to:
   - becoming confused and unclear about their position;
   - providing unreliable, misleading or incriminating information without knowing or wishing to do so;
   - accepting or acting on suggestions from others without consciously knowing or wishing to do so; or
   - readily agreeing to suggestions or proposals without any protest or question.[37]

Code C provides an important guidance to interviewers:

> Although vulnerable persons are often capable of providing reliable evidence, they may, without knowing or wanting to do so, be particularly prone in certain *circumstances* to provide information that may be unreliable, misleading or self-incriminating. Special care should always be taken when questioning such a person, and the appropriate adult should be involved if there is any doubt about a person's mental state or capacity. Because of the risk of unreliable evidence, it is important to obtain *corroboration* of any facts admitted whenever possible.[38]

The above list and description of vulnerabilities, which has been substantially refined and expanded since the previous revisions of Code C, follow the

---

[35] CODE C, 2019, para. 1.7, p. 7 and para. 1.7a, p. 7, see *supra* note 5.

[36] *Ibid.*, notes 1G and 1GB, para 1.13d, p. 9.

[37] *Ibid.*, para. 1.13(d), p. 9.

[38] *Ibid.*, para. E2, p. 82 (emphasis added).

extensive and relevant evidence-based science that has become available in recent years.[39]

Code C on vulnerability raises an important point. Misleading statements
may be made *inadvertently* (that is, 'without knowing or wishing to do so').
Inadvertent admissions or confessions, *inter alia*, occur because of reliance on
inferences in human communication and can be highly incriminating.[40] Inadvertent comments due to impulsivity or communication problems may also be
incriminating.[41]

One important remaining area of concern is the failure to provide many
vulnerable adults with an 'appropriate adult'. In a study for the Royal Commission on Criminal Procedure, Gudjonsson and colleagues found that only 4 per
cent of suspects were provided with an appropriate adult, whilst the researchers
estimated from their psychological evaluation that over 20 per cent required
one.[42]

Despite the employment of healthcare professionals at police stations in
England, a study conducted at a London Metropolitan Police station 20 years
later showed that the rate of appropriate adults remained at 4 per cent.[43] In view
of the important role that appropriate adults perform in cases of vulnerable detainees (that is, the main form of special protection), it is important that they are
suitably qualified and provided to all detainees who require them.[44]

At the end of 2019, The UK National Appropriate Adult Network
('NAAN') requested freedom of information about the use of appropriate adult
provision for adults from all 43 territorial police forces in England and Wales,
the British Transport Police and the Police Service of Northern Ireland. The results for the years 2018–2019 showed that appropriate adults were found, on

---

[39] Gudjonsson, 2018, see *supra* note 2. Gudjonsson, 2021, see *supra* note 9; Gudjonsson *et al.*,
      2021, pp. 828–850, see *supra* note 9.

[40] Luna Filipović, "Confession to Make: Inadvertent Confessions and Admissions in United
      Kingdom and United States Police Contexts", in *Frontiers in Psychology*, 6 December 2021.

[41] Gisli H. Gudjonsson and Susan Young, "An Overlooked Vulnerability in a Defendant: Atten-
      tion Deficit Hyperactivity Disorder and a Miscarriage of Justice", in *Legal and Criminologi-
      cal Psychology*, 2006, vol. 11, pp. 211–218.

[42] Gisli H. Gudjonsson, Isabel C.H. Clare, Sue Rutter and John Pearse, *Persons at Risk During
      Interviews in Police Custody: The Identification of Vulnerabilities*, Royal Commission on
      Criminal Justice, HMSO, London, 1993.

[43] Susan Young, Emily J. Goodwin, Ottilie Sedwick and Gisli H. Gudjonsson, "The Effective-
      ness of Police Custody Assessments in Identifying Suspects With Intellectual Disabilities and
      Attention Deficit Hyperactivity Disorder", in *BMC Medicine*, 2013, vol. 248, no. 11, pp. 1 –
      11.

[44] Sarah Medford, Gisli H. Gudjonsson and John Pearse, "The Efficacy of the Appropriate Adult
      Safeguard During Police Interviewing", in *Legal and Criminological Psychology*, 2003, vol.
      8, pp. 253–266.

average, to be present in 6,2 per cent in custody and 3,5 per cent in voluntary interviews. The NAAN report showed a huge variation between forces.[45]

The NAAN report makes several recommendations, including the following:

1. A national policing strategy to overcome appropriate adult barriers in investigations.
2. The development of a cross-government solution to the lack of statutory provision of appropriate adults for vulnerable adults.
3. Conduct research on PACE defined vulnerability to assist with informed criteria, responses and strategy.
4. Develop an evidence-based screening tool to assist police officers and staff in identifying people who meet the PACE threshold and definition of a 'vulnerable person' as part of risk assessment and ensure provision of appropriate adults for vulnerable adults in all areas.

3.3.5. Fitness to Be Interviewed

'Fitness to be interviewed' is a relatively recent concept in the PACE. Its introduction into Code C followed the Home Office Working Group on Police Surgeons,[46] and was an important step for a safer and fairer criminal justice system.[47]

This is a provision that helps to ensure fairness and justice for vulnerable suspects detained for an interview at a police station where the provision of an appropriate adult is insufficient.

Annex G on 'Interview Fitness' in Code C provides guidance to assist police officers and healthcare professionals ('HCPs') to assess a detainee's potential risk in an interview. A detainee is considered potentially at risk if:

(a) conducting the interview could significantly harm the detainee's physical or mental state.

(b) anything the detainee says in the interview about their involvement or suspected involvement in the offence about which they are being interviewed *might* be considered

---

[45] Chris Bath and Roxanna Dehaghani, "There to Help 3: The Identification of Vulnerable Adult Suspects and Application of the Appropriate Adult Safeguard in Police Investigations in 2018/19", National Appropriate Adult Network, September 2020.

[46] UK Home Office, *Report of the Home Office Working Group on Police Surgeons*, HMSO, London 2001.

[47] Gisli H. Gudjonsson, "Detention: Fitness to be Interviewed", in Jason Payne-James and Roger W. Byard (eds.), *Encyclopaedia of Forensic and Legal Medicine*, vol. 2, 2nd ed., Elsevier, Oxford, 2016. For an important early case study, see Gudjonsson, 1995, pp. 185–197, see *supra* note 23.

unreliable in subsequent court proceedings because of their physical or mental state.[48]

When considering the detainee's fitness for interview, the following three areas must be considered:

    (a)   how the detainee's physical or mental state might affect their ability to understand the nature and purpose of the interview, to comprehend what is being asked and to appreciate the significance of any answers given and make rational decisions about whether they want to say anything;

    (b)   the extent to which the detainee's replies may be affected by their physical or mental condition rather than representing a rational and accurate explanation of their involvement in the offence;

    (c)   how the nature of the interview, which could include particularly probing questions, might affect the detainee.[49]

The guidance stipulates:

It is essential that healthcare professionals who are consulted consider the functional ability of the detainee rather than simply relying on a medical diagnosis, for example it is possible for a person with severe mental illness to be fit for interview.[50]

The HCP should also advise on the need for an appropriate adult, whether the condition is likely to improve, need for reassessment when appropriate (for example, the interview lasting beyond a specific time) and whether a further specialist opinion may be required.

Following the mental healthcare assessment and advice, it is the custody officer who ultimately decides on the fitness of the detainee to be interviewed after considering the HCP's advice and the safeguards already available.

3.4. Conceptualization of Vulnerabilities During Suspect Interviews

The investigative interview consists of a dynamic and interactive process. This was first empirically demonstrated in several real-life studies into police interviewing conducted in the 1990s.[51] More recent real-life studies into

---

[48]   Code C, 2019, Annex G, paras. 2(a)–(b), p. 84, see *supra* note 5.

[49]   *Ibid.*, paras. 3(a)–(c), p. 84.

[50]   *Ibid.*, para. 4, p. 84.

[51]   John Pearse and Gisli H. Gudjonsson, "Measuring Influential Police Interviewing Tactics: A Factor Analytic Approach", in *Legal and Criminological Psychology*, 1999, vol. 4, pp. 221–238; John Pearse and Gisli H. Gudjonsson, "The Identification and Measurement of 'Oppressive' Police Interviewing Tactics in Britain", in Gudjonsson, 2003, pp. 75–129, see *supra* note 26; John Pearse, Gisli H. Gudjonsson, Isabel C.H. Clare and Sue Rutter, "Police Interviewing and Psychological Vulnerabilities: Predicting the Likelihood of a Confession", in *Journal of*

investigative interviewing have confirmed the interactive nature of interviewing tactics and suspects' responses.[52]

Extensive research and clinical forensic psychology practice has shown that the investigative interview process involves the interplay of five sets of key factors:[53]

1. *Background* (for example, history of sexual, physical and emotional abuse (also history of being a bully victim), creating an early cumulative disadvantage).

2. *Contextual* (for example, the nature of the crime, pressure on police to solve the crime, the strength of the evidence against the suspect, the relationship between the victim and suspect, the relationship with the co-accused).

3. *Situational* (that is, the nature and duration of the custodial and interrogative procedure and process; the suspect's understanding of the police caution and their legal rights; not having access in custody to required prescribed medication).

4. *Personal* (for example, age, mental state (or disorder), personality traits such as suggestibility and compliance).

5. *Protective* (that is, the presence of a legal representative, an independent person (when required by law), known in the UK as an appropriate adult. Any suspect under the age of 18 years and those mentally vulnerable are entitled to the presence of an appropriate adult during interviewing and

---

Community and Applied Social Psychology, 1998, vol. 8, pp. 1–21; Stephen Moston, Geoffrey M. Stephenson and Tom M. Williamson, "The Effects of Case Characteristics on Suspect Behaviour During Questioning", in *British Journal of Criminology*, 1992, vol. 32, pp. 23–40.

52 Christopher E. Kelly, Jeanneé C. Miller, Allison D. Redlich and Steven M. Kleinman, "A Taxonomy of Interrogation Methods", in *Psychology, Public Policy, and Law*, 2013, vol. 19, no 2, pp. 165–178; Christopher E. Kelly, Jeanneé C. Miller and Allison D. Redlich, "The Dynamic Nature of Interrogation", in *Law and Human Behavior*, 2016, vol. 40, no. 3, pp. 295–309; Ulf Holmberg, Sven Å. Christianson and David Wexler, "Interviewing Offenders: A Therapeutic Jurisprudential Approach", in Sven Å. Christianson (ed.), *Offenders' Memories of Violent Crimes*, John Wiley & Sons, Chichester, 2007, pp. 259–278; Michel St-Yves, "Rapport in Investigative Interviews: Five Fundamental Rules to Achieve It", in Michel St-Yves (ed.), *Investigative Interviewing: The Essentials*, Carswell, Toronto, 2014, pp. 1–27: Stavroula Soukara *et al.*, "A Study of What Really Happens in Police Interviews With Suspects", in *Psychology, Crime, and Law*, 2009, vol. 15, pp. 493–506.

53 Gudjonsson, 2018, see *supra* note 2. Gudjonsson, 2021, see *supra* note 9. Gisli H. Gudjonsson and James A.C. MacKeith, "Retracted Confessions: Legal, Psychological and Psychiatric Aspects", in *Medicine, Science and the Law*, 1988, vol. 28, pp. 187–194. Gudjonsson, 2003, see *supra* note 26. Gisli H. Gudjonsson and James A.C. MacKeith, "Disputed Confessions and the Criminal Justice System", Maudsley Discussion Paper No. 2, Institute of Psychiatry, London, 1997.

when charged with an offence. In addition, when appropriate (for example, in cases of foreign non-English speaking nationals), there is free access to interpreters.

The five-stage categorization provides a comprehensive conceptual framework for reviewing, analysing and studying the dynamics of the suspect interview process. It is particularly helpful in cases of disputed confession. *Each case of disputed confession is best understood by a rigorous analysis of all relevant material and electronic recording of interviews when these are available whilst guided by the available behavioural science.*

Gudjonsson[54] has identified 17 sets of different empirically-based vulnerabilities to false confessions, labelled 'risk factors'. These reflect the above categorization and guide the psychological evaluation in each case. It is the nature of these vulnerabilities, their relevance, number, severity and cumulative effect that determines the overall level of 'risk' and a likely underlying mechanism for false confession.

When applying the above conceptual assessment framework, it is important that the *personal* vulnerability factors are separated into *enduring factors* and *acute state factors*. Enduring factors are those present prior to the investigative interview, such as age, intellectual functioning, mental or developmental disorder and personality. In contrast, the acute state factors are those that are specific to the demand characteristics of the custodial and interrogative environment. Enduring vulnerabilities (for example, poor cognitive functioning, suggestibility, compliance, state anxiety) may become exacerbated by contextual and situational 'stress' factors, leading to accumulative disadvantage via acute state factors.

Davis and Leo[55] argue that the *primary mechanism* of resistance to suggestions and influence during custodial and confrontational investigative interview is *self-regulation* (that is, the ability to manage one's thoughts, words, emotions, impulses and decisions). *Emotional distress, discomfort* (including lack of sleep and fatigue) and *glucose depletion* are the 'big three' factors that lead to impaired self-regulation (dysfunctional coping) and unreliable (false) statement or confession.

---

[54] Gudjonsson, 2018, pp. 114–116, see *supra* note 2.

[55] Deborah Davis and Richard A. Leo, "Acute Suggestibility in Police Interrogation: Self-Regulation Failure as a Primary Mechanism of Vulnerability", in Anna. M. Ridley, Fiona Gabbert and David J. La Rooy (eds.), *Suggestibility in Legal Contexts: Psychological Research and Forensic Implications*, Wiley-Blackwell, Chichester, 2013, pp. 171–195.

3.4.1. Evidence Base for Traits of Suggestibility and Compliance

Suggestibility and compliance have long been seen as vulnerabilities that are relevant to police-induced false confessions.[56] Recently, Otgaar and colleagues[57] have provided an independent systematic review of the link between suggestibility, compliance and false confessions from 11 field and 12 experimental studies. Using Cohen's 'd', in the field studies, both suggestibility (1.09) and compliance (1.28) predicted false confession with large mean effect sizes across studies. In the experimental studies, the mean effect sizes were medium (0.33) for suggestibility and low (0.12) for compliance. The differences in the size of the effect sizes between the field and experimental studies are likely to reflect the limitations placed on interrogative pressure and its duration allowed in experimental studies for ethical approval.

3.4.2. Cumulative Disadvantage

Cumulative disadvantage can be construed in two different ways. Firstly, within the above categorization, a suspect may possess several different enduring personal vulnerabilities during an investigative interview (for example, combined intellectual disability, acquiescence, suggestibility and compliance). Secondly, the cumulative negative impact of the judicial process itself (that is, police interviews, charge, prosecution, trial and appeal).

3.5. The Gudmundur and Geirfinnur Cases and the Looming End to the 47-Year-Old 'Blame Game'

One of the most extreme cases of multiple false confessors is that of the Icelandic Gudmundur and Geirfinnur cases, which have featured on the UK's BBC web site[58] and in a BBC Four Storyville and Netflix documentary.[59] The unique feature of these two cases, which were investigated and prosecuted jointly, is the extent to which the investigators used long solitary confinement and lengthy questioning to coerce incriminating statements from six suspects to support the investigators unfounded investigative hypotheses about the disappearance of two men in 1974 and their assumed murders. One suspect's admission-confession was used to coerce incriminating statements from other co-accused and

---

[56] Gudjonsson, 2018, pp. 114–116, see *supra* note 2.

[57] Henry Otgaar *et al.*, "The Link Between Suggestibility, Compliance, and False Confessions: A Review Using Experimental and Field Studies", in *Applied Cognitive Psychology*, 2021, vol. 35, no. 2, pp. 445–455.

[58] Simon Cox, "The Reykjavik Confessions", *BBC*, May 2014.

[59] Dylan Howitt, "Out of Thin Air", Documentary, 1 May 2017.

subsequently used to extract coerced corroborative false statements from two key prosecution witnesses.[60]

3.5.1. Brief Background to the Gudmundur and Geirfinnur Cases

Gudmundur Einarsson and Geirfinnur Einarsson (unrelated men) disappeared on 27 January and 19 November 1974 respectively. Gudmundur's disappearance was not viewed as suspicious at the time; he had disappeared after leaving a night club in Hafnarfjördur late at night and walking to Reykjavík, about 10 kilometres away in heavy snow.

Geirfinnur disappeared after leaving his home in Keflavík late one evening after receiving a mysterious telephone call. He was allegedly meeting one or more people at the nearby Harbour Café. Two days before his disappearance he had visited a popular Reykjavík Club ('Klúbburinn'). Klúbburinn had previously been on the radar of an overzealous Keflavík custom officer and a Reykjavík prosecutor, both of whom later became involved in the investigation into Geirfinnur's disappearance.[61]

Very soon after the Keflavík investigation into Geirfinnur's disappearance started in November 1974, unfounded rumours began to spread that the director and the manager of Klúbburinn were responsible for Geirfinnur's disappearance. The two Klúbburinn men made a formal complaint to the Ministry of Justice about the unfounded rumours in February 1975. The Keflavík Sheriff's Department investigation was closed in June 1975 when the Ministry of Justice formally took over the case. No suspects were officially identified, but apparently the two 'Klúbburinn men' remained on the police and prosecution radar.

In December 1975, the Reykjavík police and judiciary began an investigation into Gudmundur's disappearance, apparently after having received some unsubstantiated rumour from a 'confidential' source that had been brought to their attention. Erla Bolladóttir's coerced witness statement on 20 December 1975 became the lynchpin from which the Gudmundur and Geirfinnur investigation started. Her vulnerabilities, including her separation from her infant

---

[60] Gudjonsson, 2018, see *supra* note 2. Gudjonsson, 2021, see *supra* note 9.

[61] The Reykjavík police and a senior prosecutor had taken a keen interest in the Klúbburinn in 1972 at the instigation of an overzealous Keflavík custom officer, who suspected that Klúbburinn was involved in illegal purchase of alcohol. As a result, the Chief of Police in Reykjavík temporarily withdrew the Klúbburinn's licence to sell alcohol in the autumn of 1972, effectively shutting down the Klúbburinn. The owner of the Klúbburinn made an official complaint and the Minister of Justice intervened and lifted the ban of selling alcohol and the Klúbburinn reopened. No evidence was ever found to support the Klúbburinn's involvement in smuggling of alcohol. See Gudjonsson, 2018, see *supra* note 2.

daughter, were the investigators' trump card for obtaining incriminating statements to support their speculative investigative hypotheses.

Table 1 shows the number of days in solitary confinement and the number of hours of questioning of the six suspects. Also included in the table are the number of 'face-to-face' police arranged confrontations between the suspects to improve consistency in their statements. These 'face-to-face' confrontations were used by the police by proxy to exercise pressure in order to obtain confessions. The individual numbers show the extreme lengths that the police, prosecution and judiciary went to break down resistance and obtain confessions that they could use for legal charges, prosecution and eventual convictions.

Name of defendant	Days in solitary confinement	Interviews (hours)	'Face-to-face' confrontation
Sævar Ciesielski	741	340	20
Kristján Vidarsson	682	215	18
Tryggvi Leifsson	627	124	16
Erla Bolladóttir	241	120	11
Gudjón Skarphédinsson	412	160	5
Albert Skaftason	88	17	16

Table 1: The days in solitary confinement, hours of police interviews and number of 'face-to-face' confrontations.[62]

3.5.2. Breaking the Law for the 'Greater Good' of Extracting Incriminating Statements and Confessions

One of the most important international lessons from the Gudmundur and Geirfinnur investigation is that legal regulations and guidelines regarding investigative interviewing are of no use if they are simply ignored and colluded with by the judiciary. In the 1970s, there were excellent, and for their time remarkably advanced, legal requirements for interviewing suspects in Iceland, dating back to the early 1950s.[63] The law stipulated that the interviewer must be open-minded when investigating cases (that is, focus on factors that support both guilt

---

[62] This table is adapted from Gudjonsson, 2021, see *supra* note 9. The hours of interviews figures represent an underestimate because many conversations and interviews were not recorded as legally required (for example, Bolladóttir was taken to the Síðumúli prison on three separate occasions for a total of 11 hours before her first recorded interview in the Geirfinnur case on 23 January 1976, where she indirectly implicated several people in the Geirfinnur case, including the Klúbburinn men. All these pre-statement interviews were unrecorded).

[63] For a review, see Gudjonsson, 2018, see *supra* note 2.

and innocence), it was unlawful to lie to suspects, interviewees should not be asked questions that may confuse them, the focus was on obtaining truthful answers, no threats or inducements (coercion) were allowed, and interviews should not exceed six hours without a break.[64]

The investigative law at the time was essentially an *information-gathering process* with emphasis on fairness and justice, but the process contained a highly coercive and abusive element. *This was the implicit or direct threat and use of solitary confinement to coerce incriminating statements from witnesses and suspects.*[65]

All the legal requirements regarding investigative interviews were broken during the Gudmundur and Geirfinnur investigation with the collusion of the Reykjavík Criminal Court, which presided over the entire investigation and by standard procedure in serious cases, appointed a Criminal Court lawyer to head the investigation from the 'official' beginning of the Reykjavík investigation in December 1975 (the investigators have never been open about when the investigation really commenced).[66] The approach taken was *accusatory* and *guilt-presumptive* with its inherent risks of eliciting false incriminating statements against self and others. *The risks associated with the coercive interview process were hugely exacerbated using implicit or explicit threats of almost unlimited solitary confinement.*

The Supreme Court of Iceland was unaware of the extent of those breaches in 1980 when the six defendants were convicted and given prison sentences.

Regarding the extensive police (and court) breaches in the Gudmundur and Geirfinnur cases, the investigative lawyer ('VS') who led the investigation in the Geirfinnur case from the Keflavík Sheriff's department between November 1974 and June 1975 has tried to justify the investigators breaking the rules. When he was interviewed by BBC journalist Simon Cox in 2018, VS admitted that the investigators "broke every rule, but when we did, it was a development

---

[64] The law was ambiguous about whether six hours of interviews meant six hours in a single day, or if six hours of questioning could be repeated in the same day after a break.

[65] In the 1970s, there was no stipulated upper limit for solitary confinement as can be seen from Table 1. The designated days in detention (for example, 30 days or longer at a time) was merely renewed repeatedly. There was always the looming threat for suspects who were considered 'unco-operative' to be detained in solitary confinement for almost an unlimited number of days.

[66] The investigators have never been transparent about when and why the investigation started in the first place. On two separate occasions in the District Court (January 2016 and November 2021) they claimed memory lapses about their involvement in the investigation.

of the criminal courts – it's like saying to doctor you should have used other methods on a patient 40 years ago".[67]

3.5.3. Recent Developments in the Gudmundur and Geirfinnur Cases

In March 2013, a Working Group set up by the Minister of the Interior, Ögmundur Jónasson, reported its findings that the confessions of the six convicted persons were wholly unreliable. The current author was a consultant to the Working Group and interviewed all four surviving convicted persons, jointly with a member of the Working Group.[68]

An Icelandic Court Case Review Commission ('ICCRC') argued in a report in 2017 that there were 'strong clues' from the confessions that the convicted persons had been responsible for the death of Gudmundur and Geirfinnur. This argument was based on the assumed improbability that so many persons, convicted persons and witnesses, would have confessed to the killings in a similar way. Crucially, the ICCRC failed to consider satisfactorily the evidence that many cases of false confessions involve more than one false confessor and its cumulative disadvantage across suspects and witnesses.[69]

Despite this misguided view, the ICCRC recommended that the five men's appeal applications had merit, a view shared by the special prosecutor. This was a game changer in the two cases and a credit to the ICCRC and prosecution. Surprisingly, the ICCRC had not supported the appeal application of Erla Bolladóttir, who had been convicted of perjury in the Geirfinnur case (her only conviction). She appears to have been manipulated from the beginning of the Geirfinnur investigation to implicate people of interest to the police. In May 1976, she falsely confessed to killing Geirfinnur by shooting him when placed under interrogative pressure in a coercive prison environment. Her false confession was farcical, like the other statements and confessions in the two cases.

In September 2018, on the recommendation of the ICCRC and special prosecutor the Supreme Court of Iceland quashed the convictions of all five men in connection with the two men's disappearance and death.[70]

On 4 January 2022, Bolladóttir won her appeal against the ICCRC's decision not to refer her case to the Supreme Court. A scrupulous and open-minded

---

[67] Simon Cox, *The Reykjavik Confessions*, BBC Books, London, 2018, p. 296.

[68] Tryggvi Leifsson died in Iceland on 1 May 2009, aged 57 years. Sævar Ciesielski died in Denmark on the 12 July 2011, aged 56 years. The families of the two men appealed against their convictions.

[69] Gudjonsson, 2021, see *supra* note 9.

[70] "All Found Innocent in Guðmundur and Geirfinns Case, 44 Years After the Supposed Crimes Were Committed", *Icelandic Monitor*, 27 September 2018.

Reykjavík District Court judge, Pétur Dam Leifsson, quashed the ICCRC's decision on numerous apparently well founded and argued grounds, including the ICCRC's failure to consider authoritative expert clinical psychology evidence available to the Commission in 2017 (Case no. E-6219/2019). Bolladóttir now referred her case to a newly established Court Cases Review Court.

The Icelandic judiciary now appeared to be beginning to accept that the six convicted persons were not to blame for their false confessions. Bolladóttir was the investigators' manipulative linchpin for their unfounded investigative hypotheses in both the Gudmundur and Geirfinnur cases. Continuing to blame her for this miscarriage of justice only undermined the integrity of the Icelandic police and judiciary for years to come.

In a civil compensation case of two of the wrongly convicted persons (Skarphéðinsson and Vidarsson), Iceland's Court of Appeal ('Landsréttur', Case no. 250/2020) ruled on 17 December 2021 that the false confessions of the wrongly convicted persons had been coerced by the investigators, basically exonerating the convicted persons from blame, and thereby rejecting the State's unfounded continuous reliance on the 'blame game' to avoid responsibility for this miscarriage of justice.[71] According to one of the defence lawyers, Ragnar Adalsteinsson, a veteran lawyer in the Gudmundur and Geirfinnur cases, the ruling was both historical and landmark, setting an important precedent for the professional and ethical behaviour of government officials in future cases, including that of the police, prosecutors and judges.[72] Perhaps, at last, Bolladóttir had a chance to be exonerated and the public confidence in the Icelandic judiciary restored.[73]

Unfortunatley, on 14 September 2022 the Court Cases Review Court rejected Bolladóttir's appeal on very narrow legal grounds (Case no. 8/2022).[74] Her only options now were to appeal to the European Court of Human Rights, which was a lengthy and costly process, or seek public apology and compensation from Iceland's Prime Minister, Katrín Jakobsdóttir. Bolladóttir chose the latter option and the outcome was satisfactory from her point of view (see Table 4).

---

[71] Court of Appeal of Iceland, *Skarphéðinsson and Vidarsson*, Judgment, 17 December 2021, Case no. 250/2020 (https://www.legal-tools.org/doc/iw8s0g/). Freyr Gígja Gunnarsson, "Guðjóni og Kristjáni Viðari dæmdar bætur í Landsrétti", *RÚV*, 17 December 2021.

[72] "Katrín fagnar dómsorði um bætur", *Fréttablaðið*, 18 December 2021, p. 4.

[73] She was now legally represented by Sigrún Ingibjörg Gísladóttir, a colleague of Ragnar Adalsteinsson and joint Partner at the law firm *Réttur* in Reykjavík.

[74] Brynjólfur Þór Guðmundsson, "Endurupptökudómstóll synjaði beiðni Erlu", *RÚV*, 20 September 2022.

3.6. Examples of the Processes and Mechanisms of Police-Induced False Statements

The Gudmundur and Geirfinnur cases provide excellent examples of police-induced false incriminating statements and confessions and the vulnerabilities, processes and mechanisms involved. The analysis and framework provided in this section can be readily applied to other cases internationally. Tables 2, 3 and 4 provide an in-depth behavioural science-based analysis of the three key incriminating statements that Erla Bolladóttir was coerced to make to support the investigators' speculative hypotheses in the Gudmundur and Geirfinnur cases.

Table 2 illustrates the process and mechanism of Bolladóttir's false witness statement in the Gudmundur case, followed in Table 3 by her false witness statement against several innocent men in the Geirfinnur case, and finally in Table 4 her own false confession to shooting and killing Geirfinnur. The three tables tell a remarkable story of how experienced investigators and prosecutors were apparently motivated to implicate the owner and manager of a popular Icelandic club, Klúbburinn, in Geirfinnur's disappearance by manipulating a vulnerable young woman with an infant daughter to facilitate their endeavour. The lessons learned from the flawed investigation and subsequent miscarriage of justice, as well as the detailed analysis of Bolladóttir's false incriminating statements, should be used to educate investigators about the importance of ethical interviewing and the necessity to always follow the law that guides best police practice at the time.

Table 3 shows how the content of a voluntary false confession of a troubled hospital porter in the Geirfinnur case in October 1975, three months later became a hypothesis-driven police-induced crime scene that led to false accusations against four innocent men (the Klúbburinn men), the blame game that commenced after their release from custody three months later and the eventual manslaughter convictions of three men (Ciesielski, Vidarsson and Skarphédinsson) for Geirfinnur's assumed unlawful death in the Keflavík harbour. Allegedly his death had resulted from arguments over the purchase or sale of smuggled alcohol.[75]

---

[75] Despite the alleged crime scene (Keflavík Harbour) and references to purchase of smuggled alcohol remaining reasonably consistent across the defendants, the detailed content of their statements kept changing and were riddled with inconsistencies and ambiguities. Regardless of their inherent unreliability, they were used to convict the three defendants of manslaughter.

Background:

- Bolladóttir had a history of sexual abuse in childhood and adolescence.
- On 13 December 1975, Bolladóttir was arrested on suspicion of fraud offences. Her boyfriend, Sævar Ciesielski, had been arrested the previous day. Both were placed in solitary confinement at the Sídumúli prison. At the time, Bolladóttir and Ciesielski had an eleven-week-old daughter, whom Bolladóttir had been looking after without proper support from Ciesielski or her own family. She was socially isolated and her relationship with Ciesielski was turbulent. Ciesielski had been under police surveillance for suspected drug-related offences. He had been on the police radar for a while, but always managed to stay ahead of the police and the Keflavík customs. It seems that he was a thorn in their side.
- On the seventh day in solitary confinement for the alleged fraud offences, Bolladóttir had confessed to the fraud offences and should have been immediately released from custody to go home to her infant daughter. Instead, the investigators started questioning her about Gudmundur's disappearance, which she knew nothing about, and kept her in custody for overnight stay to think about it. The following day, the investigators persuaded her that a dream she had had at the night of Gudmundur's disappearance had been real and related to witnessing his murder in her home in Hafnarfjördur. Her home, which she had shared with Ciesielski, now became a crime scene without any physical evidence.

Contextual factors:

- The 'suspects' were Bolladóttir's boyfriend (Sævar Ciesielski) and his two friends (Kristján Vidarsson and Tryggvi Leifsson).
- She had a negative mind-set with regard to Ciesielski and his friends which made it easier for her to be persuaded that they might have murdered Gudmundur (that is, there was great scope for *plausibility* and *manipulation*).

Situational factors:

- She wanted to get home after seven days in solitary confinement. All she wanted was to be with her infant daughter.
- The confession to her two fraud offences for over 25 hours in three days had left her cumulatively vulnerable, because she feared the repercussions, possibly including being further separated from her daughter or her being taken into care.
- The investigators had her under their control.
- The looming threat of further solitary confinement was always a real possibility in case she was viewed as un-cooperative.
- Persuasive questioning.
- High emotional intensity.

Enduring personal factors:	**Acute state personal factors:**
<ul><li>Emotional lability.</li><li>Low self-esteem.</li><li>Vivid imagination.</li><li>High compliance.</li><li>Susceptibility to being 'controlled' by 'significant' others.</li></ul>	<ul><li>Desperate to get out of solitary confinement.</li><li>Became distressed and confused.</li><li>Dream turned into a crime scene with the assistance of the investigators who were reportedly helping her to recover from an alleged psychogenic amnesia.</li><li>State of suggestibility.</li></ul>

Outcome of interviews: *Pressured-internalized false statements against Ciesielski and Vidarsson, later adding Leifsson to the story* after Ciesielski had mentioned him – suggesting contamination effect.
False statement process: Contextual and situational factors impact on enduring and state vulnerability factors, causing a confused state and *distinctiveness heuristic failure* (the mechanism) leading to *plausibility, acceptance and reconstruction of the alleged crime-scene*.[76]
Outcome of the case: In 1980, the Supreme Court of Iceland convicted all three men of murdering Gudmundur Einarsson in the early hours of 27 January 1974 in a flat that Bolladóttir had shared with Ciesielski. A fourth man, Albert Skaftason was convicted of interfering with the crime scene, having been the alleged driver to transport and dispose of Gudmundur's body.[77] A driver was needed in the alleged crime scene because none of the other three men had driving licences or cars.
Convictions overturned: On 27 September 2018, the convictions of Ciesielski, Vidarsson, Leifsson relating to the death of Gudmundur Einarsson, and Skaftason for interfering with the crime scene, were quashed on the recommendations of the special prosecutor and the findings of a Court Cases Review Commission in 2017.[78]

Table 2: The process and mechanism of Bolladóttir's false statements in the Gudmundur case when she implicated Sævar Ciesielski and Kristján Vidarsson (20 December 1975).

---

[76] Bolladóttir's lawyer, Ragnar Aðalsteinsson, has argued that the false statements in the Gudmundur case were merely a prelude (a form of a softening up process) to ultimately implicate the Klúbburinn men in alcohol smuggling and Geirfinnur's disappearance.

[77] For a review, see Gudjonsson, 2018, see *supra* note 2.

[78] *Icelandic Monitor*, 27 September 2018, see *supra* note 70.

Background:

- Following Bolladóttir's release from solitary confinement on 20 December 1976, the investigators from the Gudmundur case kept in touch with her and questioned her about Ciesielski's knowledge about the Geirfinnur case.[79]
- This included the investigators questioning her at home, when her mother was out, and additionally she was taken on four separate occasions to the Sídumúli prison for questioning for five (30 December), four (21 January), two (22 January) and three (23 January) hours (approximately) respectively. She had the status of a witness, which gave the investigators more freedom and scope to question her unofficially and manipulate her without legal advice or support.
- There exist handwritten notes, a narrative written in the first person of the interview on 21 January, two days prior to Bolladóttir's first written statement in the Geirfinnur case. It describes how she and Ciesielski had been driven to Keflavík Harbour where they met several people, including two of the so-called Klúbburinn men (whilst also making a vague reference to a third). Ciesielski and one other man allegedly went with Geirfinnur on a boat to collect contraband from the sea.
- After an interview in prison on 23 January 1976, Bolladóttir indirectly implicated several people of possible interest to police as having been in Keflavík Harbour on the evening of Geirfinnur's disappearance, including four Klúbburinn men (only two were directly linked to Klúbburinn; the other two by indirect association).
- Two days earlier (21 January), Ciesielski had already directly implicated three of the four Klúbburinn men during lengthy questioning on that day. That interview was not formally recorded, but handwritten notes show that Ciesielski was questioned about the Geirfinnur case and mentioned several names apparently of interest to the investigators.
- The risk of contamination between the unrecorded statements of Ciesielski and Bolladóttir was extremely high.

Contextual factors:

- Bolladóttir had already given in to pressure from the investigators and falsely implicated Ciesielski and Vidarsson in the 'death' of Gudmundur the previous month.
- The investigators had good understanding of her vulnerabilities and malleability.
- The investigators were helping her with practical matters and she misguidedly viewed them as 'friends'.
- After her arrest on 13 December 1975 for suspected fraud offences Erla Bolladóttir's flat, where she had lived with her infant daughter, was sealed and she was only allowed to go there accompanied by an investigator. Consequently, after her custody ended on 20 December, she had to move in with her mother with whom she had a turbulent relationship. This apparently unreasonable deprivation of her own independent accommodation can be construed as coercive and manipulative in relation to the Geirfinnur case.
- In October 1975, a 42-year-old hospital porter had confessed to his family during an argument about an affair he was having with an ex-partner of the owner of Klúbburinn. During the argument and whilst intoxicated, the porter claimed to have witnessed

---

[79] Ciesielski was a garrulous young man with attention deficit hyperactivity disorder who was known to have boasted to people that he knew something about the case. This may have misguided the investigators.

Geirfinnur's accidental death whilst collecting alcohol from the seabed near Keflavík Harbour. He had allegedly gone with Geirfinnur on a boat to collect the alcohol at the request of the owner of Klúbburinn. The porter told his family that he and the owner and manager of Klúbburinn had met with Geirfinnur at the Harbour Café before going out at sea to collect the alcohol.

- The Reykjavík Police interviewed the porter. He admitted to having told his family the story but claimed there was no truth to it. He was not charged with any offence related to Geirfinnur's disappearance.
- The porter's false confession to his family apparently set the scene for the subsequent false statements of Bolladóttir, Ciesielski, Vidarsson and several months later those of Skarphédinsson (the alleged driver who took them to Keflavík on 19 November 1974).[80]
- *The background to the Reykjavík investigation was heavily contaminated and misguided from the start by a botched Keflavík investigation and a subsequent false confession of a deeply troubled man.*[81]

Situational factors:

- Looming threat (and a real possibility) of being placed again in solitary confinement in Prison if she did not give the investigators what they wanted to hear.
- Unrecorded interactions with the investigators, including being questioned at her mother's home and subsequently on three previous occasions in Sídumúli Prison.
- Threatening phone calls to her home, possibly instigated by the investigators.

Enduring personal factors:	Acute state personal factors:
<ul><li>Emotional lability.</li><li>Low self-esteem.</li><li>Vivid imagination.</li><li>High compliance.</li><li>Susceptibility to being 'controlled' by 'significant' others.</li></ul>	<ul><li>Extreme fear of custody and being separated from her infant daughter.</li><li>Extreme compliance.</li><li>Fear of upsetting the investigators.</li><li>Gave the investigators what they wanted so she could go back home to her daughter.</li></ul>

Outcome of interviews: *Pressured-compliant false statements regarding the Klúbburinn men.* None of Bolladóttir's false statements directly implicated the Klúbburinn men in the disappearance and murder of Geirfinnur. This important fact appears to have been conveniently ignored by the judiciary.

False statement process: Contextual and situational factors impact on enduring and state vulnerability factors, causing *dysfunctional coping* (the mechanism), breakdown in resistance and compliance with the demands of the investigators.

---

[80] Bolladóttir, Ciesielski and Vidarsson would not have known about the previous false confession statement (that is, special knowledge), which strongly indicates contamination via the investigators.

[81] For a discussion of this first false confession in the Geirfinnur case, see Gudjonsson, 2018, Chapter 7, see *supra* note 2.

Consequences: After Bolladóttir, Ciesielski and Vidarsson had given false statements against the Klúbburinn men, the Klúbburinn men were arrested and placed in solitary confinement in the Sídumúli prison for more than three months.

Table 3: The process and mechanism of Bolladóttir's false statement against the (innocent) Klúbburinn men in the Geirfinnur case (23 January 1976).

Background:

- At the beginning of May 1975, the four Klúbburinn men had been in custody for more than three months and the investigators had failed to find any evidence against them. They all had ready access to their lawyers, unlike Ciesielski, Vidarsson and Bolladóttir. There was never any evidence to link them to Geirfinnur's disappearance and they all denied any involvement in it. Undoubtedly, this placed the entire investigation in jeopardy. Apparently to avert a disaster, the investigators again turned to their most vulnerable and malleable witness, Bolladóttir.
- At 20:30 on 3 May, Bolladóttir was taken to the Sídumúli prison for further questioning in the Geirfinnur case. She had the status of a witness. The questioning ended at 23:40, after which Bolladóttir became extremely distressed when told that she would remain in custody, requiring the attendance of the prison priest and heavy sedation to help her sleep. *Her mind was completely overborn and any statement she made would be inherently unreliable.*
- The following day at 12:38, Bolladóttir was questioned again, but this time she had the status of a suspect. The questioning was conducted by the State prosecutor in the case and two of the investigators. The purpose of the questioning was apparently to establish if Bolladóttir's involvement in the Geirfinnur case was more extensive than she had previously declared.[82] Bolladóttir gave a detailed confession statement, which included how she had shot Geirfinnur with a rifle in Keflavík Harbour at the instigation of her boyfriend Ciesielski. Following her confession, Bolladóttir remained in solitary confinement until 22 December 1976. She was now directly implicated in Geirfinnur's death.

Contextual factors:

- The imminent release of the four Klúbburinn men from custody.
- The Geirfinnur investigation was in jeopardy (and by implication also the Gudmundur case).
- Pressure on the investigators was building up to avoid professional embarrassment and avoid being blamed for incompetence.
- Bolladóttir had been in regular contact with the investigators about the Geirfinnur case since her first written false statement on 23 January 1976, including alleged crime scene visits.
- Withdrawing her false statements against the Klúbburinn men seriously risked her being charged with perjury and taken into custody. This was a tangible threat. As Sekar has cogently argued: "Perjury is a double-edged sword. It boxes witnesses in

---

[82] It seems that Bolladóttir had broken down and confessed to shooting Geirfinnur the evening before (this is consistent with what she has consistently told the author), but no statement was taken after the three hours of questioning. She was left extremely distressed in the Sídumúli prison overnight before her confession statement was taken.

to a story that, once given, leads to fear of prosecution and makes retraction unlikely".[83]

- Bolladóttir had no realistic option of retracting her false statements in the Gudmundur and Geirfinnur cases. She had to continue with the web of lies. She was doomed whatever she did.

Situational factors:

- The investigators had been in regular contact with Bolladóttir since her first incriminating statement in the Geirfinnur case, apparently trying to 'help them' with their enquiries.
- Bolladóttir was taken to the Síðumúli prison and questioned as a witness for over three hours, all unrecorded.
- She must have realized that this was serious because the questioning was led by a senior prosecutor.
- This same prosecutor had, in 1972, assiduously tried to maintain a ban of the alcohol at Klúbburinn. On 31 December 1975, he had requested the papers from the original Geirfinnur case investigation from the Keflavík Sheriff's Department, which were delivered to him a few days later.
- The prosecutor's request for the papers was the day after Bolladóttir had been taken to the Síðumúli prison (apparently for questioning in the Geirfinnur case) for five hours (all unrecorded). It is highly improbable that this was a coincidence. The Klúbburinn men were apparently again on his radar, and this time in connection with Geirfinnur's mysterious disappearance in 1974.

Enduring personal factors:	**Acute state personal factors:**
<ul><li>Emotional lability.</li><li>Low self-esteem.</li><li>Vivid imagination.</li><li>High compliance.</li><li>Susceptibility to being 'controlled' by 'significant' others.</li></ul>	<ul><li>Terrified of custody and being separated from her infant daughter.</li><li>Feelings of utter helplessness and hopelessness.</li><li>Extreme distress.</li><li>Extreme compliance.</li><li>Not wanting to upset the investigators and prosecutor.</li><li>Tried to figure out what exactly they wanted her to confess to and gave them what she thought they wanted.</li><li>Thought if she confessed to killing Geirfinnur, she would be allowed to go home.[84]</li></ul>

Outcome of interviews: *Pressured-compliant false confession to the murder of Geirfinnur.*

False confession process: Contextual and situational factors impact on enduring and state vulnerability factors, causing *dysfunctional coping* (the mechanism), breakdown in resistance and

---

[83] Satish Sekar, *The Cardiff Five: Innocent Beyond Any Doubt*, Waterside Press, Hook, 2012, p. 189.

[84] This naive belief is typically found among false confessions in high stressed (coerced) custodial and interrogative situations. See Gudjonsson, 2018, Chapter 5, see *supra* note 2.

compliance with demands of the investigators (that is, that she was directly involved in the case).

The release of the four Klúbburinn men: On 9 May 1976, the four men were released from solitary confinement after approximately three months in the Sídumúli Prison. They had all had ready access to their lawyers, there was never any evidence to link them to Geirfinnur's disappearance and they all denied any involvement in Gerirfinnur's disappearance.

Turning the tables against Ciesielski and Vidarsson: Apparently to save face and an embarrassment, after the release of the Klúbburinn men, the investigators now turned to Ciesielski and Vidarsson as suspects in Geirfinnur's disappearance and coerced false confessions out of them about them having killed Geirfinnur in the Keflavík Harbour, along with a third man, Gudjón Skarphédinsson, an educated man who late in the investigation became the 'missing' driver who had taken Ciesielski and Vidarsson to the Keflavík Harbour to purchase alcohol from Geirfinnur.

The 'Indian Technique': To assist them with the investigation of the Geirfinnur case, in July 1976, the Minister of Justice appointed a newly retired German 'Spy Catcher' from the German Federal Police ('BKA'), Karl Schütz. Schütz interviewed witnesses and the suspects in the two cases through an interpreter and taught the Icelandic investigators the 'Indian Technique' to breaking down resistance by confusing the interviewee to 'get to the truth'. The 'Indian Technique' was unlawful in Iceland but was nevertheless used by the investigators and ignored, if not informally approved, by the judiciary which was in overall charge of the investigation. References to the 'Indian Technique' in at least two of the suspects' statements should at least have alerted the judges to Schütz's unlawful technique.

Subsequently, the President of Iceland awarded Schütz and several of his ex-colleagues from the BKA with medals of honour for their assistance with the Gudmundur and Geirfinnur cases.

Outcome of the case: In 1980, the Supreme Court of Iceland convicted Ciesielski, Vidarsson and Skarphédinsson of killing Geirfinnur Einarsson in Keflavík Harbour on 19 November 1974. They all received lengthy prison sentences.

Ciesielski and Vidarsson (along with Bolladóttir), were all convicted of perjury for implicating the four Klúbburinn men (Hæstiréttur Íslands; Case no. 214/1978).[85]

Convictions overturned: On 27 September 2018, Iceland's Supreme Court quashed the convictions of Ciesielski, Vidarsson, and Skarphédinsson relating to the death of Geirfinnur Einarsson on the recommendations of the ICCRC and special prosecutor (Hæstiréttur Íslands, Case no. 521/2017).[86]

Both the ICCRC, 2017, and subsequently the Court Cases Review Court, 2022, refused to support Bolladóttir's appeal against her perjury conviction on very narrow grounds.

Iceland's Prime Minister's public apology to Erla Bolladóttir: On 22 December 2022, following Bolladóttir's constructive meeting with the Prime Minister on 30 November 2022, the government offered a public apology for the treatment of Erla Bolladóttir whilst in

---

[85] Supreme Court of Iceland, *Viðarsson et al.*, Judgment, 22 February 1980, Case no. 214/1978 (https://www.legal-tools.org/doc/v1n381/).

[86] Supreme Court of Iceland, *Skaftasyni et al.*, Judgment, 27 September 2018, Case no. 521/2017 (https://www.legal-tools.org/doc/b45dg0/).

custody in 1976 and awarded her substantial compensation. This was final resoluation in the Geirfinnur case, which Erla Bolladóttir accepted. This effectively closed the Geirfinnur case.

A 47-year battle for justice had evendually come to a satisfactory conclusion due to the humanity, courage and integrity of Iceland's Prime Minister, Katrín Jakobsdóttir, and the diligence of Bolladóttir's legal team.[87]

Table 4: The process and mechanism of Bolladóttir's false confession to murder in the Geirfinnur case (3–4 May 1976).

3.7. Conclusions

The comments of Irving and Hilgendorf in their research study for the Royal Commission on Criminal Procedure showed that in the late 1970s there was limited understanding of the vulnerabilities, processes and mechanisms that drove suspects to give false confessions to criminal offences. There was absence of a behavioural science evidence-base that could guide investigators and the judiciary and general scepticism that suspects would confess to serious crimes they had not committed.

This chapter shows the remarkable development that has taken place over the past 40 years, leaving current scientists and practitioners with a solid theoretical foundation for conceptualizing psychologically different types of false confessions, impressive empirical scientific evidence-bases to draw upon and a rigorous framework for understanding and evaluating cases of false disputed confessions.

The main conclusions for investigative practice are as follows:

1. Police-induced false confessions are a reality for most (if not all) criminal justice systems. No longer should we deny this reality. This 'closed mind-set' can be overcome by teaching and training (that is, becoming well informed of the current science-based knowledge).

2. There is incontrovertible evidence from different legal jurisdictions that both witnesses and suspects are on occasions manipulated and coerced to give false or inadvertent incriminating statements to investigators about self or others.

3. It is oversimplistic to assume that investigators always tell the truth while disputed accounts (including retractions) from defendants are merely self-serving. Extensive examination of real-life cases shows that on occasions, investigators' accounts are biased and false. The remedy here is full electronic recording of all interviews.

4. When investigators and the judiciary make mistakes, these should be discussed openly, and the lessons learned implemented. Covering up mistakes

---

[87] Gréta Sigríður Einarsdóttir, "Erla Receives Compensation and Apology over 70s Murder Investigation", *Icelandic Review*, 23 December 2022.

and malpractice and ferociously going into a counter-attack (for example, blaming the witnesses or suspects themselves which is often the investigators' fall-back position), do significant damage to the integrity and credibility of the entire legal process. This misguided practice must stop.

5. Judicial systems must be open-minded and appropriately sanction illegal and poor police practice. The Icelandic Gudmundur and Geirfinnur cases show how extensive miscarriage of justice, which became almost impossible to correct, resulted from such collusion. All criminal justice systems make mistakes. These should be corrected whenever possible, and the lessons learned used to improve investigative law and practice.

6. A recently published report by Amnesty International shows that despite the lessons that should have learned from the Gudmundur and Geirfinnur cases, "harmful and unjustified use of pre-trial solitary confinement" is still a major problem in Iceland and needs urgent attention.[88] This shows how difficult it is to change systemically flawed police and judicial practice. It takes courage and motivation to accept mistakes, learn from them, and implement appropriate legal and good practice remedies.

7. It is important that *enduring* and *state* vulnerabilities of witnesses and suspects are identified and understood prior to and during the investigative interview. The identification of vulnerabilities may require an *adjustment* to the interview (for example, asking simple questions, ensuring the interviewee understands the questions asked and the implication of answers given, frequent breaks, avoiding closed and leading questions) as well as ensuring the presence of an appropriate adult in cases of young persons (under 18 years of age) and vulnerable adults. In cases of witnesses, an intermediary may be required to assist with communication.

8. The purpose of the proper identification of vulnerabilities is to ensure fairness and justice and protect the integrity of the statement (that is, its accuracy, completeness and reliability). Vulnerabilities should never be exploited by interviewers to manipulate and trick witnesses and suspects into giving what the interviewers believe is the 'truth'.

9. The four key pillars of fairness and justice are *professionalism* (including *integrity*), *humanity*, *transparency* and *accountability*. These should drive current investigative interviewing.

---

[88] Amnesty International, ""Waking Up to Nothing": Harmful and Unjustified Use of Pre-Trial Solitary Confinement", 31 January 2023.

4

Rapport, Empathy and Relationship-Building During Interviews

Gavin E. Oxburgh, Fiona Gabbert, Lee Moffett, Libby Ashurst and Lauren Grundy[*]

4.1. Introduction

All known major interviewing and interrogation guidelines acknowledge and endorse the use of rapport-building techniques to facilitate co-operation, and the importance of rapport within the interviewing arena is regularly re-affirmed by practitioners.[1] The recently developed Méndez Principles[2] also argue that there is a need to move away from a culture of accusatory, coercive, manipulative and confession-driven practices towards rapport-based interviewing. Importantly, the Principles also include the application of legal and procedural safeguards throughout the interview process, which reduces the risks of ill-treatment, produces more reliable information, and helps to ensure a lawful outcome of the investigation or intelligence operation. Rapport-based, non-coercive methods offer an effective suite of techniques that can be successfully applied by trained

---

[*] **Gavin E. Oxburgh**, Ph.D., is a Professor of Police Science and Registered Forensic Psychologist at Northumbria University, United Kingdom ('UK'). **Fiona Gabbert**, Ph.D., is a Professor of Applied Psychology at Goldsmiths University of London, UK. **Lee Moffett**, Ph.D., is an Associate Lecturer at Northumbria University. **Libby Ashurst**, Ph.D., is a Registered Consultant Forensic Psychologist. **Lauren Grundy** is a Registered Forensic Psychologist; both are practitioners at Ashurst Associates Consultancy UK Ltd.

[1] United Kingdom Home Office, *Achieving Best Evidence in Criminal Proceedings: Guidance on Interviewing Victims and Witnesses, and Using Special Measures*, London, 2022; United States Department of the Army, *Human Intelligence Collector Operations*, FM2-22.3, Washington, D.C., 2006 (https://www.legal-tools.org/doc/wbfiw1/); Ronald P. Fisher and R. Edward Geiselman, *Memory-Enhancing Techniques for Investigative Interviewing: The Cognitive Interview*, Charles C. Thomas Publisher, Springfield, 1992; Michael E. Lamb *et al.*, "A Structured Forensic Interview Protocol Improves the Quality and Informativeness of Investigative Interviews With Children: A Review of Research Using the NICHD Investigative Interview Protocol", in *Child Abuse & Neglect*, 2007, vol. 31, nos. 11–12, pp. 1201–1231; Central Planning and Training Unit, *A Guide to Interviewing*, Harrogate, 1992.

[2] Anti-Torture Initiative, Association for the Prevention of Torture and the Norwegian Centre for Human Rights, *Principles on Effective Interviewing for Investigations and Information Gathering*, 2021 ('Méndez Principles' or 'Principles') (https://www.legal-tools.org/doc/wbfiw1/).

professionals to gather criminal and intelligence information from interviewees – including criminal suspects, victims, witnesses and intelligence sources.

However, although the benefits amongst both practitioners and academics are agreed, some uncertainty remains regarding: (i) how to define rapport; (ii) how to establish (and maintain) rapport during an interview; and (iii) the benefits of using rapport within the context of an interview. For example, many researchers draw upon theoretical models of rapport which conceptualizes rapport as having three components: (i) mutual attentiveness, (ii) positivity and (iii) coordination; but little is understood as to how these different elements can be introduced during investigative contexts. Ultimately, what constitutes sufficient and appropriate rapport in one interpersonal context is different from sufficient and appropriate rapport in another. Similar issues have been noted for the use of empathy in the interview process. In particular, with many definitions highlighted in the literature from many different professional fields, there has been much theoretical debate concerning the differences between 'empathy' and 'sympathy'. As such, the current chapter will address each of these topic areas, starting with a discussion around the definition of rapport, including consideration of the importance and function of rapport within an investigative context. It will then focus on the concepts of humanity and empathy, and the observed limitations of each being used in practice, before introducing a more defined outline of relationship-building and the concept of 'attunement'. Throughout the chapter, the relevant evidence-base will be outlined and discussed.

4.2. Rapport

The term 'rapport' can mean different things to different people, making it difficult to define.[3] Furthermore, where definitions of rapport exist, they are often vague and imprecise, leaving room for ambiguity in the ways in which they are interpreted. Perhaps because of this, there are significant inconsistencies in the ways in which researchers and practitioners describe how they build rapport. For instance, there are several listed techniques for establishing rapport,[4] which include beginning the conversation with a topic that is of interest to the interviewee, appearing interested and sympathetic towards whatever the interviewee has to say, keeping the discussion informal, displaying positive emotional responses without appearing suspicious, and, importantly, not moving onto the

---

[3]   Ariel Neuman and Daniel Salinas-Serrano, "Custodial Interrogations: What We Know, What We Do, and What We Can Learn From Law Enforcement Experiences", in United States Department of Defense, National Defence Intelligence College, *Educing Information Interrogation: Science and Art Foundations for the Future*, Washington, D.C., 2006, pp. 141–233.

[4]   Robert F. Royal and Steven R. Schutt, *The Gentle Art of Interviewing and Interrogation: A Professional Manual and Guide*, Prentice-Hall, Englewood Cliffs, 1976.

actual interviewing phase until the interviewee appears friendly and co-operative. Other commentators advise the opposite approach though, emphasizing the importance of maintaining a professional distance, appearing firm, and establishing authority by insisting that the interviewee addresses the interviewer using a title, such as mister, whilst the interviewer should address the interviewee by their first name.[5] The absence of a clear understanding of what rapport means when used in a professional setting is problematic. It leaves the term open to interpretation and difficult to measure, which has significant implications for how it is researched and practised.

Some researchers[6] draw upon a tripartite theoretical model which conceptualizes rapport as having three components: (i) mutual attentiveness, (ii) positivity and (iii) co-ordination. Mutual attentiveness can be described as focused cohesive interaction, involvement and mutual interest. Positivity includes mutual friendliness, caring and positive affect. Co-ordination can be characterized by balance, fluency of interaction and shared understanding. Importantly, this model has been developed in the context of naturally emerging rapport in a social context and relates to rapport that exists at the relationship level. Arguably, then, it is limited in the extent to which it can inform how to build rapport in a professional context, such as an interviewer attempting to build rapport with an interviewee. There are some clear differences between social and professional contexts. For example, social contexts feature the freedom to interact on an equal footing with others who share similar interests and goals, and mutual rapport can develop naturally over time. In contrast, professional contexts are often characterized by one individual purposefully attempting to develop rapport with another, sometimes within a very short period of time. In addition, professional contexts often feature imbalances of power or status, as well as differences in desired outcomes from the interaction. There can also be differences in motivation to engage, where interviewees may lack motivation to co-operate or may even deliberately resist developing rapport with the interviewer.

The fact that rapport serves a function within a particular interaction or relationship perhaps explains the discrepancies amongst academic researchers when attempting to define it.[7] Ultimately, what constitutes sufficient and appropriate rapport in one interpersonal context is different from sufficient and appropriate rapport in another.[8] For example, the level of rapport required to engender a sufficient sense of autonomy for a suspect or witness of crime to

---

[5]   United Kingdom Home Office, 2022, see *supra* note 1.
[6]   Linda Tickle-Degnen and Robert Rosenthal, "The Nature of Rapport and Its Nonverbal Correlates", in *Psychological Inquiry*, 1990, vol. 1, no. 4, pp. 285–293.
[7]   Lamb *et al.*, 2007, see *supra* note 1.
[8]   *Ibid.*

provide an account of a criminal incident, may not be sufficient to engender the additional sense of equality with other persons of interest. For example, a police informant may require to recognize shared interests with their 'handlers'.[9] Indeed, police informants need to feel sufficient autonomy not only to provide information, but also to conduct tasking in order to gather target information and may therefore require an almost peer sense of equality with their 'handler',[10] something that is unlikely to be established within a traditional police or law enforcement interview. Hence, behaviours that are suitable for establishing rapport in an interview may not be relevant or even practical within an informant–handler interaction. It is, therefore, important to understand how practitioners define rapport.

One piece of research[11] specifically asked police informant handlers for their definition, and three sub-themes emerged: (i) that rapport entails the identification of common ground and establishment of trust; (ii) that rapport involves a reciprocal relationship; and (iii) that the relationship must be based on a professional footing. This perhaps adds weight to one definition of rapport[12] which emphasizes a working relationship between the interviewer and informant based on an understanding of motivation and welfare. According to these definitions then, rapport, at least within the context of an informant–handler interaction, is long-term and relational. Whether different levels of rapport require different interpersonal skills at different stages of the relationship remains to be explored.

4.2.1. The Importance of Rapport

All known major interviewing and interrogation guidelines acknowledge and endorse the use of rapport-building techniques to facilitate co-operation and the importance of rapport within the interviewing arena is regularly re-affirmed by practitioners. For example, when researchers asked federal-level interviewers in the United States to report their perceived effectiveness of different interview techniques,[13] four of the top five reported techniques came from the *rapport and*

---

9 Daniel L. Shapiro, "Negotiation Theory and Practice: Exploring Ideas to Aid Information Eduction", in United States Department of Defense, National Defence Intelligence College, 2006, pp. 267–284, see *supra* note 3.

10 Alex Hess and Menachem Amir, "The Program of Criminal Undercover Agents Sources in the Drug Trade", in *Substance Use and Misuse*, 2002, vol. 37, nos. 8–10, pp. 997–1034.

11 Royal and Schutt, 1976, see *supra* note 4.

12 Jordan Nunan *et al.*, "The Impact of Rapport on Intelligence Yield: Police Source Handler Telephone Interactions With Covert Human Intelligence Sources", in *Psychiatry, Psychology and Law*, 2020, vol. 29, no. 1, pp. 1–19.

13 Allison D. Redlich, Christopher E. Kelly and Jeaneé C. Miller, "The Who, What and Why of Human Intelligence Gathering: Self-Reported Measures of Interrogation Methods", in *Applied Cognitive Psychology*, 2014, vol. 28, no. 6, pp. 817–828.

relationship-building domain. When asked to consider alternative interview objectives, techniques associated to *rapport and relationship-building* were perceived as more effective when gathering information or intelligence than in other interview scenarios. Other researchers[14] made a similar finding, with practitioners reporting that rapport is a critical factor in the eventual success of an intelligence interview. However, this research concluded that "[...] although interrogators recognize and emphasize the value of rapport, there is less consensus on how it might be defined, achieved, or identified".[15]

Surveys of police officers in the United Kingdom confirm the perceived importance of rapport,[16] with some researchers[17] interviewing a sample of practitioners (24 informant handlers in England and Wales) who engaged in counterterrorism investigations. They asked a series of eight directed questions relating to rapport, and found that rapport was perceived as an important component in the gathering of information. Following their survey, the researchers identified several themes. Firstly, participants reported that rapport was essential for obtaining information over the entirety of an informant–handler relationship which is generally lengthier than that formed between investigators in other crime-related interviews. Secondly, they found that rapport is a specific concept within the context of an informant–handler meeting and should, therefore, be specifically defined within that context. When asked about the ability to train rapport-building techniques, the majority of respondents seemed to imply that there may be varying levels of innate ability, linked to interpersonal skills, but that this could be enhanced through training.

4.2.2. The Function of Rapport

In a systematic review of research[18] examining the use of rapport within an information-gathering context, the verbal, non-verbal or para-verbal behaviours that had been associated with building and measuring rapport across studies were identified and reported. The underlying intention, or function, of these rapport behaviours was then considered. The researchers were able to meaningfully group the rapport behaviours according to one of three core functions, each of which has been used to support the development of rapport: (i) personalizing the

---

[14] Melissa B. Russano, Fadia M. Narchet and Steven M. Kleinman, "Analysts, Interpreters, and Intelligence Interrogations: Perceptions and Insights", in *Applied Cognitive Psychology*, 2014, vol. 28, no. 6, pp. 829–846.

[15] Cf. *ibid.*, p. 851.

[16] Jane Birkett and Graham Pike, *Exploring Rapport and Communication Methods Between Covert Human Intelligence Sources (CHIS) and CHIS Handlers Throughout a CHIS Lifecycle*, National Crime Agency, London, 2017.

[17] Royal and Schutt, 1976, see *supra* note 4.

[18] Lamb *et al.*, 2007, see *supra* note 1.

interview, (ii) presenting an approachable demeanor, and (iii) paying attention. Different behaviours can be used to achieve the same outcome. For example, engaging in active listening, including use of empathy, and using non-verbal behaviours such as appropriate use of eye-contact and head-nodding, can all be used to demonstrate that the interviewer is paying attention to the interviewee. In short, different behaviours can be used to build rapport, and it is useful (especially for practitioners) to consider not only which behaviours can be used but also what their function is and why they are effective.

Many interview models in use (for example, the PEACE model of interviewing used in England and Wales)[19] appear to adopt a rather goal-oriented interpretation of rapport as opposed to the continuous use of rapport throughout an interview. For example, within the *engage and explain* phase of the PEACE model, rapport is conceived as a means of ensuring that the procedure of the interview is adhered to by outlining objectives and expectations at the outset.[20] However, researchers have found that interviewers following the PEACE model have been able to utilize rapport throughout the majority of an interview to improve information yield. For example, researchers[21] developed a scientific tool (Observing Rapport-Based Interpersonal Techniques ('ORBIT'))[22] for measuring rapport which they used to examine a series of interviews with high-level suspects of crime. The developers of ORBIT note that prior research has generated 'task lists' to be incorporated in interviews, but that these tasks are often either poorly defined or overly specific; consequently, the concept of rapport is also poorly defined. They noted that there are parallels between a police interview and the Motivational Interview ('MI'), which is a technique utilized in clinical psychology to motivate behavioural change, and, as with a police interview, the interviewer seeks to establish an "[…] empathic, respectful, and non-judgmental atmosphere"[23] with the interviewer adopting a flexible, but goal-oriented approach. However, the MI does not propose a list of strategies or tactics to be adhered to, but emphasizes the 'spirit' of the approach, focusing on creating an atmosphere of *collaboration* over *confrontation*, and maintaining the

---

[19] See Chapter 12 of this book for more details.

[20] College of Policing, "Investigative Interviewing", 26 October 2022 (available on the College of Policing's web site).

[21] Laurence Alison *et al.*, "The Efficacy of Rapport-Based Techniques for Minimizing Counter-Interrogation Tactics Amongst a Field Sample of Terrorists", in *Psychology, Public Policy, and Law*, 2014, vol. 20, no. 4, pp. 421–430. For a full review, see Fiona Gabbert *et al.*, "Exploring the Use of Rapport in Professional Information-Gathering Contexts by Systematically Mapping the Evidence Base", in *Applied Cognitive Psychology*, 2021, vol. 35, no. 2, pp. 329–341.

[22] See Chapter 15 of this book for more details.

[23] Anti-Torture Initiative, 2021, p. 412, see *supra* note 2.

interviewee's autonomy rather than imposing the interviewer's authority. It is, however, noted[24] that police or law enforcement interviewers are advised to follow a similar approach by using open (or appropriate) questions, being non-judgmental, being empathic (see later in this chapter), goal-directed and responding flexibly to the interviewee's responses through active listening.

Researchers[25] also note that "[…] rapport building is unlikely to be appropriate or productive for every phase of the suspect interview", and so turn to the Interpersonal Behaviour Circle ('IBC') as a means of measuring the overall essence of an interaction. According to the IBC model,[26] personality is not fixed or isolated, but should be considered within the context of how people interact with each other. Alison et al., therefore, sought to combine the ethos of MI and IBC theory to build a model that could measure and analyse rapport throughout the course of a police or law enforcement interview.[27] The result is that the ORBIT model is designed to examine rapport at a macro-level, taking a holistic approach to look at the overall style and atmosphere of the interview, rather than relying on the presence or absence of a prescriptive list of techniques presumed to enhance rapport. Their findings indicated that interviewers employed rapport building and positive interpersonal behaviour throughout the interview process, and that an adaptive interpersonal technique resulted in more information being disclosed by the suspect.

However, the ORBIT model has been criticized[28] as being difficult to apply and, having been taken directly from the counselling literature, lacks specificity within the context of a police or law enforcement interview. Consequently, the model proposed by Tickle-Degnen and Rosenthal (1990)[29] was used by other researchers[30] in the only known study (to date) which measures the impact of rapport on intelligence yield specifically in informant–handler interviews. Results confirm findings from traditional police or law enforcement interviews, namely, that an increase in rapport-consistent behaviours produce greater information or intelligence yield.[31] Whilst the relational function of rapport is, without doubt, recognized, researchers have so far been limited to proposing

---

24 Cf. *ibid.*
25 Cf. *ibid.*, p. 413.
26 First proposed by Leary and Coffey in 1954 (Anti-Torture Initiative, 2021, see *supra* note 2).
27 Laurence Alison *et al.*, 2014, see *supra* note 21.
28 Kimberly Collins and Nikki Carthy, "No Rapport, No Comment: The Relationship Between Rapport and Communication During Investigative Interviews With Suspects", in *Journal of Investigative Psychology and Offender Profiling*, 2019, vol. 16, no. 1, pp. 18–31.
29 Tickle-Degnen and Rosenthal, 1990, see *supra* note 6.
30 Lamb *et al.*, 2007, see *supra* note 1.
31 College of Policing, 2022, see *supra* note 20; Lamb *et al.*, 2007, see *supra* note 1.

methods of building relational rapport based upon theories taken from other research areas, such as negotiation theory[32] and sales and marketing.[33] Again, there is some support from practitioner surveys[34] that some police officers (for example, informant handlers) do use persuasive techniques taken from sales[35] as a means of establishing collaborative rapport.

Overall then, rapport has been shown to increase information and intelligence yield in traditional police or law enforcement interviews[36] and there is also tentative support for this in a handler–informant context as well.[37] However, there is acknowledgment that rapport may serve a more relational function within an informant scenario, and there is anecdotal evidence from practitioner surveys that this is the case.[38] Consequently, rather than simply serving to facilitate specific crime interview objectives (that is, information-gathering), rapport may play a broader role within a handler–informant interaction to establish and maintain an ongoing, collaborative relationship. As outlined in the introduction of this chapter, what constitutes sufficient and appropriate rapport in one interpersonal context is different from sufficient and appropriate rapport in another.

4.3. Humanity and Empathy in Interviews

The concept of empathy has been written about and discussed by academics for many decades, most commonly within other contexts (for example, clinical and counselling psychology).[39] However, when it comes to defining empathy, as

---

[32] Shapiro, 2006, see *supra* note 9.

[33] Randy Borum, "Approaching Truth: Behavioural Science Lessons on Educing Information From Human Sources", in United States Department of Defense, National Defence Intelligence College, 2006, pp. 17–43, see *supra* note 3.

[34] Royal and Schutt, 1976, see *supra* note 4.

[35] Robert B. Cialdini, "Harnessing the Science of Persuasion", *The Harvard Business Review*, October 2001, pp. 72–80; Robert B. Cialdini, *Influence: Science and Practice*, 5th ed., Pearson Education Inc., Boston, 2009.

[36] Lamb *et al.*, 2007, see *supra* note 1; Anti-Torture Initiative, 2021, see *supra* note 2.

[37] College of Policing, 2022, see *supra* note 20.

[38] Royal and Schutt, 1976, see *supra* note 4; Redlich, Kelly and Miller, 2014, see *supra* note 13.

[39] Godfrey T. Barrett-Lennard, "The Empathy Cycle: Refinement of a Nuclear Concept", in *Journal of Counselling Psychology*, 1981, vol. 28, no. 2, pp. 91–100; Simon Baron-Cohen, *Zero Degrees of Empathy: A New Theory of Human Cruelty*, Allen Lane Publishing, 2011; David F. Barone *et al.*, "Increasing Empathic Accuracy Through Practice and Feedback in a Clinical Interviewing Course", in *Journal of Social and Clinical Psychology*, 2005, vol. 24, no. 2, pp. 156–171; Gerald A. Gladstein, "Understanding Empathy: Integrating Counselling, Developmental and Social Psychology Perspectives", in *Journal of Counselling Psychology*, 1983, vol. 30, no. 4, pp. 467–482; Mark H. Davis, "Measuring Individual Differences in Empathy: Evidence for a Multi-Dimensional Approach", in *Journal of Personality and Social Psychology*, 1983, vol. 44, no. 1, pp. 113–126; Gavin E. Oxburgh and James Ost, "The Use and Efficacy of Empathy in Police Interviews With Suspects of Sexual Offences", in *Special*

---

with rapport, there is much disagreement and confusion.[40] In particular, with many definitions highlighted, there has been much theoretical debate concerning the differences between empathy and sympathy[41] and why it is that some individuals can be moved to empathy from sympathy or *vice versa*.[42]

Indeed, in some theoretical models,[43] the two concepts are sometimes blurred and, occasionally, empathy is equated with sympathy.[44] Furthermore, there is disagreement about the individual terms. For example, some researchers regard empathy as 'perspective-taking',[45] whereas others prefer the term 'role-taking'.[46] Others argue that in order to demonstrate empathy, one self-aware person must be able to understand, un-judgementally, the subjective positive and negative experiences of another person.[47] Thus, in showing empathy, you are 'reaching out' to the other person – understanding their plight without necessarily putting yourself in their position. Sympathy, on the other hand, relates to the heightened awareness of another person's plight which needs to be alleviated. Thus, in showing sympathy, you are substituting others for yourself – imagining what it would be like if you 'were' that other person.[48] Others argue that, "It is perfectly acceptable to feel sympathy, but it is important not to allow sympathy to take charge"; the risk is of over-identifying with the individual and that "[…] empathy is a professional requirement".[49] However, we would question whether this is possible in police contexts without further specialist training, particularly because showing (and understanding) empathy is a very effortful process by all

Edition of the Journal of Investigative Psychology and Offender Profiling, 2011, vol. 8, no. 2, pp. 178–188; Stephanie D. Preston and Frans B.M. de Waal, "Empathy: Its Ultimate and Proximate Bases", in *The Behavioral and Brain Sciences*, 2002, vol. 25, no. 1, pp. 1–72.

[40] Nancy Eisenberg and Randy Lennon, "Sex Differences in Empathy and Related Capacities", in *Psychological Bulletin*, 1983, vol. 13, no. 1, pp. 100–131.

[41] Gavin E. Oxburgh, "Developing a More Effective Framework for the Investigative Interviewing of Suspected Sex Offenders", unpublished Ph.D. thesis, University of Portsmouth, 2011; Lauren Wispé, "The Distinction Between Sympathy and Empathy: To Call Forth a Concept, a Word Is Needed", in *Journal of Personality and Social Psychology*, 1986, vol. 50, no. 2, pp. 314–321.

[42] Davis, 1983, see *supra* note 39; Preston and de Waal, 2002, see *supra* note 39.

[43] S. Olinick, "A Critique of Empathy and Sympathy", in Joseph Lichtenberg, Melvin Borstein and Donald Silver (eds.), *Empathy*, Erlbaum, Hillsdale, 1984, pp. 137–166.

[44] Susanne K. Langer, *Mind: An Essay on Human Feeling*, Johns Hopkins University Press, Baltimore, 1972.

[45] Bill Underwood and Bert Moore, "Perspective-Taking and Altruism", in *Psychological Bulletin*, 1982, vol. 91, no. 1, pp. 143–173.

[46] George H. Mead, *Mind, Self and Society*, University of Chicago Press, 1934.

[47] Preston and de Waal, 2002, see *supra* note 39.

[48] *Ibid.*

[49] Eric Shepherd, *Investigative Interviewing: The Conversation Management Approach*, Oxford University Press, 2007, p. 93.

concerned. Without such training, can interviewers truly be expected to understand the full meaning of empathy and how to identify and 'communicate' empathy effectively during their interviews? To highlight the use of empathy in professional interviews, this chapter now focuses on research that has attempted to highlight its efficacy.

4.4. Understanding Empathy and Humanity

In a now very well-cited study, researchers[50] highlighted the use of a 'humane' interviewing style. That particular research aimed to explore the relationship between the behaviour of police interviewers' and whether suspects (of murder and sexual offences) chose to admit or deny the crimes they were being interviewed for. Following analyses, they categorized the interviewing styles as either *humane* or *dominant*, with the former, characterized by police officers who were reported as being more empathic, co-operative and personal towards the suspect, providing more overall admissions than the *dominant* approach. Later Australian research[51] found similar results, with offenders in these studies reporting that they would more likely confess or increase the likelihood of confessing to a crime they had committed if the interviewing officers were ethical in their approach and showed empathy and humanity towards them.

To establish what police officers understood by the concepts of a good quality interview, a study was undertaken[52] using Conceptual Analysis ('CA').[53] Although CA revealed 30 different occurrences of phrases and words overall, the results found seven main recurring phrases and words that respondents used to define a 'good quality' interview, with both empathy and rapport being high on the list (second and fourth, respectively), the highest being open questioning. Additional research[54] was then undertaken to establish what police officers

---

[50] Ulf Holmberg and Sven-Åke Christianson, "Murderers' and Sexual Offenders' Experiences of Police Interviews and Their Inclination to Admit or Deny Crimes", in *Behavioral Sciences & The Law*, 2002, vol. 20, nos. 1–2, pp. 31–45.

[51] Mark Kebbell, Emily J. Hurren and Paul Mazerolle, "Sex Offenders' Perceptions of How They Were Interviewed", in *Canadian Journal of Police and Security Services*, 2006, vol. 4, pp. 67–75; Mark Kebbell, Laurence Alison, Emily Hurren and Paul Mazerolle, "How Do Sex Offenders Think the Police Should Interview to Elicit Confessions From Sex Offenders?", in *Psychology, Crime & Law*, 2010, vol. 16, no. 7, pp. 567–584.

[52] Oxburgh and Ost, 2011, see *supra* note 39.

[53] A concept is chosen for examination (in this case, definitions of 'quality' interviews), and the analysis involves quantifying and tallying the occurrence of terms or words used within a text or texts; Richard W. Budd, Lewis Donohew and Robert K. Thorp, *Content Analysis of Communications*, Macmillan Company, New York, 1967.

[54] Gavin E. Oxburgh, James Ost, Paul Morris and Julie Cherryman, "The Impact of Question Type and Empathy on Police Interviews With Suspects of Homicide, Filicide and Child Sexual Abuse", in *Psychiatry, Psychology and Law*, 2014, vol. 21, no. 6, pp. 904–917.

---

believed to be the difference between empathy and sympathy. Unfortunately, many respondents were not able to provide a coherent distinction between the two terms. This is typified by one respondent who stated, "There is no room for empathy – it may form part of the rapport strategy, but my professionalism and experience would prevail" (participant 38).

This would tend to suggest that to show empathy would be unprofessional in some way. However, it is equally likely that this specific participant did not fully understand the meaning of empathy as a concept in professional interviewing. Indeed, a more recent study,[55] whose respondents were a group of police interviewers from seven European countries, claimed to use empathy in their interviews with suspects but varied greatly on the definitions provided.

Researchers[56] also wanted to establish the presence of empathy in actual police interviews of suspects of homicide, filicide (a person who kills their own child) and child sexual abuse. However, only 20 of the 59 interviews analysed contained any kind of meaningful, positive empathic exchange between the interviewer and interviewee. Similar results were also found[57] in the analyses of police interviews with suspects of child rape and found that the use of empathy in interviews was generally very low indeed. The latter research used a bespoke model they developed to establish the use of empathy in police interviews – this is outlined in Figure 1 below.

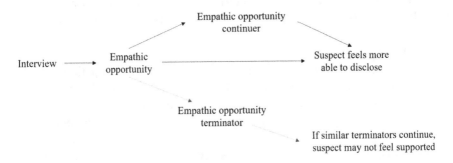

Figure 1: Model for measuring emphatic responses in police interviews.

55   Bianca Baker-Eck, Ray Bull and Dave Walsh, "Investigative Empathy: A Strength Scale of Empathy Based on European Police Perspectives", in *Psychiatry, Psychology and Law*, 2020, vol. 27, no. 3, pp. 412–427.

56   See *supra* note 54.

57   Gavin E. Oxburgh, James Ost and Julie Cherryman, "Police Interviews With Suspected Child Sex Offenders: Does Use of Empathy and Question Type Influence the Amount of Investigation Relevant Information Obtained?", in *Psychology, Crime & Law*, 2012, vol. 18, nos. 3–4, pp. 259–273.

The model above is based on the theoretical principles of the 'empathy cycle'[58] and focuses on three key variables (empathic *opportunities*, empathic *continuers* and empathic *terminators*). A fourth variable was added which the authors referred to as *spontaneous* empathy (where an interviewer could *spontaneously* make remarks of an empathic nature (for example, 'I know this must be really difficult for you, however...')).

In a 2016 study,[59] researchers wanted to establish the types of empathic behaviour police interviewers displayed in an investigative context and whether the gender of the interviewer impacted on the types of verbal empathy shown. Following analyses using Grounded Theory,[60] four distinct types of empathy emerged: (i) spontaneous comfort (offer of refreshments or comfort breaks, *et cetera*, that was offered directly by the interviewer with no preceding statement or description); (ii) continuer comfort (same verbal offerings as (i) but occurred in response to empathic opportunities concerning difficulties the interviewee was experiencing); (iii) spontaneous understanding (where the interviewer spontaneously offered some understanding of the interviewee's situation with no preceding statement); and (iv) continuer understanding (where the interviewer responded to understanding difficulties the interviewee might be having). Statistical analyses found that spontaneous comfort occurred significantly more than all other types of empathy and that females displayed significantly more empathic behaviour overall, but specifically more spontaneous empathy than men. Interestingly, female interviewers were 'offered' more empathic opportunities than their male counterparts.

Of course, empathy is not just about counting the number of times different forms of empathy are used (or counting the number of empathic *opportunities*, *continuers* and/or *terminators* plus *spontaneous* empathy within interviews), as can be seen above, it is a far more complex psychological construct. According to the psycho-medical literature, there is no doubt that empathy and humanity can be an effective tool; however, practitioners can only develop the skill if properly trained on the processes involved[61] and if they also understand what the term means. Unfortunately, there appears to be no clear understanding of the true meaning and use of the term 'empathy' by police officers[62] and

---

[58] Barrett-Lennard, 1981, see *supra* note 39.

[59] Coral J. Dando and Gavin E. Oxburgh, "Empathy in the Field: Towards a Taxonomy of Empathic Communication in Information-Gathering Interviews With Suspected Sex Offenders", in *European Journal of Psychology Applied to Legal Context*, 2016, vol. 8, no. 1, pp. 27–33.

[60] Grounded Theory is a research method concerned with the generation of theory which is 'grounded' in the data that has been systematically collected. It is used to analyse things such as social relationships and behaviours of groups.

[61] Royal and Schutt, 1976, see *supra* note 4; Redlich, Kelly and Miller, 2014, see *supra* note 13.

[62] See also Chapter 18 of this book.

despite the apparent benefits of being empathic, perhaps we should consider re-thinking how we train interviewers in conducting humane interviews using a more detailed concept of relationship-building. This is what we turn to in the next sections.

4.5. From 'Empathy' to 'Attunement'?

As highlighted above, there is no doubt that the meaning and use of empathy has been shown to be problematic for many police officers for various reasons. These include: (i) the lack of operational definitions of the construct; (ii) the failure to identify empathy in either the subjective or objective frames of reference (described below); (iii) the possibility that some interviewers believe being empathic is an effortful process, yet with the expectation that it should be utilized throughout the interview process; and (iv) that limited training in the utilization on the understanding and use of the term often means the levels of empathy shown vary considerably depending on interviewers' innate ability and interpersonal skills. Collectively, this appears to have led to interviewers having inconsistent understanding and utilization of the construct of empathy and, for some officers, an inability to differentiate between empathy and sympathy. Therefore, a common consensus of technical and professional definite language, which is a characteristic of other professions (for example, counselling and clinical psychology), is required for the field of professional interviewers (police, law enforcement, military, security and intelligence) to progress.

4.5.1. Objectivity and Subjectivity

In the preceding sections of this chapter, we allude to the fact that objectivity and subjectivity can impact and affect rapport-building and the utilization of empathy by interviewers. To be explicit, the subjective frame of reference comprises individual police practitioners' values, beliefs and sentiments – in other words, frames of reference and patterns of emotions.[63] However, the objective frames of reference are external to the police practitioner and consist of examples such as codes of practice, policies, criminal legislation and procedures. With this distinction in mind, research[64] makes clear that human service practitioners (that is, professional interviewers) should rely most heavily on their objective referents, and that a choice of constructs for a common professional language should be taken from the objective frame of reference.

---

[63] Libby Ashurst, "Emotional Intelligence and the Practitioner Working With Sexually Harmful Behaviour", in Martin C. Calder, *Contemporary Practice With Young People Who Sexually Abuse: Evidence-Based Developments*, Russell House Publishing, Lyme Regis, 2011, pp. 102–118.

[64] *Ibid.*

Previously, we defined empathy which, in reality, places it into the subjective framework of both the interviewer and the interviewee. Using an earlier exemplar orientates the reader that an example of an interviewer being empathic is 'I know this must be really difficult for you, however…'. But, in this example, 'I know' is very much a subjective assumption made by the interviewer with no objective external referent. The use of subjective frames of reference can often create a barrier with the interviewee if this subjective assumption is, in fact, wrong regarding their internal state. This makes clear that interviewers need to operate using an objective framework to promote being consciously competent (described below).

4.5.2. Professional Relationships

Interviewers, by the very nature of their roles and responsibilities, do not usually have long-term relationships with the individuals they communicate with – this is especially so in police and law enforcement interviews. Instead, their relationships are transient in nature and they have task-orientated professional interactions most commonly linked to the criminal justice system ('CJS'). Nevertheless, it is important for interviewers to be considered as professional and trustworthy and they need to be seen as authentic in their role. Authenticity requires a high level of technical and professional competence and an accurate appraisal of that competence.[65] Interviewers (or in this case, police practitioners) who are authentic will understand and accept their position fully (including the roles to be served) and, as such, will act consistently to achieve organizational and positional goals (objective) and not act in ways that are self-serving (subjective). An example of this, for professional interviewers, is that the interviewee must see the interviewer as a person of integrity, trustworthy, able to apply and understand criminal law and procedural safeguards, and sufficiently skilful to carry out the interview with confidence. The recognition of the term 'competence' has been termed[66] as being *consciously competent*. Relying more on an objective referent and being authentic in role affords the opportunity to move the field towards the use of 'attunement' as opposed to 'empathy' as it promotes growth in professional competence.

4.6. What Is Attunement?

Attunement can be described as the reactiveness we have to another person. It is the process by which we form relationships. It is a multi-faceted concept

[65] Andrew W. Halpin (ed.), *Administrative Theory in Education*, Macmillan, London, 1967.
[66] Abraham H. Maslow, "A Theory of Human Motivation", in *Psychological Review*, 1943, vol. 50, no. 4, pp. 370–396.

which some authors[67] suggest includes different components: (i) affective, (ii) cognitive, (iii) developmental and (iv) rhythmic. In terms of professional interviews (including police, law enforcement, military, security and intelligence), attunement can be described as how:

- reactive a police practitioner is to the interviewee's emotional needs and moods (affective attunement);
- the police practitioner attempts to understand the interviewee's perspective, thinking and meanings (cognitive attunement);
- the police practitioner adapts to the developmental needs of the interviewee (developmental attunement); and
- responsive they are to the interviewee's rhythmic patterns and habitual way of being, such as slow processing speed or regression (rhythmic attunement).

Affective attunement relies on conscious competence[68] because it requires a practitioner to correctly acknowledge the internal and emotional state of others, without taking them on. For example, rather than reacting when an interviewee turns the question posed by the interviewer, such as, 'Do you think I am capable of rape?', the interviewer could respond objectively with, 'Capable of rape, tell me about that'. This conscious competence and cognitive and emotional attunement can inform practice to enhance rapport and support information-gathering as it reveals when to remain silent, when to ask questions, what those questions should be and how to ask them. Attuning to an individual removes all subjective assumptions and projection of one's own perspectives and has been found to increase engagement and rapport-building in interviews.[69] This is more likely to result in a "feeling of a shared affect state without imitating the exact behavioural expression of the inner state".[70] An example of this in victim interviews is when a child cries and says, 'I knew I shouldn't have gone with him, I knew it was risky', and the interviewer does not confirm what was said, so as not to induce shame or guilt, but instead responds with the open question of, 'Tell me how you came to know it was risky'.

---

[67] Richard G. Erskine, Janet P. Moursund and Rebecca L. Trautmann, *Beyond Empathy: A Therapy of Contact in Relationships*, Taylor & Francis, London, 1999.

[68] Ashurst, 2011, see *supra* note 63.

[69] Libby Ashurst, "Developing and Testing a General Training Model for Improving Professional Practice of Case Managers: Using Practitioners Working With Young People Displaying Sexually Harmful Behaviour for an Exemplar", unpublished Ph.D. thesis, Queen's University, 2012.

[70] Daniel N. Stern, *The Interpersonal World of the Infant*, Basic Books, New York, 1985, p. 142.

4.6.1. Training in Attunement

One of the main tasks to help improve interviewer performance would be to identify a continuous improvement model of training capable of promoting the conscious competence of interviewers. A mastery model of learning would achieve this, as it is a skills-based model with clearly identified intended learning with a focus of learning to mastery. Ashurst[71] developed a mastery model for improving professional practice that was validated by a team of international experts and, to date, has been tested across environments in which frontline practitioners interact with both suspects and vulnerable victims of crime. The Ashurst Mastery Model ('AMM') transfers knowledge into practice through a 'plan-do-review' cycle which means that, with regards to an interview, it would take the skills developed during simulations within the training into practice, and then reviews of real-life interviews would take place with the trainer until the skill is fully mastered. One of the modules in this training deals with communication, in particular, interviewing for information in an objective and authentic manner and the application of attunement. Practitioners who have been trained in these skills, and their application to practice, have found increased engagement with those being interviewed, that they are able to develop rapport more quickly and effectively, and that the amount of quality and relevant information gained is increased.[72] Example feedback of the benefits for practitioners who have been trained in the AMM and utilized it to remain objective and to attune to the emotions, cognitions, development and rhythmic patterns of the interviewee are provided in Table 1.

Example 1: I had a difficult case that I had not been able to get engaged in authentic discussion. I had been using direct questions about what, how, why, when, *et cetera*, of his behaviour, but I could not get responses. In this session, I began with a brief warm-up talk with him and then when I spotted a good entry, I shifted to the tell-me-about questioning strategy. When I used that, it seemed to give him more space and he told me all about what happened and all the details for the whole day when the sexual behaviour occurred. I realized that changing from what happened and then what happened next was not working. This strategy really worked well with this client who had been in denial.

Example 2: I thought I was using the questioning method that she was teaching us, but it never worked for me. I realize that I was using something completely different. I was saying, 'Can you tell me about' rather than, 'Tell me about'. I realize now that my clients were making a semantic distinction. They interpreted my, 'Can you tell me' as an invitation which they could accept or reject. Most of them did not respond when I used that form of the question, but all do when I use the 'Tell me about' form.

Table 1: Example feedback from practitioners.

---

[71]   Ashurst, 2012, see *supra* note 69.
[72]   *Ibid.*

Should attunement be adopted, some of the skills and competences leading to attunement can be taken from the field of emotional intelligence outlined in Table 2.[73]

These four illustrative skills leading to competency in attunement are:

Self-awareness:
- recognizing your own emotions;
- recognizing how your own emotions affect language and behaviour;
- recognizing your own skills, strengths and weaknesses;
- recognizing your own values and value systems, and their foundations;
- having confidence in self.

Self-regulation:
- maintaining control over impulses and distressful emotions;
- adapting reactions and responses to those of others and to changing situations;
- acting and relating consistently and authentically;
- managing multiple tasks and interruptions;
- recognizing one's own mistakes and confronting the mistakes of others;
- working effectively and efficiently within a schedule serving both self and others;
- accepting accountability for one's own goals and task responsibilities.

Social awareness:
- appraising the emotions of others accurately;
- responding consistently with the emotional characteristics of others;
- finding and recognizing strengths of others;
- making appropriate and effective challenges to biases and intolerance of others;
- seeking and finding ways to encourage satisfaction for others.

Social skills and management of relationships:
- listening for the intentions of others;
- building bonds with interviewees and colleagues;
- working collaboratively with colleagues;
- modelling changes expected of others;
- adapting language and relationships to situations;
- dealing with situations and relationships objectively.

Table 2: Illustrative skills leading to competency in attunement.

4.7. Conclusion

There is increasing evidence that using rapport and empathy during information-gathering processes (for example, police interviewing) increases information yield from interviewees. However, we also know that there is much confusion

---

[73] Daniel Goleman, *Social Intelligence*, Bantam Books, New York, 2006.

over the terms 'rapport' and 'empathy'.[74] Focusing on the latter and its application to information-gathering practice, it appears timely for professional interviewers to consider a move towards attunement. This is because attunement is a construct of skills that demand objective practice and authenticity by practitioners. Therefore, such a move towards this concept may be in the best interests of the field. If attunement is adopted, other benefits include relying on a skill-base which can be taught to practitioners and requires conscious competence to master. To achieve this, the AMM could be adopted as it includes an interview module within which the skills of attunement are taught.

---

[74] Davis, 1983, see *supra* note 39.

5

Forget the 'Fever Dreams' of Interrogational Torture: Science, Ethics and Policy Serve Effective and Humane Interviewing

Shane O'Mara[*]

5.1. Introduction

Torture is pointless, useless and degrading for all involved – there are better ways to gather information from other human beings. Discussions and policies regarding prisoner and detainee interrogation need to be refocused as a behavioural and brain-sciences problem and not simply treated as a legal, ethical or philosophical one. The contemporary behavioural and brain sciences should have a central operational and structural role in policing and intelligence agencies. Here, I first consider the use of interrogational torture – the type of torture we see depicted most frequently in movies and television – to force the unwilling to reveal what they know. Historically, torture, as I and others argue elsewhere, has never been principally for the forced extraction of information from those who are unwilling to speak. The impulse to resort to interrogation torture is, I argue, one founded on a profound lack of knowledge regarding human cognitive and brain function, entirely bereft of an understanding of how to probe memory and disregards long-standing knowledge on how to engage the willing and unwilling in conversation. There is another and better path to effective information-gathering, one which brings science, ethics and policy in line with each other, which I discuss here.

The actual historical uses of torture – what it works best for – are rarely shown in movies and television. Torture is probably the best technique there is for forcing a confession from someone, for forcing someone to abjure their beliefs or for spreading fear and terror in a population. It is a wonderful technique for the dark imagination: the visiting of righteous vengeance and medieval punishment on 'evil-doers' and other out-groups. This latter use of torture was, of course, widespread in Europe until the late 1700s or so – the phrase 'mortification of the flesh' has real meaning as a punishment in law in the various medieval

---

[*] **Shane O'Mara**, Ph.D., is Professor of Experimental Brain Research at the School of Psychology and Institute of Neuroscience, Trinity College, University of Dublin.

states of Europe. It gives us the latter-day expression 'getting medieval', meaning to torture someone terribly.

As a veridical information-collection and information-gathering tool, torture is probably the worst technique available to an interviewer. The legal systems of the world are polluted with cases where confessions extracted under duress have been used to secure convictions – which are, of course, unsafe and unsatisfactory. And to make matters worse, the victims do not secure justice either, as the truly guilty get off scot-free (for recent examples, the cases of the 'Birmingham Six' and 'Guildford Four' are especially instructive, as they were convicted and sent to prison for bombings that killed and maimed many people on the basis of coerced confessions; they were later exonerated).[1] An honest appraisal of the evidence on interrogational torture will emphasize what the late Senator John McCain (who was tortured in Vietnam for five years) said: "I know from personal experience that the abuse of prisoners will produce more bad than good intelligence"; "I know that victims of torture will offer intentionally misleading information if they think their captors will believe it. I know they will say whatever they think their torturers want them to say if they believe it will stop their suffering".[2]

5.2. Movie Depictions of Torture

Movie and other popular depictions of torture show it as extraordinarily effective at loosening tongues and for gathering information from those depicted as unwilling to speak.[3] This is a genuine problem, for there is substantial evidence that interrogational practices depicted in television series such as *24* influenced interrogation policy in Guantánamo Bay during the early- to-mid 2000s.[4] These depictions of interrogation are likely to be the only exposure both the public and policy-makers have to interrogation – and they are fictional depictions.

I discuss here *Payback*,[5] a Mel Gibson thriller from 1999, a tough and visceral film with an extraordinary torture scene involving a hammer. *Payback*

---

[1]   Brenda J. Lutz, James M. Lutz and Georgia Wralstad Ulmschneider, "British Trials of Irish Nationalist Defendants: The Quality of Justice Strained", in *Studies in Conflict and Terrorism*, 2002, vol. 25, no. 4, pp. 227–244; Gisli H. Gudjonsson and James A.C. MacKeith, *The 'Guildford Four' and the 'Birmingham Six'. The Psychology of Interrogations and Confessions: A Handbook*, Wiley, 2002, pp. 445–457.

[2]   John McCain, "Interview", in *Legal View With Ashleigh Banfield*, CNN, 9 December 2014.

[3]   Erin M. Kearns and Casey Delehanty, "The Fast & The Furious… Torturous? Examining the Impact of Torture Scenes in Popular Films on Public Perceptions of Torture Policy", in *Studies in Conflict & Terrorism*, 2021, vol. 1, no. 16.

[4]   Shane O'Mara, *Why Torture Doesn't Work: The Neuroscience of Interrogation*, Harvard University Press, 2015; Philippe Sands, *Torture Team: Uncovering War Crimes in the Land of the Free*, Penguin, 2008.

[5]   See "Payback (1999 Film)", in *Wikipedia* ('*Payback*') (available on its web site).

shows that torture can be used to extract information, but also that the information extracted is neither complete nor useful and is in fact wholly destructive to those who forced its extraction. Gibson plays Porter, a hardened, unpleasant enforcer and killer, with a curious sense of honour (and seemingly lacking a forename). Porter is captured by his enemies, taken to a garage, tied to a chair and asked to voluntarily give up the information regarding where he has imprisoned the lead mobster's son. He refuses to do so; whereupon his shoes and socks are removed. He is menaced with a hammer and understands that non-disclosure means imminent agony. He is asked to disclose where the son is again. He refuses to do so and the small toe of his right foot is crushed irreparably with the hammer. This causes terrible pain and agony.

We are not shown his crushed toes (these are left to the imagination). Porter is again asked to give up the son's location and again refuses to disclose it. The hammer is again applied with great force, crushing another toe, again irreparably. He is, once again, asked to disclose where he has imprisoned his captor's son. This time he does so; he is removed from his chair, placed in the trunk of a car and driven to the ostensible location (a seedy hotel) where the son is allegedly held. His captors run upstairs to the room where the son is believed to be held and enter the room, whereupon a phone rings, causing a booby-trap bomb placed under the bed to explode, killing them all. Porter managed to escape from the trunk through the soft fabric back seat of the car and used the car's phone to cause the discharge of the explosives.

Payback underlines the central problem with using extreme stressors to force a captive to disclose information in what is supposedly 'real time'. Porter has lied and willingly endured terrible suffering, *to give the appearance and substance of having told the truth*, in order to lure his captors to their deaths and to save himself. In order for Porter to ensure that his lies are convincing, he knows he must endure terrible pain and suffering. He must also be able to make a reasonable estimate of the degree to which he must suffer in order for his captors to be convinced of the apparent truth of what he is about to say. Too little, and he will not be believed; too much, and he may not survive.

Thus, Porter engages in metacognition: he infers the psychological states of others and infers what others, in turn, are likely to be thinking about him. Porter uses his estimate of what others are likely to be thinking about him in order to turn the tables against them – a form of metacognitive capacity known as 'deceptive intent'. Porter is capable of enduring great pain in the present moment in order to achieve a much greater deferred reward. Porter presents a case of extreme self-control – even in the face of an imminent and terrible attack on his bodily integrity. Stubbing a toe is painful enough; having your toes systematically crushed, one-by-one, and anticipating it, will be much worse. The narrative drive here is different from the usual fictional situation with the *ticking time bomb*, but those focused on the ticking time bomb rationale will rarely, if ever, discuss other possible scenarios. Such scenarios will immediately falsify the reasoning involved which leads to torture as the only possible route to needed knowledge.

The point here really is this: the ticking time bomb scenario is most often presented with a single rationale ('a big bomb, a population centre, and now!'). But this presentation is both idealized and abstracted; to use Henry Shue's formulation in his famous paper, "Torture in Dreamland: Disposing of the Ticking Bomb".[6] In fact, there are any number of possible variations amidst the chaos of the real world. Dummy bombs, proxies, booby-traps, misdirections, lying to run down the clock, several bombs: you name it, any and all are possible. Devoting a lot of serious thinking to a single counterfactual with a single narrative drive and a singular 'a man's gotta do what a man's gotta do' storyline is to deny the actual reality of human ingenuity.

And if Porter can subvert torture with metacognition and self-control, then those who take the ticking time bomb scenario seriously need to get out to the cinema more.[7] Of course, the tortures that will be imposed by willing amateurs on prisoners in the field in order to loosen tongues in a truthful way, complex scenarios involving possible double-dealing, incomplete knowledge and deceptive intent are never specified by those who take the ticking time bomb seriously. And of the blood and filth involved in torture? They are silent on this and on the amateurs who are supposed to know 'what to do'.

5.3. Cognitive Errors Underpinning the Decision to Torture

Under many conditions (including difficult and stressful ones), people rely on *heuristics* (cognitive shortcuts that enable decisions) and are prone to effects of social processes such as groupthink. Decision-making within organizations (political institutions, law enforcement, *et cetera*) is often a difficult and ideologically charged process. Political and civil-service systems can undervalue expertise, suppress cognitive diversity and discount evidence in favour of ideology. There are persistent and enduring cognitive errors which lead to faulty decision-making by individuals (political leaders, civil servants, bankers, *et cetera*) and institutions (social systems and organizations, such as government departments, banks or churches).

---

6 Henry Shue, "Torture in Dreamland: Disposing of the Ticking Bomb", in *Case Western Reserve Journal of International Law*, 2006, vol. 37, no. 2, p. 231.

7 Michael Ignatieff, "If Torture Works...", in *Prospect Magazine*, 23 April 2006, vol. 121, pp. 3–9; Alan M. Dershowitz, "Torture of Terrorists: Is It Necessary to Do and to Lie About It?", in *id.*, *Shouting Fire: Civil Liberties in a Turbulent Age*, Little, Brown, New York, 2002.

Governing elites do not know that they do not know, nor do they even know what they need to know. Complex and difficult problems (such as how to collect valuable and useful intelligence from multiple humans under conditions where the targets are continually moving and changing) are best solved by groups with substantial intellectual strength and capacity (obvious) and substantial diversity of experience (not obvious). Absent these factors and people will rely on folk or lay intuitions as the basis for deciding courses of action – 'we need to know quick', 'let's waterboard this guy'.[8] Government decisions are taken and implemented within a group context or contexts – documents are evaluated, discussions occur and decisions are taken and then implemented (sometimes in ways that subvert the spirit and intentions of the original decision).

An interesting cognitive error during complex decision-making is to not explore *counterfactuals* – scenarios that are contrary to one's own preferred course of action – as these might falsify or invalidate a course of action. Exploring counterfactuals forces you to ask why you might be wrong ('Why might waterboarding this guy be a bad idea?')! Verificationism (also known as confirmation bias)[9] is a pervasive cognitive bias where evidence favouring a particular point of view is collected and weighted heavily and contrary evidence is discounted or ignored ('All the programmes I watch on the television show torture working'). Its opposite, falsificationism, is a difficult habit of mind to acquire. However, it is a must for any working scientist. Falsificationism requires considering what empirical evidence would invalidate (falsify) the position you are adopting. One way of avoiding this bias is to state clearly what empirical evidence would falsify your opinion or theory; another is to build an evidence-based brake into policy formation.[10] In science, this is done by international, anonymous, expert 'peer-review'. Peer-review and similar systems can be built into the process of government via policy-review boards. Arguments for interrogational torture may also pivot around the focusing illusion, a cognitive error which emphasizes only upside arguments (local benefits: 'quick and easy knowledge about terrorist networks and ticking time-bombs'), but ignores costs (the destruction of reputation and lives, and contempt for international treaties and the rule of law; acting on what is false knowledge).

---

[8] See David Cole, *The Torture Memos: Rationalizing the Unthinkable*, The New Press, New York, 2009; "Conservative General Election Manifesto 1979", Margaret Thatcher Foundation, 11 April 1979 (available on its web site), and the Torture Memos contained therein.

[9] See also Chapter 9 of this book.

[10] Shane O'Mara and John Schiemann, "Torturing Science: Science, Interrogational Torture, and Public Policy", in *Politics and the Life Sciences*, 2019, vol. 38, no. 2, pp. 180–192.

Language has the important property of *framing* arguments and discussions.[11] The crime debate at one time in the United Kingdom was dominated by the phrase 'a short, sharp shock',[12] which relied on the folk theory that quick and severe punishment would shock teenagers out of criminal tendencies (the pleasing alliteration of the successive sibilants was an important, but useless, selling point too). Short, sharp shocks, of course, predictably have no such effect, but why let data from the psychology of punishment and from criminology influence debate? The phrase 'cut and run' was used to forestall debate about the palpably failing United States ('US') military strategy in Iraq, until empirical reality forced a change of direction.[13] There are many other cognitive errors (for example, availability and affect heuristics, motivated reasoning, competence illusions, overconfidence and incentive effects) and humans are also prone to them (especially under duress, as cognition degrades under stress). Individual rationality and cognition are limited and error-prone. Institutionalized decision-making supports are vital to ensure that decisions are made using the best evidence and logic available.

5.4. Torture to Enhance Interrogation Is a Demonstrable Failure, Given Its Own Goals

The evidence is in and it is very clear: torture as an interrogational theory and practice is a complete and utter failure.[14] This seems (almost) counter-intuitive: as discussed above, we are bombarded with images and scenes from movies and television where torture is successfully used to extract information from the unwilling. Those with experience of torture take a very different view. Lavrentii Beria, the Chief of the Soviet security and secret-police apparatus (the People's Commissariat for Internal Affairs) during the Great Terror and beyond, had extensive experience of employing torture on behalf of the Politburo for political purposes. Beria subsequently testified during a secret Politburo meeting in 1953 that:

---

[11] George Lakoff and Mark Johnson, *Metaphors We Live By*, University of Chicago Press, 2008.

[12] "Conservative General Election Manifesto 1979", 11 April 1979, see *supra* note 8.

[13] Dana Milbank, "It's Time to Cut and Run From 'Cut and Run'", *The Washington Post*, 21 June 2006.

[14] Shane O'Mara, "Torturing the Brain: On the Folk Psychology and Folk Neurobiology Motivating 'Enhanced and Coercive Interrogation Techniques'", in *Trends in Cognitive Sciences*, 2009, vol. 13, no. 12, pp. 497–500; Gudjonsson and MacKeith, 2002, see *supra* note 1; Aldert Vrij *et al.*, "Psychological Perspectives on Interrogation", in *Perspectives on Psychological Science*, 2017, vol. 12, no. 6, pp. 927–955; Shane O'Mara, "On the Imposition of Torture, an Extreme Stressor State, to Extract Information From Memory: A Baleful Consequence of Folk Cognitive Neurobiology", in *Zeitschrift für Psychologie/Journal of Psychology*, 2011, vol. 219, no. 3, pp. 159–166.

a person that is beaten will give the kind of confession that the interrogating agents want, will admit that he is an English or American spy, or whatever we want, but it will never be possible to know the truth this way.[15]

There are many other such accounts available.[16] In his compelling and exhaustive historical survey of the use of torture by democracies through the ages, Darius Rejali[17] concluded:

There may be secret thorough reports of torture's effectiveness, but historians have yet to uncover them for any government. Those who believe in torture's effectiveness seem to need no proof, and prefer to leave no reports.

And here is the core problem: if there were 'off-the-shelf' procedures to support interrogational torture, we would know about them. But there are not – torture as an interrogational practice has failed throughout the ages, especially when compared with other humane, non-coercive methods.[18]

5.5. The Interrogational Torture Policy Rationale

Here, I try to depict the thinking offered by those who would use interrogational torture. Surely, the thinking goes, applying extreme pain, torment and stress to captives before (and during) interrogation will enhance their capacity and willingness to recall and reveal past events, as well as their current plans and future intentions? And, surely, the contents of their brain's long-term memory systems will remain unaffected by the extreme stressors used during torture? The flooding of the brain by stress hormones will obviously have no effect on the structure and functioning of the brain itself. And we can surely assume with certainty that the conduction mechanisms coupling the brain's memory and intention circuits to speech will be unaffected by torture.

Furthermore, the interrogators administering torture will be very well-trained, so much so that they will be especially sensitive to those they are interrogating, such that they will be able to distinguish the innocent from the guilty and they will surely only torture the guilty. More than this, they will also be able to detect lies, omissions, elisions and confabulations generated by the tortured while they carefully impose the extreme stressors used in torture. And, of course,

---

15 Anne Applebaum, *Iron Curtain: The Crushing of Eastern Europe 1944–56*, Penguin Books, 2012.

16 For extensive references, see Shane O'Mara, "Interrogating the Brain: Torture and the Neuroscience of Humane Interrogation", in Steven J. Barela, Mark Fallon, Gloria Gaggioli and Jens David Ohlin (eds.), *Interrogation and Torture: Research on Efficacy and Its Integration With Morality and Legality*, Oxford University Press, 2020, pp. 197–222.

17 Darius Rejali, *Torture and Democracy*, Princeton University Press, 2009.

18 See Chapters 5, 7, 11 and 13 of this book.

leading information provided during questioning will not be incorporated into the memories of, and the answers provided by, the tortured. We know, so the pro-torture argument goes, that the torturers will be able to precisely calibrate the degree of torment employed, ensuring minimal cruelty and suffering are employed so that the detainee speaks freely and truthfully. Unnecessary, gratuitous and vengeance-driven escalation of torment will surely not occur. After all, the interrogational torturers will have been trained carefully in what they have to do and will have substantial practice with unwilling human participants. They will possess a profound understanding of neurophysiological function: they will know how to bypass the pain gates of the thalamus and spinal cord, and they will be able to blunt the analgesic response that their body produces in response to pain, injury and suffering.

And when a murderous outrage occurs and the perpetrators are captured, the standing squads of interrogational torturers trained, practiced and maintained in democracies will be on call, ready to do their jobs. And, finally, when their day's work is done, they will go home, enjoy a normal and carefree sleep and delight in family and social life, utterly undisturbed by their day job. A day job which requires them to perpetrate continued physical and psychological assaults on the defenceless in order to gather reliable, veridical and actionable intelligence and information. After all, this is what we see in movies and television, time and again: the hero (or sometimes the anti-hero) forces someone to talk, the city is saved and the torturer heads off at the end of the session, content in the knowledge of a difficult job well done.

5.6. What Tortures Are Employed?

When put in these terms, the fatuousness of the pro-torture argument should become obvious. Even after setting ethical, moral and legal debates to one side, torture profoundly and negatively affects the tortured and, less obviously, the torturer. The range of 'white tortures' (assaults on our core psychological, neural and physiological functioning) formerly deployed by the Central Intelligence Agency and other agencies are well-known by now: oxygen deprivation through near-drowning and suffocation; shackling and stress positions; extended sleep deprivation; freezing, cooling and starving the body and brain; overloading the senses with loud noise and bright lights; drip-feed assaults on personal dignity through facial slaps and holds, enforced nakedness and the imposition of adult diapers; the slow destruction of personhood through social isolation, social deprivation and a deliberate programme of de-individualization; confinement in cramped boxes; predator threats using guns, drills and attack dogs; and pretended assaults on the loved ones of the captive.[19] Somehow, the theory goes,

---

[19] *Payback*, see *supra* note 5.

this programme of assault, when carefully calibrated and imposed, will cause the detainee to reveal the contents of their long-term memories, and to do so in a reliable, veridical and replicable fashion. It will not increase resistance, cause a hardening of the suspect or increase the rate at which confabulation, misdirection or false recall will occur: the signal-to-noise ratio of information acquired will be unaffected.

5.7.   What Do Extreme Stressors Do to the Brain?

There is overwhelming evidence that the extreme stressors employed during torture force the brain away from the relatively narrow and adaptive range that it operates within. Furthermore, these stressors attack the fabric of the brain, causing tissue loss in brain regions concerned with memory (especially in the temporal lobes, adjacent to the temples). Tissue growth is seen in brain regions especially concerned with the processing of fear and threat-related information. Hence the persistent and sustained states of hypervigilance and substantially lowered startle reflexes seen in post-traumatic stress disorder and related conditions. Finally, the brain regions concerned with intention and general behavioural control become less responsive as a result of chronic and extreme stress (the prefrontal cortices). Multiple studies of combat and elite soldiers, certain patient groups and normal populations demonstrate that these stressors substantially compromise memory, mood and cognitive function.

To take some examples: sleep deprivation is the most effective method for causing deficits in cognition, mood and memory, and it does so in direct proportion to the dose of sleep deprivation imposed. The sleep-deprived show large decrements in psychomotor and general cognitive functions, as well as profound deficits in declarative memory. Studies of persons in severe chronic pain and studies of the interaction between supervening states of pain, cognition and memory demonstrate reliably that pain impairs cognition, memory and mood. Deliberate suffocation or near-drowning is a form of predator threat, involving the repeated imposition of a near-death experience. However, oxygen restriction reliably draws activity away from brain regions concerned with higher cognitive function and memory in favour of brainstem regions concerned with reflexive responses supporting immediate survival – militating against detailed recall.

Chronic and severe stress compromises integrated psychological functioning, impairing recall and facilitating the incorporation of information contained in leading questions, and both the captive and interrogator might not know this subtle process of incorporation has occurred. Torture fails during interrogation because torture is an assault on our core integrated, social, psychological and neural functioning. Given what we know of the brain, memory, mood and cognition, it is little surprise that the signal-to-noise ratio from torture is so poor.

Finally, we have a specialized brain network (the 'pain matrix') that automatically and reflexively responds to distress, pain and despair caused to one's self – but crucially also to observing another person in distress.[20] Hence the reflexive sense of pain we experience when we see another person in distress. Politicians framing torture policies do not personally waterboard, starve or physically manhandle prisoners. They do not endure the filth of torture: the blood, detritus and effluvia from enforced nudity and prolonged stress positions (with the enforced wearing of adult diapers). But someone has to do this, and we know that those who conduct torture on behalf of the state in democracies are terribly affected by what they have done, for reasons rooted deep in our brain circuitry.

5.7.1. A Point Which Cannot Be Emphasized Enough

Torture is a useless technique for extracting information from long-term memory because imposing severe neuropsychiatric distress substantially impedes the functioning of the brain systems and sub-systems concerned with storage and recall of memory (among many other consequences). There is no good reason to expect from cognitive neuroscience that the imposition of substantial and sustained stressor states will have a positive effect on the brain systems supporting memory; quite the contrary is what should be expected.

5.8. Organizations and What Not to Do

Over a period of time in the early 2010s, suspicions arose that the largest professional association for psychologists in the world – the American Psychological Association ('APA') – had been acting in concert with the US Department of Defense ('DoD') to allow psychologists to participate as health professionals in the coercive interrogations of so-called 'high-value detainees' (although many were no such thing).[21] A subsequent investigation led by attorney David H. Hoffman had an electric effect, with high-ranking APA officials resigning, retiring or being fired. The APA investigation originally arose as a result of allegations made in James Risen's important book *Pay Any Price*[22] which

---

[20] Gian Domenico Iannetti and André Mouraux, "From the Neuromatrix to the Pain Matrix (and Back)", in *Experimental Brain Research*, 2010, vol. 205, no. 1, pp. 1–12.

[21] APA, "Report of the Independent Reviewer and Related Materials" (available on its web site); see also for further comments and notes, including the report itself, John M. Grohol, "The Hoffman Report: The Investigation into the American Psychological Association (APA)", 12 July 2015 (available on Psychcentral's web site).

[22] James Risen, *Pay Any Price: Greed, Power, and Endless War*, Houghton Mifflin Harcourt, 2014.

provided many previously unknown details on the relationship between the APA and the DoD.

A major debate has occurred within the APA regarding its participation in national security interrogations and the present position appears to be that the APA will not participate in such interrogations. It is entirely understandable that, having been burned so badly, the APA has adopted a position of non-involvement. There are a great many ethical and moral issues, in addition to legal and oversight issues, that need resolving before psychologists can contemplate participating in such interrogations, especially in what would be an adversarial role.

Among other things, the adversarial role would be that of leading, advising and assisting in the interrogation of detainees and others, with the possibility that the information so gathered might be used against the detainee in a legal process. Of course, the contrary position might arise: the psychologist might determine that the detainee has, in fact, no case to answer and should be released. This potentially adversarial role is something new for psychology. It is at the core of the legal profession and policing, for example, but it is not something psychologists have typically been involved in.

5.9. Human Interviewing Needs to Be High Status and Prioritized

Here, I elaborate a position representing an alternative way forward for both parties which I have presented previously. The behavioural and brain sciences, if allowed to, can transform interrogation.[23] The basic argument is this: the behavioural and brain sciences have the potential to transform forensic, policing, judicial and intelligence practices, and thereby enhance operational effectiveness. And they have the capacity to do so in a way that is humane, ethical and which cleaves to the importance of bowing to empirical reality as a guide to thought and action in these very important and difficult areas of human behaviour. We have seen evidence of such changes already: eyewitness testimony in court is now subject to a variety of procedural and evidential rules, given the extreme malleability of such testimony. The ease of elicitation of confession to crimes – irrespective of their accuracy, reliability, truth or veridicality – should prompt similar changes where confession evidence is concerned. The role of the interrogator needs to be completely redefined – and their role in the overall chain of information-gathering needs to be both high status and prioritized at an institutional level. This is something that is now regarded as best practice by the

---

[23] Aldert Vrij, Lorraine Hope and Ronald P. Fisher, "Eliciting Reliable Information in Investigative Interviews", in *Policy Insights from the Behavioral and Brain Sciences*, 2014, vol. 1, no. 1, pp. 129–136; Stephen Porter, Katherine Rose and Tianna Dilley, "Enhanced Interrogations: The Expanding Roles of Psychology in Police Investigations in Canada", in *Canadian Psychology/Psychologie canadienne*, 2016, vol. 57, no. 1, pp. 35–43.

United Nations.[24] Moreover, the phrase 'interrogation' should really be consigned to history, in favour of the more neutral 'investigative interview' or 'non-coercive interview', and police interrogators should be renamed as 'investigative interviewers'.

The evidence of the report of the Senate Select Committee on Intelligence is clear:[25] low-status and low-ranking individuals with little to no interrogational experience or training, markedly low-levels of self-awareness, poor impulse control, high levels of aggression and little transpersonal, psychological or situational awareness were often assigned to the supposedly signally important task of debriefing detainees. Thus, it is reasonable to conclude that no meaningful political priority was given to the signal importance of understanding human behaviour in intelligence, forensic or related contexts. Furthermore, the hard-won knowledge of interrogation obtained by the Federal Bureau of Investigation was set to one side. A clear signal of priority and urgency would then have been and would now be the creation of 'operational brain and behavioural sciences directorates' within intelligence, legal, border and policing agencies, whose leaders or directors would be of the highest status and at the executive level in terms of institutional organization. This situation has now changed to some degree with the formation of the High-Value Detainee Interrogation Group ('HIG')[26] – which funds academic research in ethical, humane and non-coercive interrogation, and which provides interrogation support in certain cases. The HIG Research Program is most welcome, but the big science, long-term and large-scale funded, integrated, interdisciplinary research and training programmes (of the type funded by the National Science Foundation or the National Institutes of Health) have not yet been created. Neither have large-scale changes in organizational structures to support this new mission been discussed (publicly, at least).

5.10. How Should Human Interviewing Be Institutionalized?

The foremost requirement is that interviewers from any organizations that communicate with others with the objective of gaining information (for example, police, law enforcement, military or security) are placed within high-status operational behavioural and brain-science directorates that report to the highest level of institutional management. In turn, this allows direct reporting to policy

---

[24] Anti-Torture Initiative, Association for the Prevention of Torture and the Norwegian Centre for Human Rights, *Principles on Effective Interviewing for Investigations and Information Gathering*, 2021 (https://www.legal-tools.org/doc/wbfiw1/).

[25] US Senate Select Committee on Intelligence, "Committee Study of the Central Intelligence Agency's Detention and Interrogation Program", 9 December 2014, S. Report No. 133–288 (https://www.legal-tools.org/doc/lbh58r/).

[26] See Chapter 22 of this book.

makers and to the government. Such directorates must have a strong ethical and moral code utterly repudiating coercive interrogation and torture as immoral, illegal and contrary to good investigative practice. Further, such directorates must sustain both strong research programmes and be invested in the conduct of research that enhances the quality of non-coercive intelligence gathering.

5.11. Training of Interviewers

Minimal standards of training, education and apprenticeship need to be mandated for would-be human information consultants. These standards should approach the level of training required for clinical interviewing by professional psychiatrists or psychologists in clinical settings. Trainees should be exposed during the course of training to the great variety and extremes of behaviour that are manifest in these and other settings; they will need training to allow them to become independent interrogators or interviewers in their own right. The personal characteristics of the interrogator are also vital: selection for training needs to focus on candidates who are personally mature and can show sensitivity and acuity in interactions with the interviewee; who are culturally-aware and are comfortable with personal reflection and expressing self-doubt; and who can engage in perspective-taking and are sensitive to the boundaries of their own capacities and knowledge. Such interrogators will have to be willing to undergo regular professional development and be able to discard aspects of their interrogational practice when the data show them to be invalid or inappropriate. There is also a considerable agenda regarding the dynamics of human interaction to be pursued, presented in part above.

5.12. The Future

There is a considerable and substantial challenge in getting the science, ethics and practice in line. It will require political, scientific and practitioner change and will present a considerable challenge to current cultural practices and norms in many areas. Rising to these challenges will increase operational effectiveness, eliminate prisoner abuse and torment, and ensure that veridical and actionable information-gathering occurs. The question of how to conduct interrogations, who should do them, what training they need and what the focus of interrogation and interviewing should be is actually a behavioural and brain-sciences problem. Empirical evidence located within the theoretical framework of the brain and behavioural sciences, dispassionately analysed and presented, should be at the heart of policy-making regarding interrogation practice and intelligence work – not ideological suppositions or barely suppressed desires for retributive punishment to be exacted against detainees. Law enforcement agencies need to be restructured to recognize that veridical human intelligence and information-gathering and -analysis are at the operational heart of what they do. The central argument here is that the science, ethics and practice of interrogation and interviewing are converging on a recurring theme: 'interrogation is for professionals and torture is for amateurs'. This message cannot be repeated enough – especially to those whose knowledge of interrogation is derived principally from the fictions of the entertainment industry.

5.13. Towards a New Science of Interviewing

One caveat: there are no royal roads to the divination of the contents of human minds, nor will there be. We need reliable, replicable, trainable and transferrable alternatives to the torture of prisoners and detainees as standard non-coercive interview procedures so that interrogational (coercive) torture is never invoked again by uninformed amateurs. These interview procedures must be ethically-sound, evidence-based and empirically-founded. Sadly, this is an area that has received little by way of direct, large-scale research funding by governments over the past decades. It is also an area in which personal intuitions are too often used as a guide, in part because our cultural imaginations are rich with images where torture is used and where, in fiction, it is done so successfully.

5.14. Interviewing as a Behavioural and Brain-Sciences Problem

During non-coercive interviews, or during a forensic interview, by definition, the interviewer minimally wishes access to the contents of the long-term memories of the detainee. A reasonable definition of long-term memory is that it is a memory of past, personally-experienced facts and events extending over at least one sleep-wake cycle (although it can, and may, extend back for decades). Long-term memories can also be of events that have not yet occurred, as memories also embrace long-held intentions for future action. The brain network supporting this form of memory consists of areas of the frontal lobes, the temporal lobes and a region deep in the centre of the brain known as the anterior thalamus.[27] Interactions between these regions, as well as regular sleep, are required for the encoding, storing and retrieval of memories.

The brain is a limited storage entity: it does not store memories faithfully or in a video-like fashion. And memories themselves are fragile, subject to revision and loss through time, fatigue, stress and pain. Stressors – depending on their severity, chronicity and type – usually impair encoding of memories, disrupt consolidation of memory, and erode retrieval of memories (even of simple, straightforward, declarative and fact-based information). This is especially the

---

[27] Shane O'Mara and John P. Aggleton, "Space and Memory (Far) Beyond the Hippocampus: Many Subcortical Structures Also Support Cognitive Mapping and Mnemonic Processing", in *Frontiers in Neural Circuits*, 2019, vol. 52, pp. 1–12. John P. Aggleton and Shane O'Mara, "The Anterior Thalamic Nuclei: Core Components of a Tripartite Episodic Memory System", in *Nature Reviews Neuroscience*, 2022, vol. 23, no. 8, pp. 505–516.

case under torture regimes that combine stressors, such as repeated suffocation (say, for example, via waterboarding), extended sleep deprivation and caloric restriction. All of the evidence gathered from combat soldiers, normal volunteers, elite athletes and a variety of neuropsychiatric patients points in the same direction: extreme stressors of the type used during torture impair cognition, memory and mood in all of their phases.

5.15. What Else Does an Interviewer Need to Know?

Additionally, the interviewer wants to understand many other things about the detainee or source: a non-exhaustive list would include how they characteristically see the world; how they reason about events in the world; the state of their mental health; what they see as especially salient about their intellectual, social, religious or familial commitments; their general mind-set; their general optimism–pessimism bias; the degree to which they are narcissistic, egotistical or grandiose about themselves and their own significance; the extent to which they have sublimated themselves within the cause to which they are affiliated; the extent to which they are knowledge-rich or knowledge-poor about the world; the list goes on and on. The extreme stressor states caused by torture need to be seen for what they are: utterly inimical to the gathering of this and other related information.

5.16. Interviewing as a Process of 'Directed Remembering'

During an interview, the interviewer wants to know what the interviewee knows: the intelligence or operational-related information that they possess; the plans and intentions that they may have; details of their past; relevant information about their social and operational networks; their skills, training, attitudes, commitment; and a whole host of other information as well. By definition, this information is stored within the networks of their brain that support long-term memory – it cannot be anywhere else. Some of this information may be wrapped up in issues of personal or group identity (for example, religious or nationalistic commitment); other information might be much less identity-bound and may be easier to elicit. Certain detainees might be profoundly motivated by reasons of religion or nationalism; others may have simply a low-boredom threshold, a sense of adventure, and enjoy getting paid for what they do; others again may be involved because of threat and coercion against their families or because of simple economic need; others still because they have been socialized into terrorism through familial links (there appears to be a strong fraternal influence involved in many recent cases, for example); or there may be other reasons entirely. Some detainees may be entirely innocent, or misidentified, or captured and sold by economically-motivated mercenaries. Stereotyping the motivations of any detainee is potentially dangerous and misleading. The foregoing underscores the need for very careful preparation prior to the undertaking of the non-coercive interview by the interviewer.

5.17. Interviewing Is a Research and Operational Problem for the Behavioural and Brain Sciences

There are a wide range of practice- and experience-derived methodologies employed by various agencies to support non-coercive interviews. There is little evidence that, until recently, interrogation and interview practices have taken account of, or cared to be rooted in, the behavioural and brain sciences. This is a significant deficit because there is a large and relevant body of research available on how the brain sustains functions such as memory, attention, mood, well-being and the like. There are also many research-based tools available within the behavioural and brain sciences that would make intelligence and infor-mation-gathering more reliable, dependable and replicable, improving, in turn, operational effectiveness.

5.18. An Interdisciplinary Science of Interviewing

At the heart of an investigative interview or a forensic interview is a conversa-tion – the use of language to elicit verbal responses to allow history-taking and information-gathering. There are well-described tools for probing memory, mood and cognition available now within the behavioural and brain sciences. Further, these tools have been tested in a wide variety of settings and with vol-unteer participants, psychiatric and neuropsychological patients and forensic and other groups. Much is now known about the stability and fragility of memory and cognition and how to optimally probe the cognitive and mood states of others. Similarly, we also now know a considerable amount about lie detection and how poor humans are at detecting lies because of systematic bi-ases in the use of cues for lying which are indistinct and undependable.

There is also a considerable research agenda to be tackled. We do not know enough, for example, about the dynamics of reconstructive and transac-tional processes occurring during remembering under non-coercive interview-ing. Equally, we know little about the inter-personal cognitive and emotional coupling that occurs during conversations. During a question and answer con-versation, the content of questions and answers and the speech systems support-ing them act on a millisecond scale – rapidly, reliably and quickly. But how and under what conditions? Self-disclosure is central to human conversation: it hap-pens quickly, effortlessly and unconsciously and comprises perhaps 40 per cent of conversational content.[28] It is also intrinsically rewarding, activating the

---

[28] Robin I.M. Dunbar, Anna Marriot and Neil D.C. Duncan, "Human Conversational Behavior", in *Human Nature*, 1997, vol. 8, no. 3, pp. 231–246.

brain's reward system, compared with making disclosures about others.[29] Interviews and police investigative interviews are, however, peculiar because they occur under artificial circumstances with an expectation of asymmetry in self-report: the interviewer expects disclosure but does not expect to engage in disclosure. We do not know if hearing disclosures from another is intrinsically biologically rewarding in the way that self-disclosure is.

Substantial research does not support current interview or interviewing practices. Techniques involving provocative or confrontational (coercive) interrogation do not have strong empirical support. Indeed, many of these techniques are better understood as historical or cultural relics, deriving from a time before much was understood about how the brain supports memory and cognition. The available evidence suggests that they might be good at eliciting confessions, but not at eliciting the truth. They therefore impair best investigative practice. Polygraphy and brain imaging for lie detection are similarly compromised as they lack empirical foundation or support.[30] There is a need for a profound cultural shift regarding these practices – they impair investigation and truth-finding, rather than facilitating it. These practices are also culture-specific: there are huge variations in interviewing practices even across the police forces of the Anglophone world.[31] There is a dearth of large-scale studies in the literature on the best interview techniques, compared with the overwhelmingly large literature on how the brain supports memory functions, for example. Any such studies must meet the appropriate empirical bar: they need to be conducted using proper experimental designs with appropriate hypotheses stated in advance or they need to be randomized control trials conducted in differing settings. There has, however, been a substantial training effort in the clinical psychological, psychiatric and related professions addressing this very issue, which can be used in this new setting.

The purpose of the non-coercive interview needs to be very clearly thought through. Is it confession-seeking or for information-elicitation and gathering? There are many possible variants to the interview: they might be assessment-based (and may be structured or semi-structured) and they might be competence-based (where a linguistic fluency and coherency analysis is undertaken, followed by tests of literacy and numeracy, where these are not known, *et cetera*). Appropriate logs and full video and sound recordings taken preferably from the point of view of both the interviewer and the detainee also need to be made. The

---

29 Diana Tamir and Jason P. Mitchell, "Disclosing Information About the Self Is Intrinsically Rewarding", in *Proceedings of the National Academy of Sciences*, 2012, vol. 109, no. 21, pp. 8038–8043.

30 O'Mara, 2015, see *supra* note 4.

31 See Chapter 8 of this book.

dual viewpoint is to allow the interviewer to develop a sense of their own personal style and to provide a focus for self-improvement, as well as providing an exterior check on the conduct of the interrogation or interview itself. Techniques giving the illusion of complete knowledge coupled with oblique and indirect questioning (for example, the Scharff technique)[32] and which will allow the detainee to be 'boxed-in' facilitate unknowing self-disclosure and boost information-gathering. The limit case here is not understood, however.

In conclusion, it should be clear, though, that there is a vast research agenda to be dealt with: we should no longer be misled by fevered intuitions and biased introspections about how to reliably gather information from other human beings.

---

[32]   See Chapter 10 of this book.

6

The Méndez Principles

Rebecca Shaeffer, Veronica Hinestroza and Sean Tait[*]

6.1. Introduction

The Méndez Principles on Effective Interviewing for Investigations and Information Gathering[1] ('Méndez Principles' or 'Principles') represent a crucial achievement in the evolution of non-coercive interviewing and interrogation as a key stage of due process, the justice process and, within them, the search for the truth. Their four-year development responded to an appeal before the 2016 UN General Assembly by Professor Juan E. Méndez, then United Nations ('UN') Special Rapporteur on Torture and Other Cruel, Inhuman or Degrading Treatment or Punishment (2010–2016). His vision was to build on the existing international momentum around ethical investigation and questioning, and promote the development of a set of guidelines to ensure that, as a matter of law and practice, no person is subjected to torture, ill-treatment or coercion while being questioned. In his report,[2] Méndez anticipated that such guidelines should be based on non-coercive techniques, ethically sound, evidence- and research-based, and empirically founded. He pointed out the importance of rendering these guidelines relevant to law enforcement and other investigative bodies, such as intelligence, security and military services, administrative bodies, during counter-terrorism operations and in situations of armed conflict, including extra-territorially.

Published in May 2021, the Principles, aim to "propose a concrete alternative to interrogation methods that rely on coercion to extract confessions. They provide guidance on obtaining accurate and reliable information in full respect of the human rights and dignity of all, including through the

---

[*] **Rebecca Shaeffer** is former Interim Global Legal Director of Fair Trials, currently attorney with National Disability Rights Network (United States), and a member of the Steering Committee for the Méndez Principles. **Veronica Hinestroza** is an independent expert on international human rights law, Senior Legal Advisor at Fair Trials, and a member of the Steering Committee for the Méndez Principles. **Sean Tait** is Director of the African Policing Civilian Oversight Forum and a member of the Steering Committee for the Méndez Principles.
[1] See Anti-Torture Initiative, Association for the Prevention of Torture and the Norwegian Centre for Human Rights, *Principles on Effective Interviewing for Investigations and Information Gathering*, 2021 (https://www.legal-tools.org/doc/wbfiw1/).
[2] Torture and other cruel, inhuman or degrading treatment or punishment, Note by the Secretary-General, UN Doc. A/71/298, 5 August 2016 (https://www.legal-tools.org/doc/luww5z/).

implementation of legal and procedural safeguards in the first hours of police custody".[3] By the time of writing, the Principles have been endorsed and welcomed by the UN Committee Against Torture, the UN Sub-committee on the Prevention of Torture, the High Representative of the European Union, the Council of Europe's Committee for the Prevention of Torture, the Organization for Security and Co-operation in Europe ('OSCE'), its Office for Democratic Institutions and Human Rights ('ODHIR'), the UN Congress on Crime Prevention and Criminal Justice, and the UN Human Rights Council, as well as by regional and domestic-level institutions such as the African Commission on Human and Peoples' Rights, which in its resolution 545 of 2022 welcomed the Principles and called on its 52 members states to support their application domestically. With time, it is hoped that they will be endorsed by the UN General Assembly and implemented by the UN Police as well as by some domestic ministries of justice, policing organizations and criminal justice, military and intelligence actors.

6.2. The Méndez Principles in the Evolution of Interview Practice

Prior to the development of the Principles, interviewing practice itself has not been informed or monitored through the lens of international standards; rather, it has been a prerogative of the different agencies themselves (for example, policing and law enforcement, military, security and intelligence). Despite its *jus cogens* status, the absolute prohibition against torture and ill-treatment has not resulted in their eradication during information-gathering stages of investigations and other forms of questioning. This is true even for States Parties to the 1984 UN Convention against Torture and Other Cruel, Inhuman or Degrading Treatment or Punishment (173 countries at the time of writing),[4] which provides that law enforcement personnel, civil or military, medical personnel, public officials and other persons who may be involved in the custody, interrogation or treatment of any individual subjected to any form of arrest, detention or imprisonment should be educated on the prohibition against torture (Article 10), as well as that each State Party shall keep under systematic review interrogation rules, instructions, methods and practices (Article 11).

Furthermore, legal standards in many countries do not effectively prohibit coercive interview practices that fall short of torture or ill-treatment, but nonetheless tend to produce false testimony and can negatively impact the mental and psychological integrity of interviewees. It is notable, for example, that the

---

[3] *Ibid.*

[4] Convention against Torture and Other Cruel, Inhuman or Degrading Treatment or Punishment, adopted 10 December 1984, entry into force 26 June 1987 ('UNCAT') (https://www.legal-tools.org/doc/713f11/).

PEACE method of interviewing,[5] as the first non-coercive method of police interview, was developed in England and Wales only after, and in response to, the passage of the Police and Criminal Evidence Act (1984),[6] the first and most significant effort to comprehensively regulate police interviews and general investigations by primary legislation. The Principles recognize the foundational role that legal norms play in establishing and reinforcing ethical and effective interview practices, and seek to link legal safeguards with evidence-based practice in a single comprehensive set of principles to which any interviewing and investigation practice (diverse and developing as they are) must cohere.

The Principles represent a paradigm shift, in which the legal safeguards long established by the international human rights frameworks are not seen as external constraints on police and law enforcement, but as integral tools to their effectiveness. In so doing, the Principles position law enforcement officials themselves as guardians of those safeguards which they recognize to be in their own interest as well as the interest of justice processes.

By establishing a common and public understanding of what constitutes lawful, effective, and ethical interviewing standards, the Principles increase the ability of independent actors playing an oversight role to effectively assess and report on interviewers' conduct, while protecting the mental integrity of individuals who enter into contact with the justice system. Stakeholders, including oversight bodies, civil society, prosecutors, defense lawyers and the judiciary, can also find in the Principles an invaluable resource to improve their questioning capabilities. Examples of oversight bodies include the National Preventative Mechanisms ('NPMs')[7] established by the UNCAT, civilian oversight boards of law enforcement[8] (also known as civilian review boards, or 'CRBs'), and prison inspectors.[9]

A second innovation of the Principles is their recognition that any non-coercive interview occurs in a context, a chain of state control which begins

---

[5] PEACE is the mnemonic acronym for the five stages of the interview process: Planning and preparation, Engage and Explain, Account, Clarify and Challenge, Closure, and Evaluation. See also Chapter 12 of this book.

[6] United Kingdom, Police and Criminal Evidence Act, 31 October 1984 (https://www.legal-tools.org/doc/b52ec0/). See also Chapters 4 and 13 of this book.

[7] See UN Office of the High Commissioner for Human Rights ('OHCHR'), Sub-Committee on the Preventnion of Torture, "National Preventive Mechanisms" (available on the OHCHR's web site).

[8] See National Association for Civilian Oversight of Law Enforcement ('NACOLE'), "Community Oversight Paves the Road to Police Accountability" (available on the NACOLE's web site).

[9] See Montgomery County, "Board of Prison Inspectors" (available on the Montgomery County's web site).

from the first contact between state actors (that is, police or law enforcement officers) and the interview subject themselves. Every element of that contact has the potential to preserve or disrupt the memory and effective testimony of the subject in a later interview.[10] For example, an arrested person may be subject to abuse that has downstream effects for memory and recall, be exposed to informal questioning[11] or receive false or inaccurate information concerning the facts about which he or she has to provide a statement, thereby contaminating his or her memory. It is therefore incumbent on the police (or other investigative actors) to ensure that safeguards are observed at every stage of contact and that any deviations are recorded and their impact on the memory and well-being of the subject are assessed. Therefore, for example, a 'clean' interview cannot compensate or legitimize breaches to due process and to the absolute prohibition of torture and ill-treatment that occurred in connection with the arrest or transfer to police custody, or indeed, during custody. The entire chain of custody is implicated in the preservation of the subject's memory and its protection from contamination, and their ability to recall it accurately and comprehensively.

The Principles recognize that part of the interviewer's role is to identify the positive or negative impact of the interviewee's immediate previous contact with the authorities on the interviewee's memory and intention to co-operate. The Principles position the interview as an instance during which the protection of the physical and mental integrity of the person to be interviewed can be realized (a positive obligation of states). Ensuring the integrity of the interview thus requires the eradication of any practice that inflicts pain or suffering on the subject, as such conduct will spoil any evidence later obtained.

International law instruments that predate the Principles – and which paved the way for the integration of ethics, science and human rights into guidelines to facilitate state compliance with their international obligations – addressed directives for the carrying out of interviews, including with victims, family members and witnesses. Both the UN Minnesota Protocol for the Investigation of Potentially Wrongful Death[12] and the UN Istanbul Protocol for the Effective Investigation and Documentation of Torture[13] placed the interview as

---

[10] See also Chapter 9 of this book.

[11] See European Court of Human Rights, *Lalik v. Poland*, Judgment, 11 May 2023 (https://www.legal-tools.org/doc/hsqpqw/).

[12] OHCHR, *The Minnesota Protocol for the Investigation of Potentially Wrongful Death (2016): The Revised United Nations Manual on the Effective Prevention and Investigation of Extra-legal, Arbitrary and Summary Executions*, September 2017 (https://www.legal-tools.org/doc/a10ntw/).

[13] OHCHR, *Istanbul Protocol: Manual on the Effective Investigation and Documentation of Torture and Other Cruel, Inhuman or Degrading Treatment or Punishment*, Rev. 2, 29 June 2022 (https://www.legal-tools.org/doc/xmw3hp/).

a central element of the investigation and emphasized the importance of conducting them under a 'do-no-harm' approach. The Principles elaborate on these developments and, while demystifying torture as a practice that produces complete or truthful information from the interviewee, present lessons from cognitive psychology and highlight the relevance of protecting the memory of all interviewees, both in relation to their mental integrity and evidence of the facts.

While cognitive psychology has made great strides in demonstrating the fragility of memories in the face of external influences – including poorly formulated questions, false statements, photographs or videos shown at the wrong time, and of course violence – memory has not been presented in any international instrument as evidence to be protected in the way that traditional forensic evidence, for example, is safeguarded from contamination. In this regard, memory is, as crime scenes, susceptible to Locard's Exchange Principle, which states that 'every contact leaves a trace'.[14]

The Méndez Principles capture this knowledge, as well as existing interviewing techniques that are compatible with human rights, and outline how to integrate this knowledge and progress with the guarantee of due process for a fair trial.

6.3. Wide Applicability

The Principles' shift in paradigm makes them a valuable resource beyond the more narrowly defined criminal justice system and into broad applicability. They apply and function effectively in multiple settings, including military, intelligence and administrative investigations; and in relation to multiple kinds of interview subjects, including victims, witnesses and suspects of crime, plus other persons of interest. They may also find applicability in the field of human rights monitoring and defense. Testimonies from victims and witnesses of an alleged human rights violation can provide both definitive evidence in individual cases and inform the identification of patterns in a series of cases. States and international investigative bodies are aware of the importance of good interviewing, and have therefore invested in, and supported, scientific efforts to develop and test techniques for obtaining accurate testimony. Unfortunately, human right defenders and monitors have, as yet, not necessarily benefitted from these developments despite the crucial importance of information that can be obtained from testimonial evidence.

While it is natural that in these types of organizations there is a focus on the 'do-no-harm' approach and the importance of protecting the mental integrity and safety of those who testify, this does not mean that their cause cannot be

---

[14] Described by Dr. Edmond Locard (1877–1966) in 1920. See Graham Gooch and Michael Williams, *A Dictionary of Law Enforcement*, Oxford University Press, 2007.

furthered through the development of more effective techniques to strengthen their work and the pursuit of justice. One of the major criticisms of police and law enforcement officials with investigative responsibilities is that they tend to fixate on investigative hypotheses that they believe to be true, and this often prevents them from maintaining objectivity when conducting interviews. However, this bias can also affect the taking of testimony by monitoring agents who may take for granted what happened and, without the proper tools and insights, be worried about re-victimizing the interviewee. This may also lead to them not being more receptive to detailed information in support of the allegations and allow them, for example, to identify patterns.

The Principles provide important guidance for the vast range of persons and disciplines who may interview. By improving interviewing techniques, monitoring organizations and bodies will be able to move away from high-level characterizations of violations to providing greater details around possible alternative hypotheses, motivations, weapons, elements of the crime under national law, direct perpetrators and chains of command.

6.4. How Do the Principles Achieve This New Paradigm Shift?

There are six principles that set out an approach to improving the efficacy, fairness and outcomes of investigations and the administration of justice. They seek to protect the inherent dignity and human rights of all persons before, during and after questioning, and do this by providing a common set of standards and an evidence-based, practice-oriented and human rights-compliant framework for those involved in investigations and conducting interviews. The Principles are grounded in the notion of legitimacy both in terms of their substance and their multi-party development, and offer a unique insight into this paradigm shift in interviewing.

An investigation is developed through collecting and analysing physical (and other forms of) evidence and through the testimony of victims, witnesses, suspects of crime and other persons of interest, and experts. Facts are established through corroborating evidence and the effectiveness of testimony, unlike physical evidence, is influenced by the willingness and level of engagement of the interviewee. Factors that negatively affect this willingness to participate include the obvious, like coercion, but also the extent to which the process might be rushed, poorly managed or badly conducted. Such factors impact on the accuracy and the detail of the information provided, and heighten the risk of the possible withdrawal of co-operation from the interviewee. An interview with a victim, witness or suspect is rarely a singular event, and if their testimony is going to be used in a hearing, their commitment to continue to be available is key to the success of the outcome. These skills, techniques and process challenges can naturally influence the person being interviewed, but can also impact on the interviewer(s) who may be affected by unconscious bias and may well miss vital information.

Legitimacy is a useful concept in understanding the motivation for full and sustained participation in an interview. Legitimacy resides in a belief that people feel obligated to and willingly participate. This, in turn, motivates co-operation and ultimately, in the case of interview evidence, increases the credibility of the testimony, being free from any inducement, positive or negative. Procedural Justice Theory[15] sets out a theoretical approach to understanding legitimacy, found both in the perceived fairness of the issue at hand and in the process of interaction between the protagonists. The substantive variables of procedural justice can thus be found in the fairness, objectivity and neutrality of the interaction; whereas being treated with dignity and respect characterize the key variables to the process. These variables: fairness, objectivity, factuality, neutrality, dignity and respect lie at the heart of the Méndez Principles. Figure 1 below show the six Principles and an explanation on each one follows.

On Foundations

Effective interviewing is instructed by science, law and ethics.

On Practice

Effective interviewing is a comprehensive process for gathering accurate and reliable information while implementing associated legal safeguards.

On Vulnerability

Effective interviewing requires identifying and addressing the needs of interviewees in situations of vulnerability.

On Training

Effective interviewing is a professional undertaking that requires specific training.

On Accountability

Effective interviewing requires transparent and accountable institutions.

On Implementation

The implementation of effective interviewing requires robust national measures.

Figure 1: The six Méndez Principles (Anti-Torture Initiative, Association for the Prevention of Torture and the Norwegian Centre for Human Rights).

---

15   See John W. Thibault and Laurens Walker, *Procedural Justice: A Psychological Analysis*, Lawrence Earbaum Associatres, Hillsdale, 1975.

6.4.1. Principle 1: On Foundations

The first principle establishes that the most effective interviews are based on empirical scientific studies, international legal standards and values-based professional duties. The increasing democratization of the interview knowledge, skill and process discussed above is underscored by including international human rights expertise and empirical research equally with the discipline of policing and the skill and experience of the investigator as grounding for new practice. While science locates the approach in an empirical knowledge of what is likely to produce the greatest success in an interview, a full re-count of the facts, ethical standards and human rights law ensure an alignment to key procedural and custodial safeguards.

These, in turn, underpin two key benefits. In the first instance, the risks of legal challenge to the testimony are greatly reduced. The legal safeguards are well known, albeit often poorly applied, and include the right to information about rights; the right to remain silent; the right to information about the reasons for arrest and any charges at the time of the arrest; access to interpretation; the right to notify a relative or third party of one's detention; the right of access to a lawyer, a doctor, an independent medical examination, and outside contact; the right to review and sign the interview record; and access to effective and independent complaints mechanisms and oversight. These procedural safeguards have the direct effect of actualizing the values of objectivity, dignity and respect essential in promoting procedural fairness, building the legitimacy of the process and, in turn, achieving the willing compliance of those being interviewed. This is reinforced by a third area of focus on the ethics of the interviewer, cautioning against the dangers of expediency and re-affirming the values of fairness, honesty and lawfulness in how interviewers carry out their duties.

6.4.2. Principle 2: On Practice

The second principle shifts our understanding from the interview as a singular event to that of a complete process encompassing all interactions between the interviewer and interviewee at all stages. Legitimacy is conditional and can be withdrawn at any point. Thus, there is paramount importance in upholding the values of fairness, honesty and lawfulness from the moment someone is identified as being 'of interest' in terms of gathering information through to the conduct of the interview, and to its conclusion. At any point along this chain, the relationship between interviewer and interviewee, and with it, the possible evidence, can be undermined through wilful actions or simple carelessness. Planning and preparation lie at the heart of managing the risks associated with poor interview techniques. The principle then sets out the processes an effective interview would likely include: thorough preparation and planning, ensuring relevant safeguards are applied throughout, establishing and maintaining rapport, and ultimately the assessment and analysis of the information gathered.

6.4.3. Principle 3: On Vulnerabilities

The third principle introduces a key valuable addition to interviews and human rights law, in pinning down the importance of risk assessment throughout the interview process. Risk assessments are recognized as critical interventions in planning complex operations and in ensuring rights are upheld. In the recently adopted African Commission Guidelines for Policing Assemblies by Law Enforcement Officials in Africa,[16] risk assessment is a key component in ensuring that rights, often competing ones, are recognized and protected. It is important to acknowledge that all persons in an interview are in a position of vulnerability. In the case of witnesses and victims, this can include very direct threats to their safety, but also the impact of secondary trauma in reliving the facts. It can also appear in how variables like age, gender and cultural differences are managed in the interview and the stress it may place on the subject. The principle makes the important distinction between the vulnerability of everyone in an interview situation, and the heightened vulnerability faced by some persons because of their circumstances, status and intersection of these. Importantly, a situation of heightened vulnerability is understood by the Principles to be dynamic and evolving, as opposed to static, and can be brought on by temporal factors like health or trauma at the time, the nature of the offence or subject-matter of the interview, being pregnant, injured, ill, under the influence of drink or drugs, breast-feeding or being a primary care giver, or migration status. These risks continually fluctuate.

This principle articulates the importance of carrying out a risk assessment to assess the vulnerability of the interviewee against a matrix of factors in order to assess the special needs that may be required to support the interview in a specific context. This sophisticated understanding of vulnerability accordingly requires a less formalistic and more individualized and adaptive assessment not only by interviewers themselves, but also by later judicial assessments of the reliability and voluntariness of any statements or evidence arising from an interview.

6.4.4. Principle 4: On Training

Building on the realization of the kinds of specialist skills that need to be available in an interview, the fourth principle locates effective interviewing as a learnt skill requiring specialist training. While some people would have the traits of

---

[16]   African Commission on Human and Peoples' Rights ('ACHPR'), "Guidelines for the Policing of Assemblies by Law Enforcement Officials in Africa", March 2017.

empathy or attention to detail which are useful for an interviewer, interviewing itself is not an intuitive endeavour. Rather, it is a discipline that requires high levels of training, practice and experience built over years.

6.4.5. Principle 5: On Accountability

Transparency and accountability are captured in the fifth principle. These values lie at the heart of promoting an organization and organizational culture accountable for its actions. It is essential to legitimacy. This principle outlines a holistic approach to accountability that includes effective record-keeping and monitoring of independent assessments and systems of accountability, remedy (including redress and non-repetition) and, linked to the latter, the importance of a regular assessment and reviews of procedures. The impact of recent measures to restrict Covid-19 transmission has included a greater move to remote interviewing. Associated limitation on some procedural safeguards, such as access to lawyers and outside contact, highlights how important it is to keep all procedures under regular review.

6.4.6. Principle 6: On Implementation

Finally, the sixth principle outlines the role of mandate holders in implementation – from a review of domestic frameworks as required by Article 11 of the UNCAT,[17] to building institutional capacity for effective interviewing and investigations. This principle articulates the broad-based, multi-institutional and legal framework necessary for the full realization of the Principles. They cannot, for example, be implemented only by changing primary legislation or police training manuals. Rather, they must be integrated into legislation, policy, oversight and judicial bodies among others, all of which are necessary for sustained and systematic changes to the way interviews are conducted.

6.5.   Putting the Méndez Principles into Practice

A practical example of such review and capacity-building is evident in East Africa. Working in parallel with the development of the Principles, some members of the Steering Committee (and the authors of this chapter) began exploring practical applications among several constituencies with whom they worked. One of these was the East African Police Commissioners Cooperation Organisation ('EAPCCO'), a forum of Chiefs of Police for Eastern Africa. An essential first step was to domesticate the principles, for instance, in the language of policing through a standard operating procedure ('SOP') for conducting interviews. This in itself is a remarkable development and provides a detailed procedure on human rights-compliant interviewing in an effort to enhance the professionalism

---

[17]   See UNCAT, see *supra* note 4.

and effectiveness of law enforcement officials and ensure that all interviews are conducted without resort to torture, ill-treatment or coercion.

Among the notable advances in the SOP are the following: (i) to clearly articulate provisions which stress that unless there are clear exceptional circumstances, interviews must only be conducted at police stations or places of detention authorized by law; (ii) no interview should be conducted unless all procedural and custodial safeguards regarding arrest and detention as contained in national law and domesticated international human rights treaties, have been upheld; (iii) interviews must be conducted by officers specifically trained, and all interviews of suspects and persons of interest must be conducted in a manner that respects the presumption of innocence; (iv) all violence during interviews and the entire investigation process, including illegal tactics like humiliation, sleep deprivation, prolonged solitary confinement, incommunicado detention, blindfolding and hooding, is prohibited and subject to criminal sanction; and (v) common manipulative techniques to be avoided include threats, inducements, misleading practices, protracted or suggestive questioning, as well as demeaning or condescending comments, or accusations based on individual qualities or cultural identities. These techniques are recognized as coercive in nature and likely to impair the free will, judgment and memory of interviewees.

As a precursor to the utility of the Principles acting as a blueprint for the systematic review of procedures and practice, EAPCCO is now developing an implementation plan for the SOP which includes assessing current regulatory and training environments of members with a view to recommending both regulatory and training alignment with the new SOP. An initiative is underway with the Kenya National Police Service to test this approach.

6.5.1. Beyond Police: Use of the Principles by Other Criminal Justice Actors

The legal profession understands the importance of a lawyer being present during the investigative interview as a safeguard against torture in the first hours of detention, as well as a safeguard of due process in relation to the right to a technical defence and the guarantee of the presumption of innocence, the right against self-incrimination and the right to remain silent. In Latin America, the Principles have been well received, especially by defence lawyers who do not yet have the possibility in all countries to be present in the interview room, as the Principles highlight, in line with pre-existing safeguards.

The Principles have also been used as a tool to improve the quality of the information collected by the lawyer from his or her client; the Federal Institute of Public Defence in Mexico included them as a working tool to obtain information on the performance of law enforcement officials during their arrest, transfer and submission to the competent authorities.[18]

Likewise, in Mexico and Brazil there has been significant interest in advancing strategic litigation to extend to coercion the scope of the exclusionary rule for evidence obtained under torture – also outlined in the Principles and implementation of which is crucial for the prevention and punishment of torture. In addition to the richness already described, the Principles reinforce principles of the right to equality before the courts and a fair trial.

Discussions on the Principles with judges and prosecutors have also led to recognizing the imminent need to work towards a cultural shift around the means, ends and limits of information-gathering. A shift that can benefit from the institutional acknowledgment that torture is not only illegal and immoral, but also ineffective for obtaining reliable information and recognizing the high social and legal cost of resorting to the infliction of pain and suffering to advance investigations.

In November 2022, the Appeal Chambers of Colombia's Special Jurisdiction for Peace, which deals with grave crimes committed during the armed conflict, drew on the Principles as guidelines for assessing the interview conducted with an applicant seeking to avail himself of the Court's jurisdiction.[19]

6.6. Lessons from the Process

The central innovation of the Principles is the integration of three fields of knowledge (science, ethics and law), with the legal safeguards understood as an indispensable element of the essential architecture of effective policing and law enforcement. On a deeper level, this integration reflects the insight that what 'works' in state-led investigations must be determined not only by professional expertise, but by democratic participation of the policed. Therefore, the multidisciplinary, inclusive and collaborative process that led to the creation of the Principles is reflected in a legal instrument that is democratic in nature. Too often, the science and strategy of non-coercive interviewing is seen as clandestine, a set of methods known only to police and siloed from scrutiny by the public. The Principles transform law-enforcement monopoly on knowledge and power by creating a common benchmark by which civil society and justice actors can assess the effectiveness and lawfulness of police and law enforcement

---

[18] Laboratorio de Litigio Estructural, Instituto Federal de la Defensoría Pública and United States Agency for International Development, *Guía Práctica para el Uso Adecuado de la Cédula de Atención para la Documentación de Hechos de Tortura y Tratos Crueles, Inhumanos o Degradantes*, 2021.

[19] Colombia, Jurisdicción Especial para la Paz, Appeals Chamber, *Nancy Conde Rubio*, Ruling Auto TP-SA 1296 de 2022 Denying the Benefit of Amnesty, 11 November 2022 (https://www.legal-tools.org/doc/wz4leh/).

behaviour in interview, a tool which is accessible, understandable and usable by everyone in society and in the entire justice system. For procedures and methods cannot be siloed within policing and law enforcement 'expertise' only – they must reflect a shared contract authorized by citizen participation and informed by evolving legal, scientific, political and popular knowledge and requirements. It follows then that all these relevant actors in society must learn from and internalize the values and strategies which the Principles proclaim, in order that they be fully realized and implemented.

The Principles recognize that the development of non-coercive interviewing and interrogation techniques is not purely a matter for professional experts from within policing and law enforcement. It is also substantially constituted by the evolving legal frameworks created by, and with, the consent of policed communities and oversight bodies. Therefore, the standards applied to state actors must similarly be products of broad consultation and consensus. The Principles bring together scientific, psychological, humanitarian and legal frameworks from civil society to create a new instrument that shifts the paradigm from an adversarial relationship between police and citizens, to a collaborative one based on shared objectives of truth-seeking, reliability, transparency, accountability, legality and safety through humane relationship. The Principles are, thus, an effort to integrate into one cohesive set of operating principles, multi-disciplinary knowledge of what makes investigative interviews effective, ethical and lawful. The process by which the Principles were developed mirrors this insight.

In order for this multi-disciplinary integration to occur, the Principles were guided into creation by a 15-person Steering Committee consisting of experts from varied backgrounds, including professional investigators in police, military and intelligence contexts, psychologists with expertise in memory and recall, and human rights experts with expertise in the legal safeguards required during interviews. The authors are four of the experts from the human rights, psychology and policing communities, and our views on the significance of the Principles are perhaps coloured by that lens. It is rare for human rights lawyers to be invited into collaboration with police and scientists. This collaboration produced an instrument which not only succeeds in capturing interviewing principles that are grounded in the evolving science of psychology and human memory, but which is also informed by the democratic principles of human rights law that reflect the perspectives of those who are subject to policing, and those who hold police to account for abuses.

6.7. Conclusion

Reaching the six Principles presented here was a rigorous process of intense discussions among a multi-disciplinary and geographically diverse Steering Committee, which came to the process with the same intention: to offer an effective alternative to the use of coercion and torture to obtain information, but with different perspectives on the reasons these illegal practices are still used around the world. We had multiple and detailed discussions about the scope of the Principles, on when they would begin to operate, primarily on whether they should be limited to the interview itself. Similarly, we discussed at length whether or not interviewers should take ownership of the guarantee of pre- and post-interview legal and procedural safeguards, and the focus of the document, whether it should be closer to a manual or be, as it is today, guiding principles applicable to any technique that seeks to be effective and lawful.

It was extremely enriching for the authors to work with the other members of the Steering Committee and to hear, in the different international meetings we held (Brazil, Tunisia and Thailand) about the opportunities and difficulties faced by those who have the responsibility to resolve cases while respecting the human rights of all those potentially involved. The Principles are not an interviewing technique or training manual *per se*, nor are they an ethics or human rights manual. They are a compilation of best practices in each area that converge in a triangulation dialogue for practical implementation by those who are responsible for conducting investigations and interviews, and monitoring by those who accompany or follow up on this work, such as lawyers and civil society.

The science and practice of law-enforcement interviewing techniques will (and should) continue to develop and change through empirical research and observation. However, no technique can be acceptable legally or professionally if it does not conform to the Principles. This overarching framework of ethical and non-coercive interviewer-behaviour is now the touchstone by which all methodologies must be assessed.

7

Forensic Linguistics and Interviewing

Nicci MacLeod and Annina Heini[*]

7.1. Introduction

While academic psychologists have had input into developments in investigative interviewing since at least the 1990s, the contribution of linguists to the field is very much still in its infancy. The field of forensic linguistics – itself only in existence since the early 1990s as a sustained organized drive to assimilate scattered attempts at applying language analysis to issues of justice – is often described as comprising two main strands: firstly, the provision of linguistic assistance and sometimes evidence in civil and criminal disputes; and secondly, the language of legal documents and processes.[1] It is into this latter subfield – sometimes referred to simply as 'language and law' – that linguistic interest in investigative interviews and interrogations falls.

This chapter sets out to distil forensic linguists' interest in the investigative interview and its role in the legal process. It reviews the linguistic processes of negotiation and transformation observable in this unique context, and it casts light on some of the ways tools from discourse analysis can help to unpick the mechanics of the interview as a discursive event and usefully inform professional practice in the area.

7.2. Institutional Talk

Interaction in the police interview room is easily characterizable as 'institutional talk', which we might define as "institutional insofar as participants' institutional or professional identities are somehow made relevant to the work activities in which they are engaged".[2] There is an obvious distance between the participants and an imbalance in the resources to which they have access. This applies both in broad practical terms (for example, in suspect interviews only one party is able to return home at the conclusion of the interview) and in discursive

---

[*] **Nicci MacLeod** is a Senior Lecturer in Forensic Linguistics at the Aston Institute for Forensic Linguistics. **Annina Heini** is a Postdoctoral Research Associate at the Aston Institute for Forensic Linguistics.

[1] Malcolm Coulthard, Alison Johnson and David Wright, *An Introduction to Forensic Linguistics: Language in Evidence*, 2nd ed., Routledge, Abingdon, 2017.

[2] Paul Drew and John Heritage, "Analyzing Talk at Work: An Introduction", in Paul Drew and John Heritage (eds.), *Talk at Work: Interaction in Institutional Settings*, Cambridge University Press, 1992, pp. 3–4.

terms (for example, the interviewer asks the questions, and the interviewee is constrained in that all they can do is answer them). It is important to emphasize here that the restriction of having to provide an 'answer' to a 'question' is not meant in the sense that content – or in this case evidence – must be given, but that the conversational *turn* that follows a 'question' is an 'answer' in terms of its function. A 'no comment' answer given by a suspect still constitutes an answer turn. This privileged access to questions as a turn type also enables the interviewer to control the topic, and thus the direction of the conversation.[3]

Institutional talk can be distinguished from ordinary conversation along several dimensions.[4] To begin with, interaction in institutional contexts is always informed by some *goal orientation*, which is to say that at least one of the participants – in our case the interviewer – is working towards a core goal or task – in our case the elicitation of information useful for either the investigation, or for the establishment of evidential details, or both (for more on the dual function of the interview, see below).[5] Secondly, there are *special and particular constraints* on what will be treated as allowable contributions by one or both participants. As mentioned above, the types of turn a participant may take are pre-allocated inasmuch as they may only respond to interviewers' questions, and do not have the power to initiate new topics. Finally, there are particular *inferential frameworks* associated with institutional talk – utterances which in ordinary conversation may be treated as fairly inconsequential may, in institutional settings, generate particular implications relating to the topic under discussion. In an interview setting, for example, a witness mentioning in passing the presence of CCTV cameras may for the interviewer constitute a highly significant direction for the investigation – this significance is unlikely to be recognized by the interviewee.

Central to the notion of constraints on talk is the concept of *asymmetry*, that is, the inequality of participants in institutional discourse as compared to 'ordinary' talk, which tends to be characterized by equality of participation.[6] Research in the area has also taken *professional lexis* – that is, vocabulary associated with particular institutions and unfamiliar to outsiders – as a key focus, and we might note that the phenomenon of 'police-speak' has drawn the

---

3   Georgina Heydon, *The Language of Police Interviewing: A Critical Analysis*, Palgrave, Basingstoke, 2005.

4   Drew and Heritage, 1992, see *supra* note 2.

5   Kate Haworth, "Police Interviews as Evidence", in Malcolm Coulthard, Alison May and Rui Sousa-Silva (eds.), *The Routledge Handbook of Forensic Linguistics*, 2nd ed., Routledge, Abingdon, 2021, pp. 144–158.

6   Drew and Heritage, 1992, see *supra* note 2. Joanna Thornborrow, *Power Talk: Language and Interaction in Institutional Discourse*, Longman, London, 2002.

attention of a number of researchers in the field.[7] A further point of interest is the highly *structured* nature of many institutional interactions – consider, for example, the phased approach to interviewing set out by the PEACE model and other frameworks discussed in this book.

An understanding of investigative interview discourse as a type of institutional talk takes us some way towards describing and understanding its interactional patterns. From a critical discourse analytical perspective, we might describe the investigative interview as being pervaded by *disorders of discourse*: "gulfs that separate insiders from outsiders, members of institutions from clients of those institutions, and elites from the normal citizen uninitiated in the arcana of bureaucratic language and life".[8]

We might also usefully describe interview discourse as an example of *legal–lay* communication.[9] While police interviewers are not as a general rule members of the legal profession, it has been shown repeatedly that the interactive practices of those working in related spheres – such as policing – are heavily influenced by the law.[10] We might thus view investigative interviewers as professionals acting on behalf of *legal* institutions, and interviewees as encountering the legal system in a non-institutional, *lay* role. The key difference between these two types of participant is a matter of awareness – while the legal participant has a high level of familiarity with the goal orientation, special interactional constraints and inferential frameworks of the context, this familiarity is unlikely to be shared by the lay interviewee.[11]

7.3. Jurisdictional Differences

As is evident from this book, there is no one universal approach to investigative interviewing. Some of the linguistic effects of these jurisdictional differences will be briefly explored in this section. In England and Wales, a number of miscarriages of justice in the 1970s, most famously the wrongful convictions of the Bridgwater Four and the Birmingham Six, led to an in-depth review of policing practices. In the case of the Birmingham Six, the questioning techniques used

---

[7] Gwyneth Fox, "A Comparison of 'Policespeak' and 'Normalspeak': A Preliminary Study", in Michael Hoey, John M. Sinclair and Gwyneth Fox (eds.), *Techniques of Description: Spoken and Written Discourse*, Routledge, Abingdon, 1993, pp. 183–195. Phil Hall, "Policespeak", in John Gibbons and M. Teresa Turell (eds.), *Dimensions of Forensic Linguistics*, John Benjamins, Amsterdam, 2008, pp. 67–94.

[8] Ruth Wodak, *Disorders of Discourse*, Longman, London, 1996, p. 22.

[9] Chris Heffer, Frances Rock and John Conley (eds.), *Legal-Lay Communication: Textual Travels in the Law*, Oxford University Press, 2013.

[10] Georgina Heydon, "From Legislation to the Courts" and Alison Johnson, "Embedding Police Interviews in the Prosecution Case in the Shipman Trial", in *ibid.*

[11] Heffer, Rock and Conley (eds.), 2013, p. 7, see *supra* note 9.

by West Midlands Police were grave cause for concern. The six men accused of murder in connection with the 1974 Birmingham pub bombings were subjected to excessively prolonged interrogations accompanied by food and sleep deprivation, beatings and mock executions. The 1981 Royal Commission on Criminal Procedure, also known as the 'Philips Commission', examined the treatment of persons suspected of crimes with a focus on the rights of the suspects and the powers of the police.[12] The Phillips Commission ultimately led to the instatement of the Police and Criminal Evidence Act 1984 ('PACE'), which broadly outlines the powers of the police.[13] PACE is accompanied by a number of Codes of Practice, with specific guidelines on the treatment of suspects. The subsequent development of the PEACE model of investigative interviewing (see Chapter 12) – based on scientific research[14] – can be seen as one of the most progressive steps of legal reform in England and Wales.

The PEACE model has been widely adopted in Norway[15] and New Zealand, with partial but growing popularity in Australia and Canada.[16] While linguists were not directly involved in the initial development of the model – a fact which is not surprising given that forensic linguistics was itself very much in its infancy at the time – PEACE interviews have enjoyed increased attention from a linguistic perspective, with a focus on analysing current practice in order to make recommendations for improvement.

The methods of interviewing in Canada have been criticized and there is a push for less confession-seeking and more information-gathering approaches.[17] More recent reviews of interview practices with suspects[18] and witnesses[19] report on the increased uses of the phased interview model and the cognitive interview. There have been linguistic insights into the discursive strategies

---

[12] Royal Commission on Criminal Procedure, "Royal Commission on Criminal Procedure (Philips Commission): Records", National Archives, 1977–1981, BS 12.

[13] UK, Police and Criminal Evidence Act, 31 October 1984 (https://www.legal-tools.org/doc/b52ec0/).

[14] Central Planning and Training Unit, *The Interviewer's Rule Book*, Harrogate, 1992.

[15] See also Chapter 12 of this book for the Structured Interviewing Model for the Norwegian police.

[16] Georgina Heydon, *Researching Forensic Linguistics: Approaches and Applications*, Routledge, Abingdon, 2019.

[17] Brent Snook et al., "Reforming Investigative Interviewing in Canada", in *Canadian Journal of Criminology and Criminal Justice*, 2010, vol. 52, no. 2, pp. 215–229.

[18] Brent Snook et al., "Challenges of a "Toolbox" Approach to Investigative Interviewing: A Critical Analysis of the Royal Canadian Mounted Police's (RCMP) Phased Interview Model", in *Psychology, Public Policy, and Law*, 2020, vol. 26, no. 3, pp. 261–273.

[19] Kate Chenier, Rebecca Milne, Andrea Shawyer and Brent Snook, "Police Victim and Witness Interviewing in a Northern Canadian Territory: Measuring Perceptions and Practice", in *Journal of Police and Criminal Psychology*, 2020, vol. 37, no. 2, pp. 258–270.

present in interviews with Canadian Aboriginal and non-Aboriginal suspects,[20] echoing previous extensive work[21] on police interactions involving Aboriginal people in Australia. In both settings, it has been shown that there is a communicative mismatch which results in the misinterpretation of crucial accounts given by Aboriginal suspects.[22] Miscommunication in this context is often based on issues with interpreting – both linguistic and cultural – as will be discussed in more detail later in this chapter.

In the United States ('US'), the widely criticized Reid Technique of Interrogation[23] continues to enjoy popularity. It can be argued that the US are unlikely to see the kind of comprehensive legal reform that England and Wales saw in the 1980s and 1990s due to the complexities of their legal system, where police guidelines are largely governed at state level. The nine steps of the Reid technique are all manifested by (persuasive) language use. One recent study used a qualitative conversation-analytic approach to explore facework, topic control and conversational structure in two Reid interrogations.[24] The study's observations in terms of the latter revealed interrogators' tendencies to formulate turns at talk as statements rather than questions, followed by silence as a means of exerting pressure on the suspect to respond. Conversational norms are furthermore infringed when interrogators ignore repeated denials from suspects and engage in rapid topic changes.

The differences between the PEACE model (and other non-coercive models) and Reid are substantial, as discussed in detail elsewhere in this book. The linguistic manifestations of these differences are perhaps best illustrated by examining the conferment of rights to suspects in the two models. In England and Wales, the following *caution* must be given to every person during the 'Engage and explain' stage of the interview:

---

[20] Lorna Fadden, "Quantitative and Qualitative Analyses of Police Interviews With Canadian Aboriginal and Non-Aboriginal Suspects", in Krzysztof Kredens and Stanislaw Gózdz-Roszkowski (eds.), *Language and the Law: International Outlooks*, Peter Lang, Frankfurt, 2007, pp. 305–322.

[21] Diana Eades, "A Case of Communicative Clash: Aboriginal English in the Legal System", in John Gibbons (ed.), *Language and the Law*, Longman, London, 1994, pp. 234–264; Diana Eades, "Taking Evidence from Aboriginal Witnesses Speaking English: Some Socio-Linguistic Considerations", in *Precedent*, 2015, no. 126, pp. 44–48.

[22] Fadden, 2007, see *supra* note 20.

[23] Georgina Heydon, *Researching Forensic Linguistics: Approaches and Applications*, Routledge, Abingdon, 2019, pp. 42–43.

[24] Marianne Mason, "The Guilt-Presumptive Nature of Custodial Interrogations in the United States: The Use of Confrontation, Appeals to Self-Interest, and Sympathy/Minimization in the Reid Technique", in Frances Rock and Marianne Mason (eds.), *The Discourse of Police Interviews*, University of Chicago Press, 2020, pp. 65–84.

> You do not have to say anything. But it may harm your defence if you do not mention when questioned something which you later rely on in court. Anything you do say may be given in evidence.[25]

Scholars[26] have identified issues with both the comprehensibility and the comprehension of the police caution. It is primarily a piece of legal language and exhibits a number of features typical of this genre, such as complex syntax in the form of the embedded adverbial clause 'when questioned', complex lexis with a specific legal meaning (for example 'mention') and overall high levels of formality. It is thus not surprising that many suspects have difficulty understanding the meaning and implications of the police caution, despite overwhelmingly answering comprehension-checking questions affirmatively.[27] This is closely connected with the concept of suggestibility,[28] where interlocutors in a weakened position of power will answer 'yes' to a question even if this does not correspond with the truth.[29] As will be discussed in Section 7.8., issues with comprehensibility of an interviewee's rights are amplified when that person is considered vulnerable.

The 'Miranda Warning' in the US covers not just the right to silence but also the right to legal representation:

> You have the right to remain silent. Anything you say can and will be used against you in a court of law. You have the right to an attorney. If you cannot afford an attorney, one will be provided for you. Do you understand the rights I have just read to you? With these rights in mind, do you wish to speak to me?

In comparison to the England and Wales caution, the Miranda Warning exhibits simpler syntax and lexis, and it can be argued that it is overall less formal in terms of its register. Having said that, there is the obvious precariousness of the double-headed question at the end, which asks for both comprehension of the rights and co-operation in the interview. The fact that comprehension

---

[25] Frances Rock, "The Caution in England and Wales", in Peter M. Tiersma and Lawrence M. Solan (eds.), *The Oxford Handbook of Language and Law*, Oxford University Press, 2012.

[26] Susanne Fenner, Gisli H. Gudjonsson and Isabel C.H. Clare, "Understanding of the Current Police Caution (England and Wales) Among Suspects in Police Detention", in *Journal of Community and Applied Social Psychology*, 2002, vol. 12, no. 2, pp. 83–93; Frances Rock, *Communicating Rights: The Language of Arrest and Detention*, Palgrave Macmillan, Basingstoke, 2007.

[27] Rock, 2012, pp. 206–207, see *supra* note 25; Annina Heini, "'Basically, I'm Gonna Ask You a Load of Questions': Cautioning Exchanges in Police Interviews With Adolescent Suspects", in *Language and Law / Linguagem e Direito*, forthcoming 2023.

[28] See also Chapter 3 of this book.

[29] Gisli H. Gudjonsson, *The Gudjonsson Suggestibility Scales Manual*, Psychology Press, Hove, 1997.

checking is part of the official Miranda wording[30] sets it apart from the caution, where it is at police officers' discretion to check suspects' understanding. In the US context, when it comes to the invocation of the right to counsel, it has been found that the police's expectations of the suspects' language can make this a highly troublesome matter: we should note that there is a strong expectation of hyper-literal language use when requesting a lawyer, where interrogators seemingly seem to ignore conversational implicature and pragmatic meaning.[31] Requests for legal representation in the form of a question (for example, 'Can I get a lawyer?') are routinely ignored by the police on the grounds that they are "formulated indirectly and thus […] equivocal".[32] The data used to illustrate linguistic phenomena in this chapter are from English-speaking jurisdictions; however, forensic linguists are examining interview discourse in other jurisdictions and languages including, for example, Dutch[33] and Chinese.[34] The increasing presence of linguists from around the world at international and interdisciplinary conferences shows that there is a promising future ahead with more international contexts being investigated.

7.4. The Police Interview in the Legal Process

The investigative interview is not, of course, a discrete and isolated discursive event. Rather, it should be seen as one crucial link in the chain of the criminal justice process. It connects to other texts, both spoken and written, backwards to pre-existing texts such as statute, associated witness statements and other relevant documents like 'statement control sheets',[35] and forwards to courtroom testimony. So-called 'silly questions' in interviews with suspects have been noted as being used by interviewers to fix certain facts on the record that ensure the reported events fit in to pre-established categories of criminal offence, often referred to as 'points to prove', and these accounts go on to have an important

---

[30] Roger Shuy, "Ten Unanswered Questions about Miranda", in *Forensic Linguistics*, 1997, vol. 4, no. 2, p. 117.

[31] Janet Ainsworth, "'You Have the Right to Remain Silent...' but Only if You Ask for It So: The Role of Linguistic Ideology in American Police Interrogation Law", in *The International Journal of Speech, Language and the Law*, 2008, vol. 15, no. 1, pp. 1–21.

[32] Mason, 2020, p. 69, see *supra* note 24.

[33] Guusje A.H. Jol and Fleur Van der Houwen, "Police Interviews With Child Witnesses: Pursuing a Response With Maar (= Dutch but) -Prefaced Questions", in *International Journal of Speech, Language and the Law*, 2014, vol. 21, no. 1, pp. 113–138.

[34] Zeng Fanjing, Huang Ching-Yu and Ray Bull, "Police Interview of Suspects in China: Developments and Analyses", in *International Journal of Police Science & Management*, 2021, vol. 23, no. 1, pp. 29–41.

[35] Frances Rock, "Every Link in the Chain: The Police Interview as Textual Intersection", in Heffer, Rock and Conley (eds.), 2013, pp. 78–103, see *supra* note 9.

function in court.[36] For example, the offence of criminal damage, as set out in the Criminal Damage Act (1971) of England and Wales,[37] requires *intent* to destroy or damage, so interviewers have a strong rationale for establishing intent through 'silly questions', such as "when you hit the door with the golf club did you intend to damage the door?".[38] This practice is a good example of interviewers' *goal orientation*, as discussed in Section 7.2. above.

There are various problems with the treatment of interview evidence throughout the England and Wales criminal justice process which have been identified and discussed from a linguistic perspective.[39] At the most basic level, the transformation of the spoken language of the interview into a written record of taped interview ('ROTI') and then back into spoken language at trial is pervaded by problems long established in linguistic research, yet is treated unproblematically by the criminal justice system. Transformations undergone by interview data on their journey from the interview room to court constitute what has been termed the 'institutional embedding of contamination': in other words, contamination that would never be tolerated in the case of physical evidence such as DNA or fibre analysis.[40] Ultimately, the inaccuracies and alterations that occur as a result of the format changes threaten the evidential integrity of the interview in ways that serve the interests of the prosecution rather than the defence.[41] This is perhaps to be expected given that the oral presentation of the interview to the court is performed solely by prosecution representatives.[42]

The process of transcribing (that is, converting spoken language into written form) has long been widely accepted in the linguistics literature as being subjective and selective. [43] Multiple scholars have observed transcribers'

---

[36] Elizabeth Stokoe and Derek Edwards, "'Did You Have Permission to Smash Your Neighbour's Door?' Silly Questions and Their Answers in Police-Suspect Interrogations", in *Discourse Studies*, 2008, vol. 10, no. 1, pp. 89–111.

[37] England and Wales, Criminal Damage Act, 14 July 1971 (https://www.legal-tools.org/doc/vpqpu6/).

[38] Stokoe and Edwards, 2008, p. 105, see *supra* note 36.

[39] Kate Haworth, "Tapes, Transcripts and Trials: The Routine Contamination of Police Interview Evidence", in *The International Journal of Evidence & Proof*, 2018, vol. 22, no. 4, pp. 428–450; Kate Haworth, "Police Interviews as Evidence", in Coulthard, May and Sousa-Silva (eds.), 2021, pp. 144–158, see *supra* note 5.

[40] Haworth, 2018, see *supra* note 39.

[41] Mary Bucholtz, "Captured on Tape: Professional Hearing and Competing Entextualizations in the Criminal Justice System", in *Text and Talk*, 2009, vol. 29, no. 5, pp. 503–523.

[42] Haworth, 2021, see *supra* note 39.

[43] Helen Fraser, "Issues in Transcription: Factors Affecting the Reliability of Transcripts as Evidence in Legal Cases", in *International Journal of Speech, Language and the Law*, 2003, vol. 10, no. 2, pp. 203–226; Robbie Love and David Wright, "Specifying Challenges in

---

tendencies to 'correct' speakers' language, for example, false starts or non-standard language use.[44] It is argued that these representations – which include that of specific language varieties – can happen on a subconscious level and that transcribers consider correcting a speaker's language use as doing them a favour.[45] Crucially, however, transcribers have a tendency to correct interviewers' and lawyers' speech, but not suspects' and defendants'.[46] Since research has revealed bias against users of non-standard varieties,[47] the selective correction of interviewers' language has the potential for the suspect, defendant or witness to be evaluated negatively by members of the jury when a transcript is read out. When it comes to capturing the official record of interview in investigative contexts, there are some key differences in the way suspect and witness interviews are preserved. While suspect interviews are routinely audio-recorded and then either a ROTI or a full transcript produced for use in court, witness interviews (with the exception of those with children or otherwise vulnerable or intimidated individuals)[48] are not routinely recorded, and instead a written statement is compiled contemporaneously. The statement is rarely used in court – instead the witness attends to provide their testimony orally.

7.5. Rapport in Linguistic Terms

Rapport[49] is a concept that is mentioned frequently in police guidance documents (for example, the description of the PEACE framework describes rapport as "being genuinely open, interested and approachable, as well as being interested in the interviewee's feelings or welfare" and states that "active listening

Transcribing Covert Recordings: Implications for Forensic Transcription", in *Frontiers in Communication*, 2021, vol. 6, pp. 1–14. Elinor Ochs, "Transcription as Theory", in Elinor Ochs and Bambi B. Schieffelin (eds.), *Developmental Pragmatics*, Cambridge Academic Press, 1979.

[44] Anne G. Walker, "Language at Work in the Law: The Customs, Conventions, and Appellate Consequences of Court Reporting", in Judith N. Levi and Anne G. Walker (eds.), *Language in the Judicial Process*, Plenum Press, New York, 1990, pp. 203–244; John Gibbons, *Forensic Linguistics: An Introduction to Language in the Justice System*, Blackwell, Malden, 2003; Diana Eades, "The Social Consequences of Language Ideologies in Courtroom Cross-Examination", in *Language in Society*, 2012, vol. 41, no. 4, pp. 471–497.

[45] Mary Bucholtz, "The Politics of Transcription", in *Journal of Pragmatics*, 2000, vol. 32, no. 10, pp. 1439–1465.

[46] *Ibid.*, pp. 1443–1444; Walker, 1990, see *supra* note 44.

[47] Emma L. Clarke, Catherine Easton and Sarah Verdon, "The Impact of Linguistic Bias upon Speech-Language Pathologists' Attitudes Towards Non-Standard Dialects of English", in *Clinical Linguistics and Phonetics*, 2020, vol. 35, no. 6, pp. 542–559.

[48] According to UK, Youth Justice and Criminal Evidence Act, 27 July 1999, Sections 16 and 17 ('Youth Justice and Criminal Evidence Act') (https://www.legal-tools.org/doc/3eb20e/).

[49] See also Chapter 4 of this book.

assists the interviewer to establish and maintain rapport").[50] The Achieving Best Evidence ('ABE')[51] guidance states: "Good rapport between the interviewer and the witness can improve both the quantity and quality of information gained in the interview". However, the police guidance does not provide definitions beyond these rather broad descriptions. The importance of building rapport for conducting effective interviews with both witnesses[52] and suspects[53] is well-documented in the psychology literature. What is not well understood is precisely what *rapport* refers to. It has been described variously as, "smooth, positive interpersonal interaction",[54] "mutual attentiveness [...] cohesiveness of shared interest and focus [...] balance and harmony between participants",[55] and "a positive and productive affect between people that facilitates mutuality of attention and harmony".[56] Juan E. Méndez, the former United Nations' Special Rapporteur on Torture, and other Cruel, Inhuman or Degrading Treatment or Punishment, echoed in his report that "[r]apport can help to reduce the interviewee's anxiety, anger or distress, while increasing the likelihood of obtaining more

[50] College of Policing for England and Wales, "Investigative Interviewing: Authorised Professional Practice", 2013.

[51] United Kingdom Ministry of Justice, National Police Chiefs' Council, "Achieving Best Evidence in Criminal Proceedings: Guidance on Interviewing Victims and Witnesses, and Guidance on Using Special Measures", 2011, p. 78.

[52] Coral J. Dando, Rachel Wilcock and Rebecca Milne, "The Cognitive Interview: Inexperienced Police Officers' Perceptions of Their Witness/Victim Interviewing Practices", in *Legal and Criminological Psychology*, 2008, vol. 13, no. 1, pp. 59–70; Zacharia Nahouli, Coral J. Dando, Jay-Marie Mackenzie and Andreas Aresti, "Rapport Building and Witness Memory: Actions May 'Speak' Louder than Words", in *PLoS One*, 2021, vol. 16, no. 8, pp. 1–20.

[53] Laurence J. Alison *et al.*, "Why Tough Tactics Fail and Rapport Gets Results: Observing Rapport-Based Interpersonal Techniques (ORBIT) to Generate Useful Information from Terrorists", in *Psychology, Public Policy, and Law*, 2013, vol. 19, no. 4, pp. 411–431; Gavin E. Oxburgh, James Ost, Paul Morris and Julie Cherryman, "The Impact of Question Type and Empathy on Police Interviews With Suspects of Homicide, Filicide and Child Sexual Abuse", in *Psychiatry, Psychology and Law*, 2014, vol. 21, no. 6, pp. 903–917; Dave Walsh and Ray Bull, "Examining Rapport in Investigative Interviews With Suspects: Does Its Building and Maintenance Work?", in *Journal of Police and Criminal Psychology*, 2012, vol. 27, no. 1, pp. 73–84.

[54] Allison Abbe and Susan E. Brandon, "Building and Maintaining Rapport in Investigative Interviews", in *Police Practice and Research*, 2014, vol. 15, no. 3, p. 208.

[55] Linda Tickle-Degnen and Robert Rosenthal, "The Nature of Rapport and Its Nonverbal Correlates", in *Psychological Inquiry*, 1990, vol. 1, no. 4, p. 285.

[56] Frank J. Bernieri and John S. Gillis, "Judging Rapport: Employing Brunswik's Lens Model to Study Interpersonal Sensitivity", in Judith A. Hall and Frank J. Bernieri (eds.), *Interpersonal Sensitivity: Theory and Measurement*, Lawrence Erlbaum Associates Publishers, 2001, p. 69.

complete and reliable information".[57] However, there is little in the literature that points to concrete communicative means by which rapport may be developed and maintained in interview situations.[58]

It is here that linguistics can help. Linguists with an interest in the discourse of investigative interviews can complement and expand upon the work of psychologists, who conceptualize rapport as matching the style of the interviewee, being polite and displaying empathy.[59] For a linguist interested in *pragmatics* – that is, the study of how context contributes to meaning – there is a good deal of work to do in fleshing out what it means to 'be polite' and 'display empathy'.

Previous research on interviews with victims of sexual assault[60] has found that, though interviewers are instructed to "communicate empathy",[61] they tend to be clinical and appear indifferent to disclosures which in a non-institutional setting would inevitably provoke an empathic response. In the context of interviews with juvenile suspects, rapport-building and maintenance can be affected by the mandatory presence of an Appropriate Adult ('AA'). An AA is a suspect's parent or guardian, a social worker or a volunteer, whose role is to advise the suspect, ensure the interview is being conducted properly and facilitate communication.[62] For example, research has found instances of interviewers addressing AAs using familial terms of endearment.[63] The extract below is from an interview with a 17-year-old suspect and the interviewer is instructing the AA – who is the suspect's mother – of her role:

---

57 Ray Bull and Bianca Baker, "Obtaining Valid Discourse from Suspects PEACE-fully: What Role for Rapport and Empathy?", in Rock and Mason (eds.), 2020, pp. 42–64, see *supra* note 24.

58 Gabrina Pounds, "Rapport-Building in Suspects' Police Interviews: The Role of Empathy and Face", in Luna Filipović (ed.), *Police Interviews: Communication challenges and solutions*, John Benjamins, Amsterdam, 2021, pp. 95–120.

59 Colin Clarke and Rebecca Milne, "National Evaluation of the PEACE Investigative Interviewing Course", Report No. PRAS/149, Police Research Award Scheme, 2001.

60 Elizabeth Stokoe, Charles Antaki, Emma Richardson and Sara Willott, "When Police Interview Victims of Sexual Assault: Comparing Written Guidance to Interactional Practice", in Mason and Rock (eds.), 2020, pp. 21–41, see *supra* note 57.

61 United Kingdom Ministry of Justice, National Police Chiefs' Council, 2011, p. 189, H.2.2.6, see *supra* note 51.

62 UK Home Office, *Police and Criminal Evidence Act 1984 (PACE): CODE C Revised Code of Practice for the Detention, Treatment and Questioning of Persons by Police Officers*, His Majesty Stationery Office, London, August 2019, Section 11.17 ('PACE Code C') (https://www.legal-tools.org/doc/1ld1rc/).

63 Annina Heini, "Discursive Manifestations of the Statutory Child–Adult Divide in Police Interviews With Suspects Aged 17 and 18", unpublished Ph.D. thesis, Aston University, 2020.

→　IR　　erm obviously **mum** in relation to why you're here…

Extract 1: Adapted from Heini, 2020, p. 114, see *supra* note 63.

In interviews with younger children, these terms of address and reference may well be appropriate and have a positive effect on rapport; however, whether the same applies in interviews with older children is questionable. Other research has found that in interviews with child witnesses, the rapport-building stage at the start of the interaction serves a number of purposes including assessing children's cognitive and linguistic abilities and building up familiarity with the types of questions that will be asked during the interview.[64] Overall, it can be said that linguistic work into pragmatics can contribute to a more comprehensive understanding of rapport. Furthermore, the issue highlights the importance of access to authentic interview data for analysis, in order to describe and explain what takes place inside the interview room when interviewers (attempt to) build and maintain rapport with a range of different interviewees.

7.6. Beyond 'Speakers' and 'Hearers': Communicative Complexities in the Interview

When one thinks of conversation, one's first instinct is to label one of the participants the 'speaker' and the other(s) the 'hearer(s)'. However, linguists working with spoken interaction have found this distinction to be problematic and the reality of the matter to be somewhat more complex. For example, it has been postulated[65] that when a speaker talks, the recipients of the message occupy different roles depending on whether they are addressed by the speaker, whether they are a ratified participant (that is, authorized to join in) and whether the speaker knows of their presence. Listeners can thus be visualized as concentric circles radiating from the speaker, with *addressees* – who are addressed, ratified and known – positioned closest to the speaker. One step out from this are *auditors*, who are known and ratified participants but to whom the speaker is not primarily targeting their talk. One step out again is a group referred to as *overhearers* whom the speaker knows are present but are not addressed nor are they ratified participants. Finally on the outer circle are *eavesdroppers*, who are not addressed, ratified or known. The roles are visualized in Table 1 below.

---

[64] Michelle Aldridge-Waddon, "Vulnerable Witnesses in Police Investigative Interviews in England and Wales", in Coulthard, May and Sousa-Silva (eds.), 2021, pp. 281–296, see *supra* note 5.

[65] Allan Bell, "Language Style as Audience Design", in *Language in Society*, 1984, vol. 13, no. 2, pp. 145–204.

	Known	**Ratified**	**Addressed**
Addressee	+	+	+
Auditor	+	+	-
Overhearer	+	-	-
Eavesdropper	-	-	-

Table 1: Hierarchy of attributes and audience roles.
Adapted from Bell, 1984, p. 160, see *supra* note 65.

The greater the distance from the 'speaker', the less influence the 'hearer' has over the design of the speaker's message. A related premise is that of *communication accommodation theory*:[66] the idea that the more we like someone or desire their approval, the closer to their language we bring our own.

Let us look at this theory in practice in relation to investigative interviews.[67] The interviewer, in carrying out their job effectively, is required to attend to the wider institutional requirements of the interview. Their day-to-day professional experience renders them fully aware of the significance of the interview in the criminal justice process; fully aware that much of what is said in the interview is to enable a charging decision to be made, defence and prosecution teams to build their cases and, ultimately, a jury to reach a verdict. They are thus attuned to the needs of these future audiences and design the content of their contributions with them in mind. None of these future audiences are present in the interview room; all are represented (in England and Wales) by the recording device.

For the interviewee on the other hand, it is feasible that these future audiences are not consciously contemplated at all. The only hearers physically present are the interviewer(s) and possibly an auditor in the form of a legal advisor or a supporter for vulnerable interviewees such as an AA or a registered intermediary.[68] The recording device, though explained by the interviewer, is nevertheless so unobtrusive as to be unlikely to keep future audiences and contexts at the forefront of the interviewee's mind. Rather, they can be heard to design their contributions for (i) the participants who are physically present; and (ii) the context in which they are produced. Thus, while interviewees produce narrative reports of events they have experienced, it is often only once the interviewer has

---

[66] Howard Giles and Peter F. Powesland, *Speech Styles and Social Evaluation*, Academic Press, London, 1975.

[67] Kate Haworth, "Audience Design in the Police Interview: The Interactional and Judicial Consequences of Audience Orientation", in *Language in Society*, 2013, vol. 42, no. 1, pp. 45–69.

[68] See also Chapters 4 and 19 of this book.

intervened that the report attends to details that are likely to be investigatively or evidentially significant: Did the reported events constitute a criminal offence as set out in statute (often referred to as 'points to prove')? Were there any mitigating factors? How reliable is the witness' account? As mentioned previously, the institutional requirement for these types of questions is likely to require explanation. Furthermore, accommodation theory holds that interviewees, a large proportion of whom are likely to be keen to impress their interviewers, will converge on their communication style; being alert to 'police-speak' coming from one's interviewees is a take-home point from linguistically-informed interview training.[69]

We have seen that the role of 'hearer' in the police interview is not exactly clear cut, and that interviewers and interviewees differ markedly in terms of whom they design their talk for. So what of the role of 'speaker'? This too has been theorized as too simplistic and in need of further delineation. When it comes to 'speakers', three distinct roles have been articulated.[70] Firstly, there is the authority behind the utterance: the person responsible for its content, known as the 'Principal'. Secondly, the 'Author' selects the words and how they are arranged. Finally, the 'Animator' is the party who physically articulates the message. Ordinarily, we as speakers occupy all three roles in relation to what we are saying. In certain contexts, however, including investigative interviews, something else is happening at each given moment, depending on the goals of that particular stretch of interview.

During information-gathering phases, of course, the advice is to have the interviewee explain 'in their own words':[71] that is, to be the Animator, Author *and* Principal of their utterances. But there are times when this framework is threatened, for example, when information is introduced by the interviewer and simply confirmed by the interviewee. In these cases, the interviewee may hold Principalship for the information – they hold the responsibility for it – but they did not select the way it was expressed nor did they physically animate it. Interviewers should be very wary, for example, of summarizing, or *formulating*, what an interviewee has said – the foregrounding of certain elements at the expense of others is an expected and natural outcome of formulation, and the phenomenon thus represents a genuine threat to the interviewee's authorship of their own

---

[69] Nicci J. MacLeod and Kate Haworth, "Developing a Linguistically Informed Approach to Police Interviewing", in Robert Lawson and Dave Sayers (eds.), *Sociolinguistic Research: Application and Impact*, Routledge, Abingdon, 2016, pp. 224–253.

[70] Erving Goffman, *Forms of Talk*, Blackwell, Malden, 1981.

[71] Nicci MacLeod, "'Tell Me in Your Own Words': Reconciling Institutional Salience and Witness- Compatible Language in Police Interviews With Women Reporting Rape", in Rock and Mason (eds.), 2020, pp. 249–267, see *supra* note 24.

narrative. Furthermore, there are occasions when interviewers invoke a participation framework whereby they are the Animators of messages on behalf of the institution they represent.[72] This occurs during the 'Engage and explain' stage, for example, where they identify themselves by rank or badge number, identify the place, date and time (in 24-hour format) of the interview and might articulate the police caution. During information-gathering too, there are clear reasons for invoking such a framework: when information is known by interviewers and they need to elicit that information from the interviewee on the record, they must misrepresent their own knowledge state by asking questions to which they already know the answer – the only way of doing so is to assume the role of Animator, and assign Author and Principal roles to the police institution.[73] Again, linguistic theory has shed light on more potential barriers to communication in the investigative interview. Any deviation from the norm, that is, a framework where speakers occupy all three roles in relation to what they say, can only add to the peculiarity as far as interviewees are concerned.

7.7. Negotiating a Final Version

A number of linguists have approached the police interview as a site where a 'police preferred version'[74] is negotiated. Research into how final versions of witness statements are produced has recommended that witness interviews, like those with suspects, should be audio-recorded. It has been claimed that this is the only way we might begin to address some of the shortcomings of the practice whereby interviewers, alert to institutional requirements for things like specificity around times and locations, potentially corrupt interviewees' narratives in which such things are not formulated specifically 'enough' on first telling.[75]

Dealing with the context of the suspect interview, some research has given particular attention to the ways in which suspects' narratives are negotiated through the evaluations of the interviewing officers, transforming the initial narrative into something of evidential value.[76] In this way, the end product of the interview is the result of a series of negotiations of meaning, wording, and so on.

---

[72]   Heydon, 2005, p. 49, see *supra* note 3.

[73]   *Ibid.*, p. 61.

[74]   Timothy Auburn, Sue Drake and Carla Willig, "'You Punched Him, Didn't You?': Versions of Violence in Accusatory Interviews", in *Discourse and Society*, 1995, vol. 6, no. 3, pp. 353–386.

[75]   Frances Rock, "The Genesis of a Witness Statement", in *International Journal of Speech, Language and the Law*, 2001, vol. 8, no. 2, pp. 44–72.

[76]   Alison Johnson, "Changing Stories: Achieving a Change of State in Suspect and Witness Knowledge Through Evaluation in Police Interviews With Suspects and Witnesses", in *Functions of Language*, 2008, vol. 15, no. 1, pp. 84–114.

One phenomenon of interest to linguists focussing on this process of negotiation is *formulation*. Formulations are essentially interviewers' paraphrases of interviewees' prior talk: points within conversation where one participant takes the opportunity to, "describe that conversation, to explain it, or characterize it, or explicate, or translate, or summarize, or furnish the gist of it [...]".[77] Thus, formulations provide a resource for participants to reach an agreement on the meaning of what has gone before: "The introduction of a formulation enables co-participants to settle on one of many possible interpretations of what they have been saying".[78] Formulations are typical of many types of institutional, audience-directed interaction,[79] and demonstrate the authority a powerful participant has to gloss the meaning of preceding talk. They can often be identified by the presence of a discourse marker such as 'so' or 'and'. In institutional contexts, they have been shown to have a variety of functions, such as displaying active listening, summarizing, probing and challenging.[80]

A further function of formulations in the police interview context, as well as in other types of institutional talk such as courtroom discourse and news interviews, is the orientation to an absent listener or 'overhearing audience',[81] as previously outlined. It is this that explains why the usual 'receipt objects' that we would expect to appear in third-turn position in ordinary conversation (for example 'good', 'really?', 'oh!', *et cetera*) are rare in the question-and-answer sequences of the interview. When present, these receipt objects align the questioner as the primary addressee of the talk – in investigative interviews, however, third-turn positions are instead typically occupied by utterances which allow questioners to "decline the role of report recipient while maintaining the role of report elicitor".[82] Formulations are directed at the overhearing audience, ostensibly to summarize the gist of preceding talk, but selectively re-presenting the

---

[77] Harold Garfinkel and Harvey Sacks, "On Formal Structures of Practical Action", in John C. McKinney and Edward A. Tiryakian (eds.), *Theoretical Sociology: Perspectives and Developments*, Appleton-Century-Crofts, 1970, p. 350.

[78] John Heritage and Rod Watson, "Formulations as Conversational Objects", in George Psathas (ed.), *Everyday Language: Studies in Ethnomethodology*, Irvington, 1974, p. 123.

[79] John Heritage, "Analyzing News Interviews: Aspects of the Production of Talk for an Overhearing Audience", in Teun A. van Dijk (ed.), *Handbook of Discourse Analysis, Vol. 3: Discourse and Dialogue*, Cambridge Academic Press, 1985, pp. 95–117.

[80] Tony Hak and Fijgje de Boer, "Formulations in First Encounters", in *Journal of Pragmatics*, 1996, vol. 25, no. 1, pp. 83–99; Heritage, 1985, see *supra* note 79; Ian Hutchby, "'Active Listening': Formulations and the Elicitation of Feelings-Talk in Child Counselling", in *Research on Language and Social Interaction*, 2005, vol. 38, no. 3, pp. 303–329.

[81] Heritage, 1985, see *supra* note 79.

[82] *Ibid.*, p. 100; Johnson, 2008, see *supra* note 76.

content in the process and inviting the interviewee to minimally confirm or deny the modified version.

The production of formulations is central to the process of negotiation[83] – by re-wording a suspect's account, interviewers increase the evidential value of the narratives. Take the example below where the participants are discussing the suspect's firearms.[84]

```
    SU    …and they don't work→
    IR    (3.0) how do you know they don't work↓
    SU    (0.6) cause I been told that they don't work↓
    IR    have you tested them in any way^ (.) to know that they don't
          work↑
    SU    no↓
→   IR    (0.8) so for all you know they could work↓
```

Extract 2: Adapted from Heydon, 2005, p. 137, see *supra* note 3.

The arrowed and bolded final turn is where we see the interviewer formulate the suspect's prior contributions, repackaging the information that has been provided into a statement about the suspect's recklessness in assessing whether or not his firearms were functional.

While translating lay accounts into institutionally useful ones, interviewers necessarily do not 'take up' all the elements that are provided. Familiarity with institutional requirements mean that more importance is attached to some details over others, so particular elements of interviewees' reports are often foregrounded and drawn out as topics for further discussion. Inevitably, this occurs at the expense of other details, which are backgrounded by virtue of exclusion from interviewers' formulations. When it comes to victims' accounts, it has been shown[85] how such practices can lead to a disproportionate amount of focus on victim behaviour while the suspects are obscured from the story – see Extract 3 below, taken from an interview with a woman reporting rape. The participants are discussing the events immediately preceding the interviewee returning home with two male acquaintances, one of whom went on to rape her.

---

[83] Heydon, 2005, see *supra* note 3; Johnson, 2008, see *supra* note 76.

[84] Heydon, 2005, p. 137, see *supra* note 3.

[85] Nicci MacLeod, "Police Interviews With Women Reporting Rape: A Critical Discourse Analysis", unpublished Ph.D. thesis, Aston University, 2010, p. 167.

```
    IE      (.) they said "ah s- can we come back to your house" (.) and
            I said "ok fine it's not very often I get company" (.)
            didn't have a problem with it.
            (5)
    IR      so how had you felt about the night so far with=
→   IE      =okay (.) no problems at all.
            (3)
→   IR      and you'd said yes because you were w- w- enjoying the
            c[company]
    IE      [ yeah ] [I felt safe.]
    IR               [ so then ] …
```

Extract 3: Adapted from MacLeod, 2010, p. 167, see *supra* note 85.

The bolded and arrowed turn in the extract above shows the interviewer fore-grounding the interviewee's behaviour at the expense of that of the men she was with. The turn not only reveals an expectation that a woman allowing two men to accompany her home is behaviour that requires explanation, but also obscures the men's role in the event – as the interviewee's original turn makes clear, it was their suggestion to join her, yet the possibility that the attack was premeditated is not explored. Furthermore, significant changes are made to the content of what the interviewee has said – she reports herself as not having "a problem with it", which is reformulated by the interviewer as "enjoying the company" – arguably something quite different. Given what we know about the importance attached by juries to the victim's prior relationship with the suspect in such cases, it is easy to see how the 'final version' negotiated from this interaction may not have been particularly close to the one the victim intended to tell. Note, however, the victim's instantaneous acquiescence to the formulation: the change may well be too subtle to be noticed, and furthermore, the words have been presented as her own, and to challenge their accuracy, particularly in such an asymmetrical setting, would be intensely face threatening.

7.8. Vulnerability

Many of the linguistic challenges outlined in this chapter are even more pronounced if the interviewee is vulnerable in one or multiple ways.[86] Perhaps the most obvious vulnerability is age. England and Wales, in line with the majority of countries in the world, consider persons under 18 years of age to be children and those aged 18 years and above to be autonomous adults.[87] Children are, by virtue of their status as vulnerable interviewees, entitled to special measures while in contact with the legal system. Child suspects are persons aged between 10–17 years; the lower limit defined by England and Wales's age of criminal responsibility.[88] A person under the age of 10 years is considered *doli incapax*,

---

[86] See also Chapter 3 of this book.

[87] UK, Children Act, 16 November 1989 (https://www.legal-tools.org/doc/dp86tx/).

[88] UK, Children and Young Persons Act, 5 July 1933 (https://www.legal-tools.org/doc/bckgja/).

that is, not capable of forming the intent to commit an offence, meaning they cannot be arrested or prosecuted for a crime.[89] England and Wales's age of criminal responsibility is the lowest in Europe, alongside Switzerland, and this has been criticized by bodies such as the Human Rights Commission and the United Nations Committee on the Rights of the Child. Most European countries have ages of criminal responsibility between 12 and 15 years.[90] In the US, the age of criminal responsibility is governed by individual states; however, many have no fixed age of criminal responsibility. Of the states that do, Massachusetts has the highest age set by statute at 12 years old,[91] and North Carolina the lowest at 6 years old.[92]

As outlined above, juvenile suspects in England and Wales must be accompanied by an AA in interviews. While the role of the AA has been analysed from a number of perspectives, including psychology[93] and legal studies,[94] this safeguard has received limited attention from forensic linguists thus far. The only qualitative research focusing on the discursive role of the AA has revealed that in interviews with 17-year-old suspects, AAs who are family members (parents, grandparents) are asked for practical information that the juvenile suspect does now know (for example, postal addresses and moped registration numbers). Furthermore, suspects ask their familial AAs to corroborate their answers by means of tag questions. Consider Extract 4 from an interview with a 17-year-old suspect whose grandfather is acting as his AA.[95] The suspect is talking about a previous encounter he had had with the police.

```
SU      ...already calling↓ 'em (0.4) and when I expected 'em to be
  →     there for my s:tatement to get across↑ (0.3) ask - didn't I
        tell↓ you that granddad↑
AA      yeah he [did yeah    ]
SU              [I did tell m]y granddad that before it happened...
```

Extract 4: Adapted from Heini , 2020, p. 237, see *supra* note 63.

[89] UK, Crime and Disorder Act, 31 July 1998 (https://www.legal-tools.org/doc/e15559/).

[90] Child Rights International Network, "Minimum Ages of Criminal Responsibility in Europe" (available on its web site).

[91] US, Massachusetts General Laws, Chapter 119, Section 52 (https://www.legal-tools.org/doc/6vezbp/).

[92] US, North Carolina General Statutes, Chapter 7B, Article 15, Section 7B-1501 (7a) (https://www.legal-tools.org/doc/bai15b/).

[93] Sarah Medford, Gisli H. Gudjonsson and John Pearse, "The Efficacy of the Appropriate Adult Safeguard During Police Interviewing", in *Legal and Criminal Psychology*, 2010, vol. 8, no. 2, pp. 253–266.

[94] Roxanna Dehaghani, *Vulnerability in Police Custody: Police Decision-Making and the Appropriate Adult Safeguard*, Routledge, Abingdon, 2019.

[95] Heini, 2020, p. 237, see *supra* note 63.

Suspects appear to do this in an attempt to lend themselves credence by having somebody backing up the story they are telling. It can be seen as a means of presenting themselves as reliable sources of information – a trait that is not usually bestowed upon children. In a similar vein, the data show instances of interviewers abandoning suspects in an interaction and putting the question to the AA instead, thereby orienting to the notion that information from (appropriate) adults is more reliable. Extract 5 below[96] follows a conversation between the interviewer and suspect where the interviewer is trying to establish the suspect's state of health.

```
    IR      but you've been d[iagnosed and tested for it]
    SU                       [    I 'ven't been tested on] for it no I
            haven't been tested [for it]
→   IR                         [ ha- ] have the doctors said that he's
            got any condition¡
            (1.0)
    AA      I don't think he's (0.5) it's not schizophrenia he's got¡
            (0.5) but he has got a problem (0.5) <with his head
```

Extract 5: Adapted from Heini, 2020, p. 245, see *supra* note 63.

The turn highlighted in bold shows the interviewer interrupting the suspect, which results in an overlap. The interviewer's question is aimed at the AA, and the suspect is only referred to by the pronoun 'he'. The one-second pause between the interviewer's question and the start of the AA's answer turn suggests that the AA himself was likely not expecting to be addressed without notice.

Perhaps unsurprisingly, familial AAs can sometimes be overprotective of the suspect, which results in them answering on behalf of their protégé – incidentally something that many AAs are explicitly instructed not to do. Given the significance of the police interview as part of an investigation, this constitutes a clear contamination of the record, for the information given is not that of the suspect but that of their parent, grandparent or guardian.

For child witnesses or victims, there is generally no lower age limit, and research shows that specially trained police officers have successfully elicited valuable information from children as young as 2 years old.[97] Analyses conducted on ABE interviews with young children have found challenges in connection with children's limited vocabulary and difficulties with concepts such as measurements.[98] The uneven power relations of the interview – reinforced by the interviewee's status as a child – mean that children often give stereotypical

---

[96] *Ibid.*, p. 245.

[97] Ruth Marchant, "How Young is Too Young? The Evidence of Children Under Five in the English Criminal Justice System", in *Child Abuse Review*, 2013, vol. 22, no. 6, pp. 432–445.

[98] Aldridge-Waddon, 2021, see *supra* note 64.

replies to questions they do not understand. All of these are factors can severely impact the type and quality of the evidence obtained.

Other types of vulnerability, such as, for example, learning disabilities, are generally considered more complex to assess than an interviewee's age[99] and thus some safeguards are less rigorously implemented than those relating to age. Having said that, some researchers argue special measures used when interviewing children can also apply to adults with learning disabilities.[100]

In England and Wales, non-native English speakers are also considered vulnerable,[101] and witnesses, victims and suspects have the right to an interpreter during a police interview.[102] As with learning disabilities, assessing somebody's linguistic competence can be a challenging matter. First, an aspect that is frequently underestimated is the correct identification of somebody's native language if they do not speak English at all. The case of Robert Dziekański illustrates this vividly: the Polish man who did not speak English was tasered by the Royal Canadian Mounted Police at Vancouver airport and subsequently died after he became agitated in the airport. Police were wrongly advised that the man spoke Russian, and the agitation fuelled by the impossibility of effective communication ultimately led to the police using force against him.[103]

Another crucial consideration in the context of non-native English speakers in the legal system is the issue of genre. As mentioned above, the legal system comes with its set of linguistic expectations and rules and legal language is hard to comprehend for many (native English-speaking) lay people. In non-native English speakers, somebody with a high proficiency in casual, informal English registers cannot automatically be expected to be able to navigate the complex linguistic landscape of the legal system. Linguistic issues in interpreting include the difficultly of conveying complex legal meanings (such as for example the police caution), and there are culture-specific concepts and pragmatic meanings that do not have an all-encompassing counterpart in the target language.

---

99 Michael A. Ventress, Keith J.B. Rix and John H. Kent, "Keeping PACE: Fitness to Be Interviewed by the Police", in *Advances in Psychiatric Treatment*, 2008, vol. 14, no. 5, pp. 369–381.

100 Aldridge-Waddon, 2021, see *supra* note 64.

101 PACE Code C, Section 13.2(a), see *supra* note 62.

102 UK Ministry of Justice, "Code of Practice for Victims of Crime in England and Wales", 2020; PACE Code C, Section 13, see *supra* note 62.

103 Krzysztof Kredens, Eloísa Monteoliva-García and Ruth Morris, "'A Shattered Mirror?' Interpreting in Law Enforcement Contexts Outside the Courtroom", in Coulthard, May and Sousa-Silva (eds.), 2021, pp. 502–520, see *supra* note 5.

Furthermore, the conversational structure is affected by the addition of an interpreter. In interviews, 'liaison interpreting' is used, which has previously been described as a 'peripheral member' of consecutive interpreting, whereby small units of discourse in the source language are delivered, followed by the production of the same unit in the target language.[104] These units of discourse often coincide with sentence or clause boundaries. Body language can also cause issues: Bulgarians, for example, nod their head to deny and shake their head to affirm, and this can cause miscommunication.[105]

Vulnerabilities often come in multitudes, and it is crucial for researchers – linguistic and otherwise – to be appreciative of the complexity that this intersectionality brings. An underage victim of a sexual offence who is also exhibiting signs of mental health issues must have all these needs attended to as they navigate the legal system. What can happen when these needs are not attended to was illustrated vividly in the case of the West Memphis Three that took place in Arkansas in the 1990s: Jessie Misskelley Jr., an underage suspect with a learning disability, confessed to the murder of three young boys and implicated his two friends in the crime.[106] In spite of little forensic evidence, all three were convicted based largely on the coerced confession. The two underage defendants received life sentences and the third defendant, who was 18 years old at the time of his arrest, was sentenced to death. All three were ultimately released after spending more than 18 years behind bars. More recently, the case of Brendan Dassey[107] became well known owing to the Netflix series "Making A Murderer". Video-taped interrogations show the 16-year-old with learning disabilities being interrogated without a parent or lawyer present. The police use tactics that are discursively coercive, such as double-headed questions and frequent repetitions, to which Dassey provides incriminating answers due to his heightened level of suggestibility. He too was ultimately convicted – again primarily based on his coerced confession – and given a life sentence.

The treatment of victims of sexual offences, defined as 'intimidated' witnesses by Section 17 of the Youth Justice and Criminal Evidence Act (1999),[108] has also been subject to scrutiny from a linguistic perspective, notably within

---

[104] Bistra Alexieva, "A Typology of Interpreter-Mediated Events", in *The Translator*, 1997, vol. 3, no. 2, pp. 153–174.

[105] Roman Jakobson, "Motor Signs for 'Yes' and 'No'", in *Language in Society*, 1972, vol. 1, no. 1, pp. 91–96.

[106] Kaytee Vota, "The Truth Behind Echols v. State: How an Alford Guilty Plea Saved the West Memphis Three", in *Loyola of Los Angeles Law Review*, 2012, vol. 45, no. 3, pp. 1003–1022.

[107] United States District Court E.D. Wisconsin, *Dassey v. Dittmann*, Judgment, 12 August 2016, ED Wis, No. 14-CV-1310 (https://www.legal-tools.org/doc/svbhjw/).

[108] Youth Justice and Criminal Evidence Act, see *supra* note 48.

the discipline of critical discourse analysis.[109] Such studies have explored the ways in which pervasive ideology around sexual violence can be manifested in the questioning of interviewers, and a driving motivation of much of this work now is to inform interviewer training from this perspective.[110]

7.9. Conclusion

This chapter has highlighted the substantive contributions made by linguists to understanding the process of investigative interviewing and the communicative obstacles that might be thrown up in this context. It has illuminated the value of viewing these interactions through a somewhat different scholarly lens than the one to which the reader might be more accustomed. Interviews are, after all, language events, and as we have seen, far more occurs in the interview room than a straightforward imparting and recording of a narrative. Rather, the account is shaped and reshaped through a series of discursive negotiations, against a backdrop of power asymmetry, differential access to discursive resources, and an imbalance between the participants in terms of their familiarity with institutional norms and requirements.

A linguist's expertise can explain the trajectory of the various re-tellings, as well as cast light on the discursive strategies manipulated by interviewers and what their various alternatives might be. We can elucidate on the multiple means by which the product that potentially arrives at court some time down the line expectedly differs from the initial story told by an interviewee and has been moulded to fit the institutional purpose which it serves. An understanding of discourse, then, is critical to unpicking the patterns we observe in the interview room, and the forensic linguist has much to offer in assisting this understanding.

---

[109] Norman Fairclough, *Critical Discourse Analysis: The Critical Study of Language*, Longman, London, 1995; Thornborrow, 2002, see *supra* note 6; MacLeod, 2010, see *supra* note 85.

[110] MacLeod and Haworth, 2016, see *supra* note 69.

8

Cultural Aspects of Interviewing

Nkansah Anakwah, Nael Sumampouw and Henry Otgaar[*]

8.1. Introduction

Society is increasingly becoming multicultural. This increase unfolds because of recent trends in migration and globalization.[1] Because of the increasing multicultural nature of society, individuals from different cultures may serve as witnesses, victims or suspects in criminal investigations.[2] Thus, investigative professionals inevitably interview individuals from different cultural backgrounds. Culture has been shown to affect the encoding, storage and retrieval of autobiographical memories.[3] Without an adequate understanding of the possible role of cultural factors in shaping police interviewing outcomes, the quality of such interviews may be compromised. Cultural understanding is, therefore, instrumental for effective interviewing.

In this chapter, we highlight cultural aspects of interviewing. Section 8.2. provides an overview of culture and several key cultural concepts, and Section 8.3. draws on previous work to highlight implications of culture for interrogations and interviewing. Section 8.4. explains the idea of culturally-competent interviewers.

---

[*] **Nkansah Anakwah**, Ph.D., is a Lecturer in Forensic Psychology at Birmingham City University. **Nael Sumampouw**, Ph.D., is a Lecturer, Researcher and Practitioner in Forensic and Clinical Psychology at Faculty of Psychology, Universitas Indonesia. **Henry Otgaar**, Ph.D., is Professor of Legal Psychology at Maastricht University, the Netherlands and a Research Professor at Katholieke Universiteit Leuven, Belgium.
[1] United Nations Department of Economic and Social Affairs, Population Division, *International Migration 2019: Report*, New York, 2019.
[2] Lorraine Hope *et al.*, "Urgent Issues and Prospects at the Intersection of Culture, Memory, and Witness Interviews: Exploring the Challenges for Research and Practice", in *Legal and Criminological Psychology*, 2022, vol. 27, no. 1, pp. 1–31.
[3] Laura Jobson, "Cultural Differences in Specificity of Autobiographical Memories: Implications for Asylum Decisions", in *Psychiatry, Psychology and Law*, 2009, vol. 16, no. 3, pp. 453–457; Wang Qi and Michael Ross, "What We Remember and What We Tell: The Effects of Culture and Self-Priming on Memory Representations and Narratives", in *Memory*, 2005, vol. 13, no. 6, pp. 594–606; Wang Qi, "Are Asians Forgetful? Perception, Retention, and Recall in Episodic Remembering", in *Cognition*, 2009, vol. 111, no.1, pp. 123–131.

8.2. The Concept of Culture

Individuals are cultural beings as they are not immune to their culture of socialization. They are socialized in a culture encompassing beliefs, norms, values and customs. In fact, in his seminal work, *Primitive Culture*, published in 1871, the anthropologist Edward Tylor defined culture as a complex whole embodying beliefs, norms, values, symbols, customs, morals and any habits that members of a social group acquire.[4] The cultural schemas acquired by members of a society guide their behaviour and social interactions.[5] Thus, the cultural context of individuals can have implications for their behaviour and psychological processes.[6] In this section, drawing on work from cross-cultural psychology, we explain some cultural concepts of relevance for the current contribution.

8.2.1. Individualism–Collectivism

One of the cultural dimensions that has been shown to be most influential pertaining to social phenomena is the individualism–collectivism cultural dimension. This is the extent to which members of a social group view the 'self' as separate from, or integrated into, the social context.[7] Specifically, whereas there tends to be a very loose relationship between individuals in individualistic cultures, in collectivistic cultures the relationship between individuals tends to be very tight.[8] The individualism–collectivism cultural dimension has been widely examined in the context of cultural differences in self-construal, [9]

4   Edward B. Tylor, *Primitive Culture*, Cambridge University Press, 1871; Jeanette Altarriba, "The Influence of Culture on Cognitive Processes", in *Advances in Psychology*, 1993, vol. 103, pp. 379–384.

5   Andrei Boutyline and Laura K. Soter, "Cultural Schemas: What They Are, How to Find Them, and What to Do Once You've Caught One", in *American Sociological Review*, 2021, vol. 86, no. 4, pp. 728–758.

6   Wang Qi, "The Cultural Foundation of Human Memory", in *Annual Review of Psychology*, 2021, vol. 72, no. 1, pp. 151–179.

7   Geert Hofstede, "Dimensionalizing Cultures: The Hofstede Model in Context", in *Online Readings in Psychology and Culture*, 2011, vol. 2, no. 1, pp. 1–26.

8   Liberty Eaton and Johann Louw, "Culture and Self in South Africa: Individualism-Collectivism Predictions", in *The Journal of Social Psychology*, 2000, vol. 140, no. 2, pp. 210–217.

9   Hazel R. Markus and Kitayama Shinobu, "Culture and the Self: Implications for Cognition, Emotion, and Motivation", in *Psychological Review*, 1991, vol. 98, no. 2, pp. 224–253.

communication style,[10] cognition[11] and autobiographical memory reports.[12] Thus, cultural context plays a crucial role in influencing psychological processes. Western cultures are typically oriented towards individualism, whereas non-western cultures are typically oriented towards collectivism.[13]

8.2.2. Self-Construal

Cultural context can shape the self-construal of members of a cultural group. Self-construal is the meaning individuals in a social context ascribe to the 'self' in relation to others.[14] The individualism–collectivism cultural dimension can lead to cultural differences in how people construe themselves.[15] Depending on whether people are socialized in individualistic or collectivistic cultures, they may develop an independent or interdependent self-construal. Individuals socialized in individualistic cultures tend to develop an independent self-construal, a schema of the self that is inherently separate and distinct from others and the social context.[16] That means that individuals with an independent self-construal view the self as more autonomous, independent and possessing unique dispositions. Consequently, individuals with an independent self-construal have a desire to assert their uniqueness in social situations.[17] Thus, individuals with an independent self-construal are more responsive to the social context, and this responsiveness is derived from a need to strategically look for the best ways to assert their internal attributes.[18] Their behaviours are mostly based on personal thoughts, feelings and preferences. Individuals socialized in collectivistic cultures tend to develop an interdependent self-construal, a schema of the 'self' that

---

[10] Bai He, "A Cross-Cultural Analysis of Advertisements from High-Context Cultures and Low-Context Cultures", in *English Language Teaching*, 2016, vol. 9, no. 8, p. 21.

[11] Angela Gutchess and Robert Sekuler, "Perceptual and Mnemonic Differences Across Cultures", in *Psychology of Learning and Motivation – Advances in Research and Theory*, 2019, vol. 71, pp. 131–174.

[12] Wang Qi, "Relations of Maternal Style and Child Self-Concept to Autobiographical Memories in Chinese, Chinese Immigrant, and European American 3-Year-Olds", in *Child Development*, 2006, vol. 77, no. 6, pp. 1794–1809.

[13] Wang, 2009, see *supra* note 3; Michael Minkov *et al.*, "A Revision of Hofstede's Individualism-Collectivism Dimension", in *Cross Cultural & Strategic Management*, 2017, vol. 24, no. 3, pp. 386–404.

[14] Susan E. Cross, Erin E. Hardin and Berna Gercek-Swing, "The What, How, Why, and Where of Self-Construal", in *Personality and Social Psychology Review*, 2011, vol. 15, no. 2, pp. 142–179.

[15] Hazel R. Markus and Kitayama Shinobu, "Culture and Selves: A Cycle of Mutual Constitution", in *Perspectives on Psychological Science*, 2010, vol. 5, no. 4, pp. 420–430.

[16] Tylor, 1871, see *supra* note 4.

[17] Altarriba, 1993, see *supra* note 4.

[18] Markus and Kitayama, 1991, see *supra* note 15.

is inextricably connected to and interdependent of others in the social context.[19] Thus, individuals with an interdependent self-construal view the self as embedded within a social context and try to fit in with others. Their behaviour may largely depend on the thoughts, feelings and actions of others in the social context.[20] Figure 1 illustrates the independent–interdependent self-construal.

A: Independent self-construal.

B: Interdependent self-construal.

Figure 1: Conceptual representation of the self.[21]

---

[19] Kwame Gyekye, "Persons and Community in African Thought", in Pieter H. Coetzee and Abraham P.J. Roux (eds.), *Philosophy from Africa: A Text With Readings*, 2nd ed., Oxford University Press, 2002, pp. 297–312; Aleksandra Pilarska, "Self-Construal as a Mediator Between Identity Structure and Subjective Well-Being", in *Current Psychology*, 2014, vol. 33, no. 2, pp. 130–154.

[20] Gutchess and Sekuler, 2019, see *supra* note 11.

[21] Markus and Kitayama, 1991, see *supra* note 15.

Figure 1A shows how for the independent self-construal, the self is viewed as independent of specific others in the social context. This self-system makes individuals with the independent self-construal more inclined to view the self as more autonomous and separate from the social context. Figure 1B shows how for the interdependent self-construal, others in the social context constitute fundamental units of the self-system. It is this self-system of the interdependent self-construal where the self is viewed as embedded within the social context that guides behaviour.

8.2.3. Self-Presentation

Differences in self-construal can lead to cultural differences in self-presentation. Individuals with independent self-construal are more inclined to self-expression – what has been referred to as self-enhancement. Self-enhancement is a tendency to be less restrained and more expressive in emphasizing one's internal attributes.[22] In contrast, individuals with an interdependent self-construal are inclined to modest or reserved responses – what has been referred to as self-effacement.[23] Self-effacement is a tendency to exercise self-restraint and be modest in emphasizing one's unique attributes.[24] This standard for self-regulation with the interdependent self-construal can constrain verbal and ideational fluency.[25] The cultural difference in self-presentation has been illustrated with a Chinese and an American proverb, representing the collectivistic and individualistic cultures respectively. The cultural disposition of self-enhancement is typified by the American proverb 'the squeaky wheel gets the grease', whereas the cultural disposition of self-effacement is typified by the Chinese proverb 'the nail that sticks out gets hammered'.[26] The Indonesian proverb 'be like the rice stalk, as it is laden with ripening grains, it bows down' also typifies the cultural disposition of self-effacement. These proverbs demonstrate differences in self-expression in social relations across the respective cultures. Evidence suggests that the independent-interdependent self-construal is correlated with

---

22 Yamagishi Toshio *et al.*, "Modesty in Self-Presentation: A Comparison Between the USA and Japan", in *Asian Journal of Social Psychology*, 2012, vol. 15, no. 1, pp. 60–68.

23 Markus and Kitayama, 1991, see *supra* note 15.

24 Steven J. Heine, Takata Toshitake and Darrin R. Lehman, "Beyond Self-Presentation: Evidence for Self-Criticism Among Japanese", in *Personality and Social Psychology Bulletin*, 2000, vol. 26, no. 1, pp. 71–78.

25 Liu In-Mao, "Chinese Cognition", in Michael H. Bond (ed.), *The Psychology of the Chinese People*, Oxford University Press, 1986, pp. 73–105.

26 Altarriba, 1993, see *supra* note 4.

expressivity norms. For example, research sampling from 31 countries showed that individualistic cultures tend to be more expressive than collectivistic cultures.[27]

8.2.4. Communication Styles

Communication is a significant component of culture as different cultures tend to have different styles of communicating. The anthropologist Edward Hall proposed high-context and low-context communication across cultures.[28] Communication in high-context ('HC') cultures tends to be indirect and implicit, whereas in low-context ('LC') cultures, communication tends to be direct and explicit. In HC cultures, many details of a message are left unsaid, allowing the context to communicate what is implied.[29] Thus, in HC cultures, most of the information is already inside the person, with few details as part of the message that is explicitly transmitted.[30] In LC cultures, most of the details are explicitly transmitted or communicated.[31] The proposition of HC and LC cultures overlaps with the individualistic–collectivistic cultural orientation. Specifically, in individualistic cultures, communication tends to be low in context, as explicitness and directness are emphasized. Communication in collectivistic cultures, however, tends to be indirect and implicit. Table 1 provides a summary of some of the main characteristics of high-context and low-context cultures.

High-context cultures	Low-context cultures
The self is embedded in a network of complex relationships (collectivism).	The self is loosely connected to the social context (individualism).
People are inclined to be connotative. Most information is implicit.	People are inclined to be denotative. Communication is mostly explicit and verbally elaborate.
Communication is indirect.	Communication is direct.
People are less confrontational in order to maintain social harmony.	People are more confrontational regardless of relationship.

Table 1: Characteristics of high-context and low-context cultures.

---

[27] David Matsumoto *et al.*, "Mapping Expressive Differences Around the World: The Relationship Between Emotional Display Rules and Individualism Versus Collectivism", in *Journal of Cross-Cultural Psychology*, 2008, vol. 39, no. 1, pp. 55–74.

[28] Edward T. Hall, *Beyond Culture*, Anchor Press, 1976.

[29] Yamagishi *et al.*, 2012, see *supra* note 22.

[30] Boutyline and Soter, 2021, see *supra* note 5.

[31] Yamagishi *et al.*, 2012, see *supra* note 22.

8.2.5. Power Distance

Cultures also differ to the extent of which they relate with authority figures. The cultural differences in relationship with authority figures has been referred to as power distance.[32] Thus, power distance is the extent of which members of a social group emphasize hierarchy in social relationships. Whilst there is more emphasis on hierarchy in social relationships in high-power distance cultures, in low-power distance cultures there is less emphasis on hierarchy in social relationships. Within work settings, for example, individuals in low-power distance cultures can freely express themselves to authority figures and express disagreement, whilst high-power distance cultures emphasize respect, obedience and fear of authority figures. Consequently, when individuals from high-power distance cultures are interacting with authority figures, free expression tends to be impeded.[33] Thus, the extent of power distance may impact behavioural dynamics when interacting with authority figures. The power distance cultural dimension is associated with the individualism–collectivism dimension, with most individualistic cultures low on power distance and most collectivistic cultures high on power distance.[34] Table 2 illustrates some main characteristics of high- and low-power distance cultures.

High-power distance cultures	Low-power distance cultures
Members of society expect and accept class divisions as part of social order.	Members of society consider each other as equal.
Parents teach children obedience, respect and fear for the elderly.	Parents teach children independence and treat them as equals.
Employees expect rules and directives from superiors.	Employees expect to be consulted and take part in decision-making.
Teacher-centred education (that is, teachers are expected to initiate communication).	Student-centred education (that is, students are expected to initiate communication).
Religions stressing hierarchy of priests are common.	Religions stressing equality of believers are common.
Individuals are less likely to openly criticize superiors, parents and other forms of authority.	Individuals are more likely to openly express their views to superiors, parents and other forms of authority.

---

[32] Wang, 2009, see *supra* note 3.

[33] Apoorva Ghosh, "Power Distance in Organizational Contexts: A Review of Collectivist Cultures", in *Indian Journal of Industrial Relations*, 2011, vol. 47, no. 1, pp. 89–101.

[34] Minkov *et al.*, 2017, see *supra* note 13.

People normally address authority figures using their titles.	People normally address authority figures using their first name.
Socialization with authority figures in informal gatherings is less common.	Socialization with authority figures in informal gatherings is common.
The powerful in the society have privileges.	Everybody in the society should have equal rights.

Table 2: Characteristics of high- and low-power distance cultures.

8.3. Cultural Aspects of Interviewing: A Review of the Literature

Cultural concepts such as those discussed above have important implications for cross-cultural interviewing (including for police, law enforcement, military, security and intelligence). In this section, we review previous research and highlight implications for interviewing in cross-cultural settings.

8.3.1. Eyewitness Reports

Culture can shape the content and nature of eyewitness memory reports. Recent research suggests cultural differences in eyewitness memory reports.[35] Using the individualistic–collectivistic cultural framework, participants were sampled from Ghana and the Netherlands. Mock witnesses viewed stimuli scenes of crimes (theft, assault, accident and robbery) and later reported what they saw. Mock witnesses with a collectivistic cultural orientation provided less elaborate reports than mock witnesses with individualistic cultural orientation. The cultural difference in elaborate provision of details could be attributed to the systematic difference in self-expression across individualistic and collectivistic cultures.[36]

Findings from the research on cultural differences in eyewitness reports are consistent with previous work in autobiographical memory reports. Specifically, research has shown that individuals with a collectivistic cultural background provide less elaborate stories of life experiences than individuals with an individualistic cultural background.[37] For example, when asked to provide earliest childhood memories and self-descriptions, North American and Chinese participants differed in their autobiographical memory reports, in that reports

---

[35] Nkansah Anakwah *et al.*, "Cross-Cultural Differences in Eyewitness Memory Reports", in *Applied Cognitive Psychology*, 2020, vol. 34, no. 2, pp. 504–515; Nkansah Anakwah *et al.*, "The Acculturation Effect and Eyewitness Memory Reports Among Migrants", in *Legal and Criminological Psychology*, 2020, vol. 25, no. 2, pp. 237–256.

[36] Gutchess and Sekuler, 2019, see *supra* note 11.

[37] Michael Ross and Wang Qi, "Why We Remember and What We Remember: Culture and Autobiographical Memory", in *Perspectives on Psychological Science*, 2010, vol. 5, no. 4, pp. 401–409; Wang, 2006, pp. 1794–1809, see *supra* note 12.

provided by Chinese participants were less elaborate and specific than those provided by North American participants.[38] This cultural difference in elaborate reporting has also been found to be present among children from different cultures.[39] Specifically, East Asian children have been found to provide generic accounts of past experiences and also to portray themselves in more modest tones than North American children.[40] Compared to East Asian children, accounts by North American children were more complex, consisting more of reference to descriptives (words that provide descriptive texture of narratives, including modifiers, adjectives and adverbs), temporal markers (words showing chronological time and temporal relations, including causal relations, conditional states and oppositional states), and internal states (words indicating emotional states and inner cognitive processes).

It has been argued that the observed cultural differences in memory reporting may be accounted for by the influence of the cultural self-construal on the accessibility, content and style of reports.[41] The autonomous (independent) self, for example, may lead to channel cognitive resources to encode and recall personal experiences elaborately. The relational (interdependent) self-construal, on the other hand, has been argued to lead to the less elaborate recall of personal experiences. Instead, social knowledge is prioritized more with the interdependent self-construal.[42] Due to the view of the self as embedded within the social context, individuals with the interdependent self-construal may prioritize details about social interactions and group activities when remembering past events.[43] Consistent with this, previous work shows that whilst individuals with the interdependent self-construal focus on social interactions, individuals with the independent self-construal focus on their own roles.[44] In view of cultural differences

---

[38] Wang Qi, "Culture Effects on Adults' Earliest Childhood Recollection and Self-Description: Implications for the Relation Between Memory and Self", in *Journal of Personality and Social Psychology*, 2001, vol. 81, no. 2, pp. 220–233.

[39] Jessica J. Han, Michelle D. Leichtman and Wang Qi, "Autobiographical Memory in Korean, Chinese, and American Children", in *Developmental Psychology*, 1998, vol. 34, no. 4, pp. 701–713; Carole Peterson, Wang Qi and Hou Yubo, ""When I Was Little": Childhood Recollections in Chinese and European Canadian Grade School Children", in *Child Development*, 2009, vol. 80, no. 2, pp. 506–518.

[40] Wang Qi, "The Emergence of Cultural Self-Constructs: Autobiographical Memory and Self-Description in European American and Chinese Children", in *Developmental Psychology*, 2004, vol. 40, no. 1, pp. 3–15.

[41] Wang and Ross, 2005, see *supra* note 3.

[42] Wang Qi and Jens Brockmerier, "Autobiographical Rembering as Cultural Practices: Understanding the Interplay Between Memory, Self and Culture", in *Culture and Psychology*, 2002, vol. 8, no. 1, pp. 45–64.

[43] Yamagishi *et al.*, 2012, see *supra* note 22.

[44] Hall, 1976, see *supra* note 28; Altarriba, 1993, see *supra* note 4.

in elaborate reporting, investigators obtaining witness accounts in cross-cultural settings should emphasize the need for detailed reporting and focus on asking open questions (for example, 'Please tell me what happened in your own words'). That is because the use of open questions allows the interviewee to give an unrestricted free narrative, thereby eliciting long and detailed information.[45] Thus, given that culture has implications for under-reporting of details, the use of open questions would be useful in prompting the reporting of detailed information.[46] Also, prompting interviewees to report as much details as possible, no matter how insignificant, may help mitigate any cultural disposition to be less elaborate in reporting witnessed events.

8.3.2. Deception Detection

One of the cues for detecting deception in law enforcement and counter-terrorism contexts is detail provision.[47] Recent research suggests that the use of detail to detect deception may be weakened in cross-cultural settings. In one study, participants were sampled from high- and low-context cultures.[48] In line with propositions on cultural differences in high-context–low-context communication styles, Arab (HC), Chinese (HC) and British (LC) participants were sampled. Interviewees from the respective cultures were interviewed in pairs about a visit to a restaurant. Overall, cultural cues were more present than deception cues. Specifically, British interviewees reported more details than Arab and Chinese interviewees, consistent with the high-context and low-context culture communication styles. Verbal cues to deception were more present in British interviewees than Arab and Chinese interviewees. Thus, deception detection in cross-cultural interviews should be done with caution to avoid mistakenly interpreting a cultural cue as a cue for deceit.

Linguistic self-presentation when deceiving may also vary culturally. The extent to which deceptive and truthful statements contain self (versus other)

---

[45] Gavin E. Oxburgh, Trond Myklebust and Tim Grant, "The Question of Question Types in Police Interviews: A Review of the Literature From a Psychological and Linguistic Perspective", in *International Journal of Speech, Language and the Law*, 2010, vol. 17, no. 1, pp. 45–66.

[46] Lorraine Hope and Fiona Gabbert, "Interviewing Witnesses and Victims", in Neil Brewer and Amy B. Douglass (eds.), *Psychological Science and the Law*, The Guildford Press, 2019, pp. 56–74; Hope *et al.*, 2022, see *supra* note 2.

[47] Pär Anders Granhag *et al.*, "Discriminating Between Statements of True and False Intent: The Impact of Repeated Interviews and Strategic Questioning", *Journal of Applied Security Research*, 2016, vol. 11, pp. 1–17; Aldert Vrij, Samantha Mann, Sharon Leal and Ronald Fisher, "'Look into My Eyes': Can an Instruction to Maintain Eye Contact Facilitate Lie Detection?", in *Psychology, Crime & Law*, 2010, vol. 16, no. 4, pp. 327–348.

[48] Sharon Leal *et al.*, "Cross-Cultural Verbal Deception", in *Legal and Criminological Psychology*, 2018, vol. 23, no. 2, pp. 192–213.

references may differ across cultures, in line with the self-construal theory. When asked to provide genuine or fabricated statements about their experiences, African, South Asian and Western European participants differed in their use of self (versus other) references: African and South Asian participants used more first-person pronouns and less third-person pronouns when lying than when telling the truth; Western European participants, on the other hand, used more third-person pronouns and less first-person pronouns when lying than when telling the truth.[49] Thus, future research should explore the use of linguistic self-presentation in detecting deception in other cultural contexts.

8.3.3. Compliance and False Confessions

The independent-interdependent self-construal has implications for suggestibility and false confessions. This is due to the role of the cultural self-construal in social influence.[50] Evidence suggests that self-construal is associated with interrogative compliance both at the individual and cultural level.[51] In that study, participants were sampled from China and Germany and completed measures of interrogative suggestibility and self-construal. Consistent with the proposition on cultural differences in independent–interdependent self-construal, Chinese participants scored higher on interdependent self-construal than German participants, who scored higher on independent self-construal than Chinese participants. Furthermore, participants from the predominantly interdependent self-construal culture (China) were more inclined to interrogative compliance than participants from the predominantly independent self-construal culture (Germany). The role of self-construal in interrogative compliance was also found at the individual level. Within the respective cultures, individuals with more interdependent and less independent self-construal were more prone to interrogative compliance. This finding at the individual level provides further support to the role of self-construal in interrogative compliance and false confessions.

Thus, although interviewees from each culture may differ from each other with regards to susceptibility to interrogative compliance, interviewees from cultures with predominantly interdependent self-construal are more prone to interrogative compliance and, likely, false confessions than interviewees from cultures where the independent self-construal is predominant. In view of previous

---

[49] Paul J. Taylor *et al.*, "Culture Moderates Changes in Linguistic Self-Presentation and Detail Provision When Deceiving Others", in *Royal Society Open Science*, 2017, vol. 4, pp. 1–11.

[50] Rod Bond and Peter B. Smith, "Culture and Conformity: A Meta-Analysis of Studies Using Asch's (1952b, 1956) Line Judgment Task", in *Psychological Bulletin*, 1996, vol. 119, no. 1, pp. 111–137.

[51] Aileen Oeberst and Wu Song, "Independent vs. Interdependent Self-Construal and Interrogative Compliance: Intra- and Cross-Cultural Evidence", in *Personality and Individual Differences*, 2015, vol. 85, pp. 50–55.

work showing the association of compliance with false confessions,[52] it is possible that interviewees from predominantly interdependent self-construal cultures would be at risk of false confessions than interviewees from cultures where the independent self-construal is predominant.

8.3.4. False Memory Creation

The role of culture in shaping cognition may have implications for the production of false memories.[53] Previous work shows that individuals socialized in individualistic cultures develop an analytic cognition, where they attend more to focal details at a visual field, whereas individuals socialized in collectivistic cultures develop a holistic cognition, where they attend more to the entire field (contextual details).[54] This cultural difference has been demonstrated using a change blindness paradigm.[55] In that study, East Asian and North American participants were sampled and presented with 30 different pairs of scenes (still photos), consisting of focal objects (for example, a foreground vehicle) and contextual objects (for example, a building in the background and clouds). For each pair of images, one of them had a slight change or modification to either the focal object (for example, a change in the colour of the vehicle) or contextual object (for example, a change in the location of clouds). Participants were then asked to indicate and report if they noticed any change. Compared to the North Americans, the East Asians were more sensitive to the contextual changes.

Research using the Deese-Roediger-McDermott ('DRM') paradigm has also demonstrated that cultural differences in holistic-analytic cognition can have implications for the production of false memories.[56] In the DRM paradigm, participants are presented with a list of words. Each list contains words that are associatively related to a critical lure (a word which is not presented as part of

---

[52] Henry Otgaar *et al.*, "The Link Between Suggestibility, Compliance, and False Confessions: A Review Using Experimental and Field Studies", in *Applied Cognitive Psychology*, 2021, vol. 35, no. 2, pp. 1–11.

[53] See Chapter 9 of this book.

[54] Masuda Takahiko and Richard E. Nisbett, "Attending Holistically Versus Analytically: Comparing the Context Sensitivity of Japanese and Americans", in *Journal of Personality and Social Psychology*, 2001, vol. 81, no. 5, pp. 922–934; Richard E. Nisbett, Choi Incheol, Peng Kaiping and Ara Norenzayan, "Culture and Systems of Thought: Holistic Versus Analytic Cognition", in *Psychological Review*, 2001, vol. 108, no. 2, pp. 291–310.

[55] Masuda Takahiko and Richard E. Nisbett, "Culture and Change Blindness", in *Cognitive Science*, 2006, vol. 30, no. 2, pp. 381–399.

[56] Wang Jianqin *et al.*, "How Culture Shapes Constructive False Memory", in *Journal of Applied Research in Memory and Cognition*, 2021, vol. 10, no. 1, pp. 24–32.

the list).[57] When asked to retrieve the list of words that were presented, participants usually include the lure word as part of words they saw or heard.

Using the DRM paradigm, Wang *et al.* (2021) examined whether individuals from an individualistic culture and a collectivistic culture differed in generating false memories about the same event. Dutch and Chinese participants watched a series of DRM pictures (focal items: for example, jam, dough, milk and butter) presented together with their own names or other people's names in different backgrounds, and their memories were later tested. Dutch participants remembered more focal DRM items, suggesting that Dutch participants had better memory for focal objects. Chinese participants also made more correct item-context bindings, suggesting they had better memory for contextual details. Furthermore, whilst Chinese participants were more likely to indicate familiarity with lure pictures, Dutch participants were more likely to indicate that they saw vivid details of lure pictures that were not presented. Results also showed that self-reference induced more item-context false bindings (creating new memory episodes by recombining memories of different episodes) for Dutch participants than it did for Chinese participants. The finding on self-reference in inducing false memory creation provides support for the role of the cultural self-construal in shaping cognition. Because the independent self-construal is prioritized in Western contexts, it is possible that Dutch participants' attention was drawn from the context to their own names. As eyewitness errors may have grave implications for the criminal justice system (for example, wrongful convictions), sensitivity to this cultural factor in interviewing can facilitate the effectiveness of cross-cultural interviews.

8.3.5. Reporting of Misleading Post-Event Information

The reporting of misleading post-event information has been shown to be shaped by self-construal. In a study using a co-witness paradigm, participants viewed footage of forensic autopsy and later discussed what they saw with a co-witness (confederate).[58] During the discussion of the footage, the confederate introduced erroneous information. Participants later completed a free recall test and their self-construal (independence and interdependence) was measured. The results showed an association between independent self-construal and conformity, with mock witnesses high on independence being less likely to report the misleading post-event information. However, no association between

---

[57] Zhu Bi *et al.*, "The Relationship Between DRM and Misinformation False Memories", in *Memory & Cognition*, 2013, vol. 41, no. 6, pp. 832–838.

[58] Bianca Petterson and Helen M. Paterson, "Culture and Conformity: The Effects of Independent and Interdependent Self-Construal on Witness Memory", in *Psychiatry, Psychology and Law*, 2012, vol. 19, no. 5, pp. 735–744.

interdependence and conformity was found. It is important to mention that while this research provides some evidence on the role of the self-construal in reporting misleading post-event information, participants for that study were sampled from the same cultural context (Western) and measured on levels of independent-interdependent self-construal. Future research should explore the role of the self-construal in intra-cultural variations of misinformation conformity in other non-Western cultures.

Recent cross-cultural investigation into the misinformation effect has provided further support for the role of culture in reporting of misleading post-event information.[59] Participants from Ghana and the United Kingdom viewed a mock crime event of a laptop theft in a travel agency and were later presented with a post-event narrative containing misleading details about the video event. For example, in the original event, the colour of the laptop was grey, but in the post-event narrative, it was indicated that the laptop was blue. Participants were later given free recall and recognition tests about the event. In their free recall, participants in both cultural groups did not differ in the reporting of misleading post-event information. However, in the recognition test, Ghanaian participants reported more misleading post-event information than the United Kingdom participants. Thus, while suggestive questioning in interviewing should be avoided, additional care should be taken when interviewing in cross-cultural contexts.

8.3.6. Investigator Authority and Detail Provision

The authority of an investigator can impact interviewees from different cultures differently. That can happen because of the cultural dimension of power distance. Power distance has been argued to impede the free and spontaneous provision of information.[60] Recent evidence suggests that cultural dimension can potentially impact the interviewing dynamics. In one research, participants were sampled from a high-power distance culture (Ghana), where there is more emphasis on hierarchy in social relationship, and a low-power distance culture (the Netherlands), where there is less emphasis on hierarchy in social relationships.[61] On Hofstede's Power Distance Index (ranging from 0 to 100), which measures the extent to which the less powerful members of society expect and accept that power is unequally distributed, the Netherlands and Ghana score 38 and 80 respectively, where a high score reflects high-power distance. In this study, participants sampled from the high- and low-power distance culture viewed a mock

---

[59] Nkansah Anakwah *et al.*, "The Misinformation Effect and Eyewitness Memory Reports: A Cross-Cultural Investigation", 2022 (manuscript submitted for publication).

[60] Liu, 1986, see *supra* note 25.

[61] Nkansah Anakwah *et al.*, "The Authority Effect and Eyewitness Memory Reports Across Cultures", 2022 (manuscript submitted for publication).

crime event of a theft and later provided written responses. These participants were then asked to assume that they were reporting to either the police or a peer. Dutch participants reported more details when reporting to police than when reporting to a peer. However, Ghanaian participants did not differ in the level of detail reported to police or a peer. Thus, there is a need for an effective rapport to enhance detail provision in cross-cultural settings. Future work could explore how best to minimize power imbalance in cross-cultural interviews. Specifically, there is a need for future research to explore culturally sensitive rapport building strategies to enhance detail provision.

8.4. Culturally-Competent Interviewers

Based on the previous sections concerning the effect of culture on interviewees' reports, it is crucial to conduct interviews in a culturally sensitive manner by culturally-competent professionals.[62] Referring to Betancourt and colleagues' definition of cultural competence,[63] interviewers are expected to be mindful of the effect of their own and their interviewee's culture, be alert of the dynamics that are created from these differences, and adapt the interview session accordingly to meet the interviewee's culturally unique needs. For example, culturally competent interviewers prefer to question interviewees such as children on alleged sexual abuse in a language in which the interviewees are proficient. As a consequence, a translator or interpreter is required when an interviewer who is proficient in the interviewee's language is not available.

Next to these linguistic issues, culturally competent interviewers should be cognizant of culturally sensitive experiential elements such as the issues of shame and guilt in sexual abuse cases that might impede the disclosure.[64] Therefore, extended rapport-building might be required not only with the interviewee but also their significant others.

In general, it is vital that the interview is conducted in a culturally sensitive manner. It starts with the interviewers' awareness as cultural beings who bring their habits of formality or informality, warmth or coolness, proximity or

---

[62] V. Barber Rioja and Barry Rosenfeld, "Addressing Linguistic and Cultural Differences in the Forensic Interview", in *International Journal of Forensic Mental Health*, 2018, vol. 17, no. 4, pp. 377–386; Lisa A. Fontes and Carol Plummer, "Cultural Issues in Disclosure of Child Sexual Abuse", in *Journal of Child Sexual Abuse*, 2010, vol. 19, no. 5, pp. 491–518.

[63] Joseph R. Betancourt *et al.*, "Defining Cultural Competence: A Practical Framework for Addressing Racial/Ethnic Disparities in Health and Health Care", in *Public Health Reports*, 2003, vol. 118, no. 4, pp. 293–302.

[64] Lorraine T. Benuto and Jena Garrick, "Cultural Considerations in Forensic Interviewing of Children", in William T. O'Donohue and Matthew Fanetti (eds.), *Forensic Interviews Regarding Child Sexual Abuse*, Springer International Publishing, 2016, pp. 351–364.

distance, and non-verbal behaviours into the interview session.[65] Moreover, planning the appropriate time (for example, ensuring that interview sessions do not interrupt praying times or cultural ceremonies), managing the environmental aspects of the interview (for example, sitting on the floor in a less formal manner) and assigning appropriate interviewers (for example, ensuring that the interview is conducted by one of similar gender or specific background because of cultural reasons) are some examples of cultural sensitivity that can be important when conducting interviews.

8.5. Conclusion

In this chapter, we drew on work in cross-cultural psychology and highlighted some key cultural concepts pertinent to police interviewing. We then provided a review of research showing the potential role of culture in impacting interviewing outcomes. It is clear that the cultural background of interviewees can impact the dynamics of interviewing. Thus, there is a need for more cultural sensitivity in interviewing contexts to enhance the quantity and quality of details. To this end, more training for legal and investigative professionals on cultural aspects of interviewing is needed. Research on interviewing should also explore non-Western contexts to provide more insight into the role of culture. Future research should explore effective strategies to enhance information provision in cross-cultural settings. There is also a need to adapt extant interviewing protocols to a wider cultural context. An understanding of cultural factors is instrumental for effective interviewing in cross-cultural contexts.

---

[65] Lorraine A. Fontes, *Interviewing Clients Across Cultures: A Practitioner's Guides*, Guilford Press, New York, 2008.

9

Does Interviewing Affect Suggestibility and False Memory Formation?

Henry Otgaar, Sanne T.L. Houben, Peter Muris and Mark L. Howe[*]

9.1. Introduction

Misinformation is ubiquitous in daily life. We can encounter it on social media in the form of fake news, but we can also be exposed to it during daily conversations. Misinformation can even transpire in police interviews or therapeutic settings, in which misleading, suggestive questions can be posed. Importantly, such suggestive questions can occur *before* or *after* a well-conducted interview.

Take for example the following scenario. A young boy goes to school where a teacher punishes him for bad behaviour. After school, the boy talks to his mother about the experience. The mother is upset and asks whether perhaps more has happened, such as physical abuse. After repeated questioning, the boy assents to the false suggestions. The mother then files a complaint against the police who interviewed the boy.[1] A pivotal question here is whether a well-conducted police interview can counteract the previous misinformation the boy had been exposed to. In this chapter, we will review the extant literature on how investigative interviewing *before* or *after* receiving suggestive information can affect suggestibility and false memory formation (see Figure 1 below).

---

[*] **Henry Otgaar**, Ph.D., is a Professor of Legal Psychology at Maastricht University and a Research Professor at KU Leuven. **Sanne T.L. Houben**, Ph.D., is a Lecturer at Maastricht University. **Peter Muris**, Ph.D., is a Professor of Developmental Psychopathology at Maastricht University. **Mark L. Howe**, Ph.D., is a Professor of Psychology at City University London. This chapter has been supported by a KU Leuven and Research Foundation – Flanders (FWO) Research Project grant awarded to the first author.

[1] Mark L. Howe, "Forensic Consequences of Creating and Shaping Children's Memories", in *Journal of Applied Research in Memory and Cognition* (forthcoming). Henry Otgaar *et al.*, "A Case Concerning Children's False Memories of Abuse: Recommendations Regarding Expert Witness Work", in *Psychiatry, Psychology and Law*, 2017, vol. 24, no. 3, pp. 365–378.

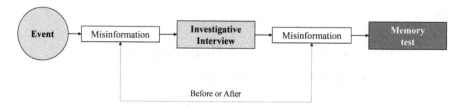

Figure 1: Schematic representation showing that misinformation can occur before or after an investigative interview.

9.2. The Creation of False Memories

The scientific interest in false memories exploded in the 1990s because of legal cases in which concerns were raised regarding suggestive therapeutic practices that led to false memories of sexual abuse.[2] Specifically, these cases frequently concerned people undergoing therapy and who needed help for their psychological problems. In these cases, therapists suggested that their mental health complaints were caused by unconscious repressed memories of trauma. Using suggestive interventions, such as hypnosis and dream interpretation, therapists attempted to excavate these buried memories, which eventually led to the formation of false memories of abuse.[3]

Such legal cases have fuelled researchers' attention into studying how such false memories can be formed in laboratory conditions. This work has revealed that false memories can be formed in myriad ways. For example, they can be produced spontaneously when relying on existing schemas (mental structures containing knowledge about a certain concept), knowledge and associations, but they can also be evoked by the power of suggestion. In this chapter, we will predominantly focus on how false memories are elicited by suggestion. Several methods have been constructed to study such suggestion-induced false memories. One of the most well-known and frequently used paradigms to elicit false memories is the misinformation paradigm.[4]

In this paradigm, participants are exposed to some stimuli such as a video of a car accident and then receive misinformation in the form of, for example,

---

[2] Elizabeth F. Loftus, "The Reality of Repressed Memories", in *American Psychologist*, 1993, vol. 48, no. 5, pp. 518–537. Henry Otgaar *et al.*, "The Return of the Repressed: The Persistent and Problematic Claims of Long-Forgotten Trauma", in *Perspectives on Psychological Science*, 2019, vol. 14, no. 6, pp. 1072–1095.

[3] Otgaar *et al.*, 2017, see *supra* note 1.

[4] Steven J. Frenda, Rebecca M. Nichols and Elizabeth F. Loftus, "Current Issues and Advances in Misinformation Research", in *Current Directions in Psychological Science*, 2011, vol. 20, no. 1, pp. 20–23. Elizabeth F. Loftus, "Planting Misinformation in the Human Mind: A 30-Year Investigation of the Malleability of Memory", in *Learning & Memory*, 2005, vol. 12, no. 4, pp. 361–366.

an eyewitness account. In the account, false details are interspersed such as stating that an ambulance arrived while this was not the case. Finally, participants receive a memory test in which they have to report what they remembered during the stimulus presentation. The default finding is that participants report having witnessed the misinformation during the encoding phase, a phenomenon that has been labelled as the misinformation effect.[5]

A plethora of studies have used the misinformation paradigm and several key findings are noteworthy. For example, various studies have found that younger children are more at risk for the misinformation effect than older children and adults.[6] Also, researchers have focused on certain individual differences that might impact on the misinformation effect and, for example, revealed that people with relatively low intelligence levels and poor perceptual abilities were especially susceptible to reporting misinformation.[7] Furthermore, and of relevance for the current contribution, there is research in which different variants of the misinformation paradigm have been used.

For instance, in the memory conformity paradigm, pairs of participants are presented with some stimuli (for example, a video of a robbery) under the impression that they are witnessing the same stimuli. However, the stimuli slightly differ from each other (for example, a video of a robbery is presented in which one participant witness a man as the perpetrator while the other participant receives the same video with a woman as the perpetrator). Following this, participants engage in a collaborative recall in which they report to each other what they observed. Because participants are unaware that different videos were presented, they inadvertently suggestively affect each other's testimony. After this phase, participants have to individually recall what they witnessed during the encoding phase. A recurrent finding is that participants report that they saw details during the encoding phase that were actually suggested to them by their paired participant.[8] Instead of presenting participants with slightly different versions of stimuli, memory researchers have also instructed confederates in collaborative recall phases to suggest details that were absent in the stimuli. This

---

5   Otgaar *et al.*, 2017, see *supra* note 1.
6   See also Henry Otgaar, Mark L. Howe, Harald Merckelbach and Peter Muris, "Who Is the Better Eyewitness? Sometimes Adults But at Other Times Children", in *Current Directions in Psychological Science*, 2018, vol. 27, no. 5, pp. 378–385.
7   ZHU Bi *et al.*, "Individual Differences in False Memory From Misinformation: Cognitive Factors", in *Memory*, 2010, vol. 18, no. 5, pp. 543–555.
8   Daniel B. Wright, Amina Memon, Elin M. Skagerberg and Fiona Gabbert, "When Eyewitnesses Talk", in *Current Directions in Psychological Science*, 2009, vol. 18, no. 3, pp. 174–178.

methodology, which is also effective in inducing misinformation effects, is called the social contagion procedure.[9]

Alternatively, in lieu of providing participants with external suggestions, in the forced fabrication paradigm, participants are forced to provide suggestions to themselves about experienced events.[10] Specifically, participants have to view some stimuli and are then forced to come up with answers to questions concerning details that were not presented in the video. Control participants are not forced to come up with fabricated answers. In the final memory test, participants are required to provide honest answers to a set of questions. Participants who had to fabricate answers are more susceptible to false memories for their fabrications than control participants are.

Paradigms that use some form of misinformation concentrate on eliciting false memories for *specific details*. On the other hand, the false memory implantation paradigm has been developed to evoke false memories for *entire autobiographical events*. In this paradigm, participants are told that they experienced several events in their childhood. One of these events is contrived by the experimenters and has been confirmed by the participant's parents to have actually never been experienced by the participant. After several suggestive interviews, about 30 per cent of participants report having experienced the false event thereby forming false memories for entire events.[11] In a recent extension of this paradigm, participants received a list of events with the instruction to indicate whether they had ever experienced these events. After a delay, participants were presented with a shortened list mainly containing the events they experienced personally. However, one critical event was added to this list, of which participants had stated to have no prior experience. Nevertheless, it was implied that participants *did* previously indicate that they had experienced the event. Similar to the standard implantation paradigm, it has been found that about 30 per cent of subjects follow this suggestion and form false memories for the never-experienced event.[12]

9   Henry L. Roediger, Michelle L. Meade and Erik T. Bergman, "Social Contagion of Memory", in *Psychonomic Bulletin & Review*, 2001, vol. 8, no. 2, pp. 365–371.

10   Jennifer K. Ackil and Maria S. Zaragoza, "Memorial Consequences of Forced Confabulation: Age Differences in Susceptibility to False Memories", in *Developmental Psychology*, 1998, vol. 34, no. 6, pp. 1358–1372.

11   Elizabeth F. Loftus and Jacquelyn E. Pickrell, "The Formation of False Memories", in *Psychiatric Annals*, 1995, vol. 25, no. 12, pp. 720–725. Alan Scoboria *et al.*, "A Mega-Analysis of Memory Reports From Eight Peer-Reviewed False Memory Implantation Studies", in *Memory*, 2017, vol. 25, no. 2, pp. 146–163.

12   Henry Otgaar, Mark L. Howe and Lawrence Patihis, "What Science Tells Us About False and Repressed Memories", in *Memory*, 2022, vol. 30, no. 1, pp. 16–21.

9.3.   False Memory Theories

Several theories can be used to explain the formation of false memories. For example, the source monitoring framework is a useful framework to explain how people decide whether memories are true or false. The framework assumes that people make attributions about their mental representations leading them to decide whether a representation refers to an experienced (external source) or imagined (internal source) event.[13] When mental representations contain many memory characteristics such as high levels of vividness, with many perceptual and auditory details, people are more likely to attribute such mental representations to an experienced event than when such memory qualities are absent. Source monitoring errors arise when mental representations of imagined events resemble those of experienced events in terms of memory qualities, and then people decide that such representations of imagined events actually refer to experienced events. When such errors occur, people create a false memory. Paradigms that use misinformation contain the necessary ingredients for such source monitoring errors to occur. Specifically, when people are falsely suggested that a certain detail or an entire event took place, this suggestion can lead to people imagining what occurred. Such imaginations amplify the phenomenology of these representations resulting in source monitoring errors.

Fuzzy-trace theory ('FTT')[14] stipulates that two opponent memory traces are formed when people experience an event (for example, a robbery). Verbatim traces support the exact details and item-specific elements of an experience (for example, the form of the weapon) while gist traces are involved in the storage of the underlying semantics of an experience (for example, that there was a weapon). When time passes, people are less likely to retrieve the exact details and items-specific elements. In other words, the verbatim traces of an event fade and so there is increased reliance on gist traces. When people rely on the underlying meaning of an event, errors might slip in leading to false memories.

While FTT can be seen as a dual process theory because it relies on the relation between two memory traces, associative-activation theory ('AAT') is a

---

[13]   Marcia K. Johnson, Shahin Hashtroudi and Stephen D. Lindsay, "Source Monitoring", in *Psychological Bulletin*, 1993, vol. 114, no. 1, pp. 3–28.

[14]   Charles J. Brainerd, Valerie F. Reyna and Stephen J. Ceci, "Developmental Reversals in False Memory: A Review of Data and Theory", in *Psychological Bulletin*, 2008, vol. 134, no. 3, pp. 343–382. Valerie F. Reyna, Jonathan C. Corbin, Rebecca B. Weldon and Charles J. Brainerd, "How Fuzzy-Trace Theory Predicts True and False Memories for Words, Sentences, and Narratives", in *Journal of Applied Research in Memory and Cognition*, 2006, vol. 5, no. 1, pp. 1–9.

single process account.[15] AAT uses the notion of spreading activation to explain the formation of false memories. According to the tenets of AAT, when people experience an event (for example, a robbery), nodes representing memories are activated which, in turn, will activate other related nodes. The more knowledge people have acquired concerning an experience, the faster and more automatic this spread of activation will be. During such associative activation, nodes can be activated that are related but were not part of the original event (for example, that there was another perpetrator involved in the crime). When such nodes are activated, false memories are formed. Misinformation is often associated to an event and hence, when people receive misinformation, they might automatically link it with their existing memory, leading to false memories.[16]

9.4. Interviewing and False Memory

Witnesses, victims and suspects of crime might be interviewed before or after they have received suggestive questions or misinformation concerning an event. Ideally, a well-conducted interview would not only maximize the reporting of correct information, but also minimize the reporting of false and suggested information. What would these above-mentioned theories predict on how such interviews would affect the propensity to produce suggestion-induced false memories? If misinformation would occur before an interview was conducted, all theories would predict that investigative interviewing would be – in general – ineffective to counteract any former exposure to misinformation. The reason is that any false memories that are created due to misinformation are experienced as true memories,[17] which would make it extremely challenging to reverse any memory-contaminating effects. Indeed, research shows that warning people that they had encountered misinformation or warning people before they receive misinformation are effective in reducing the misinformation effect and false memory levels, but do not completely abolish the memory-undermining effects of misinformation.[18]

---

[15] Mark L. Howe, Marina C. Wimmer, Nadine Gagnon and Shannon Plumpton, "An Associative-Activation Theory of Children's and Adults' Memory Illusions", in *Journal of Memory and Language*, 2009, vol. 60, no. 2, pp. 229–251. Henry Otgaar, Mark L. Howe, Peter Muris and Harald Merckelbach, "Associative Activation as a Mechanism Underlying False Memory Formation", in *Clinical Psychological Science*, 2019, vol. 7, no. 2, pp. 191–195.

[16] Otgaar *et al.*, 2017, see *supra* note 1.

[17] Daniel M. Bernstein and Elizabeth F. Loftus, "How to Tell If a Particular Memory Is True or False", in *Perspectives on Psychological Science*, 2009, vol. 4, no. 4, pp. 370–374.

[18] Hartmut Blank and Céline Launay, "How to Protect Eyewitness Memory Against the Misinformation Effect: A Meta-Analysis of Post-Warning Studies", in *Journal of Applied Research in Memory and Cognition*, 2014, vol. 3, no. 2, pp. 77–88. Katharina Schopen, Henry Otgaar, Mark L. Howe and Peter Muris, "Effects of Forewarnings on Children's and Adults'

Of course, this interpretation only applies to the situation where one assumes that misinformation and suggestive questioning lead to changes in the original *memory* itself. Support for this position originates from research on reconsolidation, which suggest that when people receive information inconsistent with past experience (for example, misinformation), memories become updated and distorted.[19] However, because misinformation and suggestibility effects are due to an amalgam of cognitive and social factors,[20] it may be the case that the original memory for the event is not contaminated by the misinformation but, rather, that a separate trace is formed, one that contains the misinformation, and this trace can interfere with the recall of the original memory of the event. If this is true, perhaps there are interviewing techniques that can minimize this interference. One such technique could be the insistence on focusing on what exactly happened during the event itself. Indeed, during investigative interviewing, people may be less likely to report the previously encountered misinformation, because such interviews oftentimes stress that people should report what they exactly remembered and that it is imperative to tell the truth.

However, it can also occur that misinformation and suggestive questions are posed *after* a well-conducted interview. The source monitoring framework would predict that if such misinformation and suggestive questions would lead to mental representations containing a high degree of phenomenology (that is, many memory characteristics), a well-conducted interview is unable to protect the witness from committing source monitoring errors. However, FTT would assume that receiving a well-conducted interview would increase verbatim traces and would increase reliance on these traces. Retrieving specific details of an experience will decrease the likelihood to fall prey to misinformation, a phenomenon also called recollection rejection.[21] Alternatively, AAT might predict that under certain circumstances, presenting misinformation after being interviewed might increase susceptibility to report misinformation. Specifically, one

---

Spontaneous False Memories", in *European Journal of Developmental Psychology*, 2022, vol. 19, no. 2, pp. 177–197. Aileen Oeberst, Merle M. Wachendörfer, Roland Imhoff and Hartmut Blank, "Rich False Memories of Autobiographical Events Can Be Reversed", in *Proceedings of the National Academy of Sciences*, 2021, vol. 118, no. 13, pp. 1–8.

[19] Alyssa H. Sinclair and Morgan D. Barense, "Prediction Error and Memory Reactivation: How Incomplete Reminders Drive Reconsolidation", in *Trends in Neurosciences*, 2019, vol. 42, no. 10, pp. 727–739.

[20] Michael McCloskey and Maria S. Zaragoza, "Misleading Postevent Information and Memory for Events: Arguments and Evidence Against Memory Impairment Hypotheses", in *Journal of Experimental Psychology: General*, 1985, vol. 114, no. 1, pp. 1–16. Stephen J. Ceci and Maggie Bruck, "Suggestibility of the Child Witness: A Historical Review and Synthesis", in *Psychological Bulletin*, 1993, vol. 113, no. 3, pp. 403–439.

[21] Otgaar, Howe and Patihis, 2022, see *supra* note 12.

might anticipate that being provided with a well-conducted interview will increase any existing links between nodes in one's knowledge. If misinformation related to the experienced event is presented afterwards, people might be more likely to accept the misinformation when the links between different memories of the event have been strengthened.

9.5. The Evidence So Far

We will now provide an overview of the body of work concerning the impact of interviewing on the susceptibility to false memory production. The evidence so far can be differentiated based on studies that have used procedures in which interviews were given prior to or after receiving information. There are also studies that have examined how interviewing can deal with misinformation given on both time points (that is, before and after; see Table 1 below).

9.5.1. Interviewing After Misinformation

One of the first experiments examining how interviewing can reduce the memory-undermining effects of misinformation was performed in 1986.[22] These researchers investigated the effect of the Cognitive Interview ('CI')[23] on adults' memory for a witnessed event for which also misleading questions were posed. In their third experiment, the CI was provided after the participants received misleading questions. The main finding was that the CI did not confer any benefits to reverse or counteract the debilitating effects of asking misleading questions.

In line with this null finding, other studies have also failed to find support that interviewing given after misinformation was beneficial to reduce its memory undermining effects. Specifically, in a study,[24] 5 to 7 year-olds and 9 to 11 year-olds were shown a videotaped story of a television series for children. Following this, some of the young participants received a misinformation narrative in which details were included that were inconsistent with the story. After a delay (that is, about three days), participants received CI instructions (for example, context reinstatement) or not. Children who received the misinformation made more errors than those who did not receive the misinformation and, most importantly, this was not affected by CI instructions.

---

[22] R. Edward Geiselman *et al.*, "Eyewitness Responses to Leading and Misleading Questions Under the Cognitive Interview", in *Journal of Police Science and Administration*, 1986, vol. 14, pp. 31–39.

[23] See Chapter 16 of this book for more details.

[24] Brett K. Hayes and Katrina Delamothe, "Cognitive Interviewing Procedures and Suggestibility in Children's Recall", in *Journal of Applied Psychology*, 1997, vol. 82, no. 4, pp. 562–577.

Another study[25] involved adult participants and presented them with a video of a bank robbery. The next day, some of them received misinformation concerning the robbery. Following the misinformation phase, half of the participants received an instruction that is also used in the CI (that is, guided memory using context reinstatement). Here too, the interview instructions did not reduce the misinformation effect. Similar results were obtained by in a later study[26] who showed adult participants a video of bank robbery after which half received misinformation. Then, half of the participants were interviewed using the CI. The authors did not find evidence that the CI minimized levels of misinformation reporting.

However, apart from these studies, there are also studies that did find that previously encountered misinformation can be reduced by follow-up interviewing. For example, in an experiment conducted on 4 and 8 year-old children,[27] they were presented with a video of a birthday party. After one day, participants were confronted with misinformation concerning the video. Following this, one group of children received a CI while another group was interviewed using a control interview (that is, Structured Interview). After this, the children received a final recognition test about the video. When the children were questioned by the CI, they were less to report misinformation than those who were not interviewed by the CI.

Others replicated this finding,[28] thereby also revealing that especially the 'report all' and 'context reinstatement' components of the CI were effective in curtailing the misinformation effect. Whereas both of the above studies focused on the CI and misinformation effects in Western children, a further study tested Arab children.[29] In their experiment, children (aged 9 to 12 years) witnessed a video of a theft and then received misinformation. Following this, half of the participants had to report what they could remember by using the CI, while the

25   Merril D. McSpadden, Jonathan W. Schooler and Elizabeth F. Loftus, "Here Today, Gone Tomorrow: The Appearance and Disappearance of Context Effects", in Graham M. Davies and Donald M. Thomson (eds.), *Memory in Context: Context in Memory*, Wiley, Chichester, 1988, pp. 215–229.

26   Antonio T. Centofanti and John Reece, "The Cognitive Interview and Its Effect on Misleading Post-Event Information", in *Psychology, Crime & Law*, 2006, vol. 12, no. 6, pp. 669–683.

27   Robyn E. Holliday, "Reducing Misinformation Effects in Children With Cognitive Interviews: Dissociating Recollection and Familiarity", in *Child Development*, 2003, vol. 74, no. 3, pp. 728–751 ('Holliday, (2003a)').

28   Robyn E. Holliday and Amanda J. Albon, "Minimising Misinformation Effects in Young Children With Cognitive Interview Mnemonics", in *Applied Cognitive Psychology*, 2004, vol. 18, no. 3, pp. 263–281.

29   Aiman El Asam and Muthanna Samara, "The Cognitive Interview: Improving Recall and Reducing Misinformation Among Arab Children", in *Journal of Forensic Psychology Practice*, 2015, vol. 15, no. 5, pp. 449–477.

other half received a control interview protocol. As found previously,[30] misinformation effects were lowered in children being interviewed by the CI.

The effect of a shorter form of the CI on susceptibility to the misinformation effect in younger and older adults was also examined.[31] Participants were presented with a video of a robbery and one day later received a summary of the event containing misinformation. Following this, participants were interviewed using a modified CI or a control interview and received a recognition test. Only in older adults, the CI was effective in reducing the misinformation effect.

Besides relying on the misinformation paradigm, researchers have also used other paradigms to study how interviewing impacts false memory generation. For example, making use of the forced fabrication paradigm to assess the effects of interviewing on false memory production, in an experiment,[32] participants first saw a clip of a robbery. One group of participants were then forced to fabricate answers to several questions. Next, these participants received a CI and then a final memory test one week later. Of importance here is that the CI was unable to reduce false memories as a result of forced fabrications.

In another study,[33] participants were involved in a memory conformity paradigm to examine how a CI could affect the negative effects of memory conformity. Specifically, participants first received a video of a road accident. After the stimulus presentation, half of the participants had to talk with a confederate about the event (co-witness condition), while in the other group participants individually recalled the event. Participants in the co-witness condition were introduced with false information by the confederate. More precisely, the confederate provided two types of false details: incorrect details referring to changing details that were presented in the video and confabulated details involving completely new, non-presented details. After one week, participants were questioned using a CI or control interview and then received some additional questions concerning the event. It was found that the CI not only led to a reduction in reporting of incorrect details but also amplified the reporting of confabulated details.

To recap, research in which investigative interviews are provided after introducing misinformation or suggestive questions yields a rather inconsistent

---

[30] Sinclair and Barense, 2019, see *supra* note 19; McCloskey and Zaragoza, 1985, see *supra* note 20.

[31] Robyn E. Holliday *et al.*, "Reducing Misinformation Effects in Older Adults With Cognitive Interview Mnemonics", in *Psychology and Aging*, 2012, vol. 27, no. 4, pp. 1191–1203.

[32] Amina Memon, Maria S. Zaragoza, Brian R. Clifford and Lynsey Kidd, "Inoculation or Antidote? The Effects of Cognitive Interview Timing on False Memory for Forcibly Fabricated Events", in *Law and Human Behavior*, 2010, vol. 34, no. 2, pp. 105–117.

[33] Magali Ginet, Nadia Chakroun, Cindy Colomb and Fanny Verkampt, "Can the Cognitive Interview Reduce Memory Conformity in an Interview Context?", in *Journal of Police and Criminal Psychology*, 2019, vol. 34, no. 4, pp. 381–391.

picture. A number of studies did not find that a CI helped in countering misinformation, while other investigations did show that misinformation and false memory effects were reduced when participants were questioned using a CI. We will now draw our attention to studies in which investigative interviewing happened prior to the presentation of misinformation and suggestion.

9.5.2. Interviewing Before Misinformation

The previously discussed study by Geiselman *et al.*[34] was one of the first to examine how investigative interviewing could affect the susceptibility to accept subsequent misinformation. In two experiments, the researchers examined the effect of the CI on adults' memory for a video of a crime for which misleading questions were also presented. The CI was presented before exposure to misinformation and misinformation effects were reduced because of the CI. Subsequent research has also identified that the CI is effective in minimizing the deleterious effects of misinformation. For example, in another study,[35] 8 to 9 year-old children watched a video clip of a magic show. After this video clip, some of them received a CI while others were questioned using a control interview. Subsequently, the children received misleading information concerning the magic show. The authors concluded that the CI, "[…] inoculates against the effects of subsequent suggestive questions".[36]

Relying on a similar procedure, other researchers[37] presented 8 to 10 year-olds with a video of a magic show. One day later, the children were questioned via a CI or a control (structured) interview. Suggestive questions were provided after or prior being interviewed. The CI only protected against the negative effects of misinformation when suggestive questions were asked after the interview. Similar protective effects of investigative interviewing towards subsequent misinformation have also been found using other evidence-based interview protocols. For example, other researchers[38] used the Self-Administered Interview ('SAI')[39] in their experiments, which is in principle a CI that witnesses can complete themselves right after an event. In two experiments, adult

---

[34] Blank and Launay, 2014, see *supra* note 18.

[35] Amina Memon *et al.*, "Reducing Suggestibility in Child Witness Interviews", in *Applied Cognitive Psychology*, 1996, vol. 10, no. 6, pp. 503–518.

[36] *Ibid.*, p. 513.

[37] Rebecca Milne and Ray Bull, "Does the Cognitive Interview Help Children to Resist the Effects of Suggestive Questioning?", in *Legal and Criminological Psychology*, 2003, vol. 8, no. 1, pp. 21–38.

[38] Fiona Gabbert, Lorraine Hope, Ronald P. Fisher and Kat Jamieson, "Protecting Against Misleading Post-Event Information With a Self-Administered Interview", in *Applied Cognitive Psychology*, 2012, vol. 26, no. 4, pp. 568–575.

[39] See Chapter 19 of this book for more details.

participants viewed a video of a crime and then had to complete the SAI or not. After a delay of one (Experiment 1) or three weeks (Experiment 2), participants received misinformation in a news report (Experiment 1) or misleading questions (Experiment 2) concerning the event. Participants who completed the SAI were less likely to report misinformation than participants who did not complete such an interview.

Otgaar and colleagues (2021)[40] used the National Institute for Child Health and Development ('NICHD')[41] protocol to interview children in their experiment. The NICHD is an evidence-based protocol that leads to reliable and detailed reports in children.[42] Specifically, in their experiment, children (5 to 11 year-olds) were involved in an interactive event (that is, a science demonstration). Following this event, one group of children were interviewed using the NICHD Protocol, one group freely recalled what happened and one group did not engage in any retrieval attempts. Next, all children received misinformation about the event, which was followed by a final memory test. The crucial finding was that the children's recall during the NICHD interview protected them against incorporating later misinformation.

Although these studies imply that investigative interviewing can inoculate against subsequent misinformation, some studies failed to detect such an 'inoculation effect'. For example, in the first experiment by Holliday,[43] 4 and 8 year-old children were presented with a video of a birthday party. After one day, one group of children were presented with a CI while another group was questioned using a control interview (that is, Structured Interview). After this, the children received misinformation concerning the event after which a final recognition test about the video was administered. It was found that the CI was ineffective to reduce the reporting of subsequent misinformation. The same null finding was also detected in a comparable study of Holliday[44] in which 4 to 5 year-old and 9 to 10 year-old children were included as participants.

---

[40] Henry Otgaar *et al.*, "Protecting Against Misinformation: Examining the Effect of Empirically Based Investigative Interviewing on Misinformation Reporting", in *Journal of Police and Criminal Psychology*, 2021, vol. 36, pp. 758–768.

[41] See Chapter 17 of this book for more details.

[42] Luis R. Benia, Nelson Hauck-Filho, Mariana Dillenburg and Lilian M. Stein, "The NICHD Investigative Interview Protocol: A Meta-Analytic Review", in *Journal of Child Sexual Abuse*, 2015, vol. 24, no. 3, pp. 259–279. Irit Hershkowitz, Sara Fisher, Michael E. Lamb and Dvora Horowitz, "Improving Credibility Assessment in Child Sexual Abuse Allegations: The Role of the NICHD Investigative Interview Protocol", in *Child Abuse & Neglect*, 2007, vol. 31, no. 2, pp. 99–110.

[43] Sinclair and Barense, 2019, see *supra* note 19.

[44] McCloskey and Zaragoza, 1985, see *supra* note 20.

Furthermore, other colleagues[45] engaged 11 to 12 year-olds in an interactive event after which some of the children completed an SAI. Two weeks later, the children were again interviewed about the event but some of them received suggestive information from an adult co-witness. Completing the SAI did not protect the children from falling prey to the suggestive pressure from the co-witness.

Interestingly, a handful of studies have also revealed that a prior investigative interview can enhance suggestibility, a phenomenon termed 'retrieval-enhanced suggestibility'.[46] One such study[47] showed adult participants a video of a crime and then half of the participants received a CI. Then, misinformation was presented in the form of a narrative after which a memory test was provided. The results indicated that prior questioning of participants with the CI made them more susceptible to the misinformation effect relative to participants who did not receive a CI.

In a child sample study,[48] researchers obtained similar results. That is, in two experiments, 5 to 10 year-old children viewed a video of a burglary. Then, one group of children was interviewed using the NICHD protocol while another group did not receive an interview. Then, all children received misinformation and a final memory test. In the second experiment, the interview, the misinformation and final memory test took place after one week. Evidence was found for retrieval-enhanced suggestibility but only when the interview was provided immediately after the event. Finally, in a recent study[49] which involved children who were interviewed by professionals from the Dutch child protection. They were interviewed because there were concerns that these children might have experienced something traumatic, such as sexual abuse. One group of children was interviewed by the NICHD Protocol while another group was questioned using a control interview. The children were interviewed about their alleged

[45] Elma Roos af Hjelmsäter, Leif A. Strömwall and Pär A. Granhag, "The Self-Administered Interview: A Means of Improving Children's Eyewitness Performance?", in *Psychology, Crime & Law*, 2012, vol. 18, no. 10, pp. 897–911.

[46] Jason C.K. Chan, Krista D. Manley and Kathryn Lang, "Retrieval-Enhanced Suggestibility: A Retrospective and a New Investigation", in *Journal of Applied Research in Memory and Cognition*, 2017, vol. 6, no. 3, pp. 213–229.

[47] Jessica A. LaPaglia *et al.*, "Misleading Suggestions Can Alter Later Memory Reports Even Following a Cognitive Interview", in *Applied Cognitive Psychology*, 2014, vol. 28, no. 1, pp. 1–9.

[48] Henry Otgaar, Mark L. Howe, Peter Muris and Harald Merckelbach, "Associative Activation as a Mechanism Underlying False Memory Formation", in *Clinical Psychological Science*, 2019, vol. 7, no. 2, pp. 191–195.

[49] Brenda Erens *et al.*, "The NICHD Interview Protocol Used by Dutch Child Protection Workers: Effects on Interview Style, Children's Reported Information and Susceptibility to Suggestion", in *Applied Cognitive Psychology*, 2022, vol. 36, no. 1, pp. 7–18.

experiences concerning trauma. After the interview, all children received several suggestions about details that did not happen at the interview (for example, 'You told me at the beginning of the interview you did not like the fact that your parents took you to Australia, right?'). Children interviewed by the NICHD Protocol were less likely to succumb to these suggestive questions than the control children.

To summarize, studies examining how investigative interviewing affects the risk of incorporating prospective misinformation have provided mixed results. Studies have shown that such interviewing can decrease or increase suggestion, or have no impact on the misinformation effect. We will now turn to the relevance of these findings.

Study	Sample	Interview before or after misinformation	Main finding of the effect of interview on false memory creation
Hayes and Delamothe (1997)	Children	After	No effect
Holliday (2003a; Experiment 2)	Children	After	Decrease
McSpadden, Schooler and Loftus (1988)	Adults	After	No effect
Holliday and Albon (2004)	Children	After	Decrease
Centofanti and Reece (2006)	Adults	After	No effect
Holliday et al. (2012)	Adults	After	Decrease (only older adults)
El Asam and Samara (2015)	Children	After	Decrease
Ginet, Chakroun, Colomb and Verkampt (2019)	Adults	After	Decreased (incorrect suggested details) but increase (reporting of confabulated suggested details)
Holliday (2003a; Experiment 1)	Children	Before	No effect
Holliday (2003a)	Children	Before	No effect
Otgaar et al. (2019)	Children	Before	Increase

Otgaar *et al.* (2021)	Children	Before	Negative correlation between recall and misinformation reporting
LaPaglia *et al.* (2014)	Adults	Before	Increase
Gabbert, Hope, Fisher and Jamieson (2012)	Adults	Before	Decrease
af Hjelmsäter, Strömwall and Granhag (2012)	Children	Before	No effect
Erens *et al.* (2022)	Children	Before	Decrease
Milne and Bull (2003)	Children	Before and after	Interview protected reporting of suggestion at a later stage
Memon *et al.* (1996)	Children	Before and after	Interview led to more correct answers on the misinformation items
Geiselman *et al.* (1986)	Adults	Before and after	Interview decreased reporting of suggestion when given before but not after the suggestion
Memon, Zaragoza, Clifford and Kidd (2010)	Adults	Before and after	Interview decreased reporting of suggestion when given before but not after the suggestion

Table 1: Studies investigating the effects of interviewing on the formation of false memories.

9.6. Concluding Remarks and Future Directions

In this chapter, we have shown what effect interviewing has on false memory formation and suggestibility. We have delineated that to address this issue, it is imperative to acknowledge that misinformation can be introduced before or after an interview has been conducted. When summarizing the different strands of research, it is obvious that there is not a coherent picture of how interviewing affects false memory production and suggestibility. Thus, it does not seem to be the case that interviewing has a reliable and replicable effect on false memory creation and suggestibility. Of course, this observation might be viewed as problematic. That is, false memories lingering on in criminal investigations and legal cases can have dramatic consequences. For example, people might misremember who was the culprit of a robbery or falsely remember being abused. When such memory aberrations are unable to be effectively corrected, they can proceed towards false accusations and even miscarriages of justice.[50]

Of course, this does mean that investigative interviewing should not be used in criminal investigations. On the contrary, they are vital as they can lead to more reliable and detailed testimonies. Therefore, we concur with colleagues who noted on their findings related to retrieval-enhanced suggestibility that, "[t]he idea that the process of conducting an effective initial interview increases eyewitnesses' sensitivity to post-interview misinformation is an unfortunate by product, but this should not deter criminal investigators from conducting the most effective initial interview possible".[51]

The fact that there is no coherent pattern on how investigative interviewing affects false memory production and suggestibility can be due to a myriad of reasons. For example, researchers have used different samples such as children,[52] young adults[53] and even older adults.[54] Since there are developmental changes in suggestibility and false memory formation,[55] such changes might have an effect on how investigative interviewing influences false memory levels and susceptibility to suggestion. Second, many of the reviewed studies used different procedures such as that some tested memory on the same day[56] while others have used a variety of delays.[57] There are many other methodological differences across studies that might have all exerted a small or large effect on how investigative interviewing impacted false memories and suggestibility.

Therefore, we believe that the following research directions are essential to pursue in this line of investigation. First and foremost, we believe that it is important that well-conducted pre-registered replications are conducted on a select set of the reviewed studies. Such replications might offer critical knowledge on the robustness of earlier detected findings. Second, it might be worthwhile to connect this line of work with research on reversing misinformation and false memories.[58] This work has revealed that when misinformation is given and

---

[50] Mark L. Howe and Lauren M. Knott, "The Fallibility of Memory in Judicial Processes: Lessons From the Past and Their Modern Consequences", in *Memory*, 2015, vol. 23, no. 5, pp. 633–656.

[51] Memon, Zaragoza, Clifford and Kidd, 2010, p. 7, see *supra* note 32.

[52] Sinclair and Barense, 2019, see *supra* note 19.

[53] Memon, Zaragoza, Clifford and Kidd, 2010, see *supra* note 32.

[54] McCloskey and Zaragoza, 1985, see *supra* note 20.

[55] Otgaar *et al.*, 2017, see *supra* note 1.

[56] Henry Otgaar, Jason C.K. Chan, Bruna Calado and David La Rooy, "Immediate Interviewing Increases Children's Suggestibility in the Short Term, But Not in the Long Term", in *Legal and Criminological Psychology*, 2019, vol. 24, no. 1, pp. 24–40.

[57] Gabbert, Hope, Fisher and Jamieson, 2012, pp. 568–575, see *supra* note 38.

[58] Oeberst, Wachendörfer, Imhoff and Blank, 2021, see *supra* note 18.

participants are afterwards informed that some of their memories are incorrect, false memory levels can significantly be reduced. It might be interesting to investigate whether evidence-based protocols could be elaborated that include such post-warnings (and forewarnings) to possibly eradicate the adverse effects of misinformation.

Taken together, misinformation can occur before or after a well-conducted investigative interview. It is significant to assess whether such misinformation can be corrected by investigative interviewing. Although our portrayal of studies indeed showed evidence for decreases in susceptibility to suggestion because of investigative interviewing, other studies did not consistently demonstrate this effect. Additional research is necessary to specifically outline whether investigative interviewing is not only the gold standard for interviewing, but also whether it can become the gold standard to eradicate the damaging effects of misinformation.

PART II: SUSPECTS

10

The Scharff Technique

Pär Anders Granhag[*]

10.1. Introduction

During World War II, Hanns Joachim Scharff worked for the German Luftwaffe. He was an interrogator at the Auswertestelle West, a camp outside Frankfurt that held captured Allied airmen.[1] Hanns Scharff has a mythical status within the military and intelligence community, but his approach to interrogation is often misunderstood and always sketchily described. In this chapter, I will explain the basic components of Scharff's approach and I will summarize the empirical research that has been done on his technique.

In legal-psychological contexts, the term *elicitation* can mean many things; for example, the Cognitive Interview[2] can be used to elicit information from a witness who tries to remember as much as possible, and the Strategic Use of Evidence technique ('SUE')[3] can be used to elicit cues to deception. But in relation to the Scharff technique, I assign a special meaning to 'elicitation' and there are three parts to the concept. The first is to subtly draw out new and reliable information. The second is to collect information without revealing what one is after, to hide one's information requirements. The third part of elicitation is to leave the source with the impression that he or she did not contribute with anything new, or at least have the source underestimate his or her contribution of new information.

For intelligence and military contexts, it rarely works to simply ask for the information needed. Sources may have loyalties to the group to which the information pertains and they are always careful not to reveal details on criminal activities in which they themselves are involved. If Scharff's prisoners had

---

[*] **Pär Anders Granhag**, Ph.D., is Professor of Psychology at the University of Gothenburg.

[1] Raymond F. Toliver, *The Interrogator: The Story of Hanns-Joachim Scharff, Master Interrogator of the Luftwaffe*, Aero Publishers, 1978.

[2] Ronald P. Fisher and Edward R. Geiselman, *Memory-Enhancing Techniques for Investigative Interviewing: The Cognitive Interview*, Charles Thomas, Springfield, 1992; see also Chapter 16 of this book.

[3] See, for example, Pär Anders Granhag and Maria Hartwig, "The Strategic Use of Evidence (SUE) Technique: A Conceptual Overview", in Pär Anders Granhag, Aldert Vrij and Bruno Verschuere (eds.), *Deception Detection: New Challenges and Cognitive Approaches*, Wiley Blackwell, Chichester, 2015, pp. 231–252; see also Chapter 14 of this book.

understood exactly what he was after, they would have probably withheld or lied about that particular information. Scharff knew that if a prisoner felt that he revealed too much, he might refuse to talk in future interrogations, therefore he left his prisoners with the impression that they did not contribute with anything new.

Both police and military interrogators must master elicitation – the persons they talk to often know more than they are willing to share. Police handlers deal with informants and are often on the hunt for specific pieces of information, but will not always reveal exactly what they are after. Undercover officers are trained to infiltrate criminal networks and terrorist organizations and their repertoire of skills must include elicitation. Elicitation is relevant also for intelligence officers who interrogate sources in custodial or more informal settings.

10.2. Who Was Hanns-Joachim Scharff?

Hanns Scharff was born 1907 in Rastenburg, East Prussia, Germany. His father, Hanns-Hermann, was killed in World War I. The Scharff family lived in Greiz, south of Leipzig. Hanns was drawn to art but had to follow the family line – he graduated from Leipzig College specializing in management, production control and economics.[4] He had a position at *Bume and Rife*, an exporting company in Hamburg. He discovered that the company had the right to export Adler automobiles to South Africa, so he bought the right with his mother's money and opened an office in Johannesburg. He married Margaret Stokes, who was South African-British, and the couple had four children. They lived a good life in South Africa. In the summer of 1939, the Scharff family travelled back to Germany for vacation, the war broke out and Hanns Scharff's exit visa was revoked.[5]

Scharff was 32 when he entered World War II. He was assigned to the Russian front, but was saved by his mother who had contacts in Berlin. As he was fluent in English, it was instead arranged that he was given a position as an interpreter. Scharff's superiors eventually selected him for a visit to the Luftwaffe Interrogation centre in Oberursel, northwest of Frankfurt. *Dulag Luft* was short for *Durchgangslager*, 'passing-through-camp', and it was composed of two separate units. The first was the *Auswertestelle West* (Evaluation Centre West), the interrogation camp where Scharff came to work. The second unit was the transit camp in the city of Wetzlar, to which the prisoners were sent before being placed in one of the permanent camps. The Auswertestelle West was the collection point for all captured airmen. The number of prisoners that passed through the camp steadily increased, from about 3,000 in 1942 to 29,000 in

---

[4]   Toliver, 1978, see *supra* note 1.

[5]   Hanns-Claudius Scharff, "Interview", Hollywood Hills, Los Angeles, 16 February 2015.

1944.[6] The idea was that Scharff should work his way through all the sections at the camp and he started as a clerk at the camp reception. Captain Horst Barth, who was the head of the fighter pilot interrogation section, noted that Scharff spoke nearly perfect English and offered him a position as an assistant interrogator.[7] Scharff had to keep track of the latest arrivals and entered their names in a ledger. Sometimes he was allowed to sit in and watch prisoners being interrogated, but more often he had to analyse the outcome. As the two interrogators assigned to the United States ('US') Army Air Forces fighter pilot section were involved in a plane crash, Scharff was transferred from the Army to the Luftwaffe. He was now an Interrogation Officer.

10.3. Scharff's Framework for Elicitation

"The first and foremost problem facing any soldier who falls into enemy hands, once he has survived, is what to say or what to not say when being questioned", said Scharff.[8] The prisoner needs to consider the potential costs of revealing or concealing particular pieces of information. The attempts that prisoners make to reach their goals are studied under the umbrella concept of counter-interrogation tactics ('CITs'):[9] that is, moves to deceive the interrogator to successfully withstand the interrogation.

10.3.1. Counter-Interrogation Tactics

Counter-interrogation tactics can be non-verbal, for example, to suppress signs of nervousness. But they can also be verbal, for example, to tell a very detailed story, but avoid critical information. Researchers have just begun to identify and categorize the CITs used by sources, suspects and detainees.[10] A prisoner's CITs can be the result of his own decision or the result of his resistance training. Furthermore, prisoners often use several CITs simultaneously, for example to avoid critical parts combined with embedding lies in the topics talked about. It is typical to shift CIT, to disengage from one CIT and adopt another.[11] The decision

---

6   Stefan Geck, *Dulag Luft, Auswertestelle West*, Peter Lang Verlag, Frankfurt am Main, 2008.

7   Toliver, 1978, see *supra* note 1.

8   Toliver, 1978, see *supra* note 1.

9   Granhag and Hartwig, 2015, see *supra* note 3.

10 Pär Anders Granhag, Franziska Clemens and Leif A. Strömwall, "The Usual and the Unusual Suspects: Level of Suspicion and Counter-Interrogation Tactics", in *Journal of Investigative Psychology and Offender Profiling*, 2009, vol. 6, pp. 129–137; Laurence Alison *et al.*, "Whatever You Say, Say Nothing: Individual Differences in Counter-Interrogation Tactics Among a Field Sample of Right Wing, AQ Inspired and Paramilitary Terrorists", in *Personality and Individual Differences*, 2014, vol. 68, pp. 170–175.

11 Pär Anders Granhag and Timothy J. Luke, "How to Interview to Elicit Concealed Information: Introducing the Shift-of-Strategy (SoS) Approach", in Peter J. Rosenfeld (ed.), *Detecting Concealed Information and Deception*, Elsevier, 2018, pp. 272–295.

to shift CIT can be a response to a change in context, for example, a new setting or a new interrogator. But it can also be due to a change in the psychological state, for example, the prisoner perceiving that he is no longer believed. Scharff used different sources to learn about his prisoners' counter-interrogation tactics; he sat in on interrogations to observe the prisoners' behaviour, he talked to the more experienced colleagues at the camp and he studied captured documents describing the resistance training that the Allied pilots had passed in the United Kingdom ('UK'). He identified several counter-interrogation tactics, the four most common were: (i) to say nothing or very little; (ii) to deny holding any secret knowledge; (iii) to talk, but avoid specific topics; and (iv) to appear co-operative by providing information that is already known by the interrogator.

"His skill to put himself into other people's mindset", said Elberskirch,[12] a colleague at the camp, describing what set Scharff apart from the other inter-rogators. Perspective-taking (simulation) is often confused with empathy, but these are two different capacities. *Empathy* is allowing someone to enter one's heart, whereas *perspective-taking* is trying to enter another's mind.[13] Scharff was empathic, but he was phenomenal at perspective-taking. But to only identify his prisoners' most common CIT had not taken Scharff very far – what made his approach so effective was that he tailored strategies and tactics to counter his prisoners' CITs. Broadly speaking, Scharff used his knowledge on his prisoners' CITs to achieve two things. First, he developed *general strategies* to involve his prisoners in relaxed conversations. Second, he tailored *specific tactics* that helped him to elicit small pieces of new information.

In everyday discussions, strategy and tactic are used interchangeably and that is, of course, fine. But in relation to the Scharff technique, a strategy is more abstract, whereas a tactic is concrete. In order to take, most strategies demand time, but their effects tend to be long-lived. One example of a strategy is when the interrogator is successfully building trust. Tactics, in contrast, tend to be in-stantaneous and their effects are often short-lived. One example is when the in-terviewer asks a question for which the answer is already known in order to understand whether the source is lying.

10.3.2. Scharff's General Strategies

Scharff used a number of general strategies, but they all had the same objective: to make the prisoner willing to engage in a conversation. Not a conversation on

---

12   Geck, 2008, see *supra* note 6.
13   Adam D. Galinsky, William W. Maddux, Debra Gilin and Judith B. White, "Why It Pays to Get Inside the Head of Your Opponent: The Differential Effects of Perspective Taking and Empathy in Negotiations", in *Psychological Science*, 2008, vol. 19, pp. 378–384; see also Chapter 4 of this book for more on empathy.

war secrets, but a conversation on what mattered to the prisoner; wives, girl-friends, children, mothers and fathers who worried for him back home. When-ever Scharff is mentioned, there is often something about how friendly he was. The effects of kindness are stronger than most people believe, but kindness de-mands a large portion of good judgment. If we want to be kind to others, we need to first know about their needs, and Scharff was a good reader of needs. After the war, many of Scharff's former prisoners testified to his friendly char-acter. Fighter pilot Hubert Zemke said that Scharff had an 'unassuming air of friendliness'. In most cases, the prisoner's impression was based on something small; a blanket, an extra slice of bread or Scharff simply asking the prisoner how he was.

"What made my father such a successful interrogator? I would say, one very important thing was that he was a gentleman", Claudius, Scharff's son ex-plained to me.[14] "He treated his prisoners with respect, right from the beginning". I believe that Claudius Scharff holds one of the keys to his father's success. A person can force him or herself to be polite and considerate, but that is not the same as respect. Respect must be unaffected. Having analysed the many testi-monies from Scharff's prisoners, I believe that they felt genuinely respected. Trust was essential to Scharff's approach and new research helps us to under-stand how he built it.[15] If a prisoner complained that his cell was cold, Scharff made sure that the temperature was set right. If Scharff said that he would for-ward a telegram or have the doctor look at the wounds, he did so. Scharff *showed trustworthiness* by keeping his promises. But he also showed that he was *willing to trust*. "If you promise not to try to escape, give your officer's honor, we will take you for a nice walk", Scharff said to fighter pilot Hub Zemke.[16] He took his prisoners skiing and he took them swimming. He accepted risks – he knew that if he showed trust, his prisoners would start to trust him back.

Laurence Alison and his colleagues at Liverpool University have devel-oped a clever framework for assessing the behaviours that occur during interro-gations: the Observing Rapport-Based Interpersonal Technique ('ORBIT').[17] Broadly speaking, ORBIT shows that successful interrogations have three trade-marks. First, there is a *collaborative* instead of a confrontational atmosphere. Second, critical information is *evoked*, rather than demanded. Finally, successful

---

[14] Hanns-Claudius Scharff, 16 February 2015, see *supra* note 5.

[15] See, for example, Laure Brimbal *et al.*, "Developing Rapport and Trust in the Interrogative Context: An Empirically Supported Alternative", in Steven J. Barela, Mark Fallon, Gloria Gaggioli and Jens David Ohlin (eds.), *Interrogation and Torture: Integrating Efficacy With Law and Morality*, Oxford University Press, 2020, pp. 141–170.

[16] Roger A. Freeman, *Zemke's Wolfpack*, Pocket Books, New York, 1988.

[17] See also Chapter 15 of this book.

interrogators honour the suspect's *autonomy*, rather than underscore their own authority. I consider this as important empirical support for Scharff's approach. Scharff found no reason to confront his prisoners. His general strategies were all designed to make his prisoners mentally engaged. He was after their attention, not their obedience. Also, Scharff never demanded information – his whole approach was about elicitation.

10.3.3. Scharff's Specific Tactics

Scharff used a number of specific tactics, but they all had the same objective: to elicit small pieces of information. It is a common misunderstanding that Scharff was able to extract plenty of information by just talking to his prisoners. There are two errors here. First, Scharff was never after a wealth of information, he was after isolated pieces of information. The second error is that having conversations with his prisoners was only the means to a larger end, to make room for specific tactics to elicit information. Below, I will first introduce the so-called knowledge-illusion that was integral to Scharff's approach. I will then review five specific tactics that Scharff used to elicit information.

10.3.4. The Knowledge-Illusion

The Auswertestelle West, the camp where Scharff worked, was organized in a sophisticated way.[18] It was divided into different sections, for example the Press section, which kept the interrogators informed on the political and social situation in the enemy countries. The section was responsible for collecting and translating information from open sources such as newspapers and radio broadcasts. The men and women working for the *Beute Und Nachrichten Auswertung* section collected and organized maps, mess tickets, photos, postcards, train tickets, private letters, wallets and forged identification papers. The smallest piece from the crash site was placed on a larger map and made available to the interrogators. But the most important section was the Interrogation section which, in turn, had different sub-sections. The Crash Report sub-section filed intercepts and reports on the enemy aircraft and crews shot down. Each aircraft was numbered together with all material captured. There was also a Card Index sub-section that kept track of all names within the enemy units, known either through interrogation or from the press.

For Scharff to build the *knowledge-illusion* – that he already had all the information that mattered – he benefited from the information that was organized and presented by the different sections, and the information gathered from previous interrogations. Scharff's knowledge-illusion was not about having scraps of information, but claiming to have a lot. It was about having plenty, but

---

[18] Toliver, 1978, see *supra* note 1.

claiming to have it all. "Somehow they had lists of the graduates of military schools, flight orders, and branches in the service that went way back", said Colonel Stark, one of the prisoners at the camp, as he was interviewed after the war.[19] "They had stuff in files. It was just amazing how much information they had." Having plenty of information, however, was not enough to sell the knowledge-illusion. For his prisoners to buy the illusion, Scharff had to present a convincing story. In order to convince, facts need to be woven into a story that grabs and holds our attention.[20] Each story that Scharff presented to his prisoners had a few small pieces missing. To get the final bricks in place, he had to use subtle tactics.

My Berlin colleague, Lennart May, and I compared the traditional way of introducing Scharff's knowledge-illusion – 'I already know what's worth to know' – against a version where the interrogator just started to present his information (the 'just-start' condition).[21] The results showed that the sources in the traditional-condition searched more actively for gaps in the interrogator's story, and they perceived the interrogator to have held comparatively less prior information. In brief, an interrogator who sticks his neck out, claiming to already know it all, will have his story more scrutinized. The sources in the traditional-condition saw the opening claim as a hypothesis that they tested against the interrogator's story, whereas the sources in the just-start condition were not provoked to do so. Our study is an example of how modern research can further sharpen Scharff's approach to interrogation.

Lulled into believing that Scharff did not want anything from him, that he already had all the information needed, the prisoner let his guard down. That made it easier for Scharff to use his subtle tactics. But to understand exactly how the knowledge-illusion was used to elicit information we need to remember the fourth counter-interrogation tactic that Scharff identified: talking about war matters, the prisoners disclosed only what they were convinced that their interrogator already knew. But if the prisoner overestimated how much Scharff already knew, he risked disclosing information that in fact was new. There is yet a positive effect of the knowledge-illusion that may not have been obvious to Scharff, but that holds for many other competitive interactions (for example, handler–source). If, for example, a handler plays the illusion, the source will not get away with simply repeating what the handler just said. To be thought of as even

---

[19] Col. Richard S. Stark, "Interview", *The Chronicle*, 1986.

[20] Steven Sloman and Philip Fernbach, *The Knowledge Illusion*, Riverhead Books, New York, 2017.

[21] Lennart May and Pär Anders Granhag, "Using the Scharff-Technique to Elicit Information: How to Effectively Establish the 'Illusion of Knowing It All'?", in *European Journal of Psychology Applied to Legal Context*, 2016, vol. 8, pp. 79–85.

minimally helpful, the source needs to provide information *beyond* what he was just told. If he does, he will provide new information.

We know that Scharff's friendly and respectful manner led to his prisoners being willing to engage in a conversation, but we also know that the prisoners rarely gave up secret information knowingly. Therefore, Scharff had to develop subtle tactics to elicit the specific pieces of information that he was after.

10.3.5. Some Examples of Scharff's Subtle Tactics

"You leave it entirely up to me to decide whether you're a spy who will be shot or a soldier who will live", Scharff said. "If I were the spy, I would claim to be a soldier exactly as you are doing." [22] Scharff made it clear that it was his obligation to make sure that the camp was free from spies. Under this guise, he asked *control questions* to establish the prisoner's identity. If the prisoner was indeed the fighter pilot claimed, he would have an easy time answering. If a prisoner refused to answer the control questions, Scharff said that it placed them both in a dilemma. Even if it would take weeks, each prisoner's identity had to be established. For the first control questions, Scharff had the answers. If the prisoner answered, Scharff was quick to confirm and expand. If the prisoner hesitated, Scharff answered his own question. Among the latter control questions, Scharff had hidden one or two for which he did not know the answer.

The bombing raid will hit either Cologne or Dresden – and there is a prisoner who knows. The most straightforward way is to ask which city, but the chance to get an answer is of course slim. And asking will inform the prisoner that we do not know. An alternative way forward is to claim that the raid will strike Cologne. If the prisoner confirms, new information has been elicited. If the prisoner disconfirms, new information has been elicited. Research from my laboratory in Gothenburg shows that sources are more willing to respond to claims than answering explicit questions. [23] Our research also lends experimental support to Scharff's idea that posing claims better mask the information objectives than asking explicit questions. [24] Furthermore, sources responding to claims tend to underestimate how much new information they actually did disclose

---

[22] Hanns-Joachim Scharff, "Without Torture", in *Argosy*, 1950, vol. 39, pp. 87–91.

[23] Pär Anders Granhag, Steven M. Kleinman and Simon Oleszkiewicz, "The Scharff Technique: On How to Effectively Elicit Intelligence from Human Sources", in *International Journal of Intelligence and Counterintelligence*, 2016, vol. 29, pp. 132–150.

[24] Simon Oleszkiewicz, Pär Anders Granhag and Steven M. Kleinman, "On Eliciting Intelligence from Human Sources: Contextualizing the Scharff-Technique", in *Applied Cognitive Psychology*, 2014, vol. 28, pp. 898–907.

during the interrogation.[25] The *claim tactic* holds a special place among Scharff's tactics as it contributes to all three aspects of elicitation; he used it to collect new information, it helped him to mask what he was after and it left the prisoner underestimating his contribution of new information. The claim tactic is a good example of how Scharff was able to circumvent his prisoners' counter-interrogation tactics. A prisoner going for 'I will not say very much' could cling to this CIT throughout the interrogation. Still, Scharff, by making a few claims, was able to elicit small pieces of new information.

"The Lieutenant may be excused, I think, for not seeing it", Scharff wrote in the *Argosy* magazine.[26] "For hours I had been telling him things about himself and his outfit which where exactly true. I did not know the truth about this critical point, so I made up a statement that was obviously a little silly", Scharff explained. "It was his almost irresistible impulse to set me straight on the error." The prisoner then gave a lengthy explanation of why Scharff was wrong. This is Scharff's *correction tactic*. When Scharff used this tactic, when he deliberately said something wrong, he had always first established the illusion of already knowing it all. The prisoners, therefore, were keen to correct him. Setting someone straight, Scharff learned, is not only pointing to what is wrong – it is also to say what is correct. The correction tactic should not be confounded with the claim tactic. For the claim tactic, Scharff did not know if his claim was correct – that was what he wanted to find out. For the correction tactic, Scharff deliberately made a false claim.

"I changed the subject to some triviality, so quickly that he did not even realize I already had got from him the answer to one of my three critical questions", Scharff said to the *Argosy* magazine.[27] Using *deliberate topic shifts*, Scharff did not acknowledge the information provided by his prisoner, he instead changed the topic. *Downplaying* is another diversionary tactic and here Scharff acknowledged the information provided by the prisoner, but downplayed its value. He either treated the information as irrelevant or as already known.

10.4. The Scharff Technique of Today: A Journey of 80 Years

The history of the Scharff technique, as it is known today within the field of legal psychology, is a journey that spans almost 80 years. This is not to say that the Scharff technique has matured over 80 years, but I think we can use this

---

[25] Simon Oleszkiewicz, Pär Anders Granhag and Sebastian Cancino Montecinos, "The Scharff-Technique: Eliciting Intelligence from Human Sources", in *Law and Human Behavior*, 2014, vol. 38, pp. 478–489.

[26] Hanns-Joachim Scharff, 1950, see *supra* note 22.

[27] Hanns-Joachim Scharff, 1950, see *supra* note 22.

timeline to mark four periods that have been critical to the development of the technique. The journey, of course, started in 1944 with Scharff's appointment as interrogator at Auswertestelle West. Scharff interrogated between 400 and 500 prisoners and, over time, he worked out an approach that made him one of the most successful interrogators at the camp.[28] In the years immediately after the war, Scharff lived in the small city of Triesberg. He, like most others in Germany, had a difficult time. He was ill, without resources and he had lost his family. He started to write about his experiences as a Luftwaffe interrogator. In 1948, he was called to the US to testify in two war trials and in connection with that he was invited to give seminars about his approach to interrogation. Scharff decided to stay in the US, and eventually he became a US citizen.

There was a contract drafted for a book and there were negotiations with a Hollywood company for a film – but nothing materialized.[29] Scharff buried his war experiences and started a career as a mosaic artist, first in New York and later in Los Angeles. This marks the end of the second relevant period. The third period starts in the mid 1970s as Scharff was approached by Raymond F. Toliver, a former pilot and war historian. Toliver had already published several books on World War II and he encouraged Scharff to bring life to the manuscript that he had begun to write 30 years before. It resulted in the book *The Interrogator*, published in 1978.[30] The publication of the book was followed by a decade of invitations; some were about promoting the book or short presentations on war reunions, but among them were also requests for seminars for military operators where Scharff presented in-depth analyses of his approach.[31] Hanns Scharff passed away in 1992.

I came across *The Interrogator* shortly after that the second edition was published in 1997. I found it fascinating, but the keys to Scharff's technique were difficult to find among all the war history, and some keys were simply not there. I started a document and named it 'The Scharff technique'. Occasionally I returned to the file, but was too busy with other projects, for example, developing the SUE technique. But in the spring of 2007, I returned to my notes and decided to pursue the project in a more serious way and this marks the start of the fourth period behind what we now call the *Scharff technique*.

In the spring of 2008, I contacted Anders Åhlén at what was then called the *National Bureau of Investigation*, within the Swedish Police in Stockholm. Anders Åhlén was the spider in the web with respect to police handlers. He was

---

[28] Toliver, 1978, see *supra* note 1.
[29] Pär Anders Granhag, *The Mosaic Man: Hanns Scharff – Master Interrogator*, 2023 (unpublished manuscript).
[30] Toliver, 1978, see *supra* note 1.
[31] Granhag, 2023, see *supra* note 29.

patient enough to listen to my ideas and together we developed a case that described an upcoming meeting with a source and this scenario was distributed to over 100 handlers. Each individual handler was asked to make a detailed plan for the meeting, write down his or her line of questioning and how to achieve the information requirements. We received answers from over 70 handlers and the most important finding for the present chapter was that none of the handlers reported a strategy that was close to Scharff's approach to elicitation.[32] Together with a small team of ambitious undergraduate students, I conducted two pilot studies on the Scharff technique; basically, we tried to develop an experimental paradigm and preliminary data was presented at a seminar in Maastricht in January 2009.[33] The pilot studies forced me to think about ways to measure the effectiveness of a technique that aims for elicitation.

In the fall of 2010, I was invited by the Federal Bureau of Investigation's ('FBI') newly established High-Value Detainee Interrogation Group ('HIG')[34] to give a two-day seminar at their headquarters in Washington, D.C. Besides my early thoughts and findings on the Scharff technique,[35] I presented work on the SUE technique and on true and false intentions. The seminar was well received and this motivated me to spend even more time on Scharff's technique. At the HIG seminar, I met Colonel (ret.) Steve Kleinman, who since then has been one of my closest and most important collaborators on Scharff's technique. A critical part of this fourth period started in 2011 where I conceptualized the technique and further developed the measures needed to map the efficacy of the technique. I tied a doctoral student to the project, Simon Oleszkiewicz, who came to play a very important role researching Scharff's technique. Later, a German Ph.D. student, Lennart May, joined our small research team. During the fall of 2012, we were granted research money from the HIG to do experimental tests of the Scharff technique and this was the starting point for a long series of studies. My initial and loose thoughts on Scharff's approach had slowly turned into a full scale research programme. One milestone of this project was the doctoral thesis

---

[32] Pär Anders Granhag, "Eliciting Information from Informants: A Survey of the Strategies used by Swedish Handlers: Classified Data", National Bureau of Investigation, 2009.

[33] Pär Anders Granhag, "Deception Detection and the Scharff Technique", E-PRODD, Critical Incident Seminar, Maastricht, 2009.

[34] See Chapter 22 of this book for further details.

[35] Pär Anders Granhag, "The Scharff Technique: Background and First Scientific Testing", Paper presented at the Professional Development Seminar, FBI HIG, Washington, D.C., 2010.

that Simon Oleszkiewicz defended in 2016: "Eliciting human intelligence: A conceptualization and empirical testing of the Scharff technique".[36]

10.5. Research on the Scharff Technique

Looking back at our 10 years of research on the Scharff technique, it is possible to identify three rounds of research (all supported by the FBI's HIG). For the first round, we conceptualized the technique and we developed measures to assess its effectiveness. For the second round, we examined the efficacy of the Scharff technique in different contexts, and for the third round, we trained professionals in the Scharff technique and compared their performance against professionals without any Scharff training. Below, I will summarize the findings from the first two rounds of research; the studies for which we trained police handlers and military intelligence officers will be discussed in the section on training.

The first round of research included three experimental studies that were structurally similar. For all three studies, the Scharff technique was conceptualized into two general strategies (friendliness and not pressing for information) and three specific tactics (the knowledge-illusion, the claim tactic and downplaying information collected). For all three studies, we tapped (i) the amount of new information collected; (ii) the extent to which the source found it difficult to read the interviewer's information objectives; and (iii) the source's subjective perception of the amount of new information revealed during the interaction. For all studies, we used mock sources that were provided with information on a planned terrorist attack. The sources were semi-co-operative. That is, they were placed in what we called a 'divided loyalty' dilemma and asked to strike a balance between not revealing too little or too much information. This set-up mirrors operational reality as many sources and detainees are not binary with respect to their decision to talk,[37] they are ambivalent and therefore the type of interview technique used is important.

For our first study, the Scharff technique was compared against the open-question technique (that is, a general invitation to talk and three follow-up questions) and the specific-question technique (that is, eight specific questions). Unexpectedly, we found no difference between the three interview techniques in

36 Simon Oleszkiewicz, "Eliciting Human Intelligence: A Conceptualization and Empirical Testing of the Scharff Technique", Ph.D. thesis, University of Gothenburg, Department of Psychology, 2016.

37 Lisa A. Kramer and Richards J. Heuer, "America's Increased Vulnerability to Insider Espionage", in *International Journal of Intelligence and Counterintelligence*, 2007, vol. 20, pp. 50–64.

terms of the amount of new information collected.[38] But we found a reason for the finding. For the Scharff condition, the claim tactic was played before the knowledge-illusion had been established. This rendered the claim tactic ineffective, the sources failed to perceive the claims as something to be commented upon. Our mistake showed how important it is to properly time the Scharff tactics.[39] As expected, the sources in the Scharff condition had a more difficult time reading the interviewer's information objectives. In hindsight, our first study was 'Bambi on ice'.

For the second study, we came better prepared and we compared the Scharff technique against the so-called 'direct approach'.[40] That is, asking a combination of open and direct questions in a business-like manner. This approach is one of the most commonly used by US military interrogators.[41] We found that the sources in the Scharff condition revealed more new information than the sources in the direct approach condition. As predicted, the sources in the Scharff condition underestimated how much new information they had disclosed. In contrast, the sources in the direct approach overestimated how much new information they had disclosed during the meeting. Our third experimental study showed that the Scharff technique resulted in more new information and that the sources underestimated how much new information they had revealed during the interaction.[42] That is, we were able to replicate the outcome of our second study. In addition, the sources in the Scharff condition had a relatively more difficult time reading the interviewer's information objectives.

For our second round of research, we examined the Scharff technique in different contexts. For the first study, we acknowledged that there is commonly a screening to assess: (i) the likelihood that the source holds critical intelligence; and (ii) the source's estimated level of co-operation.[43] We therefore compared four different types of sources: willing-able, unwilling-able, willing-unable and

---

[38] Pär Anders Granhag, Simon Oleszkiewicz and Sebastian Cancino Montecinos, "Eliciting Intelligence from Sources: The First Scientific Test of the Scharff-Technique", in *Legal and Criminological Psychology*, 2014, vol. 20, pp. 96–113.

[39] For the timing of the Scharff tactics, see also Lennart May and Pär Anders Granhag, "Techniques for Eliciting Human Intelligence: Examining Possible Order Effects of the Scharff Technique", in *Psychiatry, Psychology and Law*, 2006, vol. 8, pp. 79–85.

[40] Oleszkiewicz, Granhag and Cancino Montecinos, 2014, see *supra* note 25.

[41] Allison D. Redlich, Christopher E. Kelly and Jeaneé C. Miller, *Systematic Survey of the Interview and Intelligence Community: Final Report Submitted to the Federal Bureau of Investigation-High-Value Detainee Interrogation Group*, Washington, D.C., 2011.

[42] Oleszkiewicz, Granhag and Kleinman, 2014, see *supra* note 24.

[43] United States Headquarters, Department of the Army, *Human Intelligence Collector Operations*, Field Manual No. 2-22.3, Washington, D.C., 6 September 2006 ('*Human Intelligence Collector Operations*') (https://www.legal-tools.org/doc/wbfiw1/).

unwilling-unable.[44] We again found that the Scharff technique resulted in more new information than the direct approach. The superiority of the Scharff technique was particularly pronounced for the *less co-operative sources*. It is easy to argue that this finding is important: less willing sources are more challenging. For fully co-operative sources, the type of interview technique may not matter much. The study showed also that the sources interviewed with the Scharff technique had a more difficult time reading the interviewer's information objectives and that they consistently underestimated how much new information they had revealed.

The second study in this round accounted for the circumstance that most sources are interviewed several times. There is work showing that military detainees are interviewed on average five times and collectors of human intelligence may interact with their sources over months, or even years.[45] Half of the sources were interviewed on three occasions with the Scharff technique and the remaining half was interviewed on three occasions with the direct approach.[46] Over the three interviews, the Scharff technique resulted in significantly more new information compared to the direct approach. We again found that the sources interviewed by the Scharff technique underestimated their actual contribution of new information. Most of the Scharff tactics can be used across multiple interviews. For example, posing claims in the first interview will not render this tactic less useful for later interviews.

For the final study, we tested the extent to which the Scharff technique could be applied to small cells of sources.[47] The mock sources worked in triads and were given information about a planned terrorist attack. All sources in the cell held the exact same information. Each source was interviewed individually with either the Scharff technique or the direct approac*h*. For this study, the knowledge-illusion had a special place. For the Scharff condition, the source interviewed first was faced with a story that was built up by all the information known to the interviewer prior to the interaction. The second (third) source was

---

[44] Pär Anders Granhag, Simon Oleszkiewicz, Leif A. Strömwall and Steven M. Kleinman, "Eliciting Intelligence With the Scharff Technique: Interviewing More and Less Cooperative and Capable Sources", in *Psychology, Public Policy, and Law*, 2015, vol. 21, pp. 100–110.

[45] See for example, Robert A. Fein, Paul Lehner and Bryan Vossekuil, *Educing Information-Interrogation: Science and Art, Foundations for the Future*, National Military Intelligence College Press, Washington, D.C., 2006.

[46] Simon Oleszkiewicz, Pär Anders Granhag and Steven M. Kleinman, "Gathering Human Intelligence Via Repeated Interviewing: Further Empirical Test of the Scharff Technique", in *Psychology, Crime & Law*, 2017, vol. 23, pp. 666–681.

[47] Pär Anders Granhag, Simon Oleszkiewicz and Steven M. Kleinman, "Eliciting Information from Small Cells of Sources", in *Journal of Policing, Intelligence and Counter Terrorism*, 2016, vol. 11, pp. 143–162.

faced with an 'updated' story, the already known information plus the new information collected from the first (first and second) source. The Scharff technique and the direct approach resulted in an equal amount of new information. This was not expected and we speculated that there were two reasons for the outcome. First, the members in each cell maintained their loyalty to the group. Second, almost all sources believed that they were last in line to be interviewed, which might have lowered their motivation to reveal new information ('My fellow members have already told what should be told'). These two factors made the sources restrictive in providing new information, which left a small room for detecting differences between the two interview techniques. As predicted, the sources in the Scharff condition underestimated their own contribution of new information. The Scharff technique resulted in that the sources overestimated the amount of information revealed by their fellow group members, whereas this was not the case for the direct approach. In sum, by using the Scharff technique, we were able to *deflate* the sources' estimate of how much new information they believed to have revealed, and *inflate* the sources' estimate of how much information they believed their fellow group members to have revealed. The combined evidence showed that the Scharff technique is a promising technique for multiple sources as well.

In a recent meta-analytic overview,[48] Timothy Luke gathered all experimental studies that had been conducted on the Scharff technique. Eleven studies met the inclusion criteria and these studies reported data from 1,157 participants. In sum, the meta-analytic review lends support to the proposition that Scharff tactics are effective at (i) eliciting new information (compared to control techniques); (ii) making sources underestimate their contribution of new information; and (iii) leaving the source with a greater difficulty in understanding the interrogator's information objectives. "Viewing the existing literature at the aggregate level, a promising picture comes into focus: The experimental evidence is fairly strong that the contemporary conceptualization of Scharff's technique produces effects in the intended direction for the variables examined here", Luke concludes. The meta-analytic review points also to some shortcomings of the existing body of research. I agree that future research would benefit from increased sample sizes, designs that will increase statistical power and that there is a need to diversify the researchers involved in this strand of research. In short, I encourage other laboratories to conduct studies to see if the positive effects of Scharff's tactics replicate.

---

[48] Timothy J. Luke, "A Meta-Analytic Review of Experimental Tests of the Interrogation Technique of Hanns Scharff", in *Applied Cognitive Psychology*, 2021, vol. 35, pp. 360–373.

10.6. Training in the Scharff Technique

Below, I will first summarize my efforts with respect to training different groups of practitioners in the Scharff technique. I will then turn to, and describe, two 'training studies' that we have conducted, one involving police handlers and one involving military intelligence officers.

10.6.1. Training Professionals

Since 2014, I have had many requests with respect to the Scharff technique, some of these have been about giving a two or three hours-long lecture on Scharff's approach and the research that we have done. Other requests have been more demanding and have been about giving hands-on training in the Scharff technique, and that is what I will address next. So far, I have given training in Sweden, Norway, Denmark, the UK and the US. To date, I have given seminars on Scharff's approach to more than fifteen organizations; among them are high profile organizations such as the FBI, the Los Angeles Police Department, the New York Police Department's Intelligence Division, the MI5, and the UK Defence Intelligence. The most common target groups have been handlers within the police and the security service, undercover officers and military intelligence officers. The title of the training has often been *'How to elicit information'* – and Scharff's technique has been at the very core of the training package.

The time for the training has varied, but most often it has been two full days. These days have included an introduction to *elicitation* and a review of theoretical concepts needed to properly grasp Scharff's technique. The training has also included information on Scharff's background, how he built his framework and, of course, his general strategies and specific tactics. The training has sometimes included filmed material and exercises. Sometimes the training has been set-up to fit those who are new in the game, but more often the training has been aimed for experienced operators. I have conducted a few 'train-the-trainers' sessions, where I have taught the Scharff technique to a group of trainers already working within an organization. The basic idea behind such training is that the organization will then have in-house knowledge on the Scharff technique and can teach it at their own discretion.

The Scharff training conducted so far has not followed a strict manual – the content of the training has varied a bit depending on the needs of the receiving group. So far, I have viewed the Scharff technique as an essential part of training in how to *elicit information*. To me, the Scharff technique is not a concept that one either adopts in full or leaves behind. I instead think of the Scharff technique as a toolkit from which you select the strategies and tactics that are relevant for the current situation. The feedback that I have received on the training has been very positive. "The Hanns Scharff technique is and will continue to be the bread and butter of our investigative interview protocols", said Detective Supervisor Mark Severino, a long-time expert in covert operations working at the Major Crimes Division, Los Angeles Police Department.[49] But there are no data on how effective the training actually has been. That is, to date there are no studies comparing, for example, pre-training and post-training performance.

10.6.2. Two Quasi-Experimental 'Training Studies'

It is important to show that the Scharff technique works well in the laboratory, but to make a difference, the technique must be tested in studies involving professionals. It is necessary to examine whether the technique can be taught, and if so, will professionals who use the Scharff technique outperform colleagues who use their standard techniques? For the third round of research, my colleagues and I brought the Scharff technique back to field.

In the first 'training study', we examined handlers from the Norwegian Police, all experienced in interacting with informants.[50] Half of the handlers received training in the Scharff technique and the remaining half received no such training. The 90-minute training package consisted of a lecture and video material introducing the Scharff technique. For the first part of the lecture, the handlers were introduced to different Scharff tactics for building a friendly conversational interaction: to avoid asking explicit questions, not to press for information and to use diversionary tactics. For the second part of the lecture, the handlers were introduced to the knowledge-illusion and the claim tactic. After the lecture, the handlers were given time to individually practice building the knowledge-illusion and to formulate claims.

For the next phase of the study, all handlers (trained and untrained) received the same case file describing a source holding information about a future terrorist attack. They were all given the same three objectives: (i) to collect new critical information; (ii) not to reveal their information objectives; and (iii) to leave the source willing to meet again. Police trainees took on the role of semi-co-operative sources and were given incomplete information about the terrorist attack. Each handler interacted individually with a mock source. The trained handlers' performance was compared against the handlers who received no Scharff training and who were free to use the interview approaches as they saw fit for the situation.

---

[49] Pär Anders Granhag, "Interview With Mark Severino", Los Angeles Police Headquarters, 20 February 2018.

[50] Simon Oleszkiewicz, Pär Anders Granhag and Steven M. Kleinman, "Eliciting Information from Human Sources: Training Handlers in the Scharff Technique", in *Legal and Criminological Psychology*, 2017, vol. 22, pp. 400–419.

Our analysis showed that the trained handlers adhered to the Scharff training. They aimed to establish the knowledge-illusion, they used the claim tactic and they asked few (if any) explicit questions. In fact, more than half of the trained handlers did not ask one single explicit question. The untrained handlers used a very different approach. Broadly speaking, they tried to evoke the sources' motivation to disclose information and they asked many explicit questions. In fact, the untrained handlers asked five times as many explicit questions as did the Scharff-trained handlers. Less than 10 per cent of untrained handlers posed claims to gather new information, which indicates that the claim tactic is an underused elicitation tactic.

The Scharff-trained handlers collected significantly more new information from their sources than did their untrained colleagues. The sources that had faced Scharff-trained handlers did not find it more difficult to read their handlers' information objectives. We were surprised by this finding. One explanation may be that both trained and untrained handlers were skilled at hiding their information objectives, as this is an essential part of their training. As predicted, the trained handlers were perceived as comparatively less eager to gather information. We explained this by the trained handlers' use of the knowledge-illusion and asking very few explicit questions. Trained and the untrained handlers were equally successful in making their sources willing to meet again and in hindsight this was not surprising. The handlers were experienced in terms of recruiting and handling informants, and to leave an informant willing to meet again is again a fundamental skill.

We have conducted a second training study where we tested experienced military intelligence officers.[51] Again, half of the officers were trained in the Scharff technique, whereas the other half received no Scharff training. For this study, each officer had access to two sources. To have access to more than one source reflects operational reality.[52] We again found that the Scharff-trained officers adhered to the training; they aimed to establish the knowledge-illusion, they used the claim tactic and they asked few explicit questions. In contrast, the officers not trained in the Scharff technique asked five times as many explicit questions, they questioned the reliability of the information provided by the source, they pressured the source and displayed disappointment with respect to their sources' contribution. The Scharff-trained officers collected a similar amount of new information as their untrained colleagues. The superiority of the

---

[51] Pär Anders Granhag, Simon Oleszkiewicz, Marte Lefsaker Sakrisvold and Steven M. Kleinman, "The Scharff Technique: Training Military Intelligence Officers to Elicit Information from Small Cells of Sources", in *Psychology, Crime & Law*, 2020, vol. 26, pp. 438–460.

[52] See, for example, Peter J. Carrington, "Group Crime in Canada", in *Canadian Journal of Criminology*, 2002, vol. 44, pp. 277–315.

Scharff technique showed in that the trained officers were perceived as less eager to gather information and in that they left their sources with the impression that they had provided comparatively less new information.

Three things stand out from our two training studies. First, we showed that the Scharff tactics can be taught, learned and applied. Second, the tactics used by the two untrained groups suggested that Scharff tactics are not commonly used by handlers and intelligence officers in their day-to-day work. Third, for both studies, the Scharff-trained professionals outperformed their untrained colleagues, although partly on different measures of efficacy.

10.7. The Scharff Technique: Limitations and Possibilities

Like every other interview or interrogation technique, the Scharff technique comes with possibilities and limitations. The first limitation is that the technique is not designed to produce a wealth of information; Scharff was after isolated pieces of information. The second limitation is that the knowledge-illusion – which is central to the technique – is only possible to build if the interrogator has access to a large amount of background information. There is another problem with the knowledge-illusion. For Scharff, presenting background information to his prisoners came with little risk. For other intelligence contexts, however, presenting what is already known can be counter-productive. If the source is not in custody, he may inform the persons to which the information pertains. Networks planning future crimes could deploy sources to tap how much is known about them. A further argument against sharing is that presenting information might reveal from where it came in the first place, which might endanger the source.

For some strategic interactions, all aspects of elicitation are important. That is, the aim is not only to collect new information, but also to hide one's information objectives and leave the source underestimating his or her contribution – then the Scharff technique is the technique to use. For other contexts, some parts of the Scharff may be less relevant (for example, the knowledge-illusion), whereas other parts are highly relevant (for example, using claims). I have mentioned that the Scharff technique is relevant to handler–source interactions, military and intelligence interrogations, work within the security services and the clandestine world of undercover officers. But the Scharff technique can be useful also during traditional crime suspect interviews, where the objective may suddenly shift from a person's whereabouts to the collection of intelligence on other individuals. The technique can also be useful for interviewing witnesses, where the focus might shift from what they have seen or experienced to what they know. Giving training, I have learned that parts of the Scharff technique can be useful during security screening interviews, conducted on potential employees who will handle confidential information and for professionals working in special units within migration agencies investigating potential war criminals.

10.8. The Future of the Scharff Technique

Ten years of research have placed the Scharff technique on the map, but much work lies ahead. I mentioned that it is possible to define four periods that have led up to the Scharff technique of today. I think there is a fifth period awaiting. As I have shown in this chapter, there is a gap between what Scharff did as an interrogator during World War II and how his technique has been conceptualized and tested in modern research. For the future, the narrow version of the Scharff technique that has been empirically tested, should be broadened and incorporate more of Scharff's strategies and tactics.[53] That is a large but important undertaking. I would not be surprised if such future work will show that adding more strategies and tactics will make the Scharff technique even more effective. In line with this, I think it is important to better understand the relation between the different strategies and tactics; the effects of different orders and exactly when to play them during an interaction. Also, in this chapter, I have discussed training in the Scharff technique, but similarly to many other interview and interrogation techniques, we do not know to what extent professionals who receive training in the Scharff technique will improve in their day-to-day work.

10.9. Some Additional Observations

"In the 'we know all' approach technique, the HUMINT [human intelligence] collector subtly convinces the source that his questioning of the source is perfunctory because any information that the source has is already known": the quote is from the US Army Field Manual *Human Intelligence Collector Operations*.[54] This manual describes all interrogation approaches authorized by the US Army. The document is almost 400 pages long, and half a page is spent on the 'we know all' approach. It states that the interrogator must be familiar with the background information. "To begin the collection effort, the HUMINT collector asks questions based on this known data", the Manual states. "When the source hesitates, refuses to answer, or provides an incorrect or incomplete reply, the HUMINT collector provides the detailed answer himself." As we know, Scharff's knowledge-illusion was considerably more advanced than what we find in the Army Field Manual. Scharff, to build the illusion, used an elaborate story; in the Field Manual version, the interrogator answers his own questions.

---

[53] This future idea was also pointed out by Luke, 2021, see *supra* note 48.

[54] *Human Intelligence Collector Operations*, see *supra* note 43.

The Army Field Manual advises the interrogator to collect information by asking explicit questions. Scharff always avoided direct questions.

It is, I believe, illuminating to compare the Scharff technique to the SUE technique[55] and the more recent so-called Shift-of-Strategy ('SoS') technique.[56] The Scharff technique is, as we have seen, for eliciting small pieces of information, the SUE technique is about using the evidence strategically to better decide whether a suspect is lying or telling the truth. The SoS technique is about eliciting cues to deceit, but to use these cues as means to a larger end: to collect new information. The three techniques were developed for different situations, but they share two fundamental principles. First, all three techniques draw on the *interviewee's counter-interrogation tactics*. As I have explained, Scharff tailored his strategies and tactics in the light of his prisoners' CITs; the SUE technique profits from guilty suspects' aversive and innocent suspects' more forthcoming CITs; and the SoS technique is about making guilty suspects change their initial aversive CITs to more forthcoming. The second shared principle is that all three techniques are about playing on the *interviewee's perception of the interviewer's knowledge*. For the Scharff technique, the interviewer pretends to know more than he actually knows; for the SUE technique, the interrogator pretends to know less. The SoS technique is a hybrid: the interviewer first pretends to know less than he actually knows, and then, for a later, critical stage, pretends to know more than he actually knows. Hence, sharing the same fundamental principles, the Scharff technique, the SUE technique and the SoS technique form a triad (see Figure 1).

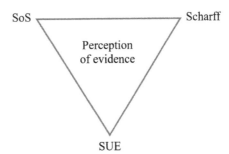

Figure 1: A triad of techniques – all drawing on the source's or suspect's perception of the interviewer's knowledge (evidence).

---

[55] Granhag and Hartwig, 2015, see *supra* note 3.
[56] See, for example, Granhag and Luke, 2018, see *supra* note 11. Timothy J. Luke and Pär Anders Granhag, "The Shift-of-Strategy Approach: Using Evidence Strategically to Influence Suspect's Counter-Interrogation Strategies", in *Psychology, Crime & Law*, 2022.

10.10. Conclusions

In the opening of this chapter, I introduced the concept of *elicitation* and made a few remarks about Scharff's background. I then spent time on the fundamentals of Scharff's approach to elicitation and explained that his insights on his prisoners' counter-interrogation tactics drove the strategies and tactics that he tailored. I tried to make it clear that the Scharff technique is not a 'bag of tricks' – instead the technique rests on advanced perspective-taking, psychologically-based strategies to make the source engage in a conversation and subtle tactics to elicit information. I also described the Scharff technique's journey from World War II to today's scientific work – a journey of over 80 years. I reviewed the outcome of a decade of empirical work on Scharff's technique and I discussed some issues related to training professionals in the technique. As proven by a recent meta-analytic review,[57] the Scharff technique has empirical support. But the journey is not over, and I predict that future empirical work, incorporating more of Scharff's strategies and tactics, will prove the technique to be even more effective. Finally, writing about Scharff and his approach to elicitation, I am not after glorifying a man who was part of the Nazi regime. But, and as I hope I have showed in this chapter, Scharff's legacy is too important to be ignored.

---

[57] Luke, 2021, see *supra* note 48.

11

The Evolution of Suspect Interview Training in United States Federal Law Enforcement

Patricia Donovan and Laura Zimmerman[*]

11.1. Introduction

The US Department of Homeland Security Federal Law Enforcement Training Centers ('FLETC'), established in 1970, provides basic and advanced training to law enforcement professionals from over 90 federal, state, local, tribal and international law enforcement agencies. To ensure these professionals receive the training necessary to meet their current operational requirements, FLETC systematically evaluates and updates training so the curriculum encompasses the latest trends, best practices and research findings. This is particularly true in the realm of investigative interviewing and interrogation.

The purpose of this chapter is to describe the evolution of suspect interview training at FLETC. This evolution reflects recent advances in empirical understanding of harmful and beneficial interview practices along with the development of new evidence-based techniques. This chapter will first present an overview of FLETC's previous training, which centred around the Five Step Interview Model. Next will be a discussion of several challenges and facilitators associated with the transition of research findings into practice. The chapter will conclude with a description of research that influenced FLETC's transition to their current evidence-based interview training along with a summary of this current training.

---

[*] **Patricia Donovan**, Ph.D., is a research engineering psychologist and interview-interrogation senior instructor at the Federal Law Enforcement Training Center in Glynco, Georgia. Her 30-year law enforcement career includes previous positions as a Special Agent investigator with the United States ('US') Secret Service, a Task Force Agent investigator at the US Drug Enforcement Administration, and a Major Felony investigator at Dekalb County, Georgia, Police Department. She holds a degree in international psychology and her research focuses on investigative interviewing and cross-cultural communications in policing. **Laura Zimmerman**, Ph.D., is a research engineering psychologist at the Federal Law Enforcement Training Center in Glynco, Georgia. She holds a degree in experimental psychology and has conducted research in the law enforcement domain for over 20 years. Her research has focused on investigative interview techniques, officer communication skills, high-stakes decision making, eyewitness identification, threat detection, and large-scale multi-agency emergency response.

11.2. Previous FLETC Five-Step Interview Model

The FLETC Five-Step Interview was designed to provide an easily adaptable guide for new trainees to use when interviewing victims, witnesses, and suspects. When interviewing suspects, the method was called the Five Step Suspect Interview ('FSSI') because Step 3 also included techniques focused on eliciting confessions. Reflecting the industry standards of the times (1970s–2000s), FLETC's suspect interview training was confession-based with the goal of obtaining self-incriminating statements that conformed to investigators' existing investigative theories. Conversely, the goal of witness or victim interviews was to obtain information. The five steps were: (i) introduction; (ii) rapport; (iii) questioning; (iv) summary; and (v) close (see Table 1 below).

Step 1	Step 2	Step 3	Step 4	Step 5
Introduction	**Rapport**	**Questioning**	**Summary**	**Close**
• Planning (prior to interview) o Examine case and suspect information o Prepare a purpose statement (prior to interview) o Develop themes based on case and suspect information o Consider interview setting: Custodial or non-custodial • Beginning the interview: o Deliver purpose statement o Initiate rapport building	• Establish common ground to build rapport • Observe baseline behaviour • Components of effective communication o Self-awareness o Clarity of expression o Self-disclosure • Active listening • Establish and maintain rapport	• Transition statement • Open-ended questions • Verbal and non-verbal cues to deception • Specific questions • *Suspect Interview* o Monologue o Disclose evidence o Themes o Handle denials o Choice/assumptive question o Seek admission o Seek confession	• Summarize information • Follow-up questions • Request written statement	• Explain forthcoming process • Acknowledge cooperation • Leave door open for additional questions

Table 1: Components of the FLETC five-step suspect interview.

Historically (and currently), the primary objective of every investigative interview was to supply prosecutors with accurate information that met the legal requirements for admission in court. Thus, in addition to the step-by-step process, the Five-Step Interview training incorporated legal considerations[1] along with verbal and behavioural communication skills. While maintaining a focus on communication, aspects of training involved criminal codes, rules and procedures (which are not discussed here). Regarding interpersonal skills, trainees learned basic elements of effective communication such as self-awareness, clarity of expression, and self-disclosure. Self-awareness involved recognizing one's own strengths, weaknesses, and biases related to interviewing. With self-awareness, trainees kept potential biases in mind and leveraged their strengths to gain information and confessions. Clarity of expression focused on speaking in a manner suspects understood to avoid confusion and build trust. Trainees also explored their willingness to self-disclose information, primarily to promote suspect reciprocation during rapport building.[2] Trainees applied these legal considerations and interpersonal skills in all steps of the FSSI.

11.2.1. Step 1: Introduction

As a part of Step 1, trainees learned how to develop a plan and create a purpose statement prior to starting the interrogation. During planning, trainees compiled case and suspect information, clarified objectives, and identified gaps in information. From this information, they developed their investigative theory about how the criminal event unfolded and who was involved. They also identified common interests and experiences for building rapport in Step 2. In addition, they chose a 'theme' they would apply in attempt to gain admissions or confessions in Step 3. The themes taught in the FSSI were rationalization, projection and minimization. These are discussed in Step 3.

Trainees also learned how to choose physical locations for their interviews by considering the interview setting and pertinent legal parameters. Suspect interviews do not always take place in interrogation rooms or even at police stations. Suspect (or any type of) interviews can take place, for example, at suspect residences, coffee shops or places of business. A key factor driving location choice is whether the suspect is under arrest (custodial) or not (non-custodial).

After finalizing the plan, trainees were ready to open the interrogation with polite and respectful introductory greetings that set a positive tone. Similar to methods used by customer service representatives, investigators start by establishing their identity and explaining the interview purpose (purpose statement). The aim in customer service is to answer the customer's first question,

---

[1] Constitution of the United States of America, 17 September 1787, Amendment V, Section 1 (https://www.legal-tools.org/doc/bc3d56/).

[2] Jaqueline R. Evans *et al.*, "Criminal versus HUMINT Interrogations: The Importance of Psychological Science to Improving Interrogative Practice", in *The Journal of Psychiatry and Law*, 2010, vol. 38 (1–2), pp. 215–249.

'Why are you talking to me?'. The same was true for trainees conducting the FSSI. They used the opening to set the tone for future rapport building, establish authority, and gain co-operation. The objective of the purpose statement was to supply suspects with enough information (without mentioning the crime under investigation) to decide whether they would speak with investigators. For example, an investigator might say, 'Hello Mr. Jones, I am Investigator Smith and I am here to talk to you about the incident that occurred yesterday. Is it OK if we talk for a moment?'.

The purpose statement, along with skills such as building rapport, are associated with police legitimacy and procedural justice theory. Procedural justice is a prescriptive pathway to police legitimacy (recognition and acceptance of authority) that promotes community member co-operation and compliance. This is done *via* dialogue (voice) that allows informed community members to decide if they will participate in criminal justice process. Procedural justice consists of four components: community member participation in dialogue, neutrality in police decision making, dignity and respect, and the trustworthy motives of authority.[3] Although the FSSI did not explicitly teach procedural justice theory, its techniques encompassed elements of procedural justice. For example, trainees learned to deliver truthful[4] purpose statements during the introduction that allowed suspects the autonomy to decide whether to participate in the encounter.

11.2.2. Step 2: Rapport

Although the FSSI emphasized rapport as an important concept, specific techniques to establish, build, and maintain rapport were not readily available in the policing domain. Unlike common social settings, rapport building during suspect interviews introduces challenges associated with the imbalance of power between investigator and suspect along with disparate motivations and goals (see also Chapter 4 of this book).[5] Thus, trainees found it difficult to put into practice common rapport-building advice such as 'engage in small talk', 'share personal information', and 'be empathetic'. A survey of US military and federal law enforcement interrogators found little consensus on the definition of rapport,

---

[3] Lorraine Mazerolle *et al.*, "Procedural Justice and Police Legitimacy: A Systematic Review of the Research Evidence", in *Journal of Experimental Criminology*, 2013, vol. 9, no. 3, p. 245.

[4] In the US, investigators are allowed to use a ruse to gain co-operation. However, FLETC training emphasized investigator truthfulness during the interview. US Supreme Court, *Frazier v. Cupp*, Judgment, 22 April 1969, 394 U.S. 731, p. 740 (https://www.legal-tools.org/doc/17vqkb/).

[5] Fiona Gabbert *et al.*, "Exploring the Use of Rapport in Professional Information Gathering Contexts by Systematically Mapping the Evidence Base", in *Applied Cognitive Psychology*, 2021, vol. 35, no. 2, pp. 329–341.

although respondents agreed rapport was crucial to interrogation success. Respondents also varied in the rapport-building strategies they thought were most effective.[6] Without a clear definition and only vague descriptions of rapport-building techniques, FLETC instructors struggled to teach trainees communication strategies that would foster co-operation and information sharing. In an examination of common interrogation practices, researchers interviewed FLETC instructors who reported struggling to teach trainees how to build rapport, however, the struggle was due, in part, to limited time available to coach trainees. Instructor opinion at the time was that rapport-building involved some innate ability, although trainees could learn skills such as conveying confidence and appearing professional while engaging in small talk.[7]

As a part of rapport building, instructors emphasized the importance of developing interpersonal communication skills. One of these skills was active listening, requiring the listener to remain neutral, listen rather than speak, clear the mind to better concentrate, and avoid interrupting. Trainees learned to show listening through non-verbal responses such as head nodding and sub-vocals ('uh-huh') and to confirm understanding by paraphrasing or summarizing the suspect responses. Active listening skills are included in current FLETC training, but the purpose shifted from observing non-verbal behaviour for deception detection to processing information for use in creating a co-operative atmosphere and fostering effective communication.

In the FSSI, trainees learned to observe suspect non-verbal behaviour and establish a baseline. Baseline behaviour is a concept espoused in the Behavioural Analysis Interview ('BAI'), a structured non-accusatory conversation in which investigators pose both investigative and behaviour provoking questions to criminal suspects. During rapport building, trainees engaged in casual conversations to prompt truthful statements from suspects. Suspect behaviours while truth-telling were considered baseline with the assumption that subsequent behavioural changes might indicate deception. This theory is linked to the physiological and behavioural responses to stress associated with polygraph testing.[8]

---

[6]   Melissa Russano, Fadia Narchet, Steven Kleinman and Christian Meissner, "Structured Interviews of Experienced HUMINT Interrogators", in *Applied Cognitive Psychology*, 2014, vol. 28, no. 6, p. 847.

[7]   Ariel Neuman and Daniel Salinas-Serrano, "Custodial Interrogations: What We Know, What We Do, and What We Can Learn from Law Enforcement Experiences", in Robert Fein, Paul Lehner and Bryan Vossekuil (eds.), *Educing Information, Interrogation: Science and Art*, National Defense Intelligence College, Center for Strategic Intelligence Research, 2006, p. 141.

[8]   John E. Reid *et al.*, *The Reid Technique of Interviewing and Interrogation*, Chicago, 1999.

It has been proposed that flaws exist in the notion that deviations from baseline are signs deception, and thus guilt. Interviews that go from low-stakes small talk (to observe baseline behaviour) to high-stakes determinations of culpability would likely induce behavioural changes in both guilty and innocent suspects. Rather than focusing on baseline behaviour, interviewers should focus on changes in verbal behaviours after implementing techniques such as reporting events in reverse order, asking unanticipated questions, and using model statements to prompt suspects to supply more detail.[9] In a study comparing the reports of truthtellers and liars after establishing baseline using small talk or a comparable truth condition (akin to investigative questioning about non-crime related activities), results showed that behaviours for both truthtellers and liars did not deviate from baseline.[10] This suggests that tracking deviations from baseline would not assist investigators in determining when suspects are lying.

11.2.3. Step 3: Questioning

11.2.3.1. Transition Statement

After trainees established rapport, or attempted to establish rapport, they transitioned to the third step, questioning. Establishing rapport with unco-operative or hostile suspects is not always possible. In these cases, investigators try to calm suspects or get them talking just enough to answer questions. However, at some point investigators must move on from their rapport building efforts and try to elicit information or admissions. The questioning phase of the FSSI generally started with a transition statement that extended the purpose statement by adding details about the suspect's alleged involvement in the crime. While the initial purpose statement opened the dialogue and built rapport, the transition statement moved the general and casual conversation to more serious topics specific to the crime under investigation.

11.2.3.2. Questioning Techniques

Trainees learned to use open-ended questions followed by specific questions. The purpose of open-ended questions was to observe suspect non-verbal and verbal behaviours during their narrative responses rather to than elicit information, which is the case with current information elicitation techniques.[11] After

---

[9] Aldert Vrij, "Baselining as a Lie Detection Method", in *Applied Cognitive Psychology*, 2016, vol. 30, p. 1112.

[10] Nicole Palena, Letizia Caso, Aldert Vrij and Robin Orthey, "Detecting Deception Through Small Talk and Comparable Truth Baselines", in *Journal of Investigative Psychology and Offender Profiling*, 2018, vol. 15, no. 3, p. 124.

[11] Ronald P. Fisher and R. Edward Geiselman, *Memory Enhancing Techniques for Investigative Interviewing: The Cognitive Interview*, Charles C. Thomas Publisher, 1992; Amina Memon, Christian A. Meissner and Joanne Fraser, "The Cognitive Interview: A Meta-analytic Review

suspects finished their free narratives, trainees asked specific questions to fill in gaps, to catch suspects lying, and to gather details for use in the accusatory stage of the interrogation.

Once trainees completed questioning, they classified their interviewees as a suspect versus a witness or bystander. If they did not uncover information or evidence that pointed to the suspect's involvement (probable cause), they shifted to gathering information using the general FLETC Five-Step Interview and ceased to presume guilt or seek confessions.

11.2.3.3. Deception Detection

Trainees learned to look for signs of deception once questioning began. They would look for deviations from baseline and clusters of behavioural cues thought to be indicative of deception, such as averted gaze, fidgeting, sweating, and hand gesturing. Instructors made clear that no one cue was proof of deception. Rather, they advised trainees to take a holistic approach and consider multiple cues simultaneously. For example, if a suspect started sweating as they averted their eyes and fidgeted, particularly if this deviated from baseline, it might imply they were withholding information or being deceitful.

Analyzing behaviours in this manner stemmed from the assumption that liars would experience internal stress and anxiety, which would affect their external actions. Standard training for evaluating verbal responses consisted of identifying truthful, omissive, evasive or deceptive statements, mainly by judging the associated non-verbal nervous behaviours. Investigators considered suspect responses truthful when they were direct and reflected the truth without evoking behaviours that signalled internal anxiety. Omissive responses meant that suspects accepted responsibility but denied criminal intent and displayed very little internal anxiety. With evasive responses, suspects implied innocence without saying so explicitly and displayed some internal anxiety. When suspects displayed a great level of internal anxiety, the investigators would consider the response deceptive.[12]

Instructor beliefs about deception detection reflected industry standards. For instance, in one study, experienced interrogators reported using verbal cues such as story contradictions, deviations from behavioural baselines, and non-verbal cues such as eye movements and fidgeting to detect deception.[13] However, research at the time tended to dispute the efficacy of these cues and showed that

---

and Study Space Analysis of the Past 25 years", in *Psychology, Public Policy, and Law*, 2010, vol. 16, no. 4, p. 34.

[12] Fred E. Inbau *et al.*, *Essentials of the Reid Technique: Criminal Interrogation and Confessions*, Jones and Bartlett Publishers, 2013.

[13] Russano, Narchet, Kleinman and Meissner, 2014, see *supra* note 6.

people, including law enforcement, were generally no better than chance at detecting deception.[14] Still, these interrogators believed the techniques worked and their abilities at detecting lies were above average.[15] Additional research has also shown that interrogators and others in law enforcement overestimate their ability to detect deception.[16] These ingrained beliefs highlight one challenge in trying to shift police practices towards more reliable methods of discerning truth from deception.

11.2.3.4. Monologue

After eliciting free narratives and asking questions, trainees transitioned from dialogue to an accusatory monologue. During the monologue, trainees would consume the conversation, stop suspect denials, use themes, and try to persuade suspects to tell truths that matched existing investigative theories. Each trainee would reveal their theory of the suspect's involvement and follow up by offering moral or psychological justifications for the suspect's behaviour. If suspects tried to talk, trainees would verbally interrupt or non-verbally cut them off (ignore, hand up, passively talk over) and request they remain silent. This action is called positive confrontation in police interviewing literature. The reason investigators accuse suspects without allowing for denials is to increase discomfort, fear of negative consequences, and to build up stress.[17] Research examining this confrontational approach has found it is associated with both true and false confessions.[18]

11.2.3.5. Factual Evidence Presentation

During the monologue, trainees presented evidence in a manner intended to overwhelm suspects so they would confess. At the time, minimal research

---

[14] Bella M. DePaulo et al., "Cues to Deception", in *Psychological Bulletin*, 2003, vol. 12, no. 9, sec. 1, pp. 74–118.

[15] Charles F. Bond and Bella M. DePaulo, "Individual Differences in Judging Deception: Accuracy and Bias", in *Psychological Bulletin*, 2008, vol. 134, no. 4, pp. 477–492.

[16] Saul M. Kassin et al., "Police Interviewing and Interrogation: A Self-report Survey of Police Practices and Beliefs", in *Law and Human Behavior*, 2007, vol. 31, no. 4, pp. 381–400; Allison Redlich, Christopher Kelly and Jeanee Miller, "The Who, What, and Why of Human Intelligence Gathering: Self-Reported Measures of Interrogation Methods", in *Applied Cognitive Psychology*, 2014, vol. 28, no. 6, p. 817; Aldert Vrij, Par Anders Granhag and Stephen Porter, "Pitfalls and Opportunities in Non-verbal and Verbal Lie Detection", in *Psychological Science in the Public Interest*, 2010, vol. 11, no. 3, p. 89.

[17] Inbau et al., 2013, see *supra* note 12.

[18] Christian Meissner et al., "Accusatorial and Information-Gathering Interrogation Methods and Their Effects on True and False Confessions: A Meta-Analytic Review", in *Journal of Experimental Criminology*, 2014, vol. 10, no. 4, p. 459; Fadia Narchet, Christian Meissner and Melissa Russano, "Modeling the Influence of Investigator Bias on the Elicitation of True and False Confessions", in *Law and Human Behavior*, 2011, vol. 35, no. 6, p. 452.

existed on evidence disclosure during interrogations. Police manuals offered mixed recommendations and common practice was to disclose evidence early. More recent research has found that early disclosure of evidence allows liars to generate plausible statements that fit the evidence.[19] This is discussed in more detail below.

11.2.3.6. Themes

Trainee monologues centered around the themes they identified during the planning phase and developed as they gained more information. The intent of themes was to alleviate the fear of confessing. Instructors focused on the themes of rationalization, projection and minimization. Rationalization was used to moralize behaviour. For example, an investigator might say, 'Sure, you took the money, but you had to feed your family'. Projection focused on deflecting responsibility by blaming other people, groups, or situations, such as 'I know it was not your idea to take the money. Your coworker was the one who planned it all'. When using minimization, investigators lessened the severity of suspect behaviour, and thus, implied less severe punishment. For example, 'It was just a few dollars from the cash register. It's not like you robbed a bank'.

When investigators present themes that morally or psychologically justify criminal behaviour, it interferes with suspects' autonomous decision making and could induce innocent suspects to confess.[20] In addition, presenting themes during interrogations is likely not necessary because, not surprisingly, guilty suspects often deny criminal involvement and rationalize their own behaviour without help from investigators. Investigators can leverage these self-preservation strategies to gain information or persuade suspects without risking undue influence by using themes.

11.2.3.7. Maximization

Although FLETC did not use the term maximization, the FSSI promoted techniques commonly associated with maximization, such as using statements that intensify the seriousness of the crime and severity of the evidence while implying that a confession will help ease a suspect's dire situation.[21] These statements also suggested that a suspect's dishonesty or lack of confession would result in

---

[19]   Maria Hartwig, Pär Anders Granhag and Timothy Luke, "Strategic Use of Evidence During Investigative Interviews: The State of the Science", in David C. Raskin *et al.* (eds.), *Credibility Assessment*, Academic Press, 2014.

[20]   Maria Hartwig, Pär Anders Granhag and Aldet Vrij, "Police Interrogation from a Social Psychology Perspective", in *Policing and Society*, 2005, vol. 15, no. 4, pp. 379–399.

[21]   Saul Kassin and Karlyn McNall, "Police Interrogations and Confessions: Communicating Promises and Threats by Pragmatic Implication", in *Law and Human Behavior*, 1991, vol. 15, no. 3, p. 233.

harsher consequences.[22] While investigators cannot make direct promises of leniency, the implication often proves true. The US justice system looks favourably upon suspects who confess, thus suspects often benefit from confessing to their crimes (if factually guilty).

11.2.3.8. Choice and Assumptive Questions

After the monologue and theme presentation, trainees transitioned to asking a choice question or an assumptive question. Choice questions offer suspects two self-incriminating choices concerning a criminal act.[23] For example, 'Did you steal the money because you wanted to feed your family or because you wanted to buy drugs?'. The purpose of a choice question is to give suspects an acceptable choice and a worse choice so they pick one option rather than denying involvement. When suspects chose an option, investigators consider it an admission of guilt. In an assumptive question, the investigator presents a question that assumes guilt.[24] For example, an investigator asks, 'Why did you take the money?' instead of, 'Did you take the money?'. If the suspect responds without denials or admits guilt, for example by saying, 'I took the money because I needed it', the investigator acknowledges co-operation and returns to the beginning of Step 2 by asking an open-ended question, such as, 'Thank you for telling me the truth, now start from the beginning and tell me everything that happened'. If the suspect denies the accusation, the investigator adjusts or changes the theme and continues communicating a certainty of guilt.

Several studies have shown the association between themes or accusatory questions and false confessions.[25] One study demonstrated how manipulating the perceived consequences of confessing, such as by exaggerating the repercussions of not confessing (maximization) and downplaying the seriousness of the offense (minimization), increased the likelihood of false confessions. In contrast, using minimization and maximization techniques without perceived consequences, such as expressions of sympathy and appeals to conscience, increased true confessions.[26] In another study, experimenters who acted as interrogators chose from several accusatorial and non-accusatorial approaches and

---

[22] Kassin *et al.*, 2007, see *supra* note 16.

[23] Inbau *et al.*, 2013, see *supra* note 12.

[24] Michael Farrell, Douglas E. Wicklander, Shane G. Sturman and L. Wayne Hoover, *Practical Aspects of Interview and Interrogation*, CRC Press, 2001.

[25] Allyson J. Horgan, Melissa B. Russano, Christian A. Meissner and Jaqueline R. Evans, "Minimization and Maximization Techniques: Assessing the Perceived Consequences of Confessing and Confession Diagnosticity", in *Psychology, Crime & Law*, 2012, vol. 18, no. 1, pp. 65–78; Narchet, Meissner and Russano, 2011, see *supra* note 18; Russano, Narchet, Kleinman and Meissner, 2014, see *supra* note 6.

[26] Horgan, Russano, Meissner and Evans, 2012, see *supra* note 25.

interviewed college students suspected of cheating. Data showed that false confessions were more likely when interrogators used minimization and maximization techniques compared to non-accusatorial methods. When interrogators believed the suspect was guilty, they applied more accusatorial techniques. They also maintained guilt biases post-interview and were more likely to believe innocent participants were guilty.[27] These studies were among several that revealed that some techniques taught in the FSSI might lead to incorrect identification of criminal perpetrators.

11.2.4. Step 4: Summary

Whether suspects continued to deny involvement, make admissions, or confesses to criminal acts, trainees had to decide when to transition to Step 4 based on failed or successful attempts to obtain a confession. The summary phrase allowed trainees to verify the details of denials, admissions or confessions. They, or a secondary trainee if present, summarized the information and asked follow-up questions. Finally, they asked the suspect to write and sign a statement of facts.

11.2.5. Step 5: Close

After the summary, trainees closed the interview by thanking the suspects for their co-operation, exchanging contact information, and explaining how and when they will make future contact.

The FSSI incorporated several techniques no longer considered sound practice. At the time, these methods of detecting deception and provoking confessions were industry standards. Investigators were not necessarily questioning the effectiveness of their methods, rather their successes supplied anecdotal evidence that supported their use of these techniques. Nonetheless, as research evidence showing the effectiveness of alternative methods increased, investigators took note and began to acknowledge that some techniques long used in policing practice were sometimes ineffective. And, as research showed, investigators often preferred using rapport-based tactics not always found in training.[28] Even with this emerging shift in mindset, modifications to training would require a more frequent and formalized collaborative effort between researchers and practitioners. The next section discusses challenges in forming these collaborative partnerships and implementing new techniques in the field. This discussion focuses primarily on the actions researchers can take to start and maintain productive partnerships and explains how the changes evolved in FLETC curriculum.

---

[27] Narchet, Meissner and Russano, 2011, see *supra* note 18.

[28] Redlich, Kelly and Miller, 2014, see *supra* note 16; Russano, Narchet, Kleinman and Meissner, 2014, see *supra* note 6.

11.3. Receptivity to Research

Around 2010, interrogation training at FLETC, and throughout the US, started to undergo significant change. While mounting evidence showed several interrogation techniques were ineffective (or effective but potentially harmful), these findings rarely made it into police training academies or practice.[29] Researchers often met resistance and skepticism when they tried to share their findings.[30] Policing culture, as well as popular culture, embraced traditional interrogation practices while investigators often relied on the 'art' of interrogation and their innate abilities to detect deception and elicit confessions. Additionally, investigators often saw the benefit of their interrogation methods reflected in their arrest and conviction rates. These positive outcomes served as evidence their techniques were effective regardless of what the science said.

Indoctrination into police culture and ties to tradition begin in the training academy.[31] New police recruits rely heavily on their training to carry out their duties and consider instructors reliable subject matter experts. Instructors are often former officers or agents with decades of first-hand experience that they pass down to their trainees. Once trainees leave the academy, their field training officers and colleagues, along with their own experiences reinforce those skills. Given this, it is foreseeable that law enforcement would be skeptical of researchers who deliver the message that their techniques and practices are wrong. Hearing suggestions from outsiders with no policing experience about better and less harmful ways to police would understandably evoke resistance, no matter how 'backed by science' those suggestions were.

In effort to remedy this, researchers have examined the challenges they face when trying to establish collaborative relationships with police agencies and when trying to transition their research findings into practice. Several academics note the relative minor influence evidence-based findings have had in

---

29   Julie Grieco, Heather Vovak and Cynthia Lum, "Examining Research–Practice Partnerships in Policing Evaluations", in *Policing: A Journal of Policy and Practice*, 2014, vol. 8, no. 4, pp. 368–378.

30   Geoffrey P. Alpert, Jeff Rojek and Andrew Hansen, "Building Bridges Between Police Researchers and Practitioners: Agents of Change in a Complex World", US Department of Justice, National Institute of Justice, 2013; Cynthia Lum, Cody Telep, Christopher Koper and Julie Grieco, "Receptivity to Research in Policing", in *Justice Research and Policy*, 2012, vol. 14, no. 1, p. 61.

31   For example, Allison T. Chappell and Lonn Lanza-Kaduce, "Police Academy Socialization: Understanding the Lessons Learned in a Paramilitary-Bureaucratic Organization", in *Journal of Contemporary Ethnography*, 2010, vol. 39, no. 2, pp. 187–214 in their examination of community policing practices in academy training.

the evolution of policing practices.[32] While a common refrain is that police organizations are particularly resistant to change,[33] researchers also play a part in the success or failure of these collaborations. The issues that waylay or facilitate successful police-researcher partnerships often centre around aligning expectations, goals and priorities while nurturing positive interpersonal relationships. The International Association of Chiefs of Police ('IACP') created a publication to aid researchers in forming partnerships with police (they also created a complementary guide for police leadership). To build effective working relationships, they suggested researchers focus on active listening, assisting police partners in seeing beyond immediate strategic concerns, and identifying shared priorities.[34]

Researchers and police practitioners often have different goals and priorities when engaging in research projects. Researchers tend to place a high value on scientific results, whereas practitioners are often concerned with immediate solutions to problems, even if those solutions have not been subject to the rigors of scientific inquiry.[35] In some cases, researchers offer data showing certain techniques are inadequate without also offering alternative solutions.[36] Other times, they deliver results that advance science but are of little value to practitioners resulting in a 'one-way street', with researchers collecting the data to satisfy their research interests without delivering results that have practical application.[37] In their guide, the IACP recommended that researchers work closely with police partners to define goals, identify practical problems associated with the

---

[32] David H. Bayley, "Policing in America: Assessment and Prospects", in *Police Foundation Series: Ideas in American Policing*, 1998; David Bradley and Christine Nixon, "Ending the 'Dialogue of the Deaf: Evidence and Policing Policies and Practices, an Australian Case Study", in *Police Practice and Research: An International Journal*, 2009, vol. 10, nos. 5–6, pp. 423–435; Lawrence Sherman, "The Rise of Evidence-Based Policing: Targeting, Testing, and Tracking", in *Crime and Justice*, 2013, vol. 42, no. 1, p. 377.

[33] Alpert, Rojek and Hansen, 2013, see *supra* note 30; Ryan Cohen, "The Force and the Resistance: Why Changing the Police Force Is Neither Inevitable, nor Impossible", in *University of Pennsylvania Journal of Law and Social Change*, 2017, vol. 20, no. 2, pp. 105–123.

[34] Ronal Serpa and Charles Wellford, "Establishing and Sustaining Law Enforcement-Researcher Partnerships: Guide for Researchers", US Department of Justice, Office of Justice Programs International Association of Chiefs of Police, 2007 (https://www.legal-tools.org/doc/tvw7cr/).

[35] Alpert, Rojek and Hansen, 2013, see *supra* note 30; Lum, Telep, Koper and Grieco, 2012, see *supra* note 30.

[36] Brian H. Bornstein and Christian A. Meissner, "Influencing Policy and Procedure With Law-Psychology Research: Why, When, Where, How, and What", in David DeMatteo and Kyle C. Scherr (eds.), *Oxford Handbook of Psychology and Law*, Oxford University Press, 2021.

[37] Dennis Rosenbaum, "Police Research: Merging the Policy and Action Research Traditions", in *Police Practice and Research*, 2010, vol. 11, no. 2, p. 144.

research topic, and discuss underlying factors that may contribute to implementation challenges and suboptimal outcomes.[38]

Another barrier to collaborative partnerships is accessibility and applicability of the research findings. Researchers often use academic language to deliver their results and publish in academic journals rather than in publications accessible to police audiences.[39] A survey of researchers who successfully collaborated with police partners found that 100 per cent of the partnerships led to academic publications while only 10 per cent reported making their findings accessible to the law enforcement community, such as through trade magazines or conferences. Over half the participants did not know the impact of their findings on police agencies or they thought their findings had no impact.[40] From the law enforcement perspective, surveys reveal that officers predominantly get their information from their own agencies, and to a lesser extent from trade magazines and organizations.[41] Other findings show that while officers often respect research, it is of little value if they cannot use the findings in practice, which highlights the need to make research 'digestible'. Researchers noted that collaborative projects need to show how research findings can be applied in the field, are cost-effective, and will have beneficial outcomes.[42]

Researchers might also overcome these barriers by working to identify effective techniques rather than focusing only on ineffective practices. Translational research can provide a useful model for interrogations as well as other topics in legal psychology. Common in the medical field, translational research focuses on moving research from basic to applied settings. It encompasses theoretically grounded basic research that progresses towards evaluation in the field.[43] When research is ready for field testing, academics should translate abstract research findings into practical strategies and engage in ongoing two-way knowledge exchanges with practitioners to disseminate findings and implement new practices.[44]

In addition, researchers should collaborate with all levels of command to foster successful relationships. They might focus particularly on the officers or investigators directly involved in the research process and those central to

---

[38] Serpa and Wellford, 2007, see *supra* note 34.

[39] Alpert, Rojek and Hansen, 2013, see *supra* note 30.

[40] Greico, Vovak and Lum, 2014, see *supra* note 29.

[41] Lum, Telep, Koper and Grieco, 2012, see *supra* note 30; Cody Telep and Cynthia Lum, "The Receptivity of Officers to Empirical Research and Evidence-Based Policing: An Examination of Survey Data from Three Agencies", in *Police Quarterly*, 2014, vol. 17, no. 4, p. 359.

[42] Lum, Telep, Koper and Grieco, 2012, see *supra* note 30.

[43] Bornstein and Meissner, 2021, see *supra* note 36.

[44] Alpert, Rojek and Hansen, 2013, see *supra* note 30.

implementing the findings.[45] Respondents in one study emphasized the importance of spending time and building rapport with personnel directly involved in the project, which included conveying intent to maintain the partnership long-term.[46] In another project, police and researchers suggested that to establish successful partnerships with law enforcement, researchers should make clear their desire to help agencies address problems or improve practices rather than serving their own research interests. They also suggested researchers reassure their police partners that they would remain objective.[47]

Finally, respecting law enforcement experience is key to forming and maintaining collaborative relationships. Partnerships are strengthened when researchers display curiosity, take the time to understand why police use current techniques, and consider practical and logistical issues when implementing projects and making recommendations.[48] One study found that both police and researcher participants stressed the importance of valuing police knowledge and incorporating that knowledge into the project.[49] Findings from another study suggested that allowing police partners the opportunity to contribute their specialized knowledge will likely increase their investment and co-operation in the project.[50] Similarly, it is important to heed the advice of police experts when discussing factors that might influence study outcomes while keeping in mind the many police experiences, situations, and practices that science has yet to study systematically. Forming good working relationships with police practitioners requires researchers to actively work at gaining trust and fostering mutual respect. This involves not just extolling the value of research but listening to the needs and practical concerns of law enforcement partners while displaying patience, empathy, and appreciation of current police practices without judgment.[51]

The work of the High-Value Detainee Interrogation Group ('HIG') exemplifies the successful transition of interrogation research into police practice. Relationship building and collaboration were embedded into the mission of the HIG from its inception in 2009. The HIG is a joint US government entity that

---

[45] *Ibid.*; Greico, Vovak and Lum, 2014, see *supra* note 29; Christian Meissner, Maria Hartwig and Melissa Russano, "The Need for a Positive Psychological Approach and Collaborative Effort for Improving Practice in the Interrogation Room", in *Law and Human Behavior*, 2010, vol. 34, no. 1, p. 43.

[46] Greico, Vovak and Lum, 2014, see *supra* note 29.

[47] Alpert, Rojek and Hansen, 2013, see *supra* note 30.

[48] *Ibid.*; Serpa and Wellford, 2007, see *supra* note 34.

[49] Alpert, Rojek and Hansen, 2013, see *supra* note 30.

[50] Lum, Telep, Koper and Greico, 2012, see *supra* note 30.

[51] Bornstein and Meissner, 2021, see *supra* note 36. See also Serpa and Wellford, 2007, *supra* note 34.

seeks to obtain reliable intelligence using science-based interrogation methods. The HIG's research program focuses on identifying effective interrogation techniques and transitioning those techniques to the field.[52] By facilitating researcher-practitioner partnerships, the HIG makes it easier for researchers to connect with law enforcement and military stakeholders and increases the legitimacy of their projects. The HIG produces research that is accessible and applicable to law enforcement (and military) and offers practical alternatives to traditional interrogation methods.

To field test the effectiveness of several non-coercive interviewing techniques studied in HIG-funded laboratory research, the HIG sought collaborative partnerships with FLETC and other US government training entities. These research efforts involved teaching instructors to use new techniques, creating training, and comparing the new training to existing training.[53] As of 2019, the HIG had produced nearly two hundred peer-review publications.[54] In addition, HIG-sponsored researchers presented their findings at conferences and held training and train-the-trainer classes for stakeholders and end-users. The prominence of these efforts along with researcher outreach at conferences was largely how FLETC became interested in updating their investigative interviewing curriculum to reflect the latest empirical evidence.

11.4. FLETC's Transition to Research-Based Interview Training

In March 2010, a FLETC interview course instructor attended the fourth International Congress on Psychology and Law, held in conjunction with the 2010 Annual Meeting of the American Psychology-Law Society. At this conference, several researchers presented findings on topics such as detecting deception, credibility assessment, and false confessions. These findings indicated that several techniques taught in the FSSI were ineffective or harmful to investigations. These presentations also proposed novel approaches to suspect interviews that FLETC did not teach. The instructor returned to FLETC and recommended to management that FLETC host a psychology consortium. The purpose of the consortium was to: (i) help FLETC, along with the agencies that send their agents to FLETC training (for example, Customs and Border Protection, Secret Service) understand emerging research on interviewing and interrogations; (ii)

---

[52] Susan E. Brandon *et al.*, "The High-Value Detainee Interrogation Group (HIG): Inception, Evolution, and Impact", in Mark A. Staal and Sally C. Harvey (eds.), *Operational Psychology: A New Field to Support National Security and Public Safety*, ABC-CLIO, 2019, pp. 263–285.

[53] Christian Meissner, Frances Surmon-Böhr, Simon Oleszkiewicz and Laurence Alison, "Developing an Evidence-Based Perspective on Interrogation: A Review of the U.S. Government's High-Value Detainee Interrogation Group Research Program", in *Psychology, Public Policy, and Law*, 2017, vol. 23, no. 4, p. 438.

[54] Brandon *et al.*, 2019, see *supra* note 52.

foster opportunity for FLETC staff to work with researchers to incorporate new and relevant material into the FLETC basic or advanced training curricula; and (iii), explore ways for FLETC to collaborate with researchers and their universities to further this type of research.

FLETC held their first Bi-Annual Psychology Consortium in August 2011. One goal of this consortium was to introduce deception detection techniques associated with cognitive load theory. Rather than focus on stress-based nonverbal indicators, researchers proposed the use of cognitive load techniques to maximize the chances of accurately detecting lies. Cognitive load techniques included describing events in reverse order, maintaining eye contact, and asking unanticipated questions.[55] Research at the time suggested the accuracy rate of traditional arousal-based approaches to detecting deception were little better than chance (54 per cent),[56] whereas the cognitive load approaches tended to show accuracy rates around 70 per cent.[57] The presentations also summarized meta-analyses that identified effective information elicitation approaches, interrogation techniques, and credibility assessment methods.[58] These presentations prompted a major step forward in improving investigative interviewing training at FLETC. For instance, instructors heard firsthand how relatively straightforward the cognitive load techniques were to implement. After hearing researchers discuss the techniques, instructors could easily explain to trainees how to use the techniques and why they tended to work.

As a result of the 2011 consortium, instructor interest in interrogation research increased. In September 2012, a group of researchers visited FLETC and presented recent findings on topics related to the cognitive interview ('CI') and social persuasion interrogation approaches. The CI is a systematic witness interviewing approach aimed at improving information elicitation.[59] It focuses on using guided memory retrieval techniques in an environment that enables communication of the memories retrieved. In a meta-analysis, the CI elicited significantly more correct details with only a small increase in erroneous details compared to control interviews.[60]

The methodology used in CI research often consisted of showing college students videos of criminal activity and interviewing them using the CI or a comparison technique. Data consistently demonstrated the CI's effectiveness,

---

[55] Vrij, Granhag and Porter, 2010, see *supra* note 16.

[56] Bond and DePaulo, 2003, see *supra* note 15.

[57] Aldert Vrij, "Interviewing to Detect Deception", in *European Psychologist,* 2014, vol. 19, no. 3, p. 184.

[58] Meissner *et al.*, 2014, see *supra* note 18.

[59] Fisher and Geiselman, 1992, see *supra* note 11.

[60] Memon, Meissner and Fraser, 2010, see *supra* note 11.

thus, researchers sought to test the CI in more realistic environments with law enforcement as interviewers. As a result, FLETC partnered with several researchers to compare the effectiveness of the FSSI to the CI using FLETC instructors as interviewers and training staff as interviewees who witnessed a live simulated event. In preparation for the study, instructors underwent intensive CI training. Results showed that the CI elicited approximately 80 per cent more relevant information than did the FSSI.[61] By participating in the study, instructors conducted the CI, applied the technique, experienced the resulting benefits, and gained insights to effectively deliver CI training. FLETC incorporated CI techniques into training and their focus started to shift from instructing trainees to spot verbal and non-verbal indicators of deception to teaching methods aimed at eliciting more information.

Another topic discussed during the 2012 visit was the use of Neurolinguistic Programming ('NLP') to elicit information and detect deception. NLP was a popular communication approach that purported the existence of a preferred representational system (one of the five senses) and claimed a relationship existed between eye movement and deception. Researchers shared with FLETC staff the fallacies surrounding NLP theory. They explained why the theories associated with NLP and stress-based lie-detection techniques were flawed and shared research that supported using techniques such as active listening and mirroring and/or matching suspect behaviours.[62] As a result, FLETC instructors removed interviewing methods consistent with NLP theories from the interviewing curriculum.

In 2013, FLETC partnered with researchers to conduct a study comparing the Strategic Use of Evidence ('SUE') technique to other interview/questioning techniques. The SUE technique is designed to improve interviewer veracity judgments by strategically asking questions about obtained evidence. The SUE technique elicits verbal responses based on the assumption that liars and truth tellers employ different strategies to convince investigators of their innocence. Results of the FLETC study showed that instructors trained in SUE asked questions and disclosed evidence in a strategic manner and were significantly more accurate at judging suspect guilt and innocence compared to untrained

---

[61] Jillian Rivard, Ronald Fisher, Belinda Robertson and Dana Hirn Mueller, "Testing the Cognitive Interview With Professional Interviewers: Enhancing Recall of Specific Details of Recurring Events", in *Applied Cognitive Psychology*, 2014, vol. 28, no. 6, p. 917.

[62] Sujeeta Bhatt and Susan Brandon, "Neurolinguistic Programming (NLP) in Investigative Interviewing: Recommended Alternative Methods", in *Investigative Interviewing: Research and Practice*, 2015, vol. 7, no. 2, pp. 51–62.

participants.[63] Based on the findings and firsthand knowledge of the technique, instructors added the SUE technique to the interviewing curriculum.

Instructors also learned about new interview training practices at the annual HIG Research Symposiums. During these symposiums, researchers present empirical findings to practitioners and stakeholders from law enforcement, the military, and other government agencies. FLETC instructors heard presentations relevant to their instruction on rapport such as the seven principles of persuasion[64] and the psychology of procedural justice.[65] Results revealed that (i) interrogators perceive fair treatment of suspects as essential to their authoritative legitimacy (procedural justice), (ii) liking and reciprocity (persuasion) were closely linked to rapport and relationship building, and (iii) social influence strategies such as rapport, principles of procedural justice and reciprocity increased information disclosure.[66] Following this, FLETC added to training the principles of persuasion along with the psychology of procedural justice to help trainees develop a mindset of social influencing behaviour.

Additional HIG symposium presentations strengthened FLETC's training on rapport and rapport-based interviewing techniques. Researchers described rapport as a smooth and positive interpersonal interaction that increased information gain, improved trust, and produced more co-operation along with faster agreement in negotiations.[67] They illustrated the importance of rapport and described concrete tactics that instructors could incorporate into training. Other researchers expanded upon these tactics by incorporating principles of motivational interviewing ('MI') and interpersonal circle theory to create Observing

---

63   Timothy Luke *et al.*, "Training in the Strategic Use of Evidence Technique: Improving Deception Detection Accuracy of American Law Enforcement Officers", in *Journal of Police and Criminal Psychology*, 2016, vol. 31, no. 4, p. 270.

64   Robert B. Cialdini and Noah J. Goldstein, "Social Influence: Compliance and Conformity", in *Annual Review of Psychology*, 2005, vol. 55, pp. 591–621.

65   Tom Tyler, Phillip Goff and Robert MacCoun, "The Impact of Psychological Science on Policing in the United States: Procedural Justice, Legitimacy, and Effective Law Enforcement", in *Psychological Science in the Public Interest*, 2015, vol. 16, no. 3, p. 75.

66   Jane Goodman-Delahunty and Loene M. Howes, "Social Persuasion to Develop Rapport in High-Stakes Interviews: Qualitative Analyses of Asian-Pacific Practices", in *Policing and Society*, 2016, vol. 26, no. 3, pp. 270–290; Jane Goodman-Delahunty, Natalie Martschuk and Mandeep K. Dhami, "Interviewing High Value Detainees: Securing Cooperation and Disclosures", in *Applied Cognitive Psychology*, 2014, vol. 28, no. 6, pp. 883–897; Jane Goodman-Delahunty, Kate O'Brien and Thea Gumbert-Jourjon, "Police Professionalism in Interviews With High Value Detainees: Cross-Cultural Endorsement of Procedural Justice", in *Journal of the Institute of Justice and International Studies*, 2013, vol. 13, p. 65.

67   Allison Abbe and Susan E. Brandon, "The Role of Rapport in Investigative Interviewing: A Review", in *Journal of Investigative Psychology and Offender Profiling*, 2013, vol. 10, no. 3, pp. 237–249.

Rapport-Based Interpersonal Techniques ('ORBIT'), a research tool initially used to study the impact of rapport-based interview techniques on information elicitation.[68] The MI is a directive, client-centred counselling style that helps clients resolve ambivalence and change behaviour. The interpersonal circle theory maps adaptive interview behaviours (responses that lead to a positive outcome) and maladaptive interview behaviours (responses that lead to negative outcome) to promote interpersonal competence and versatility.[69] Results of the ORBIT study suggested that adapting rapport-based styles of interviewing were more productive than coercive, confrontational styles. Findings from the research on rapport and social influence strategies offered a framework that instructors used to develop curriculum with concrete rapport building and social interactions skills.

The research collaborations that started in 2010 evolved into long-term relationships that continue today. These partnerships afford instructors the opportunity to raise concerns about implementing research-based techniques, such as building rapport when time is limited, providing suspects with the illusion of control during interviews, fostering information elicitation rather than forcing admissions and confessions, and decreasing reliance on nervous behaviours to detect deception. Instructors contact researchers to discuss new techniques or obtain clarification about research findings, methods of instruction, and practical application in the field. Interactions with researchers help instructors make informed decisions about existing training content (for example, NLP, microfacial expressions to detect deception) and identify emerging empirical evidence that supports new techniques (for example, CI, SUE, cognitive load).

11.5. Current Research-Based Training

As discussed above, instructors added several techniques to their suspect interview training, removed techniques, and filled gaps in training. Table 2 below lists the concepts and techniques removed from and added to FLETC's suspect interview training.

---

[68] Laurence J. Alison *et al.*, "Why Tough Tactics Fail and Rapport Gets Results: Observing Rapport-Based Interpersonal Techniques (ORBIT) to Generate Useful Information from Terrorists", in *Psychology, Public Policy, and Law*, 2013, vol. 19, no. 4, p. 411.

[69] Alison *et al.*, 2013, see *supra* note 68; William Miller and Stephen Rollnick, *Motivational Interviewing: Helping People Change*, Guilford Press, 2012.

Removed from FLETC's FSSI	Added to FLETC's Current Research-based Training
Rapport-building techniques: Non-definitive rapport building methods	Rapport-Relationship Building: ORBIT, principles of persuasion, principles of procedural justice
Questioning: Open-ended to specific, goal to observe verbal and non-verbal behaviour	Questioning: CI techniques, open-ended to specific, goal to gather information
Deception Detection: Verbal and non-verbal behavioural cues, BAI	Deception Detection: Cognitive load theory
Monologue: Block suspect communication, confrontational	Dialogue: Encourage communication, non-confrontational
Evidence Disclosure: Early, factual presentation	Evidence Disclosure: Late, SUE
Confession-Based: Use of themes such as rationalization, projection, minimalization	Rapport-Based: Motivational interviewing
Assumption of Guilt: Choice and assumptive questions	Neutrality: Non-judgmental

Table 2: Training content removed from the FSSI and content added to current FLETC suspect interview training.

While not easy, FLETC changed lesson plan development from a professional or experienced-based model reliant on industry standards, to a research-based model. Discovering new research in suspect interviewing made apparent the gaps in traditional methods. For example, the factual evidence presentation method discussed in the FSSI lacked clear and distinct strategies. The SUE technique, on the other hand, described clear strategies along with empirical evidence to support effectiveness. Similarly, traditional interview methods emphasized the importance of rapport, but without offering concrete strategies. More importantly, the contradicting message of developing rapport while using confrontational tactics was perplexing to both trainees and instructors who also struggled to maintain credibility. Researchers provided a roadmap for instructors to deliver worthwhile and effective rapport building techniques. Due, in part, to the relationships instructors formed with researchers, along with access to empirical findings, the techniques not supported by research were removed from the FSSI and replaced with effective research-based techniques. The benefit of this change is illustrated in the feedback FLETC regularly receives from former trainees who attribute their investigative successes to the techniques learned in FLETC's interview training.

11.5.1. Beyond Interview Training

Because of the successful collaborations between FLETC's interview instructors and outside researchers, FLETC implemented an initiative to develop research-based curricula across all their training subject matter. As part of this effort, instructors review lesson plans and seek out academic publications or other science-based documentation that reinforces current content or introduces promising new techniques, procedures and technology. They strive to balance knowledge gained through experience with empirical evidence and increasingly approach researchers with possible research questions. Also, the success of the research-based suspect interviewing curriculum prompted the development of a new law enforcement first responder communication training course and a communication model that incorporates rapport-based interpersonal skills, self-monitoring, procedural justice, and principles of persuasion. This model supplies first responder trainees with foundational skills to de-escalate situations, promote compliance and co-operation, and engage in productive problem solving with community members.

The shared goal of delivering to investigator trainees the best and most effective training promoted a collaborative effort between researchers and FLETC instructors. However, it took time to transition away from traditional interviewing methods widely accepted and viewed as effective across the law enforcement profession for over forty years. Since March 2010, when one FLETC instructor attended a psychology conference and had the idea to hold FLETC Bi-annual Psychology Consortiums, researchers and FLETC have maintained an exceptional collaborative relationship. FLETC's basic and advanced interviewing curriculums for investigators now incorporates research-based methods grounded in cognitive and social science. The continued communication with researchers allows instructors to obtain detailed information about ongoing, trending interview research. This, in turn, gives researchers the opportunity to frame research questions with insight into practical considerations. These relationships leave open the opportunity for more research that tests theories and validates suspect interview methods in training and applied settings.

12

Structured Models of Interviewing

John Halley, Dave Walsh, Trond Myklebust and Ole Thomas Bjerknes[*]

12.1. Introduction

Interview models differ around the world but the underlying principles are very similar.[1] These basic principles in communication are found in nearly all textbooks on the theory and practice of psychology and rhetoric, advising a phased interview beginning with rapport-building and ending with closure.[2]

In the United Kingdom ('UK'), there are two models of structured interviewing used by police forces. The PEACE model, used in England and Wales, is applied in adapted versions and used as an overarching model in the training of investigative interviewers in several countries such as Australia, New Zealand, the Nordic countries[3] (Denmark, Finland, Iceland, Norway and Sweden) and in parts of Canada. The second model is the PRICE model, used by the police in Scotland. The PRICE model has been said to be very similar to the PEACE model;[4] however, this statement is difficult to assess objectively since no written formulation of the PRICE model exists.

---

[*] **John Halley** is an advocate, a part-time sheriff (a judge with wide civil and criminal jurisdiction) and an experienced high court prosecutor (Advocate Depute, 2003–2010) in Scotland. **Dave Walsh**, Ph.D., is Professor in Criminal Investigation at Leicester De Montfort Law School, De Montfort University. **Trond Myklebust**, Ph.D., holds the position as Assistant Chief of Police and Programme Leader of the Master's in Investigation at the Norwegian Police University College. **Ole Thomas Bjerknes** is Detective Chief Superintendent and Senior Lecturer in Investigation at the Norwegian Police University College.

[1] David Walsh, Gavin Oxburgh, Allison Redlich and Trond Myklebust (eds.), *International Developments and Practices in Investigative Interviewing and Interrogation, Volume 1: Victims and Witnesses*, Routledge, London, 2015 ('Walsh, Oxburgh, Redlich and Myklebust (eds.), vol. 1'); *id.*, *International Developments and Practices in Investigative Interviewing and Interrogation, Volume 2: Suspects*, Routledge, London, 2015.

[2] See Chapter 18 of this book for further details.

[3] Ivar A. Fahsing and Asbjørn Rachlew, "Investigative Interviewing in the Nordic Region", in Tom Williamson, Rebecca Milne and Stephen Savage (eds.), *International Developments in Investigative Interviewing*, Willan Publishing, London, 2009.

[4] See, for examples, Annabel Nicol *et al.*, "Contemporary Developments and Practices in Investigative Interviewing of Witnesses and Victims in Scotland", in Walsh, Oxburgh, Redlich and Myklebust (eds.), vol. 1, see *supra* note 1; Rebecca Milne *et al.*, "The Cognitive Interview:

12.2. The PEACE Model of Interviewing in England and Wales

12.2.1. Introduction and Historical Development of PEACE

The development of the PEACE model is inextricably linked with the Police and Criminal Evidence Act ('PACE Act') 1984 (see Section 12.2.5. below) which was introduced in response to a growing perception that the public had lost confidence in the criminal justice system.[5] The media response to a 'group of sensational cases'[6] highlighted unacceptable police behaviour and revealed the existence of serious miscarriages of justice in criminal, principally terrorist, trials that took place during the 1970s.[7] High profile cases[8] involved suspects of the Irish Republican Army terrorist attacks whose convictions were largely based on forced confessions made under police interrogation and unreliable forensic evidence.[9] These cases were subsequently declared to be miscarriages of justice and all convictions were quashed.[10] It was clear that the public strongly believed that suspects had been tortured by the police,[11] that the perpetrators were still at large and that the public remained in fear of further terrorist attacks.[12] Other prominent cases, such as *R v. Lattimore et al.*, raised similar issues about confessions alleged to have been extracted by oppressive behaviour and violence during police interviews with suspects.

Applying Cognitive Principles", in Jason J. Dickinson *et al.* (eds.), *Evidence-Based Investigative Interviewing: Applying Cognitive Principles*, Routledge, New York, 2019, pp. 57–58.

[5] Clive Walker and Keir Starmer, *Miscarriages of Justice: A Review of Justice in Error*, Oxford University Press, 2004, p. 39; Michael Zander, "PACE (The Police and Criminal Evidence) Act 1984: Past, Present and Future", in *National Law School of India Review*, 2011, vol. 23, no. 1, pp. 47–62.

[6] Richard Buxton, "Miscarriages of Justice and the Court of Appeal", in *Law Quarterly Review*, 1993, vol. 109, no. 66, p. 66.

[7] *Ibid.*

[8] See the cases of the '*Birmingham Six*', '*Guildford Four*' and Judith Ward.

[9] Iann H. Dennis, "Miscarriages of Justice and the Law of Confessions: Evidentiary Issues and Solutions", in *Public Law*, 1993, no. 291.

[10] UK, Court of Appeals (Criminal Division), *R v. McIlkenny et al.*, Judgement, 27 March 1991, 93 Crim. App. R. 287; *R v. Richardson et al.*, Judgement, 19 October 1989, [1989] 10 WLUK 234; and *R v. Judith Ward*, Judgement, 4 June 1992, [1993] 1 WLR 619 ('*R v. Judith Ward*') (https://www.legal-tools.org/doc/nekxxi/). For an excellent narrative summary of the background to the introduction of the PACE Act, see LawTeacher, "Police and Criminal Evidence Act 1984" (available on the LawTeacher's web site).

[11] Dennis, 1993, p. 296, see *supra* note 9.

[12] Royal Commission on Criminal Justice, *Report of the Royal Commission on Criminal Justice*, His Majesty's Stationery Office ('HMSO'), 1991, 1991 Cm 2263, p. 6–7.

12.2.2. *R v. Lattimore et al.* (1972–1975)

Colin Lattimore, aged 18 years, Ronnie Leighton, aged 15 years, and Ahmet Salih, aged 14 years, were arrested in 1972 in a police murder investigation in London. Each made confessions in relation to the murder of the victim, Maxwell Confait, and each had been questioned by detectives with no adult present, no support and without a solicitor. Each subsequently signed a confession in the presence of a parent. At trial, in November 1972, they were variously convicted of manslaughter, murder and arson, and detained. In July 1973, the Court of Appeal refused their applications for leave to appeal; however, in June 1975, following political pressure, the then Home Secretary referred their cases to the Court of Appeal in exercise of a statutory power to do so.[13] The appeal judges allowed fresh evidence to be heard in relation to, *inter alia*, the time of the deceased's death and concluded that the essential admissions could not have been factually true. The accused had each insisted in their evidence at trial that admissions previously made by them were obtained through police violence or the threat of violence. These confessions included explicit details about a fatal assault on the deceased with a ligature and the appeal judges concluded that the substance of the confessions could not be true when tested against the medical evidence as to the deceased's time of death. The convictions were subsequently quashed on 17 October 1975 and resulting concerns about police conduct led to a public inquiry chaired by Sir Henry Fisher.

12.2.3. The Fisher Report (1977)

The Fisher Inquiry was commissioned to consider the circumstances leading to the trial of the three accused, Lattimore, Leighton and Salih. The Inquiry's Report was published on 13 December 1977[14] in which it rejected the allegations that the accused had each been subjected to, and threatened with, violence by the police.[15] However, the Inquiry made specific findings in relation to the lack

---

[13] UK, Court of Appeals (Criminal Division), *R v. Lattimore et al.*, Judgement, 17 October 1975, [1975] 10 WLUK 54 (https://www.legal-tools.org/doc/fn0ry1/).

[14] Charles H. Fisher, "Report of an Inquiry by the Hon. Sir Henry Fisher into the Circumstances Leading to the Trial of Three Persons on Charges Arising Out of the Death of Maxwell Confait and the Fire at 27 Doggett Road, London SE6", HMSO, December 1977, London (https://www.legal-tools.org/doc/j80u5c/).

[15] Fisher, 1977, see *supra* note 14, Part 1, Chapter 2:
FINDINGS:
2.1 On 24 April 1972, during separate interviews with DCS Jones (who was in charge of the investigation), Colin Lattimore and Ronald Leighton confessed to having taken part in the killing of Maxwell Confait, and Ahmet Salih confessed to having been present. All three boys confessed to having taken part in the arson at 27 Doggett Road. Later in the evening of 24 April and during the early hours of 25 April, each of the boys repeated his

of general knowledge among police officers and the legal profession about the Judges' Rules and Home Office Directions[16] which were then applicable to the conduct of police investigations and interviews with suspects.[17] In addition, the Fisher Report recommended:

> Revision of the law concerning interrogation could appropriately be considered as part of a general review of the balance between police effectiveness and individual rights aimed at the rationalisation and codification of criminal procedure [...].[18]

The Fisher Report also suggested other important safeguards that might be considered and put in place in relation to police interrogations of suspects including tape recording of interviews.[19] The Report's author, conscious of the difficulties involved in addressing systemic issues in an Inquiry focused on a single case, suggested that such matters might be considered in a systemic review in the context of a Royal Commission.[20]

12.2.4. Royal Commission on Criminal Procedure (1977–1981)

The Royal Commission on Criminal Procedure ('RCCP')[21] was duly established in 1977 to consider proposals and arrangements for safeguards in the conduct of

---

confession in a written statement made in the presence of one of his parents, and in the case of Salih in the presence also of an interpreter. Lattimore's father and Leighton's mother signed statements expressing satisfaction with the way in which the statements were taken.

2.2 In their evidence at the trial all three boys alleged on oath that they had been physically assaulted by a police officer. These allegations were repeated in evidence before me by Salih and by Lattimore. I find that the allegations were untrue. Mr Blom-Cooper, who appeared for the three boys at my Inquiry, did not invite me to accept them.

2.3 I find that no police officer deliberately falsified the record of oral answers given by the three boys to questions. The police officers tried to record as accurately as possible the questions and the answers given, and the written statements made by the boys. The records are substantially accurate in all relevant respects. Mr Blom-Cooper made it clear that, while not accepting the accuracy of the record, he did not allege fabrication in the sense of "a deliberately wicked concoction of a written record which was a travesty of what [the boys] said in the questions and answers [and] in their statements.".

16 *Ibid.*, Chapter 2; reference is made to the contents of the Judges' Rules and Home Office Directions.

17 *Ibid.*, Part 1, Chapter 2, para. 2.17:

> In the first place, some of the Rules and Directions do not seem to be known to police officers and members of the legal profession.

18 *Ibid.*, Part 1, Chapter 2, para. 2.16.

19 *Ibid.*, Part 1, Chapter 2, para. 2.24.

20 *Ibid.*, Part 1, Chapter 1, para. 1.8.

21 Royal Commission on Criminal Procedure, *Report of the Royal Commission on Criminal Procedure*, HMSO, 1981, 1981 Cmnd 8092.

---

police investigations and gathering evidence in criminal cases. The RCCP observed, examined and considered police practices during criminal investigations[22] and its recommendations were based on 12 separate research reports focusing on police station and investigation procedures and the prosecution process in general. The RCCP stated that "the issues being formulated should be the concern not only of lawyers or police officers, but of every citizen".[23] Proposals for reform were predicated on three fundamental concepts: (i) the concept of reasonable suspicion; (ii) the regulation of any use of force by the police; and (iii) the regulation of police behaviour in relation to gathering evidence.[24] RCCP researchers observed techniques used by police during interviews when questioning suspects[25] and interviewing behaviour was observed which appeared to

---

[22] Royal Commission on Criminal Procedure, "Royal Commission on Criminal Procedure (Philips Commission): Records", National Archives:

The Royal Commission on Criminal Procedure was established by Royal Warrant of 3 February 1978 under the chairmanship of Professor Sir Cyril Philips. Its terms of reference were to examine, having regard both to the interests of the community in bringing offenders to justice and to the rights and liberties of persons suspected or accused of crime, and taking into account also the need for the efficient and economical use of resources, whether changes are needed in England and Wales in:

- the powers and duties of the police in respect of the investigation of criminal offences and the rights and duties of suspect and accused persons, including the means by which these are secured;
- the process of and responsibility for the prosecution of criminal offences;
- other features of criminal procedure and evidence as relate to the above;
- and to make recommendations.

The commission held 50 full meetings, the first on 15 February 1978 and in addition set up three sub-committees - the Research Committee which engaged in the preliminary formulation of a research programme, a Law and Procedure Committee which prepared the supplementary volume of the Report describing existing arrangements, and a Drafting Committee which prepared drafts of the final Report for the approval of the full Commission.

The commission drew on evidence from four main sources, written submissions, oral evidence, visits by the Commission and research. Oral evidence was taken in late 1979 and early 1980 on the basis of a consultative paper in order to test opinion on key issues already identified and proposed changes. Commissioners visited every police force in England and Wales and also many police stations and criminal courts in the United Kingdom and abroad. In addition, they initiated twelve research studies, which were published, and some smaller research projects by Commission staff, the results of which were incorporated in the Report.

[23] *Ibid.*, para. 1.12.

[24] Richard Ward and Amanda Akhtar, *Walker & Walker's English Legal System*, 11th ed., Oxford University Press, 2011, p. 439.

[25] For examples, see Barrie Irving, "Police Interrogation. A Case Study of Current Practice", in *Research Study No. 2*, HMSO, London, 1980; Paul Softley *et al.*, "Police Interrogation: An

---

presume suspects' guilt. During interviews, police often exaggerated the strength of the available evidence or suggested that evidence existed which they did not have. Police officers were also found to be aggressive and accusatory towards suspects, often undermining the suspect's self-esteem. The researchers were driven to conclude that, often, the primary aim of police interviews with suspects was to gain confirmation of their own pre-existing beliefs in the guilt of the suspects concerned.[26] The approaches used often ran a clear risk of eliciting false confessions.

12.2.5. The PACE Act (1984)

The RCCP's recommendations were followed by a new, codified statutory regulation of police investigations and evidence gathering in relation to criminal proceedings in the PACE Act (1984). The PACE Act, and its associated Codes of Practice, provided a comprehensive procedural code for persons detained by the police as suspects in connection with investigations into alleged criminal offences. The principal intention behind the legislation was to standardize and professionalize police work.[27] The PACE Act's provisions were intended to strike a fair balance between the exercise of power by those in authority and the rights of members of the public. Those rights included: (i) the right to silence; (ii) the right to breaks for rest and refreshment during a suspect's detention; (iii) the right to legal advice before and during interviews; and (iv) a maximum period of detention (normally 24 hours) before being charged with an offence or released without charge.

12.2.6. The PACE Act and the PEACE Model of Interviewing

In relation to regulating police behaviour, the most important element of the PACE Act was a comprehensive guideline, provided in the Codes of Practice, which detail the minimum standards required to determine that evidence has been fairly obtained.[28] PACE Code C regulates the treatment of detained persons during police interviews whereas CODE E introduces the requirement for suspect interviews to be recorded. These requirements are important because the investigative process is rendered more transparent and objectively fairer. Crucially, a requirement is that there must be an accurate record of the interview[29]

Observational Study in Four Police Stations", in *Home Office Research Study No. 61*, HMSO, London, 1980.

[26] *Ibid.*

[27] Zander, 2011, p. 6, see *supra* note 5.

[28] *R v. Judith Ward*, see *supra* note 10.

[29] UK Home Office, *Police and Criminal Evidence Act 1984 (PACE): CODE C Revised Code of Practice for the Detention, Treatment and Questioning of Persons by Police Officers*, HMSO, London, August 2019, Section 11.7 ('PACE Code C') (https://www.legal-

---

which the suspect must be given the opportunity to review.[30] Two copies of the recording are required,[31] one of which must be sealed immediately after the interview in the presence of the interviewee.[32] Following the enactment of the PACE Act on 1 January 1986, the Home Office – the UK government department with responsibility for policing in England and Wales – commissioned and subsequently published, unique and ground-breaking research which provided objective information about what actually took place in police interviews with suspects.[33]

Practice was required to catch up with the ethical balance which the PACE Act was intended to establish between thorough, professional and fair investigation and prosecution of crime and the legitimate rights of citizens in a democratic society. High profile and sensitive cases demonstrated continuing difficulties for justice because of the pursuit of confessions by the police during suspect interviews. One example was the acquittal of George Heron, in 1993, after a trial for the murder of a seven-year-old girl, Nikki Allan, who had been stabbed 36 times.[34] Having heard the legal argument, the trial judge excluded from evidence heard by the jury the contents of eight (of twelve) police interview tapes. The judge concluded, as a matter of law, that the excluded tapes were inadmissible as evidence at trial on account of (i) oppressive behaviour and questioning, and (ii) misleading statements by the interviewers in relation to the state of the evidence against Heron. One of the excluded tapes allegedly contained an admission by Heron that he had killed the child. In the absence of the full evidence of the exchanges between police interviewers and Heron, the jury acquitted after

---

tools.org/doc/1ld1rc/); UK, Court of Appeals (Criminal Division), *R v. Barry*, Judgement, 5 December 1991, (1991) Cr. App. R. 384 (https://www.legal-tools.org/doc/08bb6p/).

[30] PACE Code C, Section 11.11, see *supra* note 29; UK, Court of Appeals (Criminal Division), *R v. Doolan*, Judgement, 1988, [1988] Crim LR 747.

[31] UK Home Office, *Police and Criminal Evidence Act 1984 (PACE): CODE E Revised Code of Practice on Audio Recording Interviews With Suspects*, HMSO, London, July 2018, para. 2.2 (https://www.legal-tools.org/doc/4hkowb/).

[32] *Ibid.*; see narrative summary from LawTeacher, see *supra* note 10.

[33] John Baldwin, "Police Interview Techniques: Establishing Truth or Proof?", in *British Journal of Criminology*, vol. 33, no. 3, 1993, pp. 325–352.

[34] Malcolm Pithers, "Uproar after Acquittal in Nikki Allen Murder Case: Not Guilty Verdict Ends Six-Week Trial in which Judge Refused to Admit Alleged Confession on Interview Tape as Evidence", *The Independent*, 22 November 1993 (available on its web site):

> Yesterday's verdict was not totally unexpected. There had been a long legal debate between defence and prosecution counsel and Mr Justice Mitchell, without the jury present, over the admissibility of the transcripts of police interviews with Mr Heron. The judge had allowed 4 of 12 tape recordings to be heard by the jury. One of the tapes that the jury did not hear included an alleged admission by Mr Heron that he carried out the killing, and the judge had referred to this admission during the case.

---

a six-week trial. In addition, a number of convictions which had been secured on the basis of interview evidence elicited prior to PACE being in force were subsequently quashed in light of fresh expert evidence allowed to be led in the Court of Appeal.[35]

Another recurrent issue was the apparent inability of police interviewers to effectively identify and recognize the vulnerabilities of suspects at interview, such as age, mental health or learning disability. A series of such difficulties led to the formation of the working group of senior police officers, initially established in 1991, and whose purpose was to develop interviewing training for detectives.[36] In due course, in 1992, the working party recommended the PEACE model (or approach) to investigative interviewing. All police interviewers in England and Wales were subsequently required to attend training courses and follow guidance issued in accordance with the new interviewing model. The new PEACE model was the tool or technique produced to bring about a change of focus for police interviewers: the focus was no longer to be on the pursuit of confessions; the focus in future was to be on investigative interviewing. Crucially, the driver for the PEACE model was its foundation in evidence-based research. It was recommended by the working group and has since been an influential driver in the development of structured, evidence-based and skilled investigative interviewing by police forces in England and Wales and in several other countries.[37] The PEACE framework is underpinned by its structured approach and method to elicit a detailed and accurate account from interviewees who are enabled to provide their own account of events. In these fundamental respects, the PEACE model can properly be said not to be confession-driven. It is also used as a framework for interviews with victims and witnesses.[38]

12.2.7. The PEACE Model of Interviewing

There are two fundamental aspects of the PEACE model: (i) to obtain accurate and reliable information from suspects, witnesses or victims in order to establish the truth about the matter under investigation; and (ii) interviews were to be

---

[35] Gisli Gudjonsson, *The Psychology of False Confessions: Forty Years of Science and Practice*, Wiley, Chichester, 2018.

[36] For more information, see Ray Bull, "PEACE-Full Interviewing/Interrogations: What Research Can Tell Us", in SHIGEMASU Kazuo, KUWANO Sonoko, SATO Takao and MATSUZAWA Tetsuro (eds.), *Diversity in Harmony – Insights from Psychology: Proceedings of the 31st International Congress of Psychology*, Wiley-Blackwell, 2018.

[37] Such as Australia, New Zealand, Canada, Norway and Eire; see Walsh, Oxburgh, Redlich and Myklebust (eds.), vol. 1, see *supra* note 1.

[38] Walsh, Oxburgh, Redlich and Myklebust (eds.), vol. 1, see *supra* note 1; College of Policing, "Investigative Interviewing", 26 October 2022, Witness Considerations (see the College of Policing's web site).

approached with an open mind, with information elicited from the interviewee tested against other available evidence known or capable of being reasonably established.[39]

PEACE is an acronym for the individual phases to be followed and applied in the investigative interviewing model. There are five phases in the current PEACE framework:[40]

- Planning and preparation;
- Engage and explain;
- Account clarification and challenge;
- Closure; and
- Evaluation.

Each of the five phases is described in detail in the published and freely available information detailed by the College of Policing for England and Wales.[41] The current formulation and conceptual operation of the five phases is specified in the PEACE model detailed below.

12.2.8. The PEACE Aim and Principles in Practice

The overall aim of the PEACE model is to obtain a full and accurate account and the published guidance emphasizes that to achieve this aim, the correct questions must be asked.[42] The published guidance sets out the detailed rationale for principles underlying and approach to the conduct of police investigative interviews with witnesses and suspects.

It emphasizes that public confidence and consistent performance are among the identified benefits of a well-defined, evidence-based and publicly available model for interviewing by the police.[43] The PEACE guidance specifies seven underlying principles which are sought to be maintained by its use, namely, (i) accuracy and reliability of information elicited; (ii) fairness;[44] (iii) investigative mindset having regard to all of the evidence and information

---

[39] PACE Code C, para. 10.4, see *supra* note 29.

[40] College of Policing, 2022, see *supra* note 38; a comprehensive overview of the PEACE model in detail, as it is taught to investigative interviewers, is publicly available.

[41] *Ibid.*

[42] *Ibid.*, Principles and Ethics.

[43] *Ibid.*, Benefits.

[44] *Ibid.*; Principle 2 is concerned with vulnerabilities of witnesses and requires consideration of the applicability of specialist interviewing considerations under UK, Ministry of Justice, *Achieving Best Evidence: Guidance on Interviewing Victims and Witnesses, and Guidance on Using Special Measures*, March 2011; see also UK, Ministry of Justice, *Achieving Best Evidence: Guidance on Interviewing Victims and Witnesses, and Guidance on Using Special Measures*, January 2022.

available;[45] (iv) investigative interviewing must not be oppressive interviewing;[46] (v) benefits of early admission;[47] (vi) persistent but not oppressive interviewing;[48] and (vii) requirement to put questions to suspects in the face of no comment responses.[49] The PEACE model sets out a comprehensive guide to investigative interviewing. Training for police interviewers is overseen, administered and updated by a National Strategic Steering Group on Investigative Interviewing ('NSSGII').[50] Its role is to ensure that the police service adopts a consistent and professional approach which is able to withstand judicial and academic scrutiny and instil public confidence. The overall aim of the NSSGII is to provide direction on the development of policy, practices and procedures to ensure that the interviewing of victims, witnesses and suspects supports professional investigation.

12.2.9. The PEACE Model and Formulation

The PEACE model is detailed for interviewers, and for public interest, in flowchart format for ease of understanding and application.[51] Each of the five phases is explained, with further information provided, as appropriate, in relation to specific issues and circumstances. The free and publicly available detail of the conceptualized PEACE model is set out by the College of Policing for England and Wales ('College of Policing').[52]

---

[45] Further direction is provided in relation to College of Policing, "Investigative and Evidential Evaluation" (available on the College of Policing's web site).
[46] Further guidance is provided with reference to a range of Codes of Practice under the PACE Act, see UK Home Office, "Police and Criminal Evidence Act 1984 (PACE) Codes of Practice", 22 February 2023 (available on UK Government's web site). These cover police powers in relation to stop and search, arrest, detention, investigation, identification, and interviewing detainees.
[47] The benefits for all involved are emphasized, particularly to the accused who can be entitled to up to a one-third reduction in sentence for an early guilty plea (Sentencing Council, "Reduction in Sentence for a Guilty Plea: Definitive Guideline", January 2017).
[48] As to the limits, further guidance is referenced in PACE Code C, paras. 10.9 and 11.5, see *supra* note 29.
[49] Further guidance is provided in relation to specific matters in PACE Code C, paras. 10.10–10.11, see *supra* note 29.
[50] College of Policing, 2022, see *supra* note 38.
[51] *Ibid.*, PEACE Framework.
[52] *Ibid.*

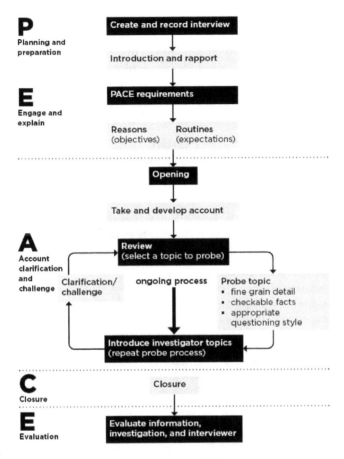

P

Planning and
preparation

E

Engage and
explain

A

Account
clarification
and
challenge

C

Closure

E

Evaluation

Create and record interview

Introduction and rapport

PACE requirements

Reasons   Routines
(objectives)   (expectations)

Opening

Take and develop account

Review
(select a topic to probe)

Clarification/   ongoing process   Probe topic
challenge   ▪ fine grain detail
                                          ▪ checkable facts
                                          ▪ appropriate
                                            questioning style

Introduce investigator topics
(repeat probe process)

Closure

Evaluate information,
investigation, and interviewer

Figure 1: The PEACE framework.[53]

12.2.10. Training and Education for Police Officers in the PEACE Model in England and Wales

The College of Policing has responsibility for the provision and teaching of necessary skills and knowledge to police recruits and has formulated and implemented a rigorous and thorough process of teaching and learning for new police recruits. The Policing and Education Qualifications Framework ('PEQF') offers three discrete programmes, or routes, for entrance to police forces in England and Wales. These are: (i) the Police Constable Degree Apprenticeship ('PCDA'), a three-year degree apprenticeship programme which is delivered by a police force in collaboration with a higher education provider; (ii) a two-year Degree

---

[53]   *Ibid.*

Holder Entry Programme ('DHEP'), again, delivered by a police force in collaboration with a higher education provider; and (iii) a three-year traditional university degree in professional policing. This comprehensive range of programmes comprises an apparently intensive blend of academic and practical learning.[54] The PEQF includes in its National Policing Curriculum, academic and practical training in the conduct of police investigations and, in particular, learning and training in the PEACE model of interviewing.[55]

12.2.11. Research on PEACE in Practice

Several studies have examined use of the PEACE model in actual interviews conducted with suspects, victims and witnesses by police officers or other criminal investigators.[56]

These studies have consistently found that difficulties identified in cases before the introduction of the PACE Act rarely occurred following the introduction of the PEACE model. Consequently, there is evidence to suggest that the

---

[54] For further details, see *ibid*.

[55] College of Policing, "Policing Education Qualifications Framework: Police Constable Degree Apprenticeship National Policing Curriculum", no. 4.0, February 2021 (available on the College of Policing's web site).

[56] Colin Clark and Rebecca Milne, *National Evaluation of the PEACE Investigative Interviewing Course: Police Research Award Scheme*, Report No. PRAS/149, Home Office, London, 2001; Andy Griffiths and Rebecca Milne, "Will It All End in Tiers? Police Interviews With Suspects in Britain", in Tom Williamson (ed.), *Investigative Interviewing: Rights, Research and Regulation*, Willian Publishing, London, 2006, pp. 167–189; Andy Griffiths, Rebecca Milne and Julie Cherryman, "A Question of Control? The Formulation of Suspect and Witness Interview Question Strategies by Advanced Interviewers", in *International Journal of Police Science & Management*, 2011, vol. 13, no. 3, pp. 255–267; Samanntha Leahy-Harland and Ray Bull, "Police Strategies and Suspect Responses in Real-Life Serious Crime Interviews", in *Journal of Police and Criminal Psychology*, 2017, vol. 32, no. 2, pp. 138–151; Gavin E. Oxburgh, Thomas Williamson and James Ost, "Police officers' Use of Emotional Language During Child Sexual Abuse Investigations", in *Journal of Investigative Psychology and Offender Profiling*, 2006, vol. 3, no. 1, pp. 35–45; Stavroulla Soukara *et al.*, "What Really Happens in Police Interviews With Suspects? Tactics and Confessions", in *Psychology, Crime & Law*, 2009, vol. 15, no. 6, pp. 493–506; Dave Walsh and Ray Bull, "The Interviewing of Suspects by Non-Police Agencies: What's Effective? What Is Effective!", in *Legal and Criminological Psychology*, 2010, vol. 15, no. 2, pp. 305–321; Dave Walsh and Ray Bull, "How Do Interviewers Attempt to Overcome Suspects' Denials?", in *Psychiatry, Psychology, and Law*, 2012, vol. 19, no. 2, pp. 151–168; Dave Walsh and Ray Bull, "Examining Rapport in Investigative Interviews With Suspects: Does Its Building and Maintenance Work?", in *Journal of Police and Criminal Psychology*, 2012, vol. 27, no. 1, pp. 73–84; Dave Walsh and Ray Bull, "Interviewing Suspects: Examining the Association Between Evidence Disclosure, Questioning Strategies, Interview Skills, and Interview Outcomes", in *Psychology, Crime & Law*, 2015, vol. 21, no. 7, pp. 661–680; David Walsh and Rebecca Milne, "Keeping the PEACE? A Study of Investigative Interviewing Practices in the Public Sector", in *Legal and Criminological Psychology*, 2008, vol. 13, no. 1, pp. 39–57.

PEACE model has resulted in improved police practice when conducting interviews with suspects, victims and witnesses. The strategic deployment of question types during the distinct phases of suspect interviews is combined with gathering, and disclosure to the interviewee, of other available evidence in order to maximize interviewing effectiveness. Narrative recall detail is maximized at every strategic opportunity by the deployment of open question types such as those beginning with 'tell', 'explain' or 'describe'.[57] Training in, and use of, such techniques has shifted the interviewing dynamic from accusatorial and confession-seeking to information-gathering and conversation management techniques.

12.2.12. Demonstrated Interviewing Issues in PEACE Practice

The deployment and use of recommended techniques within the PEACE model appear to require greater clarity and explanation to maximize their effectiveness in practice. For example, although an open questioning strategy is advised, there appears to be an absence of *consensus* in relation to what constitutes an open question.[58] The PEACE model provides no evidence-base in relation to the strategic use of particular question types during discrete interview phases.[59] There is an absence of evidence as to how different question types, methods and techniques detailed should operate in synthesis.[60] This necessarily leaves a gap which requires to be filled by the skill level of interviewers. Studies of the PEACE model in practice have also identified problems arising from the erroneous exercise of interviewers' judgement such as: (i) failure by interviewers to effectively provide intermittent or final summaries during interviews; (ii) failure to adopt and adhere to a logical structure during interviews; (iii) failure to ensure effective challenges to suspects' accounts; and (iv) failure to close interviews effectively.[61] The establishment and maintenance of rapport is identified in the PEACE model as a key component of the interview process with forensic relevance. However, the PEACE model itself provides little guidance as to what interviewers should do to build and maintain rapport.[62] Research has also

---

[57] Gavin E. Oxburgh, Trond Myklebust and Tim Grant, "The Question of Question Types in Police Interviews: A Review of the Literature from a Psychological and Linguistic Perspective", in *International Journal of Speech, Language and the Law*, 2010, vol. 17, no. 1, pp. 45–66.

[58] *Ibid.*

[59] *Ibid.*; Griffiths and Milne, 2006, see *supra* note 56.

[60] Christopher E. Kelly, Jeanneé C. Miller, Allison D. Redlich and Steven M. Kleinman, "A Taxonomy of Interrogation Methods", in *Psychology, Public Policy, and Law*, 2013, vol. 19, no. 2, pp. 165–178.

[61] Clarke and Milne, 2001, see *supra* note 56; Walsh and Bull, 2010, see *supra* note 56.

[62] See Chapter 4 of this book more details on rapport.

demonstrated that the critically important phases of planning, preparation and evaluation were not properly implemented by interviewers.[63] There is an established association between properly effective planning and preparation and eliciting a comprehensive account during an interview.[64] Lack of time was often cited as the reason for such failures.[65] Research has also found that perceived time pressures were not strongly associated with planning. In that study, there was found to be a stronger association between failure to plan and police interviewers' (usually misplaced) confidence in their own interviewing abilities.[66]

The evaluation stage of the PEACE model requires assessment by interviewers of their own interviewing skills. Research has demonstrated a consistent tendency on the part of the interviewers to exaggerate their own effectiveness when compared to the results of independent assessors.[67] Police interviewers received little or no training in the evaluation task and admitted that the evaluation phase was only rarely completed by them.[68] Research also identified that police interviewers did not receive regular feedback on their interviewing performance from superiors and supervisors.[69] All of these issues can be addressed through focused and ongoing training and empirical follow-up research to demonstrate improvements.

12.2.13. Conclusion on the PEACE Model

The PEACE model presents an interviewing formulation which is evidenced and validated by scientific research. Its formulation draws upon the research-base of the Cognitive Interview ('CI'), conversation management, psychological theories and taxonomies and a plethora of empirical findings about investigative interviewing practices.[70] The PEACE model is founded upon a philosophical approach, enunciated in the PACE Act, which seeks to balance the

---

[63] Clarke and Milne, 2001, see *supra* note 56; Dave Walsh and Rebecca Milne, "Giving PEACE a Chance", in *Public Administration*, 2007, vol. 85, no. 3, pp. 525–540.

[64] Walsh and Bull, 2010, see *supra* note 56.

[65] Walsh and Milne, 2007, see *supra* note 63; Dave Walsh and Ray Bull, "Benefit Fraud Investigative Interviewing: A Self-Report Study of Investigation Professionals' Beliefs Concerning Practice", in *Journal of Investigative Psychology and Offender Profiling*, 2011, vol. 8, no. 2, pp. 131–148.

[66] KIM Jihwan, Dave Walsh, Ray Bull and Henriette Bergstrom, "Planning Ahead? Factors Influencing Investigators' Attitudes Towards Planning for Interviews With Suspects", in *Journal of Police and Criminal Psychology*, 2018, vol. 33, pp. 158–174.

[67] Andy Griffiths and Dave Walsh, "Investigators' Reflective Portfolios: A Reflection of Their Actual Investigation Skills?", in *Psychology, Crime & Law*, 2018, vol. 24, pp. 433–450.

[68] Walsh and Bull, 2010, see *supra* note 56; Walsh and Milne, 2007, see *supra* note 63.

[69] Clarke and Milne, 2001, see *supra* note 56.

[70] Laura Fallon *et al.*, "Evaluating the Vermont State Police's PEACE Model Training Program: Phase 1", in *Psychology, Crime & Law*, 2022, vol. 28, no. 1, pp. 59–81.

(sometimes pressing) need for investigation of crime by the police with the legitimate rights of the public in general and persons who are, or may be, suspects, in particular, having regard to the interests of justice and in the public interest. While the PACE Act might legitimately be viewed as a world-leading legislative framework which requires, *inter alia,* police interviews to be conducted fairly, respectfully and objectively,[71] the PEACE model is a ground-breaking, visionary and revolutionary framework for the conduct of police interviews. Its adoption and influence in jurisdictions beyond England and Wales are eloquent of the PEACE model's unique and legitimate claim to be the first police interview training framework of its kind.

12.3. The PRICE Model of Investigative Interviewing in Scotland

12.3.1. Introduction and Historical Development of the PRICE Model

Scotland has a devolved parliament, government and legal system within the UK.[72] Scotland also has a single police force, the Police Service of Scotland ('Police Scotland'), formed in 2013 when the original eight forces were merged.[73] Police Scotland serves the largest geographical area of any UK police force. The Scottish legal system and court structure differ in nature, origin, structure and approach from other UK systems. For example, there is no right of appeal in criminal cases beyond the High Court of Justiciary Appeal Court ('HCJAC') in Edinburgh. This is important when considering the development of investigative interviewing of suspects by the police in Scotland because the HCJAC definitively determines all issues of fairness and legality, applying the criminal law of Scotland. There is very limited scope for cross-fertilization of concepts, jurisprudence or practice from the criminal courts of England and Wales. Legislative competence for police functions, powers and duties is largely devolved to the Scottish Parliament.[74]

12.3.2. The Development of Interviewer Training

There is evidence of suspect interview training for detectives in Scotland from 1960.[75] The availability of tape-recording for suspect interviews in the late

---

[71] See also Chapter 6 of this book on the Méndez Principles.

[72] UK, The Scotland Act, 19 November 1998, 1998 c. 46 ('The Scotland Act, 1998') (https://www.legal-tools.org/doc/vun5wt/).

[73] Scotland, Police and Fire Reform Act, 1 May 2012, 2012 asp 8.

[74] The Scotland Act, 1998, Section 30, see *supra* note 72.

[75] For an informed summary of the history and development of investigative interviewing by police in Scotland, see Neil Drummond, "Investigative Interviewing – The PRICE Model in Scotland", in *International Investigative Interviewing Research Group Bulletin*, 2008, vol. 1, no. 1, pp. 24–32. Neil Drummond records a brief, but valuable, history and development of

1970s and 1980s was the catalyst for introducing a tape-recording instruction course for detectives in 1988.[76] In 1989, the need for a structured approach to training for suspect interviews was identified. Scottish detectives attended interview training courses in England where one week of training was devoted to this 'primary skill of a detective officer'.[77] Interview training at West Midlands Police in the early 1990s included teaching of the RIDES model ('Rapport, Information, Development, Evaluation and Sensitivity') developed by psychologist Peter Marshall. He subsequently developed the RICE model ('Rapport, Information, Confirmation and Evaluation') which was introduced into detective training in Scotland in 1993.[78] This structured approach to police interviewing sought to draw on the CI approach and was undoubtedly influenced by the requirements of the PACE Act and the development of the PEACE model in England and Wales.[79] Subsequently, the RICE model was further developed with the addition of the 'Planning and Preparation' stage, resulting in what is now known as the PRICE model,[80] which provides a structured interview technique that has subsequently evolved through practice-based learning, shaped by comments from, and decisions of, the HCJAC and criminal trial courts.[81]

12.3.3. The PRICE Model

The acronym 'PRICE' denotes the phases in a structured approach to suspect, victim and witness interviews although, as yet, no empirical evaluation of the PRICE model has been undertaken.[82] These are: (i) Planning and Preparation; (ii) Rapport building; (iii) Information gathering; (iv) Confirming the content; and (v) Evaluation and action. No written formulation of the PRICE model has previously been published; however, the principal sources documenting the

---

the PRICE model in Scotland and details a synoptic tabluar comparison of its theoretical stages and approach with the PEACE model operated in England and Wales.

[76] *Ibid.*, p. 25.

[77] *Ibid.*, p. 25, quoting Scottish Police College records.

[78] *Ibid.*, p. 26.

[79] Ronald P. Fisher and Edward R. Geiselman, *Memory Enhancing Techniques for Investigative Interviewing: The Cognitive Interview*, Charles C Thomas, Springfield, 1992.

[80] Drummond, 2008, p. 26, see *supra* note 75.

[81] See, for examples, Scotland, Criminal Appeals Court, *Luke Muir Mitchell v. H.M. Advocate*, Judgement, 16 May 2008, [2008] HCJAC 28 ('*Luke Muir Mitchell v. H.M. Advocate*') (https://www.legal-tools.org/doc/jwgeoy/); and Scotland, High Court of Justiciary, *H.M. Advocate v. Jake Hawkins*, Judgement, 10 September 2017, [2017] HCJ 79 ('*H.M. Advocate v. Jake Hawkins*') (https://www.legal-tools.org/doc/lu8ytf/).

[82] Drummond, 2008, p. 31, concluding paragraph, see *supra* note 75. See also Amina Memon, *Modifying the Cognitive Interview for Suspect Interviews*, conference presentation for the Scottish Institute for Policing Research Evidence & Investigation Network Seminar, 18 February 2009 (available on the Scottish Institute for Policing Research's web site).

PRICE model's formulation, development, attributes, ethos and application are the teaching materials from the Scottish Police College.[83] Suspect interviewing in Scotland is viewed by police interviewers as an art form in which interviewers are said to be engaged in a constant learning process, with informal review expected through discussion between peers and with superiors.[84]

12.3.4. The PRICE and PEACE Models

The essential elements of the PEACE model appear to have influenced the development and application of the PRICE model in practice through shared training and teaching for Scottish detectives with other UK police forces over decades.[85] Shared teaching and learning may well have influenced police interviewing practice in Scotland. Comparison to date has been superficial.[86]

12.3.5. The PRICE Model Training

The PRICE model is currently taught as the central component of the five-day Initial Investigative Interview Skills Course ('IIISC') by the Detective Training Unit at the Scottish Police College.[87] A distilled PRICE model is taught to uniformed police officers during a one half-day course. There is no refresher training offered to detectives or uniformed police officers.[88]

12.3.6. The PRICE Model Formulation in Detail

- Phase 1: Planning and Preparation: Interviewers plan using all of the available information. They should be dynamic and adapt questioning in light of information provided by the interviewee.[89] Interviewers should consider evidence from all sources, including how aspects of available circumstantial evidence can support other evidence.[90] A further acronym is applied, MAGICOP, which summarizes preparatory considerations. These are related to assessing Motive; Ability; Guilty intention; Identification; Conduct (before and after crime); Opportunity; and Preparation.

---

[83] Drummond, 2008, p. 30, see *supra* note 75:
    PEACE or PRICE model? The following is a summary of the key points of both models. The PEACE model is taken from the Practical Guide to Investigative Interviewing (2004) published by CENTREX (now the National Policing Improvement Agency in England and Wales) while the PRICE model is taken from the training notes found within the Detective Training Unit at the SPC.

[84] *Ibid.*

[85] *Ibid.*

[86] *Ibid.*, p. 30 details a tabulated synoptic comparison of the PEACE and PRICE models.

[87] Scottish Police College, "Price Model Interview Training", 2021.

[88] Information obtained directly in discussion with IIISC leadership, Scottish Police College.

[89] Scottish Police College, 2021, pp. 19–21, see *supra* note 87.

[90] *Ibid.*, p. 22.

Interviewers are encouraged to consider which aspects of circumstantial evidence can be 'ticked-off' (that is, as proved).[91] Planning for the interview includes a review of the suspect's rights which must be explained not more than one hour prior to the interview.[92] The interviewer prepares to explain the general nature of the suspected offence; that there is no obligation to say anything other than give his or her name, address, *et cetera*; that the suspect has a right to have a solicitor present during the interview; that the suspect has a right to have another person informed; and that a pre-interview review of rights *aide memoire*, in prescribed form,[93] is to be read *verbatim* to every person in the interview room prior to every interview. The interviewer must then consider the sequence of the interview: the introduction (circumstances surrounding arrest); the caution; the impact question (an implicit, 'impactive' accusation put to the suspect at the beginning of the information-gathering stage); the suspect's account (before, during and after approach to each factual scenario); the police agenda (before, during and after approach to each factual scenario); 'Yes/No Spiral' (confirm the impact question and/or cover relevant material); knowledge of DNA (if relevant); challenges (weakest to strongest); and finally, the need to arrest or release from custody, as appropriate.[94]

- Phase 2: Introduction to the Interview and Rapport Building: Interviewers are encouraged to consider questioning styles. They should elicit free narrative by asking open questions, such as those beginning with 'Tell', 'Explain' or 'Describe' ('TEDs'). Interviewers are encouraged to build rapport. IIISC teaching materials state the requirement for "Building a rapport with both Suspect and Solicitor".[95] Interviewers are encouraged to explain procedures to the suspect and to develop a working relationship "with both suspect and solicitor".[96] Interviewers are directed to ensure that they have thought out and can deliver a common law caution. This focuses on the necessary elements such as specifics of time and locus; specification of victim; and details of alleged crime including, for example, alleged assault and any relevant aggravations, such as "repeatedly" or "to severe injury and permanent disfigurement".[97] The caution is said

---

[91] *Ibid.*, p. 23.
[92] Scotland, Criminal Justice Act, 6 April 2020, 2016 asp 1, Section 31.
[93] Scotland, Police Form No. 051-035.
[94] Scottish Police College, 2021, p. 27, see *supra* note 87.
[95] *Ibid.*
[96] *Ibid.*, p. 29.
[97] *Ibid.*, p. 30.

to be "Human Rights informed" and interviewers must "Ensure understanding using appropriate terms". They are encouraged to test the suspect's understanding of the caution. They must use correct legal terminology and ensure "that the caution contains enough information to allow the suspect to understand the crime under investigation, i.e. Crime Type, Locus, Date and Victims Name if appropriate".[98]

- Phase 3: Information Gathering: The information gathering stage always begins with the 'Impact Question'. This is a central and important feature of a Police Scotland suspect interview. Interviewers spend time learning how to formulate impact questions. Typically, the impact question begins with an implicit accusation, such as 'Tell me about your involvement in the murder of X at Y locus on Z date?'. Interviewers are instructed to obtain the suspect's account; movements at the material time; and to elicit "good detail". Interviewers are instructed not to interrupt and to "Build up a timeline" with as much detail as possible according to the '80–20 rule' (the suspect should talk for 80 per cent of the interview and the interviewer for only 20 per cent). Questions should be asked which elicit answers that anchor events in time. Interviewers are instructed to explore time sequence by applying a 'before, during and after' approach to time segmented questioning, with as much detail as possible elicited from the interviewee. The interviewee's account is not challenged at this stage, but key topics are identified and probed in time sequence.[99] The suspect's account in response to the impact question is probed in this manner. Any admission requires exploration of the motivation for doing so, in order to eliminate the possibility of a false confession. If the suspect chooses to make no comment, interviewers must follow the prepared plan.[100] Interviewers are taught to be aware of the 'Police Agenda' comprised of the relevant investigative areas and lines of enquiry ('what we need to know'). These matters are probed with, "appropriate closed questions". All essential elements must be covered.[101] For 'no comment' interviews, interviewers are taught: "There is still evidence within a 'no comment' interview that can be presented in court". Matters such as body language; professional approach by the interviewer; accused's reaction, including to triggers (images, CCTV, *et cetera*); and non-verbal communication (hands behind head, shrug of shoulders, *et cetera*) are all emphasized as relevant.

---

98   *Ibid.*, p. 31 [sic.].
99   *Ibid.*, p. 32.
100   *Ibid.*, p. 34.
101   *Ibid.*, p. 35.

Interviewers are also invited to read an article entitled "Silence looks like an admission of guilt" by the Daily Mail Reporter.[102]

- Phase 4: Confirming the Content: This is also described as the "Clarification ('Yes/No Spiral') Stage".[103] The 'Yes/No Spiral' describes a funnelling questioning strategy of closed questions which seeks clarification of information already elicited from the interviewee. The interviewer is required to explain to the suspect "the interviewer's expectation of the clarification stage of the interview […]". The first question is the impact question during this phase. It should be clear and concise. The interviewer does not cover every question asked and answered, but clarification of the points to be included in the subsequent 'challenges' must be covered.[104] The interviewer begins with the 'suspect agenda' and probes all material detail of events elicited, without challenge. Then the interviewer probes the suspect's version of events from the perspective of the 'police agenda', based on the whole evidence available. Essential evidential elements are put to the suspect for comment. No challenge is made to the suspect's comments on the available evidential aspects put. Clarification of essential detail is sought using time segmentation (before, during or after) and the 'Yes/No Spiral' approach.

- Phase 5: Evaluation and Action: This phase is described in the teaching materials as "evaluation/challenges".[105] Interviewers are taught that: "Presentation of investigative material must be 'Impactive'; must not be opinion; must be structured; and must be accurate [and] capable of being used in court".[106] Challenges are made to the suspect's account, as appropriate, starting with the weakest challenges and ending with the strongest. Interviewers are encouraged to use challenging body language during this phase. If any further admission is made interviewers are instructed to revert to phase three and elicit the suspect's account, thereafter again following the model described.

12.3.7. Further Focus on the PRICE Training

Following focus on the model and common interviewing challenges, such as the formulation of current hypotheses and questions,[107] common interviewing errors are highlighted such as: (i) lack of preparation; (ii) 'attitude to burst people'; (iii)

---

[102] *Ibid.*, pp. 36–37.
[103] *Ibid.*, p. 40.
[104] *Ibid.*, p. 40.
[105] *Ibid.*, p. 41.
[106] *Ibid.*, p. 41.
[107] Oxburgh, Myklebust and Grant, 2010, see *supra* note 57.

negative comments such as, 'this is your only chance to tell us […]'; (iv) oppressive tone and body language; (v) lack of time; and (vi) lack of plan for the interview.[108]

Finally, interviewers are taught that it is essential to carefully consider the role of each of the two interviewers who are required to conduct each suspect interview. Both must work as a team in compiling the interview plan, and in deciding tactics for the interview such as who will be the first (lead) and second interviewer. It is said to be essential that every interview must be led by one interviewer with the other taking notes and it is considered good practice for the lead interviewer to ask the second interviewer at intervals during the interview if there is anything to add. Interview notes are submitted as an evidential production and must be clear, concise and accurate. The importance of the role of the second interviewer is emphasized as is the need for an agreed sign to use in case anything has been missed so that it can be discussed prior to concluding the interview. The second interviewer's notes must be in order in the event of equipment failure.[109]

12.3.8. The Effectiveness of the PRICE Model in Practice

In the absence of empirical assessment of (i) whether the PRICE model is an effective, evidence-based method for conducting investigative interviews, and (ii) whether, if effective in theory, the model is adhered to by police interviewers in practice, it is not possible to comment accurately on its effectiveness in practice. The absence of any scientific review (see following sections below) or formal refresher training for detectives and uniformed officers assumes the risk that interviewers depart from the PRICE model in their interviewing practices. The duration, intensity and structure of the IIISC may only provide detectives, at best, with adaptable structures, advice and techniques which each practitioner may use to develop his or her own unique interviewing method and skills. In this sense, the PRICE model may assist interviewers in practical development to achieve their own version of investigative interviewing, viewed by interviewers as a form of art. However, it is not self-evident from the current formulation of the PRICE model that key aspects such as (i) the impact question; taken together with (ii) a possible misapprehension of the nature, conduct and forensic value of rapport,[110] (said to be established and maintained with suspect and

---

[108] Scottish Police College, 2021, p. 42, see *supra* note 87.
[109] *Ibid.*, pp. 43–44.
[110] See, for example, Aldert Vrij, Lorraine Hope and Ronald P. Fisher, "Eliciting Reliable Information in Investigative Interviews", in *Policy Insights from Behavioral and Brain Sciences*, 2014, vol. 1, no. 1, pp. 129–136:

solicitor), operate as parts of an effective, evidence-based method for investigative interviewing. The effect of the impact question on successfully establishing and maintaining meaningful rapport with the suspect may warrant empirical investigation.

12.3.9. Assessment of PRICE by the Courts

Aspects of the PRICE model of police interviewing practice have been assessed by the criminal courts in Scotland in specific cases in which challenges have been made to the fairness or legality of police interviewing practice. Statements by accused persons in Scotland form one exception to the general rule against the admissibility of hearsay evidence in criminal trials.[111] The issue for a criminal court is whether the accused's statement was obtained fairly by police interviewers. A statement by a suspect is not regarded as having been fairly obtained unless it was 'spontaneous' and 'voluntary'.[112] The classic formulation of this rule is as follows:

> [a] voluntary statement is one which is given freely, not in response to pressure and inducement, and not elicited by cross-examination. This does not mean that, if a person elects to give a statement, it becomes inadmissible because he is asked some questions to clear

---

Developing rapport. Rapport has been described as the "heart of the interview" (St. Yves, 2009, p. 104). Rapport is the most critical element of investigative interviewing, according to a US Intelligence Science Board report on gathering information, and the most effective way to obtain accurate information from interviews, according to the FBI (Driskell, Blickensderfer, & Salas, 2013).

Quintan Crough, Cassandre D. Larivière, Mark D. Snow and Joseph Eastwood, "Reflections on the Nature of Rapport Within Suspect Interviews", in *Current Issues in Criminal Justice*, 2022, vol. 34, no. 2, pp. 219–228.

[111] UK, Criminal Procedure (Scotland) Act, 1 April 1996, 1995 c. 46, Section 21ZA. See also Tony Convery, "The Limits of Questioning in Police Interviews", in *Criminal Law Bulletin*, 2018, vol. 153, pp. 4–6 and Robert S. Shiels "Undermining the Advice of a Solicitor", in *Journal of Criminal Law*, 2019, vol. 83, no. 2, pp. 125–127 for recent commentaries by legal practitioners.

[112] Scotland, High Court of Justiciary, *H.M. Advocate v. William Alexander Mair*, Judgement, 11 February 1982, 1982 SLT 471, per Lord Hunter ('*H.M. Advocate v. Mair*') (https://www.legal-tools.org/doc/93o3yw/):

> In the case of *Hartley v. H.M. Advocate* at p. 28 Lord Avonside described the objectionable method in terms which almost exactly cover the course of events during the interview in the present case. 'Firstly, police officers may question a suspect so long as they do not stray into the field of interrogation. Secondly, and most importantly, cross-examination is just what it means. It consists in questioning an adverse witness in an effort to break down his evidence, to weaken or prejudice his evidence, or to elicit statements damaging to him and aiding the case of the cross-examiner.

up his account of the matter, but such questions as he is asked must
not go beyond elucidation.[113]

The application of these principles depends on the circumstances in individual cases.[114] However, objectively, there appears to be at least some degree of uncertainty between the clear expression of the fundamental principles and their application in any particular case.[115] In addition, there may appear to be some difficulty in distinguishing between phases three, four and five of the PRICE model, as currently taught, and what amounts to cross-examination:

> Secondly, and most importantly, cross-examination is just what it means. It consists in questioning an adverse witness in an effort to break down his evidence, to weaken or prejudice his evidence, or to elicit statements damaging to him and aiding the case of the cross-examiner.[116]

12.3.10. Conclusion on PRICE

The absence of (i) any evaluation of the PRICE model in practice, (ii) any empirical evidence base demonstrating its effectiveness, and (iii) the apparent tension between the applicable Scottish legal principles and police interviewing practice, might all be taken to illustrate that there is a need to re-visit and perhaps update the PRICE model. As much was suggested by an informed Scottish police interviewer and teacher as long ago as 2008:

> With criticism of police interviewing aired on national television recently, and an increase in interest from COPFS, perhaps it is time that an honest assessment of investigative interviewing in Scotland took place, and the lessons learned from the evaluations and research in England and Wales considered as part of that process.[117] Such an assessment has yet to happen.

12.4. Structured Interview Models in Other Countries

In the development of structured interview protocols, the PEACE model has been applied in adapted versions and used as an overarching interview model in

---

[113] Scotland, High Court of Justiciary, *Chalmers v. H.M. Advocate*, Judgement, 5 March 1954, 1954 JC 66 (https://www.legal-tools.org/doc/rljy91/), per Lord Justice Clerk Thomson.

[114] See, for example, *Luke Muir Mitchell v. H.M. Advocate* and *H.M. Advocate v. Jake Hawkins*, see *supra* note 81. In *Mitchell*, police questioning of a 15-year-old youth was described by the Lord Justice General as "outrageous" and "to be deplored", but answers to particular questions which the Crown founded upon were held to be admissible. In *Hawkins*, a preliminary objection to the admissibility of statements made during a police interview was upheld pre-trial in circumstances in which the police interviewers sought to undermine the advice of a solicitor to make exercise the suspect's right to silence.

[115] College of Policing, 2022, see *supra* note 38.

[116] *H.M. Advocate v. Mair*, see *supra* note 112.

[117] Drummond, 2008, p. 31, see *supra* note 75.

several countries.[118] Both the PEACE and PRICE models are focused on their structured interview approaches. Other adaptions focus on the values and principles as applied in each jurisdiction. For example, one of the programmes developed and applied in Norway is KREATIV. The acronym denotes the overarching values and principles which require to be adhered to in implementing PEACE-structured interviews. The acronym denotes the following principles: (K) Communication, (R) Rule of law, (E) Ethics and Empathy, (A) Active consciousness, (T) Trust through openness, and (I) Information (V) Verified through science. The Structured Interviewing Model for the Norwegian Police is based on the PEACE-structure, and a part of the basic three-year Bachelor's degree programme[119] to become a police officer in Norway.

Based on these principles, the most significant enhancement in the development of the Norwegian approach to the PEACE model is the focus upon the 'alternative hypothesis', based on the pragmatic model for the testing of evidence by the Swedish professor Christian Diesen,[120] who believed the focus in every investigation and evaluation should be to identify alternative hypotheses, reasonable alternative explanations for the evidence pointing towards the suspect and to actively test them by pursuing information liable to challenge or support the alternative explanations.[121] These fundamental principles are also found in other structured models and techniques which are taught at the Norwegian Police University College, such as the Strategic Use of Evidence[122] and the CI.[123] Similarly adapted versions of the PEACE model, with additional components, are applied in other jurisdictions around the world.[124] The majority of

---

[118] Walsh, Oxburgh, Redlich and Myklebust (eds.), vol. 1, see *supra* note 1.

[119] Included in the (i) Psychology, (ii) Law and (iii) Investigative Procedures lectures of the three-year Bachelor's programme. The Norwegian Structured Interviewing Model is also taught in several of the post-graduate studies in investigations at the Norwegian Police University College.

[120] Christian Diesen, *Examination of Evidence in Criminal Cases*, Norstedts Juridik, Stockholm, 2015; Christian Diesen, "Beyond Reasonable Doubt. Standard of Proof and Evaluation of Evidence in Criminal Cases", in *Scandinavian Studies in Law – Legal Theory*, 2000, vol. 40, pp. 179–180.

[121] Diesen, 2015, see *supra* note 120; Diesen, 2000, see *supra* note 120; Andy Griffiths and Asbjørn Rachlew, "From Interrogation to Investigative Interviewing", in Andy Griffiths and Rebecca Milne (eds.), *The Psychology of Criminal Investigation: From Theory to Practice*, Routledge, 2018.

[122] See Chapter 14 of this book.

[123] See Chapter 16 of this book.

[124] For analysis of a mixed approach with PEACE elements, see Brent Snook *et al.*, "Challenges of a 'Toolbox' Approach to Investigative Interviewing: A Critical Analysis of the Royal Canadian Mounted Police's (RCMP) Phased Interview Model", in *Psychology, Public Policy, and Law*, 2020, vol. 26, no. 3, pp. 261–273.

---

police officers and investigators in different jurisdictions are trained in the theory and practice of one or several structured interview models. The most influential models are presented throughout this book.

12.5. The Way Forward

In order for interviewing training and practical forensic questioning skills to be effective, there are three essential requirements that require to be met.[125] Firstly, the delivery and content of training must be based on methods that have been tested in scientific study and have been proved to work. Secondly, training in the required methodology, interview structure and technique should be supported with information about the research base demonstrating the required approach. Thirdly, training programmes should be continuous and ongoing so that the quality of questioning is maintained at the highest possible standards.[126] It appears that the first and second identified criteria may be met in the operation of the PEACE model, and possibly also the principal elements of the PRICE model. However, whether police interviewers routinely adhere to the conceptual methodology, interview structure and technique formulated in the PEACE, PRICE or other structured models can only be established through continuous empirically demonstrated assessment and training of interviewers in their respective organizations. Future research might focus on the need for an integrated approach between the interview and all aspects of police investigations, including the optimal interviewing environment and interviewing practices which anticipate subsequent court procedures and requirements. Future focus on such aspects will most likely lay the foundations for the further improvement of forensic interviewing practices and the structured models, such as the PEACE model.

---

[125] Michael E. Lamb, "Difficulties Translating Research on Forensic Interview Practices to Practitioners: Finding Water, Leading Horses, but Can We Get Them to Drink?", in *American Psychologist*, 2016, vol. 71, pp. 710–718.

[126] Heather Stewart, Carmit Katz and David J. la Rooy, "Training Forensic Interviewers", in Michael E. Lamb, David J. La Rooy, Lindsay C. Malloy and Carmit Katz (eds.), *Children's Testimony: A Handbook of Psychological Research and Forensic Practice*, Wiley-Blackwell, Chichester, 2011, pp. 199–216.

13

The Cylinder Model

Mattias Sjöberg, Paul J. Taylor and Stacey M. Conchie[*]

13.1. Introduction

Imagine interviewing a suspect accused of committing a serious crime. Before going into the interview room, you plan meticulously: be factual, begin with questions about their whereabouts, challenge their answer with closed-circuit television evidence. You have it sorted, or so you think. As the suspect starts talking, they express fear that their family will be harmed if they co-operate. What should you do? Ignore the distraction and stick to your plan? Or re-evaluate, letting the suspect drive the conversation? The answer is not straightforward. Your response depends on how you interpret the suspect and their intentions, a process of social inference known as *interpersonal sense-making*.[1]

Despite the centrality of sense-making to social interaction, it was largely ignored by early literature on interviewing, which focused on identifying effective forms of questioning. Implicit in this early literature and the continuing search for effective tactics is a cooking pot view of interviews:[2] start with some relationship development, add open questions and memory prompts and, if desired, reveal some evidence strategically. The idea that there are 'right ingredients' for good interviews still persists in the literature, though any researcher and practitioner worth their salt – cooking idiom intended – acknowledges that

---

[*] **Mattias Sjöberg** is a Ph.D. student in psychology at Lancaster University. **Paul J. Taylor**, Ph.D., is a Professor of Psychology at Lancaster University and Professor of Human Interaction at University of Twente. **Stacey M. Conchie**, Ph.D., is Professor of Psychology at Lancaster University. The authors are funded by the Centre for Research and Evidence on Security Threats ('CREST') (Economic and Social Research Council Award No. ES/N009614/1), which is funded in part by the United Kingdom ('UK') Home Office and security and intelligence agencies. The funding arrangements required this paper to be reviewed to ensure that its contents did not violate the Official Secrets Act (UK) nor disclose sensitive, classified or personal information.

[1] Ellen Giebels, Miriam S.D. Oostinga, Paul J. Taylor and Joanna L. Curtis, "The Cultural Dimension of Uncertainty Avoidance Impacts Police–Civilian Interaction", in *Law and Human Behavior*, 2017, vol. 41, pp. 98–102; Shaun Nichols and Stephen P. Stich, *Mindreading: An Integrated Account of Pretence, Self-Awareness, and Understanding of Other Minds*, Clarendon Press, Oxford, 2003.

[2] Michael E. Holmes, "Phase Structures in Negotiation", in Linda L. Putnam and Michael E. Roloff (eds.), *Communication and Negotiation*, Sage Publications, 1992, pp. 83–105.

interviewing cannot be boiled down to a recipe. The 'how' of a good interview is entirely dependent on the suspect and the context.

Some empirical examples demonstrate this point well. Beune *et al.*[3] found that statements made in Dutch police interviews that intimidate, warn or accuse a suspect can, in certain contexts, be effective at eliciting information. Oostinga *et al.*[4] found that denying a mistake can, on occasion, lead a suspect to offer more information than if the interviewer offered an apology. Neither of these studies suggests that intimidation or mistakes should be mixed into all interviews. What they demonstrate is that no approach, no tactic and no type of question is always 'good' or always 'bad'. What matters is knowing what to use and when.

13.2. The Cylinder Model

To know what to use and when, we must understand the various ways in which people use and interpret communication. Early research on this question of 'communication structure' took its influence from game theory and examined interactions through the lens of negotiating gains and losses.[5] But authors soon argued that interactions are not devoid of emotional content. Donohue and Roberto,[6] for example, took a relational stance, emphasizing how speakers relate to one another and use language to modify the 'closeness' of the relationship. Still others stressed the importance of the speakers' dispositions and identities, using the term 'facework' to describe how speakers use dialogue to attack, defend and restore a person's identity.[7]

Taylor[8] argued that all these perspectives are correct and that their different foci – the relational, the identity and the instrumental – reflect a different 'frame' that will dominate an interaction at any one time. "The challenge", he wrote, "[...] is to develop and establish a model that explicates the conceptual dimensions or facets necessary to provide a comprehensive understanding of the

3   Karlijn Beune, Ellen Giebels and Paul J. Taylor, "Patterns Of Interaction in Police Interviews: The Role of Cultural Dependency", in *Criminal Justice and Behavior*, vol. 37, 2010, pp. 904–925.

4   Miriam S.D. Oostinga, Ellen Giebels and Paul J. Taylor, "Communication Error Management in Law Enforcement Interactions: A Sender's Perspective", in *Criminal Justice and Behavior*, 2020, vol. 47, pp. 39–60.

5   Thomas C. Schelling, *The Strategy of Conflict*, Harvard University Press, Cambridge, 1980.

6   William A. Donohue and Anthony J. Roberto, "Relational Development as Negotiated Order in Hostage Negotiation", in *Human Communication Research*, 1993, vol. 20, pp. 175–198.

7   Randall G. Rogan and Mitchell R. Hammer, "Crisis Negotiations: A Preliminary Investigation of Facework in Naturalistic Conflict Discourse", in *Journal of Applied Communication Research*, 1994, vol. 22, pp. 216–231.

8   Paul J. Taylor, "A Cylindrical Model of Communication Behaviour in Crisis Negotiations", in *Human Communication Research*, 2002, vol. 28, no. 1, pp. 7–48.

interrelationships among behaviors".[9] The result of addressing this challenge is the cylinder model, which captures the ways in which people communicate and the motivations that underpin these ways. Initially supported by analyses of crisis negotiations,[10] the cylinder model has subsequently been used to study and understand interviews and interrogations.[11]

13.2.1. Orientation

As shown in Figure 1 below, the spine of the cylinder differentiates a person's overall orientation to interaction as either avoidant, competitive or co-operative. An avoidant orientation is characterized by 'no comments', retractions from substantive discussion and a refusal to accept responsibility for events. This can occur because the suspect is overwhelmed by the situation or because they strategically wish to stonewall progress. Vrij and Mann[12] report an example of a murder suspect who talked about his actions in the morning but avoided giving specific details of his whereabouts in the afternoon when the murder took place. Blending a false story with truthful elements is a strategy used by a suspect to portray an image of being forthcoming while avoiding incriminating details.[13]

---

[9]   *Ibid.*, p. 8.

[10] Wolfgang Bilsky, Beate Liesner and Denise Webel-Therhorn, "Escalation and Deescalation in Hostage-Negotiation", in Randall G. Rogan and Frederick J. Lanceley (eds.), *Contemporary Theory, Research and Practice of Crisis and Hostage Negotiation*, Hampton Press, Cresskill, 2010, pp. 119–140; Taylor, 2002, see *supra* note 8; Paul J. Taylor and Ian Donald, "The Structure of Communication Behaviour in Simulated and Actual Crisis Negotiations", in *Human Communication Research*, 2004, vol. 30, pp. 443–478; Paul J. Taylor and Ian Donald, "Testing the Relationship Between Local Cue-Response Patterns and Global Dimensions of Communication Behaviour", in *British Journal of Social Psychology*, vol. 46, 2007, pp. 273–298.

[11] Lucy Arnold, "Strategies Used by Suspects During Police Interview", Ph.D. thesis, University of Portsmouth, 2021; Giebels, Oostinga, Taylor and Curtis, 2017, see *supra* note 1; Mattias Sjöberg, Paul J. Taylor and Stacey M. Conchie, "Sensemaking and Cooperation in Interrogations: The Role of Matching", manuscript in preparation, 2021 ('Sjöberg, Taylor and Conchie, 2021a').

[12] Aldert Vrij and Samantha Mann, "Telling and Detecting Lies in a High-Stake Situation: The Case of a Convicted Murderer", in *Applied Cognitive Psychology*, 2001, vol. 15, no. 2, pp. 187–203.

[13] Simon Wells and Susan E. Brandon, "Interviewing in Criminal and Intelligence-Gathering Contexts: Applying Science", in *International Journal of Forensic Mental Health*, 2019, vol. 18, no. 1, pp. 50–65.

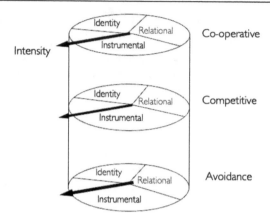

Figure 1: The cylinder model.

When suspects do engage, they often begin in a competitive orientation. This can be expressed by behaviours that attack the interviewer's position or credibility, while simultaneously restoring a personal position through positional arguing, boasting and the rejection of compromises. These behaviours often form the bulk of interactions in unco-operative suspects whose natural response is to push back – a phenomenon characterized as the 'one-down effect'.[14] Arnold[15] found this to be particularly true of suspects being interviewed about domestic offences compared to theft or violence offences.

Finally, a suspect in a co-operative orientation engages proactively with the interviewer and provides information that may act as evidence in a potential trial.[16] They may make concessions, agree to provide other forms of evidence (for example, draw the scene), express a common goal and even compliment the interviewer on their approach. When a suspect is in this orientation, the result is often the establishment of a 'common ground', which is a single agreed way of describing actions and an agreed timeline of events.[17] Although adopting a co-operative orientation is associated with good outcomes and is likely to be the default approach for interviewers, there are instances where it is detrimental.

---

[14] William A. Donohue and Paul J. Taylor, "Testing the Role Effect in Terrorist Negotiations", in *International Negotiation*, 2003, vol. 8, pp. 527–547.

[15] Arnold, 2021, see *supra* note 11.

[16] Wells and Brandon, 2019, see *supra* note 13.

[17] Paul J. Taylor, "The Role of Language in Conflict and Conflict Resolution", in Thomas M. Holtgraves (ed.), *The Oxford Handbook of Language and Social Psychology*, Oxford University Press, 2014, pp. 459–470.

For example, revealing information in the hope of an agreement can be used strategically by the suspect to damage the interaction.[18]

An interesting, empirically demonstrated aspect of the cylinder model is the linear ordering of the orientations. To get from avoidance to co-operation, one moves through competition. For example, if a suspect is adopting an avoidant orientation towards the interview, a skilled interviewer may try to slightly provoke the suspect by highlighting inconsistencies in their behaviour (for example, "You say you are a good father, but what father would treat their children like this?").[19] Consistent with this observation, Alison *et al.*[20] found that police interviewers sometimes used competitive language at key moments in the interview to maximize information gain. Similarly, in their analysis of transcripts from police responders, Sikveland, Kevoe-Feldman and Stokoe[21] found challenges were a productive way to prompt a positive shift in suicidal persons' behaviour. Finally, Sjöberg, Taylor and Conchie[22] observed that shifting to a more competitive orientation was at times successful in making a suspect who was resolutely denying everything to open up.

13.2.2. Motivations

While the three orientations capture a person's inclination towards the interaction, they say little about the goal or purposes behind it. The second distinction in the cylinder model characterizes a person's communicative goals, as instrumental, relational or identity framed. At any one point in time, a speaker will typically focus on one of these frames, moving among them either in response to their interlocuter or because their own priority has shifted. A suspect in an instrumental frame will focus on information provision, laying out interests, bargaining and discussing who, what, where and when.[23] Since the main purpose of an interview is to transmit information, this is often the dominant frame. Encouraging a witness to report everything that they can remember without

---

[18] J. Keith Murnighan, Linda Babcock, Leigh Thompson and Madan Pillutla, "The Information Dilemma in Negotiations: Effects of Experience, Incentives, and Integrative Potential", in *International Journal of Conflict Management*, 1999, vol. 10, no. 4, pp. 313–339.

[19] Wells and Brandon, 2019, see *supra* note 13.

[20] Laurence J. Alison *et al.*, "Why Tough Tactics Fail and Rapport Gets Results: Observing Rapport-Based Interpersonal Techniques (ORBIT) to Generate Useful Information from Terrorists", in *Psychology, Public Policy, and Law*, 2013, vol. 19, no. 4, pp. 411–431.

[21] Rein O. Sikveland, Heidi Kevoe-Feldman and Elizabeth Stokoe, "Overcoming Suicidal Persons' Resistance Using Productive Communicative Challenges During Police Crisis Negotiations", in *Applied Linguistics*, 2020, vol. 41, pp. 533–551.

[22] Mattias Sjöberg, Paul J. Taylor and Stacey M. Conchie, "Communication Behaviours in Military Investigative Interviews", manuscript in preparation, 2021 ('Sjöberg, Taylor and Conchie, 2021b').

[23] Wells and Brandon, 2019, see *supra* note 13.

filtering any details is one example of an instrumental approach, and a useful one too.[24]

However, far more occurs in an interview than instrumental exchanges. As Donohue and Roberto[25] recognized, we often use dialogue to manage the interdependencies and relationships between ourselves and the other person. This might be making a promise, expressing a joke or challenging the relationship that exists through appeals or excuses.[26] This kind of language is often associated with building rapport, which has emerged as an important facilitator of co-operation and information gain. For example, Mindthoff, Meissner, Hess and Vallano[27] conducted a meta-analysis on the use of rapport-building techniques on information disclosure and found a moderately strong positive effect on suspect co-operation. Similar results of rapport on co-operation and information gain have also been observed among children and adolescents.[28] Thus, early relational dialogue can build a degree of connection that allows the interviewer and suspect to move into more instrumental discussions.

Finally, suspects may boast and issue criticisms and insults to belittle the interviewer or may use compliments and empathy to achieve the opposite. These behaviours are less focused on an instrumental goal and more focused on self and the perceptions that others have of 'face'.[29] Within investigative interviews, Pounds[30] looked at a corpus of suspect interviews and found that they often contained both face-enhancing (for example, "I just want to give you the opportunity to explain", p. 108) and face-challenging statements (for example, "My concern is that you are telling us things that other people aren't going to be able to confirm", p. 112). This shows how identity concerns are often at the forefront

24 Ronald P. Fisher, R. Edward Geiselman and Michael Amador, "Field Test of the Cognitive Interview: Enhancing the Recollection of Actual Victims and Witnesses of Crime", in *Journal of Applied Psychology*, 1989, vol. 74, no. 5, pp. 722–727. Günter Köhnken, Rebecca Milne, Amina Memon and Ray Bull, "The Cognitive Interview: A Meta-Analysis", in *Psychology, Crime & Law*, 1999, vol. 5, no. 1, pp. 3–27.

25 Donohue and Roberto, 1993, pp. 175–198, see *supra* note 6.

26 Taylor, 2002, see *supra* note 8.

27 Amelia Mindthoff, Christian A. Meissner, Karen M. Hess and Jonathan P. Vallano, "The Effect of Relational Methods on Fostering Cooperation and Information-Elicitation: A Systematic Review of Rapport in the Investigative Interviewing Literature", online conference presentation, International Investigative Interviewing Research Group, 6 September 2021.

28 Jennifer Lavoie, Joshua Wyman, Angela M. Crossman and Victoria Talwar, "Meta-Analysis of the Effects of Two Interviewing Practices on Children's Disclosures of Sensitive Information: Rapport Practices and Question Type", in *Child Abuse & Neglect*, 2021, vol. 113, pp. 1–12.

29 William A. Donohue and Robert Kolt, *Managing Interpersonal Conflict*, Newbury Park, 1992.

30 Gabrina Pounds, "Rapport-Building in Suspects' Police Interviews: The Role of Empathy and Face", in *Pragmatics and Society*, 2019, vol. 10, no. 1, pp. 95–121.

of suspect interviews, and adequately addressing them can be a priority for interviewers.

Critically, an individual can pursue each of these motivational goals while adopting an avoidant, competitive or co-operative orientation to dialogue. This creates nine regions that form the cylinder model. At any one time, individuals tend to adopt an avoidant, competitive or co-operative orientation to interaction and pursue either an identity, instrumental or relational goal with varying degrees of intensity. So, for example, a couple in a child custody dispute may yell abuse and insults as they compete over identity issues that stem from their mistrust and dislike of their ex-partner. But they may revert to more co-operative, instrumental behaviour such as compromises and promises when discussing what is best for their child.

13.2.3. Intensity

The final distinction is the intensity to which individuals communicate about a particular issue. The intensity of a speaker's messages may seem like an obvious clue to make sense of, but it is easily overlooked. High intensity dialogue includes anger and threats, profanity, obscure metaphors and dramatic changes in paralinguistic cues that reflect a deviation from neutrality. It is associated with threat conviction and emotional stress,[31] but simply, it means the issue being described is important to the speaker. The cylinder model predicts that high intensity dialogue will always be focused on one of the three motivational frames, hence intensity moves from the middle to the outer rim of each orientation. To move frame, it is necessary to reduce intensity and bring the suspect back into the middle of the orientation, at which point other frames become 'available'. For example, relentlessly threatening action if a demand is not met signifies a high degree of concern from a suspect, which is unlikely to dissipate until some form of acknowledgement or agreement is made.[32]

What is quite remarkable about the cylinder structure is how universal it is as a description of the communication that occurs in many contexts. It is possible to take a recording of an interaction and quite literally plot each speaker moving in and out of these different frames over time.[33] This is not to suggest that any one utterance or message is exclusively attached to one frame.

---

[31] John W. Bowers, "Language Intensity, Social Introversion, and Attitude Change", in *Speech Monographs*, 1963, vol. 30, pp. 415–420.

[32] Susan E. Brandon, Simon Wells and Colton Seale, "Science-Based Interviewing: Information Elicitation", in *Journal of Investigative Psychology and Offender Profiling*, 2018, vol. 15, pp. 133–148.

[33] Figure 6.1 in Arnold, 2021, see *supra* note 11; Figure 5-5 in Paul J. Taylor, "Intra-Individual Communication Behaviour in Conflict Negotiations", Ph.D. thesis, University of Liverpool, 2004.

Conversation is more dynamic than that. But what it does suggest is that the process of co-operating with others is structured around the cylinder structure, and seeking to interpret a suspect's dialogue through this framework can be a useful way to gain insights.

13.3. The Cylinder Model and Interaction Success

While the original intent of the cylinder model was descriptive, researchers and practitioners soon questioned what characterized good outcomes in the model. Experimental and field research converges to suggest two primary answers to this question. The first answer is that interviewers should stay above the suspect in their orientation. If the suspect is competitive, the interviewer should, in all but the most exceptional circumstances, act co-operatively. Any matching of the suspect's competition risks conflict spiralling, while taking an avoidance orientation gives room for the suspect to dominate the interaction.[34] If the suspect is avoidant, then the interviewer has the freedom to either judiciously use competition to simulate interaction[35] or to co-operate.

The second answer is that interviewers should seek to match the suspect's motivational frame. Ormerod, Barrett and Taylor[36] observed that such matching was associated with peaceful resolutions in crisis negotiations. More recently, across studies of both simulations and real interactions, Taylor, Curtis, Giebels and Oostinga[37] found that officers often inadvertently matched suspects' orientations rather than their motivational frames, but when they matched frames, co-operation was more likely to ensue. Over time, adhering to the 'frame matching' finding becomes easier as the interviewer and the suspect become 'entrained'. Entrainment is when the interviewer and suspect have established a common understanding of the dialogue and often follow each other's communicative frame. As Richardson et al.[38] show, the effect of entrainment on interviewer-suspect co-operation can manifest at the basic level of language matching.

---

[34] Paul Christiansen, Laurence J. Alison and Emily Alison, "Well Begun Is Half Done: Interpersonal Behaviours in Distinct Field Interrogations With High-Value Detainees", in *Legal and Criminological Psychology*, 2017, vol. 23, pp. 68–84.

[35] Alison *et al.*, 2013, see *supra* note 20.

[36] Thomas C. Ormerod, Emma C. Barrett and Paul J. Taylor, "Investigative Sense-Making in Criminal Contexts", in Laura Militello, Thomas C. Ormerod, Jan M. Schraagen and Raanan Lipshitz (eds.), *Naturalistic Decision Making and Macrocognition*, Ashgate Publishing, Farnham, 2008, pp. 81–102.

[37] Paul J. Taylor, Joanna L. Curtis, Ellen Giebels and Miriam S.D. Oostinga, "Interpersonal Sensemaking in Crisis Negotiations", unpublished manuscript.

[38] Beth H. Richardson *et al.*, "Language Style Matching and Confessions in Police Interrogations", in *Law and Human Behavior*, 2014, vol. 38, pp. 357–366.

Ormerod *et al.*'s[39] analysis also gave us the first insight into what good sense-making looks like. They found that in transitional periods, where the officer and the suspect were not matching one another's frames (that is, they were 'out of sync'), officers spoke 40 per cent less than during matching periods. This, they argue, suggests that successful officers recognize when they were speaking at cross-purposes with the perpetrator and switch to listening to assess the suspect's motivation. Once they had successfully re-evaluated the situation, they engage in a manner that matches the motivational frame of the suspect. How they do this effectively, and how this skill can be trained, remains a topic of active research.

13.4. Learning to Use the Cylinder Model

The cylinder model is part of many training curricula around the world, taught since 2013 to over 4,000 personnel in 5EYES (an intelligence alliance between Australia, Canada, New Zealand, the UK and the United States ('US')), the European Union and eight other countries. For example, the 2016 tri-agency (that is, the Central Intelligence Agency, the Department of Defense and the Federal Bureau of Investigation) High-Value Detainee Interrogation Group ('HIG') Interrogation Best Practices Guidelines, commissioned by the US Congress, recommends the cylinder model for ensuring "the interrogator and detainee are in-sync with respect to how they are communicating".[40] Similarly, the UK Eliciting Information Framework[41] includes sense-making as a foundation level skill contributing to Engage. A 2018 independent review concluded that interviewed practitioners identify the cylinder model as having "contributed directly to changes in practice, clearly demonstrated by the Hypercacher Supermarket siege in Paris" (p. 12).[42]

Rather than train the model through an 'accredited' course, Taylor has offered materials to all who wish to use the model at no cost. Consequently, the length of cylinder model training depends on who is teaching and the precise audience. In European, US and UK courses, the cylinder forms part of the foundation-level provision for advanced interviewers. It is taught by combining a short overview with a range of exercises that encourage interviewers to recognize a speaker's frame, adapt their own behaviour to different frames and do both within the interview room. As trainees become more proficient, they are

---

[39] Ormerod, Barrett and Taylor, 2008, see *supra* note 36.

[40] HIG, "Interrogation: A Review of the Science", September 2016.

[41] Anna Leslie, "The Eliciting Information Framework: A Vehicle for Research into Practice", in *Crest Security Review*, 15 October 2021.

[42] Jo Edwards, "Impact Review: A Review of the Impact of CREST Research Projects", Lucidity Solutions, September 2019.

introduced to suspects with different cultural backgrounds and way of interacting, thus further challenging their sensemaking skills. The training is designed to move interviewers toward being able to use the cylinder intuitively, recognizing and reacting to dialogue through the lens of the cylinder model in real time.

The efficacy of sense-making training has been the subject of review and direct experimental testing. A partnership between the HIG and the US Air Force sought to develop interview skills among experienced interviewers.[43] Analysing interviews both pre- and post-training revealed that interviewers who had received training displayed more active listening and interpersonal rapport, which, in turn, was associated with increased co-operation and information elicitation.[44] Giebels, Oostinga, Taylor and Curtis[45] taught Dutch and German negotiators to adapt their behaviour to match the expectations, and thus sense-making, of Dutch or German suspects. Trainees then faced suspects of different cultures and were able to achieve more motivational frame matching than otherwise, with the result being more co-operation.

13.5. Operational Uses of the Cylinder Model

The cylinder model[46] has been adapted by negotiators, interviewers and intelligence teams globally to suit their operational needs. This is as it should be. The evolution of the model reflects the important synergy between theory and practice, between researcher and user. For example, one national training course teaches the 'flat cylinder' that juxtaposes orientation and motivation frame in a grid composed of three rows and three columns, allowing users to capture 'scores' (that is, higher scores indicate more of a particular orientation and frame) and notes in each of the cylinder's nine regions. The flattening is partly pragmatic – it is easier to draw onto a flipchart – but also partly strategic. For their purposes, intensity of dialogue is self-evident by the centre of gravity of notes within the grid.

In other areas, only one dimension of the model has been adopted. Prentice et al.[47] report an analysis of online texts that advocate violent extremism

---

[43] Susan E. Brandon et al., "The High-Value Detainee Interrogation Group (HIG): Inception, Evolution, and Impact", in Mark A. Staal and Sally C. Harvey (eds.), *Operational Psychology: A New Field to Support National Security and Public Safety*, ABC-CLIO, 2019, pp. 263–285.

[44] Brandon, Wells and Seale, 2018, see *supra* note 32.

[45] Giebels, Oostinga, Taylor and Curtis, 2017, see *supra* note 1.

[46] As described in Taylor, 2002, see *supra* note 8.

[47] Sheryl Prentice et al., "Analyzing the Semantic Content and Persuasive Composition of Extremist Media: A Case Study of Texts Produced During the Gaza Conflict", in *Information Systems Frontiers*, 2011, vol. 13, pp. 61–73; See Sheryl Prentice, Paul Rayson and Paul J. Taylor, "The Language of Islamic Extremism: Towards an Automated Identification of Ideas,

---

within the UK. They classified statements within each text as either instrumental (for example, explicit or implicit promise of a reward, defined as 'exchanging'), relational (for example, use of social comparisons to provide 'social proof') or identity (for example, messages that intimate the commitments demanded by a religious identity). They showed that over half of the statements across the texts promoted violent extremism through relational messages, contrasting the 'war on terror' instrumental narrative that was dominant in counter-extremism efforts at the time. Watson *et al.*[48] also focus on the motivational dimension in their exploration of the influence behaviours used by suspects accused of control and coercion offences. They found that the frames captured the forms of denial, dominance, justifications, trustworthiness displays, deflections and arguments used by these offenders; denials of the victim and denial of injury being the most often used to persuade interviewers of their innocence.

13.5.1. Guiding Dialogue

Anecdotes from interviewers who have structured their inferences using the cylinder model are common. Some report doing this during dialogue when they recognize the suspect's focus and try to respond accordingly. Others report doing so 'out of the booth' as they recap and plan for future sessions with their team. One of the interesting reports made by those who use the model regularly is that they have begun to recognize their own strengths. Some interviewers find it easy to interact in an instrumental mode but find it more difficult to engage a suspect with identity concerns. Others find relational dialogue and the development of rapport natural, but can struggle to switch to an information-gathering mode. A 12-item questionnaire is available to help interviewers self-assess their communicative preferences,[49] though what people self-report as their strengths in not always congruent with how they interview. The value of recognizing a personal preference is at least two-fold. First, interviewing teams can deploy interviewers strategically, matching team member strengths against their expectations regarding the suspect's preferences. Second, interviewers can target their professional development to build skills and expertise in areas that do not come naturally.

Beliefs, Motivations and Justifications", in *International Journal of Corpus Linguistics*, 2012, vol. 17, pp. 259–286.

[48] Steven J. Watson *et al.*, "Controlling the interview: The Influencing Techniques of Suspects of Control and Coercion", Eleventh International Investigative Interviewing Research Group conference, Porto, 2018.

[49] Sjöberg, Taylor and Conchie, 2021a, see *supra* note 11.

13.5.2. Message Design

While the model's original purpose was to guide dialogue, the result of several high-profile kidnapping investigations in the early 2000s gave recognition to the idea that the model could support efforts to interpret and craft 'messages' sent as part of the investigation. The model provides a framework for the investigator and analyst to systematically consider the motivation behind the messages they are receiving (for example, in a threat to life scenario) and construct messages that either align to the framing or strategically take a different tact. The result is an evidence-based set of decisions that can be referenced back to strong underpinning research literature.

For example, on 19 October 2004, Margaret Hassan was kidnapped outside the gates of the humanitarian relief organization CARE International, located in Baghdad, where she provided shelter and care for all, but particularly young people impacted by the war. Margaret Hassan was born in Ireland but had become an Iraqi citizen, having lived in Baghdad for several decades with her husband.[50] How best, then, to frame messages to seek her release? An instrumental approach could offer medical aid and other permissible items to the kidnappers as an exchange. A relational approach could emphasize Margaret Hassan's key role in supporting the local sick and wounded; the very people the kidnappers may be seeking to help. An identity approach could emphasize Margaret Hassan's Iraqi identity, her family and her clear dedication of several decades to the region. All approaches seek the same outcome, but they do so in different forms.

13.5.3. Planning

Although workloads often make it a challenge, interviewers will wherever possible want to plan how they are going to approach the suspect. Training encourages interviewers to use the cylinder in two ways. First, to assess where the suspect 'is' within the cylinder, asking questions such as 'where would they place themselves', 'what is their dominant orientation', and 'what their prominent motivation goal will be and why'. Second, to assess how the suspect will view the interview, asking questions such as 'who do they expect us to be', 'how shall we confirm or challenge their expectation', and 'what do they think our goal is likely to be'.

One area where planning has come to the fore is in relation to cross-cultural and second language interactions. Cross-cultural conversations start with a lower natural frame alignment because each party brings a different set of

---

[50] "Charity Worker Kidnapped in Iraq", *The Guardian*, 19 October 2004.

expectations and norms.[51] Giebels and Taylor[52] found that crisis negotiators who use tactics consistent with the cultural frame of the suspect secured more concessions. Low-context (individualistic) rather than high-context (collectivistic) suspects tended to respond in a compromising way toward the use of culturally normative persuasive arguments. Interestingly, low-context suspects also tended to give a more co-operative response to direct pressure (for example, 'we need to resolve this now') compared to high-context suspects, who immediately reciprocated the challenge. Similarly, Beune et al.[53] found that individualistic suspects are more co-operative when confronted with instrumental rather than relational dialogue, with the opposite pattern of co-operation evident for collectivistic suspects. Most interesting of their findings is the relatively negative reaction to being kind (for example, showing of empathy) shown by high-context suspects compared to low-context suspects. The authors attribute this response to empathy being interpreted by high-context suspects as a face threat rather than a show of concern.

It can be useful for an interviewer to think about these findings and what they imply for their future interview. One of the challenges of planning in this way is the sheer complexity of evidence and theory an interviewer could draw on to inform their approach. As Hope et al.[54] note, "How best [...] to shepherd the growing number of case studies and non-Western replications into a coherent, practical body of knowledge?" In an effort to make this evidence tractable, Vrij, Taylor and Picornell[55] introduced a common misunderstandings framework that highlights eight of the most robust findings in relation to cross-cultural communication. They point to small talk, role differences, storytelling, emphasizing, persuasion, ultimatums, resistance and issues of face as being issues for interviewers to consider when trying to make sense of the suspect's behaviour.

---

[51] Giebels, Oostinga, Taylor and Curtis, 2017, see *supra* note 1.

[52] Ellen Giebels and Paul J. Taylor, "Interaction Patterns in Crisis Negotiations: Persuasive Arguments and Cultural Differences", in *Journal of Applied Psychology*, 2009, vol. 94, pp. 5–19.

[53] Beune, Giebels and Taylor, 2010, see *supra* note 3.

[54] Lorraine Hope *et al.*, "Urgent Issues and Prospects: Examining the Role of Culture in the Investigative Interviewing of Victims and Witnesses", in *Legal and Criminological Psychology*, 2021, vol. 17, p. 20.

[55] Aldert Vrij, Paul J. Taylor and Isabel Picornell, "Verbal Lie Detection", in Gavin E. Oxburgh, Tim Grant, Trond Myklebust and Rebecca Milne (eds.), *Forensic Communication: Integrated Approaches from Psychology, Linguistics and Law Enforcement*, Wiley, 2015.

13.6. What's Next for Sense-making?

13.6.1. Experimental Demonstrations

While promising, the evidence regarding the benefit of motivational frame matching on interaction outcomes has largely been correlational. In an effort to address this potential limitation, Sjoberg, Taylor and Conchie[56] manipulated suspect interview interactions to either be motivationally matched or non-matched in order to look at the effect on co-operation and trust. They found that participants within a matched interaction trusted, felt more understood and identified more with the interviewer. However, this was only true for an interaction where both the suspect and interviewer adopted a co-operative orientation towards the interaction. When the suspect and interviewer both adopted a competitive orientation towards the interaction, motivational frame matching led to less willingness to co-operate and identify with the interviewer (but not feelings of being understood or an intention to trust the interviewer). This shows the criticality of the interaction between orientation and frame matching on suspects' behaviour.

13.6.2. Handling Mistakes

An area where interviewer sensitivity and flexibility ought to be especially important relates to communication mistakes. Interviewing police negotiators, Oostinga, Giebels and Taylor[57] found that these types of communication errors often could be attributed to a lack of success on the part of the negotiator to actively listen and align the communication with the perpetrator. Interestingly, when an error did occur, some negotiators stressed that active listening could be used as a strategy to re-assess how the other party understood the message, and depending on their reaction to it, either to address the error or to choose to ignore it completely. This speaks to successful sensemakers as being not only zealous listeners, but skilled and adaptable communicators who are able to quickly react to the suspect and respond appropriately.

13.6.3. Interpersonal Sensitivity

As described above, Ormerod, Barrett and Taylor's[58] analysis of frame matching and success revealed that police negotiators almost halved the amount they speak during transitional periods where the frame of the perpetrators' speech and their own speech was not aligned. By doing so, they gave themselves the opportunity to retune their sense of the perpetrator's communication and re-engage them with the appropriate frame. This finding begs the question of how these successful officers achieve this effect and whether or not one can train

---

[56] Sjöberg, Taylor and Conchie, 2021b, see *supra* note 22.
[57] Oostinga, Giebels and Taylor, 2018, pp. 17–30, see *supra* note 4.
[58] Ormerod, Barrett and Taylor, 2008, see *supra* note 36.

others to do the same. Recently, Oleszkiewicz, Weiher and Mac Giolla[59] developed a paradigm for observing and measuring adaptability within officers. Their findings show how levels of adaptability are strongly related to trustworthiness and rapport, and the paradigm may provide new insights into sense-making in years to come.

13.7. The Cylinder Model: A Common Language

Arguably the greatest operational value of the cylinder model, unanticipated by the authors, is that it provides a common, working language for making sense of complex interviews. Teams from various countries have described how interviewer, analyst, interpreter and command come together using the cylinder frames to quickly deliver views during planning, delivery and debriefs. Over time, for example, regular debriefs using the cylinder model begins to beget patterns and variations that allow the team to grow a common expertise. At least one interviewer has used the cylinder in a more explicit way; having it translated to the language of their suspect and introducing it explicitly to them, using a conversation about the model to better understand their position and to aid interaction.

13.8. Conclusion

It is perhaps ironic that the cylinder model has become a language to aid sense-making within teams, given its origins in helping make sense of dialogue with suspects. Yet, this usage reinforces a conclusion that echoes where this chapter began: at the heart of interrogation is the need to make sense of a suspect's dialogue before considering any tactic or response. To make sense of the interaction between interviewer and suspect; to make sense of team members' perspectives and use their insights effectively; to make sense of the many models and tactics in the literature so that their use aligns with the complex, dynamic nature of dialogue. These questions – our need to make sense of sense-making – are not going away any time soon.

---

[59] Simon Oleszkiewicz, Lynn Weiher and Erik M. Giolla, "The Adaptable Law Enforcement Officer: Exploring the Adaptability in a Covert Police Context", in *Legal and Criminological Psychology*, 2022, vol. 27, no. 2, pp. 265–282.

14

Strategic Use of Evidence:
A Review of the Technique and Its Principles

Maria Hartwig and Pär Anders Granhag[*]

14.1. Introduction

Interviewing and interrogation is a fascinating phenomenon, and it is a ubiquitous one. Interrogations occur in criminal investigations, and most forms of other investigations too (for example, in civil cases and other branches of the legal system). Furthermore, it occurs in enterprises of war, in intelligence-gathering and in counter-intelligence. At its core, we here define interrogation as the questioning of one person by another, where the person being questioned may or may not be concealing information (for example, on their guilt). Interrogation is thus a complex phenomenon in that it involves an epistemic problem of determining the truthfulness of the person and what they are saying, along with the intricate social dynamic that occurs between the questioner and the person being questioned. It makes sense to make a distinction between two basic elements that need to be judged. First, if the person being interrogated is a criminal suspect, the central question is whether the person is indeed guilty (or has information regarding the guilt of others). This is a question of the *credibility* of the person. Second, a more general question is whether a given piece of information is true or not – this is a question about the *reliability* of the information yielded.

Interrogators must make numerous such judgments during the course of an interrogation. They also need to manage the social dynamic of the interrogation and pose questions in such a manner that they elicit reliable information. Here, we describe a system of interrogation called the 'strategic use of evidence' ('SUE') technique. In brief terms, the SUE technique is a method of interrogation that relies on strategic considerations of the available case information or evidence. It deals with how interrogators 'play' these pieces of information – not only how they manage the evidence and pose questions around it during the interrogation, but also how they strategize and plan what information to use, and how, prior to interrogation. Before describing the SUE technique in greater detail, we will briefly review past research in order to set the stage.

---

[*] **Maria Hartwig**, Ph.D., is a Professor of Psychology at John Jay College of Criminal Justice, New York. **Pär Anders Granhag**, Ph.D., is a Professor of Psychology at the University of Gothenburg.

14.2. Judgments of Reliability and Credibility

As we discussed above, judgments of reliability and credibility are central during questioning. A now massive body of research shows that lie detection is a very difficult enterprise. When presented with a given piece of information or a statement and asked whether it is true or not, people would obtain an accuracy rate of 50 per cent by merely guessing. How good are we – that is, with what degree of accuracy – at distinguishing between statements that are true and statements that are false? One of the most stable findings in social psychological research is that people obtain an accuracy rate barely above the level of chance.[1] More specifically, meta-analyses[2] show a hit rate (that is, success or accuracy rate) of roughly 54 per cent. This hit rate applies to professional lie-catchers – for example, researchers have studied law enforcement officers' attempts at making judgments both of credibility and reliability, and found that they too make many errors when attempting to distinguish between truth and deception. In fact, contrary to common sense and the intuition of police officers themselves, they too perform just slightly above chance. However, police officers do make judgments in different ways compared to ordinary people: while lay people display a truth bias, that is, a tendency to judge statements as true, law enforcement officers (at least American samples) display a lie bias and are more confident in their judgments, a phenomenon that has been labelled investigator bias.[3]

It may be that it is to incorrectly frame things to say that people's performance at detecting lies is poor. Alternatively, it may be that the near-chance hit rates shown in the literature are, in fact, not due to the person making the judgment, but rather to the judgment itself being difficult. Research strongly supports this view: despite a large body of research investigating all sorts of elements of behaviour,[4] there appear to be very few behavioural signs of deception, leaving the judge with very little to material to work with.[5] In other words,

[1] Aldert Vrij, Maria Hartwig and Pär Anders Granhag, "Reading Lies: Nonverbal Communication and Deception", in *Annual Review of Psychology*, 2019, vol. 70, pp. 295–317.

[2] Charles F. Bond Jr. and Bella M. DePaulo, "Accuracy of Deception Judgments", in *Personality and Social Psychology Review*, 2006, vol. 10, no. 3, pp. 214–234; *id.*, "Individual Differences in Judging Deception: Accuracy and Bias", in *Psychological Bulletin*, 2008, vol. 134, no. 4, p. 477; Valerie Hauch, Iris Blandón-Gitlin, Jaume Masip and Siegfried L. Sporer, "Are Computers Effective Lie Detectors? A Meta-Analysis of Linguistic Cues to Deception", in *Personality and Social Psychology Review*, 2015, vol. 19, no. 4, pp. 307–342.

[3] Jaume Masip, Hernán Alonso, Eugenio Garrido and Antón Concha, "Generalized Communicative Suspicion (GCS) Among Police Officers: Accounting for the Investigator Bias Effect", in *Journal of Applied Social Psychology*, 2005, vol. 35, no. 5, pp. 1046–1066.

[4] Bella M. DePaulo *et al.*, "Cues to deception", in *Psychological Bulletin*, 2003, vol. 129, no. 1, pp. 74–118.

[5] Maria Hartwig and Charles F. Bond Jr., "Why Do Lie-Catchers Fail? A Lens Model Meta-Analysis of Human Lie Judgments", in *Psychological Bulletin*, 2011, vol. 137, no. 4, p. 643.

scientific research shows that detecting deception through behaviour is difficult because the indicators of deceptions are simply too weak.

The scientific research is at odds with people's beliefs about deceptive behaviour. People across the world actually express the belief that lies show and that they show in particular ways.[6] Most commonly, people express the belief that liars are nervous and uncomfortable and that these emotions show in behaviour – for example, that they cannot look you in the eye and that they move their body and fidget in a way that is indicative of discomfort. However, studies of actual behaviour show that these are baseless stereotypes: liars and truth-tellers do not differ in terms of gaze and eye behaviour, and liars do not engage in fidgety and nervous behaviour more than truth-tellers.

It is an interesting question as to where these beliefs come from. One set of culprits is the many manuals and training programmes directed at professionals who have to make judgments of deception and truth as part of their everyday work.[7] These manuals frequently reference non-verbal behaviour and how to use it in order to detect deception. Another possibility is that false stereotypes about deceptive behaviour are part of a shared cultural belief system which coincides with the belief in a just world.[8] This belief holds that good things happen to good people and bad things to bad people. It is firmly in line with this belief to think that a liar (who presumably is up to no good) will betray themselves, possibly through non-verbal behaviour.

14.3. Passive and Active Lie Detection

Most research on lie detection is passive, in the sense that they involve a sender who delivers either a truthful message or a lie – the task of the judge is to correctly classify these statements. However, an interrogation is dynamic, where the interrogators pose questions in order to ferret out the truth (more technically speaking, in order to elicit cues to deception). Researchers have conducted studies where presumably proficient interrogators, armed with a case file,

---

[6] Global Deception Research Team, "A World of Lies", in *Journal of Cross-Cultural Psychology*, 2006, vol. 37, no. 1, pp. 60–74.

[7] Nathan J. Gordon and William L. Fleisher, *Effective Interviewing and Interrogation Techniques*, 2nd ed., Academic Press, San Diego, 2006; Warren D. Holmes, *Criminal Interrogation: A Modern Format for Interrogating Criminal Suspects Based on the Intellectual Approach*, Charles C Thomas, Springfield, 2002; Fred E. Inbau, John E. Reid, Joseph P. Buckley and Brian C. Jayne, *Criminal Interrogation and Confessions*, Jones & Bartlett Publishers, 2013; John Walkley, *Police Interrogation: Handbook for Investigators*, Police Review Publication, London, 1987; Stan Walters, *Principles of Kinesic Interview and Interrogation*, 2nd ed., CRC Press, Boca Raton, Florida, 2003.

[8] Melvin J. Lerner, *The Belief in a Just World: A Fundamental Delusion*, Plenum Press, New York, 1980.

interrogated a mock suspect.[9] Even though these interrogators were seasoned, they obtained an accuracy rate no higher than chance, and they did not manage to elicit behavioural differences between truth-tellers, a pattern replicated in other samples.[10]

How can it be that there are no discernable signs of deception? Some have questioned the generalizability of what is largely a body of laboratory research and argued that when the stakes of the situation are high,[11] liars will give themselves away through leakage of cues to emotion and stress, which an observer can presumably utilize in order to make judgments on deception. However, a meta-analysis on accuracy in deception judgment compared judgments made under conditions where participants told lies and truths in low-stake situations to those told in high-stake settings, and found no significant difference in accuracy.[12] It is possible that this is due to what is called *context overshadowing*: when the stress of the situation (for example, a police interrogation) is high, the pressure is high on liars. But it is equally important to recognize that the pressure on truth-tellers would also be high in such a situation. That is, the more stressful the situation for liars, the more stressful it is for truth-tellers. Indeed, Bond and DePaulo's meta-analysis (2006) shows that more motivated liars and truth-tellers are perceived as less honest compared to their less motivated counterparts. The authors speculate that because of high motivation, both liars and truth-tellers come to resemble the stereotype of deceptive behaviour, that is, displaying cues to nervousness and stress.

One of the most compelling theories that can explain why there are barely any signs of deception in passive displays is Bella DePaulo's *self-presentational theory of deception*. According to this theory, liars and truth-tellers share the goal to be perceived as truthful and both put effort into the enterprise of generating an impression of honesty. If liars and truth-tellers attempt to control their behaviour in order to not resemble a stereotypical liar, we can assume that their displays of behaviour will be similar. As Goffman's original *self-presentational theory* holds (1978), people are practiced at editing and grooming the behaviours they give off depending on what is situationally appropriate or required; since we know self-presentation and impression management are central enterprises

9   Maria Hartwig, Pär Anders Granhag, Leif A. Strömwall and Aldert Vrij, "Police Officers' Lie Detection Accuracy: Interrogating Freely Versus Observing Video", in *Police Quarterly*, 2004, vol. 7, no. 4, pp. 429–456.

10 Timothy J. Luke *et al.*, "Training in the Strategic Use of Evidence Technique: Improving Deception Detection Accuracy of American Law Enforcement Officers", in *Journal of Police and Criminal Psychology*, 2016, vol. 31, no. 4, pp. 270–278.

11 Mark Frank and Elena Svetieva, "Lies worth Catching Involve Both Emotion and Cognition", in *Journal of Applied Research in Memory and Cognition*, 2012, vol. 1, no. 2, pp. 131–133.

12 Bond Jr. and DePaulo, 2006, pp. 214–234, see *supra* note 2.

in ordinary life, we can assume that people are proficient in 'putting on a show'.[13]

Because of the weakness in cues to deception, researchers have argued that lie-catchers must move beyond passive observation to the use of systematic questioning techniques which generate different behaviours from truth-tellers and liars.[14] Such techniques rest on the assumption that while liars and truth-tellers might have the same goal (to be believed to be truthful), they might be in different states of mind. One notion is that liars are experiencing heavier *cognitive load* – simply put, that lying requires more effort than telling the truth. Furthermore, this fact can be exploited purposefully by an interviewer – if further cognitive load is imposed. For example, by asking the interviewee to provide their statement in reverse chronological order or to maintain eye contact, this load will be harder to deal with for a liar than a truth-teller.[15] A line of research supports the cognitive load perspective, in that either cues to deception become increasingly available or that accuracy in deception judgment increases when targets of judgment are subjected to cognitive load.[16] Another line of research, the *unanticipated questions* approach, is based on the premise that liars prepare more than truth-tellers. Further, it holds that liars prepare some, but not all aspects of their cover story. This approach suggests that by asking liars about aspects of their cover story that they have not planned, their responses may be less detailed, plausible and consistent.[17]

The strategic use of evidence technique is a method of eliciting verbal differences between truth-tellers and liars – in particular, the extent to which their statements are consistent with the evidence. It, too, is based on the notion that liars and truth-tellers operate with different mindsets. We will now move to describe the theoretical underpinnings of the technique, after which we will describe the technique itself. The theory underlying the SUE technique is important to understand in order for the technique to be used and applied in a flexible manner.

---

[13] DePaulo *et al.*, 2003, pp. 74–118, see *supra* note 4.

[14] For a review, see Aldert Vrij and Pär Anders Granhag, "Eliciting Cues to Deception and Truth: What Matters Are the Questions Asked", in *Journal of Applied Research in Memory and Cognition*, 2012, vol. 1, no. 2, pp. 110–117.

[15] Aldert Vrij, Ronald P. Fisher, Samantha Mann and Sharon Leal, "A Cognitive Load Approach to Lie Detection", in *Journal of Investigative Psychology and Offender Profiling*, 2008, vol. 5, nos. 1–2, pp. 39–43.

[16] Erik Mac Giolla and Timothy J. Luke, "Does the Cognitive Approach to Lie Detection Improve the Accuracy of Human Observers?", in *Applied Cognitive Psychology*, 2020, vol. 35, pp. 385–392.

[17] Vrij, Hartwig and Granhag, 2019, see *supra* note 1.

14.4. The Psychology of Self-Regulation

The SUE technique has its theoretical basis partly in the psychology of self-regulation. Self-regulation theory is a social cognitive framework that focuses on how people control their behaviour in order to steer away from undesirable outcomes and instead approach those that are desirable.[18] In general, people outline goals and use planning and self-regulatory strategies in order to reach those goals.[19] Some aspects of self-regulation occur automatically and without conscious input,[20] while some other situations call for deliberate control of behaviour. The focus of the SUE technique is primarily on *conscious approaches* to reach desired goals.

Self-regulatory behaviours are activated by threatening situations, in particular those in which a person is operating without full knowledge about a forthcoming event. The SUE technique postulates that both liars and truth-tellers will view a forthcoming interview as a possible threat, with the threatening element here being that one might not be able to convince the interviewer of one's honesty. There is plenty of uncertainty in this situation – for example, the person may not know what the interviewer knows or what questions they will ask.

An aversive and threatening event will trigger self-regulatory strategies.[21] People have a number of such strategies to choose from, with the shared goal to restore control over the situation and steer oneself toward the desired outcome. Researchers have made a distinction between two basic categories: *behavioural* and *cognitive* strategies. A behavioural strategy might be to try to physically avoid the threatening event altogether, and a cognitive strategy can entail forming a mental plan for coping with the threatening situation. In an interview setting, a behavioural strategy could be to invoke one's right to silence and an attorney during the interview, while a cognitive strategy might be to generate a plan for what to say, what to deny, what to avoid talking about, what to say if accused, *et cetera*. The SUE technique focuses primarily on liars' and truth-tellers' cognitive strategies, which we call *counter-interrogation strategies*. We

---

[18] Chales S. Carver and Michael F. Scheier, *On the Self-Regulation of Behaviour*, Cambridge University Press, 2001.

[19] Joseph P. Forgas, Roy F. Baumeister and Dianne M. Tice, "The Psychology of Self-Regulation: An Introductory Review", in *id.* (eds.), *Psychology of Self-Regulation: Cognitive, Affective, and Motivational Processes*, Psychology Press, New York, 2009, pp. 1–17.

[20] For example, routinized non-verbal behaviour when greeting a friend, see John A. Bargh and Tanya L. Chartrand, "The Unbearable Automaticity of Being", in *American Psychologist*, 1999, vol. 54, no. 7, p. 462.

[21] Kathleen D. Vohs and Roy F. Baumeister (eds.), *Handbook of Self-Regulation: Research, Theory, and Applications*, Guilford Publications, 2016.

shall return to the available literature on counter-interrogation strategies later in this chapter.

14.5. Self-Regulatory Differences Between Liars and Truth-tellers

Earlier in this chapter, we discussed self-presentational theory as a framework for understanding how liars and truth-tellers facing an interview share a common goal: to be judged as innocent. However, they differ in several ways. On the most basic levels, liars and truth-tellers by definition differ when it comes to their claims to honesty – which in the case of a liar are bogus.[22] Furthermore, they differ in terms of the critical information that they hold. Liars who are guilty of some sort of transgression are attempting to conceal the true state of affairs in order to implant a false belief in the other that they are innocent. Innocents who have nothing to hide do not have the motivation to distort the receiver's belief system. The primary threat being evoked in an interview for a guilty person is that the interviewer will come to know the true state of affairs which they are motivated to conceal. In a critical sense, the opposite is true for truth-tellers – the main threat is that the interviewer will not come to know the true state of affairs (that they are innocent). Liars and truth-tellers thus differ in their relation to crime-relevant information, and we can expect that they will have different cognitive strategies (that is, pertaining to planning what to say before the interview) as well as different behavioural strategies (that is, managing what to say, what to avoid mentioning, what to deny, *et cetera*, during the interview) with regards to the crime-relevant information. To sum up, because an interview represents a threat (that one will not be believed), self-regulatory strategies likely kick in for both truth-tellers and liars. However, because liars possess information that they aim to conceal (as opposed to truth-tellers), we can expect that liars and truth-tellers will differ in their counter-interrogation strategies in important ways that can be exploited for the purpose of lie detection.

14.6. Counter-Interrogation Strategies

We can make a distinction between *impression management strategies* and *information management strategies*, both of which are counter-interrogation strategies (that is, strategies to prevail in the interview). Impression management strategies are Goffman-like attempts by the interviewee to control others' views of them by using both verbal and non-verbal means. In this case, the desired impression is that of honesty. Interestingly, and in line with Bella DePaulo's original ideas, research mapping liars' and truth-tellers' counter-interrogation strategies shows that truth-tellers too are concerned about the impression they

---

give off and put effort into seeming credible.[23] In one study on counter-interrogation strategies, the two most commonly reported non-verbal strategies for truth-tellers was to avoid moving too much and to maintain eye contact (note that this is exactly the same stereotype as the one we discussed above).[24] However, as one would expect, truth-tellers do not seem to be concerned with the management of information, again as they, per definition, do not have 'guilty knowledge'.[25]

Liars, on the other hand, must make a number of strategic decisions during interviews and interrogations about how to manage the information they have (that is, the guilty knowledge). They must balance multiple risks regarding what to admit, what to deny, what information to offer, *et cetera*. Liars who wish to give a statement must make sure that what they say is both internally consistent and consistent with the knowledge held by the interviewer. For example, denying visiting the Temple Bar on Third Street when the interviewer knows for a fact that they have would hamper their credibility.

In some ways then, liars have to be like game-players, who make numerous strategic moves. This is a decision-making model derived from Hilgendorf and Irving's (1981)[26] classic research, where they highlight the number of strategic decisions a person must make during interrogation. In the SUE technique view, and in line with game theory, knowledge about the counterparts' strategies allows for an exploitation of those strategies, much like in a game of chess.

There are two basic responses to the critical information that a liar must conceal – avoidance and escape or denial. For example, imagine that a person committed a crime at a given location. When asked to provide a free narrative, a liar can refrain from mentioning anything about being at the crime scene. This would be avoidance. If the option of avoiding the topic is not available – for example, if the suspect is asked a direct question about whether they have been to the scene of crime – the suspect could deny (escape). It is interesting to note

---

[23] Maria Hartwig, Pär Anders Granhag, Leif A. Strömwall and N. Doering, "Impression and Information Management: On the Strategic Self-Regulation of Innocent and Guilty Suspects", in *The Open Criminology Journal*, 2010, vol. 3, no. 1, pp. 10–16.

[24] Leif A. Strömwall, Maria Hartwig and Pär Anders Granhag, "To Act Truthfully: Nonverbal Behaviour and Strategies during a Police Interrogation", in *Psychology, Crime & Law*, 2006, vol. 12, no. 2, pp. 207–219.

[25] Maria Hartwig and Pär Anders Granhag and Leif A. Strömwall, "Guilty and Innocent Suspects' Strategies During Police Interrogations", in *Psychology, Crime & Law*, 2007, vol. 13, no. 2, pp. 213–227.

[26] E. Linden Hilgendorf and Barrie Irving, "A Decision-Making Model of Confessions", in Sally M.A. Lloyd-Bostock (ed.), *Psychology in Legal Contexts: Applications and Limitations*, Macmillan, London, 1981, pp. 67–84.

that avoidance and escape responses are very basic forms of behavioural responses to threats that apply to both humans and animals.[27]

When it comes to truth-tellers, they are not in the same information management dilemma as liars as they are not facing a situation where incriminating information must be withheld and false information put forth. Because of this, we expect that truth-tellers will have straightforward counter-interrogation strategies regarding information (they may not even perceive telling the truth to be a strategy). It is likely that truth-tellers believe that if they only tell the truth as it happened, they will be believed. Several psychological mechanisms may contribute to this naive belief. First, truth-tellers may fall victim to the *belief in a just world* – the pervasive notion mentioned above that good things happen to good people.[28] In line with this belief, truth telling suspects might believe that they will be believed simply because they deserve it. Also, people have a general tendency to overestimate the extent to which their inner state shows – a phenomenon that has been dubbed the *illusion of transparency*. For example, a person who engages in a public performance may be very nervous, but tends to overestimate the degree to which this nervousness is evident in behaviour and detectable to others.[29] Research shows that people overestimate the extent to which their mindsets can be read across a number of situations.[30] Interestingly, research on false confessions has shown that innocent people often behave naively in the context of interrogation – for example, by waiving their right to silence, and they justify this behaviour by stating that they had nothing to hide and that if they were able to talk to an interrogator their innocence would show.[31] It thus seems that people not only believe that lying shows (as discussed above), but also that truth-telling shows. Based on this, we can expect truth-tellers to be forthcoming with information, in contrast to liars.

There have been a number of empirical tests of the reasoning outlined here regarding liars' and truth-tellers' counter-interrogation strategies. The typical methodology for these studies is to have some research participants commit a mock crime and then ask them to deny it in an interrogation, while other

---

[27] Neil R. Carlson and William Buskist, *Psychology: The Science of Behavior*, 5th ed., Allyn & Bacon, Boston, 1996.

[28] Lerner, 1980, see *supra* note 8.

[29] Thomas Gilovich, Kenneth Savitsky and Victoria Husted Medvec, "The Illusion of Transparency: Biased Assessments of Others' Ability to Read One's Emotional States", in *Journal of Personality and Social Psychology*, 1998, vol. 75, no. 2, pp. 332–346.

[30] Jacquie D. Vorauer and Stephanie-Danielle Claude, "Perceived Versus Actual Transparency of Goals in Negotiation", in *Personality and Social Psychology Bulletin*, vol. 24, no. 4, pp. 371–385.

[31] Saul M. Kassin, "On the Psychology of Confessions: Does Innocence Put Innocents at Risk?", in *American Psychologist*, 2005, vol. 60, no. 3, p. 215.

research participants commit a similar but innocuous act and are asked to convince the interrogator that they are innocent of the mock crime. This generates a group of lying suspects as well as truth-telling suspects, who prior to interrogation are asked (i) whether they had a strategy to convince the interrogator of their innocence; and (ii) if no, why not, and if yes, what that strategy was.

The available data supports that liars strategize more than truth-tellers – for example, in previous research,[32] the majority of liars (60.5 per cent) reported having a strategy to convince the interrogator of their innocence, while only a minority of truth-tellers did so (37.5 per cent). In line with the expectations outlined above, liars' strategies were primarily revolving around information management strategies (for example, avoid providing incriminating information and staying as close to the truth as possible).[33] Interestingly, when liars' reported having no strategy, this was often a strategic choice to attempt to come across as spontaneous and unrehearsed ('keep it simple').[34] Also in line with our expectations, research on counter-interrogation strategies of truth-tellers show that they indeed report having a strategy less often and that their principal strategy tended to be to tell the truth like it happened ('keep it real').[35]

14.7. From Psychological Principles to Interrogation Strategy

So far, we have reviewed the principal theories on which the SUE technique rests. We have emphasized the importance of considering suspects' strategies, and we have discussed the different strategies reported by liars and truth-tellers. We now turn to how the differences in verbal counter-strategies of information management can be exploited in order to elicit differences in truth-tellers' and liars' statements. We previously described interrogation as having game-like properties. In technical terms, the SUE technique consists of a sort of double-cross, where liars' attempts to deceive are led to backfire on them. In order to understand how the basic principles of the SUE technique can be used to generate different statements from liars and truth-tellers, we will describe the paradigm used in the first test of the SUE principles.[36]

---

[32] Hartwig, Granhag and Strömwall, 2007, pp. 213–227, see *supra* note 25.

[33] Kevin Colwell *et al.*, "Strategies of Impression Management Among Deceivers and Truth-Tellers: How Liars Attempt to Convince", in *American Journal of Forensic Psychology*, 2006, vol. 24, no. 2, pp. 31–38; Amber Hines *et al.*, "Impression Management Strategies of Deceivers and Honest Reporters in an Investigative Interview", in *European Journal of Psychology Applied to Legal Context*, 2010, vol. 2, no. 1, pp. 73–90.

[34] Hartwig, Granhag, Strömwall and Doering, 2010, see *supra* note 23.

[35] Strömwall, Hartwig and Granhag, 2006, see *supra* note 24.

[36] Maria Hartwig, Pär Anders Granhag, Leif A. Strömwall and Aldert Vrij, "Detecting Deception Via Strategic Disclosure of Evidence", in *Law and Human Behavior*, 2005, vol. 29, no. 4, pp. 469–484.

In this study, participants were randomly assigned to either commit a mock crime or to carry out a similar but innocent act. More specifically, liars went to a store in order to look for a briefcase in the corner of that store. They were instructed to open the briefcase and steal a wallet from it. Truth-tellers were asked to go to the very same store and look for an object in the corner where the briefcase was left. In order to look for the object, they had to move the briefcase. This scenario generated several pieces of 'evidence' or information that suggested (but did not conclusively prove) that the participants might have committed the crime. First, there was a witness outside the store who saw the participants enter; second, there was a worker in the store who observed the participants in the corner of the store; third, there was evidence that the participants had touched the briefcase. Note that this evidence was true both for innocent and guilty suspects. All participants were then told that there had been a theft and that they were to be interviewed about their recent activities and that it was their goal to deny involvement in the theft.

There were two types of interviews: one in which the interviewer disclosed the available evidence (the two witnesses and the fingerprint on the briefcase) in the beginning of the interview, while, in others, this evidence was withheld until the end of the interview. Some have misunderstood this to mean that the SUE technique is simply about withholding the evidence – this is missing the point, since the SUE technique revolves around the questions being asked while the suspect is in a state of ignorance about what information the interviewer has. In this study, participants were first asked to provide a broad free recall of their activities over the last hours. They were then asked a series of questions that pertained to the evidence but did not disclose it; these questions were increasingly specific in a structure called the *funnel-line of questions*. For example, they were asked whether they had been to the store in question, where in that store they had been, whether they had been in the corner of the store, whether they had seen a briefcase and whether they had handled the briefcase.

The point of these questions is to highlight the difference in counter-interrogation strategies resulting in forthcoming responses from innocent suspects and avoidant or denial strategies from guilty suspects. Indeed, in the condition where the evidence was disclosed right away, liars and truth-tellers' statements were in line with the evidence. This makes sense – providing liars with information about what incriminating evidence one has gives the liars the opportunity to spin a narrative that is innocent but explains the evidence. In the condition where suspects were questioned without knowing what the evidence was, liars and truth-tellers showed notable differences in verbal behaviour. In the free recall phase, liars were less likely to volunteer information relating to the evidence (for example, not mentioning the store where the theft occurs) than truth-tellers.

Further, in the funnel-line of questions, liars contradicted the evidence more than truth-tellers (for example, saying that they indeed went to the store but that they were never in the corner of the store, or that they saw but never touched the briefcase), a cue to deception we call statement–evidence inconsistency. In this study, it was significantly easier to distinguish between truth-tellers and liars in the so called late disclosure condition compared to the control condition.[37]

The SUE model consists of two layers: first, there are the principles behind the technique – these are theory-based and abstract as well as independent of particularities of a case (this is the *strategic level*).[38] Further, Granhag outlines the *tactical level* as the more concrete and points to two particular forms of tactics – questioning tactics and disclosure tactics. Here, we will use the nomenclature 'techniques' instead of 'tactics'.

14.8. Questioning Techniques

The questioning element of the SUE technique is critical. As we have already stated, withholding the evidence during the questioning phase of the suspects is key. When liars know what the evidence is, they provide statements in line with that evidence. When they are unaware or unsure of what the interviewer knows, their counter-interrogation strategies of verbal avoidance and denial become apparent.

Further, as the experiment we described makes clear, different questions result in different forms of cues to deception. The primary cue that emanates from broad, open-ended questions is avoidance – that is, the lying suspects tend to omit crime-relevant information such as being at the scene of the crime. This kind of information is less often withheld by innocent suspects, presumably precisely because they are innocent and do not perceive such admissions as incriminating. As questions become increasingly specific, in the funnel-line of questions, liars can no longer resort to avoidance. For example, if they are asked directly if they handled the briefcase, they must either admit or deny. Admission is risky as it incriminates them – indeed, the pattern from research is that liars are likely to resort to denials in response to such direct questions. These denials are easy to see through – that is, if we know X to be true and a suspect claims X is not true, we know that what they are saying is not true.

We should insert the caveat here that all behaviour is probabilistic and not all suspects interviewed with the SUE technique behave exactly like we have described here. Also, statement–evidence inconsistencies can result from lapses

---

[37] *Ibid.*

[38] Pär Anders Granhag, "The Strategic Use of Evidence (SUE) Technique: A Scientific Perspective", presented at the High Value Detainee Interrogation Group Research Symposium "Interrogation in the European Union", Washington, D.C., 2010.

in attention or memory on behalf of truth-tellers. For example, if the suspect did not register handling the briefcase while looking for the item in the innocent condition, the statement would contradict the evidence. The important point here is that we, in general terms, can expect differences in the statements when the SUE questioning techniques are used; however, no method is fool-proof. It is also worth noting that an empirical investigation showed that statement–evidence consistency is robust against memory decay – truth-tellers were more consistent with the evidence even after several months.[39]

In investigative interviewing literature there is a strong emphasis on open-ended questions as being preferrable to narrower probes.[40] In another mock crime study utilizing the briefcase paradigm but placing it in a library,[41] we examined the effect of free recall separately from the funnel-line of questioning. There are two take-home messages from this study: unless liars were asked specific questions (for example, whether they went to the crime scene), cues to deception tended to be vague because their statements were vague. It thus seems necessary to ask pointed, direct questions in order to elicit strong statement–evidence (in)consistency. Second, the pattern of response from liars in this study was such that the closer the questions came to the bottom of the funnel (that is, the final questions about the briefcase) the more liars were prone to deny – expressed differently, the more incriminating the question, the more likely liars were to contradict the evidence. This makes sense but is nevertheless critical to note.

Let us expand some more on the funnel-line of questioning that is integral to the SUE technique. In practice, how would an interviewer go about eliciting both avoidance and denial responses from guilty suspects? Expressed differently, exactly how should one plan and pose a line of questions in order to elicit statement–evidence inconsistencies from liars and consistencies from truth-tellers. We have proposed a funnel-like structure as the backbone of the SUE line of questioning. At the top of the funnel are the broadest possible probes for information, consisting of prompts for free recall. Following this are more narrow but still broad questions that pertain to the evidence that the interviewer holds (for example, in the library mock crime above, such a question could be 'Have you been to the library in the last couple of hours?'). Following this is a further

[39] Divya Sukumar, Kimberley A. Wade and Jacqueline S. Hodgson, "Truth-Tellers Stand the Test of Time and Contradict Evidence Less than Liars, Even Months After a Crime", in *Law and Human Behavior*, 2018, vol. 42, no. 2, pp. 145–155.

[40] Rebecca Milne and Ray Bull, *Investigative Interviewing: Psychology and Practice*, Wiley, 1999.

[41] Maria Hartwig *et al.*, "Detecting Deception in Suspects: Verbal Cues as a Function of Interview Strategy", in *Psychology, Crime & Law*, 2011, vol. 17, no. 7, pp. 643–656.

narrowing down of the questions to the key evidence, so that the questions at the bottom of the funnel would be specifically about the briefcase and whether the suspect handled it.

Within an interview, it is possible to create multiple funnels surrounding pieces of evidence that are independent of each other. For example, let us say that a person first stole a car on Main Street, and later that evening used the car to drive to another place where they committed theft in a store. Let us further imagine that there is some evidence pointing to a suspect: (i) multiple independent eye-witnesses seeing the suspect by the car on Main Street; and (ii) CCTV footage of the person in the store in which the theft occurred. In an instance like this, it would make sense to run multiple lines of questions, that is, to create a funnel-line of question for evidence (i) and another for evidence (ii). On a more general note, this phase of the SUE technique is not only about formulating questions, but also about formulating goals that the questions should help to reach. The broader point here is that the basic principles of the SUE technique – the strategic level – allow interviewers to creatively use the principles in order to deploy the technique in ways that are suitable for cases of varying nature and complexity.

14.9. Training in the SUE Technique

Does the SUE technique work in more naturalistic settings – outside the laboratory? In fact, training in the SUE technique seems to result in higher accuracy rates in judging deception and truth. In one study,[42] researchers trained a group of police academy students in the basic principles of the SUE technique and how to use the funnel-line of questions, and then tested their performance during an interview with a mock suspect who had committed a theft in a store. The performance of these trainees was compared to that of a group of students who did not receive the same training. Training affected interview performance in several critical ways. First, the SUE-trained group was more likely to withhold the evidence during questioning – the untrained group disclosed the evidence at significantly earlier stages of the interview. Second, the SUE-trained group asked more funnel-like questions (that is, more specific questions about the evidence (without disclosing it)). Third, the trained group generated far more differences in statement–evidence consistency compared to their untrained counterparts (that is, they managed to elicit a strong, reliable cue to deception). Finally, the average accuracy rate in distinguishing truthful from deceptive statements was 85 per cent after receiving SUE training, significantly better than the untrained

---

[42] Maria Hartwig, Pär Anders Granhag, Leif A. Strömwall and Ola Kronkvist, "Strategic Use of Evidence During Police Interviews: When Training to Detect Deception Works", in *Law and Human Behavior*, 2006, vol. 30, no. 5, pp. 603–619.

group and far better than the 54 per cent hit rates found in meta-analyses on lie detection accuracy.[43]

Perhaps the reader objects to the use of police students as interviewers due to their lack of experience in interviewing. It is possible to argue that seasoned interviewers would be able to elicit statement–evidence inconsistencies because of their experience of interviewing. We do not think this argument is plausible for several reasons. First, a study using a similar paradigm with highly experienced Swedish interviewers (with an average experience of conducting interviews and interrogations of 21.7 years) who had received no training in the SUE technique showed accuracy rates at chance level, and found no evidence of systematic use of the evidence in order to elicit statement–evidence inconsistencies.[44] Second, a replication of Hartwig *et al.*'s training study using a variety of American law enforcement officers shows that the SUE technique is not a mode of interviewing in general, but that training in the technique generates higher hit rates in detecting lies and truths.[45]

14.10. Disclosure Techniques

Although the SUE technique emphasizes systematic questioning as a strategy while the evidence is withheld, there are phases when an interviewer wants to disclose parts or all the evidence to the suspect. Here, we discuss strategic considerations regarding evidence disclosure derived from the basic framework of the SUE technique.

Why would an interviewer disclose the evidence at all? An obvious answer is if they have conducted a funnel-line of questions and have elicited an inconsistency with the evidence. For example, after a series of increasingly specific questions about a suspect's travels, a liar might have denied being in a certain city, even though there are travel records indicating that it is a lie. Disclosing the evidence here could start a discussion about the cause of the inconsistencies between the statement and the facts held by the interviewer.

The body of work on the SUE technique has focused on two aspects of evidence disclosure: the *timing* of the disclosure and the *manner* in which the evidence is disclosed. Starting with the timing element, a number of studies have manipulated when the evidence is disclosed, most typically dichotomously as either early or late disclosure. A meta-analysis showed clearly that cues to deception are stronger when the evidence has been withheld until the end of the

---

[43] Bond Jr. and DePaulo, 2006, pp. 214–234, see *supra* note 2; Bond Jr. and DePaulo, 2008, p. 477, see *supra* note 2.

[44] Hartwig, Granhag, Strömwall and Vrij, 2004, pp. 429–456, see *supra* note 9.

[45] Luke *et al.*, 2016, see *supra* note 10.

interview.[46] A few studies have examined 'drip-feeding' of the evidence (that is, disclosing it gradually) with mixed results. One study showed that drip-feeding and late disclosure both improved hit rates compared to early disclosure.[47] However, other research[48] found that drip-feeding of the evidence led to higher accuracy rates than late disclosure. The totality of the literature thus strongly advises against early disclosure, but research on timing beyond the operationalization of late disclosure is underdeveloped both theoretically and empirically.

When it comes to the manner in which the evidence is disclosure, the SUE technique incorporates a framework called the Evidence Framing Matrix ('EFM').[49] In order to understand the utility of the EFM, it must be recognized that a given piece of evidence can be framed in different ways when it is disclosed. For example, surveillance photographs from the entrance showing a person at Union Station in Washington, D.C., where a crime was committed can be framed in its most straightforward way just as such: 'We have photographs from surveillance cameras showing you entering the train station in Washington, D.C.'. However, the very same piece of evidence can, in terms of what it shows, be framed more generally – for example, 'We have information that you have been to Washington, D.C.'.

14.10.1. The Evidence Framing Matrix

The EFM has two dimensions on which evidence can be framed. First, there is the source of the information, which can be presented on a dimension ranging from vague to precise. Another way to put this is *how do we know* what it is that we know? Using the example above, the source here is surveillance photographs. This can be framed either as precise – surveillance photography from the entrance – or vaguely – in its most vague form, the interviewer can merely frame this as 'information'. The second dimension of the Matrix consists of the content of the evidence – exactly *what is it that we know*. This too can be framed specifically – 'We know you have gone through the entrance of Union Station in Washington, D.C.' – to more vaguely – 'We know you have been at Union Station' – to even more vaguely – 'We know you have visited Washington, D.C.'.

---

[46] Maria Hartwig, Pär Anders Granhag and Timothy J. Luke, "Strategic Use of Evidence During Investigative Interviews: The State of the Science", in *Credibility Assessment*, 2014, pp. 1–36.

[47] Marina Sorochinski *et al.*, "Interviewing to Detect Deception: When to Disclose the Evidence?", in *Journal of Police and Criminal Psychology*, 2014, vol. 29, no. 2, pp. 87–94.

[48] Coral J. Dando and Ray Bull, "Maximising Opportunities to Detect Verbal Deception: Training Police Officers to Interview Tactically", in *Journal of Investigative Psychology and Offender Profiling*, 2011, vol. 8, no. 2, pp. 189–202.

[49] First proposed by Granhag, 2010, see *supra* note 38.

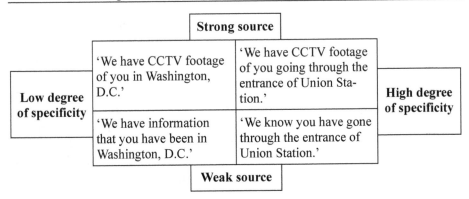

Figure 1: The Evidence Framing Matrix.

How is an interviewer supposed to use the EFM? The basic purpose is to be able to strategize regarding evidence disclosure in such a way that it complicates liars' efforts at keeping their story straight. Imagine that a liar who indeed went to Union Station has given a statement in which he denies being in the Washington, D.C., area altogether (because of the counter-interrogation strategies of avoidance and denial). If the evidence is presented in a vague form, both in terms of source and content ('We have information that you have actually been to Washington, D.C.'), the liar has two options: deny the information (rendering their statements even more inconsistent with the evidence) or revise their story so that it fits with the evidence as it has been presented but still leaving them innocent ('I forgot that I did go to Washington, D.C., but I was only in the suburbs and never went to the station'). Now a new cue has emerged – the suspect has begun to contradict their own statement. We call this cue within-statement consistency. In a test of gradual evidence disclosure using the EFM, there were three interview conditions: SUE Basic, where the evidence was disclosed in its most precise form at the end of the interview; SUE Incremental, where the evidence was disclosed gradually, using the EFM to move from general to more specific disclosure; and an early disclosure condition where the evidence was disclosed before questioning began.[50] Indeed, when the evidence was disclosed using the EFM, the differences between liars and truth-tellers in terms of within-statement consistency were the most pronounced, showing support for this method of disclosure. However, more empirical research is needed on how to optimally use the EFM. For now, it is worth noting that it can function as an important tool in the planning and execution of a SUE-style interview. The broad

---

50 Pär Anders Granhag, Leif A. Strömwall, Rebecca M. Willén, Maria Hartwig, "Eliciting Cues to Deception by Tactical Disclosure of Evidence: The First Test of the Evidence Framing Matrix", in *Legal and Criminological Psychology*, 2013, vol. 18, no. 2, pp. 341–355.

conclusions we would like to draw here are that not only *when* but *how* the evidence is disclosed matters for the outcome of the interview.

In a recent study, we used computer-generated avatars, driven by empirically-based algorithms of suspect behaviour, to train naive participants in using the EFM.[51] Each participant interviewed two different avatars, and we found that those who had received EFM training before the first interview, or feedback after the first interview (or both training and feedback), outperformed a control group receiving no training or feedback in assessing the veracity of the avatars' statements (88 per cent accuracy versus 42 per cent accuracy, respectively). We can draw two conclusions from this study. First, it is possible to teach naive participants to strategically disclose the evidence during an interview using the EFM. Second, with avatars the training can be done cost effectively; there is no need for role-playing suspects and the training can be done remotely.

14.11. The Shift of Strategy Approach

In a new line of research, we have tested what we call the *Shift of Strategy* ('SoS') approach. As the name indicates, the approach is about interviewing in a way which will make the suspect change his or her counter-interrogation strategy – from aversive to forthcoming. This approach was foreshadowed by Serra Tekin and her colleagues[52] and, during the recent years, we have developed the approach further. Beyond a set of evidence disclosure tactics, the SoS approach is a collection of strategies for managing information and social principles to guide interviewers.

For the SoS approach, the interviewer gives the suspect the impression that he or she is substantially knowledgeable about the suspect's activities, and this is done by initially withholding information and then, after they provide a partial account of their activities, alerting suspects to the fact that their statements have contradicted the evidence (or have been consistent with the evidence). As the interview proceeds, the suspect can gradually learn the pattern: that the interviewer typically knows more than they initially let on. The suspect then overestimates the interviewer's knowledge and, later in the interview, is more likely to reveal truthful information about their activities to avoid damaging their credibility by contradicting something that the interviewer knows but has not yet revealed. Thus, the purpose of the SoS approach is to induce guilty

---

[51] Siyu Li *et al.*, "A Serious Game With Avatar Suspects Can Be Used to Train Naïve Participants in the Strategic Use of Evidence (SUE)", 2022 (manuscript under review).

[52] Serra Tekin *et al.*, "Interviewing Strategically to Elicit Admissions from Guilty Suspects", in *Law and Human Behavior*, 2015, vol. 39, no. 3, pp. 244–252; Serra Tekin, Pär Anders Granhag, Leif A. Strömwall and Aldert Vrij, "How to Make Perpetrators in Denial Disclose More Information About Their Crimes", in *Psychology, Crime & Law*, 2016, vol. 22, no. 6, pp. 561–580.

suspects to change their strategy from a generally withholding one to a more forthcoming one, while also providing an opportunity for innocent suspects to give a statement that is in line with the evidence.

In a recent study, we test the effectiveness of two variations of the SoS approach, one in which the interviewer responded immediately to any discrepancies with the evidence (Reactive), and one in which the interviewer only responded to severe discrepancies (Selective). We predicted that the SoS approach conditions would be more effective at eliciting new information from mock suspects, compared to direct questioning.[53] In a laboratory experiment, 300 mock suspects committed a simulated crime and were interviewed using one of the two versions of the SoS approach or with an interviewing approach that did not involve the presentation of evidence. We found that the Reactive version was significantly more effective than direct questioning at eliciting new information from the suspects. The Reactive technique also led the suspects to change their strategies during the interview.

The SoS approach is an extension of the SUE technique; it is based on the same foundational understanding of suspects' strategies, but it differs in its focus and scope. Whereas many SUE interviews have deception detection as a main objective, the main purpose of the SoS approach is to obtain previously unknown information.[54] Differently put, for the SoS approach, the cues to deceit are means to a larger end.

14.12. SUE Applied to Real-World Settings

Before closing the chapter, we would like to underscore that not only does the SUE technique rest on a solid theoretical base, there are by now over 20 individual empirical examinations of the different parts or stages of the technique. A critical examination by Aldert Vrij and Ronald P. Fisher in 2016[55] showed that the SUE technique was one of very few deception detection techniques that were assessed as having enough empirical support to be recommended to the criminal justice system. The SUE technique has proven successful for single suspects, but also for groups of suspects. The technique works for questioning suspects

---

[53] Timothy J. Luke and Pär Anders Granhag, "The Shift-of-Strategy Approach: Using Evidence Strategically to Influence Suspect's Counter-Interrogation Strategies", in *Psychology, Crime & Law*, 2022, pp. 1–26.

[54] Pär Anders Granhag and Timothy J. Luke, "How to Interview to Elicit Concealed Information: Introducing the Shift-of-Strategy (SoS) Approach", in J. Peter Rosenfeld (ed.), *Detecting Concealed Information and Deception*, Elsevier, 2018, pp. 272–295.

[55] Aldert Vrij and Ronald P. Fisher, "Which Lie-Detection Tools Are Ready for Use in the Criminal Justice System?", in *Journal of Applied Research in Memory and Cognition*, 2016, vol. 5, no. 3, pp. 302–307.

about the past, but also for questioning suspects about their future intentions.[56] We have been teaching the SUE technique world-wide for more than 15 years and the technique has been picked up by many police departments and organizations, such as the Federal Law Enforcement Training Centers, the High-Value Detainee Interrogation Group, and the Los Angeles Police Department ('LAPD'). Recent communication with the LAPD shows that over 100 agencies in California alone are to receive training in the SUE technique.

14.13. Concluding Remarks

We opened this chapter by outlining the principal theories on which the SUE technique rests. We then moved from the theoretical underpinnings to concrete counter-interrogation strategies and we made clear that: (i) liars and truth-tellers differ in terms of their counter-interrogation strategies; and (ii) the SUE technique exploits these differences. In the latter part of the chapter, we closed in on the tactical level of the SUE technique and spent time discussing the funnel approach to questioning and the EFM which helps the interviewer to disclose evidence as tactically as possible. Finally, we introduced the SoS approach, a recent and promising extension of the SUE technique that utilizes SUE tactics to elicit new information from suspects.

---

[56] For a summary, see Pär Anders Granhag and Maria Hartwig, "The Strategic Use of Evidence Technique: A Conceptual Overview", in Pär Anders Granhag, Aldert Vrij and Bruno Verschuere (eds.), *Detecting Deception: Current Challenges and Cognitive Approaches*, Wiley-Blackwell, 2015, pp. 231–251.

15

Observing Rapport-Based Interpersonal Techniques for Research and Training in Suspect Interviewing

Frances Surmon-Böhr, Laurence J. Alison and Emily Alison[*]

15.1. Introduction

Observing Rapport-Based Interpersonal Techniques ('ORBIT') is the first and by far and away the largest empirically-grounded and comprehensive model of field-based law enforcement interviews. Deriving its theory-driven pedigree from over 70 years of interpersonal, social psychological research from the personality and counselling domains, ORBIT is the most theory-rich approach to suspect and human source interviewing. It has carefully reconstructed, synthesized and empirically validated humanistic and interpersonal theories of human relating to form a model of rapport-based interaction. ORBIT is also unique insofar as it is based on by far the largest dataset globally of real interviews with real detainees. The size and scope of the sample grows each year as more data is added with the dataset now in excess of 2,000 hours of carefully coded material. In addition to law enforcement interviews, it now also includes imminent threat interviews and what might more appropriately be called interrogations since some of this material includes objectives different to law enforcement agencies (that is, search for truth and evidence) and may instead be directed at, for example, time-sensitive intelligence or information rather than material obtained for court or criminal justice goals.

An extensive research programme over the past 10 years has culminated in a series of publications in internationally recognized journals,[1] as well as a

---

* **Frances Surmon-Böhr**, Ph.D., is a post-doctoral research associate at the School of Psychology at the University of Liverpool. **Laurence J. Alison**, Ph.D., is a Professor of Forensic and Investigative Psychology and Director of the Centre for Critical and Major Incident Research at the School of Psychology, University of Liverpool. **Emily Alison**, Ph.D., is a behavioural consultant psychologist and research associate at the School of Psychology, University of Liverpool.

1 Laurence J. Alison *et al.*, "Why Tough Tactics Fail and Rapport Gets Results: Observing Rapport-Based Interpersonal Techniques (ORBIT) to Generate Useful Information from Terrorists", in *Psychology, Public Policy, and Law*, 2013, vol. 19, no. 4, pp. 411–414; Laurence J. Alison *et al.*, "Whatever You Say, Say Nothing: Individual Differences in Counter Interrogation Tactics Amongst a Field Sample of Right Wing, AQ Inspired and Paramilitary Terrorists",

book on the ORBIT model.[2] ORBIT now forms the central approach to interviewing terrorist suspects in the United Kingdom ('UK'), having been directly embedded in the UK National Counter Terrorism Advanced and Specialist Interviewer Training Programs. It has been used by the Central Intelligence Agency ('CIA'), the United States ('US') Department of Defense ('DoD'), the Federal Bureau of Investigation ('FBI') and the US Department of Agriculture in the US, by the UK military interrogation unit, the UK National Crime Agency ('NCA'), the UK War Crimes unit, the UK Border Force Intelligence Directorate, by intelligence agencies in Israel and by law enforcement and military agencies across Europe such as the Netherlands' police and military intelligence units. Other sectors that have been trained in ORBIT include international banks, trade compliance and audit teams and the International Committee of the Red Cross.

To understand the development and application of the ORBIT framework, it is essential to follow the genesis and approach taken by the research team. Reflective of the solutions-focused and field-based collaboration adopted by the original researchers, it is worth outlining the journey taken in terms of the dataset, the background literature on rapport and interpersonal communication, and the critical review of techniques and skills that yield the most effective results in challenging interviews.

15.2. The Genesis of ORBIT

ORBIT was developed to research the most effective methods of conducting sensitive, high-stakes interviews where individuals may be resistant or reluctant to co-operate. Although its origins go as far back as 2005, it gained considerable traction after 2012 when the High-Value Detainee Interrogation Group ('HIG'; formed by the Obama Administration in the US) funded work for assessment of its application in the context of interviews with high-value targets (that is,

---

in *Personality and Individual Differences*, 2014, vol. 68, pp. 170–175 ('Alison *et al.*, 2014a'); Laurence J. Alison *et al.*, "The Efficacy of Rapport Based Techniques for Minimizing Counter Interrogation Tactics Amongst a Field Sample of Terrorists", in *Psychology, Public Policy, and Law*, 2014, vol. 20, pp. 421–430 ('Alison *et al.*, 2014b'); Paul Christiansen, Laurence J. Alison and Emily Alison, "Well Begun Is Half Done: Interpersonal Behaviours in Distinct Field Interrogations With High-Value Detainees", in *Legal and Criminological Psychology*, 2018, vol. 23, pp. 68–84; Frances Surmon-Böhr, Laurence J. Alison, Paul Christiansen and Emily Alison, "The Right to Silence and the Permission to Talk: Motivational Interviewing and High-Value Detainees", in *The American Psychologist*, 2020, vol. 75, no. 7, pp. 1011–1021.

[2] Laurence J. Alison, Emily Alison, Neil D. Shortland and Frances Surmon-Böhr, *ORBIT: The Science of Rapport-Based Interviewing for Law Enforcement, Security, and Military*, Oxford University Press, 2020.

terrorist suspects). As part of this work, Alison and Alison[3] developed ORBIT as a taxonomic classification framework to code interpersonal behaviour and rapport-based skills in investigative interviews or interrogations. Based on extensive research over the past 10 years, ORBIT has evolved as an evidence-based approach to both analysis and research, as well as a training framework for interviewing for law enforcement, security services and the military.

What makes ORBIT unique is that it is based on the analysis of real interviews, involving real interviewers with real suspects and real consequences. In 2012, working in close co-operation with the UK Counter Terrorism ('CT') Police Unit, a research team at the University of Liverpool, led by the second author of this chapter, were granted unprecedented access to 878 hours of real-world police interviews with terrorism suspects. The dataset comprised suspects with a wide range of religious, ideological and political affiliations including Al-Qaeda, Irish paramilitaries and right-wing extremist groups. Access to further CT police interviews, comprising a large sample of suspects affiliated with Islamic State ('IS'), was later granted and added to the existing dataset. Securing this data was laborious and involved extensive negotiation and communication that satisfied the many concerns and regulations associated with CT police interviewing.

After obtaining an initial dataset, Alison *et al.*[4] sought to understand why certain interviewers were more successful at communicating with suspects, subsequently gaining more evidentially useful information from them, than others. The authors identified similarities between effective and ineffective interviewer–suspect interactions and therapist–client interactions. Thus, the first part of ORBIT focuses on how to build rapport and draws heavily on the principles of humanistic psychology and person-centred counselling, where the concept of rapport, or 'therapeutic alliance' between the therapist and client (that is, the connection and relationship between a therapist and their patient), has been well studied.

15.3. The Humanistic Paradigm of Rapport Building

Rapport is covered at length in Chapter 4 of this book; however, as a reminder, the ability to build rapport and form a human connection with a suspect is regarded as the foundation of successful interviews.[5] This can be considered a

---

[3] Laurence J. Alison and Emily Alison, "ORBIT: Observation of Rapport-Based Interview Techniques (version 16)", University of Liverpool, 2012 (internal document).

[4] Alison *et al.*, 2013, see *supra* note 1.

[5] Ulf Holmberg and Kent Madsen, "Rapport Operationalized as a Humanitarian Interview in Investigative Interview Settings", in *Psychiatry, Psychology and Law*, 2014, vol. 21, no. 4, pp. 591–610; Allison Abbe and Susan E. Brandon, "The Role of Rapport in Investigative

relationship based on respect, trust, empathy and a shared understanding of one another's goals.[6] Whilst there is a clear consensus amongst practitioners and researchers on the importance of rapport, the concept has proved difficult to define and measure in law enforcement, military and security contexts.[7]

To be clear, rapport is not about being nice or being the suspect's friend, it is not something you just do at the beginning of an interview and then get to the 'real stuff' later, nor does it just emerge in response to certain tactics or specific sets of words. Instead, rapport requires management of your own responses and fluidly responding to the other person. Rapport is based on an authentic connection with someone which requires maintaining respect, dignity, and compassion for others, regardless of how they are behaving towards you.[8] It can be lost and found over time and can go up and down over a single session, over night or over the course of weeks or months. It must be conceptualized as an organic process rather than a distinct stage of the interview.

The concept of rapport has been well defined and studied in the therapeutic-counselling arena where the relationship between the therapist and client is considered critical to successful therapeutic outcomes.[9] Much of this work originates from the so-called humanistic paradigm.[10]

Interviewing: A Review", in *Journal of Investigative Psychology and Offender Profiling*, 2013, vol. 10, pp. 237–249.

[6] Laurence J. Alison and Emily Alison, "Revenge vs. Rapport: Interrogation, Terrorism and Torture", in *American Psychologist*, 2017, vol. 72, no. 3, pp. 266–277; Jacqueline R. Evans *et al.*, "Criminal Versus HUMINT Interrogations: The Importance of Psychological Science to Improving Interrogative Practice", in *Journal of Psychiatry and Law*, 2010, vol. 38, pp. 215–249; Christopher E. Kelly, Jeaneé Miller, Allison D. Redlich and Steven M. Kleinman, "A Taxonomy of Interrogation Methods", in *Psychology, Public Policy, and Law*, 2013, vol. 19, no. 2, p. 165.

[7] But see Alison, Alison, Shortland and Surmon-Böhr, 2020, *supra* note 2, and Jonathan P. Vallano and Nadja S. Schreiber Compo, "Rapport-Building With Cooperative Witnesses and Criminal Suspects: A Theoretical and Empirical Review", in *Psychology, Public Policy, and Law*, 2015, vol. 21, pp. 85–99 for a comprehensive review.

[8] Alison, Alison, Shortland and Surmon-Böhr, 2020, *supra* note 2.

[9] Adam O. Horvath and Dianne B. Symonds, "Relation Between Working Alliance and Outcome in Psychotherapy: A Meta-Analysis", in *Journal of Counseling Psychology*, 1991, vol. 38, no. 2, p. 139; Daniel J. Martin, John P. Garske and M. Katherine Davis, "Relation of the Therapeutic Alliance With Outcome and other Variables: A Meta-Analytic Review", in *Journal of Consulting and Clinical Psychology*, 2000, vol. 68, no. 3, p. 438.

[10] Abraham H. Maslow, "Preface to Motivation Theory", in *Psychosomatic Medicine*, 1943; Carl R. Rogers, *Client-Centered Therapy*, Houghton Mifflin, 1943; Carl R. Rogers, "A Theory of Therapy, Personality and Interpersonal Relationships as Developed in the Client-Centered Framework", in Sigmund Koch (ed.), *Psychology: A Study of a Science: Vol. 3. Formulations of the Person in the Social Context*, McGraw-Hill, 1959, pp. 184–256.

Humanistic psychology emerged during the 1950s as an alternative to the two approaches that dominated psychology at the time: (i) psychoanalysis (focused on unconscious forces that drive human thought and behaviour); and (ii) behaviourism (focused on how behaviour is learned and shaped by the environment through a process called 'conditioning'). Unlike the deterministic nature of these approaches, humanistic psychology stressed the importance of taking a holistic view of people and their ability to exercise free will.

Influential humanistic psychologist Carl Rogers pioneered a therapeutic approach based on what he had learned and observed from clinical experience, initially called 'non-directive' but which later became known as 'client-centred' and 'person-centred' therapy. Rogers believed effective therapist–patient relationships should be more egalitarian, built on mutual trust and respect.[11] Rather than focusing on skills to be acquired, it was argued[12] that a strong therapeutic relationship or *therapeutic alliance* was based on a therapist's attitude toward the client, later describing it as a 'way of being'.[13] This attitude is also known as therapist 'core conditions', which include being genuine or real with the client, providing unconditional positive regard to the client (that is, being non-judgmental and accepting of the person) and expressing accurate empathy (that is, trying to accurately understand the other person's world). As such, success is based on the therapeutic value system of the therapist and their macro-level approach to communication.

Whilst the ORBIT framework is based broadly on humanistic principles, it specifically draws on strategies from Motivational Interviewing ('MI')[14] to define and operationalize rapport in an investigative interview context. Pioneered by William Miller and Stephen Rollnick in the 1980s and 1990s, MI is an evidence-based clinical intervention that evolved from Roger's non-confrontational, person-centered approach.[15] It was originally developed as an approach to encourage behavioural change in problem drinkers. Like client-centred

---

[11] Carl R. Rogers, "The Necessary and Sufficient Conditions of Therapeutic Personality Change", in *Journal of Consulting Psychology*, 1957, vol. 21, no. 2, p. 95.

[12] Carl R. Rogers, "The Therapeutic Relationship: Recent Theory and Research", in *Australian Journal of Psychology*, 1965, vol. 17, no. 2, pp. 95–108.

[13] Carl R. Rogers, "Growing Old – or Older and Growing", in *Journal of Humanistic Psychology*, 1980, vol. 20, no. 4, pp. 5–16.

[14] William R. Miller and Stephen Rollnick, *Motivational Interviewing: Preparing People for Change*, Guilford Press, 1992.

[15] William R. Miller and Theresa B. Moyers, "Motivational Interviewing and the Clinical Science of Carl Rogers", in *Journal of Consulting and Clinical Psychology*, 2017, vol. 85, no. 8, p. 757.

therapy, MI evolved from intuitive clinical practice and the author[16] recognized that for behavioural change to occur, motivation to change needed to come from the client rather than being imposed by the therapist.

In line with a client-centred approach, MI is underpinned by a particular 'spirit' that promotes collaboration between the therapist and client, aims to evoke the client's own thoughts and ideas about behavioural change, and recognizes that ultimately it is up to the client to choose to make the change or not.[17] It is within the presence of this spirit that rapport is likely to emerge. However, unlike the non-directive nature of traditional client-centred therapy, MI is very goal-directed insofar as the therapist intentionally targets the client's ambivalence (that is, simultaneous motivations for making a change and for not making that change) about behavioural change. Therapists deliberately guide the conversation using specific skills so that it is the client, not the therapist, who voices any reasons for change in order to enhance the client's motivations to make this change. The efficacy of MI for encouraging behavioural change has now been shown in a wide range of settings (for example, from reduction or abstinence from alcohol or drugs and eating more healthily to violence reduction). To date, over 600 clinical trials and numerous meta-analyses and systematic reviews have been conducted on it.[18]

Alison and Alison (2012)[19] were the first to formally adopt and adapt specific MI principles and skills for use within the context of investigative interviewing and interrogation. Specifically, they identified five Global MI principles that were applicable to this context – acceptance, adaptation, autonomy, empathy and evocation. The reason for adopting some of the thinking behind MI relates to its capacity to provide an empathic and non-coercive atmosphere that, where relevant and appropriate, allows individuals to discuss things that they may be ambivalent about revealing. As in a therapeutic context, whilst observing police interviews with terrorism suspects, it was noticed[20] that when interviewers used approaches like those used in MI, even though they were not trained in these techniques, suspects were more engaged with the interviewers

---

[16] William R. Miller, "Motivational Interviewing With Problem Drinkers", in *Behavioural and Cognitive Psychotherapy*, 1983, vol. 11, no. 2, pp. 147–172.

[17] Miller and Rollnick, 1992, see *supra* note 14.

[18] Carlo C. DiClemente *et al.*, "Motivational Interviewing, Enhancement, and Brief Interventions Over the Last Decade: A Review of Reviews of Efficacy and Effectiveness", in *Psychology of Addictive Behaviors*, 2017, vol. 31, no. 8, p. 862; Petra Lawrence, Paul Fulbrook, Shawn M. Somerset and Paula Schulz, "Motivational Interviewing to Enhance Treatment Attendance in Mental Health Settings: A Systematic Review and Meta-Analysis", in *Journal of Psychiatric and Mental Health Nursing*, 2017, vol. 24, nos. 9–10, pp. 699–718.

[19] Alison and Alison, 2012, see *supra* note 3.

[20] Alison *et al.*, 2013, see *supra* note 1.

and willing to talk. In particular, interviewers (i) who came across as open-minded about the investigation and did not show any judgment towards the individual in front of them, (ii) who showed interest in the suspect and focused on drawing out their values and beliefs, (iii) who were able to adapt fluidly to what was being said by the suspect (instead of rigidly controlling the agenda), and (iv) who emphasized the suspect's right to choose to talk or not usually had a good relationship with the suspect and gained more evidentially useful information.

These notions are operationalized in ORBIT's six cornerstones of rapport known as the HEEAAR principles: (i) honesty; (ii) empathy; (iii) evocation; (iv) adaptation; (v) autonomy; and (vi) reflection, see Table 1 for definitions of each of these concepts). The original ORBIT framework contained 'acceptance' (providing unconditional positive regard) as a key principle, however, more recently this was replaced by the concept of 'honesty' to encourage being non-judgmental but also being clear, objective and direct about the circumstances; and the key skill of reflective listening was added to form the HEEAAR principles.

Skill	Definition
Honesty	Being direct, clear and objective – that is, not being judgmental or avoidant of asking difficult questions or raising difficult topics.
Empathy	Displaying genuine understanding of the suspect's actions or mindset.
Evocation	Eliciting statements from the suspect about their thoughts, feelings and the underlying core values or beliefs.
Adaptation	Altering agenda in response to the suspect rather than rigidly adhering to interview plan.
Autonomy	Respecting or emphasizing the suspect's right to choose to co-operate, speak, engage or not.
Reflection	Repeating back strategic elements of what has been said or implied by the suspect.

Table 1: ORBIT global rapport-based strategies (HEEAAR) developed by Laurence J. Alison and Emily Alison.

Like client-centred counselling, we observed that attempts at listening to and genuinely trying to understand a suspect's perspective without judgement can lead to a respectful, empathic atmosphere that facilitates co-operation. However, even more pronounced was the observation that interviewers who engaged in approaches antithetical to those outlined above seemed to have very poor relationships with the suspect and were often met with suspect resistance (for example, silence, 'no-comment' or aggression) (see Table 2 for details of approaches considered inconsistent with rapport-building).

Skill	MI-Consistent Definition	MI-Inconsistent Techniques
Reflective Listening	*Accurate understanding*: demonstration that the interviewer has accurately heard and understood the detainee; using simple or complex reflections without judgment.	*Assumptive questioning*: inaccurate or exaggerated interpretations of what the detainee has said; providing unsolicited advice; interrupting the detainee; being dismissive, argumentative or accusatorial.
Summaries	*Balanced summary without judgment*: information is summarized using the suspect's own words and then clarification or further detail is sought; summaries that include both positive and negative content.	*Judgmental summary*: focus is on the negative aspects of the account; summaries that introduce the interviewer's view rather than the detainee's; summaries with a tone of sarcasm or disbelief.
Rapport and Resistance	*Rolling with resistance*: use of evocative prompts; statements that reflect positive and negative content; using three prompts when met with resistance, then shifting to an area of less resistance.	*Fighting resistance*: use of tactics that inhibit rapport such as threatening, ordering, use of sarcasm or judgment; warning the detainee of consequences; misleading or forced questions.
Developing Discrepancies	*Neutral challenge*: inconsistencies presented to the detainee for explanation without providing excuses or passing judgment; use of the detainee's own speech or specific details of forensic reports to ensure no misunderstanding; inviting an explanation.	*Judgmental challenge*: inconsistencies are presented in a confrontational, accusatory or judgmental manner such as: demanding explanations, shaming or blaming; focus on police or victim's perspective rather than the detainee's.

Table 2: Motivational Interviewing of detainees: Assessment of skills coding framework (adapted from Alison and Alison, 2012, see *supra* note 3).

In addition to the observation that humanistic therapeutic approaches seem to be effective at encouraging suspects to disclose evidentially useful information, taking such an approach is beneficial for several other reasons. Firstly, regardless of whether the suspect co-operates or not, adoption of such approaches will do no harm to the suspect. ORBIT opposes the use of deception or persuasion through its commitment to both honesty and honouring suspect autonomy. Hence, ORBIT's rapport-based strategies are entirely ethically and legally compliant with interviewing guidelines and honour suspects' basic human and legal rights (for example, PACE, 1984;[21] the Méndez Principles, 2021).[22]

Secondly, innocent suspects are protected as there is no pressure (from persuasion or coercion) to reveal false information. Any pressure to reveal information will be generated in a suspect who is experiencing internal ambivalence through increased awareness of it. It was hypothesized[23] that in contexts where the suspect has guilty knowledge, the atmosphere created will increase the internal conflict they feel over revealing information. It is then up to the suspect whether to talk or to maintain silence or deception. The goal is to create an environment conducive to open communication where any internal conflict with the suspect (if there is any) will emerge without deceit or trickery. If the suspect has no ambivalence or knows nothing about the investigation, no internal pressure will emerge. This negates any issues with false confessions that can emerge from pressurizing or persuasive interrogations.[24]

Thirdly, if a suspect is lying, withholding or concealing information, and evidence can prove this, humanistic approaches will demonstrate to the jury that the police have consistently provided the suspect an opportunity to talk without pressure. However, accomplishing this rapport-based approach is not an easy task. It is hard for interviewers to consistently remain flexible and respond fluidly to suspects, whilst considering the needs of the suspect, especially in the face of aggressive or demanding behaviour. Furthermore, some suspects will require a different approach to others (for example, a highly dominant Taliban commander compared to a scared farmer). Thus, to begin, interviewers need to figure out how the person they are dealing with wants to be dealt with.

15.4. Interpersonal Relating and Managing Difficult Behaviour

This brings us to the second part of ORBIT which focuses on understanding how to manage difficult suspect behaviour based on theories of personality and interpersonal relating. It is our view that for the interviewer to get to a point of productive conversation and opportunity to build rapport, they must first manage the suspects' behaviour. In ORBIT, this is called interpersonal style and relates to the behaviours that are present between individuals when interacting

---

[21] United Kingdom, Police and Criminal Evidence Act, 31 October 1984 (https://www.legal-tools.org/doc/b52ec0/).

[22] Anti-Torture Initiative, Association for the Prevention of Torture and the Norwegian Centre for Human Rights, *Principles on Effective Interviewing for Investigations and Information Gathering*, 2021 ('Méndez Principles') (https://www.legal-tools.org/doc/wbfiw1/); see also Chapter 6 of this book.

[23] Alison and Alison, 2012, see *supra* note 3.

[24] See Brandon L. Garrett, "The Substance of False Confessions", in *Stanford Law Review*, 2009, vol. 62, p. 1051.

with each other. ORBIT draws on the ideas proposed by psychologists Timothy Leary and Moulton Marsden in the late 1950s in relation to personality. They reasoned that personality, previously considered a fixed, person-specific state, was something that could be best observed when an individual interacts with another individual. Additionally, Marsden and Leary identified two driving motivations that occur when people interact: desire for power over other people and the desire for intimacy or love. The interpersonal circumplex model[25] provides a visual representation of this. The model maps interpersonal behaviours and characteristics along two axes: a vertical axis of dominance–submission and a horizontal axis of hostility–friendliness. The theory is that the vertical axis works on a rule of correspondence (that is, dominant behaviour invites submissive behaviour and *vice versa*) and the horizontal axis works on the rule of reciprocity (that is, friendliness invites friendliness and hostility invites hostility).

Forty years later, building on Leary's theory of interpersonal behaviour, the 'interpersonal octagon' was developed[26] which allowed for behaviour in between the two axes to be mapped. Birtchnell's most important contribution though was his observation that communication styles could be done either adaptively (likely to promote communication) or maladaptively (likely to impede communication).

Based on both Leary and Birtchnell's behavioural circumplex and octagon, an interrogation-specific version known as the interpersonal behaviour circles ('IBC'; informally called the 'interpersonal wheel') was developed as part of the ORBIT model (see Figure 1 for a schematic representation of the IBC). The ORBIT IBC allows the dyadic interaction between interviewer and suspect to be measured. The inner circle represents adaptive behaviours and the outer circle represents the maladaptive variants of these areas on the wheel.[27] For example, an interviewer might be adaptively in charge and advising, but, if they stray too far, they might become bossy and demanding.

ORBIT training encourages increased self-awareness and emotion regulation to manage one's own behaviour, recognizing that any behaviour, if too intense, can become problematic. It also focuses on three key interpersonal skills – interpersonal *sensitivity* (for example, to be able to accurately judge the nature of the person they are dealing with); interpersonal *competence* (that is, to be able to avoid negative forms of interaction and 'stay off' the maladaptive areas); and

[25] Timothy Leary, *Interpersonal Diagnosis of Personality*, Ronald Press, 1957.

[26] John Birtchnell, "The Interpersonal Octagon: An Alternative to the Interpersonal Cycle", in *Human Relations*, 1994, vol. 47, pp. 511–529.

[27] The original ORBIT framework contained two wheels, one adaptive and one maladaptive, but we have since updated the visual representation of this to form a single wheel.

interpersonal *versatility* (for example, to be able to deploy a range of different behaviours when they are needed).

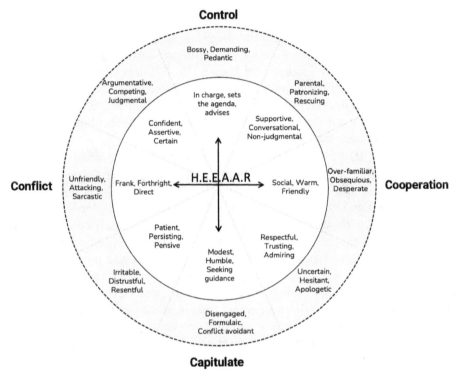

Figure 1: Schematic representation of the ORBIT interpersonal wheel.

15.5. Measuring Success

All of what has been discussed thus far is focused on how to understand and measure the interaction between the interviewer and suspect based on the interviewer's behaviour. The aim is to create an environment that is conducive to establishing rapport and securing information. However, the ultimate end-goal of an investigative interview or interrogation is to gain an account from a suspect which contains verifiable information and intelligence (either provable facts or disprovable lies). As such, when understanding the effectiveness of building rapport with suspects, the main dependent variable (that is, the thing that is being measured) is operationalized as *yield*. The ORBIT framework provides an Interview Yield Assessment ('IYA') for coding yield that captures the amount of information obtained during an interview. Specifically, the IYA captures information relating to four categories: (i) capability (the suspect's ability to commit the offence); (ii) opportunity (the suspect's circumstances allowing commission of the offence); (iii) motive (any reasons for the suspect to commit the offence); and (iv) descriptions (any details about people, locations, actions and times that may be related to the offence).

In addition to the amount of yield disclosed in an interview, also of interest is how engaged or disengaged the suspect is with the interviewers, as it indicates the suspect's level of attention and willingness to co-operate. Thus, ORBIT contains a Suspect Engagement Rating ('SER') designed to capture this. SER is scored on an eight-point scale where '1' reflects that the suspect refuses to engage with the interviewers at any point in the session and '8' represents the suspect answering all questions fully and thoroughly, providing new information and outlining their role in the events.

Finally, ORBIT also contains a measure of the degree to which the suspect was resisting the interview through the Suspect Resistance Behaviour Scale ('SRBS'). Some suspects engage in behaviours used to resist co-operation or communication and these may be intentional or unintentional. Individuals who are experienced with police interviews or have been deliberately coached to employ strategies within police interviews use a range of tactics that can be broadly categorized into three types: distractions, disengagement and provocation. The SRBS thus categorizes resistance based on these categories: (i) distractions (that is, strategies that attempt to disrupt the flow of the interview to delay or derail the line of questions); (ii) disengagement (that is, strategies that switch the suspect off from the interaction); and (iii) provocation (that is, the most overt resistance and aggressive strategies to upset and derail the interview process).

15.6. ORBIT Research Overview

Since the creation of the ORBIT framework in 2012, Alison and colleagues have conducted a series of studies to examine how interviewer behaviours impact suspect behaviour and the subsequent amount of evidentially useful information disclosed in interviews. Much of this research, as well as an extensive overview of the development of the ORBIT model and its application in the field, can be found in a recent book.[28] For completeness, a summary of the key findings is provided below.

In their first study,[29] ORBIT was used to examine interviews with 29 individuals convicted of terrorism-related offences. For the first time, they provided empirical evidence for the effectiveness of adopting an interpersonally skilled, rapport-based approach with terrorism suspects, in which the suspects are treated with respect, dignity and integrity. Specifically, they examined interviewer–interviewee rapport based on the interviewers' use of five global MI

---

[28] Alison, Alison, Shortland and Surmon-Böhr, 2020, see *supra* note 2.
[29] Alison *et al.*, 2013, see *supra* note 1.

skills – acceptance, empathy, evocation, adaptation and providing autonomy. They found that the use of these strategies was significantly associated with increased information yield. Similar findings were reported in a recent study examining a sample of South Korean investigative interviews with victims of sexual offences.[30]

Further exploration of rapport-based strategies with additional data from the National CT Police Unit was conducted with a sample of interviews with 75 terrorist suspects.[31] The findings revealed that suspect engagement was a strong driver of yield. The authors also reported that interviewer use of specific MI core skills (that is, reflective listening, rolling with resistance or balanced summaries) was associated with increased suspect engagement, but, importantly, they found that even minimal use of behaviours antithetical to MI (that is, being assumptive, judgmental or accusatorial) led to a significant decrease in suspect engagement. Thus, it is imperative that interviewers focus on eliminating any maladaptive behaviours they might have which could impede communication with the suspect.

Research has also begun to explore the dynamic nature of rapport-building and suspect engagement. For example, Christiansen, Alison and Alison (2018)[32] found an association between suspect engagement in the first and last interviews, as well as certain adaptive interviewer interpersonal behaviours that were associated with adaptive suspect behaviours in the first and last interviews. Additionally, another study[33] examined the impact of the interviewer's use of rapport-based strategies on suspect engagement and interview yield within a particular interview and across a series of interviews conducted over a number of days. The results revealed that two rapport-based strategies (acceptance and adaptation) were particularly effective at engaging suspects, but the positive impact of using these strategies was only seen on that day. This suggests that interviewers must engage in rapport-building efforts on each day of interviewing and not assume that the positive influences will carry forward to further interviews on other days. Further research is needed to explore the dynamic nature of rapport investigative interviews.

---

[30] Sunghwan Kim, Laurence J. Alison and Paul Christiansen, "Observing Rapport-Based Interpersonal Techniques to Gather Information from Victims", in *Psychology, Public Policy, and Law*, 2020, vol. 26, no. 2, p. 166.

[31] Surmon-Böhr, Alison, Christiansen and Alison, 2020, see *supra* note 1.

[32] Christiansen, Alison and Alison, 2018, see *supra* note 1.

[33] Frances Surmon-Böhr, Laurence J. Alison, Paul Christiansen and Emily Alison, "Securing Continued Engagement With High Value Suspects at the Start of Each New Day: The Benefits of Humanistic Psychological Approaches", University of Liverpool (unpublished manuscript).

Research using ORBIT has also looked at the issue of suspect resistance and suspects' use of Counter Interrogation Tactics ('CITs').[34] The authors identified: (i) patterns in the use of CITs among different groups of terrorists,[35] and (ii) found that interviewer use of rapport-based strategies was directly associated with decreases in certain CITs, including silence and 'no comment' responses.[36] At present, our research team is working on an HIG-funded research project aimed at furthering our understanding of extreme resistance in terrorist suspects utilizing ORBIT.

More recently, in partnership with the UK NCA, ORBIT has been validated in police interviews with individuals suspected of child sex offences. Looking at interviews of 25 individuals convicted of child sexual abuse offences,[37] another study replicated previous findings[38] in relation to the impact of rapport-based strategies and increased yield. Although rarer in this sample of offenders, the results highlighted that with a highly entrenched maladaptive responder, any positive adaptive approaches on the interviewer's part may fail to have any effect. Nonetheless, these results reinforce the idea that it may not always be possible to improve engagement, but it is always possible to make it worse.

15.7. Application to Real-Life Settings

The development of ORBIT and the subsequent research programme that ensued made a significant contribution to the area of investigative interviewing which, in turn, has had important implications in the field. Although ORBIT's primary research base is interviews conducted by police officers with terrorist suspects, its practice sample is much wider and includes military interrogations, interviews with suspected war criminals and interviews with individuals suspected of murder, rape, Child Sexual Abuse ('CSA') and Exploitation ('CSAE') and domestic abuse. It has also been used in many live cases in the field, which, in some instances, has led to interviewers obtaining life-saving intelligence. Furthermore, it has had significant implications for interviewer–interrogator training. For example, the ORBIT model of interviewing is now the subject of training for interviewers around the world, including CIA, DoD and FBI officers in the US, the UK Joint Force Intelligence Group, as well as Shin Bet in Israel and

---

[34] Alison *et al.*, 2014a, see *supra* note 1; Alison *et al.*, 2014b, see *supra* note 1.

[35] Alison *et al.*, 2014a, see *supra* note 1.

[36] Alison *et al.*, 2014b, see *supra* note 1.

[37] Michael Humann *et al.*, "Motivational Interviewing in Child Sexual Abuse Investigations – Approaches Shown to Increase Suspect Engagement and Information Gathering During Police Interviews" (under review).

[38] Alison *et al.*, 2013, see *supra* note 1; Surmon-Böhr, Alison, Christiansen and Alison, 2020, see *supra* note 1.

law enforcement agencies across Europe. In the UK, ORBIT sits at the centre of the national CT police specialist and advanced interviewer training courses and the NCA's national specialist training programme, as well as the US HIG core training programme (for FBI, CIA and DoD officers).

15.8. Emerging Evidence Relating to Training

As mentioned earlier, the initial research on ORBIT was made possible by the UK CT Police Unit providing interviews for analysis, and this has since been expanded owing to collaboration with the NCA and access to interviews with CSA or CSAE suspects. In return for providing this data, practitioners were assured an evidence base to design training programmes that could hone specialist interviewer skills. Consequently, all findings and publications were shared directly with the relevant units first. Further, ensuring that findings make their way into practice, we have worked closely with various professional development units to re-embed learning into revised or new training programmes. Working together, both psychologists and practitioners have contributed to the development and facilitation of various specialist courses to ensure the effective transfer of the research findings to practice for interviewing officers.

ORBIT training programmes range from half-day lecture inputs to five-day immersive scenario-based courses. The objective of training is to enable individuals from a wide range of organizations, and with varying levels of experience, to obtain comprehensive, detailed and direct information in a way that is legal, sensitive, compassionate, respectful, professional and, most critically, effective. Courses cover the interpersonal skills and rapport-based methods that have been empirically tested in extremely difficult environments. Workshops include a series of detailed talks on ORBIT. Following this, participants are put through a series of exercises to develop and hone key skills to use the ORBIT model. It is recommended that training environments closely replicate real-world complex problems, and that the acquisition of these complex multi-faceted skills can then be scaffolded and supported by both the trainers during training and by more experienced staff when they are back in service.[39] Hence, for more advanced participants, these skills are then deployed across a series of immersive role-plays, based on scenarios designed specifically for each organization, with input from practitioners. Participants are provided with immediate

---

[39] Elizabeth L. Bjork and Robert A. Bjork, "Making Things Hard on Yourself, But in a Good Way: Creating Desirable Difficulties to Enhance Learning", in Morton A. Gernsbacher, Richard W. Pew, Leaetta M. Hough and James R. Pomerantz (eds.), *Psychology and the Real World: Essays Illustrating Fundamental Contributions to Society*, Worth Publishers, 2011, pp. 56–64; Selen Turkay *et al.*, "Toward Understanding the Potential of Games for Learning: Learning Theory, Game Design Characteristics, and Situating Video Games in Classrooms", in *Computers in the Schools*, 2014, vol. 31, nos. 1–2, pp. 2–22.

feedback and coaching by psychologists and field professionals to accelerate learning. To avoid training decay, subsequent 'top up training' is also available through both face-to-face work as well as online support packages that include modelling best practices, aide memoires and 'flashcard' challenges.

The longest-running ORBIT training course is 'Alcyone', which is a comprehensive, six-day, specialist interviewer training course for police interviewers in the UK who work within the CT unit. The course was significantly revised in 2013 to incorporate most recent findings and fully integrate recommendations, resulting in a six-day course that provides the following: (i) psychological training in ORBIT; (ii) input on pre-interview briefing; and (iii) legislation and input on safety interviewing. The course begins with theoretical lectures outlining the key concepts and underlying philosophy of ORBIT. Initially, there is a strong focus on interviewers' mindset and on understanding the approach before the more tactical elements are taught. Based on the research findings, there is a strong emphasis on officers first eliminating any maladaptive interviewing behaviours they might have, before attempting to acquire new skills. Approximately 80 per cent of the course involves immersive scenario-based role-play for participants to practice deploying the skills, with additional knowledge checks and short lecture inputs. Due to the intensity and complexity of the course, all officers who attend Alcyone have already completed a specialist suspect interviewer training course (previously named 'Tier 3' but now called the specialist interviewer course under 'PIP level 2', in line with the College of Policing's Professionalising Investigation Programme ('PIP') of 2018).[40] Officers can either be nominated, or nominate themselves, to be considered for the course. The course runs twice a year and usually consists of 12 officers that are then split into three teams of four persons. To date, nearly 200 officers from across the six CT Units in the UK, as well as individuals from the UK military, War Crimes Unit and the HIG have been trained across 17 courses.

Two studies have been conducted to examine the efficacy of ORBIT training on the Alcyone course with very promising results. First, a field-based study examined 31 sets of real-life CT interviews conducted between 2012–2017, of which, all interviewers had undertaken a specialist suspect interviewing course (under PIP 2), but 16 interviewers had also undergone Alcyone training.[41] Alcyone-trained officers were found to use significantly more rapport-based strategies than untrained officers and were significantly less likely to use maladaptive behaviours. Importantly, the findings showed that interviewers who were

---

[40] College of Policing, *Professionalising Investigations: Programme Policy*, 2018.

[41] Laurence J. Alison *et al.*, "How to Build Rapport: Assessing the Effectiveness of ORBIT Training With Police Interviewers", in Alison, Alison, Shortland and Surmon-Böhr, 2020, see *supra* note 2.

Alcyone-trained yielded significantly more information from their interviews than those who were not trained. The Alcyone-trained interviewers had received their training between three and 30 months prior to conducting the interviews included in the dataset, which suggests that Alcyone training is not only effective but has an enduring impact.

Another study[42] provides evidence for the short-term effects of Alcyone training. The authors examined the impact of training across the duration of an Alcyone course based on measures of 29 officers' rapport-based interview performance on the first and last day of the course. The results showed significant increases in the use of rapport-based strategies and decreases in approaches that may impede rapport by the end of the course. Again, the results indicated powerful effects of the training, with all officers making significant improvements in their use of rapport-based strategies from day one to day five.

15.9. Financial Impact of Using ORBIT in the Field

We have recently conducted the first economic evaluation of the value of rapport-based interviewing based on ORBIT-specific approaches[43] which examined a sample of interviews with offenders convicted of CSAE. Giles *et al.* wanted to explore the impact of interviewer interpersonal behaviours (adaptive and maladaptive) and their use of rapport-based strategies on extracting information of investigative value. Specifically, the authors were interested in two types of economic yield: (i) 'case strengthening' yield (that is, passwords and pin codes, evidence of involvement, usernames on social media, information on victim devices, presence of digital evidence, information on areas and movements, knowledge of other devices, knowledge of other significant people); and (ii) 'safeguarding' yield (that is usernames of associates, information about associate devices, knowledge of other undisclosed plans, other offenders, culpability for other offences, knowledge of other victims). Procuring this information would reduce resource requirements elsewhere (that is, taking the burden off data analytics, digital forensics, house to house enquiries, victim identification, identification of networks, facilitation of safeguarding and strengthening of legal cases). The findings revealed that adaptive interpersonal behaviours increased case strengthening and safeguarding yield, with rapport-based interviewing strategies having the largest impact on safeguarding yield. Conversely, maladaptive interviewer strategies reduced case strengthening and different

---

[42] Laurence J. Alison, Nicole Plummer and Michael Humann, "Motivational Interviewing Training of Practitioners Who Interview Terrorists: Assessing the Effectiveness of ORBIT Training on an Advanced CT Interviewer Course", University of Liverpool (unpublished dissertation).

[43] Susan Giles *et al.*, "An Economic Evaluation of the Impact of Using Rapport-Based Interviewing Approaches With Child Sexual Abuse Suspects", in *Frontiers in Psychology*, 2021, vol. 12, pp. 1–14.

types of economic yield. Economic modelling estimated that ORBIT training in adaptive interpersonal behaviours and rapport-based interviewing could contribute cost savings between GBP 19–78 million (annual unit costs) increasing to GBP 238–972 million (lifetime costs) for online CSA across England and Wales; and GBP 157–639 million (annual unit costs) increasing to GBP 2–8 billion (lifetime costs) for all CSA. The authors conclude that failure to commit training resource to this, or an alternative strategy, could mean the cost burden attributable to maladaptive interviewing (between GBP 1–6 million for online CSA and GBP 12–48 million for all CSA) is not successfully averted.

15.10. Limitations and Future Directions

Whilst ORBIT has proven highly effective as an approach to research and training, and as a practical method for interviewers to use in the field, there are some limitations that should be discussed. Firstly, nearly all of the research into ORBIT has been conducted on real-world police interviews with suspects. The strength of this applied approach to research lies in its ecological validity and generalizability to real world contexts. However, as highlighted by other scholars,[44] real life data is necessarily limited by the lack of control of extraneous variables. For example, strength of evidence and, crucially, the suspect's perception of the evidence against them have been found to be two of the most frequent and important reasons why suspects confess.[45] The presentation of evidence has not been controlled for any of the research into ORBIT, which is an important limitation of the work and future research should control for this.

Secondly, the majority of research into ORBIT has analysed the data as a static model with a lack of sequencing. Some studies have begun to examine the dynamic nature of rapport-based strategies on suspect engagement,[46] however, further research is needed to explore this, especially in cases where multiple interviews are conducted over a long period of time. Future research could also examine the potential impact of a suspect's behaviour on an interviewer's behaviour.

Thirdly, one aspect of ORBIT that could be improved is the coding framework used to code interviewer and suspect behaviour in investigative interviews. Generally, inter-rater reliability of the various coding scales in the coding framework are good but some coding sub-scales have only achieved 'fair' scores.[47] It

---

[44] Maria Hartwig, Pär Anders Granhag and Aldert Vrij, "Police Interrogation from a Social Psychology Perspective", in *Policing and Society*, 2005, vol. 15, no. 4, pp. 379–399.

[45] Gisli H. Gudjonsson, *The Psychology of Interrogations and Confessions: A Handbook*, John Wiley & Sons, 2003.

[46] Christiansen, Alison and Alison, 2018, see *supra* note 1.

[47] Surmon-Böhr, Alison, Christiansen and Alison, 2020, see *supra* note 1; Alison *et al.*, 2014b, see *supra* note 1.

is important to note though that when using dichotomous categories (presence or absence of behaviours) rather than ordinal scales (0–3, 0–5), all scales were found to have very good reliability. This indicates that small differences in interpretation of behaviour (for example, mild to moderate) may make it more difficult to apply subtler coding to some of the scales. As such, the ORBIT coding framework would benefit from being simplified to ensure better consistency in coding among researchers.

Lastly, whilst there is evidence to support the use of ORBIT in the field, interviewers are often trained in the use of a range of different interviewing approaches[48] (for example, the Cylinder model and sensemaking;[49] the Strategic Use of Evidence ('SUE');[50] the Scharff Technique;[51] the Cognitive Interview ('CI') technique;[52] Cognitive-based Credibility Assessment).[53] Currently, there is a lack of research into how ORBIT can be most effectively used alongside other interviewing methods. Whilst there is evidence to support the use of the different interviewing methods as standalone entities (that is, SUE, the Scharff Technique, the CI, *et cetera*), further research is needed to determine the best way to integrate the different approaches for practitioners to use in the field.

15.11. Conclusions

ORBIT is the first empirically-grounded and comprehensive model of investigative interviewing and interrogation based on an analysis of the largest sample of interviews with terrorism suspects in the world. The model is unique in that it is based on the analysis of real interviews, involving real interviewers with real suspects and real consequences. Bringing together over 70 years of

---

48 Susan E. Brandon *et al.*, "The High-Value Detainee Interrogation Group (HIG)", in Mark A. Staal and Sally C. Harvey (eds.), *Operational Psychology: A New Field to Support National Security and Public Safety*, ABC-CLIO, 2019, p. 263.

49 Paul J. Taylor, "A Cylindrical Model of Communication Behavior in Crisis Negotiation", in *Human Communication Research*, 2002, vol. 28, pp. 7–48; see also Chapter 13 of this book.

50 Maria Hartwig, Pär Anders Granhag, Leif A. Strömwall and Ola Kronkvist, "Strategic Use of Evidence During Police Interviews: When Training to Detect Deception Works", in *Law and Human Behavior*, 2006, vol. 30, no. 5, p. 603; see also Chapter 14 of this book.

51 Pär Anders Granhag, Simon Oleszkiewicz, Leif A. Strömwall and Steven M. Kleinman, "Eliciting Intelligence With the Scharff Technique: Interviewing More and Less Cooperative and Capable Sources", in *Psychology, Public Policy, and Law*, 2015, vol. 21, pp. 100–110; see also Chapter 10 of this book.

52 Ronald P. Fisher and R. Edward Geiselman, "The Cognitive Interview Method of Conducting Police Interviews: Eliciting Extensive Information and Promoting Therapeutic Jurisprudence", in *International Journal of Law and Psychiatry*, 2010, vol. 33, pp. 321–28; see also Chapter 16 of this book.

53 Aldert Vrij, Ronald P. Fisher and Hartmut Blank, "A Cognitive Approach to Lie Detection: A Meta-Analysis", in *Legal and Criminological Psychology*, 2017, vol. 22, pp. 1–21.

combined research on humanistic therapeutic approaches and interpersonal relating, ORBIT provides a theoretically-rich model of communicating with resistant individuals in difficult settings. At the heart of the ORBIT approach is a mindset that is honest, empathic and honours suspects' right to choose whether to co-operate or not, as well as commitment to always treat suspects with respect, dignity and integrity. Hence, ORBIT rejects all notions of coercion, persuasion and manipulation. As an internationally recognized model, ORBIT has now been trained to a range of organizations including UK and US law enforcement and military, the UK War Crimes Unit, the UK Border Force, international banks and international humanitarian organizations.

PART III: VICTIMS AND WITNESSES

16

The Cognitive Interview in Laboratory and Field Tests of Crime and Terrorism

Ronald P. Fisher and Tzachi Ashkenazi[*]

16.1. Introduction

Solving and thwarting crimes or acts of terrorism requires that investigators acquire information, the lifeblood of all investigations. They need information about the perpetrators, their support system, the methods used, the event's planning and a host of other facts. If investigators are fortunate, the relevant information will be stored on physical media (for example, fingerprints, remnants of other physical paraphernalia and electronic devices); more often, the information will be stored only in the minds of people (for example, victims, eyewitnesses and informants). Securing the information from co-operative people will then become the focal point of the investigation, and the focus of this chapter.

Given the importance of eliciting information from these sources, it is surprising that law enforcement receives so little training on interviewing co-operative people. Law enforcement training academies either omit completely or spend minimal time on the topic.[1] Similarly, the United States ('US') Army Field Manual,[2] a comprehensive guide to information-gathering, allocates minimal space to eliciting information from co-operative sources – although it covers extensively how to interrogate unco-operative sources. Perhaps we should

---

[*] **Ronald P. Fisher**, Ph.D., is a Professor of Psychology at the Florida International University. He co-developed the Cognitive Interview ('CI') protocol, and has conducted extensive research to test the CI. He has conducted many training programmes in the United States and internationally with law enforcement agencies (such as the Federal Bureau of Investigation), the military and national security organizations. **Tzachi Ashkenazi** founded and headed the Operational Behavioral Science Unit in the Israeli Prime Minister's Office where he served for 20 years. He researched and developed various methods in investigative interviewing, including memory-enhancing techniques and deception detection methods, gained extensive experience in their operational use and has conducted extensive training programmes in these areas. He is an Adjunct Professor at Bar Ilan University and Ashkelon Academic College.

[1] Peter F. Molinaro, Ronald P. Fisher, Alexandra E. Mosser and Geri E. Satin, "Train-the-Trainer: Methodology to Learn the Cognitive Interview", in *Journal of Investigative Psychology and Offender Profiling*, 2019, vol. 16, no. 4, pp. 32–43.

[2] United States Department of the Army, *Human Intelligence Collector Operations*, Field Manual No. 2-22.3, Washington, D.C., 6 September 2006 (https://www.legal-tools.org/doc/wbfiw1/).

---

not be so surprised, as criminal investigators and military interrogators receive minimal training on interviewing co-operative human sources in many domains (for example, vehicular and industrial accidents, military encounters, insurance fraud, *et cetera*). The training they do receive tends to focus on the respondent's motivation to co-operate and on the content of the investigation: the case-related details that need to be uncovered. Rarely does the training emphasize the respondent's cognitive processes (for example, memory retrieval).

As a result of the poor training given to investigators, and their general insensitivity toward witnesses' memory retrieval processes, investigators make many avoidable errors when interviewing co-operative witnesses (see the analyses of American police,[3] Canadian police[4] and German police[5]). Common errors include interviewers: (i) failing to develop adequate rapport; (ii) asking too many closed questions and too few open-ended questions; (iii) asking suggestive questions; (iv) interrupting witnesses during their narrations; and (v) not providing memory-retrieval assistance when witnesses fail to remember critical details. These errors contribute to witnesses either providing less information than is potentially available (omission errors) or reporting their experiences incorrectly (commission errors).

The goal of the present chapter is to examine how researchers and investigators have contributed to improving investigative interviews of co-operative witnesses by incorporating the science of cognition (thinking, memory, communication and other mental activities). Specifically, we focus here on the CI protocol. We describe how the CI evolved from its simple beginnings to its current state, which is more comprehensive but also more effective. As we expect our readers to demand empirical evidence, we describe the traditional, controlled experimental studies conducted in the laboratory and then present, in greater detail, how the CI fared in real-world investigations of crime and, most recently, in its role to investigate acts of terrorism. Sprinkled throughout the chapter are brief anecdotal accounts of how specific CI techniques were implemented in real-world criminal, military and security-related investigations (some details were altered to protect innocent people and to avoid disclosing sensitive

---

[3] Ronald P. Fisher, R. Edward Geiselman and David S. Raymond, "Critical Analysis of Police Interviewing Techniques", in *Journal of Police Science and Administration*, 1987, vol. 15, no. 3, pp. 177–185.

[4] Brent Snook and Kathy Keating, "A Field Study of Adult Witness Interviewing Practices in a Canadian Police Organization", in *Legal and Criminological Psychology*, 2011, vol. 16, no. 1, pp. 160–172.

[5] Alexander Berresheim and Anette Weber, "Die Strukturierte Zeugenvernehmung und Ihre Wirksamkeit" [Structured witness interviewing and its effectiveness], in *Kriminalistik*, 2003, vol. 57, no. 12, pp. 757–771.

information). Finally, we offer some observations on the importance of conducting field research, and we offer suggestions about future research.

16.2. Evolution of the Cognitive Interview

16.2.1. Original Version of the Cognitive Interview

The beginnings of the CI date back to the mid-1980s and reflect Edward Geiselman and Ronald Fisher's beliefs that witness reporting of criminal events was limited primarily by their memory retrieval processes.[6] Geiselman and Fisher therefore developed the CI by incorporating into the interview a set of mnemonic instructions that were known from basic memory research to enhance memory retrieval. Specifically, they instructed witnesses to use three guiding principles. First, reinstate the context of the original experience (encoding specificity principle:[7] memory retrieval is enhanced when the context at retrieval (the interview) is the same as the original encoding experience (for example, the crime); being in the exact same location as the original event is optimal, but often impractical; in such cases, mentally reinstating the original experience is a good alternative). Second, report everything the witnesses remembered (multi-component view of memory:[8] the memory record of an event is composed of many components (for example, visual, spatial, auditory and temporal), which link to other related events; requesting witnesses to 'report everything' may activate several related events). Third, recall the event in different ways (varied retrieval),[9] either in different chronological orders (forward and backward) or from different spatial or personal perspectives, as each retrieval cue may activate a different aspect of the critical event; hence, additional retrieval cues activate a more complete representation and description of the critical event.

Whereas it was shown[6] that the CI worked in a laboratory test, how well does it fare in real-world investigations? We describe one specific technique,

---

[6] R. Edward Geiselman *et al.*, "Enhancement of Eyewitness Memory: An Empirical Evaluation of the Cognitive Interview", in *Journal of Police Science and Administration*, 1984, vol. 12, no. 1, pp. 74–80.

[7] Endel Tulving and Donald M. Thomson, "Encoding Specificity and Retrieval Processes in Episodic Memory", in *Psychological Review*, 1973, vol. 80, no. 5, pp. 352–373.

[8] Gordon H. Bower, "A Multicomponent Theory of the Memory Trace", in Kenneth W. Spence and Janet T. Spence (eds.), *The Psychology of Learning And Motivation: Vol. 1*, Academic Press, New York, 1967, pp. 229–325.

[9] Richard C. Anderson and James W. Pichert, "Recall of Previously Unrecallable Information Following a Shift in Perspective", in *Journal of Verbal Learning and Verbal Behavior*, 1978, vol. 17, no. 1, pp. 1–12.

context reinstatement, that was used to enhance the memory of a soldier after his platoon was attacked.[10]

> The interviewee was a soldier who survived an attack on his platoon while being in a vehicle that ended in many casualties. The surviving soldier was hospitalized in a military hospital located in a military base. Upon arriving at the hospital, the interviewer asked the physicians if he can interview the soldier in and around a similar vehicle (to reinstate context). [...] The interview took place in and outside the vehicle, and it replicated the actual event, e.g., for the first 5 minutes of the real attack the soldier was sitting inside the vehicle and then got out and did a sort of 8-shape path around the vehicle that ended in hiding in the bushes. That space and time series of events were re-enacted exactly within the interview, with the interviewer sitting with him at the beginning inside the vehicle, and then walking side by side with the soldier. [...] Many new pieces of information were remembered by the soldier compared to an earlier conducted conventional military interview. These details, which helped to build up the intelligence picture and to take other actions, were corroborated later through additional pieces of intelligence [...] only in the CI it was found out exactly why the vehicle was separated from the other group of three other vehicles in the preliminary part of the event and consequently corrective actions were taken. [...] Holding the CI inside and around the vehicle helped the soldier to communicate clearly what he saw, from which distance and angle, what was hidden from him and why.[11]

A second case combines the use of context reinstatement with the technique of varied retrieval.

> My assignment as a federal investigator was to gather information about where an important narco-trafficker lived and operated from, and any activities planned for the future. As we later learned, these activities included developing future distribution routes and paramilitary style attacks against counter-narcotics investigators. I interviewed an informant who had worked with me in the past. The informant had been driven a few times to the critical location by two escorts, who discussed important details about other narco-traffickers who were visiting the same location. My informant only had limited spatial information, though, as the informant was

---

[10] Taken from Tzachi Ashkenazi in Ronald P. Fisher and R. Edward Geiselman, "Expanding the Cognitive Interview to Non-Criminal Investigations", in Jason J. Dickinson *et al.* (eds.), *Evidence-Based Investigative Interviewing: Applying Cognitive Principles*, Routledge, New York, 2019, pp. 1–28.

[11] The text that appears here is based on our formulation in Fisher and Geiselman, 2019, see *supra* note 10. We thank Routledge Publishers (Taylor & Francis Group).

blindfolded before each trip. [...] I tried to recreate the context of the drive to elicit information about the escorts' conversations. I [...] used the [...] concept of varied retrieval cues to gather information about the drive to the critical location. These (non-visual) cues targeted temporal details (the drive started in the afternoon and ended at dusk), olfactory details (smoggy odor initially, turning to cleaner air at the destination), auditory-proprioceptive details (sounds of other cars initially, but dissipated in time; road surface changed from paved to unpaved; speed of the car decreased considerably during the drive). Based on the information I gathered from the informant, and other information gathered from another federal agency, we were able to find the target location (taken from the description provided by John Gervino, retired Special Agent with Immigration and Customs Enforcement, appearing in Fisher and Geiselman, 2019).[12]

16.3. Enhanced Cognitive Interview

After several laboratory experiments confirmed the effectiveness of the original version of the CI – to be described in Section 16.3.3. – it became obvious that, although the CI was more effective than a typical law enforcement interview, witnesses were still failing to report many important details in the critical event. That motivated Fisher and Geiselman to consider how they might improve on the original version of the CI.

Many different forces influenced Fisher and Geiselman to enhance the original version of the CI (called, appropriately, the Enhanced Cognitive Interview, sometimes written as 'ECI'). Fisher and Geiselman carefully perused dozens of tape-recorded interviews from laboratory studies and real-world police investigations to determine which interview techniques seemed to assist witnesses and which techniques either did not work, or worse, disrupted witness recall. They spoke to the most effective police interviewers – those who elicited the greatest amount of information – about their strategies for conducting interviews. They surveyed the literature in other, non-criminal domains (for example, oral history, psychotherapy and journalism) to find gems not found in the eyewitness literature. Most importantly, they realized that interviews are not limited exclusively by witness memory retrieval. The interview is a complex activity that reflects several underlying psychological processes, including: (i) how the interviewer and witness interact with one another as people (social dynamics); (ii) cognitive processes in addition to memory retrieval (for example, the witness must make a meta-cognitive decision whether to volunteer an answer or to

---

[12] Ronald P. Fisher and R. Edward Geiselman, *Memory-Enhancing Techniques in Investigative Interviewing: The Cognitive Interview*, Charles C Thomas, Springfield, 1992.

say 'I don't know'); (iii) the cognitive processes of the interviewer (for example, attempting to do multiple tasks concurrently: listening to the witness, notating the witness' response, thinking about the next interview question, *et cetera*); and (iv) both the witness and the interviewer communicating to one another, the interviewer communicating their investigative needs (for example, 'I need to learn about the perpetrator's appearance') and the witness communicating their knowledge ('How can I describe in words the perpetrator's odour?').

The above concepts were incorporated into Fisher and Geiselman's book,[13] which described the enhanced version of the CI. The ECI included the original CI techniques, but also several new techniques that were intended to improve: (i) the social dynamics between witness and interviewer (for example, 'develop rapport' and 'active witness participation'); (ii) the witness' memory retrieval and general cognition (for example, 'witness-compatible questions' – asking questions that are compatible with the witness' currently activated knowledge – 'close eyes', 'multiple and varied retrieval' and 'don't guess'); (iii) the interviewer's cognition (for example, instructing the witness to draw a sketch); and (iv) communication between the witness and interviewer (for example, code-compatible output – encouraging witnesses to output their knowledge in a format that is compatible with how the information is stored, such as drawing a sketch to convey a visual or spatial memory). Other generally desirable interviewing elements were also included, including asking open-ended questions primarily, funnelling the questions from a broader scope to a narrower scope, asking follow-up questions, *et cetera*. See Table 1 for a description of the major CI elements and the psychological processes influenced.

CI Element	Description	Psychological Processes Enhanced[14]
Rapport	Develop rapport between the respondent and interviewer.	Social Dynamics
Active respondent participation	Respondent actively generates information (that is, does not merely answer the interviewer's questions).	Social Dynamics

---

[13] *Ibid.*

[14] These are the psychological processes Fisher and Geiselman *intended* to enhance. We do not know which psychological processes were *actually* enhanced. Some of the CI elements were intended to influence more than one process.

Report everything	Include all recollections in response; do not edit out unimportant details.[15]	Memory and Communication
Reinstate context	Reinstate the context of the original experience.	Memory
Describe in detail; Model statement	Instruct respondents to provide a detailed account. Provide respondents a very detailed description of a different event as an example of the level of detail requested.	Communication
Close eyes	Instruct respondents to close their eyes.	Cognition
No interruptions	Do not interrupt the respondent's narration.	Social Dynamics and Cognition
Don't guess	Instruct respondents not to guess (allowing them to say 'I don't know').	Cognition
Open-ended questions; Funnel: broad to narrow questions	Ask primarily open-ended questions; progress from broader to narrower open questions, ending with closed questions.	Social Dynamics and Cognition
Multiple retrieval	Search through memory more than once.	Memory
Varied retrieval	Search through memory in different ways.	Memory
Respondent-compatible questions	Ask questions that are compatible with the respondent's currently accessible information.	Memory
Avoid suggestive questions	Avoid asking questions that suggest a specific answer.	Memory
Code-compatible output	Allow the respondents to output their knowledge in the same form as it is stored (often non-verbal, for example sketches).	Communication

---

[15] Sometimes this is misinterpreted to mean that respondents are encouraged to guess. Respondents are not encouraged to guess (see 'Don't guess' instruction). This instruction encourages respondents to report all facts, whether the respondents consider the facts important or not or whether in chronological order or not.

| Timeline | Construct a timeline marked by personally significant events. Focus on each time segment (or epoch). | Memory |

Table 1: Major CI elements.[16]

A recent terrorism case illustrates the value of the CI technique of making the witness an active participant who generates information and does not merely answer the interviewer's questions. A woman had taken a ride as a hitchhiker from a person she did not know. During the ride, the driver indicated that he intended to attack people from a targeted group (that is, a hate crime). The woman called the Anti-Terrorism Division ('ATD') of National Security and said that she wanted to report a possible planned terror event. The ATD investigator conducted a conventional law enforcement interview with the woman, asking many specific questions about the driver, their conversation, the car, and the route driven. The woman answered as many questions as she could, but she could not provide enough descriptive information for the ATD to identify the driver. Later, when the woman was given a CI, and she was encouraged to freely narrate everything that was related to the experience, she indicated that she had spoken to her sister immediately after returning home from the hitchhike, and that her sister knew immediately who she was referring to. This opened an important new lead for the investigation, starting with interviewing the sister and eventually thwarting that potential terror event.

16.3.1. Recent Updates to the Cognitive Interview

In the 30 years since the ECI was originally described,[17] we have had several opportunities to learn about and devise new techniques to improve it. One source was the traditional scientific literature on memory and cognition, but other ideas emerged from the literature on detecting deception, where one tactic is to encourage respondents to provide more verbal information.[18] Our most prolific source of new ideas came from conducting training programs for law enforcement and other investigative agencies (such as for the military, national security or organizations that investigate accidents). During these training programs, we had the opportunity to meet with trainees who were professional investigators and who, much to our good fortune, were willing to share their insights with us. In addition, operational police officers who had been trained in the CI reported their experiences of conducting CIs: which techniques worked, and which did

---

[16] Part of this table was reprinted from Fisher and Geiselman, 2019, see *supra* note 10.

[17] Fisher and Geiselman, 1992, see *supra* note 12.

[18] Sharon Leal *et al.*, "You Cannot Hide Your Telephone Lies: Providing a Model Statement as an Aid to Detect Deception in Insurance Telephone Calls", in *Legal and Criminological Psychology*, 2015, vol. 20, no. 1, pp. 129–146.

not work or were difficult to implement. Finally, we had some opportunities to peruse videotapes or read transcripts of excellent interviews conducted by police, from which we learned much.

As a result of these opportunities, several new techniques were added to the ever-developing CI to bring it to its current status. The techniques added in this last phase of the CI's development have mainly addressed the communication component of the CI, and specifically, how to assist witnesses to provide a more detailed description of their experience. It became obvious to us, but only after listening to several tape-recorded police interviews, that civilian witnesses often provide less information than they have available because they are not aware of how much detail is required in a law enforcement investigation. To overcome this misperception, we encouraged interviewers to provide a model statement of what a desirable response sounds like (namely, a very detailed description of the critical event).[19] So that the model statement does not alter the witness' memory of the event under investigation, the content of the model statement should differ considerably from the content of the actual investigation (for example, the model statement could be about the interviewer making breakfast whereas the critical event is about a bank robbery). After providing the model statement, the interviewer should instruct the witness to provide a similarly detailed description when narrating his or her own experience, if possible. Moreover, it will take a long time (such as 30–40 minutes) to provide such a detailed narration. Indicating that the narrative description will take a long time helps to overcome witnesses' mistaken belief that their narrations should be short – and hence, uninformative. Witnesses might easily adopt that mistaken belief either because: (i) they see on television that witnesses, who invariably play a secondary role, provide relatively brief answers; or (ii) they have learned over the course of their lives that they should not dominate conversations with authority figures.

Another technique that we have found remarkably effective is to encourage witnesses to draw a sketch – or multiple sketches – of their experience and to narrate while they are sketching.[20] We believe that sketching works for many reasons. The sketch: (i) helps the witness to remember by reinstating the original experience;[21] and (ii) allows the witness to use a non-verbal modality to output

---

[19] Sharon Leal *et al.*, "The Effectiveness of Different Model Statement Variants for Eliciting Information and Cues to Deceit", in *Legal and Criminological Psychology*, 2021, vol. 27, no. 2, pp. 247–264.

[20] Aldert Vrij *et al.*, "Sketching While Narrating as a Tool to Detect Deceit", in *Applied Cognitive Psychology*, 2020, vol. 34, no. 3, pp. 628–642.

[21] Coral J. Dando, Rachel Wilcock, Claudia Behnkle and Rebecca Milne, "Modifying the Cognitive Interview: Countenancing Forensic Application by Enhancing Practicability", in *Psychology, Crime & Law*, 2011, vol. 17, no. 6, pp. 491–511.

their knowledge, in addition to conveying their knowledge verbally. The sketch also helps the interviewer to understand the witness' experience, and it provides many opportunities (from the elements of the sketch) to ask follow-up questions that may elicit additional details (for example, "I see that you included a car in your sketch; who was in the car?").[22] Sometimes, in the midst of drawing, the witness reflects on the sketch, which, in turn, brings on new recollections. This is demonstrated in the following incident, in a recent terrorism-related investigation.

A witness was interviewed about a terror-planning meeting that took place in an open area. He described several of the participants, and other objects that were around, such as a warehouse, a closet full of weapons, some shrubs, and a tree. When he drew the sketch of the scene, he included a car that he had not mentioned before. He noted that he remembered the car because he wanted to draw the trunk of the tree and then realized that he did not actually see the tree trunk because a car was situated in front of the tree blocking his view. After the witness commented on the sketch, he also remembered that at the end of the meeting a man got into the car (prior to that, the interviewee had not mentioned anything about the man). The man was an important participant in the meeting – but not previously known by intelligence officials as a terrorist. The new sketch-aided information led to the capture of the man, his sentencing and imprisonment, thus preventing his participation in possible future terrorist incidents.

When temporal information is critical, and the investigator needs to learn either the absolute time when a critical event occurred (that is, the date and time) or the relative time of an event's occurrence (that is, before or after another critical event), a valuable technique is to use a timeline.[23] To make the timeline even more effective, the witness should mark the timeline by events that are personally significant for them (for example, 'When I moved to Washington' or 'I started to work at the grocery store'), rather than the investigator marking the line with canonical dates, for instance, the first of January.[24] A related non-verbal

---

[22] Kirk Luther, Brent Snook, Joseph Eastwood and Ronald P. Fisher, "Sketching: The Effect of a Dual-Modality Technique on Recall Performance", in *Journal of Police and Criminal Psychology*, 2022.

[23] Drew A. Leins *et al.*, "Interview Protocols to Facilitate Human Intelligence Sources' Recollections of Meetings", in *Applied Cognitive Psychology*, 2014, vol. 28, no. 6, pp. 926–935.

[24] Tzachi Ashkenazi and Ronald P. Fisher, "Field Test of the Cognitive Interview to Enhance Eyewitness and Victim Memory, in Intelligence Investigations of Terrorist Attacks", in *Journal of Applied Research in Memory and Cognition*, 2022, vol. 11, no. 2, pp. 200–208; Elizabeth F. Loftus and Wesley Marburger, "Since the Eruption of Mt. St. Helens, Has Anyone Beaten You Up? Improving the Accuracy of Retrospective Reports With Landmark Events", in *Memory & Cognition*, 1983, vol. 11, no. 2, pp. 114–120.

---

technique to enhance witnesses' reporting of temporal information is to label each of several remembered actions on a small piece of paper (for example, with yellow 'sticky' notes), then to place the several pieces of paper in their appropriate order and then, afterwards, to elaborate on each of the labelled actions.[25]

Other changes that are reflected in the most recent version of the CI are not novel techniques, but constraints on implementing earlier-suggested techniques.[26] Feedback from the British police suggests that they were uncomfortable to implement some of the original CI techniques, specifically 'reverse order' and 'change perspective'.[27] Others have suggested that these instructions might be particularly difficult for young children.[28] Also, some British police officers have found it difficult or awkward to implement the 'mental context reinstatement' element of the CI; as a substitute, drawing a sketch of the scene may serve a similar function,[29] where investigators had more positive reactions to mental context reinstatement. In keeping with the dynamic nature of the CI, we recommend that interviewers gauge either their own reactions or the witness' ability to implement any specific technique, and, if necessary, either deleting or modifying it.

16.3.2. Cognitive Interview as a Toolbox

If various techniques can be deleted or modified for a specific interview, the CI is better considered as a toolbox rather than as a fixed technique that must be implemented exactly the same way under every circumstance.[30] That is, the CI is a collection of memory- and communication-enhancing techniques only some of which are likely to be used in any situation. As such, the skill of conducting a CI reflects, in part, the interviewer's knowledge of which CI tools are most

---

[25] Lorraine Hope, Rebecca Mullis and Fiona Gabbert, "Who? What? When? Using a Timeline Technique to Facilitate Recall of a Complex Event", in *Journal of Applied Research in Memory and Cognition*, 2013, vol. 2, no. 1, pp. 20–24.

[26] Coral Dando, Rachel Wilcock and Rebecca Milne, "The Cognitive Interview: Novice Police Officers' Witness/Victim Interviewing Practices", in *Psychology, Crime & Law*, 2009, vol. 15, no. 8, pp. 679–696; Dando, Wilcock, Behnkle and Milne, 2011, see *supra* note 21.

[27] Mark R. Kebbell, Rebecca Milne and Graham F. Wagstaff, "The Cognitive Interview: A Survey of Its Forensic Effectiveness", in *Psychology, Crime & Law*, 1999, vol. 5, nos. 1–2, pp. 101–115.

[28] Karen J. Saywitz, R. Edward Geiselman and Gail K. Bornstein, "Effects of Cognitive Interviewing and Practice on Children's Recall Performance", in *Journal of Applied Psychology*, 1992, vol. 77, no. 5, pp. 744–756.

[29] Luther, Snook, Eastwood and Fisher, 2022, see *supra* note 22; Cindy Colomb *et al.*, "Back to the Real: Efficacy and Perception of a Modified Cognitive Interview in the Field", in *Applied Cognitive Psychology*, 2013, vol. 27, no. 5, pp. 574–583.

[30] Ronald P. Fisher, Rebecca Milne and Ray Bull, "Interviewing Cooperative Witnesses", in *Currrent Directions in Psychological Science*, 2011, vol. 20, no. 1, pp. 16–19.

appropriate for the specific situation and how to implement the tool for the specific situation. No two interviews will be identical as the witnesses and the specific conditions of all interviews will differ from one another. Note that the skilled carpenter – or plumber or surgeon – has an array of tools to use to build a cabinet – or fix a leaky faucet or do surgery on a patient – and we would not expect them to use exactly the same tools, or in exactly the same fashion, for all tasks. Similarly, we should not expect the cognitive interviewer to use exactly the same cognitive tools, or in the same fashion, for every investigative interview.

Some will find the 'flexibility' of the CI to be burdensome as it does require making more on-line decisions than conducting a standardized interview with a fixed protocol, which is to be used identically in all situations. But it is precisely the CI's flexibility that contributes toward its effectiveness.

Because a properly conducted CI will likely vary from one interview to another, experimental tests of the CI do not examine whether the CI enhances witness reporting – as the CI is never implemented in its entirety. Rather, experimental tests examine whether *exposure* to the principles of the CI (that is, CI training) enhances witness reporting. We turn now to the extensive body of research on whether being trained in the CI allows interviewers to elicit more, and better, information from witnesses than being exposed to an alternative method of interviewing.

16.3.3. Empirical Tests of the Cognitive Interview

Most tests of the original version of the CI and the ECI followed the same plan. Volunteer participants were exposed to a simulated event and were interviewed later with the CI/ECI or with a control interview, intended to resemble either a typical law enforcement interview, or a 'Structured Interview' ('SI': the CI minus the specific memory-enhancing techniques). The participants were usually college students, but sometimes they were community members,[31] young children[32] or older adults.[33] Usually, the participants were told before viewing the event that they would be asked questions about the observed event. The event was often a videotape of a simulated crime, but, in some instances, the event was a staged crime and sometimes a staged, live innocuous event. The delay between the event and the interview usually varied from almost immediate to a

---

[31] Geiselman *et al.*, 1984, see *supra* note 6.
[32] Robyn E. Holliday and Amanda J. Albon, "Minimising Misinformation Effects in Young Children With Cognitive Interview Mnemonics", in *Applied Cognitive Psychology*, 2004, vol. 18, no. 3, pp. 263–281.
[33] Allison M. Wright and Robyn E. Holliday, "Enhancing the Recall of Young, Young-Old and Old-Old Adults With Cognitive Interviews", in *Applied Cognitive Psychology*, 2007, vol. 21, no. 1, pp. 19–43.

few hours (very few tested after a few days). The interviewers were usually undergraduate or graduate research assistants, although in a few instances, the interviewers were professional police officers.[34] The interviews were recorded, transcribed and coded for the number of details reported by the witness, and also their accuracy (number of correct details, number of incorrect details and the accuracy rate). The initial experiments were conducted by Geiselman and Fisher and their colleagues in the mid-1980s in the US, but several studies were done shortly thereafter and in the 1990s by Köhnken and colleagues in Germany and by Bull, Memon and Milne and their colleagues in England. More recently, Py and Ginet (France), Paulo (Portugal) and Campos and Alonso-Quecuty (Spain) have contributed to the research base.

The typical finding was that the CI elicited between 25–50 per cent more information than the control interview – a robust finding, found not just in the US[35] and the United Kingdom ('UK'),[36] but also in non-English-speaking countries such as Germany,[37] Italy[38] and Portugal,[39] as well as in developing countries, such as Brazil,[40] Mexico[41] and Iran.[42] In some studies, the number of errors elicited was greater in the CI than in the control interview, but, in other studies, the

---

[34] Kebbell, Milne and Wagstaff, 1999, see *supra* note 27; Jillian R. Rivard, Ronald P. Fisher, Belinda Robertson and Dana Hirn Mueller, "Testing the Cognitive Interview With Professional Interviewers: Enhancing Recall of Specific Details of Recurring Events", in *Applied Cognitive Psychology*, 2014, vol. 28, no. 6, pp. 917–925.

[35] R. Edward Geiselman, Ronald P. Fisher, David P. MacKinnon and Heidi L. Holland, "Enhancement of Eyewitness Memory With the Cognitive Interview", in *The American Journal of Psychology*, 1986, vol. 99, no. 3, pp. 385–401; Saywitz, Geiselman and Bornstein, 1992, see *supra* note 28.

[36] Dando, Wilcock, Behnkle and Milne, 2011, see *supra* note 21.

[37] Günther Köhnken, Claudia Thürer and Dirk Zoberbier, "The Cognitive Interview: Are the Interviewers' Memories Enhanced Too?", in *Applied Cognitive Psychology*, 1994, vol. 8, no. 1, pp. 13–24.

[38] Luca Bensi, Raffaella Nori, Elisa Gambetti and Fiorella Giusberti, "The Enhanced Cognitive Interview: A Study on the Efficacy of Shortened Variants and Single Techniques", in *Journal of Cognitive Psychology*, 2011, vol. 23, no. 3, pp. 311–321.

[39] Rui M. Paulo, Pedro B. Albuquerque and Ray Bull, "Improving the Enhanced Cognitive Interview With a New Interview Strategy: Category Clustering Recall", in *Applied Cognitive Psychology*, 2016, vol. 30, no. 5, pp. 775–784.

[40] Lilian M. Stein and Amina Memon, "Testing the Efficacy of the Cognitive Interview in a Developing Country", in *Applied Cognitive Psychology*, 2006, vol. 20, no. 5, pp. 597–605.

[41] Marisol Elizalde Monjardin, "The Cognitive Interview, Exploring Its Effectiveness in the UK and Mexico", Ph.D. thesis, University of Leicester, 2016.

[42] Ahmad Shahvaroughi *et al.*, "Testing a Modified Cognitive Interview With Category Clustering Recall in Iran", in *Applied Cognitive Psychology*, 2021, vol. 35, no. 1, pp. 148–159.

number of errors was either not different or the CI generated fewer errors.[43] In almost all cases, the accuracy rate (number of accurate statements divided by the total number of statements) was approximately the same or minimally higher in the CI compared to the control interviews.[44] In overview, the CI elicited more information, of comparable quality, than did control interviews across a wide range of people, events and test conditions.[45]

The research studies described thus far all took place in the laboratory (or a room that functioned like a laboratory (such as a school classroom)). Clearly, such a controlled setting is important for maintaining experimental control. However, it is also important to demonstrate that the CI works in real-world investigations, like criminal investigations, where (i) the victims' or witnesses' arousal levels are much higher than in a laboratory-simulation setting; (ii) the witnesses and victims are average people as opposed to college students, who likely have better cognitive and communication skills; (iii) the interviewers are professional investigators as opposed to students; and (iv) several other critical differences. Also, because the 'consumers' of the research are likely to be professional investigators, who are more attuned to findings in real-world settings than laboratory findings, it is important to show that the CI works in settings that investigators are familiar with.

We describe here three such real-world investigations of crime, one in the US, one in the UK and one in France. Fisher *et al.* (1989)[46] worked with 16 experienced detectives in the Robbery Division of the Dade County (Miami, Florida) Police Department (US). Approximately half of the participating

---

[43] Amina Memon, Christian A. Meissner and Joanne Fraser, "The Cognitive Interview: A Meta-Analytic Review and Study Space Analysis of the Past 25 Years", in *Psychology, Public Policy, and Law*, 2010, vol. 16, no. 4, pp. 340–372.

[44] For an interesting discussion of the relative value of number of errors versus accuracy rate, see Amina Memon and Sarah V. Stevenage, "Interviewing Witnesses: What Works and What Doesn't?", in *Psycoloquy*, 1996, vol. 7, no. 6, and Ronald P. Fisher, "Misconceptions in Design and Analysis of Research With the Cognitive Interview", in *Psycoloquy*, 1996, vol. 7, no. 6.

[45] For reviews of the CI research, see Ronald P. Fisher and R. Edward Geiselman, "Investigative Interviewing", in Vincent B. Van Hasselt and Michael L. Bourke (eds.) *Handbook of Behavioral Criminology*, Springer, Cham, 2018, pp. 451–465, and Lorraine Hope and Fiona Gabbert, "Expanding the Legacy of the Cognitive Interview: Developments and Innovations in Evidence-Based Investigative Interviewing", in Dickinson *et al.* (eds.), 2019, pp. 42–55, see *supra* note 10. For meta-analyses of the findings, see Günther Köhnken, Rebecca Milne, Amina Memon and Ray Bull, "The Cognitive Interview: A Meta-Analysis", in *Psychology, Crime & Law*, 1999, vol. 5, nos. 1–2, pp. 3–27 and Köhnken, Thürer and Zoberbier, 1994, see *supra* note 37.

[46] Ronald P. Fisher, R. Edward Geiselman and Michael Amador, "Field Test of the Cognitive Interview: Enhancing the Recollection of Actual Victims and Witnesses Of Crime", in *Journal of Applied Psychology*, 1989, vol. 74, no. 5, pp. 722–727.

---

detectives (N=7) were trained on the ECI; the other detectives (N=9), who were equally experienced, were not trained on the ECI. Training entailed four 60-minute sessions composed of background lecture material, demonstrations and feedback on the detectives' field interviews of robbery victims. All detectives audio-recorded several of their interviews with robbery victims and witnesses before ECI training and then several additional interviews (different cases) after training. The audiotaped interviews were transcribed and coded for the number of details provided by the respondents. The trained detectives elicited 63 per cent more details than the untrained detectives. Almost identical benefits of the ECI were found when the trained detectives were compared to themselves after versus before training (a 47 per cent increase in details after training). Interestingly, of the seven detectives in the trained group, all except one changed his interviewing style after going through the training – in general to ask fewer questions, but more open-ended questions, and to encourage respondents to participate more actively; and all those detectives showed large gains compared to their pre-training levels. One detective did not change his interviewing style, and he was the only detective in the trained group who did not increase the quality of his interviews compared to pre-training levels. The moral of the story: investigators need to be capable and motivated to adopt the CI for it to be effective.

Of course, we do not know whether the reported details were correct or not, because there was no formal record of what actually occurred during the crimes (the 'gold standard') – one of the advantages of conducting laboratory research. In 22 of the robbery cases, there was a second person (another victim or witness) who provided information to the police about the crime, thereby allowing us to compare the answers across witnesses. We looked at the corroboration rate (consistency between the primary witness and the second witness) as a proxy for accuracy. Such proxy measures are not perfect measures of accuracy, but they are likely the best we can do in real-world cases. Two findings are illuminating: (i) the corroboration rates were generally very high (94 per cent) – suggesting that, perhaps, eyewitnesses are more accurate than is commonly believed;[47] and (ii) the corroboration rate was slightly higher in the interviews conducted after CI training (94.5 per cent) than those conducted before CI training (93 per cent). This finding mirrors laboratory studies, where the accuracy rates in CI-elicited interviews are either comparable or minimally higher than in SIs.[48]

---

[47]   See also Nicholas B. Diamond, Michael J. Armson and Brian Levine, "The Truth Is Out There: Accuracy in Recall of Verifiable Real-World Events", in *Psychological Science*, 2020, vol. 31, pp. 1544–1556.

[48]   Köhnken, Thürer and Zoberbier, 1994, see *supra* note 37; Stein and Memon, 2006, see *supra* note 40.

That is, the CI elicits more information than SIs, but not because the CI entices witnesses to guess.

A second field study of an early version of the CI was conducted in the UK.[49] They assigned 28 police officers to one of four training conditions: CI, Conversation Management ('CM'), combined (CI and CM) and a control (no formal interview training). The researchers compared transcripts of (tape-recorded) real-world interviews before and after training. Only the CI-trained investigators elicited considerably more information after training than before training (72 per cent increase); the other three groups did not improve. Interestingly, and perhaps the explanation for the CI's success, only the CI group changed its interviewing tactics, asking fewer question, but more open-ended questions, after training than before training. No measures were reported about the accuracy of the gathered information or the interviewers' reactions to conducting the interviews.

A more recent study of the ECI was conducted in France, with French military police conducting interviews of witnesses and victims of various crimes, ranging from less violent (such as robbery and fraud) to more violent (such as murder, domestic and sexual violence).[50] Twenty-seven experienced investigators were assigned evenly to one of three interview groups: Standard Police ('SPI': no specialized training beyond their professional experience), SI (basic social and communication skills of the ECI, but not including any memory-enhancement skills) and a minimally revised ECI (ECI minus the 'change-perspective' and 'change-order' elements). Overall, the ECI elicited about 50 per cent more information than did either the SPI or SI, which did not differ from one another. Interestingly, the ECI was more effective for interviewing victims than for witnesses, and the ECI was more effective for more violent crimes than for less violent crimes. No measures of accuracy or proxies of accuracy were reported. The study did, however, assess the investigators' reactions to conducting the ECI. In general, they found it useful, usable and institutionally acceptable.

16.3.4. Terrorism

We turn next to two very recent field studies that applied the CI to real-world cases of terrorism in Israel. These studies are particularly important for two reasons. First, the version of the CI that was implemented included many elements that were introduced only in the past few years, long after the ECI was

---

[49] Brian R. Clifford and Richard George, "A Field Evaluation of Training in Three Methods of Witness/Victim Investigative Interviewing", in *Psychology Crime and Law*, 1996, vol. 2, no. 3, pp. 231–248.

[50] Colomb *et al.*, 2013, see *supra* note 29.

established[51] and, as far as we know, are the only published studies to test the most recent version of the CI.[52] Second, the events were real-world acts of terrorism which posed threats to the nation, and thus extensive resources were available to conduct the investigations. Also, because some of the witnesses were interviewed many times and over several months – in some cases, years – we were able to examine the CI's effect in repeated interviews and over very long retention intervals.

In the first study, we examined 60 cases in which Jewish and Arab witnesses, victims and occasional sources of intelligence information were interviewed about terrorist acts (such as stabbings, shootings and explosions) that took place in Israel between the years 2010–2020.[53] The interviewees were interviewed initially by experienced Israeli investigators who used generally recommended techniques (SI), including developing rapport, asking primarily open-ended questions, not interrupting, avoiding suggestive questions, *et cetera*. In all cases, the interviewees were interviewed a second time to try to elicit new information not gathered on the first interview. In half of the cases, the initial SI was followed by a second SI (SI/SI), and in half of the cases, the initial SI was followed by a CI (SI/CI). The interviewers took handwritten notes during the interviews of facts they considered to be important to advance the investigation and included them in a final report. We analyzed the final reports for (i) the number of new facts elicited in the second interview that were not contained in the first interview; (ii) the investigative utility of the new facts; and (iii) the consistency between the facts reported in the two interviews.

16.3.4.1. Number of New Facts

The average number of facts recalled on the initial SI was 21.53 (20.23 for the SI/SI; 22.83 for the SI/CI). Of the 60 people being interviewed, almost everyone (N=58) recalled some facts on the second interview that they had not recalled earlier (reminiscence), a finding often found in the laboratory[54] and consistent with the CI principle of 'multiple retrieval' (additional retrieval attempts yield new information). More important for the CI protocol as a whole in the terrorism investigation, the amount of new information gathered by the follow-up CI

---

[51]   Fisher and Geiselman, 1992, see *supra* note 12.

[52]   Ronald P. Fisher and R. Edward Geiselman, "Memory-Enhanced Interviewing Techniques for Investigating Critical Events: The Cognitive Interview" (manuscript in preparation).

[53]   Vrij *et al.*, 2020, see *supra* note 20.

[54]   Julian A.E. Gilbert and Ronald P. Fisher, "The Effects of Varied Retrieval Cues on Reminiscence in Eyewitness Memory", in *Applied Cognitive Psychology*, 2006, vol. 20, no. 6, pp. 723–739.

(42.43 new facts) was more than 3.5 times greater than the amount of new information gathered by the follow-up SI (11.83).

16.3.4.2. Investigative Utility of New Facts

The new information's utility was assessed by two 'blind' professional investigators who rated: (i) the intelligence contribution of the new information; (ii) how much the new information can help 'solve' the investigated event or prevent it from occurring in the future; and (iii) how much the new intelligence information enables constructing questions for a Concealed Information Test to detect deception.[55] The results showed that the new information elicited by the follow-up CI (mean utility=8.16 on a 0–10 Likert scale) was judged to be substantially more useful than the new information elicited by the follow-up SI (5.07).

16.3.4.3. Consistency Between Facts Reported on the Two Interviews

How accurate were the facts provided in the interviews? In real-world investigations, we generally do not have an independent measure of what actually occurred in order to determine whether a witness' description is accurate. We can, however, judge whether a witness' description is *inaccurate* by noting whether the witness changes some details from the first interview (for example, explosion occurred in the morning) to the second interview (for example, explosion occurred in the evening), because at least one version of the description must be wrong. Such measures of within-witness inconsistency are often used to assess accuracy in real-world situations.[56] In the current study, of the 666 potentially consistent facts reported across the 60 investigations, only three were inconsistent. We have little reason to believe that interviewees were guessing or that their descriptions were incorrect.

The above aggregated scores across the 60 investigations clearly showed the value of the CI. Two specific cases illustrate more powerfully the benefit of the CI. In one case, a 31-year-old Jewish victim who survived an improvised explosive device attack was interviewed with an SI two days after the event and reported 15 facts. When interviewed nine days later with a CI, he reported 87 facts, of which 78 were new facts. In another case, a 20-year-old Arab man who witnessed Molotov bottle bombs being thrown at a passing car was interviewed 77 days after the event and reported 28 facts. When interviewed nine days later

---

[55] Galit Nahari and Gershon Ben-Shakhar, "Psychophysiological and Behavioral Measures for Detecting Concealed Information: the Role of Memory for Crime Details", in *Psychophysiology*, 2011, vol. 48, no. 6, pp. 733–744.

[56] Ronald P. Fisher, Neil Brewer and Gregory Mitchell, "The Relation Between Consistency and Accuracy of Eyewitness Testimony: Legal Versus Cognitive Explanations", in Ray Bull, Tim Valentine and Tom Williamson (eds.), *Handbook of Psychology of Investigative Interviewing: Current Developments and Future Directions*, Wiley-Blackwell, 2009, pp. 121–136.

with the CI, he reported 119 facts, of which 105 were new facts. The perceived utility of the new information elicited for both cases was evaluated as 10 (on a 0–10 scale).

In contrast with the first study, which examined witnesses who experienced a single, isolated event, the second study[57] examined witnesses who experienced repeated events of the same type (for example, attended several meetings with terrorists, or bought or sold weapons frequently). Recalling individual episodes of repeated, similar events is known to be difficult,[58] and so we modified the CI to better access specific acts of terrorism. The major changes entailed: (i) personalizing a timeline and developing a parallel procedure for locations, combined with context reinstatement; (ii) encouraging respondents to think about different salient properties of terrorism experiences; and (iii) combining the technique of sketching with semantic memory.

Specifically, we encouraged interviewees to construct a 'personalized' timeline by dividing it into meaningful periods of time (epochs), demarcated by personally meaningful events. After creating such a personalized timeline, interviewees were instructed to reinstate the context of each epoch by thinking about their appearance at the specific time, their thoughts and emotional state at the time, their physical locations (for example, their dwelling or workplace), the typical activities they used to do and the people they used to meet. After the interviewees indicated that they had reinstated the context, they were asked if they remembered any new events that had not yet been mentioned before, and they named each such event. After all epochs were exhausted, the same procedure was repeated for locations, with the interviewee first listing the different locations, and then the interviewer helping them in the process of context reinstatement for each location.

The interviewees were also presented with a series of salient properties of terrorism events to see if these properties brought up other events they had not yet reported. Some of the properties were general and therefore were used for all events (for example, numerosity: events in which few or many people were present; emotional state: events in which the interviewee felt especially happy, sad, surprised or worried); other properties were suitable for some events but not others (for example, for arms trafficking: events in which guns, rifles or missiles were involved).

Finally, interviewees sketched a conceptual map that included the names of people (or organizations or weapons) that may have been involved in the

---

[57]   Ashkenazi and Fisher, 2022, see *supra* note 24.

[58]   Sonja P. Brubacher, Martine B. Powell and Kim P. Roberts, "Recommendations for Interviewing Children About Repeated Experiences", in *Psychology, Public Policy, and Law*, 2014, vol. 20, no. 3, pp. 325–335.

various to-be-remembered events. After sketching the conceptual map – in whatever format the interviewee chose (for example, tree diagram, linear arrangement, *et cetera*) – the interviewee then focused on each of the named people (or organizations or weapons) to see if it reminded them of other events that they had not yet remembered. For example, the interviewee drew a sketch that included the names of members of a terrorist organization, and the hierarchical connections between them, and then focused on each named person to see whether they remembered any new arms deals conducted with that person.

The study examined 35 cases of terrorism that occurred in Israel between the years 2013–2020. Arab men (mostly) who served as informants were interviewed repeatedly (2–20 times) with an SI over a long period of time (weeks, months or years), and then once more with a CI. The primary dependent measure was the number of new events that were elicited on each interview that were not reported on any of the preceding interviews (all preceding interviews were SIs.) The study findings showed that the number of new events elicited by the one CI (6.37) was considerably greater than the number of new events reported in each of the preceding individual SIs (0.69) – and in several cases, greater than the *total* number of new events reported when summed across *all* the preceding SIs. For example, in one case, a witness reported no events on the initial SI, and then was interviewed 12 more times (all SIs), generating a total of three new events; when this witness received the one CI, 132 days after the first interview, he reported five new events. In a second case, a witness reported six events on the initial SI, and then in the ensuing eight SIs, the witness reported only one new event; when this witness received the one CI, 740 days after the first interview, he reported 13 new events.

In this study, too, as in the first terrorism study, we were interested in the accuracy of the interviewee's reports. This time, we were able to locate other, independent sources of information (other people who attended the named event or electronic sources, for example, hidden cameras or microphones) that could either corroborate or refute the interviewees' statements. Of the 223 CI-elicited events, corroborating (or refuting) evidence was available for 90 events. Of those, all 90 events were corroborated; none were refuted.

In sum, the two terrorism studies, using the most up-to-date version of the CI, found that, for real-world investigations of highly arousing events: (i) the CI elicited considerably more facts and events than an SI conducted by professional investigators who used generally accepted interviewing techniques; (ii) the CI effect was found under a variety of conditions (short, medium and long retention intervals) and for assorted interviewees (male and female, Arab and Jewish and also civilians, informants and soldiers); (iii) the CI-elicited facts were evaluated to be highly useful for the investigation; and (iv) although we have no definitive measure of accuracy, the proxy measures (such as within-witness consistency and cross-witness corroboration) suggest that we have no compelling reason to suspect that the witness reports were inaccurate.

16.3.5. Non-Criminal Investigations

Because the CI is a process-oriented technique, it should be adapted easily to non-criminal investigations, including (i) events of military and security value; (ii) debriefing hostages, spies and other informants;[59] (iii) contact-tracing investigations of infected patients[60] and other medical and health-related events;[61] (iv) vehicular and industrial accidents;[62] (v) debriefing police officers and other law enforcement agents after a critical incident; and (vi) a host of others.[63]

As an example of the CI's use in a non-criminal investigation, the following describes how the CI was used to debrief former hostages to learn about the hostage-takers' actions:

> After more than 30 years in federal law enforcement, counterintelligence and counterterrorism, I became an international security consultant in 2010 [...] in which I often interview information sources to recall specific details of prior experiences. A client hired me to gather information about a hostage situation for the purpose of developing and executing a strategy for the safe return of the hostage. The hostage was taken from an area where al-Qaeda and affiliated groups operated. To ensure that my client was making informed decisions about their hostage, I interviewed two former hostages that had been safely released from captivity from the same area after being held for an extended period. I used the cognitive interview, in conjunction with other emerging research,

---

[59] Colomb *et al.*, 2013, see *supra* note 29; Ashkenazi and Fisher, 2022, see *supra* note 24. Department of Criminology, Bar Ilan University, and Department of Criminology, Ashkelon Academic College.

[60] Jacqueline R. Evans *et al.*, "Enhancing the Effectiveness of Contact Tracing Interviews: A Randomized Controlled Experiment of an Enhanced Cognitive Interview Protocol", in *American Journal of Infection Control*, 2022, vol. 5, no. 6, pp. 631–637.

[61] Ronald P. Fisher and Kathryn L. Quigley, "Improving the Accuracy of Food Consumption Histories in Foodborne Outbreak Investigations", in Judith M. Tanur (ed.), *Questions About Survey Questions: Inquiries into the Cognitive Bases of Surveys*, Russell Sage Foundation, New York, 1992, pp. 154–169; Ronald P. Fisher, Karen L. Falkner, Maurizio Trevisan and Michelle R. McCauley, "Adapting the Cognitive Interview to Enhance Long-Term (35 Years) Recall of Physical Activities", in *Journal of Applied Psychology*, 2000, vol. 85, no. 2, pp. 180–189.

[62] Oliver Dodier *et al.*, "Using the Cognitive Interview to Recall Real-World Emotionally Stressful Experiences: Road Accidents", in *Applied Cognitive Psychology*, vol. 35, no. 4, pp. 1099–1105.

[63] For a review, see Fisher and Geiselman, 1992, see *supra* note 12.

including embodied cognition, and environmental priming. [...] [I] asked the persons interviewed to offer a birds-eye view and draw sketches of areas I was interested in, including where they were kidnapped from, areas held in, and conditions of captivity. On both occasions, the persons interviewed advised they were able to recall more information, about their captors, their locations, travel patterns and the mindsets of their captors, than they had previously provided during other interviews by trained interviewers. The reported details were confirmed by others observing, who had also been privy to previous debriefings of the persons I interviewed. When the hostage was eventually released, I interviewed him/her in the same manner as the two former hostages. The now-freed hostage was surprised at the level of recall and specific details conveyed during the interview.[64]

The only context in which the CI has failed repeatedly to enhance witness recall is in a person- or face-recognition test, as would typically occur in a live or photographic lineup after a crime. Researchers conducted several experiments in which, following a critical event, a live or photographic line-up was conducted under CI instructions or neutral instructions.[65] Although witnesses were able to *describe* the perpetrator better when given a CI than an SI,[66] performance in the line-up (*recognition*) test was not improved (or made worse) by giving a CI. It was not obvious to us why the CI was ineffective in the person or face recognition task.

16.4. The Importance of Conducting Field Research

Most of the CI research has been conducted in the laboratory, where: (i) the critical event is a simulation or in some other way non-threatening; (ii) witnesses often know before experiencing the critical event that they will be tested later about the event; (iii) interviewers are inexperienced undergraduate or graduate

---

[64] The text that appears here is based on our formulation that appeared in Fisher and Geiselman, 2019, see *supra* note 10, and is taken from the description provided by Mark Fallon, Director of ClubFed, LLC, a strategic consultancy, and former Naval Criminal Investigative Service Director and Department of Homeland Security Senior Executive. We thank Routledge Publishers (Taylor & Francis Group).

[65] Ronald P. Fisher and Nadja Schreiber, "Interviewing Protocols to Improve Eyewitness Memory", in Michael P. Toglia, J. Don Reed, David F. Ross and Roderick C.L. Lindsay (eds.), *The Handbook of Eyewitness Psychology: Volume One: Memory for Events*, Erlbaum Associates, Mahwah, 2007, pp. 53–80. See also Patrick Gwyer and Brian R. Clifford, "The Effects of the Cognitive Interview on Recalling Identification, Confidence and the Confidence/Accuracy Relationship", in *Applied Cognitive Psychology*, 1997, vol. 11, no. 2, pp. 121–145.

[66] Geri E. Satin and Ronald P. Fisher, "Investigative Utility of the Cognitive Interview: Describing and Finding Perpetrators", in *Law and Human Behavior*, 2019, vol. 43, no. 5, pp. 491–506.

students; (iv) there are no dire consequences for suspects as a result of the witness' testimony; and (v) many other differences with real-world investigations. All of these differences limit the ability to generalize to real-world conditions, and especially the real world of crime and terror. We suggest that more balance is needed in the empirical literature, which can be accomplished only by conducting more field research on real-world cases. Obviously, researchers lose valuable experimental control in real-world testing and are sometimes unable to determine whether a witness statement is accurate or not. However, statistical and design techniques can often reduce those costs. More important, conducting real-world field research has benefits that are not possible to capture in the pristine laboratory, including: (i) conducting ethically responsible research on highly arousing and objectively dangerous and emotional experiences; (ii) testing people in conditions that are, logistically, almost impossible to produce in the lab (for example, interviewing people repeatedly and after several years have passed); and (iii) including practitioners working as interviewers in their own real-world cases. We encourage other CI researchers to set the research balance more evenly by conducting research in the field.

16.5. Comments on the Research and Future Directions

We offer here some personal comments on the past CI research, and where we see future research most profitably heading.

1. The original version of the CI was superseded by the ECI in the late 1980s, almost 35 years ago. Nevertheless, some researchers are still testing the original version. Researchers should focus on the more recent versions of the CI. For the sake of clarity, researchers should indicate exactly which CI elements they used in the study, rather than just labelling the procedure as a 'CI'.

2. Almost all of the research on the CI assesses its value on two measures: the number of details elicited and the accuracy of those details. That approach treats all details as equally valuable. Clearly, some details are more valuable than others, either because they are more precise (as compared to coarse-level details) or because they are more relevant to the investigation's goal. Researchers should try to include a measure that assesses the utility of the gathered evidence and not only the number of details and their accuracy. Measuring utility likely will require including an expert (for example, an experienced detective) on the research team.

3. Given the large number of studies that have validated the CI, it is no longer in doubt that the CI is effective. Researchers could use their resources more profitably by developing new techniques into an ever-

developing CI[67] than by conducting yet more validation tests. A quick caveat: it is valuable to show that the CI does not work in specific contexts (for example, in identification testing).

4. The original version of the CI treated witness interviews exclusively as being limited by the witness' mental functions. But the interviewer also has cognitive limitations. A valuable research direction will be to devise new techniques that will allow interviewers to be more efficient – perhaps by not overloading their capacity to process information or by making them better listeners of the witness' statements.

5. The CI has been developed to improve the interviewer's efficiency to elicit information from interviewees. We suspect that interviewees also might be trained to be more effective generators of information. It is unlikely that civilians can be trained to encode or learn experiences more effectively – and especially in highly arousing and unexpected crimes – but it is likely that they can be trained to play their role as interviewees more productively.

6. The CI was developed by incorporating techniques that Fisher and Geiselman believed would influence one of three underlying psychological processes: social dynamics between the interviewer and respondent, memory and cognition, and communication. Two caveats: first, there may be other psychological processes that contribute to the interview's success, or failure, and it is worthwhile to explore these other processes. Second, that Fisher and Geiselman believed that a specific technique would influence one underlying process is not the same as demonstrating empirically that the technique does, in fact, influence the specific process. Fisher and Geiselman might be – almost assuredly are – wrong. Researchers should devise methods to examine which underlying process are, in fact, influenced by specific techniques.

7. Dando, Milne and colleagues have made good strides to note some of the impractical aspects of the CI (for example, the CI takes a long time; investigators are uncomfortable to implement some CI techniques) and to develop new techniques to overcome some of these limitations. The field can benefit from additional research to modify the CI and make it more practical for real-world use.[68]

8. Successful transmission of the CI to practitioners requires proper training. We suspect that the British system of a tiered approach is a step in the right direction. Nevertheless, research can profit by examining

---

[67] Rivard, Fisher, Robertson and Hirn Mueller, 2014, see *supra* note 34.
[68] Dando, Wilcock, Behnkle and Milne, 2011, see *supra* note 21.

systematically how best to conduct training on the CI so that it will be transmitted efficiently.

9. It is likely that some investigators will learn to conduct the CI more effectively than others. A worthwhile research goal is to devise a test that will discriminate between those people who will become good CI interviewers versus those will become poor or mediocre CI interviewers.

10. In many law-enforcement interviews, interviewers have to: (i) gather information from an interviewee; and (ii) decide if the interviewee is truthful. Currently, these two goals are explored by different researchers: some explore eliciting information and others explore detecting deception. The research community would do well to try to develop techniques with both goals in mind, such as eliciting information efficiently from truth-tellers and also detecting deception (or detect truthfulness). Some initial inroads have already taken place in exploring the dual goals.[69]

11. Researchers should make better use of experienced practitioners both in conducting the research and also in imparting the CI to law enforcement. We suspect that most research teams do not include law enforcement investigators. Incorporating investigators into the research team can provide at least three benefits: (i) they can guide researchers to be aware of real-world conditions that the researchers are missing and to help shape research designs so that they take into account real-world conditions; (ii) they can assist researchers to code experimental data in a more meaningful fashion by providing guidance about how witness statements might be used during an investigation and/or during a trial; and (iii) on a practical level, other law enforcement personnel will be more likely to resonate to research projects that have fellow practitioners on the research team.

12. As noted earlier, investigators often consider only the respondent's motivation to participate, and they overlook the memory-retrieval components of the respondent's task. Failure to consider memory-retrieval limitations naturally leads to respondents providing less information than is available, and especially when they have extensive knowledge. Such less-than-complete reporting might occur when interviewing: (i) suspects who have committed many crimes (such as, serial killers); or (ii) informants who

---

[69] C.J. Koolmees, "The Cognitive Interview for Deception Detection: An Investigative Interviewing Method for Information Gain and Veracity Assessment", Master's thesis, Florida International University, 2021; R. Edward Geiselman, "The Cognitive Interview for Suspects (CIS)", in *American Journal of Forensic Psychology*, 2012, vol. 30, no. 3, pp. 5–20; Sharon Leal, Aldert Vrij, Haneen Deeb and Kevin Kamermans, "Encouraging Interviewees to Say More and Deception: The Ghostwriter Method", in *Legal and Criminological Psychology*, 2019, vol. 24, no. 2, pp. 273–287.

know many members of large terrorist cells; or (iii) hostages held in captivity many months (for example, see, earlier in Section 16.3.5., Mark Fallon's anecdotal description of using the CI to debrief hostages). We recommend that investigative agencies consider other interviewing contexts that might profit from incorporating memory-enhancing elements into the interview.

We hope we have made some contributions toward these aims.

17

The National Institute of Child Health and Human Development Protocol

Trond Myklebust, David J. La Rooy and Carlos E. Peixoto[*]

17.1. Introductory Comment

The National Institute of Child Health and Human Development ('NICHD') Protocol was developed in the mid-1990s to address perceived shortcomings in the quality of interviews that were being conducted.[1] It was developed by United States ('US') government scientists at the National Institutes of Health with collaboration and input from a wide range of professionals including forensic interview trainers, lawyers, defence expert witnesses, police, social workers and alike. The main objective of the NICHD Protocol was to target the area of forensic interviewer training and develop a training tool that would assist in improving the skills of forensic interviewers and the quality of interviews they conducted. In this chapter, we discuss the development of the NICHD Protocol and its subsequent revisions, the uniqueness of the underpinning research, the influence it has had on forensic interviewing practice worldwide and the challenges that have been faced along the road to becoming one of the most influential interview protocols developed to date. The authors are child forensic interview experts and have been closely involved in the development, implementation and training of the NICHD Protocol.

17.1.1. Basic Lessons from Suggestibility Research

The 1980s heralded an explosion of research aimed at understanding the factors involved in children's suggestibility in legal contexts.[2] Much of this research

---

[*] **Trond Myklebust**, Ph.D., holds the position as Assistant Chief of Police and Programme Leader of the Master's in Investigation at the Norwegian Police University College. **David J. La Rooy**, Ph.D., is an Honorary Senior Research Fellow at the Department of Psychological Medicine, University of Otago. **Carlos E. Peixoto**, Ph.D., is a forensic psychologist and holds the position as Invited Auxiliary Professor at the Faculdade de Educação e Psicologia of the Universidade Católica Portuguesa, Porto.

[1] Kathleen J. Sternberg *et al.*, "Effects of Introductory Style on Children's Abilities to Describe Experiences of Sexual Abuse", in *Child Abuse & Neglect*, 1997, vol. 21, no. 11, pp. 1133–1146; Yael Orbach *et al.*, "Assessing the Value of Structured Protocols for Forensic Interviews of Alleged Abuse Victims", in *Child Abuse & Neglect*, 2000, vol. 24, no. 6, pp. 733–752.

[2] Stephen J. Ceci and Maggie Bruck, "Suggestibility of the Child Witness: A Historical Review and Synthesis", in *Psychological Bulletin*, 1993, vol. 113, no. 3, pp. 403–439; Thomas D.

---

was stimulated in the wake of many high-profile cases in which children made fantastic allegations of abuse that many commentators doubted could have ever happened.[3] Research on suggestibility made it clear that interviewer bias in forensic investigations of child abuse, particularly around the questioning of children, would, with a high probably, lead to the production of inaccurate information about what did or did not happen. The take-home message from suggestibility research at the time the NICHD Protocol was initially developed was that children could easily fall foul of suggestive influence and that suggestive questioning in investigations should be avoided at all costs. This stimulated experts in the field to look for ways in which the forensic interviewing of children could be improved.

17.1.2. Basic Lessons from Memory Research

Developmental psychologists and memory researchers had also begun to learn much about the ways that reliable information *can* be extracted from children about their experiences if children were questioned in an open and unbiased manner.[4] These basic insights slowly began to shape recommendations about how forensic interviews with children should be conducted and how forensic interviewers should be trained. Early forensic interview guidelines, for example the Memorandum of Good Practice[5] and the StepWise model,[6] were clearly influenced by the work of the early memory researchers.[7] However, even with

---

Lyon, "The New Wave in Children's Suggestibility Research: A Critique", in *Cornell Law Review*, 1999, vol. 84, no. 4, pp. 1004–1087.

[3] Nadja Schreiber *et al.*, "Suggestive Interviewing in the McMartin Preschool and Kelly Michaels Daycare Abuse Cases: A Case Study", in *Social Influence*, 2006, vol. 1, no. 1, pp. 16–47.

[4] Gail S. Goodman and Jennifer M. Schaaf, "Over a Decade of Research on Children's Eyewitness Testimony: What Have We Learned? Where Do We Go from Here?", in *Applied Cognitive Psychology*, 1997, vol. 11, no. 7, pp. 5–20; Margaret-Ellen Pipe and J. Clare Wilson, "Cues and Secrets: Influences on Children's Event Reports", in *Developmental Psychology*, 1994, vol. 30, no. 4, pp. 515–525.

[5] United Kingdom ('UK') Home Office, *Memorandum of Good Practice on Video Recorded Interviews With Child Witnesses for Criminal Proceedings*, His Majesty's Stationery Office ('HMSO'), 1992; Kathleen J. Sternberg, Michael E. Lamb, Graham M. Davies and Helen L. Westcott, "The Memorandum of Good Practice: Theory Versus Application", in *Child Abuse & Neglect*, 2001, vol. 25, no. 5, pp. 669–681.

[6] John C. Yuille, Robin Hunter, Risha Joffe and Judy Zaparniuk, "Interviewing Children in Sexual Abuse Cases", in Gail S. Goodman and Bette L. Bottoms (eds.), *Child Victims, Child Witness: Understanding and Improving Testimony*, Guilford Press, New York, 1993, pp. 669–681.

[7] Debra A. Poole and Michael E. Lamb, *Investigative Interviews of Children: A Guide for Helping Professionals*, American Psychological Association, Washington, D.C., 1998.

---

such clear recommendations coming to the forefront of professional thinking,[8] the quality of forensic interviewing still contained many shortcomings including the persistence of biased interviewing, lack of open questioning and the use of 'techniques' that that were known to reduce the reliability of testimony.[9] It was perplexing that the quality of forensic interviewing was so low given the clarity of research findings and professional recommendations.

17.2. What Is the NICHD Protocol?

The NICHD Protocol was developed to maximize the conditions in which children would be most likely to accurately describe their experiences of abuse in legal contexts. The NICHD Protocol has at its core developmentally appropriate expectations about children's capabilities and seeks to help interviewers avoid suggestive practices while at the same time capitalizing on cognitive strengths.

17.2.1. The Basic Structure of the NICHD Protocol

The NICHD Protocol is structured and characterized by the following phases of the investigative interview.

17.2.1.1. Introduction and Ground Rules

In this phase, interviewers inform children that they should tell the truth and that they will be required to describe events in detail because the interviewer was not present and therefore does not know what happened. This initial phase is designed to remove potential pressure that could manifest itself as suggestive influence later in the interview. The number and type of ground rules used can differ across jurisdictions due to legal requirements. One of the core aspects of the NICHD Protocol is that it is flexible enough to permit variation in these procedures. Typical ground rules that interviewers should communicate include: (i) that it is important to tell the truth; (ii) asking the child to promise to tell the truth; (iii) a demonstration of 'truth and lies'; (iv) 'if you do not understand me, say so'; (v) 'it is OK to say 'I don't know''; (vi) 'correct me if I make a mistake'; (vii) 'tell me everything'; (viii) 'tell me if you cannot remember'; (ix) 'do not guess'; and (x) 'sometimes we will ask questions again to clarify what you mean'.

---

[8]   Michael E. Lamb, "The Investigation of Child Sexual Abuse: An Interdisciplinary Consensus Statement", in *Child Abuse & Neglect*, 1994, vol. 18, no. 12, pp. 1021–1028.

[9]   Sternberg, Lamb, Davies and Westcott, 2001, see *supra* note 5; Jan Aldridge and Sandra Cameron, "Interviewing Child Witnesses: Questioning Techniques and the Role of Training", in *Applied Developmental Science*, 1999, vol. 3, no. 2, pp. 136–147; Amye Warren *et al.*, "Assessing the Effectiveness of a Training Program for Interviewing Child Witnesses", in *Applied Developmental Science*, 1999, vol. 3 no. 2, pp. 128–135.

17.2.1.2. Rapport Building and Practice Interview

In this phase, the interviewer uses open prompts to get acquainted with the child and to familiarize the child with the questioning style that will be used later in the interview to discuss alleged abuse. The interviewer begins by inviting the child to provide some 'neutral topics' about things that they have done recently. Typically, an interviewer might ask a child 'What are some things that you like to do?'. Once the child has provided some topics the interviewer can follow up with open prompts such as 'Tell me more about that' to convey that they are interested in 'getting to know' the child. Sometimes the interviewer will have some pre-prepared topics that they can use if the child is not able to provide suitable topics to talk about (for example, a recent celebration such as Matariki or Thanksgiving) which are also followed up with open prompts.

The rapport building phase feeds directly into what we know as the 'practice interview'. The interviewer continues to encourage the child to retrieve memories about neutral topics. The continued use of open prompts by the interviewer helps the child 'practice' their memory retrieval skills which further helps the child become familiar with the communication style that will continue throughout the interview. During this phase, the interviewer can get a feel for the child's language and developmental abilities, how reluctant or worried they are and their overall level of comfort and can adapt their style accordingly.

17.2.1.3. Transition to Substantive Phase

The interviewer uses a series of prompts to assist the child in transitioning to the topic of concern. These prompts are ranked on a continuum using a funnel approach, with interviewers beginning with open prompts such as 'Now that I know you a little better, it is time to talk about why you came to see me today'. Children who have previously made an outcry will often know that this is the time to discuss the alleged abuse. Should the child not be forthcoming, the interviewer may need to resort to more direct prompting, with the specificity of the prompting required varying case-by-case.

17.2.1.3.1. Investigating the Incident(s)

If the child does make a clear disclosure, the interviewer follows up with open prompts to allow the child to tell them more about what happened (for example, 'Tell me what happened'). If the interviewer suspects that there may be multiple instances of abuse to investigate, they may need to separate the incidents by asking '*Did X happen one time, or more than one time?*'. If there are multiple incidents, the interviewer explores details for as many specific incidents as the child can remember. The incidents that are likely to be best remembered are 'the first time' and 'the last time'. The interviewer can also enquire about 'another time' but it should be remembered that in cases of multiple incidents children can find it difficult to provide detailed information about each time that they were abused.

17.2.1.4. Focused Questions

Once the child has provided their account in response to open prompts, the interviewer must address forensically relevant information that the child has not spontaneously provided using focused questions. Sometimes additional information obtained using focused questions can also be followed up using open prompts, what has been called the 'pairing principle'.

17.2.1.5. Break

During the break, the interviewer leaves the room and confers with colleagues about ideas for follow-up questions. This provides a chance to make sure important details are not missed. A skilled colleague observing the interview may have spotted aspects of a child's account that need to be clarified to get a clearer picture about what happened or to satisfy legal requirements. Typical follow up questions can include, 'When you said he touched you, was that above the clothes or below the clothes?', or 'When you said he touched you, was that before or after your birthday?'. If new information is introduced the interviewer may again follow up with additional open prompts.

Interviewers may take as many breaks as the child, or they, need. If the child is reluctant, the interviewer can use the break to discuss potential barriers to communication, how they might be addressed or whether to abort the interview altogether.

17.2.1.5.1. Disclosure Information

The interviewer explores the circumstances of the initial disclosure made by the child. Who did the child initially tell? Who else knows what happened?

17.2.1.5.2. Closure

The interviewer thanks the child for talking and leaves the door open for future interviews if necessary (for example 'Anything else you want to tell', 'Do you have any questions to ask me? If you remember anything else, ask a grown-up to give me a call'). It is good practice to then end the interview on a neutral topic not related to the abuse or allegations that have been made.

17.3. The Development of Approaches to Interview Protocols Past and Present: Differences and Common Ground

17.3.1. Quintilian

The historical roots of our approach to forensic interviewing goes back to around 95 AD when Quintilian wrote at length about 'interviewing' in the famous *Institutio Oratoria*, a 12-volume textbook on the theory and practice of rhetoric and training of the 'orator', or what we today call the 'interviewer'.[10] The basic principles are remarkably like the approach we take today. Quintilian wrote that interviews should have the following aspects:

- Have a purpose and a plan for the interview;
- to engage with the interviewee;
- be aware of the formal and informal setting of where and when the communication (interview) is taking place;
- getting the interviewee to provide the information and to clarify and challenge the information presented;
- summarize what has been presented and close the communication; and
- examine and reflect upon how well the interview went and what could have been done differently.

17.3.2. Stern

More than a hundred years ago, Stern[11] argued that the quality of a witness statement was dependent upon how the interviewer phrased their questions. Stern made the distinction between two kinds of interviewing styles termed 'Bericht' and 'Verhör'. The Bericht style of questioning was characterized as one that allowed a witness to provide their account in a manner that was unhampered by leading and suggestive questions, and interviewer expectation and bias. We now often refer to these types of accounts as 'free narratives' that are elicited by the interviewer using open prompts. By contrast, the Verhör style of questioning was characterized as one that included 'closed' and 'suggestive' questions. These core principles in communication are now found in nearly all textbooks on the theory and practice of interviewing, especially those in legal contexts.

17.3.3. Modern Interview Guidelines and Protocols

The communication principles theorized by Quintilian and Stern are like those we see in most interview structures today. For example, the interviewing protocols listed below (in alphabetical order) all have a similarly phased approach to interviewing, beginning with rapport-building, opportunities to obtain accounts of events of interest and ending with closure:

- Achieving Best Evidence in Criminal Proceedings;[12]

---

[10] *The Institutio Oratoria of Quintilian*, Harvard University Press, William Heinemann, 1920–1922 (translation).

[11] L. William Stern, *Beiträge zür Psychologie der Aussage*, Verlag von Johann Ambrosius Barth, Leipzig, 1903/1904.

[12] UK Ministry of Justice, *Achieving Best Evidence in Criminal Proceedings Guidance on Interviewing Victims and Witnesses, and Guidance on Using Special Measures*, 2011; see also Chapter 18 of this book.

- Advanced Interview Mapping for Child Forensic Interviewers;[13]
- APSAC Practice Guidelines on "Investigative Interviewing in Cases of Alleged Child Abuse";[14]
- ChildFirst® Forensic Interview Protocol;[15]
- Cognitive Interview;[16]
- CornerHouse Forensic Interview Protocol;[17]
- Dialogical Communication Method (DCM);[18]
- Interviewing children and recording evidence (Queensland Family Services);[19]
- KREATIV principles and programme;[20]
- Learning to listen;[21]

---

[13] Mark D. Everson, Scott Snider and Scott M. Rodriguez, "Taking AIM: Advanced interview Mapping for Child Forensic Interviewers", in *American Professional Society on the Abuse of Children ('APSAC') Advisor*, 2020, vol. 31, no. 2.

[14] APSAC Taskforce, "Forensic Interviewing in Cases of Suspected Child Abuse", APSAC, 2012.

[15] Rita Farrel and Victor Vieth, "ChildFirst® Forensic Interview Training Program", in *APSAC Advisor*, 2020, vol. 32, no. 2, pp. 56–62.

[16] Ronald P. Fisher and R. Edward Geiselman, *Memory-Enhancing Techniques for Investigative Interviewing: The Cognitive Interview*, Charles C Thomas Publisher, Springfield, 1992; see also Chapter 16 of this book.

[17] Jennifer Anderson, "The CornerHouse Forensic Interview Protocol: An Evolution in Practice for Almost 25 Years", in *APSAC Advisor*, 2013, vol. 25, no. 4, pp. 2–7; CornerHouse, "The CornerHouse Protocol", 2018.

[18] Kari Trøften Gamst and Åse Langballe, "Barn som vitner. En empirisk og teoretisk studie av kommunikasjon mellom avhører og barn i dommeravhør. Utvikling av en avhørsmetodisk tilnærming", Ph.D. thesis, Institutt for spesialpedagogikk, University of Oslo, 2004; Norwegian Ministry of Justice and Public Security, *Avhør av særlige sårbare personer i straffesaker. Rapport fra arbeidsgruppen sor gjennomgang av regelverket om domemravhør og observasjon av barn og psykisk utviklingshemmede*, 2012; Trond Myklebust, "The Nordic Model of Handling Children's Testemonies", in Susanna Johansson, Kari Stefansen, Elisiv Bakketeig and Anna Kaldal (eds.), *Collaborating Against Child Abuse*, Palgrave Macmillan, Cham, 2017.

[19] Queensland Family Services, "Interviewing Children and Recording Evidence: Education, Health and Police Services", 1992.

[20] Ole Thomas Bjerknes and Ivar A. Fahsing, *Etterforskning – Prinsipper, metoder og praksis*, Fagbokforlaget, Bergen, 2018; Andy Griffiths and Asbjørn Rachlew, "From Interrogation to Investigative Interviewing", in Andy Griffiths and Rebecca Milne (eds.), *The Psychology of Criminal Investigation: From Theory to Practice*, Routledge, London, 2018; see also Chapter 12 of this book.

[21] Patti Toth, "APSAC's Approach to Child Forensic Interviews: Learning to Listen", in *APSAC Advisor*, 2019, vol. 32, no. 2, pp. 9–18.

- Memorandum of Good Practice;[22]
- NICHD Protocol;[23]
- PEACE model;[24]
- RADAR Child Interview Models;[25]
- Step by Step: Sixteen Steps Toward Legally Sound Sexual Abuse Investigations;[26] and
- StepWise Protocol.[27]

17.3.4. Differences Between Approaches

Some of these approaches were largely influenced by academic researchers, whereas other approaches were more heavily influenced by practitioners working for government, non-governmental or private organizations. Depending on the context in which these approaches were developed, some have received copyright protection of intellectual property, whereas other protocols have been made freely available to any person or agency that wants to use them.

There are also notable differences in the content and focus. For some approaches, the focus has been on the values and principles that underpin them. For example, the KREATIV approach[28] adopted in Norway, emphasizes: (K) Communication, (R) Rule of law, (E) Ethics and Empathy, (A) Active consciousness, (T) Trust through openness and (I) Information (V) Verified through science.[29] For others, the content is more focused on the actual structure of the interview approach. For example, the PEACE model[30] originally adopted in England and Wales uses a mnemonic for emphasize the structure of the

---

22 UK Home Office, *Memorandum of Good Practice on Video Recorded Interviews With Child Witnesses for Criminal Proceedings*, HMSO, London, 1992; see also Chapter 18 of this book.

23 Michael E. Lamb, Irit Hershkowitz, Yael Orbach and Philip W. Esplin, *Tell Me What Happened: Structured Investigative Interviews of Child Victims and Witnesses*, Wiley-Blackwell, Hoboken, 2008; David J. La Rooy *et al.*, "The NICHD Protocol: A Review of an Internationally-Used Evidence-Based Tool for Training Child Forensic Interviewers", in *Journal of Criminological Research, Policy and Practice*, 2015, vol. 1, no. 2, pp. 76–89.

24 See Chapter 12 of this book.

25 Mark D. Everson, Scott Snider, Scott M. Rodriguez and Christopher T. Ragsdale, "Why RADAR? Why Now? An Overview of RADAR Child Interview Models", in *APSAC Advisor*, 2020, vol. 31, no. 2, pp. 36–47.

26 Jan Hindman, *Step by Step: Sixteen Steps Toward Legally Sound Sexual Abuse Investigations*, AlexAndria Associates, Ontario, 1987.

27 Yuille, Hunter, Joffe and Zaparniuk, 1993, see *supra* note 6.

28 Bjerknes and Fahsing, 2018, see *supra* note 20.

29 For further details, see Chapter 12 of this book.

30 *Ibid.*

---

interviewing approach – (P) Planning and preparation; (E) Engage and explain, (A) Account, (C) Closure and (E) Evaluation.

Another difference between these different approaches is length of training required for an interviewer to be considered competent.[31] Some training programmes involve only a few hours while other training programmes can last for several days or weeks.

An important question over recent decades for researchers and practitioners alike has been – how effective are the different approaches to interviewing? Some commentators have taken the stance that it is important to validate interviewing approaches and systematically evaluate their effectiveness by examining real-life forensic interviews conducted with children.[32] Without developing a 'perfect' way to measure the effectiveness of a forensic interview, many researchers decided that a good place to start is by examining the post-training questioning styles used by interviewers conducting real-life forensic interviews.

A less ecologically valid, yet equally important, approach to assessing the effectiveness of various interview approaches has been to conduct analogue experimental research.[33] Much of the research literature that supports current approaches to forensic interviewing relies on memory and suggestibility research conducted on non-abused children who assent to participate in the research.

Some of the modern approaches to forensic interviewing listed above do not rely heavily on scientific research and are guided by the professional experience of the developers.

17.4. Research Underpinning the NICHD Protocol

17.4.1. Early Field Research

What makes the NICHD Protocol so unique is that, unlike many other interview approaches that have been developed, the NICHD Protocol was, and continues to be, the subject of rigorous ecologically-valid scientific evaluation. Beginning in 1997, Sternberg and collaborators, using an Israeli sample of real-life forensic interviews, evaluated the relative effectiveness of two rapport-building techniques for eliciting information from children. Israeli youth investigators who participated in the research were also trained using two different structured

---

31   Heather Stewart, Carmit Katz and David J. La Rooy, "Training Forensic Interviewers", in Michael E. Lamb, David J. La Rooy, Lindsay C. Malloy and Carmit Katz (eds.), *Children's Testimony: A Handbook of Psychological Research and Forensic Practice*, 2nd ed., Wiley-Blackwell, Chichester, 2011, pp. 199–216.

32   Michael E. Lamb, "Difficulties Translating Research on Forensic Interview Practices to Practitioners: Finding Water, Leading Horses, but Can We Get Them to Drink?", in *American Psychologist*, 2016, vol. 71, no. 8, pp. 710–718.

33   Deirdre A. Brown *et al.*, "The NICHD Investigative Interview Protocol: An Analogue Study", in *Journal of Experimental Psychology: Applied*, 2013, vol. 19, no. 4, pp. 367–382.

interview protocols. One was primarily based around using direct prompts, while the other was based around using open prompts. In that process, consistent with the findings of experimental research,[34] researchers demonstrated that using open prompts, particularly when combined with narrative elaboration training, increased the total amount of information provided by children alleging abuse. It also appeared that the information elicited was more useful from an investigative perspective. That said, the research also showed that interviewers did not persist using open prompts for long, and often ceased using them soon after the substantive phase of the interview had begun.

17.4.2. Testing of a Structured Protocol

Subsequent research focused on ways that would help interviewers use open prompts more effectively. Sternberg and collaborators[35] focused primarily on the use of a *structured* interview protocol (later to become known as the NICHD Protocol) to improve the overall quality of forensic interviews. Using a US sample of experienced police officers, the quality of post-training structured interviews was compared with the quality of pre-training interviews. Specifically, the training involved police officers undertaking a 40-hour training programme. In addition to being provided with information about children's testimony, memory development and suggestibility, they also received training in the use of a highly structured interview protocol. During their training, they received detailed feedback from their trainers following role-play interviews, reflected on their own interviewing techniques and participated in group discussion sessions. Role-play interviews were also recorded, re-watched and reviewed. This study showed that interviewers trained to use a structured protocol, particularly the one based around facilitating the use of open prompts, were able to obtain greater amounts of uncontaminated information from the children they interviewed.

17.4.3. Field Research Using the NICHD Protocol

In 2000, Orbach and colleagues[36] conducted the first 'official' field trial of the NICHD Protocol. Real-life interviews using the NICHD Protocol were

---

[34] Helen R. Dent, "An Experimental Study of the Effectiveness of Different Techniques of Questioning Mentally-Handicapped Child Witnesses", in *British Journal of Clinical Psychology*, 1986, vol. 25, no. 1, pp. 13–17; Hellen R. Dent and Geoffrey M. Stephenson, "An Experimental Study of the Effectiveness of Different Techniques of Questioning Child Witnesses", in *British Journal of Social and Clinical Psychology*, 1979, vol. 18, no. 1, pp. 41–51.

[35] Kathleen J. Sternberg, Michael E. Lamb, Phillip W. Esplin and Laila P. Baradaran, "Using a Scripted Protocol in Investigative Interviews: A Pilot Study", in *Applied Developmental Science*, 1999, vol. 3, no. 2, pp. 70–76.

[36] Yael Orbach *et al.*, "Assessing the Value of Structured Protocols for Forensic Interviews of Alleged Abuse Victims", in *Child Abuse & Neglect*, 2000, vol. 24, no. 6, pp. 733–752.

compared to a sample of non-protocol forensic interviews. This study demonstrated that the NICHD Protocol facilitated an interview style based on open prompts and better stimulated children's ability to provide uncontaminated free narrative; the research also showed the suggestive questioning by interviewers was reduced; and that this change was achieved in the first interviews after training. The same research design was later replicated in three more countries: (i) the US in 2001; (ii) the UK in 2006; and (iii) Canada in 2006, and provided consistent findings that were subsequently published.[37]

Using this quasi-experimental methodology, subsequent research was also able to explore other aspects of forensic interviewing, for example, credibility assessment, effects of interview delay and the dynamics of the disclosure process.[38]

17.5. Further Development of the NICHD Protocol

17.5.1. Reluctant Children

Subsequent research has also facilitated a revision of the NICHD Protocol now termed the 'NICHD-R'. In a study of the interviews with children in cases that had been independently corroborated, Hershkowitz et al.[39] observed that interviewers tended to respond to reluctant children counter-productively by (i) putting pressure on reluctant children rather giving them support; (ii) shifting the discussion to sensitive issues before the children seemed comfortable; and (iii) using intrusive rather than open questions when exploring the possibility that abuse might have occurred. A related study revealed that reluctant disclosers (those who disclosed in response to focused recognition memory prompts, rather than to open prompts) reported fewer abuse-related details than non-reluctant

---

[37] Kathleen J. Sternberg et al., "Use of a Structured Investigative Protocol Enhances Young Children's Responses to Free Recall Prompts in the Course of Forensic Interviews", in *Journal of Applied Psychology*, 2001, vol. 86, no. 5, pp. 997–1005; Michael E. Lamb et al., "Use of a Structured Investigative Protocol Enhances the Quality of Investigative Interviews With Alleged Victims of Child Sexual Abuse in Britain", in *Applied Cognitive Psychology*, 2009, vol. 23, no. 4, pp. 449–467; Mireille Cyr and Michael E. Lamb, "Assessing the Effectiveness of the NICHD Investigative Interview Protocol when Interviewing French-Speaking Alleged Victims of Child Sexual Abuse in Quebec", in *Child Abuse & Neglect*, 2009, vol. 33, no. 5, pp. 257–268.

[38] La Rooy, 2015, see *supra* note 23.

[39] Irit Hershkowitz et al., "Dynamics of Forensic Interviews With Suspected Abuse Victims Who Do Not Disclose Abuse", in *Child Abuse & Neglect*, 2006, vol. 30, no. 7, pp. 753–769.

children.[40] Accordingly, Hershkowitz *et al.*[41] recommended that interviewers should refrain from raising abuse-related issues until children appear comfortable and co-operative, and that they should invest greater effort in establishing rapport to support reluctant children. The NICHD Protocol in its original form clearly helped children report information about experienced events, but it did not specifically address important and complicated motivational obstacles that make some children unwilling or unable to talk about suspected abuse.

17.5.2. The Revised NICHD Protocol

The NICHD-R was designed to (i) assist interviewers in building better rapport with the children at the outset, and (ii) provide children with more emotional support throughout the investigative interview.[42] Specifically, the NICHD-R includes a friendlier version of the pre-substantive phase and provides guidance for interviewers to use non-suggestive, supportive comments, especially in response to reluctant behaviour. In a comparison to the original Protocol, research has shown that the revised Protocol was associated with increased support and decreased reluctance to talk.[43]

The specific modifications made to the NICHD-R were designed to enhance the children's emotional comfort, trust and co-operation. The rapport-building phase of the interview preceded, rather than followed, the explanation of the ground rules and expectations. Furthermore, interviewer training shifted focus to place greater emphasis on the use of non-suggestive, supportive comments, which included:

- expressions of interest in the child's experiences ('I really want to know you better');

- using the child's name while echoing their feelings ('You say you were (sad, angry or the feeling mentioned)');

- acknowledging the child's feelings ('I see' or 'I understand what you are saying') and exploring them ('Tell me more about (the feeling)');

---

[40] Yael Orbach, Hana Shiloach and Michael E. Lamb, "Reluctant Disclosers of Child Sexual Abuse", in Margaret-Ellen Pipe, Michael E. Lamb, Yael Orbach and Ann-Christin Cederborg (eds.), *Child Sexual Abuse: Disclosure, Delay, and Denial*, Erlbaum, Mahwah, 2007, pp. 115–134.

[41] Hershkowitz *et al.*, 2006, see *supra* note 39.

[42] Irit Hershkowitz, Michael E. Lamb and Carmit Katz, "Allegation Rates in Forensic Child Abuse Investigations: Comparing the Revised and Standard NICHD Protocols", in *Psychology, Public Policy, and Law*, 2014, vol. 20, no. 3, pp. 336–344.

[43] Elizabeth C. Ahern *et al.*, "Support and Reluctance in the Pre-Substantive Phase of Alleged Child Abuse Victim Investigative Interviews: Revised Versus Standard NICHD Protocols", in *Behavioral Sciences & the Law*, 2014, vol. 32, no. 6, pp. 762–774; Hershkowitz, Lamb and Katz, 2014, see *supra* note 42.

- positively reinforcing the child's efforts ('Thank you for letting me listen' or 'You are really helping me understand') but not what they said; and
- expressing empathy about the interview experience ('I know (it is a long interview, there are many questions or other difficulties the child expressed)').

17.6. Training in Israel and the Research-Led Approach

17.6.1. The Opportunity in Israel

The implementation of the NICHD Protocol and training model requires a well-organized and supporting institutional context. In many ways, the early research on the NICHD Protocol conducted in Israel was greatly facilitated by the political, legal and organizational context in Israel in the mid-1990s. Since 1955, Israeli law had specified that children under 14 years of age who were victims or witnesses of crimes should be interview by trained forensic interviewers.[44] Therefore, a nationwide network of youth investigators had already been established and overseen by the Ministry of Social Affairs.[45]

In the the early 1990s, Professor Michael Lamb contacted the Israeli Minister of Social Affairs to explore the possibility of implementing the Protocol in Israel. Since then, Israeli child forensic interviewers started to be trained to use the NICHD Protocol, which, in 1998, became mandatory nationwide.[46]

17.6.2. The Research-Practice Connection

The connection between the NICHD research team and Israeli forensic interviewing practitioners became not just a role model in interview training but also an excellent example of an action-research methodology. This approach seeks transformative change through the simultaneous process of taking action and doing research that is linked together by critical scientific reflection. The method was based on a continual loop between planning, implementation, description and evaluation of forensic interviews, aimed to improve and support interviewer practice, and providing an expectation that there will be ongoing scientific evaluation and inquiry. In Israel, every forensic interview conducted using the NICHD Protocol is, and has been, recorded so the possibility of conducting research is greatly facilitated with a database of tens of thousands of interviews available.

---

[44] Carmit Katz, "Investigative Interviews With Alleged Victims and Witnesses in Israel: Consequences of the 1955 Law for Practice", in David Walsh, Gavin E. Oxburgh, Allison D. Redlich and Trond Myklebust (eds.), *International Developments and Practices in Investigative Interviewing and Interrogation*, Routledge, 2016.

[45] *Ibid.*

[46] *Ibid.*

17.7. Training With the NICHD Protocol

17.7.1. Challenges

Despite the clarity of the research findings and training methods discussed above, professional forensic interview trainers employing the NICHD Protocol have encountered some common difficulties and challenges in training environments. Of course, there are challenges faced by anyone delivering training regarding child forensic interviewing, most notably around the content and subject matter of the training itself, but some issues have arisen that are particular to training using the NICHD Protocol. These challenges center around the perception that the NICHD Protocol is a 'script', and that, because every child is different, a 'one-size-fits-all' approach is not appropriate.

17.7.2. The NICHD Protocol Is Not a 'Script' to Be Read to Children

The most common difficulty to overcome is the perception that the NICHD Protocol is a 'script' that should be simply read to children in a forensic interview. Because the NICHD Protocol contains very specific guidance about what interviewers should say in a forensic interview, some argue that it will lead to a lack of spontaneity on the part of the interviewer, and lead to the interview itself seeming robotic and detached.

Ideas like this, when expressed in an interview training session, should be dealt with as they arise. They should be taken seriously by interview trainers as they bring to the forefront a major misunderstanding about the role that the NICHD Protocol plays in improving the quality of forensic interviews. The NICHD Protocol functions primarily as a training tool designed to provide the necessary interviewing skills to professionals, who may have never interviewed a child about abuse before, within a few days. As a training tool the NICHD Protocol allows interviewers to familiarize themselves with the language, questioning style and phases of the forensic interview. Trying to remember what to say in all the different phases of the interview is difficult so interviewers benefit from having very clear guidance. It is important to remember that the language of the NICHD Protocol was decided through consultation with psychologists, legal experts and experienced forensic interviewers so that it is developmentally appropriate and meets legal standards in the jurisdictions that it is used. With training and feedback, interviewers manage to quickly learn the 'basics' before, over time, settling on a more personal and relaxed approach while still following the structure of the NICHD Protocol. In practice, no two interviews are ever the same and interviewers will still need to make many decisions about the direction their interviews lead and take a flexible, rather than a rigid, approach. Using the NICHD Protocol provides a standardized starting position for training and provides, as research shows, better outcomes in the long term.

17.7.3. The NICHD Protocol Is Not Designed as a 'One-Size-Fits All' Approach

Another criticism has been that the NICHD Protocol is not appropriate for all children, with trainees often pointing out that 'every child is different' and that a standard approach is not appropriate in every case. This is a very valid concern, but it does not mean that the NICHD Protocol should not be used in training contexts as a valuable training tool. The NICHD Protocol was primarily developed and tested in research studies on children who have made a clear initial disclosure and/or when abuse is strongly suspected to have occurred. In these situations, children are often 'ready to talk' and the NICHD Protocol provides the techniques for forensic interviewers to obtain detailed accounts about what happened. So, in practice, the NICHD Protocol is appropriate to use in most cases.

That said, experienced interviewers will still recognize cases where modifications to the approach may be warranted, for example, when children are very young, have intellectual disabilities, suffered repeated abuse or are traumatized. Changes to the NICHD Protocol have been made to support children in cases with particularly difficult dynamics and are reflected in the NICHD-R discussed in Section 17.5.2.

Thus, the NICHD Protocol should be considered a training tool that can be used for interviewers to quickly learn the basic approach, and over time they will be able to use it more flexibly in a larger variety of cases.

17.8. Perceived Credibility of the NICHD Protocol in Legal Contexts

17.8.1. Legal Outcomes Are Improved

Although the NICHD Protocol improves the quality of forensic interviews, a related question has centered around whether it improves legal outcomes in cases of child abuse when it is used. In a study of more than 1,000 interviews, Pipe and collaborators[47] demonstrated that charges were more likely to be filed by the police when the NICHD Protocol had been used by investigators. In addition, in cases where the NICHD Protocol had been used by investigators, a greater number of guilty pleas were obtained. It was also notable that in the minority of the cases studied by Pipe and collaborators[48] that proceeded all the way to trial, there were higher rates of conviction, presumably because the accounts provided by the children interviewed using the NICHD Protocol appeared more compelling and accurate. Further, forensic interviews conducted

---

[47] Margaret-Ellen Pipe *et al.*, "Do Case Outcomes Change when Investigative Interviewing Practices Change?", in *Psychology, Public Policy, and Law*, 2013, vol. 19, no. 2, p. 179.

[48] *Ibid.*

using the NICHD Protocol yielded more investigative leads (that is, information that suggests new directions in which to seek corroborative evidence) that facilitated the verification of allegations. In fact, NICHD Protocol interviews produced leads that were clearer and more easily verifiable compared to the leads produced in non-NICHD Protocol interviews.

17.8.1.1. Credibility Is Improved

Additional research[49] found that interviews conducted using the NICHD Protocol facilitated credibility assessment by eliciting statements that were richer in the Criteria-Based Content Analysis scale, hypothesized to differentiate between plausible and implausible event reports.[50] Hershkowitz and Lamb also showed that the NICHD Protocol impacted on credibility assessment and observed that the use of the NICHD-R increased the chances that interviews would be deemed to be more credible.[51] We may therefore surmise that structured forensic interviews help to frame children's narratives so they appear more credible.

17.9. Overcoming Language Barriers

17.9.1. Translated Versions of the NICHD Protocol

Over the course of the last few decades, as the popularity of the NICHD Protocol grew, so too did the need for the Protocol to be translated into languages other than English and Hebrew. Developing translated versions of the NICHD Protocol has been undertaken largely on an *ad hoc* basis. Professionals around the world, sensing the need for the NICHD Protocol to be available to non-English speaking jurisdictions, took it on themselves to prepare new translated versions. Sometimes proposals for translated versions were supported by the developers of the original NICHD Protocol, whilst other times translated versions appeared, by necessity, out of the blue!

When the developers were contacted about proposals to translate the NICHD Protocol, a question often asked has been how 'close' the translation should be to its original form in English? The advice from those involved in developing the NICHD Protocol was that the literal translations would probably not work and that translations of the NICHD Protocol should focus on

---

[49] Irit Hershkowitz, Sara Fisher, Michael E. Lamb and Dvora Horowitz, "Improving Credibility Assessment in Child Sexual Abuse Allegations: The Role of the NICHD Investigative Interview Protocol", in *Child Abuse & Neglect*, 2007, vol. 31, no. 2, pp. 99–110.

[50] Michael E. Lamb *et al.*, "Assessing the Credibility of Children's Allegations of Sexual Abuse: A Survey of Recent Research", in *Learning and Individual Differences*, 1997, vol. 9, no. 2, pp. 175–194.

[51] Irit Hershkowitz and Michael E. Lamb, "Allegation Rates and Credibility Assessment in Forensic Interviews of Alleged Child Abuse Victims: Comparing the Revised and Standard NICHD Protocols", in *Psychology, Public Policy, and Law*, 2020, vol. 26, no. 2, pp. 176–184.

preserving the 'spirit' of the original version and be faithful to the structured approach to interviewing. Of course, this meant that the NICHD Protocol needed to be translated by professionals who were also knowledgeable about the underpinning logic and psychology of the NICHD Protocol. We have the most confidence in translations that have been 'back translated' into English for inspection to make sure that the spirit of the NICHD Protocol is preserved.

To date, there are versions of the NICHD Protocol translated into Bahasa, Bulgarian, Chinese, Dutch, English, Finnish, French, Georgian, German, Greek, Hebrew, Italian, Japanese, Portuguese, Romanian, Russian, Slovene, Spanish and Swedish. The advantage of having these translated versions is that the reach of the NICHD Protocol research has been greatly extended, and it has also paved the way for the possibility of more research in a larger variety of countries and cultures. These translated versions can be found on the NICHD Protocol web site. There is still a need for even more translations of the NICHD Protocol.

17.9.2. Interpreter-Mediated Interviews

One additional advantage of having ready access to translated versions of the NICHD Protocol was that it became apparent that it would be helpful in interpreter mediated interviews, where a child may be most fluent in a different language from the jurisdictions where they live. The role of an interpreter in any forensic setting is challenging, but even more so when interviewing children and developmental issues come to the fore. Interpreters are very familiar with the linguistic 'rules' when interpreting but may be less aware of the underlying psychology that underpins the NICHD Protocol, in particular, the ways in which question types from a psychology standpoint invoke different memory processes. Being able to provide interpreters with a translated version of the NICHD Protocol may indeed help them more closely adhere to the very sensitive and critical nature of the questioning, although this should be the subject of future evaluation.

17.10. The Use of Additional Techniques

17.10.1. Body Diagrams

Alternative techniques are often used when it is suspected that a child's account might be incomplete and that they require additional ways to be able to communicate abuse experiences. The use of 'body diagrams', for example, emerged due to the difficulty of preschool-age children to verbally identify and communicate body touches. The body diagrams could, in this way, potentially facilitate body touch clarification during a forensic interview, as well as help to characterize the type of body touch experienced by the child. This technique could also be useful in cases where children show emotional constraints that make it difficult to verbalize the type and location of the body touch experienced. Although widely used in various forensic interview approaches (for example 'RATAC'),[52] the use of body diagrams in forensic interviews is still controversial. Pipe and Salmon, in a review,[53] indicated that the usefulness of body diagrams depends on how they are used, when they are used and who uses them. So, despite apparent advantages, there are clearly risks.

17.10.2. Field Research With Body Diagrams

Studies[54] with the NICHD Protocol have pointed to improvements in the quality and quantity of information when body diagrams are used. Aldridge and collaborators[55] found that body diagrams generated a greater amount of information regarding body touches, helping to clarify their location. This effect was particularly salient in school-age children. These findings were also supported by Teoh and collaborators,[56] who found that the use of body diagrams, after exhaustive inquiry through open questions, lead to the verbalization of new touches, as well as the clarification of the body touches already described. However, the authors of this study cautioned that because they studied real-life forensic interviews, it was not possible to verify whether the additional information provided was accurate.

Empirical studies[57] have also pointed to the existence of risks in the use of these methodologies because gains in the amount of information obtained is a combination of both correct and incorrect information. Therefore, the use of body diagrams in forensic practice may be problematic, as there is a risk of eliciting false information and errors. Research on body diagrams has also shown

---

[52] Jennifer Anderson *et al.*, "The Cornerhouse Forensic Interview Protocol: RATAC®", in *Thomas M. Cooley Journal of Practical and Clinical Law*, 2010, vol. 12, no. 2, pp. 193–332.

[53] Margaret-Ellen Pipe and Karmen Salmon, "Dolls, Drawing, Body Diagrams, and Other Props: Role of Props in Investigative Interviews", in Kathryn Kuehnle and Mary Connell (eds.), *The Evaluation of Child Sexual Abuse Allegations: A Comprehensive Guide to Assessment and Testimony*, Wiley, Hoboken, 2009, pp. 365–395.

[54] Jan Aldridge *et al.*, "Using a Human Figure Drawing to Elicit Information from Alleged Victims of Child Abuse", in *Journal of Consulting and Clinical Psychology*, 2004, vol. 72, no. 2, pp. 304–316; Deirdre A. Brown *et al.*, "Supportive or Suggestive: Do Human Figure Drawings Help 5- to 7-Year-Old Children to Report Touch?", in *Journal of Consulting and Clinical Psychology*, 2007, vol. 75, no. 1, pp. 33–42; Teoh Yee-San *et al.*, "Do Human Figure Diagrams Help Alleged Victims of Sexual Abuse Provide Elaborate and Clear Accounts of Physical Contact With Alleged Perpetrators?", in *Applied Cognitive Psychology*, 2010, vol. 24, no. 2, pp. 287–300.

[55] Aldridge *et al.*, 2004, see *supra* note 54.

[56] Teoh *et al.*, 2010, see *supra* note 54.

[57] Aldridge *et al.*, 2004, see *supra* note 54; Brown *et al.*, 2007, see *supra* note 54; Teoh *et al.*, 2010, see *supra* note 54.

that little additional information is gained when they are used with preschool-age children.[58]

Due to the risks pointed out with the use of body diagrams, the developers of the NICHD Protocol have consistently recommended that they should only be used as a last resort and only after obtaining the child's full account about the alleged incidents through open questions. Therefore, the diagrams would be best used to clarify information already provided by the child and never to trigger disclosure.

17.11. Research Challenges

17.11.1. Negative Research Findings

When researchers want to test the efficacy of the NICHD Protocol, there is often a phase in research projects that involves collecting some 'baseline data' to determine the quality of forensic interviews prior to the introduction of the NICHD Protocol. Scientifically speaking, having some access to baseline data allows researchers to determine the amount of improvement in the quality of forensic interviews after the NICHD Protocol has been introduced into training programmes.

From the perspective of researchers, studies like these are viewed as being very important because they 'prove' that there are problems with existing training methods for forensic interviewers and offer a solution to be able to improve the quality of forensic interviews. With such clear data, researchers have sometimes been perplexed as to why the NICHD Protocol was not more quickly adopted by forensic interviewers, and sometimes researchers even sensed reluctance to change existing methods.[59] On the surface, it appeared that there sometimes existed a lack of desire to change existing training methods and improve the quality of forensic interviews.

17.11.2. Research Relationships

When organizations agree to allow researchers to scrutinize the quality of work of their forensic interviewers, they are often not expecting the outcome of the research to show that they have such low standards of quality. Once research findings are published, the repercussions within organizations can be extensive and there can be ensuing 'blame games' that result in ill feelings and questions asked as to why the research was allowed to be undertaken in the first place. Sometimes organizations regret their involvement and become reluctant to continue to co-operate in further research studies.

---

[58] Teoh *et al.*, 2010, see *supra* note 54.
[59] Lamb, 2016, see *supra* note 32.

Sensitivities around nature and the way research is conducted and the relationship between researchers and organizations needs to be managed carefully, and, over time, researchers have become better at building trust and putting measures in place to mitigate any ill feelings that research findings might understandably cause. It is important for researchers to be very up-front about the sorts of results that their research might uncover – this includes negative findings regarding the quality of forensic interviews. This might mitigate the 'shock' when research is finally published and give individual organizations time to start thinking about possible solutions at a much earlier stage. It is also important to provide organizations with early insights into what the research is uncovering well in advance of the formal publication of research results. Of course, all research in these forensic contexts will adhere to ethical standards and findings are published anonymously. However, some organizations, interviewers and trainers may nonetheless take the research results personally – researchers should be mindful of this when contributing to training and organizational change.

17.12. Future Directions and Conclusions

Since the initial development of the NICHD Protocol, there have been continuing developments in the approach taken to training forensic interviewers. Early training was often provided by academics knowledgeable about the relevant research, communication-principles, developmental psychology and other relevant topics. Practitioners sometimes found it hard to take training provided by academics seriously when they realized that the academics delivering the training did not actually conduct forensic interviews themselves, or even investigate crimes! Over time, there has been a gradual, and welcomed, shift towards involving greater numbers of professionals (for example, police and youth investigators) in the delivery of forensic interviewer training. This has improved the perceived credibility of training programmes and will continue to do so in the future.

Moreover, while much interviewer training still focuses on developing the individual skills of interviewers, we have also seen organizations themselves taking greater responsibility for training at an individual, group, leadership and organizational level. This allows a more team-based approach.[60] This change has been paralleled by a more international focus, for example, the European Union Agency for Law Enforcement Training works together with universities, police

---

[60] Mohan P. Pokharel and Choi Sang Ok, "Exploring the Relationships Between the Learning Organization and Organizational Performance", in *Management Research Review*, 2015, vol. 38, no. 2, pp. 126–148 (pp. 122 ff.); David Weisburd and Peter Neyroud, "Police Science: Toward a New Paradigm", in *New Perspectives in Policing*, Harvard Kennedy School, National Institute of Justice, 2011.

university colleges and many other different organizations to further develop training. The Israeli experience implementing the NICHD Protocol is also another example of how academics and practitioners can positively work together. Co-operation like this has been achieved despite significant national, legal and cultural differences.

The international Covid-19 pandemic has also caused professionals to put greater focus on conducting remote interviews using digital platforms and recordings. It is likely that advances in artificial intelligence will also have a major impact on how interviewers are trained and how interviews are conducted in the future.[61] How this will impact on forensic interviewing, and the future development of the NICHD Protocol, remains to be studied.

The future will also see forensic interview training continue to be expanded to include greater numbers of professionals involved in other aspects of child abuse investigation, for example, lawyers, judges, intermediaries, forensic psychologists and alike. We have already seen extensive training in these professions in England and Wales,[62] Chile, Georgia, Scotland and Taiwan. The need for ongoing training, evaluation and research of all aspects of forensic interviewing, including the NICHD Protocol, will remain an important endeavour.

We hope that this chapter has contributed to the understanding of the development of the NICHD Protocol and some of the challenges that have been faced in both research and training. The future involves continuing to bring practitioners and academics together to improve the quality of forensic interviewing as times change. This must involve the continued development of interview education programmes, robust interviews protocols such as the NICHD and be accompanied by scientific research.

---

[61] Francesco Pompedda, Zhang Yikang, Haginoya Shumpei and Pekka Santtila, "A Mega-Analysis of the Effects of Feedback on the Quality of Simulated Child Sexual Abuse Interviews With Avatars", in *Journal of Police and Criminal Psychology*, 2022, vol. 37, no. 3, pp. 485–498; Francesco Pompedda, Angelo Zappalà and Pekka Santtila, "Simulations of Child Sexual Abuse Interviews Using Avatars Paired With Feedback Improves Interview Quality", in *Psychology, Crime & Law*, 2015, vol. 21, no. 1, pp. 28–52; Pegah Salehi *et al.*, "Synthesizing a Talking Child Avatar to Train Interviewers Working With Maltreated Children", in *Big Data and Cognitive Computing*, 2022, vol. 6, no. 2, pp. 1–22.

[62] Joyce Plotnikoff and Richard Woolfson, *Intermediaries in the Criminal Justice System: Improving Communication for Vulnerable Witnesses and Defendants*, Bristol University Press, 2015.

18

Achieving Best Evidence
from Victims and Witnesses

Laura D. Farrugia and Katie Maras[*]

18.1. Introduction

The evidence of victims and witness ('witnesses') is pivotal for successful criminal prosecutions; the quality of their evidence is often relied upon by the prosecution in proving their case. However, the reality is that many witnesses are children, vulnerable or intimidated and so require assistance in providing their best evidence, both at the investigation stage and during the trial. As such, there is a reliance on the criminal justice system to be able to understand and accommodate their needs. Historically, the legal and procedural systems were not considered to be adequate in doing so, and it was following a number of inquiries and revisions of guidance that has led to the development of current guidance for vulnerable witnesses.

In England and Wales, the interviewing of children and vulnerable witnesses is underpinned by guidance produced by the UK's MoJ, *Achieving Best Evidence in Criminal Proceedings* ('ABE').[1] In this chapter, we outline the rationale and development of the ABE framework within its policy and legislative context, what it entails and for whom, and the research that underpins it. We conclude with sections on recent update and limitations, highlighting both strengths and areas of concern of the framework, supported by research to date.

18.1.1. Early Developments: The Memorandum of Good Practice

The predecessor to the ABE, the Memorandum of Good Practice[2] ('MoGP'), was borne out of an advisory group chaired by His Honour Judge Thomas Pigot KC. The group had been set up to consider the admissibility of video-recorded

---

[*]   **Laura Farrugia**, Ph.D., is an Assistant Professor at the Department of Psychology, Northumbria University and works as a Registered Intermediary, accredited with the United Kingdom's ('UK') Ministry of Justice ('MoJ'). **Katie Maras**, Ph.D., is a Senior Lecturer and Deputy Director of the Centre for Applied Autism Research at the University of Bath.
[1]   MoJ, *Achieving Best Evidence in Criminal Proceedings*, UK Home Office, London, 2022 ('ABE').
[2]   UK Home Office, *Memorandum of Good Practice*, His Majesty's Stationary Office London, 1992.

interviews with children in criminal cases. The Pigot Report (1989)[3] recommended that such interviews, conducted by a police officer or social worker, should be used as a substitute for the child's live examination-in-chief evidence at trial. Initially, the Report recommended that a 'Code of Practice' be drawn up to govern the conduct in which the interviews should be carried out in relation to rules of evidence. Recommendations extending the videotape principle to cross-examination and the use of intermediaries[4] were also proposed. In compiling a draft Code of Practice, the UK Home Office commissioned a number of professionals to assist. Following a number of revisions, the title changed from 'Code' to 'Memorandum of Good Practice' – this was done to reflect the guidance of the document, rather than it being viewed as containing inflexible rules. The MoGP was published by the UK Home Office in 1992 to assist and guide those responsible for conducting video-recorded interviews with children or vulnerable witnesses. The MoGP provided a number of recommendations; including that the interview should be conducted as soon as possible after the alleged offence is reported in an informal setting, and that it should last no more than one hour. Other recommendations related to interviewers being trained to interact with children. During the interview, the guidance suggested that children should be given every opportunity to tell their own story before being asked direct questions regarding the alleged offence and that questioning should use open questions to begin with and more direct questions towards the end of the interview, if necessary. The MoGP was launched in 1992 to coincide with the implementation of the Criminal Justice Act (1991).[5] This Act permitted the used of the videoed interview to serve as a child witness' evidence-in-chief at trial. Whilst the Act adopted the admissibility of video-recorded interviews as evidence-in-chief, it did not incorporate recommendations regarding cross-examination and the use of intermediaries in assisting the witness.[6]

Since the implementation of the MoGP, several research studies have been conducted regarding its use and impact. Butler (1993)[7] reported that of

---

[3] UK Home Office, *Report of the Advisory Group on Video Evidence*, London, 1989.

[4] Intermediaries are self-employed communication specialists who assist vulnerable victims, witnesses and defendants to give their evidence during a police interview or trial. Registered Intermediaries are accredited by the MoJ and generally assist with victims and witnesses. See MoJ, "Ministry of Justice Witness Intermediary Scheme", 4 April 2022 (available on the UK government's web site) for more information.

[5] UK, Criminal Justice Act, 15 July 1991 (https://www.legal-tools.org/doc/uahqyr/).

[6] Graham H. Davies and Helen L. Westcott, "Interviewing Child Witnesses Under the Memorandum of Good Practice: A Research Review", Police Research Series Paper No. 115, UK Home Office, Policing and Reducing Crime Unit and Research, Development and Statistics Directorate, 1999.

[7] Anthony Butler, "Spare the Child", in *Police Review*, 2003, no. 14.

nearly 15,000 videotaped interviews conducted in its first nine months of operation, less than a quarter had been submitted to the Crown Prosecution Service ('CPS') and only 44 were known to have been played at trial. Legal delays and late guilty pleas were known to have impacted upon the figures, although the author did also note wide variations in video-recorded interviews being conducted and submitted to the CPS between police force areas. What followed was an evaluation commissioned by the UK Home Office.[8] They reported that 75 per cent of cases at trial included an application to show a video-recorded interview and a general acceptance of the value of recording evidence in this manner amongst police officers, social workers and judges. They also found that children who provided their evidence via video-recording were more relaxed than those who had testified at court. However, interviewers were not always found to follow the guidance regarding free narrative and open-ended questions.

Subsequent research has reported further mixed findings in its support of the MoGP. Some reported that the values of the Memorandum were doubted,[9] and that it failed to address the needs of children with special needs.[10] Whilst these criticisms have been reiterated, other research has found support for the principles included in the MoGP.[11]

18.1.2. Developing 'Achieving Best Evidence in Criminal Proceedings'

In 1998, the UK Home Office tasked an inter-departmental working group with examining the barriers faced by vulnerable or intimidated witnesses in having their voices heard in court. Their resulting report, *Speaking Up for Justice*,[12] highlighted the high rates of attrition between initial police contact and court when vulnerable witnesses were involved.[13] The report produced wide-ranging recommendations to better support and assist vulnerable or intimated witnesses.

---

[8] Graham H. Davies, Clare Wilson, Rebecca Mitchell and John Milsom, *Videotaping Children's Evidence: An Evaluation*, UK Home Office, London, 1995.

[9] Beverley Hughes, Howard Parker and Bernard Gallagher, *Policing Child Sexual Abuse: The View from Police Practitioners*, Home Office Police Research Group, London, 1996.

[10] Helen L. Westcott and Jocelyn Jones (eds.), *Perspectives on the Memorandum: Policy, Practice and Research in Investigative Interviewing*, Ashgate Publishing, 1997.

[11] Graham H. Davies, Emma Marshall and Noelle Robertson, "Child Abuse: Training Investigating Officers", Police Research Series Paper No. 94, UK Home Office Policing and Reducing Crime Unit, London, 1998.

[12] UK Home Office, *Speaking Up for Justice: Report of the Interdepartmental Working Group on the Treatment of Vulnerable or Intimidated Witnesses in the Criminal Justice System*, UK Home Office Procedures and Victims Unit, London, 1998.

[13] Graham H. Davies and Helen L. Westcott, "Preventing the Withdrawal of Complaints and Psychological Support for Victims", in Mark R. Kebbell and Graham H. Davies (eds.), *Practical Psychology for Forensic Investigations and Prosecutions*, Wiley, Chichester, 2006, pp. 183–202.

To legislate these recommendations, the Youth Justice and Criminal Evidence Act (1999)[14] set out a range of 'special measures' to enable vulnerable witnesses to give improved evidence which may be allowed by the court if they are likely to improve the quality of a witness' evidence. These include:

- Section 23: allowing witnesses to give evidence in court from behind a screen;
- Section 24: the use of live link for cross-examination (including from within the court building where the trial is taking place or from an alternative, authorized remote location);
- Section 25: evidence being provided in private, which involves the public gallery being closed and only one media representative having permitted access;
- Section 26: removal of court dress (wigs and gowns);
- Section 27: allowing evidence-in-chief to be presented in the form of a pre-recorded investigative (police) interview, usually an ABE interview;
- Section 28: pre-recorded cross-examination (via video link);
- Section 29: communication through a 'Registered Intermediary'; and
- Section 30: aids to communication (such as communication boards, signs or symbols) to enable the witness to give their best evidence.

Some of these measures were already available to children prior to this through the Criminal Justice Act (1991) and accompanying MoGP. However, this neglected a large proportion of vulnerable people, such as adults with psycho-social difficulties who are at greater risk of victimization.[15] As the Youth Justice and Criminal Evidence Act (1999) extended the option of video-taped evidence-in-chief, along with providing for further special measures (as mentioned above) to all groups of vulnerable witnesses, a small team of specialists were commissioned by the government to draft a new set of guidelines for interviewing vulnerable adults as well as children. The ABE is largely consistent with the MoGP in terms of the style of interviewing it advises, and that its primary purpose is to capture on video the vulnerable witness' evidence for use in the investigation. However, the ABE further differs from the MoGP in that it offers additional guidance regarding support for vulnerable witnesses prior to police interviews and at court. As such, ABE guidance is intended not just for

---

[14] UK, Youth Justice and Criminal Evidence Act, 27 July 1999 (https://www.legal-tools.org/doc/267f70/).

[15] Louise Ellison, Vanessa E. Munro, Katrin Hohl and Paul Wallang, "Challenging Criminal Justice? Psychosocial Disability and Rape Victimization", in *Criminology & Criminal Justice*, 2015, vol. 15, no. 2, pp. 225–244.

police but for all those involved in the legal process, including lawyers and judges.

Following the Youth Justice and Criminal Evidence Act (1999), special measures are all now available (at the discretion of the court) to both children and vulnerable adult witnesses, who are defined by the Act as:

- children under 18 years of age;
- any witness whose quality of evidence is likely to be diminished because they:
  - o are suffering from a mental disorder (as defined by Section 1(2) of the Mental Health Act (1983) and amended into a single definition by Section 1(2) of the Mental Health Act (2007) as any disorder or disability of the mind);[16]
  - o have a significant impairment of intelligence and social functioning;
  - o have a physical disability or are suffering from a physical disorder; or
  - o are suffering from fear or distress in relation to testifying in the case (complainants in sexual offences are automatically defined as falling within this category unless they wish to opt out).

One of the key measures that can be implemented for these groups is the ABE interview which is set out in the guidance document, *Achieving Best Evidence in Criminal Proceedings: Guidance for Vulnerable or Intimidated Witnesses, including Children.*[17]

18.2. Overview of the ABE Framework

The ABE framework provides overall guidance on interviewing victims and witnesses that may require special measures. Although the framework provides extensive guidance, it focusses specifically on four main areas: (i) planning and preparation; (ii) conducting the interview; (iii) witness support and preparation for court; and (iv) witnesses in court. For the purposes of this chapter, each aspect will be discussed in more detail below.

---

[16] UK, Mental Health Act, 9 May 1983 (https://www.legal-tools.org/doc/zrz03a/); *id.*, Mental Health Act, 19 July 2007 (https://www.legal-tools.org/doc/vum89x/).

[17] MoJ, *Achieving Best Evidence in Criminal Proceedings: Guidance on Interviewing Victims and Witnesses, and using Special Measures*, UK Home Office, London, 2011 ('ABE: Guidance on Interviewing Victims and Witnesses, and using Special Measures'); *id.*, *Achieving Best Evidence in Criminal Proceedings: Guidance on Interviewing Victims and Witnesses, and using Special Measures*, UK Home Office, London, 2022.

18.2.1. Planning and Preparation for the ABE Interview

Planning and preparation prior to the ABE interview are well documented as critical for the success of an interview and thus also the subsequent investigation.[18] Indeed, the ABE guidance highlights that "a well-conducted interview will only occur if appropriate planning has taken place".[19] Historically, however, officers' planning and preparation of interviews has been found to be satisfactory at best,[20] highlighting the need for more emphasis on the importance of planning and preparation ahead of an interview.[21] The ABE guidance highlights key areas in planning and preparing for the ABE interview, from making initial contact with the witness to using planning information to inform an interview plan.

18.2.1.1. Initial Contact With Witnesses

ABE guidance on planning and preparation includes early witness contact. Prior to the ABE interview, there will inevitably be some form of initial contact with the victim or witness; for example, to take immediate action regarding the securing of forensic evidence or obtaining medical attention. Some preliminary questioning may also be necessary to elicit a brief account of what the victim or witness is alleging to have occurred. The ABE guidance recommends that only a brief account should occur at this stage, focussing specifically on where and when the alleged offence took place and who was involved or present at the time. Such initial accounts should be brief and obtained using appropriate questioning strategies such as open questions, to avoid contaminating the witness' original memory trace.[22] The initial account should also be documented and subsequently made available to assist in the planning of the formal interview conducted at a later stage.

---

[18] Rebecca Milne and Ray Bull, *Investigative Interviewing: Psychology and Practice*, Wiley, Chichester, 1999; Kevin Smith and Rebecca Milne, "Planning the Interview", in Michael E. Lamb, David J. La Rooy, Lindsay C. Malloy and Carmit Katz (eds). *Children's Testimony: A Handbook of Psychological Research and Forensic Practice*, Wiley, Chichester, 2011, pp. 87–107.

[19] ABE: Guidance on Interviewing Victims and Witnesses, and using Special Measures, p. 17, para. 2.1, see *supra* note 17.

[20] David W. Walsh and Rebecca Milne, "Keeping the PEACE? A Study of Investigative Interviewing Practices in the Public Sector", in *Legal and Criminological Psychology*, 2008, vol. 13, pp. 39–57.

[21] Smith and Milne, 2011, see *supra* note 18.

[22] Elizabeth Loftus, "Make-Believe Memories", in *American Psychologist*, 2003, vol. 58, no. 11, pp. 867–873.

18.2.1.2. Planning Information

Collating relevant information about the individual witness is critical in order to plan an appropriate and effective interview with them. This will usually be gathered through a witness assessment carried out by the interviewing officer in the first instance, although specialist advice (for example, from a Registered Intermediary or psychologist) may be necessary, particularly if the witness has (or is suspected to have) a learning disability or developmental or mental health condition. A mental health assessment by a psychiatrist or psychologist may also take place if such issues are identified, with the aim of informing the childcare planning process (where applicable) and/or assessing the witness' ability to provide reliable evidence and the effect that this might have on mental and physical health. However, these assessments can also (with the agreement of the mental health professional) be used to assist the planning of the video interview, if applicable.

The interviewer should have clear objectives for the assessment and not encourage the witness to talk about the alleged event during the interview (although the witness should not be interrupted if they do freely recall significant events). The focus should be on collating relevant information about the witness' circumstances and individual characteristics that may impact on the interview. These include factors such as age, gender, culture and religion, language and communication, social and cognitive functioning, mental health, welfare and social care issues (and the impact that these, in turn, may have on their mental and emotional state), their relationship to the alleged offender, the need for safeguarding, and whether they have any physical disability. Other factors to be explored include the witness' ability and willingness to talk within a formal interview setting (either to a police officer, social worker or any other trained interviewer), potential issues around compliance, whether communication aids are needed (for example, for witnesses with hearing and communication difficulties) and whether there are any special requirements (for example, if they have separation anxiety). The ABE guidance sets out the importance of establishing the witness' ability to give informed consent to the interview; if not, parent or guardian consent will be required. It is imperative that a witness is able to understand the implications of them being interviewed and, if videoed, how their videoed interview will be used. A full explanation and discussion of the possible special measures that may be implemented must also be explained to a vulnerable witness.

As noted in the ABE guidance, identifying vulnerability (and hence the need for support) in adults can be more difficult because of the fluctuating nature of many mental disorders and often hidden vulnerabilities in conditions such as autism[23] and mild learning disabilities. It is also problematic to generalize the nature and extent of difficulties across (and indeed within) different mental health, learning and developmental conditions. Currently, there is no accepted or consistent approach to the assessment of witness competence for those with mental health conditions and, as noted in the ABE guidance, varying criteria may be used by experts to make assessments. It is also important to note that some people may be reluctant to disclose that they have a learning disability or mental health condition, highlighting the importance of establishing positive early contact with a witness to ensure that they feel comfortable in – and understand the potentially positive implications of – disclosing their diagnosis.[24]

There are also other issues around potential discrimination (perceived or real and implicit or explicit) based on factors such as the witness having a previous history of abuse and neglect, domestic violence, disability or racism. For example, possible side effects of having experienced abuse and neglect include poor self-esteem and heightened anxiety[25] and decreased cognitive functioning,[26] which, in turn, can result in episodic memory difficulties[27] and heightened compliance.[28] Being sensitive to such issues and preparing the witness for the interview and establishing rapport is an essential step towards mitigating against such effects. Ensuring the witness is familiar with the interviewer and other personnel present (including the intermediary) and providing a safe and non-judgemental environment for the witness is crucial. Similarly, intimated witnesses (that is, those whose quality of evidence is likely to be diminished by reason of fear or distress) particularly need to feel safe and may require support and encouragement to participate in an interview. This may include an interview supporter, enrolment in a protection scheme and special measures such as the use of screens in court or giving their evidence in court via live television link.

---

23 Nicholas Chown, "Do You Have Any Difficulties That I May Not Be Aware of? A Study of Autism Awareness and Understanding in the UK Police Service", in *International Journal of Police Science & Management*, 2010, vol. 12, no. 2, pp. 256–273.

24 Laura Crane *et al.*, "Experiences of Autism Spectrum Disorder and Policing in England and Wales: Surveying Police and the Autism Community", in *Journal of Autism and Developmental Disorders*, 2016, vol. 46, no. 6, pp. 2028–2041.

25 Çiğdem Berber Çelik and Hatice Odacı, "Does Child Abuse Have an Impact on Self-Esteem, Depression, Anxiety and Stress Conditions of Individuals?", in *International Journal of Social Psychiatry*, 2020, vol. 66, no. 2, pp. 171–178.

26 Andrea L. Roberts *et al.*, "Childhood Abuse and Cognitive Function in a Large Cohort of Middle-Aged Women", in *Child Maltreatment*, vol. 27, no. 1, pp. 100–113.

27 Eija Airaksinen, Maria Larsson and Yvonne Forsell, "Neuropsychological Functions in Anxiety Disorders in Population-Based Samples: Evidence of Episodic Memory Dysfunction", in *Journal of Psychiatric Research*, 2005, vol. 39, no. 2, pp. 207–214.

28 Robert J. Chandler, Ailsa Russell and Katie L. Maras, "Compliance in Autism: Self-report in Action", in *Autism*, 2019, vol. 23, no. 4, pp. 1005–1017.

The ABE guidance also discusses issues around competency to give evidence. This is broadly defined as the witness' ability to understand questions put to them and to give answers which can be understood, bearing in mind the various special measures that are available to support them in this. Where a witness is competent to give evidence, they are usually also compellable and thus *may* be legally required to attend trial (although they are not necessarily also legally required to provide a preliminary statement to the police). The interviewer will need to have *some* contextual knowledge of the alleged offence (for example, the type of offence(s), its approximate time and location and how it came to the notice of the police) in order to plan the areas for general investigation during the interview. Although more specific details about case may be made available at a later stage (after an attempt has been made to elicit and clarify the witness' about), it is critical to ensure there is no potential contamination from the interviewer when eliciting the witness' initial account(s).

18.2.1.3. Use of Planning Information

The information gathered during the planning and preparation stage should then be used to inform decision-making about *what* should be covered in the interview (usually the responsibility of an interview advisor) and *how* to elicit and probe the account.[29] The decision to complete an ABE interview with a vulnerable witness is usually made at a strategy meeting. This will involve setting the objectives for the interview, which is particularly important in giving direction and structure to the interview, and determining specific interview techniques. Generally, this will be governed according to the witness and the type of offence and may include techniques used in the Cognitive Interview ('CI') (see Chapter 16) and the National Institute of Child Health and Human Development (see Chapter 17). The use of drawings, pictures, photographs, symbols, dolls, figures and props may also be considered to help assess level of understanding but also to support the verbal recall of a witness' account. Although research has indicated that such communicative aids can assist,[30] the ABE guidance indicates that interviewers need to be aware of pitfalls or risks. This can relate to legal challenges at trial, the use of props and dolls leading the witness to provide an inaccurate account or encouraging fantasy play.[31] The format of the interview

---

[29] Smith and Milne, 2011, see *supra* note 18.

[30] Michelle L.A. Mattison, Coral J. Dando and Thomas C. Ormerod, "Sketching to Remember: Episodic Free Recall Task Support for Child Witnesses and Victims With Autism Spectrum Disorder", in *Journal of Autism and Developmental Disorders*, 2015, vol. 45, no. 6, pp. 1751–1765.

[31] Michael E. Lamb, Irit Hershkowitz, Yael Orbach and Phillip W. Esplin, *Tell Me What Happened: Structured Investigative Interviews of Child Victims and Witnesses*, Wiley-Blackwell, Chichester, 2008.

including who will conduct the interview, the location and timing will also be determined, as well as support for the witness post-interview.

A witness' account can be obtained via either a written statement or, in order for it to be later considered as evidence-in-chief, a video-recorded interview. However, a video interview is only usually allowed if the witness is vulnerable or intimidated as per the definitions in Sections 16 and 17 of the Youth Justice and Criminal Evidence Act (1999), and if any special measures are likely to improve the quality of the witness' evidence. It should be noted that this is also the choice of the witness; where a witness does not consent to be visually recorded, a written statement should be taken.

Early qualitative work examining the perceptions of police officers, lawyers and members of the judiciary regarding the use of video and audio taped evidence suggested unanimous support for videoed interviews as a method of obtaining evidence.[32] However, concerns were nevertheless raised regarding the frequent absence of a coherent account and the level of detail required to prove the various offences, as well as the inability to scrutinize questions asked prior to the recording of the interview. However, other scholars have highlighted advantages of recording the interview. Archambault and Lonsway (2020)[33] report that recording interviews allows for more details to be recorded and more accurately when compared to a written statement, and that interviewers are able to actively listen to witnesses rather than interrupt their narrative to write down their recall. Furthermore, the recording of an interviews conveys the impact that an alleged offence has had on a witness.

18.2.2. Conducting the ABE Interview

In England and Wales, the ABE guidance emphasizes the importance of the following four phases during any interview conducted with a witness. These are: (i) rapport; (ii) free recall; (iii) questions; and (iv) closure (see Figure 1). Each of these will be discussed, in turn, in relation to the ABE guidance and the psychological literature.

---

[32] Martine B. Powell and Rebecca Wright, "Professionals' Perceptions of Electronically Recorded Interviews With Vulnerable Witnesses", in *Current Issues in Criminal Justice*, 2009, vol. 21, no. 2, pp. 205–218.

[33] Joanne Archambault and Kimberly A. Lonsway, *Recording Victim Interviews*, End Violence Against Women International, 2020.

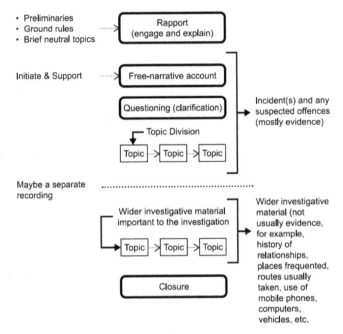

- Preliminaries
- Ground rules
- Brief neutral topics

Rapport
(engage and explain)

Initiate & Support

Free-narrative account

Questioning (clarification)

Incident(s) and any
suspected offences
(mostly evidence)

Topic Division

Topic → Topic → Topic

Maybe a separate
recording

Wider investigative material
important to the investigation

Wider investigative
material (not
usually evidence,
for example,
history of
relationships,
places frequented,
routes usually
taken, use of
mobile phones,
computers,
vehicles, etc.

Topic → Topic → Topic

Closure

Figure 1: Typical interview structure provided in current ABE guidance.[34]

18.2.2.1. Rapport

Establishing good rapport with a witness is key and critical aspect of investigative interviewing. It helps to gain trust, which, in turn, leads to more co-operation from the interviewee and the recall of more information.[35] This can be especially crucial for vulnerable witnesses, who may feel shame, embarrassment or fear about disclosing information (particularly on personal matters) and may worry about the potential negative adverse implications this might have for themselves or others on whom they are dependant.[36]

There is not a firm consensus on the definition of rapport, although there is general agreement that it consists of mutual attention, positivity, like and respect. Researchers have attempted to manipulate rapport in different ways, including voice tone, body posture, level of engagement and the use of the

---

[34] ABE, see *supra* note 1.

[35] Allison Abbe and Susan E. Brandon, "The Role of Rapport in Investigative Interviewing: A Review", in *Journal of Investigative Psychology and Offender Profiling*, 2013, vol. 10, no. 3, pp. 237–249; *id.*, "Building and Maintaining Rapport in Investigative Interviews", in *Police Practice and Research*, 2014, vol. 15, no. 3, pp. 207–220.

[36] Michael E. Lamb, "Difficulties Translating Research on Forensic Interview Practices to Practitioners: Finding Water, Leading Horses, But Can We Get Them to Drink?", in *American Psychologist*, 2016, vol. 71, no. 8, p. 710.

interviewee's name by the interviewer.[37] As noted by Hope and Gabbert (2019),[38] the lack of a precise definition of rapport limits the extent to which it can be robustly tested, trained and used in practice.

There is also a balance between ensuring the witness feels comfortable enough with the interviewer to disclose information, without the supportiveness being potentially viewed as suggestive and thus undermining the credibility of the interviewee's account. It should not therefore be contingent on specific responses, but instead be a more generic supportive social environment.[39] This can be achieved through the interviewer engaging with the interviewee about neutral topics that are not related to the event in question and which can be answered positively in order to foster a positive mood. The ABE guidance also advises that interviews be similarly open in nature to those that will be used during the rest of the interview, so that the interviewee becomes familiar with this style of interaction and practises proving elaborative responses. The rapport phase should not, however, be so long as to exhaust the interviewee or confuse them regarding the purpose of the interview. If the interview plan suggests that a lengthy discussion of neutral topics may be beneficial for that witness then this should take place as part of witness preparation before the interview session itself.

The witness should receive an explanation of the outline of the interview and the ground rules for what is expected of them. An investigative interview is an unusual social interaction in that it requires a significant level of specific detail that would not be appropriate in other social situations. Most witnesses will therefore naturally withhold reporting of information that they consider irrelevant,[40] but certain vulnerable witnesses (such as those with intellectual disability) may be particularly reluctant to recall a high level of detail due to insecurities about their own cognitive ability.[41] Providing explicit instructions about

---

[37] Roger Collins, Robyn Lincoln and Mark G. Frank, "The Effect of Rapport in Forensic Interviewing", in *Psychiatry, Psychology and Law*, 2002, vol. 9, no. 1, pp. 69–78; Holmberg and Madsen, "Rapport Operationalized as a Humanitarian Interview in Investigative Interview Settings", in *Psychiatry, Psychology and Law*, 2014, vol. 21, no. 4, pp. 591–610.

[38] Lorraine Hope and Fiona Gabbert, "Interviewing Witnesses and Victims", in Neil Brewer and Amy Bradfield Douglass, *Psychological Science and the Law*, The Guidlford Press, 2019, pp. 56–74.

[39] Walsh and Milne, 2008, see *supra* note 20.

[40] Fiona Gabbert *et al.*, "The Role of initial Witness Accounts Within the Investigative Process", in Gavin Oxburgh, Trond Myklebust, Tim Grant and Rebecca Milne (eds.), *Communication in Investigative and Legal Contexts: Integrated Approaches from Forensic Psychology, Linguistics and Law Enforcement*, Wiley-Blackwell, 2015, pp. 107–132.

[41] Katie Maras and Rachel Wilcock, "Suggestibility in Vulnerable Groups: Witnesses With Intellectual Disability, Autism Spectrum Disorder, and Older People", in Anne M. Ridley, Fiona

---

the level and type of detail required (including a reminder that the interviewer was not present at the event and does not yet know what happened) is therefore important in overcoming this. At the same time, however, it is crucial for the interviewer to emphasize the importance of the witness saying 'I don't know' or 'I can't remember' in order to preserve the accuracy of information reported.[42] They should also inform the witness that they can ask for a break at any time. This is especially important for vulnerable witnesses who may have limited attentional and cognitive resources and become tired more easily.

Ensuring understanding of truth and lies should be carried out with children and some (but not all) vulnerable adult witnesses. If applicable, this should be carried out towards the end of the rapport phase, after the ground rules have been established. This usually takes the form of a short story, whereby the witness demonstrates their understanding of the difference between a truth and a lie. Where they show no appreciation of the distinction between truth and lies, an expert assessment should be commissioned before proceeding with the interview to avoid jeopardizing the evidential value of the interview.

18.2.2.2. Free Narrative Account

The interviewer should invite the witness to provide a free narrative account of the event using open-ended prompts such as 'Tell me what happened' and 'Is there any more you can tell me?'. A witness must be allowed to provide their account without interruptions to avoid disrupting their flow. The ABE guidance encourages interviewers to use non-specific prompts such as 'Did anything else happen?' or 'Is there more you can tell me?'. In addition, 'active listening' is recommended (for example, by reflecting back on what the witness has just said in their account) to let the witness know that the interviewers are attending to their account. Concerns relating to compliance, acquiescence and reticence are documented though.

18.2.2.3. Questioning

The aim of the questioning phase is to ask the witness to expand and clarify upon the account they provided during free recall. Emphasizing again the importance of saying 'I don't know' or 'I can't remember' is crucial for vulnerable witnesses, who may be more prone to guessing due to heightened compliance or suggestibility.[43]

Gabbert and David J. La Rooy (eds.), *Investigative Suggestibility: Theory, Research and Applications*, Wiley-Blackwell, Oxford, 2013, pp. 149–170.

[42] Ronald P. Fisher and R. Edward Geiselman, *Memory-Enhancing Techniques in Investigative Interviewing: The Cognitive Interview*, Charles C Thomas, Springfield, 1992.

[43] Roberts *et al.*, 2020, see *supra* note 26.

The gold standard here is the use of more open of 'TED' (*Tell*, *Explain* and *Describe*) questions, in order to elicit more detailed and accurate responses that would be achieved through more closed or specific questions.[44] However, for some vulnerable witnesses (for example, children, autistic witnesses, the elderly and those with intellectual disability), this may elicit information that is accurate, but not particularly detailed. Thus, more focussed but still open and non-leading prompting may then be required. This can be achieved using 'WH' questions (*Who*, *What*, *Where*, *When* and *How*). Although these types of questions tend to produce shorter responses than more open questions,[45] they can be useful for focussing on and clarifying investigation-relevant information. Finally, if TED and WH questions fail to produce sufficient information that the witness is believed to remember about the event, closed questions (for example, that only require a 'yes/no' type response) may be used. However, given that these types of questions can force witnesses to guess, they should only be based on what the witness has already said (for example, asking 'Was his hat red?' only if they had already mentioned that the perpetrator was wearing a hat). Closed questions should only be used as a last resort if absolutely necessary and at the end of the interview, as vulnerable witnesses are more likely to acquiesce to them and they may contaminate the witness' subsequent account.[46]

Other question types should be avoided altogether. Questions with multiple parts (for example, 'On the night of June 12th, were you in the park and on the following morning did you see Beth?') and leading, tag and negative questions (for example, 'Nick didn't tell you he was home all evening, did he?') and can be difficult for most witnesses, resulting in heightened suggestibility.[47] However, they are particularly problematic for those with executive function and language processing difficulties and often result in acquiesce or heightened suggestibility.[48] The use of jargon and technical terminology can cause confusion, and some vulnerable witnesses may struggle to grasp concepts such as dates, times, weights and heights. An interview that moves back and forth between topics may also confuse the witness and should be avoided; instead, topics should be probed in turn, that is, one at a time, using simple language (see Figure 1).

---

[44] Gavin Oxburgh, Trond Myklebust and Tim Grant, "The Question of Question Types in Police Interviews: A Review of the Literature from a Psychological and Linguistic Perspective", in *International Journal of Speech, Language and the Law*, 2010, vol. 17, no. 1, pp. 45–66.

[45] Airaksinen, Larsson and Forsell, 2005, see *supra* note 27.

[46] Roberts *et al.*, 2020, see *supra* note 26.

[47] Airaksinen, Larsson and Forsell, 2005, see *supra* note 27.

[48] Roberts *et al.*, 2020, see *supra* note 26.

The interviewer should ensure witnesses have ample time to process a question and allow them space to formulate their response. This is important for all witnesses, but especially for children, elderly witnesses and adults with cognitive and developmental conditions, who may have executive function and language processing difficulties.[49] Moreover, rapid-fire closed questions tend to result in witnesses becoming more passive question answerers, which is at odds with the witness compatible questioning advocated by the CI.[50]

After the witness' account of the incident has been probed, the interviewer can move on to probing about case-specific information that was identified as important to the investigation at the planning and preparation stage. The ABE guidance recommends that this is done separately at the end to avoid distracting the witness from recounting their version of events, and that it may only relevant to the investigation (but not trial) in any case.

18.2.2.4. Closure

Once the free narrative and questioning phases appear to have finished, the interviewer should, if appropriate, summarize the witness' account. This is particularly important as it assists the witness in ensuring that what the interviewer has recalled is accurate. Summarizing the witness' account may also lead to further retrieval from the witness. It is not recommended to complete this if the witness is showing signs of fatigue, has a short attention span or is particularly emotional. Here, the interviewer may return to the more neutral topics discussed in the rapport-building phase. Regardless of how the closure stage is conducted, it is important that it is completed so that the witness does not feel that they have disappointed the interviewer.

18.2.3. Witness Support and Preparation for Court

Many witnesses will have neither attended court nor given evidence as part of a trial. As such, it is imperative that they are provided with the appropriate support and preparation. This may take the form of providing appropriate information about the process including the explanation of special measures. It is recommended that in doing so, the support and preparation provided is tailored to the witness' specific needs and users of the ABE guidance are recommended to also read the statutory Code of Practice for Victims of Crime[51] to ensure that witnesses receive the enhanced level of service they are entitled to.

---

[49] Laura Farrugia, *Interviewing of Suspects With Mental Health Conditions and Disorders in England and Wales: A Paradigm Shift*, Routledge, London, 2022.

[50] Hope and Gabbert, 2019, see *supra* note 38.

[51] MoJ, *The Code of Practice for Victims of Crime in England and Wales and Supporting Public Information Materials*, London, 2020.

18.2.3.1. Support during the Investigation

As part of the investigation, information may emerge that indicates that expert assistance is required for the witness to give their best evidence, particularly during the interview. For example, the witness may have communication difficulties. Here, the ABE guidance recommends the assistance of an interpreter (where English is not the first language) or the use of a Registered Intermediary. The latter conducts an assessment regarding the communication abilities of the vulnerable witness and will provide advice and recommendations to the interviewing officer on how best to communicate effectively with the witness to ensure that best evidence is obtained. The Registered Intermediary will also provide a report to the court communicating their recommendations for the witness to give their best evidence during trial.[52]

In the interval between the interview and the trial, a witness care officer will provide the witness with regular updates regarding the progression of the case. In addition, an early special measures discussion between the investigating officer and the CPS may take place where relevant to ensure that the witness' needs are taken into account when considering special measures. The ABE guidance highlights how it is the responsibility of both counsels (prosecution and defence) to communicate any special needs the witness may have.

18.2.3.2. Support before the Trial or Hearing

As well as support during the investigation, it is helpful for support to be provided before the trial so that the witness feels equipped to deal with the demands this stage can bring. This occurs in a number of ways but perhaps the most important is the plea and case management hearing. This hearing provides the opportunity for the court to discuss applications for special measures so that all necessary directions are given by the judge in preparation of the trial starting. These may include (but are not limited to) a pre-trial visit, the use of a supporter, the use of a Registered Intermediary to assist whilst the witness gives their evidence (including when the ground rules hearing will be), how the witness will refresh their memory (for example, re-reading their statement or viewing their video-recorded interview), how the witness will access the court and any reporting restrictions on the trial and any use of electronic equipment (for example, the use of a video link room). The witness care officer will continue to provide updates regarding the progression of the trial and any significant developments.

---

[52] Joyce Plotnikoff and Richard Woolfson, *Intermediaries in the Criminal Justice System: Improving Communication for Vulnerable Witnesses and Defendants*, Policy Press, Bristol, 2015.

18.2.4. Witnesses in Court

Generally, if the ABE guidance is followed, the needs and wishes of the vulnerable witness and the necessary preparations will have been identified and put in place. In cases where a Registered Intermediary is to be used, ground rules will have been set to ensure the quality of the witness' evidence is maximized. As before the trial, the court has a duty to ensure that all witnesses are enabled to give their best evidence; this is usually enacted through the directions of special measures, but the ABE guidance also recommends the active role that the court plays in ensuring distress is minimized.

This is also the case for the legal representatives involved in the case. The ABE guidance indicates that their responsibilities include putting the witness at ease as much as possible; one way of doing so may be to meet the witness prior to them giving their evidence. Legal representatives are expected to assist the court to make informed decisions about special measures. Whilst the defence counsel's duty is to promote the best interests of the defendant they represent, the manner in which they cross-examine a witness must not be inappropriate. Indeed, there exists much guidance and assistance on how to cross examine vulnerable witnesses[53] and it is expected that all legal representatives maintain their current knowledge and expertise.

18.2.4.1. Other Protections for Witnesses

In addition to the special measures that vulnerable and intimated witnesses are entitled to, there are other protections that are afforded for this type of witness too. For example, protection from cross-examination by the defendant in certain circumstances such as cases whereby sexual offences are alleged. This ensures that the witness is not intimidated any further. Defendants are not able to cross-examine children in cases involving offences of a violent or sexual nature. The courts can also prohibit any defendant from cross-examining any type of witness if they are satisfied that the direction be made in the interests of justice. Restrictions relating to evidence and questions about the witness' sexual behaviour can also be made; this not only ensures that the witness is protected from humiliation and invasion of privacy, but also that the jury is not distracted by information that may not be relevant to the case. When this direction is made, only questions relating to the alleged offence can be asked. Other protections include reporting restrictions. Whilst the general rule is that justice must be enacted in public, the court can impose restrictions if it is felt that the reporting will lead to the identification of witnesses or if the witness is experiencing fear and distress

---

[53] See, for example, the Advocate Gateway's web site.

in giving their evidence. There is an automatic ban on the reporting of witnesses involved in sexual offences.

18.3. Does the Framework Achieve Best Evidence?

It was initially thought that vulnerable witnesses were unable to provide evidence. This may be in part due to the age of the witness, vulnerabilities including mental illness and learning disabilities of adult witnesses and the impact of trauma.[54] Thus, they were rarely given the help they required.[55] However, since the implementation of the ABE guidance, vulnerable witnesses are now able to participate within the judicial system and provide their evidence via the special measures made available to them.

However, early research work suggested that the use of rapport, closure and free recall were found to be variable,[56] little preparation had been conducted and the interview did not tend to follow the four-phased approach set out in the ABE guidelines.[57] More recently, research has continued to suggest mixed findings. Hill and Davies (2013)[58] identified the positive effects of ABE guidance on the rapport-building phase of the interview, in addition to setting ground rules and using appropriate examples of lying. But when comparing interviews conducted under the MoGP and the ABE guidance, there were little differences observed and there was a failure to include all four phases of the interview as well as inappropriate question typologies being used. Such findings were echoed to some extent when researchers examined what worked well in ABE interviews with child witnesses in Northern Ireland.[59] Whilst their results suggested an overall positive view of the ABE practice including high levels of awareness, high levels of engagement with specialist training and refresher courses and regular use of cognitive interviewing techniques, they also identified barriers that may prevent good practice from happening. These included:

---

[54] Julia C. Davidson and Antonio Bifulco, "Investigating Police Practice in the UK: Achieving Best Evidence in Work With Young Victims of Abuse", in *Pakistan Journal of Criminology*, 2009, vol. 1, no. 3, pp. 19–46.

[55] Camilla Macpherson, "The Youth Justice and Criminal Evidence Act 1999: Achieving Best Evidence?", in *Medicine, Science and the Law*, 2001, vol. 41, no. 3, pp. 230–236.

[56] Helen L. Westcott and Sally Kynan, "Interviewer Practice in Investigative Interviews for Suspected Child Sexual Abuse", in *Psychology, Crime & Law*, 2006, vol. 12, no. 4, pp. 367–338.

[57] Brenda Robinson, "ABE Interviews: Is the Child's 'Best Evidence' Being Achieved in Alleged Sexual Abuse Cases? (Part 1)", in *Family Law Week*, 2008 (available on its web site).

[58] Emily Hill and Graham M. Davies, "Has the Quality of Investigative Interviews With Children Improved With Changes in Guidance? An Exploratory Study", in *Policing: A Journal of Policy and Practice*, 2013, vol. 7, no. 1, pp. 63–71.

[59] Lisa Bunting, Nicola Carr, David Hayes and James Marshall, *Good Practice in Achieving Best Evidence Interview With Child Witnesses in Northern Ireland – Criminal Justice Perspectives*, Northern Ireland Department of Justice, April 2015.

1. *Planning, preparation and flexibility*: Participants identified that the specialist skills and time required for ABE interviewers were not recognized or understood by some, in addition to very few interviewers being available;

2. *Practice and rapport*: Participants were worried that the use of practice interviews could be considered as 'coaching' and others indicated that there was not enough time to conduct practice interviews or build rapport;

3. *Interview skills and techniques*: The use of techniques including mental reinstatement of context was not well understood by some participants, with others feeling concerned about what is allowed in the formal interview; and

4. *Feedback and review*: Participants highlighted that there is a lack of ongoing monitoring and review process and those that are in supervisory roles may not have the knowledge to evaluate such interviews.

Despite detailed ABE guidance emphasizing the importance of using more open-ended questions, in practice interviewers rarely maintain this, often reverting back to the use of closed questions.[60] Nevertheless, there are other specialized interview techniques that are not covered in the ABE guidance that may be acceptable to the courts as an alternative method. For example, the CI has been shown to be ineffective for autistic witnesses, reducing the accuracy of their accounts[61] and free recall questions, in particular, are difficult for autistic people.[62] This is problematic because questions should be based on what a witness has already said; if free recall is reduced then there is less for the interviewer to follow-up on. To circumvent this problem, an alternative 'Witness-Aimed First Account' ('WAFA') interview technique was recently developed,[63] in which the witness is asked to self-segment their memory of the event into their own discrete parameter-bound 'topic boxes' at the outset, before engaging in an exhaustive free recall retrieval attempt (followed by interviewer probing)

---

[60] Graham M. Davies, Helen L. Westcott and Noreen Horan, "The Impact of Questioning Style on the Content of Investigative Interviews With Suspected Child Sexual Abuse Victims", in *Psychology, Crime & Law*, 2000, vol. 6, no. 2, pp. 81–97; Kathleen J. Sternberg, Michael E. Lamb, Graham M. Davies and Helen L. Westcott, "The Memorandum of Good Practice: Theory Versus Application", in *Child Abuse & Neglect*, 2001, vol. 25, no. 5, pp. 669–681; Lamb, 2016, p. 710, see *supra* note 36.

[61] Katie L. Maras and Demot M. Bowler, "The Cognitive Interview for Eyewitnesses With Autism Spectrum Disorder", in *Journal of Autism and Developmental Disorders*, 2010, vol. 40, no. 11, pp. 1350–1360.

[62] Katie L. Maras, "Obtaining Testimony from People With ASD", in Fred R. Volkmar, Rachel Loftin, Alexander Westphal and Marc Woodbury-Smith (eds.), *Handbook of Autism and the Law*, Springer, Cham, 2021, pp. 145–183.

[63] Katie L. Maras *et al.*, "The Witness-Aimed First Account (WAFA): A New Method for Interviewing Autistic Witnesses and Victims", in *Autism*, 2020, vol. 24, no. 6, pp. 1449–1467.

within the parameters of each topic box in turn. Displaying the topic boxes on post-it notes serves as a reminder of the structure of the event and reduces the amount of event information that they have to hold 'online', freeing up cognitive resources and allowing the witness to focus their search and retrieval strategies within individual segments. Findings indicate that the WAFA interview elicits more detailed and accurate recall from both autistic and 'typically developing' witnesses than a standard best practice interview.[64]

18.4. Recent Updates: Achieving Best Evidence (2022)

The ABE framework has recently been updated and is now in its fourth edition. Whilst much of the main framework remains the same, there have been some key changes that give witnesses more choice as they progress through the criminal justice system. For example, witnesses are now able to choose the gender of their interviewer during the ABE interview given the Code of Practice for Victims[65] that came into force in April 2020. Vulnerable and intimidated witnesses are now able to provide their evidence at court via pre-recorded cross-examination, and the revised Witness Charter[66] states that the standards that can be expected as part of the journey through the criminal justice system. In addition, more understanding around trauma and witness support is included based on advancements in research recently and to ensure that witnesses remain engaged with the process. However, perhaps the most significant update is that the ABE guidance now extends to witnesses of modern slavery and domestic abuse.

18.5. Limitations: Achieving Best Evidence (2022)

Although the ABE framework has recently been updated, there still remains some limitations that are yet to be addressed. These relate to how key concepts, such as rapport, empathy and questioning typologies are explained in the ABE guidance and the interview techniques that are suggested for vulnerable witnesses.

Developing rapport and empathy is central to conducting an effective interview. Indeed, all major interviewing and interrogation guidelines advocate for the use of rapport-building techniques to assist with co-operation and achieving best evidence.[67] Similarly, the recently updated ABE framework makes

---

[64] Abbe and Brandon, 2013, see *supra* note 35.

[65] MoJ, 2020, see *supra* note 51.

[66] MoJ, *The Witness Charter: Standards of Care for Witnesses in the Criminal Justice System*, London, 2013.

[67] Fisher and Geiselman, 1992, see *supra* note 42; Michael E. Lamb *et al.*, "A Structured Forensic Interview Protocol Improves the Quality and Informativeness of Investigative Interviews With Children: A Review of Research Using the NICHD Investigative Interview Protocol", in *Child Abuse & Neglect*, 2007, vol. 31, nos. 11–12, pp. 1201–1231.

reference to this and indicates that establishing and maintaining a good rapport is central (see para. 2.25), that the lead interviewer should be the individual who has established rapport with the interviewee (see para. 2.43), and that preparing the witness for interview and a rapport stage prior to formal questioning is essential (see para. 2.103). Thus, the concept of rapport is mentioned throughout the ABE guidance and interviewers are directed to use topics established during the rapport stage in the closing phase of the interview (see para. 3.90). However, the ABE framework does not offer any definition of what rapport is, how it can be developed and how it can be maintained despite recent publications, including a systematic review, in the psychological literature.[68] This is also true regarding empathy. The current ABE framework makes brief mention of empathy by indicating that in order to develop rapport, empathy must be communicated (see para. H.2.2.6). However, there is no further mention of empathy, how to identify and interpret it and the importance of using empathy during the interview.[69]

Perhaps one of the biggest issues in the recently updated ABE guidance is the conceptualization of question typologies. The general consensus in the psychological literature and, indeed, which drives most of the contemporary guidance regarding interviewing, is that open questions and probing questions are best practice in eliciting accurate and reliable information.[70] Open questions are generally understood as TED questions. The ABE framework advocates for the use of open questions, for example, in initiating a free-narrative account (see para. 3.29), and provides appropriate examples of such questions (paras. 3.51–3.53). But, confusion lies with how probing questions are described. Within the psychological literature, probing questions are described as the five WH questions.[71] However, in the ABE framework, these are defined as 'specific-closed questions' and no reference is made to 'how' questions. In addition, the ABE guidance refers also to these types of questions (specific-closed) as open questions (para. 3.56). Thus, there appears to be confusion regarding what constitutes an open question and a specific-closed question (or probing) in the recently updated ABE framework. Perhaps more concerning is that reference is made to

[68] Fiona Gabbert *et al.*, "Exploring the Use of Rapport in Professional Information-Gathering Contexts by Systematically Mapping the Evidence Base", in *Applied Cognitive Psychology*, 2021, vol. 35, no. 2, pp. 329–341.

[69] Garry E. Oxburgh, James Ost, Paul Morris and Julie Cherryman, "The Impact of Question Type and Empathy on Police Interviews With Suspects of Homicide, Filicide and Child Sexual Abuse", in *Psychiatry, Psychology and Law*, 2014, vol. 21, no. 6, pp. 904–917.

[70] Brent Snook, Kirk Luther, Heather Quinlan and Rebecca Milne, "Let 'Em Talk! A Field Study of Police Questioning Practices of Suspects and Accused Persons", in *Criminal Justice and Behaviour*, 2012, vol. 39, no. 10, pp. 1328–1339.

[71] Oxburgh, Myklebust and Grant, 2010, see *supra* note 44.

using forced-choice questions and leading questions as a last resort (para. 3.51), thus appearing to contradict existing literature that indicates that a vulnerable individual may exhibit an increased risk of suggestibility, compliance and acquiescence if interviewed using such questions.[72]

Aside from issues with how key concepts are defined and operationalized in the updated ABE framework, the interview techniques suggested for use with vulnerable witnesses warrant some attention, primarily, the recommendation for the use of the Enhanced CI.[73] Generally, this evidence-based interview technique is widely used and has been shown to increase the amount of correct information recalled by witnesses.[74] However, this technique has been proven ineffective with vulnerable individuals even when components have been changed (such as sketching to reinstate the context).[75] For example, those with autism require specific parameters when providing their recall due to their set of difficulties they experience.[76] The ABE framework does not appear to take into account recently developed interview models that seek to accommodate the most vulnerable individuals.[77]

18.6. Conclusion

There is doubt that the ABE framework is a key development in England and Wales. Building on previous guidance developed for interviewing children (such as, the MoGP), the ABE was first introduced in 2011 and its fourth iteration was recently published in 2022. It offers a framework for supporting vulnerable victims and witnesses (both children and vulnerable adults) to provide evidence from the initial investigative interviewing stages through to court. This includes consideration of an individual's specific vulnerabilities, adapted interviewing techniques, communication support and special measures that can be made to alleviate some of the stresses associated with providing evidence in court (such as allowing the witness to be cross-examined via a live link or in a pre-recorded cross-examination). Research to date generally supports the recommendations outlined in the ABE guidance, and the recently updated version allows more

---

[72] Gisli H. Gudjonsson, *The Psychology of False Confessions: Forty Years of Science and Practice*, John Wiley & Sons Ltd., London, 2018; Farrugia, 2022, see *supra* note 49.

[73] Fisher and Geiselman, 1992, see *supra* note 42.

[74] Amina Memon, Christian A. Meissner and Joanne Fraser, "The Cognitive Interview: A Meta-Analytic Review and Study Space Analysis of the Past 25 Years", in *Psychology, Public Policy, and Law*, 2010, vol. 16, no. 4, pp. 340–372.

[75] Michelle Mattison, Coral J. Dando and Thomas C. Ormerod, "Drawing the Answers: Sketching to Support Free and Probed Recall by Child Witnesses and Victims With Autism Spectrum Disorder", in *Autism*, 2018, vol. 22, no. 2, pp. 181–194.

[76] Maras *et al.*, 2020, see *supra* note 63.

[77] *Ibid.*

choice for witnesses as they navigate their way through the criminal justice system. It is positive to see more understanding around trauma and the inclusion of witnesses of modern day slavery and domestic abuse. However, there remain some concerns regarding limited explanations relating to key concepts of rapport and empathy, especially given recent publications in the psychological literature. Furthermore, how questions are defined and conceptualized and the suggestion for use of questions that are likely to increase the vulnerability of an interviewee require some further attention. The ABE framework must be able to provide appropriate guidance for interviewers to implement it, and so consideration should also be given to the recommendations for interview techniques that are not entirely suitable for vulnerable witnesses.

19

The Self-Administered Interview

Fiona Gabbert and Lorraine Hope[*]

19.1. Introduction

When multiple witnesses are present at a crime scene, it is unlikely that there will be enough interviewers available to gather information from each available person. This is particularly evident in chaotic situations such as a terrorist attack in a crowded city, where emergency responders like the police prioritise recovering victims and securing the area against further attacks. Many co-operative witnesses who are keen to assist may not be interviewed immediately. Follow-up investigations may take several weeks or even months. During this delay, important details may be forgotten and witnesses have more opportunity to encounter potentially misleading post-event information (for example, from news reports and social media). If witnesses are not interviewed promptly, both the amount and accuracy of information reported from memory is at risk, which can subsequently risk the efficacy of the investigation.

A solution for officers who do not have the resources in terms of time, expertise, or personnel to conduct interviews with witnesses shortly after an incident, is to use a Self-Administered Interview ('SAI').[1] The SAI is an interview method that helps witnesses provide a detailed initial account independently, without the requirement for a police officer to conduct the interview or, indeed, be present. It can be used as a triage to identify key witnesses to prioritize for follow-up enquiries and has been shown to preserve and protect witness memory until a formal interview can be conducted. Due to the many advantages of the SAI, it has been adopted into police policy and procedure in an increasing

---

[*]   **Fiona Gabbert**, Ph.D., is a Professor of Psychology at Goldsmiths University of London. **Lorraine Hope**, Ph.D., is a Professor of Applied Cognitive Psychology at the University of Portsmouth.

[1]   The SAI© is a copyrighted tool, but subsequently will be referred to as SAI (without the copyright symbol); Fiona Gabbert, Lorraine Hope and Ronald Fisher, "Protecting Eyewitness Evidence: Examining the Efficacy of a Self-Administered Interview Tool", in *Law and Human Behavior*, 2009, vol. 33, pp. 298–307; Ruth Horry *et al.*, "A Meta-Analytic Review of the Self-Administered Interview: Quantity and Accuracy of Details Reported on Initial and Subsequent Retrieval Attempts", in *Applied Cognitive Psychology*, 2021, vol. 35, no. 2, pp. 428–444.

number of countries worldwide, including the United Kingdom ('UK').[2] The current chapter describes what the SAI is, why it was developed, theoretical underpinnings, key research findings, applications and recent developments. In addition, we consider gaps in knowledge and future directions for research and application.

19.2. What Is the SAI?

The SAI is an empirically tested investigative tool that can be used quickly and efficiently to elicit comprehensive initial accounts from witnesses. It was originally designed as a generic tool, suitable for reporting a range of different types of crime. The SAI takes the form of a standardized protocol of clear instructions, retrieval facilitation techniques including mnemonics from the Cognitive Interview ('CI')[3] and open questions that guide witnesses through the process of producing their own account without the need for a trained interviewer to be present. It is, therefore, ideal for use when restricted resources mean that a traditional verbal interview is not possible. By enabling cooperative individuals to provide their own initial accounts, valuable resources are freed up for deployment elsewhere.[4]

During its development, the SAI format and instructions were piloted through several iterations for clarity, ease of understanding and simplicity. The current version of the SAI tool comprises eight sections containing information and instructions designed to facilitate both recall and reporting of memories for a witnessed event:

- Section 1 provides witnesses with clear background information regarding what the SAI is and how to engage with it. Emphasis is placed on the importance of following the instructions and working through the SAI sections in sequential order.

- In Section 2, an open-ended free recall instruction to 'Report Everything' ('RE') is preceded by a 'Mental Reinstatement of Context' ('MRC') instruction which guides the witness through the process of mentally revisiting the scene of the incident, with instructions to focus on different aspects of their experience and information about how this activity will assist them in recalling their account. Witnesses are encouraged to "Give

---

[2] College of Policing, "Obtaining Initial Accounts from Victims and Witnesses: Guidelines for First Responders", 2019 (available on the College of Policing's web site).

[3] Ronald P. Fisher and Edward R. Geiselman, *Memory-enhancing Techniques for Investigative Interviewing: The Cognitive Interview,* Charles C. Thomas Publisher, Springfield, 1992.

[4] Lorraine Hope, Fiona Gabbert, Ronald P. Fisher and Kat Jamieson, "Protecting and Enhancing Eyewitness Memory: The Impact of an Initial Recall Attempt on Performance in an Investigative Interview", in *Applied Cognitive Psychology*, 2014, vol. 28, pp. 304–313.

yourself plenty of time to concentrate, and visualize what happened in your mind". In order to fully support the self-generated context reinstatement procedure, it is suggested that they consider the following: "Where were you; What were you doing, Who were you with; How were you feeling; What was happening; Who was involved; What you could see; What you could hear". Witnesses are also advised that they may find it helpful to shut their eyes while engaging in this procedure. Witnesses are then asked to 'Report Everything' and provide the most complete and accurate account possible, but to avoid guessing about details they cannot remember.

- Section 3 focuses on gaining detailed person descriptor information by asking witnesses to provide as much detail as possible about the appearance of the perpetrator(s), including physical characteristics (height, build, distinguishing features, *et cetera*) as well as descriptions of clothing and accessories.
- Section 4 asks witnesses to generate a sketch of the scene to preserve important spatial information. Instructions here assure witnesses that this is not a test of drawing ability, but rather a request for a graphical representation of the general layout of the scene including positions of themselves in relation to other persons present (perpetrators and other witnesses) and details relating to direction of movement or travel if relevant, which may be particularly pertinent for the investigation of road traffic incidents or direction of escape routes.
- Section 5 asks witnesses to report details about people they have spoken to about the incident, and what was discussed.
- Section 6 asks whether the witness has any photos or recordings, and if so, whether they have shared these, for example, on social media.
- Section 7 focuses on gaining detailed descriptor information about any vehicles involved.
- Section 8 contains a series of questions relating to the 'ADVOKATE' acronym which is used by UK police officers to assess the quality of encoding the incident. It asks witnesses to report information that they might not previously have thought to mention, for example, details of the viewing conditions at the scene of the event (for example, time of day, lighting, whether their view was clear or obstructed, weather conditions, *et cetera*).

19.3. Why Was the SAI Developed?

The quality of eyewitness accounts has been shown to be time-critical.[5] As the delay increases between witnessing a crime and reporting information in a formal investigative interview, so too does the likelihood of forgetting.[6] The passing of time can also pose a serious threat to recall accuracy as there is greater opportunity for a witness' memory to be contaminated by inaccurate information encountered between witnessing the event and providing the police with an account of the incident. Exposure to post-event information from co-witnesses, friends, family, local or national news and social media can negatively influence an individual's original memory of what actually happened.[7] A significant problem for investigators is, therefore, the delay incurred between individuals witnessing a crime and providing their statement. Ideally, witnesses should be interviewed as soon as possible, however, this is not always achievable.

The SAI provides a simple and effective way to reduce the risks associated with delay by enabling witnesses to independently report a crime at the scene of an incident or shortly afterwards, without the need for an officer to be present. The tool was initially developed in 2006 following a meeting with a local UK police force who described a particular challenge they faced when an incident occurs for which there are multiple eyewitnesses and limited officers available to conduct interviews. The original research team[8] then worked closely with police forces to further develop and implement the SAI into practice. Feedback from investigators has been positive:

> Notably, the SAI© is the first empirically-derived interviewing practice development that has been presented to the police in almost 20 years, probably the most valuable additional tool placed at our disposal in the world of investigative interviewing since the

5   Ruth Horry, Lisa-Marie Colton and Paul Williamson, "Confidence-Accuracy Resolution in the Misinformation Paradigm Is Influenced by the Availability of Source Cues", in *Acta Psychologica*, 2014, vol. 151, pp. 164–173.

6   John W. Turtle and John C. Yuille, "Lost but Not Forgotten Details: Repeated Eyewitness Recall Leads to Reminiscence but Not Hypermnesia", in *The Journal of Applied Psychology*, 1994, vol. 79, pp. 260–271.

7   Fiona Gabbert and Lorraine Hope, "Suggestibility in the Courtroom: How Memory Can Be Distorted During the Investigative and Legal Process", in Henry Otgaar and Mark L. Howe (eds.), *Finding the Truth in the Courtroom: Dealing With Deception, Lies, and Memories*, Oxford University Press, 2018, pp. 31–57.

8   The original research team comprises Dr. Fiona Gabbert (Goldsmiths University of London), Dr. Lorraine Hope (University of Portsmouth) and Dr. Ronald Fisher (Florida International University).

adoption of the 'PEACE' model of interviewing in the early 1990s, and the introduction of the enhanced cognitive interview model.[9]

19.3.1. Theoretical Underpinnings

In the absence of an interviewer being present to probe for information by asking follow-up questions, it is important that any self-administered interview facilitates the reporting of reliable information at a sufficient level of detail via well-crafted instructions and questions. The SAI draws on well-established cognitive theories to support eyewitnesses when recollecting and reporting their memories of an incident. The first of these is the Encoding Specificity Hypothesis[10] which posits that reinstating the original encoding context at the point of retrieval can lead to increased recall. This idea underpins one of the most effective components of the CI,[11] the MRC instruction. In the context of an investigative interview, the MRC mnemonic requires eyewitnesses to mentally place themselves back in the context of the crime event before reporting what they can remember. This 'context resinstatement' is achieved by providing simple instructions that encourage the witness to think back to the physical context (what can be seen, heard, who else was present, *et cetera*) and personal context (how was the witness feeling at the time, *et cetera*) from the time at which the crime was witnessed. By facilitating the feature overlap between encoding and retrieval, remembering is supported. In the SAI, as in the CI, the MRC mnemonic is paired with the RE instruction. The RE mnemonic encourages witnesses to 'report everything' by asking them to mention as many details as possible, regardless of whether they seem important, without any editing. Not only does this protect against the omission of potentially crucial information, but it can also help jog a witness' memory for additional details via associative memory cueing.[12]

Further sections of the SAI probe for specific investigation-relevant information, such as eliciting detailed descriptions of the perpetrator(s), vehicle(s) and any other potential witnesses. Non-leading cues are used in each of these sections to facilitate recollection by prompting memory. For example, a witness might provide a physical description but not mention clothing, or *vice versa*, without cues prompting them to consider both types of details. Witnesses are

---

9   Ian Hynes, "Personal Communication", January 2014 (on file with the authors). See also "The Self-Administered Interview: Using Applied Memory Research to Help Improve the Police Interview", Impact case study (REF3b), University of Abertay Dundee (available on the Research Excellence Framework's web site).

10   Endel Tulving and Donald M. Thomson, "Encoding Specificity and Retrieval Processes in Episodic Memory", in *Psychological Review*, 1973, vol. 80, pp. 352–373.

11   See Chapter 16 of this book for further details.

12   John R. Anderson, "A Spreading Activation Theory of Memory", in *Journal of Verbal Learning and Verbal Behavior*, 1983, vol. 22, pp. 261–295.

also asked to draw the general layout of the scene, including their position in relation to other features of the scene and/or individuals present. Drawing a scene from memory requires the witness to activate their memory for the special layout, thus facilitating feature overlap between encoding and retrieval.[13] Research on the use of sketching has demonstrated its effectiveness for aiding recollection via spatial cueing.[14]

The various components of the SAI are effective not only in supporting witnesses to report relevant information at a sufficient level of detail, but also in helping to protect memory. Research shows that the act of retrieval can increase the activation level of items of information in memory as well as the associations between them, thus strengthening their representation in memory and enhancing the degree to which they are bound with one another to form an integrated episodic trace.[15] Retrieval attempts can also facilitate subsequent remembering by creating different retrieval routes to access the originally encoded information. The associated benefits are that retrieving an item from memory can increase the likelihood that it is recalled again.[16] In fact, a large body of research on the 'testing effect' which shows that taught material is better remembered if students are given a memory test shortly after the learning (encoding) episode.[17] Further, interviewing witnesses as soon as possible after an incident has been found to

---

[13] Coral J. Dando, "Drawing to Remember: External Support of Older Adults' Eyewitness Performance", in *Plos ONE*, 2013, vol. 8, no. 7, pp. 1–8; Coral J. Dando, Fiona Gabbert and Lorraine Hope, "Supporting Older Adults' Episodic Remembering: The Self-Administered Interview and Sketch Reinstatement of Context", in *Memory*, 2020, vol. 28, pp. 712–723; Coral J. Dando, Rachel Wilcock and Rebecca Milne, "The Cognitive Interview: The Efficacy of a Modified Mental Reinstatement of Context Procedure for Frontline Police Investigators", in *Applied Cognitive Psychology*, 2009, vol. 23, no. 1, pp. 138–147; Fisher and Geiselman, 1992, see *supra* note 3.

[14] Matsuo Kayo and Miura Hiroshi, "Effectiveness of the Self-Administered Interview and Drawing Pictures for Eliciting Eyewitness Memories", in *Psychiatry, Psychology and Law*, 2017, vol. 24, no. 5, pp. 643–654.

[15] See Chapter 16 of this book for further details; Michael Ayer and Lynne Reder, "A Theoretical Review of the Misinformation Effect: Predictions from an Activation-Based Memory Model", in *Psychonomic Bulletin & Review*, 1998, vol. 5, no. 1, pp. 1–21; Antonio R. Damasio, "Time-Locked Multiregional Retroactivation: A System Level Proposal for the Neuronal Substrates of Recall and Recognition", in *Cognition*, 1989, vol. 33, pp. 25–62.

[16] Robert A. Bjork, "Retrieval Practice and the Maintenance of Knowledge", in Michael M. Gruneberg, Peter E. Morris and Robert N. Skyes (eds.), *Practical Aspects of Memory: Current Research and Issues, Vol. 1: Memory of Everyday Life*, Wiley, New York, 1988, pp. 396–401; John S. Shaw, Robert A. Bjork and Allison Handal, "Retrieval-Induced Forgetting in an Eyewitness-Memory Paradigm", in *Psychonomic Bulletin & Review*, 1995, vol. 2, pp. 249–253.

[17] Pooja K. Agarwal, Ludmiler D. Nunes and Janell R. Blunt, "Retrieval Practice Consistently Benefits Student Learning: a Systematic Review of Applied Research in Schools and Classrooms", in *Educational Psychology Review*, 2021, vol. 33, pp. 1409–1453.

---

protect against forgetting.[18] In sum, an early recall attempt can increase the activation level of items of information in memory as well as the associations between them, enhancing subsequent retention and recall of information and protecting against forgetting.

The quality of the initial recall, in terms of the amount and accuracy of information retrieved, is also important for subsequent retrieval attempts. It is not simply the act of engaging in retrieval at an early stage that preserves episodic memory, but the act of engaging in good quality initial recall. In contrast, a poor quality initial recall attempt may impair later recall. Some research suggests that recalling an incomplete subset of information from an episodic memory may impair one's ability to subsequently recall the remaining (unrecalled) items of information.[19] Thus, subsequent retrieval attempts are likely to be facilitated by a good quality initial recall.[20] A poor quality initial recall can also be detrimental as recall errors made in an initial retrieval attempt may be repeated in future retrievals.[21]

Strengthening memory via retrieval practice can also offer some protection against exposure to misleading post-event information encountered in the form of suggestive questions or from other sources, such as discussions with other witnesses. Individuals with stronger memories are more likely to notice discrepancies between their original memories for the event and any post-event

---

[18] Ebbe B. Ebbesen and Cynthia Rienick, "Retention Interval and Eyewitness Memory for Events and Personal Identifying Attributes", in *Journal of Applied Psychology*, 1998, vol. 83, pp. 745–762; Horry *et al.*, 2021, see *supra* note 1.

[19] Malcolm MacLeod, "Retrieval-Induced Forgetting in Eyewitness Memory: Forgetting as a Consequence of Remembering", in *Applied Cognitive Psychology*, 2002, vol. 16, no. 2, pp. 135–149; Shaw, Bjork and Handal, 1995, see *supra* note 16.

[20] Elizabeth J. Marsh, Barbara Tversky and Michael Hutson, "How Eyewitnesses Talk About Events: Implications for Memory", in *Applied Cognitive Psychology*, 2005, vol. 19, pp. 1–14; Barbara Tversky and Elizabeth Marsh, "Biased Retellings of Events Yield Biased Memories", in *Cognitive Psychology*, 2000, vol. 40, pp. 1–38.

[21] Amina Memon, Maria Zaragoza, Brian R. Clifford and Lynsey Kidd, "Inoculation or Antidote? The Effects of Cognitive Interview Timing on False Memory for Forcibly Fabricated Events", in *Law and Human Behavior*, 2010, vol. 34, pp. 105–117; Kerri L. Pickel, "When a Lie Becomes the Truth: The Effects of Self-Generated Misinformation on Eyewitness Memory", in *Memory*, 2004, vol. 12, pp. 14–26.

information received.[22] An early series of studies[23] found that participants were less susceptible to the effects of misleading questions when a CI had been administered prior to the misleading questions being encountered. In contrast, a CI given after the misleading questions conferred no benefits with respect to attenuating suggestibility. Similar conclusions have been reached by researchers[24] who found that participants who were interviewed with a CI prior to (but not following) a suggestive interview reported significantly more accurate information in a second interview one week later. These findings support the idea that participants are better able to be vigilant against discrepancies if their memory for a target event is strengthened. It is of no surprise then that research has found that witnesses who complete an SAI are less suggestible when faced with items of misleading post-event information or leading questions.[25] Across two studies, Gabbert *et al.*[26] found a significant negative correlation between the number of accurate items of information reported and the number of items of misinformation reported.

19.3.2. Key Research Findings

In early tests of the SAI, mock witnesses (comprising a sample of community volunteers of all ages and background) viewed a simulated crime event and were required to report as much as they could about what they had seen. Witnesses who completed the SAI tool reported 42 per cent more correct details than those participants who were simply asked to report what they had seen.[27] In subsequent tests, mock witnesses who had completed the SAI tool shortly after witnessing the event provided almost 30 per cent more correct details when

---

[22] Elizabeth Loftus, "Planting Misinformation in the Human Mind: A 30-Year Investigation of the Malleability of Memory", in *Learning & Memory*, 2005, vol. 12, pp. 361–366; Elizabeth Loftus, Bjorn Levidow and Sally Duensing, "Who Remembers Best? Individual Differences in Memory for Events that Occurred in a Science Museum", in *Applied Cognitive Psychology*, 1992, vol. 6, pp. 93–107.

[23] Edward R. Geiselman, Ronald P. Fisher, Gina Cohen and Heidi Holland, "Eyewitness Responses to Leading and Misleading Questions Under the Cognitive Interview", in *Journal of Police Science and Administration*, 1986, vol. 14, pp. 31–39.

[24] Memon, Zaragoza, Clifford and Kidd, 2010, see *supra* note 21.

[25] Fiona Gabbert, Lorraine Hope, Ronald P. Fisher and Kat Jamieson, "Protecting Against Susceptibility to Misinformation With the Use of a Self-Administered Interview", in *Applied Cognitive Psychology*, 2012, vol. 26, pp. 568–575; WANG Emyo, Helen Paterson and Richard Kemp, "The Effects of Immediate Recall on Eyewitness Accuracy and Susceptibility to Misinformation", in *Psychology, Crime & Law*, 2014, vol. 20, no. 7, pp. 619–634.

[26] Gabbert, Hope, Fisher and Jamieson, 2012, see *supra* note 25.

[27] Gabbert, Hope and Fisher, 2009, see *supra* note 1.

interviewed after a delay than those who had not made an earlier recall attempt.[28] Subsequent research has replicated and extended these findings. Specifically, we have found that mock witnesses who complete the SAI are more resistant to the misleading effects of exposure to post-event information.[29] More recently, across two studies, we have demonstrated that administering the SAI online (via a computer or mobile device as opposed to using a paper-based format) is not detrimental to witness reporting.[30] This is an an important finding given the increasing use of technology to communicate coupled with the additional functionality that digital presentation may afford.

More than 15 years on, these initial findings have been replicated and extended by research labs around the world. For example, some interesting research by Gawrylowicz and colleagues[31] observed a 'transfer effect', whereby reporting about one event using the SAI enhanced subsequent reporting about another unrelated event. Here, participants with prior SAI experience reported significantly more correct details for a new event for which the SAI was not used, without a decrease in accuracy rates. A follow-up study[32] replicated this finding with older adults. Together, these findings suggest that the beneficial effects of the SAI are not only due to rehearsal, but that it may equip witnesses with transferable skills to use when providing reports about subsequent events. Other researchers have examined whether the SAI may increase reports of psychological distress when the witnessed event is stressful.[33] Despite finding increases in anxiety after its completion, the SAI was not found to have an effect on stress symptoms at a follow-up conducted one week later.[34] Other researchers have examined the utility of the sketch component of the SAI, finding that

---

28 Lorraine Hope, Fiona Gabbert and Ronald P. Fisher, "From Laboratory to the Street: Capturing Witness Memory Using a Self-Administered Interview", in *Legal and Criminological Psychology*, 2011, vol. 16, pp. 211–226.

29 Gabbert, Hope, Fisher and Jamieson, 2012, see *supra* note 25.

30 Fiona Gabbert *et al.*, "Examining the Efficacy of a Digital Version of the Self-Administered Interview", in *Computers in Human Behavior Reports*, 2022, vol. 5, pp. 1–7.

31 Julie Gawrylowicz, Amina Memon and Alan Scoboria, "Equipping Witnesses With Transferable Skills: the Self-Administered Interview©", in *Psychology, Crime & Law*, 2013, vol. 20, no. 4, pp. 315–325.

32 Julie Gawrylowicz *et al.*, "Enhancing Older Adults' Eyewitness Memory for Present and Future Events With the Self-Administered Interview", in *Psychology and Aging*, 2014, vol. 29, no. 4, pp. 885–890.

33 Thomas L. Mackay and Helen Paterson, "How Does Timing of Recall Affect Eyewitness Memory and Psychological Distress?", in *Journal of Police and Criminal Psychology*, 2015, vol. 30, pp. 242–253.

34 Though see Catherine Gittins, Helen Paterson and Louise Sharpe, "How Does Immediate Recall of a Stressful Event Affect Psychological Response to It?", in *Journal of Behavioral Therapy and Experimental Psychiatry*, 2015, vol. 46, pp. 19–26.

when information reported within the sketches was coded, the SAI achieved better results than the CI and Free Recall in terms of information reported.[37]

In a recent meta-analysis,[35] researchers compared the quantity and quality of information reported in the SAI with that reported in other initial reporting formats, such as in response to cued and free recall prompts. Compared to alternative recall formats, initial SAI reports were associated with a large increase in the number of correct details reported and a slightly smaller increase in the number of incorrect details. The overall accuracy rate was slightly lower for the SAI than for other reporting formats. This slight increase in the number of incorrect details reported is likely to be a direct consequence of relaxing the reporting threshold via the use of the RE instruction from the CI. Indeed, a meta-analysis of studies featuring the CI found very similar results, whereby the CI was associated with a large increase in correct details and a smaller increase in incorrect details.[36]

In a second set of analyses, researchers[37] examined how, and to what extent, subsequent accounts differed between witnesses who had and had not completed an initial SAI. Here it was found that witnesses who had completed an initial SAI reported more correct details on a subsequent report than witnesses who did not complete an initial SAI, and further, that the accuracy of their subsequent reports was higher overall. A further tentative finding was that exposure to misleading post-event information did not significantly moderate the effect sizes for correct details, incorrect details or overall accuracy. These results suggest that the SAI allows witnesses to produce full and accurate accounts even after they have been exposed to misinformation. In sum, research has largely confirmed that witness accounts obtained via the SAI result in more detailed accounts than other reporting formats. Further, completing the SAI soon after witnessing an event protects the memory of that event from memory decay and distortion over time, leading to more detailed and accurate subsequent accounts.[38]

19.4. Adapting the SAI for Use in Different Contexts

While a key strength of the SAI is eliciting reliable information in a timely manner, there are a number of additional ways in which it can add value to an

---

[37] Matsuo and Miura, 2017, see *supra* note 14.

[35] Horry *et al.*, 2021, see *supra* note 1.

[36] Amina Memon, Christian Meissner and Joanne Fraser, "The Cognitive Interview: A Meta-Analytic Review and Study Space Analysis of the Past 25 Years", in *Psychology, Public Policy, and Law*, 2010, vol. 16, pp. 340–372.

[37] Horry *et al.*, 2021, see *supra* note 1.

[38] *Ibid.*

investigation. First, the format is standardized which serves to overcome idiosyncrasies and other variations in interview training, style, and quality. Second, the SAI enables speed and efficiency in collecting information from multiple individuals simultaneously, likely preserving limited practitioner resources. Third, the SAI can be administered remotely. Fourth, the SAI is simple to translate, thus making the tool accessible across different countries or within countries where there might be delays in accessing an interpreter.

As a result of recognized benefits, the original SAI research programme has been significantly extended in recent years through the development of bespoke versions for application in different contexts. These new SAI tools have been developed to assist specific investigative needs identified by end-users, including workplace accidents,[39] missing persons investigations[40] and road traffic collisions.[41] Importantly, these new SAI tools have been developed in collaboration with stakeholders and end-users to ensure context-relevant adaptations. For example, the SAI-Missing includes the use of targeted retrieval cues designed to elicit unique personal details about the missing person, while the SAI for Road Traffic Collisions ('SAI-RTC') prompts for information about precipitating factors in road traffic collisions. Data from experimental research and live trials with police forces confirm the efficacy and versatility of these new SAI tools, relative to existing reporting formats. For example, there was a reported average increase of 35 per cent for missing persons descriptions[42] and an average increase of 57 per cent for details relating to road traffic incidents in comparison to the standard forms.[43] Below, we summarize some of the key bespoke versions of the SAI that have been developed.

19.4.1. SAI for Workplace Accident and Incident Investigations

Accident and incident investigation is vital for an effective occupational health and safety culture.[44] The prevention of workplace accidents begins with

---

[39] Carla MacLean, Fiona Gabbert and Lorraine Hope, "The Self-Administered Witness Interview Tool (SAW-IT™): Enhancing Witness Recall of Workplace Incidents", in *Applied Cognitive Psychology*, 2019, vol. 33, no. 6, pp. 1212–1223.

[40] Fiona Gabbert *et al.*, "Examining the Efficacy of a Self-Administered Report Form in Missing Person Investigations", in *Legal and Criminological Psychology*, 2020, vol. 25, pp. 1–16.

[41] Ruth Horry, Chelsea Hughes, Lorraine Hope and Fiona Gabbert, "Capturing Best Evidence from Witnesses to Serious Road Traffic Collisions: A Field Trial of the Self-Administered Interview for Road Traffic Collisions", Final Report for the Road Safety Trust, 2022 (available on the Road Safety Trust's web site).

[42] Gabbert *et al.*, 2020, see *supra* note 40.

[43] Horry, Hughes, Hope and Gabbert, 2022, see *supra* note 41.

[44] Kevin Kelloway, Veronica Stinson and Carla MacLean, "Eyewitness Testimony in Occupational Accident Investigations: Towards a Research Agenda", in *Law and Human Behavior*, 2004, vol. 28, no. 1, pp. 115–132.

understanding what is causing them, and knowledge of causation can facilitate the identification and correction of the weak or failing elements. The information gleaned from the post-incident investigation is fundamental to (i) comprehensively understanding how and why the incident occurred, (ii) preventing future similar adverse occurrences and (iii) pursuing criminal investigations or inquiries if appropriate.[45] Obtaining detailed and reliable accounts from the people involved in an accident or incident is therefore of primary importance when investigating workplace incidents. Yet, the incident investigation literature suggests that there is great variability in the training and techniques used by workplace investigators and offers only basic suggestions on interview techniques.[46] Further, research that has examined the quality of evidence reported in a health and safety investigation shows that there is frequently insufficient information obtained to provide a complete picture of the conditions under which the accidents or incidents have taken place.[47]

Against this backdrop, the Self-Administered Witness Interview Tool ('SAW-IT') was developed for generic use in health and safety investigations to obtain high quality evidence quickly, efficiently and in a standardized manner. As per the original SAI, the SAW-IT tool takes the form of a standardized protocol of clear instructions, best practice question formats and targeted retrieval support that guide the respondent through the process of remembering and reporting relevant information. Prior to the development of SAW-IT, there was no single standardized witness statement form in use for incident investigations. Where organizations had developed their own forms, they typically lacked theoretical background or evidence-based best practice techniques.[48]

To test the efficacy of the SAW-IT, researchers[49] showed mock witnesses a simulated industrial incident and asked them to provide a detailed statement about what had happened using either the SAW-IT report form or a self-administered standard incident report form. Results indicated that the SAW-IT tool

---

[45] "Incident Investigation", Det Norske Veritas, Duluth, 2003; Jeffrey W. Vincoli, *Basic Guide to Accident Investigation and Loss Control*, John Wiley and Sons, New York, 1994.

[46] Kelloway, Stinson and MacLean, 2004, see *supra* note 44; James Montgomery and Edward Kevin Kelloway, "Management of Occupational Health and Safety", 2nd ed., Nelson Thomas Learning, 2002.

[47] John Stoop, "Accident Scenarios as a Tool for Safety Enhancement Strategies in Transportation Systems", in Bernhard Wilpert, Matthias Freitag and Andrew Hale (eds.), *After the Event: From Accident to Organisational Learning*, Elsevier Science, Oxford, 1997, pp. 77–93.

[48] Kathryn Mearns *et al.*, "Factoring the Human into Safety: Translating Research into Practice, the Development and Evaluation of a Human Factors Accident and Near Miss Reporting Form for the Offshore Oil Industry", Health and Safety Executive ('HSE') Research Report No. 60, HSE Books, Suffolk, 2003.

[49] MacLean, Gabbert and Hope, 2019, see *supra* note 39.

significantly enhanced the quality of witness reports in comparison to a traditional incident report form. Specifically, the SAW-IT tool elicited 31 per cent more correct details at a consistent accuracy rate (proportion of accurate details to all details reported). This increase of reporting correct details was seen across all content categories explored, such as the environment, people and equipment. The information retrieved yielded 35 per cent more fine-grained (precise rather than general) details. In a real-world context, this information could be used to reliably classify incidents and inform root cause analyses. This, in turn, could generate targeted responses, such as identifying specific training needs that could help prevent similar incidents reoccurring.

19.4.2. The SAI for Missing Persons Investigations

A missing person is "anyone whose whereabouts cannot be established [...] and their well-being or otherwise confirmed".[50] During 2019 and 2020, police forces in England and Wales received 359,240 calls relating to missing persons; this equates to six calls per 1,000 residents.[51] When searching for a missing person, the police only have a finite number of resources available. Thus, they must allocate resources according to the level of perceived risk to the missing person and the public more generally.[52] The success of a missing persons investigation often centres on the quality of information obtained in the early stages.[53] Reliable information can not only inform the search but might also become vital evidence if the case broadens into a criminal investigation relating to a sexual offence, abduction or even murder. Key information to obtain includes a detailed description of the missing person, what they have with them and whether they prepared for leaving. It is also useful for officers to examine whether there have been any recent changes to the person's normal routine or mood that might provide a clue to their whereabouts or well-being. Obtaining information from individuals experiencing high stress often means that a second interview is required as it is difficult and overwhelming to remember and report all potentially relevant items of information in the initial stages; this further adds to resourcing

---

[50] College of Policing, "Major Investigation and Public Protection: Missing Persons" (available on the College of Policing's web site).
[51] United Kingdom Missing Persons Unit, *Missing Persons Data Report 2019/20*, National Crime Agency, 2021.
[52] College of Policing, see *supra* note 50.
[53] Charlie Hedges and Karen Shalev-Greene, "Managing a Missing Person Investigation", in Karen Shalev-Greene and Llian Alys (eds.), *Missing Persons: A Handbook of Research*, Taylor & Francis, London and New York, 2016.

demands.[54] The sheer volume of people reported missing on a daily basis presents a serious challenge for the police to conduct thorough interviews while also managing the worries of those who have reported the missing person.

In response to these challenges, an adapted version of the SAI was developed in collaboration with practitioners from the National Crime Agency for use in missing persons investigations. As per the original version, the SAI for Missing Persons Investigations ('SAI-Missing') takes the form of a standardized protocol of clear instructions, best practice question formats and targeted retrieval support that guide the respondent through the process of remembering and reporting relevant information. In this context, the form is designed to obtain reliable information that would meaningfully inform the missing persons investigation while at the same time providing a means for family and friends to be actively involved. The SAI-Missing tool can be used to collect key information prior to initial police contact. Alternatively, officers can conduct the initial interview and risk assessment and then ask the reporting person to complete the SAI-Missing tool in his or her own time, returning it later to further inform the investigation.

The SAI-Missing tool comprises of three core sections that each reflect key areas for a missing persons investigation outlined in best practice guidelines.[55] These sections focus on obtaining (i) a detailed and accurate physical description of the missing person, including (if relevant) a description of what they were wearing and any personal effects that they had with them; (ii) circumstances surrounding the disappearance of the missing person, including who they were with and their intentions (if known); and (iii) information about the missing person's normal routine, moods, and behaviours, alongside instructions to consider and report any recent changes to these. The SAI-Missing tool also provides respondents with a list of tasks that could enable them to further help. For example, finding a clear and recent photo and creating a list of relevant contacts, passwords and significant items missing.

To test the efficacy of the form, two laboratory studies were conducted.[56] In the first experiment, participants were tested individually and asked to provide a description of a person they knew well but had not seen for 24 hours. In the second experiment, participants were tested in pairs, but immediately separated into different rooms and instructed to imagine that the person they came with has gone missing. In both experiments, participants completed either the

---

[54] Nicholas R. Fyfe, Olivia Stevenson and Penny Woolnough, "Missing Persons: The Processes and Challenges of Police Investigation", in *Policing and Society*, 2015, vol. 25, no. 4, pp. 409–425.

[55] College of Policing, see *supra* note 50.

[56] Gabbert *et al.*, 2020, see *supra* note 40.

SAI-Missing or a self-administered control reporting form. Across the two experiments, those completing the SAI-Missing tool provided significantly more accurate information about physical descriptions and descriptions of clothing and personal effects than the comparison control form (an average increase of 35 per cent of information reported).

In sum, experimental research has confirmed the efficacy of the SAI-Missing tool in eliciting detailed and useful information for the missing persons investigation. In addition, the tool enables the police to respond to a report of a missing person immediately and efficiently, as well as providing a means for the individuals reporting the missing person to be actively involved and engaged in the investigation. Many elements of the SAI-Missing have been incorporated into the 'Report a Missing Person' online form, used by the UK police forces.[57]

19.4.3. The SAI for Road Traffic Collision Investigations

The aftermath of a road traffic incident is often busy and frontline roads policing officers have to contend with many competing demands. Critical evidence in road collision cases is often provided by eyewitnesses, yet frontline officers often have to prioritize safety and well-being concerns and so have limited resources for interviewing and taking detailed statements from witnesses. This is especially true when there are multiple injured persons and witnesses at the scene. Vital information can therefore be forgotten or distorted in the period between the incident and a subsequent follow-up contact from the police. To address this, a bespoke version of the SAI, the SAI-RTC, was developed and field-tested between 2019 and 2021.

The SAI-RTC draws heavily upon the original SAI, following a similar structure and incorporating similar retrieval support. However, the SAI-RTC incorporates new sections and instructions designed specifically for the roads policing context. There are specific prompts and cues relating to vehicles, drivers and road conditions (including traffic, visibility and weather). A recent field trial tested the efficacy of the tool with adults who witnessed or were involved in a road traffic collision that was attended by road traffic police officers. At the end of the trial period, almost 300 statements were available for analysis. Witnesses who provided their account via an SAI-RTC provided significantly more details than witnesses who completed the standard form. This was true overall (57 per cent increase) and for each category of detail analysed (for example, person details, vehicle details and spatial details). Witnesses who completed the SAI-RTC were also much more likely to report additional personal and contextual information that might prove to be important, such as whether they had discussed the collision with anyone else, the road and weather conditions at the time of the

---

[57] UK Metropolitan Police, "Report a Missing Person" (available on its web site).

collision and whether they had corrected or normal vision. Feedback from officers was also positive with all (100 per cent) reporting that the SAI-RTC produced reports that were as detailed or more detailed than the standard reporting form. Further, 71 per cent of surveyed officers considered the SAI-RTC to be as useful or more useful than the standard form. Regarding witness feedback, 84 per cent reported that the SAI-RTC was either very easy or quite easy to complete, and 71 per cent reported that the SAI-RTC definitely or probably helped them remember the incident in more detail. Additional feedback from end-users of the SAI-RTC has prompted further work in this area. For example, several officers indicated that completing the SAI-RTC at the scene was often impractical and many witnesses reported that they would have preferred an online format. Thus, work is underway to develop an online version of the SAI-RTC.

19.4.4. The SAI for Aviation Incidents

The most recent adaptation of the SAI involved a collaboration between the members of the Directorate of Flight Safety in Canada and one of the co-developers of the SAI, Dr. Ronald Fisher. Aviation accidents often occur at remote locations, which inevitably leads to a delay between the time of an accident and when the first in-person interview of witnesses can be conducted. Therefore, the 'SAI for Aviation Incidents' was developed to be used by aircraft accident investigators. A case study detailing the use of the SAI following a helicopter crash in the Ionian Sea was reported by Ikede and Fisher.[58] The crash occurred during the Covid-19 global pandemic, resulting in a delay of at least 72 hours between the time of the accident and the arrival of the investigators to begin witness interviews. As per the flight safety protocol within the Royal Canadian Air Force, witnesses of the accident were initially asked to give a written statement within 24 hours of the accident. They were subsequently asked to complete an SAI the next day, thus resulting in two sets of statements that were available for the investigators to review prior to arriving to conduct in-person interviews. Eighteen witnesses completed both the written statement from day one and the SAI from day two. Redacted versions were then analysed by the investigators. It was found that the average number of words reported in the SAI was 420 (range: 106 to 1,018), in comparison to an average of 246 words reported in the traditional written statement (range: 107 to 593); this relates to a 70.7 per cent increase. Further, more key themes were reported in the SAIs than in the written statements, which helped investigators prepare for the face-to-face interviews and also facilitated triage decisions regarding which witnesses to interview

---

[58] Ajiri Ikede and Ronald Fisher, "The Self-Administered Interview: A Case Report from a Helicopter Crash", in *Forum, Journal of the International Society of Air Safety Investigators*, 2022, vol. 55, no. 2, pp. 21–24.

immediately and which to interview later. Given the nature of the accident, not all details provided by the witnesses could be objectively verified. However, of the statements and observations that could be verified, almost all were consistent with the findings of the investigation. While being cautious about conclusions drawn from case studies, these initial findings are positive and demonstrate an advantage of the SAI over the traditional written statement method.

19.5. Gaps in Knowledge and Future Directions

While the SAI has numerous advantages and can be adapted for use in different investigative contexts, there are certain areas for which research is needed to determine its suitability and efficacy. For example, following a critical incident such as a violent terrorist attack, many witnesses might be traumatized. The majority of SAI studies have used videos of non-violent mock crimes as encoding stimuli, rather than immersive and stressful experiences. Given that the SAI is recommended for use following critical incidents, it is vital that ecologically valid research is conducted to examine the effects of the SAI when completed by witnesses displaying a range of emotions including trauma, stress and general upset. Future research should seek to recreate the immersive, stressful experience of witnesses more faithfully to examine how witnesses respond to the SAI when they are still experiencing an acute physiological stress reaction from witnessing an unexpected and arousing event.

Another area in need of research is to examine how the SAI performs with a more diverse range of participants than currently sampled. For example, as noted in a meta-analysis,[59] the majority of studies examining the SAI have recruited healthy young adult participants. Research with younger or older participants is currently limited; however, the available studies examining the efficacy of the SAI with older adults has confirmed the typical SAI effect.[60] For example, in one study,[61] older adults (more than 65 years old) witnessed an unexpected live event, following which half immediately completed an SAI and half did not. After a 48-hour delay, participants received a face-to-face interview using one of three techniques: Sketch Reinstatement of Context, MRC or no support control. Those who had completed the SAI recalled more correct information in the face-to-face interview irrespective of the technique used.

Research is also needed to examine whether the SAI is suitable for use with witnesses that have specific difficulties with language and cognition. A

---

[59] *Ibid.*
[60] Dando, Gabbert and Hope, 2020, see *supra* note 13; Gawrylowicz *et al.*, 2014, see *supra* note 32.
[61] Dando, Gabbert and Hope, 2020, see *supra* note 13.

study by Maras and colleagues[62] examined the effectiveness of the SAI for witnesses with autism spectrum disorder ('ASD'). It was hypothesized that the SAI might be particularly suitable for witnesses with ASD for three reasons: (i) it removes the social component of interview administration; (ii) it provides instructions via a different sensory modality; and (iii) it allows the witness to control the pace both at which they (self) administer the instructions and at which they recall details of the event. However, no specific advantages were found when compared with a comparison structured interview that had no retrieval support. These findings are consistent with previous research showing that mnemonics, such as the MRC, are not effective for people with ASD.[63] This observation highlights that the SAI is not effective for all witnesses, yet at present there is insufficient research to identify the boundary conditions.

Another potential barrier to the efficacy of the SAI is a witness' level of literacy. Indeed, a limitation of the current format of the SAI is that it requires witnesses to be able to read the instructions and then write their own account. Its applicability may therefore be limited in countries with high illiteracy rates. Even if witnesses have basic literacy skills, they might choose to write less or use only words which they can confidently spell, therefore restricting the quantity and quality of the information reported. One unpublished study[64] examined whether administering the SAI orally might overcome this potential problem. Participants watched a mock crime event and provided an account of the incident after a short interval, either through the written SAI or an oral version. Results showed no significant difference between conditions in either the amount or accuracy of information reported by witnesses. Thus, when witnesses have difficulty responding to the written protocol, the spoken version of the SAI may be used without incurring a loss in terms of the quantity and quality of information.

19.6. Conclusion

Since its development 15 years ago, the SAI has proven to be a versatile and effective investigative tool for capturing detailed initial accounts and preserving

[62] Katie Maras *et al.*, "Evaluating the Effectiveness of the Self-Administered Interview© for Witnesses With Autism Spectrum Disorder", in *Applied Cognitive Psychology*, 2014, vol. 28, pp. 693–701.

[63] Katie L. Maras and Dermot M. Bowler, "The Cognitive Interview for Eyewitnesses With Autism Spectrum Disorder", in *Journal of Autism and Developmental Disorders*, 2010, vol. 40, pp. 1350–1360; Katie L. Maras and Dermot M. Bowler, "Context Reinstatement Effects on Eyewitness Memory in Autism Spectrum Disorder", in *British Journal of Psychology*, 2012, vol. 103, pp. 330–42.

[64] Luciano H. Pinto, Lilian M. Stein, Fiona Gabbert and Lorraine Hope (manuscript in preparation).

witness memory until a formal interview can be conducted. It has added value to a range of investigations including shootings, violent assaults, missing persons investigations and workplace incidents.[65] It has been embedded into police policy and procedure in an increasing number of countries worldwide including the Netherlands and Norway. In 2019, it was officially adopted into UK professional practice police guidelines as a strategic-level recommendation for senior officers in charge of managing serious crimes involving high numbers of witnesses.[66]

While the SAI has proven to be adaptable for use in a range of investigations, further research is needed to understand the boundary conditions to inform guidance as to who will benefit most, and least, from self-administered reporting formats. Furthermore, while the SAI was originally developed for use following critical incidents involving multiple witnesses, it is increasingly acknowledged that there is value in using the SAI to investigate single-victim crimes, as some individuals might prefer this format of self-administered reporting. With the recent move for police forces to offer capability for the remote reporting of crimes, there is a need for further research to inform best practice procedure.

---

[65] Hope, Gabbert and Fisher, 2011, see *supra* note 28.
[66] College of Policing, 2019, see *supra* note 2.

20

The Timeline Technique

Lorraine Hope, Wayne Thomas and Feni Kontogianni*

20.1. Introduction

Consider a situation in which an intelligence agent is tasked with debriefing an important co-operative informant who, over the course of a few months, has gleaned valuable intelligence about a terrorist network after having spent time embedded in training camps overseas, perhaps in hostile, war-torn or otherwise inaccessible regions. During that period, the informant (or source) had the opportunity to visit different locations and encounter key targets and other associates, suppliers or 'fixers' involved in the network in several different situations, including formal meetings, informal interactions and incidental observations. Without doubt, given their experiences, the informant has valuable information stored in memory. This information may well include actionable intelligence about the future plans of the network. However, sources of this kind are also likely to have encoded a significant amount of information about the people encountered – from details about their appearance, status and role in the network to specifics about their relationships with others and the activities they have engaged in. They may know information about relevant locations and how they are reached, arranged or operationalized. They will also know information about how daily schedules are organized, how time is spent, and when, where and with whom different activities occur. They might have encountered relevant information about weapons, bomb-making, operational tactics and previously unknown key actors. They may have insights into the main source of finances and how they are managed or, in other contexts, information about online activities, including grooming, sourcing of illicit materials or even surreptitious planning. They may have gleaned first-hand insights into ideology, motivation,

---

* Lorraine Hope, Ph.D., is a Professor of Applied Cognitive Psychology at the University of Portsmouth. Wayne Thomas is an instructor in science-based interviewing with over 30 years of operational experience. Feni Kontogianni, Ph.D., is a Lecturer in Psychology at the University of Winchester. It is acknowledged that Lorraine Hope and Feni Kontogianni's work on the writing of this chapter has been funded by the Centre for Research and Evidence on Security Threats (ESRC Award no. ES/N009614/1), which is funded in part by the United Kingdom ('UK') Home Office and security and intelligence agencies (see the public grant decision on the UK Research and Innovation web site). The funding arrangements required this chapter to be reviewed to ensure that its contents did not violate the Official Secrets Act nor disclose sensitive, classified or personal information.

cohesiveness, preparedness for action and potential for infiltration. Given this potential wealth of intelligence information, the task for the source handler is to conduct the most thorough debriefing possible.

As is clear from the scenario above, obtaining detailed, accurate, reliable and relevant information is a challenge not just in intelligence-gathering contexts as outlined, but also in criminal investigations. This challenge is particularly exacerbated in contexts where the full scope of information known to the interviewee is not necessarily known to the interviewer. A source may have *several* critical experiences or facets of knowledge to report but may not be able to discriminate which experiences or details are of interest to the interviewer and which are not. Finally, information may have been gained over an extended period of time – maybe months, but often years. Such information may be difficult to recall in the absence of effective retrieval cues.

The Timeline Technique[1] was developed for use in information-gathering contexts involving complex or extended debriefings, where the interviewee likely has a large amount of relevant information to impart, the full scope of which may not be entirely known to the interviewer. Specifically, it was designed to facilitate obtaining a comprehensive initial account from a co-operative interviewee and, in doing so, inform the conduct of an efficient, productive and focused follow-up interview.

In this chapter, we outline the development of the Timeline Technique, including the theoretical underpinning and empirical testing. Recent developments and novel applications of the Timeline Technique are discussed as well as limitations of the Technique. We explore practical aspects of using the tool, its application in the field and the routes for future development.

20.1.1. What Is the Timeline Technique?

The Timeline Technique is a self-administered reporting format that uses a 'timeline' to provide a structure for remembering in information-gathering contexts. Drawing on memory theory and, importantly, responding to specific challenges identified by operational personnel in intelligence-gathering and law enforcement, this Technique is designed to enable interviewees to provide detailed information about complex events involving multiple people or repeat incidents occurring over extended periods of time. The Timeline Technique dispatches with the conventional idea that witnesses should provide an account in a linear narrative, starting 'at the beginning'. Instead, the self-administered timeline

---

[1] Lorraine Hope, Rebecca Mullis and Fiona Gabbert, "Who? What? When? Using a Timeline Technique to Facilitate Recall of a Complex Event", in *Journal of Applied Research in Memory and Cognition*, 2013, vol. 2, no. 1, pp. 20–24.

format used in the Timeline Technique enables witnesses to report and structure information as they remember it and to best reflect what actually happened.

In its original format, the materials used to administer the Timeline Technique comprised a visual timeline (for example, a piece of card with a line running across the mid-point to each end to represent the conceptual temporal space along which the incident 'took place' from start to finish, oriented horizontally) and a set of reporting cards to record person descriptions and actions. Description cards were blank, white, lined record cards. Action cards were blank and yellow with a semi-adhesive strip on the back to facilitate removal and re-ordering during use on the timeline.

In a debriefing using the Timeline Technique, following instructions by the interviewer, the interviewee is free to begin documenting the details of their account along the timeline by using a record card to describe either a person involved or activity that took place, and then placing this card at the relevant point on the timeline representing the incident. This process continues until the interviewee has exhausted the information they can report on the timeline.

Beyond promising insights from the wider memory literature supporting the beneficial effects of timeline reporting (see Section 20.2.), it is evident that the use of timelines to organize information is a common-sense practice in many investigative contexts. A visitor to any major incident room will likely see several large-scale visual timelines describing not only the status of live investigations but also the information about the target incident, including the sequence of events, key individuals and other relevant information. Given that investigators regularly use timeline formats to both represent available information, identify gaps and visually represent a period of interest, the concept of allowing cooperative interviewees to provide their own accounts of complex events using timelines, while simultaneously using the format to capitalize on the well-known retrieval processes, seems entirely intuitive.

In summary, the Timeline Technique is a self-administered recall and reporting technique designed to optimize an interviewee's ability to recall information from a particular time period in sequence, to identify and describe the people involved and to link those people with their specific actions or other relevant information. As such, it provides an effective means of gaining an initial account from an interviewee where other approaches falter due to the scope of knowledge, complexity of events or their extended duration. This initial account can then be more effectively and productively explored during more focused further interviews.

20.2. Theoretical Background

The development of the Timeline Technique relied on a rich theoretical background located in memory science that not only draws on the structure and organization of memory but also accounts for the role of encoding, retrieval and meta-cognitive processes in memory reporting. In this section, we outline the key theoretical principles underpinning the Technique.

20.2.1. Temporal Nature of Memory

By virtue of its format, the Timeline Technique exploits theoretical accounts contending that episodic memory is temporally ordered and that temporal context plays an important role in the retrieval process. For instance, information in episodic memory is associated with the temporal-spatial context in which it was encoded.[2] Basic memory literature also demonstrates that temporal context plays an important role in the retrieval process during free recall.[3] Indeed, the fact that items encoded in close temporal proximity tend to be recalled in close proximity suggests that the temporal clustering of items is a 'ubiquitous property' of sequence recall.[4]

One obvious organizing principle in any episodic event is that it occurs within a particular time-frame.[5] Consider a witnessed event: witnesses will retrieve some point at which they believe an incident commenced (for example, 'two armed men ran into the jewellery store') and concluded (for example, 'the getaway car sped off through the traffic lights'). Between these two points, witnesses might also recall information about the sequence of events, including who did what, when and to whom. Thus, one way to conceive of – and retrieve – the witnessed event is with reference to a conceptual timeline between the start and end points.

Retrieval tasks and investigative interview techniques, in laboratory or field settings, rarely explicitly exploit temporal context when educing witness

---

[2]   For example, see Endel Tulving, *Elements of Episodic Memory*, Clarendon, Oxford, 1983.

[3]   Marc W. Howard and Michael J. Kahana, "Contextual Variability and Serial Position Effects in Free Recall", in *Journal of Experimental Psychology: Learning, Memory and Cognition*, 1999, vol. 25, no. 4, pp. 923–941; Michael J. Kahana, "Associative Retrieval Processes in Free Recall", in *Memory & Cognition*, 1996, vol. 24, no. 1, pp. 103–109; Nash Unsworth, "Exploring the Retrieval Dynamics of Delayed and Final Free Recall: Further Evidence for Temporal–Contextual Search", in *Journal of Memory and Language*, 2008, vol. 59, no. 2, pp. 223–236.

[4]   Sean M. Polyn, Kenneth A. Norman and Michael J. Kahana, "A Context Maintenance and Retrieval Model of Organizational Processes in Free Recall", in *Psychological Review*, 2009, vol. 116, no. 1, pp. 129–156.

[5]   Lu Shulan, Derek Harter and Arthur C. Graesser, "An Empirical and Computational Investigation of Perceiving and Remembering Event Temporal Relations", in *Cognitive Science*, 2009, vol. 33, no. 3, pp. 345–373.

recall. Indeed, many interviews simply involve a question-and-answer exchange with the question order determined by the interviewer. Only one technique, the Cognitive Interview,[6] actively promotes witness-compatible questioning and implicitly draws on temporal context and temporal ordering to facilitate recall (that is, mental reinstatement of context ('MRC') and reverse order recall mnemonics) with no constraints on the witness' account. Nonetheless, many interview approaches oblige witnesses to 'start at the beginning' and produce, initially at least, a linear narrative account of what they saw. While this type of linear reporting provides an organizing narrative structure, it is unlikely to be an optimal approach for facilitating the retrieval and reporting of complex or extended events involving multiple actors. Providing such an account necessarily involves selecting which information to report first (for example, descriptions, actions or sequences of events) and switching between elements at different times while differentiating between who did what and when. Planning, organizing and maintaining these different elements in memory places heavy demands on cognitive resources. Indeed, switching between episodic elements and 'holding' information in limited working memory is likely to disrupt retrieval strategies and curtail output.[7]

Although research on witnesses' episodic memory has not explored the use of timelines to facilitate recall, work in the autobiographical memory domain has focused on how events are organized across longer time periods, such as across the lifespan.[8] Timeline-type methods have been used previously as a survey methodology to elicit information about autobiographical events,[9]

6   Ronald P. Fisher and R. Edward Geiselman, *Memory-Enhancing Techniques for Investigative Interviewing: The Cognitive Interview*, Springfield, Charles C Thomas, 1992. See also Chapter 16 in this book.

7   Klaus Oberauer and Svetlana Bialkova, "Accessing Information in Working Memory: Can the Focus of Attention Grasp Two Elements at the Same Time?", in Journal of Experimental Psychology: General, 2009, vol. 138, no. 1, pp. 64–87.

8   Gordon D.A. Brown and Nick Chater, "The Chronological Organisation of Memory: Common Psychological Foundations for Remembering and Timing", in Christoph Hoerl and Teresa McCormack (eds.), *Time and Memory: Issues in Philosophy and Psychology*, Clarendon Press, Oxford, 2001, pp. 77–110; Alex Fradera and Jamie Ward, "Placing Events in Time: The Role of Autobiographical Recollection", in *Memory*, 2006, vol. 14, pp. 834–845.

9   Robert F. Belli, "The Structure of Autobiographical Memory and the Event History Calendar: Potential Improvements in the Quality of Retrospective Reports in Surveys", in *Memory*, 1998, vol. 6, no. 4, pp. 383–406; Robert F. Belli, Ipek Bilgen and Tarek Al Baghal, "Memory, Communication, and Data Quality in Calendar Interviews", in *Public Opinion Quarterly*, 2013, vol. 77, pp. 194–219; Robert F. Belli, Frank P. Stafford and Duane F. Alwin (eds.), *Calendar and Time Diary Methods in Life Course Research*, Sage Publications, Thousand Oaks, 2009; Wander van der Vaart, "The Time-Line as a Device to Enhance Recall in Standardized Research Interviews: A Split Ballot Study", in *Journal of Official Statistics*, 2004, vol. 20, no. 2, pp. 301–317.

including experiences of violence.[10] Drawing on Conway's[11] multi-level model of autobiographical memory, Belli and colleagues found that respondents in social, medical and economic surveys provided higher quality information when interviewed using techniques incorporating a temporal component, such as event history calendars (compared against standard interviews).[12] In such interviews, calendars are usually only available to the interviewer who uses the temporal reference point.[13]

Extending the methodology, van der Vaart (2004)[14] and van der Vaart and Glasner (2007)[15] provided a timeline as a simple visual aid during telephone interviews in which respondents were asked to recall purchasing over a seven-year period. Recall accuracy was higher when a timeline was present during interviews and the beneficial effects of a timeline as a visual aid were particularly pronounced when the recall task was difficult. Survey methodologies incorporating a temporal component are likely to activate points of association along a rich network of retrieval pathways resulting in enhanced quality and quantity of information regarding extended life periods.[16]

In short, although timeline interview methodologies had not been explicitly adapted for investigative or intelligence-gathering purposes prior to the development of the Timeline Technique, there is ample evidence in the wider literature for the beneficial memorial effects of timeline formats, especially for complex retrieval tasks.

---

[10] Yoshihama Mieko *et al.*, "Does the Life History Calendar Method Facilitate the Recall of Intimate Partner Violence? Comparison of Two Methods of Data Collection", in *Social Work Research*, 2005, vol. 29, pp. 151–163.

[11] Martin A. Conway, "Autobiographical Knowledge and Autobiographical Memories", in David C. Rubin (ed.), *Remembering Our Past: Studies in Autobiographical Memory*, Cambridge University Press, 1996, pp. 67–93.

[12] Belli, 1998, see *supra* note 9; Robert F. Belli, Sangeeta Agrawal and Ipek Bilgen, "Health Status and Disability Comparisons Between CATI Calendar and Conventional Questionnaire Instruments", in *Quality and Quantity*, 2012, vol. 46, pp. 813–828; Belli, Stafford and Alwin (eds.), 2009, see *supra* note 9.

[13] Robert F. Belli, William L. Shay and Frank P. Stafford, "Event History Calendars and Question List Surveys: A Direct Comparison of Interviewing Methods", in *Public Opinion Quarterly*, 2001, vol. 65, no. 1, pp. 45–74.

[14] van der Vaart, 2004, see *supra* note 9.

[15] Wander van der Vaart and Tina J. Glasner, "Applying a Timeline as a Recall Aid in a Telephone Survey: A Record Check Study", in *Applied Cognitive Psychology*, 2007, vol. 21, no. 2, pp. 227–238.

[16] Belli, 1998, see *supra* note 9; John R. Anderson, "A Spreading Activation Theory of Memory", in *Journal of Verbal Learning and Verbal Behavior*, 1983, vol. 22, no. 3, pp. 261–295.

20.2.2. Associative Nature of Episodic Memory

Beyond facilitating retrieval via temporal context, encouraging interviewees to recall and organize their memories freely and without external input from an interviewer capitalizes on other important aspects of how our memories work. In particular, this approach is likely to maximize the performance of associative memory and facilitate effective self-cuing.

Episodic memory is thought to comprise multiple features bound together to reflect a cohesive representation of an event (*multi-component view of memory*).[17] As such, memory can be usefully conceptualized as a network of concepts connected by associated links. Spreading activation models propose that recall of a target item is facilitated by recalling other information associated with the target through a process of activation across the network.[18] These associative networks are formed of two different types of 'nodes': generic nodes that represent concepts or categories and episodic nodes that represent specific instances with nodes connected by associative links.[19] Original spreading activation theories[20] contended that information is organized around semantically similar information and, as activation spreads between related memory information, the recall of one item can prime the recall of related items. As activation spreads, information associated with the sources of activation is remembered.[21] In the context of remembering using a timeline format, it is reasonable to suggest that this approach facilitates a focus on a particular detail, located in time and the associated activation of other information relevant or otherwise associated with that detail.

Salient cues are most likely to facilitate accurate retrieval and this kind of high-quality retrieval cue typically has a strong association with the target memory while also providing sufficiently unique or idiosyncratic information to prompt *only* the target memory. For this reason, cues that are 'self-generated' by the rememberer (as opposed to those provided by some external source) are

---

[17] Gordon Bower, "A Multicomponent Theory of a Memory Trace", in Kenneth W. Spence and Janet T. Spence (eds.), *The Psychology of Learning and Motivation*, vol. 1, Academic Press, Oxford, 1967, pp. 230–325; Donald M. Thomson and Endel Tulving, "Associative Encoding and Retrieval: Weak and Strong Cues", in *Journal of Experimental Psychology*, 1970, vol. 86, no. 2, pp. 255–262.

[18] Anderson, 1983, see *supra* note 16.

[19] Michelle R. Tuckey and Neil Brewer, "The Influence of Schemas, Stimulus Ambiguity, and Interview Schedule on Eyewitness Memory Over Time", in *Journal of Experimental Psychology: Applied*, 2003, vol. 9, no. 2, pp. 101–118.

[20] For example, M. Ross Quillian, "Word Concepts: A Theory and Simulation of Some Basic Semantic Capabilities", in *Behavioral Science*, 1967, vol. 12, no. 5, pp. 410–430.

[21] John R. Anderson and Peter L. Pirolli, "Spread of Activation", in *Journal of Experimental Psychology*, 1984, vol. 10, pp. 791–798.

likely to be particularly powerful. Such cues can capitalize on how an individual's memory is organized and are most likely to be compatible with their own encoding of target material. Self-selected cues are also more likely to provide the strongest associative link to the target memory[22] (see also Section 20.3.2.1. for further discussion). As such, cues that are actively generated by the individual have a strong cue–target overlap and are likely to facilitate a more complete retrieval of the target memory.

From a retrieval perspective, the Timeline Technique involves a reporting activity (that is, recording one's memories on a timeline for the target event) that requires interviewees to generate and work with their own cues when remembering an event. As the Technique is entirely self-administered, cues are not provided by an external source, such as an interviewer, in the form of questions or other prompts. These types of 'other-generated' cues tend to be broad or based on the 'gist' or general meaning of target information, unlike more focused self-generated cues. While working into the timeline, the interviewee can use whatever cues that come to mind to initiate their account of what happened. In this way, and due to the spreading activation of relevant and associated memories, the initial cues committed to the timeline prompt the retrieval of further details which can then be added, as they come to mind, to the account. As such, the timeline reporting format – unlike interviews which require the production of a verbal linear narrative – provides a free and open 'space' for the interviewee to capitalize on the organization, cuing and reporting of their own memories. A further benefit of this self-cuing and self-reporting procedure is that it avoids the contamination of memory associated with the use of suggestive questioning techniques, unintentionally or otherwise, by an interviewer.

20.2.3. Effortful Retrieval and Cognitive Demand

Finally, there is an inherent feature of the timeline reporting format that could well underpin at least some of the memorial benefits, from a theoretical perspective. As noted above, the timeline format dispatches with the requirement for production of a linear narrative while retrieving information (that is, different report elements can be added at any point). This likely has beneficial implications for performance, particularly when cognitive demands are high. To provide a coherent linear narrative verbally, the interviewee must not only retrieve information but also organize and output the retrieved information in a way that adheres to conventional 'story' structures. In a verbal interaction with an interviewer, conversational maxims may make it difficult for the interviewee to suddenly introduce information which has been retrieved spontaneously but is not

---

[22] Rebecca L. Wheeler and Fiona Gabbert, "Using Self-Generated Cues to Facilitate Recall: A Narrative Review", in *Frontiers in Psychology*, 2017, vol. 8, pp. 18–30.

relevant to the current phase of the narrative. As a result, information that is recalled out of sequence, or comes to mind at the 'wrong time', may not be reported because it disrupts the narrative flow of the 'story' and so may be resisted.[23] In the context of retrieving detailed or complex information while engaging in effortful retrieval, this additional requirement likely exerts additional demands and places cognitive constraints on information flow.[24] For instance, if a particular detail comes to mind but is not immediately relevant to the information being described at that moment, then the interviewee likely attempts to retain that piece of information until it can be reported. Permitting interviewees to report anything they want at any time is likely to reduce demand on cognitive resources, in that retrieved details no longer have to be effortfully rehearsed in working memory. Instead, details that come to mind can be recorded (externally) immediately and integrated into the sequence later. Spontaneously identifying this advantage, a research participant using the Timeline Technique observed:

> It was good because you could write down what you thought of immediately on the cards and then you could go through what you had already written down and re-do it or think 'wait something happened before that' and correct or re-arrange it (Experiment 1: Hope *et al.*, 2013).[25]

Additionally, a timeline format "keeps time in view"[26] and enables interviewees to relate, visually or mentally, to different features of the event.

20.3. Empirical Development of the Timeline Technique

20.3.1. Development of the Timeline Technique

The first iteration of this novel approach to obtaining information from a cooperative interviewee was tested and reported by Hope, Mullis and Gabbert (2013).[27] This proof-of-concept set of experiments used a mock witness paradigm in which participants viewed a multi-perpetrator simulated crime incident involving theft and assault on a female victim by a group of five men. Unlike typical timeline methodologies used in the survey domain,[28] the timeline format used here did not provide generic personal cues but instead presented a visual 'timeline' on which the witness could plot their recollection of the individuals,

---

[23] Paul Grice, "Logic and Conversation", in Peter Cole and Jerry L. Morgan (eds.), *Syntax and Semantics*, Academic Press, New York, 1975, pp. 41–45.

[24] Wallace Chafe, "Cognitive Constraints on Information Flow", in Russell Tomlin (ed.), *Coherence and Grounding in Discourse*, John Benjamins, Amsterdam, 1987, pp. 21–51.

[25] Hope, Mullis and Gabbert, 2013, see *supra* note 1.

[26] Joanna Sheridan, Kerry Chamberlain and Ann Dupuis, "Timelining: Visualizing Experience", in *Qualitative Research*, 2011, vol. 11, p. 560.

[27] Hope, Mullis and Gabbert, 2013, see *supra* note 1.

[28] van der Vaart and Glasner, 2007, see *supra* note 15.

actions and sequence of events. One group of mock witnesses provided their account of the witnessed incident on a physical 'timeline' while the other group provided a free report. Different groups of mock witnesses provided their account, using either the timeline format or free report, immediately or after a two-week delay. Participants in all experimental conditions received the same overall recall instructions requiring them to report as much information as they could about the incident including detailed descriptions of the people involved. Participants were also instructed to make clear in their account which actions were associated with individual perpetrators. No time restrictions were imposed in either reporting condition. Mock witnesses who provided their accounts using a timeline provided more (i) person description details, (ii) person-action details, and (iii) sequence details than those using a free report format, at no cost to accuracy. Specifically, compared to the free recall control condition, the timeline reporting format extracted 47 per cent more correct information when participants provided their account shortly after witnessing an incident and 32 per cent more correct information when accounts were provided after a two-week delay. The additional information reported in the Timeline Technique conditions was not associated with an increase in errors at either retention interval.

A second experiment examined whether any single component of the Timeline Technique (that is, instructions, reporting cards or visual timeline) might account for the observed reporting advantage described above. Results indicated that optimal performance was achieved when the complete timeline format was used. In other words, no single component appeared to underpin the beneficial effects.

These initial findings paved the way for a programme of research examining the adaptability of the Timeline Technique in different contexts, including the development of the Technique to include additional cues and mnemonics.

20.3.2. Recent Developments in Timeline Technique Research

20.3.2.1. The Timeline Technique and Self-Generated Cues

Building on the original Timeline Technique research, an experiment conducted by Kontogianni *et al.* (2018)[29] tested the use of a theory-driven, self-generated mnemonic in conjunction with the Timeline Technique to facilitate retrieval of an incident witnessed under optimal and sub-optimal conditions, respectively. As outlined in Section 20.2., self-generated cues are (the most) salient or memorable details which are actively generated by an individual.[30] Cues can facilitate

---

[29] Feni Kontogianni *et al.*, "The Benefits of a Self-Generated Cue Mnemonic for Timeline Interviewing", in *Journal of Applied Research in Memory and Cognition*, 2018, vol. 7, no. 3, pp. 454–461.

[30] Wheeler and Gabbert, 2017, see *supra* note 22.

the process of retrieval if they increase the overlap between the conditions that were present when one first encoded an event and during recall (*encoding-specificity principle*).[31] For cues to be highly effective in facilitating retrieval, they should also be sufficiently distinctive to identify a specific target memory rather than match with multiple related memory traces (*principle of cue overload*).[32] Previous research has shown that the use of different types of self-generated cues are more reliable than generic descriptions or cues that are generated by someone other than the individual recalling the to-be-remembered information.[33] In applied contexts, the idea of self-generated cues is rather intuitive as being witness to an incident is a subjective experience and investigators cannot know what information is most salient to the interviewee.

In the experiment reported by Kontogianni *et al.* (2018),[34] one group of mock-witnesses was asked to generate their own cues (self-generated cues) by listing the first six things that they remembered seeing or thinking when viewing the event and by focussing on each one to see if that cue helped them remember more details. Another group was provided with MRC instructions[35] wherein they were instructed to think back to when they witnessed the incident and to focus on what their surroundings were, what they could see, hear, think and feel at the time. The MRC was used as a comparison to the self-generated cues as it is an established mnemonic that allows for witness-compatible retrieval but relies on the use of prompts that are generated by the interviewer to guide the witness. A third group of mock witnesses received no additional mnemonics. All participants used the Timeline Technique to provide their account. Mock witnesses who used self-generated cues reported a higher number of correct details than mock witnesses who used the MRC instructions or no cognitive mnemonics. The number of errors reported across conditions was similar. The effectiveness of self-generated cues in conjunction with the Timeline Technique was observed under the condition where participants could pay full attention to the event.

---

[31] Endel Tulving and Donald M. Thomson, "Encoding Specificity and Retrieval Processes in Episodic Memory", in *Psychological Review*, 1973, vol. 80, no. 5, pp. 352–373.

[32] James S. Nairne, "The Myth of the Encoding-Retrieval Match", in *Memory*, 2002, vol. 10, nos. 5–6, pp. 389–395.

[33] Timo Mäntylä and Lars-Göran Nilsson, "Cue Distinctiveness and Forgetting: Effectiveness of Self-Generated Retrieval Cues in Delayed Recall", in *Journal of Experimental Psychology: Learning, Memory, and Cognition*, 1988, vol. 14, no. 3, pp. 502–509; Jonathan G. Tullis and Aaron S. Benjamin, "Cue Generation: How Learners Flexibly Support Future Retrieval", in *Memory & Cognition*, 2015, vol. 43, no. 6, pp. 922–938; Rebecca M. Willén, Pär A. Granhag, Leif A. Strömwall and Ronald P. Fisher, "Facilitating Particularization of Repeated Similar Events with Context-Specific Cues", in *Scandinavian Journal of Psychology*, 2015, vol. 56, no. 1, pp. 28–37.

[34] Kontogianni *et al.*, 2018, see *supra* note 29.

[35] Fisher and Geiselman, 1992, see *supra* note 6.

Perhaps unsurprisingly, and consistent with findings reported in the wider literature, participants whose attention was divided at encoding did not benefit from the use of additional cues, self-generated or otherwise. Future research might focus on testing recall for events encoded in more naturalistic settings to establish any boundary conditions for the use of additional cues.

Overall, these results provide support for the idea that self-generated cues facilitate retrieval more than other-generated cues (such as MRC) and, importantly, can be used effectively in conjunction with the Timeline Technique to improve reporting.

20.3.2.2. The Timeline Technique and Repeated Events

Interviewees might have information about experiences which took place over a period of time, and which follow a certain pattern or are characterized by a common theme. Such repeated events might include incidents of domestic abuse, sexual assault, common gang activities or recurring daily activities in terrorist training camps. There are distinct challenges in eliciting information about repeated events, particularly as the stakes may be high with respect to obtaining specific and accurate details.

Memory for recurring details is stronger relative to memory for unique experiences due to prolonged exposure.[36] Individuals tend to develop scripts based on what typically happens in certain contexts; for instance, one's morning bus commute or the structure of weekly workplace meetings and the standing items on the agenda. However, it is challenging to remember details that consistently vary across occurrences, such as what was discussed in a specific weekly meeting (particularization). Some details that strongly deviate from the script might be more memorable (for example, having to drive to work because of a public transport strike), but memory for variations of what usually happens is not as strong as for details that occur in unique experiences.

Due to repeated exposure to a general routine across repeated events, it becomes more difficult to remember 'what happened when'. Research shows that there is increased likelihood for interference or confusion of details across repeated events, especially if they are highly similar (*Source Monitoring Framework*).[37] Yet, in applied contexts, investigators may need witnesses to report information with high levels of precision, including dates of events or the specific actions of a perpetrator in a criminal network, to correctly target and prosecute

---

[36] Heather L. Price and Deborah A. Connolly, "Suggestibility Effects Persist After One Year in Children Who Experienced a Single or Repeated Event", in *Journal of Applied Research in Memory and Cognition*, 2013, vol. 2, no. 2, pp. 89–94.

[37] Marcia K. Johnson, Shahin Hashtroudi and Stephen D. Lindsay, "Source Monitoring", in *Psychological Bulletin*, 1993, vol. 114, no. 1, pp. 3–28.

the guilty party in a trial.[38] However, research shows that 'what happened when' type of errors can be reduced if appropriate cues are available during retrieval.[39]

To examine reporting and particularization of specific instances of repeated events, Kontogianni *et al.* (2021)[40] tested the combined use of self-generated cues, the Timeline Technique and open-ended follow-up prompts. As described in Section 20.3.2.1., research suggests self-generated cues can be used effectively with the Timeline Technique, while in other research the use of follow-up open prompts for depth of information ('Tell me more about X') or to seek clarification ('Explain in more details what you mean by Y') educed up to 22 per cent additional information on top of an already detailed spontaneous timeline account.[41] In Kontogianni *et al.* (2021),[42] participants witnessed four simulated terrorism planning events on separate occasions over the course of a week. Each event depicted four perpetrators who met to plot an attack and distribute explosives to different locations. Participants were instructed to imagine that they were an undercover agent who had infiltrated the group and could, therefore, attend these meetings and operations. The overall pattern of actions remained similar across meeting events, but the roles assigned, plan details and selected locations varied across events. One week after witnessing the final event, participants were asked to provide information about each of the events they had witnessed.

More correct details about specific instances (increased particularization) were reported when the Timeline Technique and self-generated cues were both used (compared against free recall) with no cost to accuracy or increased confusion between instances. The use of the Timeline Technique also improved the reporting of 'who did or said what and when' attributions across events relative to the use of the free recall format. Also, the use of follow-up prompts produced new information that had not been spontaneously reported before, indicating that open prompts following an initial retrieval can serve as a cue to increase reporting. However, the results also suggest that caution is necessary when

---

[38] For example, Andrew J. Roberts, "Questions of Who Was There and Who Did What: The Application of Code D When a Suspect Disputes Participation but Not Presence", in *Criminal Law Review*, 2003, pp. 709–716.

[39] For example, Marcia K. Johnson, Tracey L. Kahan and Carol L. Raye, "Dreams and Reality Monitoring", in *Journal of Experimental Psychology: General*, vol. 113, no. 3, pp. 329–344.

[40] Feni Kontogianni *et al.*, "Facilitating Recall and Particularisation of Repeated Events in Adults Using a Multi-Method Interviewing Format", in *Memory*, 2921, vol. 29, no. 4, pp. 471–485.

[41] Feni Kontogianni *et al.*, "'Tell Me More About This…'": An Examination of the Efficacy of Follow-Up Open Questions Following an Initial Account", in *Applied Cognitive Psychology*, 2020, vol. 34, no. 5, pp. 972–983.

[42] Kontogianni *et al.*, 2021, see *supra* note 40.

asking further questions after an extensive free report as, predictably, accuracy progressively decreases when interviewees sacrifice accuracy for informativeness – particularly if they are not confident about their memory.[43]

In summary, these findings show that the Timeline Technique is bolstered by the use of self-generated cues and follow-up prompts and can be flexibly used to facilitate retrieval and reporting of both unique and repeated events. These findings are noteworthy in the context of repeated events as, due to a high risk of interference across instances, interviewees are likely to be more suggestible about details that they are less certain about.[44] For this reason, using an interviewee-led approach when interviewing individuals about repeated events may be particularly important.

20.3.2.3. The Timeline Technique and Memory for Conversations

Research has also examined whether the Timeline Technique might support the reporting of conversational details. Most interviewing focuses on eliciting information about *what happened*. However, the verbal content of interactions (*what was said* and *who said what*) can be equally important as evidence and intelligence. First, there are criminal and civil cases that can revolve around the content of interpersonal verbal interactions (for example, harassment, bullying, stalking or bribery). Second, crimes may take place under conditions where only overheard information is available because the witness was unable to see the perpetrators (for example, a hooded or blindfolded hostage). Third, intelligence gleaned from clandestine groups or terrorist organizations may take the form of recalled accounts of meetings and conversations during which the details of plots or other plans were discussed. Yet memory for conversations has not been a focus of much research and there have been only limited attempts to develop or adapt interviewing techniques to enhance the recall and reporting of *who said what* and *when did they say it*.

The limited available research on memory for *criminal conversations* illustrates both the transformation of such conversations into gist-based free recall reports and the superior recall of the 'gist' of criminal conversations (compared against verbatim recall).[45] Research also broadly confirms that a high-quality

---

[43] Kontogianni *et al.*, 2020, see *supra* note 41; Kontogianni *et al.*, 2021, see *supra* note 40.

[44] Johnson, Hashtroudi and Lindsay, 1993, see *supra* note 37; D. Stephen Lindsay, Bem P. Allen, Jason Chan and Leora C. Dahl, "Eyewitness Suggestibility and Source Similarity: Intrusions of Details from One Event into Memory Reports of Another Event", in *Journal of Memory and Language*, 2004, vol. 50, no. 1, pp. 96–111.

[45] Laura Campos and Maria L. Alonso-Quecuty, "Remembering a Criminal Conversation: Beyond Eyewitness Testimony", in *Memory*, 2006, vol. 14, no. 1, pp. 27–36; Kathy Pezdek and Matthew Prull, "Fallacies in Memory for Conversations: Reflections on Clarence Thomas, Anita Hill, and the Like", in *Applied Cognitive Psychology*, 1993, vol. 7, no. 4, pp. 299–310.

---

interviewing approach can elicit more information about conversations[46] but has not explored whether an alternative retrieval format might (i) provide more effective cues to enable participants to access verbatim details and (ii) capitalize on the structure of a conversation during retrieval. There are a number of reasons that reporting conversations from memory might be facilitated through a timeline reporting approach. Like any other episodic event, conversations occur within a particular time-frame and, as such, witnesses can identify a start point, a finish point and a sequence of information, including who said what, when and to whom. Given that the timeline reporting format facilitates enhanced reporting of 'who did what' for a multi-perpetrator event, it may be the case that the recall of a conversation, in particular remembering *'who said what'*, might benefit from a format that focuses on the reporting of specific details in the order in which they occurred. Another contextual feature of contemporary social interaction might also be relevant. Given the prevalence of text and in-app messaging (such as through SMS, instant messaging or WhatsApp) and the availability of online formats for synchronous and asynchronous communication, communicating via real-time text chat is commonplace.[47] As such, it is possible that visualizing a conversation along a timeline is now intuitive for many people.

Across three empirical studies, using methodologies designed to analogue the experiences of both witnesses to overheard criminal conversations and undercover sources operating in organized crime contexts, Hope *et al.* (2019)[48] examined whether an adapted timeline reporting format might facilitate recall of overheard conversations. Experiment 1 examined the information reported about an overheard conversation between two perpetrators (with no visual information present). In Experiment 2, mock witnesses were exposed to a simulated conversation involving several gang members and provided an account using an extended version of the Timeline Technique that also enabled them to provide descriptions of the target individuals. In Experiment 3, mock witnesses, in the role of undercover officers acting as members of a gang, witnessed three

46   Laura Campos and Maria L. Alonso-Quecuty, "Language Crimes and the Cognitive Interview: Testing Its Efficacy in Retrieving a Conversational Event", in *Applied Cognitive Psychology*, 2008, vol. 22, no. 9, pp. 1211–1227.

47   Andrew J. Flanagin, "IM Online: Instant Messaging Use Among College Students", in *Communication Research Reports*, 2005, vol. 22, no. 3, pp. 175–187; Darren Gergle, David Millen, Robert E. Kraut and Susan Fussell, "Persistence Matters: Making the Most of Chat in Tightly-Coupled Work", in *Proceedings of the SIGCHI Conference on Human Factors in Computing Systems*, ACM, New York, 2004, pp. 431–438; Anabel Quan-Haase, "Instant Messaging on Campus: Use and Integration in University Students' Everyday Communication", in *The Information Society*, 2008, vol. 24, no. 2, pp. 105–115.

48   Lorraine Hope *et al.*, "Who Said What and When? A Timeline Approach to Eliciting Information and Intelligence About Conversations, Plots, and Plans", in *Law and Human Behavior*, 2019, vol. 43, no. 3, pp. 263–277.

different conversations between gang members on three separate occasions over a seven-day period and then provided an account of these conversations using the Timeline Technique to provide their report.

Across all experiments, participants using the Timeline Technique to report their memories provided more information about the conversations they heard or observed, including more verbatim details than participants who reported via free recall. Notably, in the most complex test of the format in Experiment 3, overall recall of both the conversations (verbatim, gist, speaker attributions) and the people involved in these conversations was significantly enhanced when the timeline format was used to elicit information about these conversations despite a one-week delay.

20.3.3. Summary

Grounded in basic memory literature and contemporary cognitive approaches to survey methodology, the experiments conducted to date largely confirm the benefits of a novel timeline approach to eliciting information about complex events. Even though all mock interviewees across studies were provided with the same general instructions emphasizing the recall of the actions and descriptions of the people involved, interviewees providing their accounts using the Timeline Technique typically reported significantly more correct information than their counterparts in control conditions. Furthermore, particular aspects of accounts were notably enhanced through use of the Technique. Specifically, participants provided significantly more correct details about the actions of individual perpetrators in a multiple perpetrator incident. Timeline participants were also less likely to make sequencing errors when reporting the order of events. In sum, the Timeline Technique facilitated the reporting of information about 'who did what?' and 'when did they do it?'. Importantly, and in contrast to previous interview and timeline methodologies, performance increments were achieved in timeline conditions without externally generated memory cues or prompts.

20.4. Future Research

Although reports from the field reflect successful use of the Timeline Technique in a number of different contexts with diverse co-operative interviewees and for different types of investigative or intelligence-gathering purposes, there are many routes for future research to explore in order to examine the performance of the Technique across a range of contexts, both when used alone and in conjunction with other tools and techniques.

In this section, we outline a number of potentially interesting areas for wider future research, including development for use in different cultural contexts, expanding use for the reporting of extensive autobiographical information in extended debriefings, potential use in credibility assessment and integration with other tools and techniques. Of course, we should also note that the Timeline Technique, like all techniques developed and tested under laboratory conditions, should also be systematically evaluated in more naturalistic or field environments.

20.4.1. Timeline Technique and Culture

With respect to culture, to date only limited research has examined the extent to which existing interviewing and elicitation techniques, generally developed and tested in Western and broadly individualistic contexts, are effective in non-Western and broadly collectivistic contexts. Culture might be defined as a dynamic and complex set of shared systems, meanings and practices within a social group, emerging from the histories and experiences of that group and shaping social interactions and relationships at all levels from the individual to the wider society.[49] Indeed, memory has been described as "an open system saturated in cultural contexts"[50] that is shaped by the dynamic forces of culture, as indeed are many other cognitive processes associated with memory. Therefore, irrespective of whether a witness interview involves a cross-cultural component in the interview room or not, differences in reports between cultures may reflect differences in processing, interpretation or prioritization of information concerning a witnessed event. In a preliminary cross-cultural examination of the Timeline Technique, memory accounts provided by mock witnesses drawn from a UK sample were compared with those provided by mock witnesses drawn from an Arabic-speaking Lebanese sample.[51] Lebanon offered an interesting contrast to an English-speaking sample as we were also keen to test a sample where the language takes a different form to that of the Latin alphabet used in many European languages. A notable feature of reading and writing in Arabic is that it runs from right to left whereas to date the timeline has only been tested on samples using writing forms that run from left to right. Although the timeline format does not impose a specific reporting direction consistent with any particular conceptual flow of time (that is, interviewees can report any detail at any time anywhere on the timeline), it does by virtue of format fundamentally assume a linear left to right representation of time. Research has shown that the direction of writing in

---

[49] Lorraine Hope *et al.*, "Urgent Issues and Prospects at the Intersection of Culture, Memory, and Witness Interviews", in *Legal and Criminological Psychology*, 2022, vol. 27, no. 1, pp. 1–31.

[50] Wang Qi, "The Cultural Foundation of Human Memory", in *Annual Review of Psychology*, 2021, vol. 72, pp. 151–179.

[51] Lorraine Hope *et al.*, "Cultural Differences in Eyewitness Reports: Is a Self-Administered Reporting Technique Beneficial for Arabic-Speaking Lebanese Witnesses", 2023 (manuscript under review).

an individual's native language affects how they represent time spatially.[52] Specifically, native English speakers arrange temporal sequences from left to right, while native Hebrew speakers arranged them from right to left, in accordance with the direction of writing in their native tongue. Consistent with previous research,[53] mock witnesses in the UK group provided significantly more correct information overall in their recall reports than the Lebanese group, irrespective of the reporting format. Comparing between reporting conditions, UK participants who provided their accounts using the timeline format reported significantly more information than those UK participants who provided a free recall of what they had seen. However, a comparable effect of reporting format was not mirrored in the Lebanese sample. Lebanese participants reported roughly the same amount of correct information, irrespective of reporting format. There were no overall differences between the cultural groups in terms of the reporting of incorrect details. However, as overall accuracy rate is a function of quantity, the UK group provided more accurate information overall. These results are interesting and highlight the need for further research with more diverse samples.[54]

There are a number of theoretical and pragmatic factors which might well underpin these finding. For instance, research suggests that there are interesting cross-cultural differences in memory specificity and that diverse cultural groups 'segment' memory for events in different ways.[55] It may also be the case that in a culture associated with high context communication where social interactions are more indirect and reliant on the context to communicate what is implied, a format reflecting linear temporal organization is not optimal. To date, none of these issues have been empirically examined in the context of applied memory, such as witness interviewing or source debriefing (although see Hope *et al.*, 2021 for review and discussion).[56] Given that such differences may affect reporting and the extent to which tools and techniques serve as facilitative, adaptations to the timeline methodology may be needed to capitalize on different cultural features or preferences. Other considerations pertain to the methodological challenges of conducting cross-cultural research, particularly where reporting takes place in different languages or where normative attitudes to the investigative context vary. While unrelated to the Timeline Technique *per se*, these

---

[52] Orly Fuhrman and Lera Boroditsky, "Cross-Cultural Differences in Mental Representations of Time: Evidence from an Implicit Nonlinguistic Task", in *Cognitive Science*, 2010, vol. 34, no. 8, pp. 1430–1451.

[53] Nkansah Anakwah *et al.*, "Cross-Cultural Differences in Eyewitness Memory Reports", in *Applied Cognitive Psychology*, 2020, vol. 30, no. 2, pp. 505–515.

[54] For further discussion, see Hope *et al.*, 2022, see *supra* note 49.

[55] Khena M. Swallow and Wang Qi, "Culture Influences How People Divide Continuous Sensory Experiences into Events", in *Cognition*, 2020, vol. 205, p. 205.

[56] Hope *et al.*, 2022, see *supra* note 49.

observations highlight some of the difficulties of conducting meaningful cross-cultural comparisons.

20.4.2. Timeline Technique and Extended Debriefings

A key area for future research on the Timeline Technique pertains to its use as a method for conducting extended debriefings. Again, while successful use in the context of eliciting wide-ranging information about extended histories has been reported, more research is needed to optimize the Technique for such debriefings. In this context, the main challenge facing interviewees is that the sheer volume of information they have to report may be overwhelming. For example, an informant who decides to report on several decades of involvement in individual criminal activity, international terrorism or organized crime gangs will have a wealth of both semantic knowledge (for example, information about people) and episodic information (for example, recall of what happened in certain incidents) to report. In such cases, the onus is on the interviewer to provide an organizing frame or structure to assist with the remembering, reporting and organization of extensive detailed information.

One approach to an extended debriefing of this nature that has been used in operational settings is to use a 'scoping' timeline to capture key periods or life chapters initially, each of which can then be examined using individual timelines, and follow-up targeted questioning, focused on specific periods or events. This approach draws on our current understanding of the structure of autobiographical memory, with particular reference to the Self Memory System,[57] Transition Theory[58] and chapter thinking.[59] The objective of this approach is to allow the interviewee to use their own subjective life chapter labels to improve autobiographical recall and recall of associated episodic events. While a preliminary test of this scoping procedure has been successfully implemented for the reporting of repeated events[60] and effective use has been reported in the field, further testing is necessary to determine if this approach is indeed the best way to facilitate recall and reporting of extended periods using the timeline format.

---

[57] Martin A. Conway and Christopher W. Pleydell-Pearce, "The Construction of Autobiographical Memories in the Self-Memory System", in *Psychological Review*, 2000, vol. 107, no. 2, pp. 261–288.

[58] Norman R. Brown, "Transition Theory: A Minimalist Perspective on the Organization of Autobiographical Memory", in *Journal of Applied Research in Memory and Cognition, 2016, vol. 5*, no. 2, pp. 128–134.

[59] Dorthe K. Thomsen, "Autobiographical Periods: A Review and Central Components of a Theory", in *Review of General Psychology*, 2015, vol. 19, no. 3, p. 294.

[60] Kontogianni *et al.*, 2021, see *supra* note 40.

20.4.3. Timeline Technique and Deception

To date, the Timeline Technique has not been empirically tested in the context of interviewee deception. As such, the strategies that might be used to deceive using this format are, as yet, undocumented. However, reporting using a timeline format in an initial interview commits the interviewee to a particular (written) version of events. If this version of events represents a true account, it should not be difficult for interviewees to remember, and indeed expand on, the information originally provided in follow-up interviews. If, however, the initial account is deliberately inaccurate (that is, deceptive) or has deceptive elements, the interviewee now must remember what exactly they reported initially and ensure they are consistent subsequently to avoid suspicion or further questioning. This activity alone is likely to be mentally taxing for the interviewees – and indeed anecdotal reports suggest that interviewees who are merely presenting themselves as co-operative shy away from the task when given the requirement to provide extensive information. For interviewees who are deliberately deceptive, 'cognitive load' could be further increased by not permitting interviewees to review their timeline account before any follow-up interviews. Finally, if there are some weaknesses in the account (for example, apparent deception, inconsistency, deliberate omissions or 'glossing over'), these can be robustly explored by the interviewer via direct questions later. Dedicated research might uncover particular strategies deployed by deceptive interviewees tasked with providing a comprehensive timelined account.

20.4.4. Extending the Timeline Technique

Since the original development of the Timeline Technique, it has become clear that the retrieval 'space' made available by this flexible, self-administered reporting format provides the opportunity for the integration of the Technique with other mnemonics and reporting tools. Indeed, research to date has explored the use of some other techniques in conjunction with the Timeline Technique (for example, self-generated cues;[61] 'family tree' mnemonic).[62]

One of the most promising tools for integration with the Timeline Technique, particularly in the context of terrorism and organized crime, is the Reporting Information about Networks and Groups ('RING') technique.[63] The

---

[61] Kontogianni *et al.*, 2018, see *supra* note 29.

[62] Hope *et al.*, 2019, see *supra* note 48; Drew A. Leins *et al.*, "Interview Protocols to Facilitate Human Intelligence Sources' Recollections of Meetings", in *Applied Cognitive Psychology*, 2014, vol. 28, no. 6, pp. 926– 935.

[63] Lorraine Hope, Feni Kontogianni, Kristoffer Geyer and Wayne Thomas, "Development of the Reporting Information About Networks and Groups (RING) Task: A Method for Eliciting Information from Memory About Associates, Groups, and Networks", in *The Journal of Forensic Practice*, 2019, vol. 21, no. 4, pp. 240–247.

RING technique was developed to improve recall and reporting of information about people involved in groups and networks. Much like the Timeline Technique, and drawing on the associative nature of memory and concept of 'keeping memory in view', this technique is based on the notion that visually representing the links between people will (i) facilitate recall of individuals who associate with that particular group or network and (ii) prompt recall of additional individuals who might otherwise go unmentioned. First, memory for one member of a network should serve as a cue for other relevant individuals and prompt a more comprehensive retrieval of information. Second, a visual representation of the network capitalizes on how memory is organized and should prompt additional recall as a result. Beyond benefits for memory, a visual description of complex relationships and networks should also provide an interviewer with enhanced understanding of relevant information about complex or extended relationships and allow a more thorough interrogation of these relationships in further questioning. The RING technique might also be used to probe for information about specific gatherings or meetings. As such, the RING technique is a reporting format designed to elicit as much information as possible about individuals involved in a group or network, the links (that is, relationships) between those individuals, and the strength, direction and proximity of such relationships. At the most basic level, this instruction can be used to prompt a source to work on a paper-and-pen diagram of the network during a debriefing (although usability trials of an app-based electronic format have also been conducted).

In an extended timeline debriefing involving descriptions of people involved in a gang or criminal network, it is easy to see how the RING technique might be integrated as a beneficial supplementary task. Future research might examine when the best time is to introduce such supplementary tasks to facilitate optimal retrieval.

20.5. Applications of the Timeline Technique

20.5.1. Use in the Field

To date, the Timeline Technique has been used in a number of field settings, mainly in intelligence debriefing contexts. This has included debriefing of those involved in fighting overseas in recent conflicts, the examination of radicalization pathways and criminal histories, the documentation of experiences, routes and locations in human trafficking and illegal migration contexts, and the debriefing of hostages that have been held for extended periods of time. In an independent review conducted in 2019 for the UK intelligence agencies,[64] use of the Timeline Technique was cited as "[...] providing greater insights into key

---

[64] Jo Edwards, *Impact Review: A Review of the Impact of CREST Research Projects*, Lucidity Solutions, September 2019.

national security issues and significant information relating to recruiting techniques and locations used by a terrorist organisation". This review also confirms effective use of the Technique in the context of hostage debriefing noting that, "[…] the use of this technique has shown that more information can be obtained from those who are released or escape having been held hostage, as opposed to a straight forward question and answer session". The Timeline Technique is part of the interview and negotiation process and toolkit within the United States High-Value Detainee Interrogation Group and has been integrated into operational practice.

Beyond the benefits of promoting autonomy and associated rapport with a co-operative source, anecdotal reports from end users have observed a reduction in the fatigue often experienced in the early stages of debriefing while obtaining a comprehensive overview. For example, it has been noted in practice that when using the Timeline Technique, interviewers are able to concentrate on the welfare of the interviewee rather than using attentional resources on questioning strategies. Tactics such as encouraging the interviewee to use their autonomy to take breaks when necessary have been used to bolster interviewee confidence in their role and participation in the debriefing process. Used as part of the initial stages of an extended debrief, feedback suggests the Timeline Technique allows a more structured approach to subsequent interviews while minimizing the cognitive strain on both interviewer and interviewee. Additionally, the autonomy aspect has been used innovatively to structure debriefs with interviewees who are willing to co-operate in providing information about certain topics but have reservations about others. Although further research is needed, it is possible these features of this Technique have positive implications for the interviewer–interviewee relationship.

While the Timeline Technique has been used extensively in intelligence-gathering contexts, it has only recently been introduced into evidence-gathering contexts, including cold case investigations. Although evidential rules have varied across jurisdictions, in general the original (physical) timeline account produced during the debrief has been treated like interviewer notes. In some cases, the original timeline account has been preserved as unused material, while, in others, a time and dated digital photograph has been sufficient for disclosure or court requirements.

20.5.2. Training and the Timeline Technique

The Timeline Technique is an advanced technique and is designed mainly for use in debriefing contexts with co-operative interviewees when sufficient time is available in an appropriate context. As such, the Technique should only be used by experienced interviewers who are knowledgeable about relevant memory science and trained with respect to use of the format. The Timeline

Technique is a flexible, adaptable and intuitive format but lack of knowledge, appropriate training and ill-informed 'creativity' is likely to result in the misuse (abuse) of the Technique to the detriment of outcomes.

Training for informed use of the Timeline Technique has been designed by the developers and takes on average two to three days, including exercises and consideration of complementary retrieval techniques.

20.6. Conclusion

Empirical research and observations from the field suggest that the Timeline Technique provides interviewees with an intuitive organizing structure that facilitates reporting about complex, multi-faceted knowledge and experiences while reducing various demands on both the interviewee and interviewer. In addition to promoting autonomy, permitting reporting flexibility and attenuating pressure to maintain sequence or inhibit information recalled at the wrong time in a linear narrative, the Technique also works to maximize cueing of associated memories. Importantly, as the Timeline Technique is entirely self-directed, the potential for inadvertent influence on the interviewee's account (for example, through suggestive questioning) is largely eliminated. In the context of extended debriefings in intelligence-gathering contexts, the Timeline Technique offers interviewers an approach with which to establish a detailed and comprehensive initial account with a co-operative source before pursuing more focused and productive questioning.

PART IV: RELEVANT ORGANIZATIONS

21

The International Investigative Interviewing
Research Group (iIIRG)

Trond Myklebust and Gavin E. Oxburgh[*]

21.1. Brief History and Development of Investigative Interviewing

21.1.1. Introduction

The 1980s saw the start of substantial research by academics into police interviewing of victims, witnesses and suspects of crime. Initially, there was little guidance for serving police officers regarding the most effective way of conducting such interviews, with training typically provided 'on the job' by more experienced colleagues.[1]

Prior to the 1980s, there were several handbooks to aid officers in their interviewing, and one of these well-used sources of guidance was the American text, 'Criminal Interrogation and Confessions'.[2] The first version of this manual was published in 1962, although, either separately or together, both of its authors had a long tradition of publishing books on this topic commencing in 1942.[3] The book became an influential interviewing guide for police officers in England and Wales pre-1984.[4] Inbau and Reid claimed that their interrogation process was and is an effective method for obtaining confessions from guilty suspects.[5]

---

[*]   **Trond Myklebust** holds the position of Assistant Chief of Police and Programme Leader of the Master's in Investigation at the Norwegian Police University College. He was the Deputy Chair and Co-Director of the International Investigative Interviewing Research Group ('iIIRG') from April 2007 to June 2019 and a member of their Executive Committee until June 2022. **Gavin E. Oxburgh** is a Professor of Police Science and Registered Forensic Psychologist at Northumbria University. He was the Chair and Co-Director of the iIIRG from April 2007 to June 2019 and a member of their Executive Committee until June 2022.

[1]   David Walsh and Gavin E. Oxburgh, "Investigative Interviewing of Suspects: Historical and Contemporary Developments in Research", in *Forensic Update*, 2008, vol. 9, no. 2.
[2]   Fred E. Inbau, John E. Reid and Joseph P. Buckley, *Criminal Interrogations and Confessions*, 2nd ed., Williams and Wilkins, Baltimore, 1986.
[3]   Gisli H. Gudjonsson, *The Psychology of Interrogations and Confessions*, Wiley, Chichester, 2003.
[4]   Walsh and Oxburgh, 2008, see *supra* note 1.
[5]   Inbau, Reid and Buckley, 1986, see *supra* note 2; Fred E. Inbau, John E. Reid, Joseph P. Buckley and Brian C. Jayne, *Criminal Interrogations and Confessions*, 4th ed., Aspen, Gaithersburg, 2001; *id.*, *Criminal Interrogations and Confessions*, 5th ed., Jones & Bartlett Learning, Burlington, 2001.

Characteristics of the model include manipulation of the suspect (via persuasion), minimization (of the seriousness of the offence) and maximization (both of the severity of not confessing and the benefits of confession). Interrogators are also encouraged to inform suspects that any denials would be futile as they are sure of the suspect's guilt. It is also permissible for interrogators trained in this approach to lie to suspects about the nature and strength of the evidence against them – something that other interviewing models (such as the PEACE model developed in England and Wales)[6] and some legal systems prohibit.

Not surprisingly, psychologists around the world were (and still are) deeply concerned with this approach, arguing that such oppressive and coercive methods are, in fact, likely to lead individuals, especially those who are vulnerable, to falsely confess to crimes that they did not commit.[7] Nonetheless, despite these serious misgivings, interrogation models using coercive techniques still remain in use today in many parts of the world.

21.1.2. Interviewing in England and Wales

In England and Wales in 1981, a Royal Commission on Criminal Procedure, precipitated by judicial concerns over police interviewing techniques, brought about legislation which paved the way for a change in approach away from the coercive interviewing styles that were felt to be prevalent in practice at that time.[8] One effect of this legislation was the introduction of the Police and Criminal Evidence Act (1984)[9] which, amongst many other legislative changes, mandated that all interviews with suspects had to be audio-recorded. This, in turn, gave rise to the opportunity for a detailed examination of subsequent audiotapes to establish what was actually occurring in real-life interviews. Since then, there have been other models of non-coercive interviewing[10] together with research studies conducted across the world, many in collaboration with practitioners.

However, despite such excellent advances, it became apparent to the authors of this chapter that the vast majority of research was only being published in formats that were, in reality, unavailable to many practitioners. This was primarily due to academic journals not being freely available to practitioners from which new techniques could be learnt and included in future training courses.

---

[6] See Chapter 12 of this book.

[7] See Saul M. Kassin, *Duped: Why Innocent People Confess and Why We Believe Their Confessions*, Prometheus Books, Guilford, 2022; see also Chapter 3 of this book.

[8] Barrie L. Irving, "Police Interrogation: A Case Study of Current Practice", Research Study No. 2, Royal Commission on Criminal Procedure, London, His Majesty's Stationery Office, 1980.

[9] See UK, Police and Criminal Evidence Act, 31 October 1984 (https://www.legal-tools.org/doc/b52ec0/).

[10] See Chapter 12 of this book for more details of these models.

Thus, following a conference by the International Investigative Interviewing Network ('IIIN') (see also below in this chapter for more details about this group) at the University of Portsmouth in 2006, the idea of creating an international organization to conduct scientific research and bridge the gap between research and practice was formed.

21.1.3. Background and 'Roots' of the iIIRG[11]

Whilst studying for a Master's degree in Forensic Psychology at the University of Portsmouth (2002 to 2004), Oxburgh (who was a serving police officer in the Royal Air Force at that time) first encountered Tom Williamson,[12] who not only became his supervisor for his forensic psychology dissertation, but latterly a friend. Numerous discussions took place around the area of interviewing and the impact of negative emotional language during police interviews with suspects of sexual offences – this was ultimately to be the topic of Oxburgh's dissertation which was completed and subsequently published in 2006.[13] The findings of this research were presented at the European Association of Psychology and Law Conference, 2005, in Vilnius, where the authors of this chapter met and became academic colleagues and good friends.

Whilst at the Vilnius conference, Oxburgh and Myklebust became very much aware of the importance of research-based practice and practice-based research – the 'dialogue of the deaf'[14] was very much in play! The mutual interest in investigative (or non-coercive interviewing) led to regular discussions between Oxburgh, Myklebust and Tom Williamson after Vilnius. Williamson clearly saw the importance, a definite need and potential for a more formalized group to be established that focussed on robust scientific research (as opposed to a network of interested parties). For Williamson, such a group would continue his drive for what he called 'ethical policing', which dominated his work from his time as a young police officer in the Metropolitan Police anti-corruption branch in the early 1970s to his later role as a thinker, writer and reformer after his retirement from the service in 2001.

In his second career as a senior research fellow at the University of Portsmouth, Williamson brought his skills as an operational detective *par excellence* to the table and into various discussions. Building from the analysis of

---

[11] Note that this is *not* the same group as the International Investigative Interviewing Network ('IIIN') which is discussed in more detail later in this chapter.

[12] David Rose, "Obituary: Tom Williamson", in *The Guardian*, 14 March 2007 (available on its web site).

[13] Gavin E. Oxburgh, Thomas Williamson and James Ost, "Police Officers Use of Emotional Language During Child Sexual Abuse Investigations", in *Journal of Investigative Psychology and Offender Profiling*, 2006, vol. 3, no. 1, pp. 35–45.

[14] See the Preface to this book.

mishandled interrogations and miscarriages of justice contained in his 1990 Ph.D. from the University of Kent, Williamson was at the forefront of a radical shift in police interview techniques and training. As Commander of the Hendon Police Training College in the early 1990s, he fostered the development of extramural diplomas (at the University of Portsmouth) in policing that gave ordinary constables new opportunities for personal development.

With Oxburgh now a Ph.D. candidate at the University of Portsmouth and Myklebust likewise in Oslo, Myklebust and Oxburgh had the pleasure to meet and discuss various topics with Williamson on several occasions. During these conversations, he always underlined the importance of the old miscarriage cases being replaced by a neutral search for reliable evidence by all officers and investigators. He encouraged Myklebust and Oxburgh to think internationally and expand the contact-base for practitioners devoted to investigative interviewing. Unfortunately, Williamson had been diagnosed with mesothelioma, the cancer linked with exposure to asbestos, and passed away far too early at the age of 59 years on 25 February 2007.

In the name of Williamson, Myklebust and Oxburgh worked on an ambitious plan of forming an organization to try and avoid 'the dialogue of the deaf'[15] and bring together practitioners and academics to conduct joint scientific research together. With this background and both their Ph.D. projects taking shape, under the auspices of the European Forensic Psychology Interviewing Research Group, Oxburgh invited a small group of practitioners and academics to an initial seminar at Teesside University (where he was a Senior Lecturer in Forensic Psychology) on 2 and 3 April 2007. The event was attended by around 50 participants and the keynote talk entitled, *Investigative interviewing: The future is up to you*, was presented by Dr. Julie Cherryman, formerly University of Portsmouth. Following a tour of the facilities, the rest of that first day was devoted to invited talks from:

- Gavin Oxburgh, Teesside University: *Investigative interviews with suspected sex offenders: Current perspectives, future directions*;
- Dr. David J. La Rooy, Kingston University: *New developments in our understanding of repeated interviews with children*;
- Trond Myklebust, Norwegian Police University College ('NPUC'): *What you ask for is what you get: Structured analyses of investigative interviews*;
- Dave Walsh, University of Derby: *Interviewing suspects in UK non-police agencies: Current perspectives*;
- Heike Schmidt, University of Cape Town: *Facial recognition*;

---

[15] See the Preface to this book.

- Coral Dando, London South Bank University: *The cognitive interview: A modified procedure for frontline police investigators.*

It is important to highlight the experts listed above because they were the founding members of this unique group. The second day was devoted to attending participants discussing ideas, methodologies and other aspects of interviewing in a relaxed and informal setting. It was after this meeting at Teesside that the decision was made to change the name to the International Investigative Interviewing Research Group and sincere thanks go to Professor Elizabeth Barnes, previously Dean of the School of Sciences and Law, Teesside University (and formerly Vice Chancellor at the University of Staffordshire) and Hans Sverre Sjøvold, then the Director of the NPUC, who both clearly saw Myklebust and Oxburgh's vision where others could not.

In September 2007, Myklebust and Oxburgh met at NPUC, and in addition to holding presentations to the police bachelor students, were also asked by Sjøvold and Grete-Ba Flaaten to plan for a conference for the European Union Agency for Law Enforcement Training – Norway ultimately arranged this (together with their Swedish counterparts) in Stockholm in February 2008. At this conference, the key topics from central studies in the area of investigative interviewing were presented. The conference was a success, and Myklebust and Oxburgh were asked where and when the next iIIRG conference would be arranged as they had generated much interest from delegates.

21.1.4. Initial iIIRG Conferences

It is important to note that the iIIRG was initially developed and run through Teesside University, but it was decided that, for logistical reasons, the first formal Annual Conference would be held at the University of Derby in March 2008. This was organized by Professor Dave Walsh (now at De Montfort University) and around 80 participants attended from across the United Kingdom ('UK'), Australia, the Netherlands, Norway and Sweden. In April 2009, the second Annual Conference was held at Teesside University which saw over 130 international delegates attending. The conference was supported by key partners including Teesside University, NPUC, Centre for Forensic Linguistics at Aston University (UK), Indico Systems (Norway), Neal (UK), Wiley Publishers and Willan Publishing.

The second Annual Conference was important for the iIIRG's development as the decision was made that Myklebust and Oxburgh should be independent and not linked to any academic institution. Thus, realizing that funds would be needed to support the iIIRG going forward, an approach was made to Indico Systems to sponsor the iIIRG. Following detailed discussions, they were happy to oblige and continued to support the organization. In July 2010, to formalize the initiative, Myklebust and Oxburgh registered the iIIRG at the UK's Companies House as a *not-for-profit* organization with Myklebust and Oxburgh as the chairs and directors of the group. The word spread very quickly and soon the group expanded to over 600 members worldwide. It was clear to the directors and founding members that many academics and practitioners in the field of interviewing around the world saw the potential of the iIIRG to be the focal point, internationally, for practice and research around the area of investigative (or non-coercive) interviewing.

21.2. Research and Collaboration

Given the rapid expansion of members to over 600 worldwide and the iIIRG's new-found independence and expectations from potential members, Myklebust and Oxburgh realized that they had to organize the group more formally including through the formation of an Executive Committee[16] and a Scientific Committee.[17] Their objective was to improve non-coercive interviewing worldwide and ensure that all practices and improvements were underpinned by a robust evidence-base. To achieve this aim, their main objectives were to:

- support and facilitate a worldwide network of professionals in order to promote and enhance interview best practice worldwide in relation to victims, witnesses and suspects of crime;
- ensure that the iIIRG worked with all international bodies who were committed to improving investigative interviewing and ensuring all practices and improvements are underpinned by a robust evidence-base;
- hold annual conferences and specialist masterclasses to underpin the aims of the group; and
- maintain a publicly accessible web site, online journal and newsletter to disseminate relevant research and other material to the membership.

The areas of collaboration and research interest grew equally quickly and included such areas as:

- counter-terrorism;
- domestic abuse;
- investigative interviewing training programmes;
- detecting deception;
- enhanced cognitive interviewing and cognitive interviewing;
- establishing credibility within police suspect interviews;

---

[16] To oversee the day-to-day management of the group.
[17] To oversee all aspects of science and its application to interviewing relevant to the group and to review all abstract submissions for talks at the annual conferences.

- evidence-based approach to major investigations;
- eyewitness memory (recall, recognition and interviewing procedures);
- false confessions;
- false and recovered memory;
- forensic linguistics;
- fraud;
- non-recent sexual offences;
- individual differences;
- influence of life events on susceptibility to suggestion;
- interviewing vulnerable groups;
- investigative decision-making;
- interrogative suggestibility;
- linguistic markers of effectiveness in police suspect interviews;
- major enquiry interview co-ordination, policy and procedure;
- organized crime;
- repeated interviews with victims, witnesses and suspects;
- sexual offending;
- social cognition;
- structured interviews with registered sex offenders in order to identify risk; and
- training in advanced investigative interview techniques and their effectiveness.

Given the vast range of research interests, a decision was made to hold a two-day Masterclass at each annual conference immediately preceding the three-day conference.

21.3. The iIIRG Masterclasses and Annual Conferences

The details of each subsequent Masterclass (limited to a maximum of 30 participants), together with the venue of the annual conferences, are detailed in Table 1 below.

No.	Date	Location	Keynotes	Topic	Host
3	20–24 June 2010	Norwegian Police University College, Stavern (Norway)	Professor Laurence Alison (UK); Professor Ray Bull (UK); Professor Pär Anders Granhag (Sweden); Professor Günter Köhnken (Germany); Professor Martine Powell (Australia)	Investigative interviewing of child witnesses	Professor Michael Lamb, University of Cambridge (UK); Dr. Philip Esplin (United States ('US'))
4	30 May–3 June 2011	University of Abertay, Dundee (Scotland)	Professor Ronald Fisher (US); Professor Saul M. Kassin (US); Mr. John Halley (Scotland)	Cognitive interviewing	Professor Amina Memon, Royal Holloway, University of London (UK)
5	22–26 May 2012	Toronto (Canada)	Dr. James Ost (UK); Professor Rod Lindsay (Canada); Professor Deborah Poole (US)	Suspect interviewing utilizing the PEACE model	Dr. Brent Snook, Memorial University (Canada); Todd Barron, Royal Newfoundland Constabulary (Canada)
6	1–5 July 2013	Maastricht University (the Netherlands)	Professor Christian A. Meissner (US); Mr. Iyavar Chetty (South Africa); Dr. Coral Dando (UK); Professor Taru Spronken (the Netherlands)	Interviewing of sex offenders	Professor Mark Kebbell, Griffith University (Australia)

7	2–6 Jun 2014	University of Lausanne (Switzerland)	Professor Eric Shepherd (UK); Professor Pierre Margot (Switzerland); Professor Vicki Bruce (UK); Colonel (ret'd) Steve Kleinman (US); Michel St-Yves (Canada)	The investigation of historical cases of child abuse	Dr. James Ost, Department of Psychology, University of Portsmouth, UK; Detective Sergeant Gary Pankhurst, New Scotland Yard, UK
8	22–26 June 2015	Deakin Management Centre, Melbourne (Australia)	Professor Martine Powell (Australia); Professor Carolina Navarro (Chile); Mrs. María Paz Rutte and Mr. Alejandro Espinoza (Chile)	Interviewing in context: A case study from disclosure to trial	Professor Martine Powell (Australia); Mr. Mark Barnett (Australia); Dr. Kimberlee Burrows (Australia); Ms. Mairi Benson (Australia)
9	20–24 June 2016	London (UK)	Professor Mark Kebbell (Australia); Professor Maria Hartwig (Sweden/US); Michel De Smedt (International Criminal Court ('ICC'), The Hague)	The use of intermediaries in the Criminal Justice System (in England and Wales)	Judge Leslie Cuthbert (UK); Professor Penny Cooper, Advocates Gateway (UK)
10	3–7 July 2017	Monterey Bay, California (US)	Mr. Mark Fallon (US); Dr. Christopher Kelly (US); Detective Mark Severino (US)	Intelligence interviewing	Colonel (ret'd) Steve Kleinman (US); Mr. Mark Fallon (US)
11	2–6 July 2018	Universidade Catolica, Porto (Portugal)	Professor Irit Hershkowitz (Israel); Dr. David J. La Rooy (UK)	1. Child interviewing, 2. Judicial decision-making	Irit Herschkowitz (Israel); Mr. John Halley (Scotland); Dr. Carlos Piexeto (Portugal)

| 12 | 26–28 June 2019 | Norwegian Police University College, Stavern, Norway | Professor Juan E. Méndez, former UN Special Rapporteur on Torture (2010–2016); Professor Lorraine Hope (UK); Professor Laurence Alison (UK) | Intelligence debriefing: Co-operation, memory and elicitation techniques | Professor Lorraine Hope (UK); Mr. Wayne Thomas (UK) |

Table 1: Details of masterclasses and conferences from 2010 to 2019.

21.3.1. The iIIRG Awards

The iIIRG prides itself in supporting and facilitating a worldwide network of professionals to promote and enhance interview best-practice in any area of work. Indeed, Myklebust and Oxburgh have continued to work with all international bodies who are committed to improving non-coercive interviewing and ensuring all practices and improvements are underpinned by a robust evidence-base. To this end, in 2009, it was decided that four different awards should be introduced and awarded at each annual conference thereafter: (i) Senior Academic Award; (ii) Senior Practitioner Award; (iii) Junior Academic Award; and (iv) Junior Practitioner Award.

In 2009, Professor Ray Bull (UK) was presented with the first Senior Academic Award and Mr. Gary Shaw MBE (UK) was presented with the first Practitioner Award. Dr. Coral Dando (UK), Lancaster University (now Professor of Psychology at Westminster) was presented with the Junior Academic Award for her work on the further development of the cognitive interview with the use of sketch plans, with Inspector Marlene Prenzler (Australia) receiving the Junior Practitioner Award for her tireless work on paving the way for Queensland (and other forces within Australia) to adopt the PEACE model of interviewing more widely across Australia.

The recipient for the Senior Academic Award in 2010 was presented to Professor Günter Köhnken, University of Kiel, for his significant lifetime contribution to the field of investigative interviewing. The Senior Practitioner Award went to ex-Detective Superintendent Andy Griffiths (UK) for his contribution to the development of national policy and training in England and Wales on investigative interviewing. The recipient of the Junior Academic Award 2010 was Dr. Lindsay C. Malloy for her work on children's and adolescents' disclosure of negative or traumatic experiences, investigative interviewing and interrogation techniques and implications of research findings for the legal system.

In 2011, the iIIRG Executive Committee decided to adapt the process and introduced the following three Awards, replacing the previous ones:

(i) *Academic Excellence Award*: reserved for an individual from an academic background who has displayed academic 'excellence' in their specialist field;

(ii) *Practitioner Excellence Award*: reserved for an individual from any practitioner background who has displayed 'excellence' in their specialist field; and

(iii) *Lifetime Achievement Award*: reserved for an individual who has made a *significant* contribution to interviewing either nationally or internationally. The award is given to a person who, during his or her career, is distinguished in an exceptional way through work, practice or teaching, which complies with the mission pursued by the iIIRG and in respect of fundamental human rights.

The 2011 Academic Excellence Award was presented to Dr. Fiona Gabbert, University of Abertay, Dundee (later Professor of Psychology at Goldsmiths College, University of London) for her work and development of the self-administered interview.[18] The Practitioner Excellence Award was presented to Ole Thomas Bjerknes of the Norwegian Police who had worked on numerous high-profile investigations including air crashes, health services and sexual abuse. He has edited books on investigative interviewing in 2003, 2005 and 2009, the latter being on tactical investigations, used by all police officers at the NPUC. The Lifetime Achievement Award was presented to two distinguished iIIRG members for their outstanding achievements in psychology: (i) Distinguished Professor Saul M. Kassin, John Jay College, for his continuing work on false confessions and the many cases he has worked on with the Innocence Project; and (ii) Professor Ronald P. Fisher[19] for his continued work on human memory and why it is sometimes inconsistent, together with examining the implications for impeaching witnesses.

In 2012, the Academic Excellence Award was presented to Dr. Julia Korkman (Finland) whose dedication to training and educating police officers, prosecutors, judges and healthcare professionals has profoundly changed the way forensic interviews are conducted in her country today and was one of the driving forces in introducing, developing and executing the first and only evidence-based and practically-oriented training programmes for forensic child interviewers in her country. The Practitioner Excellence Award was presented to three practitioner members from Greater Manchester police: (i) Detective Sergeant

---

[18] See the *Self-Administered Interview* web site.
[19] See also Chapter 16 of this book.

(ret'd) Mick Confrey; (ii) Mr. Steve Retford (now retired); and (iii) Mr. Ian Hynes (now retired), who were all Interview Advisors within their force. Between them, they have assisted a great deal of academic researchers from across the world in developing research protocols throughout the spectrum of investigative interviewing. The year 2012 was very important for another reason. Professor Ray Bull retired from the University of Leicester and became an Emeritus Professor. To mark that occasion, Oxburgh was asked to provide a presentation at Ray's retirement lecture where he was awarded with the honorary lifetime membership of the iIIRG. This was the first time such an award had been made and no others have been made since.

Following a strategic merger with the IIIN outlined earlier in the chapter, it was agreed that the iIIRG would adopt the IIIN's Tom Williamson Award which replaced the iIIRG's Lifetime Achievement Award. Thus, in 2013, the first-ever iIIRG Tom Williamson Award was presented to Professor Michael Lamb for his outstanding and continued work on interviewing children. Myklebust and Oxburgh would like to thank the IIIN for all its hard work and endeavours over the previous years to the cause of ethical interviewing worldwide, especially to its chairperson, Michel St. Yves, Psychologue Judiciaire, École Nationale de police du Québec, who has written various articles and co-edited numerous books on interviewing. The Academic Excellence Award in 2013 was presented to Professor Christian A. Meissner for his continued work on non-coercive interviewing and interrogations and the Practitioner Excellence Award was presented to Colonel (ret'd) Steven M. Kleinman for his outstanding work on intelligence interviewing.

In 2014, the iIIRG Tom Williamson Award was presented to Professor Peter van Koppen, Maastricht University, for his lifetime achievement in the field of legal psychology and for his outstanding and extensive record of publications since 1978. The Academic Excellence Award was presented to Dr. David J. La Rooy (New Zealand) for his work on child interviewing across the world and for many different organizations. Dr. La Rooy was also the founding editor of the original iIIRG Bulletin (before the journal). The 2014 Practitioner Excellence Award was presented to Dr. Nina Westera who although was an academic researcher, was a previous police officer in Australia. Nina Westera changed the interviewing of witnesses in New Zealand by developing and implementing an evidence-based approach to interviewing. Unfortunately, she passed away in May 2017 at the very young age of 42 years from a particularly aggressive form of ovarian cancer.[20]

---

[20] See "In Memory of Nina Westera", SARMAC News for Summer 2017 (available on the Society for Applied Research in Memory and Cognition's web site).

For 2015, the iIIRG Tom Williamson Award was awarded to Professor Martine Powell for her exceptional work, research and indefatigable promotion of best practice in investigative interviewing techniques. The Academic Excellence Award was presented to Emily Henderson (UK) for her outstanding legal work on cross-examination in court and the ways in which individuals are 'interviewed' in court settings. The Practitioner Excellence Award was presented to Cameron Gardner, Queensland Police Service ('QPS'), for being a tireless advocate for investigative interviewing to be a central component of detective training and for it to be of 'World Class' standard for QPS.

The iIIRG Tom Williamson Award was presented to Professor Aldert Vrij (UK) in 2016 for his continued and excellent work which refutes the widespread, erroneous belief that lies can effectively or reliably be detected from the non-verbal behaviours of an interviewee. Instead, he pioneered the innovative 'cognitive load' approach to deception detection which is now the basis for ethical information-gathering by police, military and intelligence agencies worldwide. The Academic Excellence Award was presented to Assistant Professor Chris Kelly, St. Joseph's University, for his outstanding work on changing the culture of interviewing and interrogation practices with suspected offenders within the US judicial system. The Practitioner Excellence Award for 2016 was presented to Mr. Alistair Graham, ICC, for his tireless work on leading the progression of foundation and advanced interview training within the then Investigation Division of the ICC.

In 2017, the iIIRG Tom Williamson Award was presented to Professor Gisli H. Gudjonsson, King's College London. He is viewed worldwide as having developed forensic psychology as a scientific discipline and his work, including his testimony in landmark cases in Britain and abroad, has significantly enhanced legal practice regarding the human rights of the accused, police training and confession evidence. He is internationally recognized for his pioneering research into the measurement and application of interrogative suggestibility, psychological vulnerabilities and false confessions. The Academic Excellence Award was presented to Professor Richard A. Leo who is renowned in multiple academic disciplines for his path-breaking conceptual and empirical research on the social psychology of police interrogation, the phenomena of false confessions and the causes and consequences of the wrongful conviction of the innocent in the American criminal justice system. The Practitioner Excellence Award was presented to Mr. Mark Fallon who is a tenacious advocate for lawful, effective and humane interrogation techniques. He has made numerous representations to representatives of the US government and presentations on Capitol Hill opposing torture. He consistently argues for the use of evidence-based research to inform and improve the practice of interrogation to better protect national security and public safety.

For 2018, the iIIRG Tom Williamson Award was presented to Dr. Philip Esplin who has conducted numerous national and international training seminars worldwide on proper interviewing and investigative techniques in child molestation cases. He has testified in over 500 court matters involving children and adolescents and has consulted or testified in a number of major sex abuse cases. The Academic Excellence Award was presented to Dr. Sonja Brubacher (Canada) for her work on conducting experimental research on topics relevant to the forensic interviewing of children. She has extensively examined issues around the use of practice interviews, retrieval of information for repeated events and how children can better remember specific experiences. The Practitioner Excellence Award was presented to Staff Sergeant Greg Yanicki, Royal Canadian Mounted Police, who has been central to the development and implementation of the 'phased interview' model.

The 2018 Conference also saw the resignation of Myklebust and Oxburgh. Having served tirelessly and voluntarily for over 11 years, they made a conscious decision to stand down as chairs and directors of the iIIRG to allow new ideas to flourish in the organization. Thus, at the 2019 Conference, they said farewell and handed over the reins to the new incumbents, voted in by the iIIRG membership.

At their farewell 2019 Conference, the iIIRG Tom Williamson Award was presented to Emeritus Professor Graham Davies who has been a stalwart of ethical interviewing practices spanning over four decades. He has published over 120 articles in peer-refereed academic journals and has written, and been involved in, many reports for major organizations including on the training needs of police officers involved in child abuse investigations (1998) and has served as an editor of the Achieving Best Evidence document in 2002. He was also the founding editor (in 1986) of the highly regarded and much-respected journal, *Applied Cognitive Psychology*. The Academic Excellence Award was presented to Professor Lorraine Hope, University of Portsmouth, who has introduced innovative and effective interview techniques to the field, inspired by practitioner need and informed by psychological science. Her research has made an enormous impact to the field of investigative interviewing. She was a member of the iIIRG Executive Committee for many years until 2022. The recipient of the Practitioner Excellence Award for 2019 was Judge Leslie Cuthbert for his outstanding work in helping legal professionals understand the effects of psychology on interviewing and the courtroom more deeply. He is currently engaged in a number of different roles in England including judicial work, sitting as a recorder in the Crown Court, tribunal judge of both the Mental Health Tribunal and Special Education Needs and Disability Tribunal, acting as one of the independent adjudicators for Companies House and being a legally qualified chair for the Police Misconduct Panel.

Myklebust and Oxburgh's farewell conference in 2019 also saw the introduction of the Exceptional Contribution Award to one of the conference delegates. This award was presented to Professor Juan E. Méndez (Argentina) in recognition of his lifelong contribution and achievements in ethical interviewing and procedural safeguards, for his work on international human rights and for being the co-chair of the Steering Committee that developed the Méndez Principles.[21]

21.4. Other Developments of the iIIRG Between 2007 and 2019

21.4.1. The iIIRG Bulletin and Journal

From the iIIRG's inception in 2007, its research and case study outlet for its membership was the iIIRG Bulletin. Given its success, it was decided by the Executive Committee to rename it to make it more focused on the group's main activities (for example, research and practice). As such, from April 2012, the Bulletin was rebranded as the iIIRG's official journal (hosted by EBSCO Industries) and subsequently renamed as *Investigative Interviewing: Research and Practice* ('II-RP'). Initially, the II-RP, was available online to members only, but since 2020, it is now available as an open-access journal. Given the multi-disciplinary nature of the iIIRG, the worldwide circulation and strong practitioner focus, a wide range of articles are considered for inclusion by members and non-members including individual research papers or practitioner case studies.

21.4.2. Specialist Training and Consultancy

From 2012 to 2019,[22] the iIIRG (through the Executive Committee) provided specialist training and consultancy services to various international organizations including the:

- South African Police Service (in collaboration with the Kids Internet Safety Alliance ('KINSA');
- South African Prosecution Services in collaboration with KINSA;
- ICC;
- United Nations High Commissioner for Refugees;
- United Nations Development Programme;
- World Bank; and the

---

[21] See Chapter 6 of this book.
[22] When the authors of this chapter stood down as chairs and directors.

- European Investment Bank.

Broadly speaking, such training programmes included an introduction to the PEACE model of interviewing (and other models of non-coercive interviewing) with foundation-level training for active investigators, followed by advanced-level training for those dealing with vulnerable victims and witnesses and reluctant witnesses.

21.4.3. Sponsors of the iIIRG

As outlined previously in this chapter, when the iIIRG became independent of the Teesside University, there was a need for financial help and Indico Systems were the first main sponsors for the iIIRG and they remain sponsors to this day.[23] In addition to Indico Systems, the iIIRG has had various main sponsors over the years[24] including: Forensic Interview Solutions (2013 to 2015); Interview Management Solutions (2014 to present day); and Intersol Global (2016 to 2019, and who also separately sponsored the annual conferences during this time). Without the help and financial assistance of the valued sponsors, the iIIRG could not have flourished in the way it has in order to become a truly international organization.

---

[23] In 2023, Indico Systems rebranded into 'Davidhorn'.
[24] Up to 2019 when the authors of this chapter stood down as chairs and directors.

22

From Research to Practice:
The High-Value Detainee Interrogation Group

Susan E. Brandon and Christian A. Meissner[*]

22.1. Interrogation in the United States: A Legacy of Coercion and Torture

Through the 1930s, interrogation practices in the United States ('US') involved overt elements of physical and psychological coercion (known as the 'third degree'). Such tactics included physical assault, incommunicado detention and other 'deniable' coercive methods that would leave little evidence of abuse (beatings with a rubber hose, standing for hours, *et cetera*).[1] Questions regarding the efficacy and unethical nature of such approaches were highlighted in volume 11 of the Wickersham Commission's 1931 publication, *Report on Lawlessness in Law Enforcement*.[2] With the brutality of such methods exposed to the American public, the use of third-degree tactics declined over the next two decades.

In its place, law enforcement was offered training on accusatorial interrogation tactics.[3] These approaches relied upon psychological pressure, manipulation and deception to secure confessions or admissions.[4] Such methods included prolonged *isolation* of the subject in a small, windowless room; *confrontation* of the subject with false evidence and accusations of guilt; *maximization* of the subject's perception of the consequences associated with the illegal act; and *minimization* of the subject's perceptions of their culpability using *themes* that

---

[*] **Susan E. Brandon**, Ph.D., provides interview and interrogation training to local and state law enforcement in New York and New Jersey. **Christian A. Meissner**, Ph.D., is Professor of Psychology at Iowa State University, Ames.
[1] Richard A. Leo, *False Confessions: Police Interrogation and American Justice*, Harvard University Press, 2009, pp. 195–236.
[2] National Commission on Law Observance and Law Enforcement, *Report on Lawlessness in Law Enforcement*, US Government Printing Office, Washington, D.C., 1931.
[3] Cf. Fred E. Inbau and John E. Reid, *Criminal Interrogation and Confession*, Williams & Wilkins, Baltimore, 1963; Worth R. Kidd, *Police Interrogation*, R.V. Basuino, New York, 1940.
[4] Saul M. Kassin *et al.*, "Police-Induced Confessions: Risk Factors and Recommendations", in *Law and Human Behavior*, 2010, vol. 34, no. 1, pp. 3–38; Christopher E. Kelly and Christian A. Meissner, "Interrogation and Investigative Interviewing in the United States: Research and Practice", in David Walsh, Gavin E. Oxburgh, Allison D. Redlich and Trond Myklebust (eds.), *International Developments and Practices in Investigative Interviewing and Interrogation*, vol. II, Routledge, Oxfordshire, 2015, pp. 11–25.

implicated leniency to absolve the subject of responsibility in exchange for a confession.

Cases involving false confessions elicited via the use of these accusatorial tactics began to emerge throughout the 1980s and 1990s.[5] During the same period, social science research demonstrated that accusatorial tactics play a causal role in producing such coerced confessions[6] and that some subjects (as a function of their age, cognitive ability or psychological state) may be especially vulnerable to the increased suggestibility that is associated with false confessions.[7]

Similar cases of wrongful conviction in the United Kingdom ('UK') (for example, the 'Birmingham Six' and 'Guildford Four' cases)[8] led to a series of reforms in the interrogation of criminal suspects, and ultimately to the adoption of the UK PEACE model of interviewing in 1992.[9] An information-gathering approach, exemplified by the PEACE model, has been shown to improve the diagnostic value of confessions when compared with accusatorial approaches.[10] Nevertheless, law enforcement practitioners within the US largely eschewed

---

[5]   See Steven A. Drizin and Richard A. Leo, "The Problem of False Confessions in the Post-DNA World", in *North Carolina Law Review*, 2004, vol. 82, pp. 891–1007; Barry Scheck, Peter Neufeld and Jim Dwyer, *Actual Innocence*, Doubleday, New York, 2000. To date, more than 25 per cent of 325 wrongful conviction cases documented by the Innocence Project have been shown to involve false confessions or admissions. See Innocence Project, "The Causes of Wrongful Conviction" (available on its web site).

[6]   Inbau and Reid, 1963, see *supra* note 3; Christian A. Meissner, Chistopher E. Kelly and Skye A. Woestehoff, "Improving the Effectiveness of Suspect Interrogations", in *Annual Review of Law and Social Sciences*, 2015, vol. 11, pp. 211–233.

[7]   Saul M. Kassin and Gisli H. Gudjonsson, "The Psychology of Confessions: A Review of the Literature and Issues", in *Psychological Science in the Public Interest*, 2004, vol. 5, no. 2, pp. 33–67; Henry Otgaar, Mark L. Howe and Lawrence Patihis, "What Science Tells Us About False and Repressed Memories", in *Memory*, 2022, vol. 30, no. 1, pp. 16–21.

[8]   The Guildford Four were four Irish citizens who had been arrested and charged with murder and other offenses arising out of the bombing of two Irish pubs in 1974. They were released 15 years later after concerns were uncovered about the methods used by the police to obtain their confessions. The Birmingham Six were six men arrested after two bombs went off in the center of Birmingham in 1974, killing 21 people and injuring 182. Following beatings, threats and sleep and food deprivation to elicit confessions, they were imprisoned until being released in 1991. Gisli H. Gudjonsson and James A.C. MacKeith, "The 'Guildford Four' and the 'Birmingham Six'", in Gisli H. Gudjonsson, *The Psychology of Interrogations and Confessions: A Handbook*, John Wiley & Sons, Chichester, 2002, pp. 445–457.

[9]   See Chapter 12 of this volume for more details; Ray Bull and Asbjørn Rachlew, "Investigative Interviewing: From England to Norway and Beyond", in Steven J. Barela, Mark Fallon, Gloria Gaggioli and Jens D. Ohlin (eds.), *Interrogation and Torture: Integrating Efficacy With Law and Morality*, Oxford University Press, 2020, pp. 171–196.

[10] Christian A. Meissner *et al.*, "Accusatorial and Information-Gathering Interrogation Methods and Their Effects on True and False Confessions: A Meta-Analytic Review", in *Journal of Experimental Criminology*, 2014, vol. 10, pp. 459–486.

similar changes to interrogation practices through the early 2000s, often rejecting the notion that such accusatorial tactics were problematic or produced wrongful convictions.[11]

Interrogation practice within the US military and intelligence communities has been similarly accusatory and guided by customary practices.[12] In general, there has been considerable overlap in interrogation practices and beliefs across the law enforcement, military and intelligence communities,[13] with an escalation of abusive tactics in the Bush Administration's 'enhanced interrogation programme',[14] where even worse coercion – physical as well as psychological – was used by interrogators at Central Intelligence Agency's ('CIA') black sites, prisons in Iraq and Afghanistan, and the US military detention facility at Guantánamo Bay, Cuba.[15] This occurred despite historical accounts describing the use and ineffectiveness of torture in previous engagements[16] and the then available social science that showed such techniques were likely to produce confabulations and coerced information that simply confirmed what was believed, not what was true.[17]

---

[11] Kassin *et al.*, 2010, see *supra* note 4.

[12] Susan E. Brandon, "Impacts of Psychological Science on National Security Agencies Post-9/11", in *American Psychologist*, 2011, vol. 66, pp. 495–506; Maria Hartwig, Christian A. Meissner and Matthew D. Semel, "Human Intelligence Interviewing and Interrogation: Assessing the Challenges of Developing an Ethical, Evidence-Based Approach", in Ray Bull (ed.), *Investigative Interviewing*, Springer, New York, 2014, pp. 209–228.

[13] Jacqueline R. Evans *et al.*, "Criminal Versus HUMINT Interrogations: The Importance of Psychological Science to Improving Interrogative Practice", in *Journal of Psychiatry & Law*, 2010, vol. 38, nos. 1–2, pp. 215–249; Allison D. Redlich, Christopher E. Kelly and Jeaneé C. Miller, "The Who, What, and Why of Human Intelligence Gathering: Self-Reported Measures of Interrogation Methods", in *Applied Cognitive Psychology*, 2014, vol. 28, no. 6, pp. 817–828; Melissa B. Russano, Fadia M. Narchet, Steven Kleinman and Christian A. Meissner, "Structured Interviews of Experienced HUMINT Interrogators", in *Applied Cognitive Psychology*, 2014, vol. 28, no. 6, pp. 847–859.

[14] Cathy Scott-Clark and Adrian Levy, *The Forever Prisoner: The Full and Searing Account of the CIA's Most Controversial Covert Program*, Atlantic Monthly Press, New York, 2022.

[15] US Senate and US Senate Armed Services Committee, "Inquiry Into the Treatment of Detainees in U.S. Custody", in *Report of the Committee on Armed Services, United States Senate*, 110th Congress, 2nd Session, vol. 20, US Government Printing Office, Washington, D.C., 2008.

[16] Alfred W. McCoy, *A Question of Torture: CIA Interrogation, From the Cold War to the War on Terror*, Metropolitan Books/Henry Holt and Company, New York, 2006; Michael Otterman, *American Torture: From the Cold War to Abu Ghraib and Beyond*, Melbourne University Publishing, 2007.

[17] Elizabeth F. Loftus, "Intelligence Gathering Post-9/11", in *American Psychologist*, 2011, vol. 66, no. 6, pp. 532–541; Aldert Vrij *et al.*, "Psychological Perspectives on Interrogation", in *Perspectives on Psychological Science*, 2017, vol. 12, no. 6, pp. 927–955.

22.2. Out of the Ashes: A Science-Based Approach to Interrogation Is Born

In September 2004, the US Intelligence Science Board convened a group of scholars and practitioners to evaluate the historical and empirical legacy of US interrogation practices.[18] Led by Robert Fein, the group published the *Educing Information* report in 2006,[19] offering a substantive critique of interrogation training and practice. Based on its review, the report concluded:

> Training manuals, materials, and anecdotes contain information about common and recommended practices and the behavioral assumptions on which they are based, but virtually none of those documents cites or relies upon any original research. It even appears that some of the conventional wisdom that has guided training and policy for half a century is at odds with existing scientific knowledge (p. 18).

Further, the report offered this recommendation:

> Experience and lessons learned offer a necessary, but insufficient, basis for determining the effectiveness of [interrogation] practices. A program of scientific research on [interrogation] practices is both necessary and highly feasible. [...] Such a research program should combine experimental research with a substantial effort to perform independent and objective analyses of specific interrogation results (p. 310).

Reflecting aspects of the *Educing Information* report, Barack Obama signed Executive Order ('EO') 13491, 'Ensuring Lawful Interrogations', on the seventh day of his first Presidential term.[20] The EO set up a "Special Interagency Task Force [...] on Interrogation and Transfer Policies (Special Task Force) to review interrogation and transfer policies", to be staffed by the Attorney General (Chair), the Directors of National Intelligence and the CIA, the Secretaries of Defense, State and Homeland Security, and the Chair of the Joint Chiefs of Staff. The mission of the Special Task Force on Interrogation ('Task Force') was:

---

[18] The Intelligence Science Board was chartered in August 2002 to advise the Office of the Director of National Intelligence ('DNI') and senior intelligence community leaders on emerging scientific and technical issues of special importance to the intelligence community. It was disbanded by the DNI in 2010 (Federation of American Scientists, "Intelligence Science Board" (available on its web site)).

[19] Robert A. Fein, Paul Lehner and Bryan Vossekuil (eds.), *Educing Information-Interrogation: Science and Art, Foundations for the Future*, National Defense Intelligence College, Center for Strategic Intelligence Research, 2006.

[20] US, Executive Order No. 13491: Ensuring Lawful Interrogations, 27 January 2009, 74 Fed. Reg. 16 (https://www.legal-tools.org/doc/5axj6m/).

to study and evaluate whether the interrogation practices and techniques in Army Field Manual (AFM) 2–22.3,[21] when employed by departments or agencies outside the military, provide an appropriate means of acquiring the intelligence necessary to protect the Nation, and, if warranted, to recommend any additional or different guidance for other departments or agencies [...].

EO 13491 also limited interrogation tactics used "in any armed conflict" to those described by the 2006 Army Field Manual ('AFM'),

individuals detained in any armed conflict [...] shall in all circumstances be treated humanely [...] [and] shall not be subjected to any interrogation technique or approach [...] that is not authorized by and listed in Army Field Manual (AFM) 2-22.3,

with an exception for "the Federal Bureau of Investigation, or other Federal law enforcement agencies", who were allowed "to use authorized, non-coercive techniques of interrogation that are designed to elicit voluntary statements and do not involve the use of force, threats, or promises".[22] This EO was intended, in part, to prohibit the use of abusive interrogation techniques by any US personnel in the CIA and the US Department of Defense ('DoD').

The Task Force issued its report within the year. Its conclusions regarding whether the interrogation techniques listed in the AFM 2-22.3 provide appropriate means is an exemplar of bureaucratic non-committal. It stated that "[n]o federal agency [...] believed that it was necessary or appropriate to national security to use any interrogation practice or technique not listed in the AFM or currently used by law enforcement".[23] This was followed by:

Although there may be some lawful and effective interrogation practices and techniques that are not listed in the Army Field Manual or currently used by law enforcement agencies, the Task Force did not consider whether it was appropriate or legal for any agency of the federal government to use any specific technique not contained in the Army Field Manual. [...] Experienced intelligence

---

[21] US Headquarters, Department of the Army, *Human Intelligence Collector Operations*, Field Manual No. 2-22.3, Washington, D.C., 6 September 2006, was published by the Department of the Army ((https://www.legal-tools.org/doc/wbfiw1/). It replaced US Headquarters, Department of the Army, *Intelligence Interrogations*, Field Manual No. 34-52, Washington, D.C., published in 1987 and reissued in 1992.

[22] The requirement that intelligence and military interrogation methods be limited to those of AFM 22.3 was made law with the US National Defense Authorization Act of 2016, 25 November 2015, Public Law 114-92, Section 1045 ('NDAA') (https://www.legal-tools.org/doc/or0k6w/).

[23] Special Task Force on Interrogations and Transfer Policies, US Department of Justice ('DoJ'), "Report of the Special Task Force on Interrogation and Transfer Policies", 24 August 2009, Press Release Number: 09-835, p. 2.

and law enforcement interrogators do not rely solely on particular interrogation techniques but instead develop lawful interrogation strategies based on extensive knowledge of the detainee and his organization, guile and deception, the use of incentives, and other factors. [...] Additional research is needed on the science of interrogation and the potential to develop new and more effective interrogation practices [...].[24]

The Task Force went further than to comment on the 'appropriateness' of the AFM interrogation techniques. It recommended: (i) the creation of the High-Value Detainee Interrogation Group ('HIG') that would collect intelligence to protect national security; (ii) in such a manner that, where possible, the information so collected could be used in a criminal prosecution. In addition; (iii) the HIG should develop, identify and disseminate "a set of best practices for interrogation"; while also (iv) "study[ing] the effectiveness and propriety of existing practices, techniques and strategies" as well as "try[ing] to develop new ones that meet the requirements of domestic law and the United States obligations under international law".[25]

The HIG was chartered in April 2010.[26] It was to be administered by the Federal Bureau of Investigation ('FBI') and staffed with personnel detailed from law enforcement (including special agents from the FBI and the US Department of Homeland Security), the CIA and DoD. Legal advice was provided by an attorney permanently detailed from the DoJ. Policy guidance and oversight were co-ordinated by the National Security Council.[27] There were two primary tasks: (i) to deploy "mobile teams of experienced interrogators, analysts, subject matter experts, and linguists to conduct interrogations of high-value terrorists if the United States obtains the ability to interrogate them" (the HIG had neither capture nor detention authorization or capability); and (ii) to "develop a set of best practices and disseminate those for training purposes among agencies that conduct interrogations" and establish a "scientific research program [...] to study the comparative effectiveness of interrogation approaches and techniques, with the goal of identifying the existing techniques that are most effective and developing new lawful techniques to improve intelligence interrogations".[28]

---

[24] US Special Task Force on Interrogations and Transfer Policies*Ibid.*, pp. 2–3.

[25] *Ibid.*, p. 3.

[26] US DoD, "DoD Directive No. 3115.13: DoD Support to the High-Value Detainee Interrogation Group (HIG)", 26 August 2020.

[27] US DoJ, Office of Public Affairs, "Special Task Force on Interrogations and Transfer Policies Issues Its Recommendations to the President", 24 August 2009 (available on the DoJ's web site).

[28] *Ibid.*

22.3. The HIG Research Program[29]

The HIG Research Program released its first request for research proposals (Broad Agency Announcement ('BAA')) in early 2010 with the intent to fund such proposals within the same fiscal year.[30] The FBI procurement process, an infrastructure more tuned to technical acquisitions than the funding of basic or applied behavioural science, was modified by HIG personnel to ensure that: (i) proposers did not have to be US citizens; (ii) the research would be unclassified; and (iii) the products of the research could be published in publicly available scientific journals.[31] In addition, all HIG-supported contracts that included participation by human subjects had to be reviewed and approved by the contractor's own human subjects Institutional Review Board ('IRB') as well as by the FBI's IRB. These steps were deemed necessary to attract proposals from world-renowned scientists with deep, previously established knowledge of topics relevant to interrogations. Susan E. Brandon, who had managed research contracts focused on interrogation methods at DoD since 2007, was detailed to serve as the HIG Research Program manager in March 2010[32] and Christian Meissner was awarded the first HIG contract in September 2010. The HIG has regularly issued BAAs since 2010 and maintained an active portfolio of sponsored research, though budget constraints have sometimes limited what new work could be supported.

Both EO 13491 and the Task Force report mandated research on "the comparative effectiveness of interrogation approaches and techniques, with the goal of identifying the existing techniques that are most effective". What might

---

[29] HIG operations, budget and policy are classified. Details regarding those are therefore outside the scope of this chapter, which is limited to description of the HIG research and interrogation training programs, the activities and products of which were unclassified.

[30] A 2010 query by the HIG to other US government agencies (both research-oriented agencies such as the National Science Foundation and intelligence agencies such as the CIA) found that no other agency at the time reported conducting or supporting research on interrogations. Whether this was in fact true or whether the topic 'interrogations' had become so toxic that it was systematically avoided and/or whether related research was labeled differently (for example, as 'research on debriefing methods') was difficult to know.

[31] There was some concern that making the research unclassified and publicly available would 'provide aid to the enemy,' who could better resist in an interrogation. The counter-argument was made that this would require their: (i) access to scientific journals; (ii) expertise to understand the technical reports; (iii) substantive training on the methods; and (iv) resistance to the fundamental processes of human memory, motivation, persuasion and social dynamics inherent to the science-based methods. In addition, the AFM 2-22.3 was publicly available by law (and remains so).

[32] Susan E. Brandon served in that role until December 2017. She was joined by Sujeeta Bhatt, Ph.D., from June 2010 to December 2014. The number of research personnel within the HIG varied between one and three between 2010 and 2019.

such a "comparative effectiveness" look like, and what is necessary to identify the "most effective" existing techniques? The gold standard in the US for the evaluation of evidence is randomized, double-blind placebo control studies. Such studies, for example, are required for approval of a new drug by the Federal Drug Administration and experimental protocols have become important for evaluating policies and practices by the Department of Education and the National Institute of Justice. While it might be possible to randomly assign an interrogatee to an interrogator, with some interrogators using Method X and others using Method Y, a double-blind control (where the administrator of the treatment, here, the interrogator, is blind as to what methods are being used) is impossible. Clinical psychologists confronted a similar problem (that is, the clinician had to know what therapeutic method they were using) and decided that an acceptable standard is good experimental designs and comparison of the intervention with another treatment.[33] Non-experimental methodologies, which provide less definitive outcomes, could include surveys, in which interrogators are asked what success they have had with Method X or Method Y, and observational studies, in which assessments are made of Method X versus Method Y by independent observers. Surveys suffer from the limitations of humans to accurately report their own behaviour,[34] and observational studies suffer from the confounds of situational variables (for example, the characteristics of the interrogatee and interrogator, the timing and context of the interrogation) with the interrogation method.[35]

In conceptualizing its research program, the HIG categorized interrogation approaches and techniques used in the US within two broad categories: those of military and intelligence agencies (whose personnel are limited to those of the 2006 AFM) and those of federal, state and local law enforcement. The HIG mandate was to evaluate the AFM – and, as noted, there had never been any empirical studies of the effectiveness of AFM interrogation approaches and techniques. There was (and is), however, a rich scientific literature on interrogation techniques used by law enforcement. As a result, the immediate concern of the research program was the relevance of this literature to the HIG as an intelligence-collection entity. And important to that early effort were surveys and observations within military and intelligence contexts that indicated

---

[33] Task Force on Promotion and Dissemination of Psychological Procedures, "Training in and Dissemination of Empirically Validated Treatments: Report and Recommendations", in *The Clinical Psychologist*, 1995, vol. 48, pp. 3–23.

[34] Elizabeth F. Loftus and Geoffrey R. Loftus, "On the Permanence of Stored Information in the Human Brain", in *The American Psychologist*, 1980, vol. 35, no. 5, pp. 409–420.

[35] Thomas D. Cook, Donald T. Campbell and William R. Shadish Jr., *Experimental and Quasi-Experimental Designs for Generalized Causal Inference*, Houghton Mifflin, Boston, 2002.

considerable similarity of interrogation approaches and techniques within the two domains – despite their different histories and policies.

22.4. Law Enforcement Interrogations

Interrogation approaches and techniques used by federal, state, local or tribal law enforcement agencies are rooted in customary practices developed in the field by investigative professionals, and future generations of investigators are trained in them either formally or informally.[36] State and local criminal investigators usually receive on-the-job training or some formal training (for example, provided by state-level Peace Officer Standard Training ('POST')). Many have been trained by private firms such as John E. Reid & Associates or Wicklander-Zulawski & Associates. There are also many books – written by former law enforcement or intelligence personnel – relating their experiences and perceptions of the effectiveness of certain interrogation practices and cues to deception. Federal investigators are typically trained at the Federal Law Enforcement Training Center ('FLETC') in Glynco, Georgia, or by their own agencies such as the FBI.

What is known about interrogations conducted by US law enforcement agencies comes almost exclusively from the research community. These data include not only descriptions of these traditional methods but analyses of their effectiveness. As alluded to previously, accusatorial interrogation methods have pervaded US interrogation practices since the 1960s. Such tactics have been widely adopted at the federal, state and local levels, and are commonly endorsed in surveys of interrogation professionals.[37] Research has shown that while accusatorial tactics can increase the likelihood of confessions, such practices also increase the likelihood that innocent individuals will falsely confess.[38]

In this context, the HIG Research Program sought to identify effective interrogation practices that might replace the prevailing accusatorial model.[39] The Program accomplished this by evaluating current practice via observations

---

[36] Christian A. Meissner *et al.*, "Investigative Interviewing: A Review of the Literature and a Model of Science-Based Practice", in David Dematteo and Kyle Scheer (eds.), *Oxford Handbook of Psychology and Law*, Oxford University Press, 2022.

[37] Saul M. Kassin, "Police Interviewing and Interrogation: A Self-Report Survey of Police Practices and Beliefs", in *Law and Human Behavior*, 2007, vol. 31, no. 4, pp. 381–400.

[38] Kassin *et al.*, 2010, see *supra* note 4; Meissner *et al.*, 2014, see *supra* note 10.

[39] Christian A. Meissner, Frances Surmon-Böhr, Simon Oleszkiewicz and Laurence J. Alison, "Developing an Evidence-Based Perspective on Interrogation: A Review of the US Government's High-Value Detainee Interrogation Group Research Program", in *Psychology, Public Policy, and Law*, 2017, vol. 23, no. 4, pp. 438–457.

of interrogations conducted by law enforcement personnel,[40] as well as surveys and semi-structured interviews of interrogation professionals.[41]

---

[40] Laurence J. Alison *et al.*, "Why Tough Tactics Fail and Rapport Gets Results: Observing Rapport-Based Interpersonal Techniques (ORBIT) to Generate Useful Information From Terrorists", in *Psychology, Public Policy, and Law*, 2013, vol. 19, pp. 411–431; Laurence J. Alison *et al.*, "The Efficacy of Rapport-Based Techniques for Minimizing Counter-Interrogation Tactics Amongst a Field Sample of Terrorists", in *Psychology, Public Policy, and Law*, 2014, vol. 20, pp. 421–430; Christopher E. Kelly and Esteban J. Valencia, "You Ask and Do Not Receive, Because You Ask Wrongly", in *International Journal of Police Science & Management*, 2021, vol. 23, no. 1, pp. 42–54; Christopher E. Kelly, Allison D. Redlich and Jeaneé C. Miller, "Examining the Meso-Level Domains of the Interrogation Taxonomy", in *Psychology, Public Policy, and Law*, 2015, vol. 21, no. 2, pp. 179–191; Christopher E. Kelly, Melissa B. Russano, Jeaneé C. Miller and Allison D. Redlich, "On the Road (To Admission): Engaging Suspects With Minimization", in *Psychology, Public Policy, and Law*, 2019, vol. 25, no. 3, pp. 166–180; Christopher E. Kelly, Evan Dawson and Maria Hartwig, "Context Manipulation in Police Interviews: A Field Experiment", in *Journal of Experimental Criminology*, 2021, vol. 17, no. 1, pp. 67–86; Nathan Meehan, Christopher E. Kelly and Michael McClary, "The Snitching Hour: Investigations and Interviewing in a County Jail", in *Security Journal*, 2021, vol. 32, no. 3, pp. 198–217.

[41] Jane Goodman-Delahunty and Loene M. Howes, "High-Stakes Interviews and Rapport Development: Practitioners' Perceptions of Interpreter Impact", in *Policing and Society*, 2019, vol. 29, no. 1, pp. 100–117; Jane Goodman-Delahunty, Natalie Martschuk and Mandeep K. Dhami, "Interviewing High Value Detainees: Securing Cooperation and Disclosures", in *Applied Cognitive Psychology*, 2014, vol. 28, no. 6, pp. 883–897; Kelly and Meissner, 2014, see *supra* note 4; Jeaneé C. Miller, Allison D. Redlich and Christopher E. Kelly, "Accusatorial and Information-Gathering Interview and Interrogation Methods: A Multi-Country Comparison", in *Psychology, Crime & Law*, 2018, vol. 24, no. 9, pp. 935–956; Fadia M. Narchet, Melissa B. Russano, Steven M. Kleinman and Christian A. Meissner, "A (Nearly) 360 Perspective of the Interrogation Process: Communicating With High-Value Targets", in Gavin E. Oxburgh, Trond Myklebust, Tim Grant and Rebecca Milne (eds.), *Communication in Investigative and Legal Contexts: Integrated Approaches from Forensic Psychology, Linguistics, and Law Enforcement*, John Wiley & Sons, New York, 2016, pp. 159–178; Redlich, Kelly and Miller, 2014, see *supra* note 13; Russano, Narchet, Kleinman and Meissner, 2014, see *supra* note 13.

The Program also supported both laboratory experiments[42] and field studies,[43] as well as systematic reviews and meta-analyses of research literature.[44]

---

[42] Laure Brimbal, Rachel E. Dianiska, Jessica K. Swanner and Christian A. Meissner, "Enhancing Cooperation and Disclosure by Manipulating Affiliation and Developing Rapport in Investigative Interviews", in *Psychology, Public Policy, and Law*, 2019, vol. 25, no. 2, pp. 107–115; Evan Dawson, Maria Hartwig and Laure Brimbal "Interviewing to Elicit Information: Using Priming to Promote Disclosure", in *Law and Human Behavior*, 2015, vol. 39, no. 5, pp. 443–450; Rachel E. Dianiska, Jessica K. Swanner, Laure Brimbal and Christian A. Meissner, "Conceptual Priming and Context Reinstatement: A Test of Direct and Indirect Interview Techniques", in *Law and Human Behavior*, 2019, vol. 43, no. 2, pp. 131–143; *id.*, "Using Disclosure, Common Ground, and Verification to Build Rapport and Elicit Information", in *Psychology, Public Policy, and Law*, 2021, vol. 27, no. 3, pp. 341–353; Sarah Ewens *et al.*, "The Effect of Interpreters on Eliciting Information, Cues to Deceit and Rapport", in *Legal and Criminological Psychology*, 2016, vol. 21, no. 2, pp. 286–304; Pär A. Granhag, Sebastian C. Montecinos and Simon Oleszkiewicz, "Eliciting Intelligence From Sources: The First Scientific Test of the Scharff Technique", in *Legal and Criminological Psychology*, 2015, vol. 20, no. 1, pp. 96–113; Pär A. Granhag *et al.*, "Discriminating Between Statements of True and False Intent: The Impact of Repeated Interviews and Strategic Questioning", in *Journal of Applied Security Research*, 2016, vol. 11, no. 1, pp. 1–17; Hwang Hyisuing and David Matsumoto, "The Effects of Liking on Informational Elements in Investigative Interviews", in *Journal of Investigative Psychology and Offender Profiling*, 2020, vol. 17, no. 3, pp. 280–295; Timothy J. Luke, Evan Dawson, Maria Hartwig and Pär A. Granhag, "How Awareness of Possible Evidence Induces Forthcoming Counter-Interrogation Strategies", in *Applied Cognitive Psychology*, 2014, vol. 28, no. 6, pp. 876–882; David Matsumoto and Hwang Hyisuing, "Social Influence in Investigative Interviews: The Effects of Reciprocity", in *Applied Cognitive Psychology*, 2018, vol. 32, no. 2, pp. 163–170; *id.*, "An Initial Investigation Into the Nature and Function of Rapport in Investigative Interviews", in *Applied Cognitive Psychology*, 2021, vol. 35, no. 4, pp. 988–998; Simon Oleszkiewicz, Pär A. Granhag and Steven M. Kleinman, "On Eliciting Intelligence From Human Sources: Contextualizing the Scharff-Technique", in *Applied Cognitive Psychology*, 2014, vol. 28, no. 6, pp. 898–907; *id.*, "Gathering Human Intelligence via Repeated Interviewing: Further Empirical Tests of the Scharff Technique", in *Psychology, Crime & Law*, 2017, vol. 23, no. 7, pp. 666–681; Aldert Vrij *et al.*, "Detection of Concealment in an Information-Gathering Interview", in *Applied Cognitive Psychology*, 2014, vol. 28, no. 6, pp. 860–866; Aldert Vrij *et al.*, "'Please Tell Me All You Remember': A Comparison Between British and Arab Interviewees' Free Narrative Performance and Its Implications for Lie Detection", in *Psychiatry, Psychology and Law*, 2021, vol. 28, no. 4, pp. 546–559.

[43] Kelly, Dawson and Hartwig, 2021, see *supra* note 40; Drew A. Leins, Laura A. Zimmerman and Emily N. Polander, "Observers' Real-Time Sensitivity to Deception in Naturalistic Interviews", in *Journal of Police and Criminal Psychology*, 2017, vol. 32, no. 4, pp. 319–330; Annelies Vredeveldt and James D. Sauer, "Effects of Eye-Closure on Confidence-Accuracy Relations in Eyewitness Testimony", in *Journal of Applied Research in Memory and Cognition*, 2015, vol. 4, no. 1, pp. 51–58.

[44] Timothy J. Luke, "A Meta-Analytic Review of Experimental Tests of the Interrogation Technique of Hanns Joachim Scharff", in *Applied Cognitive Psychology*, 2021, vol. 35, no. 2, pp. 360–373; Erik Mac Giolla and Timothy J. Luke, "Does the Cognitive Approach to Lie Detection Improve the Accuracy of Human Observers?", in *Applied Cognitive Psychology*, 2021,

---

Training studies have also assessed the effectiveness of various interrogation strategies and tactics when compared with customary practices, including developing rapport,[45] eliciting information from memory using the Cognitive Interview ('CI'),[46] leveraging information or evidence to motivate engagement[47] and assessing deception using cognitive cues and strategic questioning approaches.[48] The primary findings are likely best summarized by considering these key interview processes: developing rapport and co-operation, eliciting information from memory, presenting evidence or information and detecting deception.[49]

22.4.1. Developing Rapport and Co-operation

Research funded by the HIG has evaluated the efficacy and effectiveness of rapport-based tactics for developing co-operation and eliciting information,

---

vol. 35, no. 2, pp. 385–392; Simon Oleszkiewicz and Steven J. Watson, "A Meta-Analytic Review of the Timing for Disclosing Evidence When Interviewing Suspects", in *Applied Cognitive Psychology*, 2021, vol. 35, no. 2, pp. 342–359; Vrij *et al.*, 2017, pp. 927–955, see *supra* note 17; Christian A. Meissner, "What Works? Systematic Reviews and Meta-Analyses of the Investigative Interviewing Research Literature", in *Applied Cognitive Psychology*, 2021, vol. 35, no. 2, pp. 322–328.

[45] Laure Brimbal *et al.*, "Evaluating the Benefits of a Rapport-Based Approach to Investigative Interviews: A Training Study With Law Enforcement Investigators", in *Law and Human Behavior*, 2021, vol. 45, no. 1, pp. 55–67; Laurence J. Alison, Emily Alison, Neil Shortland and Frances Surmon-Böhr, *ORBIT: The Science of Rapport-Based Interviewing for Law Enforcement, Security, and Military*, Oxford University Press, 2020.

[46] Peter F. Molinaro, Ronald Fisher, Alexandra E. Mosser and Geri E. Satin, "Train-the-trainer: Methodology to Learn the Cognitive Interview", in *Journal of Investigative Psychology and Offender Profiling*, 2019, vol. 16, no. 1, pp. 32–43; Jillian R. Rivard, Ronald P. Fisher, Belinda Robertson and Dana Hirn Mueller, "Testing the Cognitive Interview With Professional Interviewers: Enhancing Recall of Specific Details of Recurring Events", in *Applied Cognitive Psychology*, 2014, vol. 28, no. 6, pp. 917–925.

[47] Pär A. Granhag, Simon Oleszkiewicz, Marthe Lefsaker Sakrisvold and Steven M. Kleinman, "The Scharff Technique: Training Military Intelligence Officers to Elicit Information From Small Cells of Sources", in *Psychology, Crime & Law*, 2020, vol. 26, no. 5, pp. 438–460; Timothy J. Luke *et al.*, "Training in the Strategic Use of Evidence Technique: Improving Deception Detection Accuracy of American Law Enforcement Officers", in *Journal of Police and Criminal Psychology*, 2016, vol. 31, no. 4, pp. 270–278; Simon Oleszkiewicz, Pär A. Granhag and Steven M. Kleinman, "Eliciting Information From Human Sources: Training Handlers in the Scharff Technique", in *Legal and Criminological Psychology*, 2017, vol. 22, no. 2, pp. 400–419.

[48] Aldert Vrij *et al.*, "Translating Theory Into Practice: Evaluating a Cognitive Lie Detection Training Workshop", in *Journal of Applied Research in Memory and Cognition*, 2015, vol. 4, no. 2, pp. 110–120; Tuule Sooniste, Pär A. Granhag and Leif A. Strömwall, "Training Police Investigators to Interview to Detect False Intentions", in *Journal of Police and Criminal Psychology*, 2017, vol. 32, no. 2, pp. 152–162.

[49] Meissner, Surmon-Böhr, Oleszkiewicz and Alison, 2017, see *supra* note 39.

---

including scales and indicators from which to assess the development of rapport[50] and examining rapport when multiple interviewers are present[51] and in interpreter-mediated interviews.[52] Studies have highlighted the important role of certain influence strategies such as liking and reciprocity,[53] and the value of self-disclosure and developing common ground for building relationships with the interview subject.[54] Studies have also highlighted the value of developing trust and distinguishing it from rapport-based strategies.[55] HIG research has uncovered the mechanisms by which rapport tactics facilitate information elicitation: namely, rapport approaches lead an interview subject to a fundamental decision to co-operate with (or resist) the interviewer, and it is this decision to co-operate that mediates the exchange of information.[56]

HIG-sponsored studies have also evaluated the value of motivational interviewing skills[57] for application in interview and interrogation contexts.[58] Research on terrorist suspects has shown that when interviewers used rapport-based Motivational Interviewing skills (including autonomy, adaptation,

---

[50] Misty C. Duke *et al.*, "Development of the Rapport Scales for Investigative Interviews and Interrogations (RS3i), Interviewee Version", in *Psychology, Public Policy, and Law*, 2018, vol. 24, no. 1, p. 64; James Driskell, "Investigative Interviewing: A Team-Level Approach", in *Electronic Theses and Dissertations, 2004–2019*, 2013, pp. 1–165.

[51] Tripp Driskell, Elizabeth L. Blickensderfer and Eduardo Salas, "Is Three a Crowd? Examining Rapport in Investigative Interviews", in *Group Dynamics: Theory, Research, and Practice*, 2013, vol. 13, no. 1, p. 1.

[52] Kate A. Houston, Melissa B. Russano and Elijah P. Ricks, "'Any Friend of Yours is a Friend of Mine': Investigating the Utilization of an Interpreter in an Investigative Interview", in *Psychology, Crime & Law*, 2017, vol. 23, no. 5, pp. 413–426; Mandeep K. Dhami, Jane Goodman-Delahunty and Saoirse Desai, "Development of an Information Sheet Providing Rapport Advice for Interpreters in Police Interviews", in *Police Practice and Research*, 2017, vol. 18, no. 3, pp. 291–305; Ewens *et al.*, 2016, pp. 286–304, see *supra* note 42; Sarah Ewens *et al.*, "Using the Model Statement to Elicit Information and Cues to Deceit From Native Speakers, Non-Native Speakers and Those Talking Through an Interpreter", in *Applied Cognitive Psychology*, 2016, vol. 30, no. 6, pp. 854–862.

[53] Hwang and Matsumoto, 2020, see *supra* note 42; Matsumoto and Hwang, 2018, see *supra* note 42; Matsumoto and Hwang, 2021, pp. 988–998, see *supra* note 42.

[54] Brimbal, Dianiska, Swanner and Meissner, 2019, see *supra* note 42; Dianiska, Swanner, Brimbal and Meissner, 2021, see *supra* note 42.

[55] Laure Brimbal, Steven M. Kleinman, Simon Oleszkiewicz and Christian A. Meissner, "Developing Rapport and Trust in the Interrogative Context: An Empirically Supported and Ethical Alternative to Customary Interrogation Practices", in Barela, Fallon, Gaggioli and Ohlin (eds.), 2019, pp. 141–196, see *supra* note 9.

[56] Brimbal, Dianiska, Swanner and Meissner, 2019, see *supra* note 42; Brimbal *et al.*, 2021, see *supra* note 45; Dianiska, Swanner, Brimbal and Meissner, 2021, see *supra* note 42.

[57] William R. Miller and Stephan Rollnick, *Motivational Interviewing: Helping People Change*, Guilford Press, New York, 2012.

[58] Alison, Alison, Shortland and Surmon-Böhr, 2020, see *supra* note 45.

empathy, evocation and acceptance), they achieved greater co-operation and engagement from subjects, including key investigative information.[59] Further, such rapport-based skills were also shown to reduce the likelihood of resistance and the use of counter-interrogation tactics by interview subjects.[60] Application of this rapport-based framework to victim interviews showed similar benefits to increasing information disclosures.[61]

22.4.2. Eliciting Information From Memory

Systematic research in the cognitive domain has documented the fragility of memory and the profound influence that interviewers can have on a subject's memory of an event.[62] As a result, best practices for interviewing adults and children have been assessed over the years.[63] Likely the most significant advance in improving the recall of interview subjects has been the CI, first developed by Fisher and Geiselman.[64] More than 30 years of research on the CI has demonstrated its profound benefits to increasing recall of event memory.[65]

HIG research has demonstrated that the CI can be easily integrated into an information-gathering interview context and used effectively with less co-operative subjects, leading to greater information gain when compared with accusatorial interrogation approaches.[66] Further, the CI was extended to include

---

[59] Alison *et al.* 2014, pp. 421–430, see *supra* note 40; Frences Surmon-Böhr, Laurence Alison, Paul Christiansen and Emily Alison, "The Right to Silence and the Permission to Talk: Motivational Interviewing and High-Value Detainees", in *American Psychologist*, 2020, vol. 75, no. 7, pp. 1011–1021.

[60] Alison *et al.*, 2013, see *supra* note 40.

[61] Sunghwan Kim, Laurence Alison and Paul Christiansen, "Observing Rapport-Based Interpersonal Techniques to Gather Information From Victims", in *Psychology, Public Policy, and Law*, 2020, vol. 26, no. 2, pp. 166–175.

[62] Charles J. Brainerd and Valerie F. Reyna (eds.), *The Science of False Memory*, Oxford University Press, 2005; Elizabeth F. Loftus, "Planting Misinformation in the Human Mind: A 30-Year Investigation of the Malleability of Memory", in *Learning & Memory*, 2005, vol. 12, no. 4, pp. 361–366; Eryn J. Newman and Maryanne Garry, "False Memory", in Timothy J. Perfect and D. Stephen Lindsay (eds.), *The SAGE Handbook of Applied Memory*, SAGE, Los Angeles, 2013, pp. 110–126.

[63] Martine B. Powell, Ronald P. Fisher and Rebecca Wright, "Investigative Interviewing", in Neil Brewer and Kipling D. Williams (eds.), *Psychology and Law: An Empirical Perspective*, Guilford Publications, New York, 2005, pp. 11–42.

[64] Ronald P. Fisher and R. Edward Geiselman, *Memory Enhancing Techniques for Investigative Interviewing: The Cognitive Interview*, Charles C Thomas Publisher, Springfield, 1992.

[65] Amina Memon, Christian A. Meissner and Joanne Fraser, "The Cognitive Interview: A Meta-Analytic Review and Study Space Analysis of the Past 25 Years", in *Psychology, Public Policy, and Law*, 2010, vol. 16, no. 4, pp. 340–372.

[66] Jacqueline R. Evans, Stephen Michael, Christian A. Meissner and Susan E. Brandon, "Validating a New Assessment Method for Deception Detection: Introducing a Psychologically

---

mnemonics that facilitate the retrieval of discrete events (to include people, conversations, actions and setting details).[67] The introduction of a model statement was shown to significantly increase the amount of detail provided by interview subjects[68] and the utility of eye-closure and context reinstatement instructions was shown to enhance recollection.[69] In an evaluation study, the CI was shown to elicit 80 per cent more event details when compared with a standard interview protocol trained at the US FLETC.[70]

22.4.3. Presenting Evidence or Information

One of the most challenging phases of an interrogation relates to an investigator's use of evidence or information to confront a subject and challenge any inconsistencies in their account. Accusatorial tactics generally involve an emotional confrontation of a suspect's claims of innocence and the presentation of evidence intended to overwhelm a suspect's perception of an interviewer's knowledge.[71] Such tactics also frequently involve the use of evidence bluffs or the presentation of false evidence, which have been shown to elicit false confessions by the innocent.[72] HIG-supported research has demonstrated that accusatorial presentations of evidence actually increase suspect resistance and reduce the likelihood of confession.[73]

In contrast, a strategic presentation of evidence that considers both the timing and order of evidence disclosure has been shown to reveal aspects of a suspect's account that may appear inconsistent with the available evidence and, in some cases, to facilitate co-operation and disclosure of new case-relevant

---

Based Credibility Assessment Tool", in *Journal of Applied Research in Memory and Cognition*, 2013, vol. 2, no. 1, pp. 33–41.

[67] Drew A. Leins *et al.*, "Interview Protocols to Facilitate Human Intelligence Sources' Recollections of Meetings", in *Applied Cognitive Psychology*, 2014, vol. 28, no. 6 , pp. 926–935.

[68] Ewens *et al.*, 2016, pp. 854–862, see *supra* note 52; Sharon Leal, Aldert Vrij, Haneen Deeb, and Louise Jupe, "Using the Model Statement to Elicit Verbal Differences Between Truth Tellers and Liars: The Benefit of Examining Core and Peripheral Details", in *Journal of Applied Research in Memory and Cognition*, 2018, vol. 7, no. 4, pp. 610–617.

[69] Dianiska, Swanner, Brimbal and Meissner, 2019, see *supra* note 42; Vredeveldt and Sauer, 2015, see *supra* note 43.

[70] Rivard, Fisher, Robertson and Hirn Meuller, 2014, see *supra* note 46.

[71] Christopher E. Kelly, Jeaneé C. Miller, Allison D. Redlich and Steven M. Kleinman, "A Taxonomy of Interrogation Methods", in *Psychology, Public Policy, and Law*, 2013, vol. 19, no. 2, pp. 165–178; Meissner, Kelly and Woestehoff, 2015, see *supra* note 6.

[72] Kassin *et al.*, 2010, see *supra* note 4.

[73] Kelly and Valencia, 2021, see *supra* note 40; Kelly, Redlich and Miller, 2015, see *supra* note 40; Christopher E. Kelly, Jeaneé C. Miller and Allison D. Redlich, "The Dynamic Nature of Interrogation", in *Law and Human Behavior*, 2016, vol. 40, no. 3, pp. 295–309.

information.[74] HIG research examined the strategies that suspects engage in when they become aware of an interviewer's knowledge of evidence[75] and showed that framing of the evidence from general to specific and using a late disclosure with an incremental presentation of evidence was most effective.[76]

22.4.4. Detecting Deception

HIG funding has also helped to facilitate an important paradigm shift in research on deception detection. Accusatorial practices have traditionally included an anxiety-based model of deception in which non-verbal cues to nervousness, anxiety and feelings of guilt were believed to be indicative of deceptive responses; however, research has generally found little support for such cues to deception.[77] An alternative 'cognitive' approach to deception has emerged over the past decade in which liars have been found to experience greater cognitive load (or effort) when attempting to create and maintain a lie while simultaneously suppressing the truth.[78] Research on cognitive credibility assessment has identified three important interviewing approaches that can facilitate the discrimination of lies and truths: (i) using interview techniques that impose cognitive load, particularly on lie-tellers, including reverse-order recall;[79] (ii) encouraging interviewees to say more by providing a model statement,[80] introducing a supportive second

---

[74] Maria Hartwig, Pär A. Granhag and Timothy J. Luke, "Strategic Use of Evidence During Investigative Interviews: The State of the Science", in David C. Raskin, Charles R. Honts and John C. Kircher (eds.), *Credibility Assessment*, Elsevier, 2014, pp. 1–36; Oleszkiewicz and Watson, 2021, see *supra* note 44.

[75] Luke, Dawson, Hartwig and Granhag, 2014, see *supra* note 42.

[76] Pär A. Granhag, Leif A. Strömwall, Rebecca M. Willén and Maria Hartwig, "Eliciting Cues to Deception by Tactical Disclosure of Evidence: The First Test of the Evidence Framing Matrix", in *Legal and Criminological Psychology*, 2013, vol. 18, no. 2, pp. 341–355; Timothy J. Luke *et al.*, "Interviewing to Elicit Cues to Deception: Improving Strategic Use of Evidence With General-to-Specific Framing of Evidence", in *Journal of Police and Criminal Psychology*, 2013, vol. 28, no. 1, pp. 54–62.

[77] Bella M. DePaulo *et al.*, "Cues to Deception", in *Psychological Bulletin*, 2003, vol. 129, no. 1, pp. 74–118.

[78] Aldert Vrij, "Interviewing to Detect Deception", in *European Psychologist*, 2014, vol. 19, no. 3, pp. 184–194; *id.*, "Deception and Truth Detection When Analyzing Nonverbal and Verbal Cues", in *Applied Cognitive Psychology*, 2019, vol. 33, no. 2, pp. 160–167; Aldert Vrij and Pär A. Granhag, "Eliciting Information and Detecting Lies in Intelligence Interviewing: An Overview of Recent Research", in *Applied Cognitive Psychology*, 2014, vol. 28, no. 6, pp. 936–944.

[79] Evans, Michael, Meissner, and Brandon, 2013, pp. 33–41, see *supra* note 66.

[80] Ewens *et al.*, 2016, see *supra* note 52; Leal, Vrij, Deeb and Jupe, 2018, see *supra* note 68.

interviewer,[81] or enhancing memory recall via eye closure instructions;[82] or (iii) asking unanticipated questions that take advantage of lie-tellers' strategies.[83] HIG-supported research has shown that these approaches are effective in enhancing the cognitive or story-based cues (for example, amount of detail provided, complications in the story, verifiable details, *et cetera*) that differentiate lies and truths[84] and that individuals trained in such cues and interview tactics can better distinguish lies and truths.[85]

22.5. Military and Intelligence Interrogations

AFM 2-22.3 (2006), largely similar to its predecessors (AFM 34-52, 1987, 1992), describes 19 authorized interrogation approaches (with some restrictions, such as those for separation).[86] These approaches can be roughly clustered into a *Direct* approach (the interrogator asks direct questions), an *Incentive*-based approach (the interrogator "trades something that the source wants for information"), three positively valenced and four negatively valenced *Emotional* approaches, and ten other approaches (such as *Rapid Fire*, where the interrogator asks "a series of questions in such a manner that the source does not have time to answer a question completely before the next one is asked"[87] and *Silent*, when the interrogator "says nothing to the source, but looks him squarely in the eye, preferably with a slight smile on his face […] [to] force him to break eye contact first. The source […] may ask questions, but the [interrogator] should not answer until he is ready to break the silence").[88]

---

[81] Samantha Mann, "Two Heads Are Better Than One? How to Effectively Use Two Interviewers to Elicit Cues to Deception", in *Legal and Criminological Psychology*, 2013, vol. 18, no. 2, pp. 324–340; Dominic J. Shaw *et al.*, "Expect the Unexpected? Variations in Question Type Elicit Cues to Deception in Joint Interviewer Contexts", in *Applied Cognitive Psychology*, 2013, vol. 27, no. 3, pp. 336–343.

[82] Vrij *et al.*, 2014, see *supra* note 42.

[83] Shaw *et al.*, 2013, see *supra* note 81; Tuule Sooniste, Pär A. Granhag, Leif A. Strömwall and Aldert Vrij, "Statements About True and False Intentions: Using the Cognitive Interview to Magnify the Differences", in *Scandinavian Journal of Psychology*, 2015, vol. 56, no. 4, pp. 371–378; *id.*, "Discriminating Between True and False Intent Among Small Cells of Suspects", in *Legal and Criminological Psychology*, 2016, vol. 21, no. 2, pp. 344–357.

[84] Vrij *et al.*, 2017, see *supra* note 17.

[85] Mac Giolla and Luke, 2021, pp. 385–392, see *supra* note 44.

[86] AFM 2-22.3 is largely similar to AFM 34-52 (1987, 1992); these were superseded by AFM 30-15 (1969, revised and reissued in 1978 and 1982). Anecdotes of archival records are that the approaches described are the product of after-action reports and formal reviews from both World War II and the Korean War. None of the interrogation approaches or techniques described in these AFMs had been systematically evaluated prior to the HIG.

[87] *Ibid.*, pp.8–7.

[88] *Ibid.*, pp. 8–16.

A 2010 HIG in-house review of the 19 approaches, as described in AFM's Chapter 8, "Approach Techniques and Termination Strategies", examined the extent to which each of the 19 techniques was supported by extant science, unsupported by such science or for which no known science was available – while recognizing that any approach might be effective at some point in time, depending on contextual (including personal) factors impinging on the success of an interrogation.[89] The review found three approaches consistent with the available evidence base, one moderately consistent, three moderately inconsistent, and ten contraindicated. It was noted that much of the science that contradicted so many of the approaches had been publicly available for decades. These findings raised the question of how much of the research program should be dedicated to the evaluation of the AFM methods, especially since so many of the methods were inconsistent with relevant science.

22.5.1. Experiments

Given the overall inconsistency of the AFM with extant psychological science, only two experimental studies were sponsored that focused directly on the AFM approaches and techniques. Each examined different clusters of approaches. The first found some support for approaches based on positive emotions versus those based on negative emotions (that is, more support for *Fear-Down*, *Pride and Ego-Up* than for *Fear-Up*, *Futility*, and *Pride and Ego-Down*)[90] while the second found strong support for *We Know All*.[91] Such findings were broadly consistent with what was already known about the impact of rapport-building[92] and with previous data demonstrating the influence of a subject's perception of relevant evidence.[93]

---

[89] Susan E. Brandon, Sujeeta Bhatt, Brandi P. Justice and Steven M. Kleinman, *Army Field Manual 2-22.3 Interrogation Methods: A Science-Based Review*, National Defence Intelligence College Press, Washinton, D.C., 2010; Susan E. Brandon, Steven M. Kleinman and Joeanna C. Arthur, "A Scientific Perspective on Army Field Manual 2-22.3", in Mark A. Stall and Sally C. Harvey (eds.), *Operational Psychology: A New Field to Support National Security and Public Safety*, Praeger Publishers, 2019, pp. 287–326.

[90] Jacqueline R. Evans *et al.*, "An Empirical Evaluation of Intelligence-Gathering Interrogation Techniques From the United States Army Field Manual", in *Applied Cognitive Psychology*, 2014, vol. 28, no. 6, pp. 867–875.

[91] Misty C. Duke, James M. Wood, Justin Magee and Hector Escobar, "The Effectiveness of Army Field Manual Interrogation Approaches for Educing Information and Building Rapport", in *Law and Human Behavior*, 2018, vol. 42, no. 5, pp. 442–457.

[92] Roger Collins, Robyn Lincoln and Mark G. Frank, "The Effect of Rapport in Forensic Interviewing", in *Psychiatry, Psychology, and Law*, 2002, vol. 9, no. 1, pp. 69–78.

[93] Stephen Moston and Terry Engelberg, "The Effects of Evidence on the Outcome of Interviews With Criminal Suspects", in *Police Practice and Research*, 2011, vol. 12, no. 6, pp. 518–526; Gisli H. Gudjonsson and Hannes Petursson, "Custodial Interrogation: Why Do Suspects

---

Anecdotes of notable interrogation successes reported by Hanns-Joachim Scharff, a World War II German Luftwaffe interrogator, prompted HIG-sponsored experimental studies relevant to the AFM's *We Know All* approach. This research facilitated an understanding of how managing information and a subject's perception of the interviewer's knowledge can facilitate information disclosure.[94] Scholars identified five interrelated tactics that Scharff used to facilitate his elicitation efforts: (i) a friendly approach in which rapport and trust are built with the interview subject; (ii) managing the conversation using narrative questioning that does not press the subject for information that the interviewer is seeking; (iii) demonstrating extensive knowledge regarding certain topics so as to create an 'illusion of knowing all'; (iv) using claims to lure an interviewee into confirming or disconfirming target information; and (v) not acknowledging an interviewee's disclosure of new information in order to mask questioning objectives and interests. HIG-supported research has demonstrated the rather impressive benefits of this approach for eliciting more new information and, in doing so, for the subject to underestimate the amount of new information that they had revealed and to remain unaware of the interviewer's information objectives.[95] Studies also have shown that source handlers can be successfully trained in the Scharff technique.[96]

22.5.2. Surveys

Several HIG contracts produced surveys of interrogators for their perceptions of 'best practices'.[97] One of these focused on interrogators with military

---

Confess and How Does It Relate to Their Crime, Attitude and Personality?", in *Personality and Individual Differences*, 1991, vol. 12, no. 3, pp. 295–306.

[94] Luke, Dawson, Hartwig and Granhag, 2014, see *supra* note 42.

[95] Granhag, Montecinos and Oleszkiewicz, 2015, see *supra* note 42; Pär A. Granhag, Jenny Rangmar and Leif A. Strömwall, "Small Cells of Suspects: Eliciting Cues to Deception by Strategic Interviewing", in *Journal of Investigative Psychology and Offender Profiling*, 2015, vol. 12, no. 2, pp. 127–141; Oleszkiewicz, Granhag and Kleinman, 2014, see *supra* note 42; *id.*, 2017, see *supra* note 42; Simon Oleszkiewicz, Pär A. Granhag and Sebastian C. Montecinos, "The Scharff-Technique: Eliciting Intelligence From Human Sources", in *Law and Human Behavior*, 2014, vol. 38, no. 5, pp. 478–489. For a meta-analysis of this research, see Luke, 2021, see *supra* note 44.

[96] Oleszkiewicz, Granhag and Kleinman, 2017, see *supra* note 47. To date, seminars on Scharff's technique have been provided to more than 15 organizations, including the FBI, the Los Angeles Police Department (LAPD), the Intelligence Division of the New York Police Department, MI5 and UK Defence Intelligence ("Personal Communication", 17 December 2021 (on file with the authors)).

[97] Jane Goodman-Delahunty, Kate O'Brien and Thea Gumbert-Jourjon, "Police Professionalism in Interviews With High Value Detainees: Cross-Cultural Endorsement of Procedural Justice", in *Journal of the Institute of Justice and International Studies*, 2013, vol. 13, pp. 65–82; Redlich, Kelly and Miller, 2014, see *supra* note 13; Jane Goodman-Delahunty and Loene M.

experience,[98] where there was consensus among the 42 survey participants on the importance of interpersonal skills and rapport building. The most commonly reported interrogation tactics were *rapport and relationship building* (87.8 per cent) and *emotional provocation*[99] (87.8 per cent). Notably, "few discernible response patterns emerged between military and law enforcement participants".[100]

22.5.3. Observations

An opportunity to systematically observe interrogations conducted by the US military was made possible via a partnership with DoD psychologists who supported theater-level interrogation operations.[101] In 2009, several Behavioral Science Consultants ('BSCs') (in this instance, Ph.D. clinical psychologists), located initially at Camp Cropper, Iraq, approached interrogation instructors at the Human Intelligence Training Joint Center of Excellence ('HT-JCOE') in Ft. Huachuca, Arizona, seeking guidance and support to conduct systematic observations of interrogations to which BSCs were already privy.[102] HT-JCOE instructors then reached out to the HIG to help construct an appropriate protocol for such observations.

Howes, "Social Persuasion to Develop Rapport in High-Stakes Interviews: Qualitative Analyses of Asian-Pacific Practices", in *Policing and Society*, 2016, vol. 26, no. 3, pp. 270–290.

[98] Russano, Narchet, Kleinman and Meissner, 2014, see *supra* note 13.

[99] This was a term used to describe techniques specifically designed to target the source's raw emotions (including anger, anxiety, fear, guilt, hope, love, pride and sadness), any real or perceived evidence against the source, appealing to the source's self-interest, conscience, religion or capitalizing on the stress of being captured and exaggerating or alleviating the source's fear. See Kelly, Miller, Redlich and Kleinman, 2013, pp. 165–178, see *supra* note 71.

[100] Russano, Narchet, Kleinman and Meissner, 2014, p. 849, see *supra* note 13.

[101] US DoD, "Instruction No. 2310.08E: Medical Program Support for Detainee Operations", 6 June 2006, described the role of such psychologists:

BSCs [Behavioral Science Consultants] are authorized to make psychological assessments of the character, personality, social interactions, and other behavioral characteristics of detainees, including interrogation subjects, and, based on such assessments, advise authorized personnel performing lawful interrogations.

This Instruction was rescinded in 2019, effective 2021, following extensive public and classified reviews. The 2021 Instruction prohibits psychologists from "consult[ing] in relation to, supervis[ing], conduct[ing] or direct[ing] interrogations" (US DoD, "Instruction No. 2310.08: Medical Program Support for Detainee Operations", 5 September 2019, p. 4). The previous Instruction, issued in 2006, also prohibited psychologists from conducting or directing interrogations.

[102] HT-JCOE was the only DoD facility to provide interrogation instruction for all DoD-certified interrogators as of 2006 (HT-JCOE, "Military Intelligence Professional Bulletin, PB 34-10-4", in *Military Intelligence*, October–December 2010, vol. 36, no. 4, pp. 1–40). The Joint Training Center continues to offer human intelligence ('HUMINT') training. One goal of the observational studies described here was to provide feedback to the HT-JCOE instructors on the effectiveness of their interrogator training.

This collaboration resulted in three studies, two conducted at Camp Cropper, Iraq (2009–2010) and a third conducted at a detention facility in Parwan, Afghanistan (2010). Interrogators who participated in all three studies completed an informed consent process and the observation methodology was approved by an IRB and by the Command Staff at each facility. The data were anonymized and there was no "intervention" or "interaction" that would have forced categorization of the studies as "research".[103] Observers coded each interrogation session via a one-way mirror or video feed at the facility, absent any interaction with the interrogator or detainee. More than 1,000 observations were analyzed by the HIG for the frequency with which various AFM approaches were used and their association with key interrogation outcomes, including the development of rapport, achieving co-operation by the interrogation subject and the elicitation of intelligence information. There were two particularly salient outcomes of these studies. First, many of the 19 AFM approaches and techniques were never used; although there was some variance across studies, interrogators most often used *Direct, Incentive, Emotional-Love* and *Emotional Fear-Down* (in descending order of frequency). The second was that positively valenced approaches (*Emotional-Love, Emotional Fear-Down* and *Emotional-Pride and Ego-Up*) were consistently associated with the development of rapport between the detainee and the interrogator, and therein positively predicted both increased co-operation and the elicitation of intelligence. In contrast, negatively valenced approaches (*Emotional Fear-Up, Emotional-Pride and Ego-Down, Emotional-Futility* and *We Know All*) were likely to limit rapport and co-operation.[104]

Other direct observational data were available but could not be accessed. As of 2012, the DoD had required audio-video recordings of strategic intelligence interrogations conducted at theater-level detention facilities "or at any other location to the extent required by law or DoD policy".[105] These recordings were encrypted and stored in secure locations within the US. Given the large

---

[103] US, Code of Federal Regulations ('CFR'), Title 45, Section 46.102(e)(1).

[104] Stoney Trent, Colin Burchfield, Christian A. Meissner and Susan E. Brandon, "A Field Study of U.S. Military Interrogations in Iraq and Afghanistan", unpublished manuscript, 2018; HIG personnel visited the detention facility in Parwan, Afghanistan, in January 2012, to provide support for the continuation of these observations. However, further collection of data was not supported by the local US Commander and subsequently was prohibited by DoD, "Instruction No. 3216.02", 8 November 2011, that stated that, "[r]esearch involving a detainee or a prisoner of war as a human subject is prohibited". Arguments that the data were anonymized, and that data collection involved no interactions or interventions with the subject so that human subjects regulations could be adhered to, were not effective.

[105] US DoD, "Directive No. 3115.09: DoD Intelligence Interrogations, Detainee Debriefings, and Tactical Questioning", 29 October 2020.

number of interrogations conducted in such facilities in Iraq and Afghanistan, and that it would have been possible to analyze these recordings while still adhering to human subjects regulations, these recordings could have provided unique opportunities to assess the AFM approaches and techniques. However, a more than five-year attempt by the HIG to access these recordings proved unsuccessful.

It might be asked why HIG research personnel did not systematically observe HIG interrogations to assess effectiveness. The reasons are multiple and they illustrate, perhaps, the difficulty of knowing what intelligence interrogation methods are actually used in the field (as opposed to what methods are shown by science to be most effective, what interrogation manuals describe or prescribe, what methods are trained or what interrogators say they do). For example:

- Security issues prohibited HIG interrogations from being audio or video recorded, even after the DoD required video recordings of all strategic interrogations of persons in their custody as of 2012,[106] and DoJ policy mandated that the FBI "will electronically record custodial interviews" in 2014.[107]

- There was an early attempt to ask the HIG Mobile Interrogation Team ('MIT') interrogators to complete a questionnaire (created by HIG research personnel) following each interrogation. Each participant signed a consent form upon deployment and the data collection was approved by the FBI's IRB. The questionnaire asked about methods used and challenges faced. The effort was hampered both because DoD-certified interrogators and FBI agents did not share a common language to describe what they did and because participation was rare, most likely given that it was voluntary. The effort was abandoned after two years.

- The argument could have been made, especially once the HIG initiated its own interview and interrogation training, that systematic observations of HIG interrogations could fall under the rubric of 'programme evaluation' and therefore would not meet the definition of research (research is defined as "a systematic investigation, including research development, testing, and evaluation, designed to develop or contribute to generalizable knowledge").[108] The challenge was in designating who might conduct such programme evaluation: HIG research personnel did occasionally deploy with the MIT, but observations made by such individuals could not be characterized as 'independent', and including 'independent observers'

---

[106] *Ibid.*

[107] US DoJ, Office of Public Affairs, "Attorney General Holder Announces Significant Policy Shift Concerning Electronic Recording of Statements", 22 May 2014.

[108] US, CFR, Title 45, Section 46.102(l).

on an MIT was never considered both because there were no HIG personnel who could fill that role and because there was always a need, for logistic and security reasons, to keep the MITs as small as possible.

- If such data had been collected, it could not have been shared with HIG-sponsored researchers unless they agreed to the considerable restrictions inherent in security clearances, including prohibitions against publication of the data. This virtually eliminated sharing the data with the several HIG-sponsored researchers who were not US citizens and risked creating a two-tiered community, with some 'in the know' and some 'in the dark'. It was also contrary to the effort to keep the research programme unclassified.

- There were concerns that the HIG Research Program might be perceived as conducting research on detainees that, despite being within the federal guidelines regarding human subjects' protections, might be misconstrued by members of the public as both illegal and immoral. A report by Physicians for Human Rights ('PHR'), published in June 2010, asserted that the CIA had conducted research on detainees and explicitly referenced the 'Nuremberg Code':[109]

> Health professionals working for and on behalf of the CIA monitored the interrogations of detainees, collected and analyzed the results of those interrogations, and sought to derive generalizable inferences to be applied to subsequent interrogations. Such acts may be seen as the conduct of research and experimentation by health professionals on prisoners, which could violate accepted standards of medical ethics, as well as domestic and international law. These practices could, in some cases, constitute war crimes and crimes against humanity (p. 3).

The HIG thus faced the quandary that research on 'real life' interrogations, especially those conducted by its own MITs, was difficult and, given the political milieu, unwise.

22.6. Dissemination of Research Findings

The dissemination of HIG-sponsored research was both inward (to HIG personnel) and outward (to US and international scholars, practitioners and the public). Different mechanisms were created for each. Of fundamental importance to the

---

[109] The 'Nuremberg Code' (International Military Tribunal, *US v. Karl Brandt et al.*, Judgment, 19 August 1947 (https://www.legal-tools.org/doc/2975dc/)) is reprinted in International Military Tribunal, *Trial of the Major War Criminals before the Nuremberg Military Tribunals Under Control Council Law No. 10*, vol. 2, US Government Printing Office, Washington, D.C., 1949, pp. 181–182.

success of dissemination efforts was that the research was unclassified and thus could be shared and distributed in unclassified channels and venues.

22.6.1. Inward Dissemination

Perhaps because the HIG was chartered while consisting of less than 10 personnel and remained relatively small, everyone occupied the same office space (within a Sensitive Compartmented Information Facility), and all personnel held similar high-level security clearances. This meant that the day-to-day functions of the HIG were available to everyone. Such face-to-face contact was likely instrumental in helping to close the gap between research and practice, including researchers and practitioners. Both began to see what the other did and the peculiar challenges each faced. And although research personnel could not share HIG operational details with HIG contractors (who were primarily academic scholars situated in universities in the US and abroad), the challenges that the MITs faced could be accurately characterized by the research personnel in the language and findings of psychological science: for example, how to know if a statement is true; how to persuade a reluctant detainee to talk; how to build and maintain sufficient rapport; how to work with personnel from other government agencies; and so on.

In 2012, HIG research personnel were supported by the HIG Director to establish an in-house interview and interrogation training programme. The content of such a course was determined primarily by the research personnel, but a highly experienced former UK Detective Chief Inspector and Course Director of the UK National Hostage Crisis Negotiation Course, Simon Wells, served as the (contract) instructor for an initial four-week course. All HIG operational personnel were required to take the course, which was offered several times a year. In 2014, a full-time HIG instructor position was filled by FBI Special Agent Colton Seale, who taught the HIG course with Wells for several years and served as programme manager for the training programme until 2019.

22.6.2. Outward Dissemination

The HIG training programme evolved into an outward dissemination mechanism, perhaps inadvertently at first. With considerable resources spent towards developing and offering the in-house HIG interview and interrogation training course (which had been shortened to a one-week 'Core Course'), HIG personnel often could not attend because they were deployed. To ensure greater attendance, the HIG first reached out to FBI training instructors and subsequently to instructors at other federal agencies, which resulted in attendance by a wide range of additional participants. By 2015, the programme was training nearly 1,000 students each year. Initially, demand for the course was primarily from within the FBI, but that quickly expanded to a broader section of the US Intelligence and

Special Operations communities. Components of the FBI, CIA and DoD all had completion of the Core Course as a mandatory component of their internal training. Demand also expanded outside the US, with requests coming from FBI Legal Attachés and other overseas offices of the US government. The HIG Core Course was delivered to close allies of the US in the 'war on terrorism', including (but not limited to) the 'Five Eye' partners.[110] Within several years, HIG training personnel received more requests for training than they could support. In 2017, FBI Director Christopher Wray offered the following comments at an HIG Research Symposium:

> To date, the HIG has trained personnel from more than 50 government agencies. In this most recent fiscal year, the HIG trained 800 students across multiple agencies, including 90 foreign partner participants – including folks from both Canada's Security Intelligence Service and Britain's MI5. The HIG training and research units also work closely with the staff of FLETC – the Federal Law Enforcement Training Center in Georgia – and Fort Huachuca – the military training facility in Arizona.[111]

The first HIG Research Symposium (2011) provided a venue for HIG-sponsored researchers to share the results of their one-year HIG contracts with one another and to help co-ordinate overlapping efforts. Symposia subsequently were offered annually. By 2015, when the event was held at the National Academy of Sciences in Washington, D.C. and one of the speakers was then FBI Director James Comey, pre-registration for the event became necessary and attendance averaged between 200–350 each year. There was a considerable synergy between HIG training courses and attendance at HIG symposia, as each attracted participation in the other.

HIG-sponsored researchers were encouraged to publish their work in peer-reviewed, open-source scientific journals. As of 2021, the HIG reported more than 220 HIG-sponsored publications.[112] HIG research personnel also created a mechanism for the distribution of research findings within the intelligence community, referred to as Research Dissemination Reports ('RDRs') to appeal to a community accustomed to reading Intelligence Information Reports. Each RDR, written by HIG research personnel, described the findings from an HIG-contracted project or projects in non-technical terms and noted the extent to

---

[110] 'Five eye' is an intelligence alliance comprising Australia, Canada, New Zealand, the UK, and the US. "Personal Communication", 24 September 2021 (on file with the authors).

[111] Christopher Wray, "HIG: Using Science and Research to Combat National Security Threats", Seventh Annual HIG Research Symposium, 16 October 2017 (available on the FBI's web site).

[112] "Personal Communication", 24 November 2021 (on file with the authors).

which the findings were immediately applicable (or not) to real-world interrogation contexts.

22.7. HIG Best Practices

While it remains critical that accusatorial interrogation techniques be held to account for instances of false confessions and wrongful convictions, only pointing out what is done wrong is not as persuasive as offering alternatives. HIG or HIG-based training did *not* begin by describing to the participants all 'the errors of their ways' but rather relied upon the inherent appeal of science-based methods. The 'HIG model', writ large, was offered as a credible alternative to traditional tactics. This model was based on the sciences of decision-making, cognition, memory, motivation (both implicit and explicit), persuasion (again, both implicit and explicit), communication, resistance, co-operation and trust, strategic use of evidence or information and credibility assessment.[113]

Three aspects of the HIG model were critical. One was that it was not offered as a checklist or 'toolbox',[114] but as a coherent plan (from planning for an interview, to conducting an interview, to post-interview reflection). A second was that no distinction was made between an 'interview' and an 'interrogation', in contrast to what was traditionally taught and assumed by American law enforcement.[115] Third, both interviews and interrogations were presumed to be oriented towards the collection of information (as opposed to the elicitation of confessions or admissions). Recognizing a common goal in both law enforcement and intelligence or HUMINT domains[116] had the fortunate outcome of making the decades of research on law enforcement contexts (as described above) relevant to military and intelligence contexts.

---

[113] For descriptions of the HIG model see: Susan E. Brandon, Simon Wells and Colton Seale, "Science-based Interviewing: Information Elicitation", in *Journal of Investigative Psychology and Offender Profiling*, 2018, vol. 15, no. 2, pp. 133–148; Susan E. Brandon and Simon Wells, "Commonalities and Complementarities Among Science-Based Interview Methods: Towards a Theory of Interrogation", in Jason J. Dickinson *et al.* (eds.), *Evidence-Based Investigative Interviewing*, Routledge, Oxfordshire, 2019, pp. 134–155; Susan E. Brandon and Simon Wells, *Science-Based Interviewing*, BookBaby, 2019; Simon Wells and Susan E. Brandon, "Interviewing in Criminal and Intelligence-Gathering Contexts: Applying Science", in *International Journal of Forensic Mental Health*, 2019, vol. 18, no. 1, pp. 50–65.

[114] Brent Snook *et al.*, "Challenges of a 'Toolbox' Approach to Investigative Interviewing: A Critical Analysis of the Royal Canadian Mounted Police's (RCMP) Phased Interview Model", in *Psychology, Public Policy, and Law*, 2020, vol. 26, no. 3, pp. 261–273.

[115] Fred E. Inbau, John E. Reid, Joseph P. Buckley and Brian C. Jayne, *Criminal Interrogations and Confessions*, 4th ed., Aspen Publishers, Frederick, 2001; Inbau and Reid, 1963, see *supra* note 3.

[116] Evans *et al.*, 2010, see *supra* note 13.

The HIG Core Course provided not only strategies and tactics, but also a description of the science underlying these as they might be relevant to an individual interview. Descriptions of the science were included in the training so that the practitioner could understand *why* a method worked (or did not) and how to usefully adapt a method to a particular circumstance while not violating underlying core psychological principles. The protest, sometimes made by the highly experienced HIG interrogators, that 'I know all this already', was countered with the argument that 'all experts have coaches'.[117] Coaches were included in the training to provide individual feedback on performance in multiple training scenarios and practical exercises. A significant accomplishment of the HIG Core Course was to provide members of the MITs with a common language to describe what they did and what they observed, which proved invaluable not only in real time as an interrogation proceeded, but also for after-action reports.

22.8. HIG Influence on US Training and Practice

Perhaps the greatest impact of the HIG to date has been on interview and interrogation training by federal law enforcement agencies and departments. Multiple federal agencies participated in the HIG Core Course and subsequently changed their internal training to reflect the 'HIG model', which can be described in broad strokes as planning, building and maintaining rapport, eliciting a narrative, strategic questioning and presentation of evidence (if available), dealing with possible resistance and assessing credibility.[118] A notable example is the US Air Force Office of Special Investigations ('AFOSI'), which partnered with the HIG to provide one-week training to more than 100 of its Special Agents in 2014–2015. The perceived success of this training led to a similar course being incorporated within the internal training offered by AFOSI in 2016.[119] Another example involves the substantively modified training offered to FBI Agents by the FBI Training Academy as of 2018. Similarly, the Advanced Interviewing Course offered by FLETC currently reflects the HIG Core Course.[120]

---

[117] Atul Gawande, "Top Athletes and Singers Have Coaches. Should You?", *The New Yorker*, 26 September 2011.

[118] Evans *et al.*, 2014, see *supra* note 90; Susan E. Brandon *et al.*, "An Interdisciplinary Partnership to Assess the Efficacy of Science-based Investigative Interviewing", in Stall and Harvey (eds.), 2019, pp. 263–286, see *supra* note 89.

[119] Heather L. Morris and David G. Ray, "Investigative Psychology. Applying Psychological Science to Military Criminal Investigations", in Stall and Harvey (eds.), 2019, pp. 185–209, see *supra* note 89.

[120] See FLETC, "Advanced Interviewing for Law Enforcement Investigators" (available on its web site).

· There has been less impact at state, local and tribal levels, though efforts are underway.[121] The Intelligence Division of the New York Police Department has incorporated the CI[122] into its interview and debriefing training,[123] and the Los Angeles Police Department, an early partner with the HIG research and training programs,[124] has plans to base its interviewing course on the HIG model as offered via the California POST program. The Wichita Police Department, which participated in a training research study funded by the HIG, has now focused its approach to training exclusively on science-based interviewing methods.

Private companies that offer interrogation training are now incorporating practices that HIG-supported researchers have developed. For example, a well-known interrogation training company Wicklander-Zulawski & Associates.[125] now offers a somewhat modified curriculum to reflect a less confrontational approach.[126] New companies have also been developed via partnerships between HIG researchers and practitioners from the field who have established science-based training programmes. The latter include former HIG interrogators (for example, Special Agent (ret.) John Gervino at Truth Intelligence Consulting) and former police detectives with extensive exposure to HIG training (for example, Detective (ret.) Mark Severino and Detective (ret.) Matt Jones at Evocavi). The impacts of such training are difficult to assess, of course, as changes in training curricula do not guarantee changes in practice. Nevertheless, there is increasing demand for science-based interview training among federal, state and local law enforcement agencies in the US, as well as by companies interested in training their corporate investigations teams on such methods.

Even more difficult to quantify are the impacts of HIG-funded publications in scientific journals. Since 2010, the cumulative number of interrogation-related research studies has shown a marked increase, in large measure due to HIG-sponsored research. Perhaps equally significant have been the partnerships between HIG researchers and practitioners.[127] In contrast to the frequently

---

[121] As noted, the HIG had no mandate to train any agencies outside its intelligence partners.

[122] Fisher and Geiselman, 1992, see *supra* note 64.

[123] "Personal Communication", 24 September 2021 (on file with the authors).

[124] Robert Kolker, "A Severed Head, Two Cops, and the Radical Future of Interrogation", *Wired*, 24 May 2016 (available on its web site).

[125] See the Wicklander-Zulawski & Associates' web site.

[126] "Wicklander-Zulawski Discontinues Reid Method Instruction After More Than 30 Years", *PRWeb*, 6 March 2017.

[127] A precedent for such a partnership was a conference co-organized by G. Daniel Lassiter and Chris A. Meissner in 2007, attended by academics and law enforcement personnel, intended to provide "a unique forum in which social scientists, legal scholars, and practitioners

---

adversarial relationship between US academics and the intelligence and law enforcement communities, HIG researchers have presented jointly with HIG practitioners at both academic and practitioner conferences (for example, 2014–2016 meetings of the International Association of Chiefs of Police), published journal articles and edited volumes together[128] and conducted joint training (as discussed above). The trainings conducted by researcher-practitioner teams, the proliferation of research publications and the HIG's annual research symposia have all facilitated active collaborations and open communication in these contexts.

22.9. Lessons Learned

The successes of the HIG have largely been due to the efforts towards pushing against a number of constraints imposed by the US intelligence community (and some fortuitous circumstances). From this experience comes a number of lessons learned that can be shared.

- First, an unclassified research program allowed the HIG to access worldrenowned scholars and scientists who otherwise would not have contributed to the body of research. It also allowed that research to be transitioned into training programmes outside of the US intelligence community, which has increased its impact on how interviews and interrogations are conducted within the US.

- HIG research personnel were co-located with HIG operational personnel and occasionally deployed with interrogation teams. This allowed the former to serve as a 'bridge' between the science and intelligence operations which affected the nature and course of the research program. As a result of the relationships fostered, operational personnel also became instrumental in the review and selection of research topics and contracts on a yearly basis.

- HIG research personnel worked closely with HIG contract researchers, forming a partnership and collegial relationship rather than a more distanced 'supervision' of 'work for hire' as is often the case in governmentcontractor relations. HIG researchers contributed significantly to the

---

critically examine the current state of research on interrogations and confessions and assess whether policy recommendations might be developed", in G. Daniel Lassiter and Christian A. Meissner, *Police Interrogations and False Confessions: Current Research, Practice, and Policy Recommendations*, American Psychological Association, Washington, D.C., 2010, p. xvii.

[128] Barela, Fallon, Gaggioli and Ohlin (eds.), 2020, see *supra* note 9; Leins, Zimmerman and Polander, 2017, see *supra* note 43; Meehan, Kelly and McClary, 2019, see *supra* note 40; Haneen Deeb *et al.*, "Mapping Details to Elicit Information and Cues to Deceit: The Effects of Map Richness", in *European Journal of Psychology Applied to Legal Context*, 2022, vol. 14, no. 1, pp. 11–19.

direction and growth of the research programme, and HIG-sponsored researchers modified their research methods and measurement processes to be more useful in the field as a function of their interactions and conversations with practitioners.

- As noted above, several aspects of the HIG training programme were advantageous. First, the curriculum was developed via a partnership between the scientists and HIG operational personnel (both interrogators and analysts), and these same individuals provided the instruction in training sessions. The practitioner had the 'street credibility' and the scientist had the scientific expertise. Second, coaches served an important role in the HIG's scenario-based training to provide individualized feedback to trainees. And third, the HIG MITs were trained together, meaning that the analysts, interpreters, and support staff understood the strategies and tactics used during an interrogation and could provide appropriate and often vital insights as it occurred.

- The HIG Research Program set up a mechanism to receive feedback from an *ad hoc* committee of individuals who would represent key constituencies. These included individuals with relevant research expertise or experience as intelligence, military or law enforcement interrogators; an ethicist with a deep expertise and understanding of military culture; and representatives from the human rights community, some of whom had been instrumental in the Obama Administration's EO 13491. The impetus for this 'research committee' was, in part, the 2010 PHR report described above: the committee, whose proceedings were unclassified, was intended to serve as the 'public face' of the research programme and as a way to gauge and reflect public perceptions of the programme (such as those reflected in the PHR report), which could impact the willingness of researchers (as members of the public) to participate. One example of the issues discussed was the use of nonconscious priming.[129] The committee had no policy or budgetary authority and its members served voluntarily.

22.10. Challenges Remain: Moving Forward

While the HIG has made an indelible impact on interrogation training and practice in the US and abroad, there remain significant issues that must be addressed. Importantly, a review and a revision of the interrogation approaches described in the 2006 AFM are necessary. The NDAA of 2016 required that the HIG submit to the Secretary of Defense, the Director of National Intelligence, the Attorney General and other officials "a report on best practices for interrogation that

---

[129] Kelly, Dawson and Hartwig, 2021, see *supra* note 40; Endel Tulving and Daniel L. Schacter, "Priming and Human Memory Systems", in *Science*, 1990, vol. 247, no. 4940, pp. 301–306.

do not involve the use of force" within 120 days of enactment.[130] The language of the NDAA stated that the HIG report "may include recommendations for revisions to AFM 2-22.3 based on the body of research commissioned by the High-Value Detainee Interrogation Group". However, the HIG (under the direction of the FBI) declined to offer such recommendations. Nevertheless, it is critical that research inform future amendments to the AFM and the training of military interrogators, debriefers and intelligence officers.[131]

Private industries within the US typically employ and train their own security teams to investigate policy violations and illegal activities at their sites. The HIG is neither funded nor chartered to provide interview and interrogation training to such entities, or (for that matter and as noted) to US federal, state, local and tribal law enforcement agencies and departments. While HIG training has reached the latter entities in some ways, both private industries and federal, state and local government agencies often turn to commercial training companies to support their interview and interrogation training efforts. An effective and sustainable transition from government-supported science institutions to private industries is critical in this arena – and has precedent: the US government supports the basic science that industries see no profit in until such time that profit may incur, at which time private industries deliver a product.[132]

Federal, state and local law enforcement also receive their training via relevant police training academies and professional associations. To further reforms within the US, it will be critical to work with such academies and associations to facilitate change from the training of customary, accusatorial tactics to that of a rapport-based, information-gathering approach. Police officer training varies widely in the US and there are no federally mandated minimum training requirements. A 2018 DoJ report counted 681 state and local law enforcement training academies that provided basic training instruction to 59,511 recruits.[133] In 2021, California passed Senate Bill 494[134] that would have required that California law enforcement officers be trained in 'science-based interviewing'. This

---

[130] Two reports were released as of 2016, one written by HIG operational personnel (HIG, "Interrogation Best Practices", 26 August 2016) and one written by HIG research personnel (HIG, "Interrogation: A Review of the Science", September 2016).

[131] Susan E. Brandon and Mark Fallon, "The Méndez Principles: The Need to Update the Army Field Manual on Interrogation for the 21st Century", in *Just Security*, 11 June 2021 (available on its web site). For the Méndez Principles in general, see Chapter 6 in this book.

[132] Mikko Packalen and Jay Bhattacharya, "NIH Funding and the Pursuit Of Edge Science", in *Proceedings of the National Academy of Sciences*, 2020, vol. 117, no. 22, pp. 12011–12016.

[133] Emily E. Buehler, *State and Local Law Enforcement Training Academies, 2018 – Statistical Tables*, US DoJ, Office of Justice Programs, Bureau of Justice Statistics, 2018.

[134] US, California Legislature, Senate Bill No. 494, Law Enforcement: Training, 9 October 2021, SB 494 (https://www.legal-tools.org/doc/4pniy9/).

bill specifically mentioned the HIG as a precedent for such training, and efforts are now underway to modify California's POST training curriculum based on the available science and best practice recommendations. Similar efforts in other states are necessary to make a substantive departure from accusatorial interrogation methods that remain prevalent in the US.

Finally, military and law enforcement training should be multidisciplinary. The first HIG training instructor was a former UK police officer. HIG interrogator trainees were recruited from various federal agencies: FBI, DoD and DHS. The 'outsider status' of the instructor was a deliberate selection: it meant the trainees could not dismiss what he said based on their own prejudices regarding their sister federal agencies. At the same time, when HIG instructors were FBI agents instructing DoD personnel, or DoD personnel instructing FBI agents, there was a tendency to dismiss what was said as 'not relevant to what I do'. Special Agent Seale had the expertise and experience to overcome this challenge, but a diverse training team would have facilitated his efforts and, perhaps more importantly, made overseas interrogations more efficient because these often occur in the context of multiple agencies working together.

23

The Centre for Research and Evidence
on Security Threats

Paul J. Taylor and Stacey M. Conchie[*]

23.1. Origins

The United Kingdom's ('UK') Centre for Research and Evidence on Security Threats ('CREST' or 'Centre') was set up in October 2015 following an Economic and Social Research Council competition to establish a world-class interdisciplinary research and evidence hub with a focus on understanding, countering and mitigating security threats. It was a unique partnership with UK security and intelligence agencies whose leadership understood how the Centre's knowledge integration, financial gearing, and community engagement would drive forward research and innovation at a pace not achievable by conventional contracting.

Today, CREST brings together the world's foremost expertise in understanding the psychological and social drivers of the threats, skills and technologies that enable its effective investigation, and the protective security measures that help counter the threat in the first place. It does so within a rich context of stakeholder and researcher engagement that spans five continents (approximately 2,500 people receive CREST's newsletter). Since its inception, its researchers have addressed interviewing topics that include cross-cultural dynamics, interpersonal trust, memory enhancement, motivation and intent, online elicitation, rapport, recovery from errors, sense-making, and the underlying narratives and ideologies of suspects.[1] Their focus has always been the whole interview process – not simply what happens 'in the booth', but also how practitioners can best deliver planning, debriefing and other intelligence activities.

23.2. The Structure of CREST

Although CREST has adapted over the years to meet the changing needs of its stakeholders, its mission has remained consistent: to deliver world-leading behavioural and social science research, knowledge exchange that enhances the

---

[*] **Paul Taylor** is Professor of Psychology at Lancaster University and was the founding director of CREST. **Stacey Conchie** is Professor of Psychology at Lancaster University and is the current Director of CREST.

[1] The research and researchers who have contributed on each of these topics can be found on the CREST web site by searching the keywords given in this sentence.

understanding and skills of researchers and practitioners, and activities that foster the capability and capacity of a shared community. Consistent too has been its approach. CREST delivers solution-focused research born out of practitioner–researcher co-working, making results accessible to users beyond the domain experts, including to senior decision-makers and the public.

CREST organizes its approach around three agendas:

1. Activities that deliver high-quality synthetic and original research with a rich diversity of methods and disciplinary perspectives, remaining responsive to funders' changing needs and balancing basic discovery with field validation and implementation;

2. activities that combine direct researcher–stakeholder interaction with print and online dissemination, delivering an accessible knowledge base that impacts practice. These activities include the collaborative development of knowledge management tools that curate CREST products for specific practice and training needs; and

3. activities that reinforce and grow collaborations across the international researcher–stakeholder community. This includes running events for the early career researcher community and growing industry partnerships to diversify funding and deliver impactful innovation.

To deliver these agendas, CREST has funded 195 academics, post-doctorals, Ph.D. students, and independent researchers from 45 universities and small-medium enterprises. Their disciplinary expertise includes computer science, crime science, international relations, law, linguistics, management science, politics, religious studies, sociology and psychology. They work in institutions across the UK, as well as in Australia, Canada, the Netherlands, Norway, Sweden and the United States. Approximately 40 per cent are 'Early Career Researchers' (defined as being no more than three years post-Ph.D.) and 45 per cent are women.

Those funded by CREST contribute in different ways. Approximately one-third of the researchers contribute to multi-year programmes that deliver 'driving' research. These small teams – typically a few academics, a post-doctoral researcher and a Ph.D. student (or two) – lay a theoretical foundation and initial evidence-base in an area of significant practitioner relevance.

They have been responsible for new paradigms, such as Ashenden's participatory approach to cyber threat prevention;[2] new methodologies, such as

---

[2]   Debi Ashenden, "In Their Own Words: Employee Attitudes Towards Information Security", in *Information and Computer Security*, 2018, vol. 26, no. 3, pp. 327–337.

Hope *et al.*'s app for group identity mapping;[3] new statistics, such as Taylor *et al.*'s review of interviewing effect sizes;[4] cornerstone reviews, such as Knott *et al.*'s work on counter *jihad*;[5] and new approaches, such as Shaw *et al.*'s demonstration of using digital traces to identify users.[6]

The remaining researchers contribute to 47 six-to-twelve-months projects, commissioned through five open competitions offering collectively GBP five million in funding. This commissioning emulates the Economic and Social Research Council's model of soliciting proposals – that is, having proposals reviewed by experts and using the reviews to support the decisions of a six-person, independent panel, chaired by CREST's Director.[7] CREST uses a reviewer web site and solicits, for all proposals, four academic reviews and a fifth 'stakeholder' review that comments on impact potential. All reviews are returned to submitters. Some of the successful commissioned projects deliver to here-and-now challenges. Others break ice on new topics, providing resilience for the future.

Unusually for a national research centre, CREST invests in a 'core' team of administrative, communication and security specialists – known as 'Research-to-Practice Fellows'. They support researchers' engagement with stakeholders by ensuring the complex research portfolio delivers with quality, value for money and on time; by running events, over 230 to date, including 65 symposia and workshops; and by bridging the gap between academia and practice,

---

3   Lorraine Hope, Feni Kontogianni, Kris Geyer and Wayne D. Thomas, "Development of the Reporting Information About Networks and Groups (RING) Task: A Method for Eliciting Information from Memory About Associates, Groups, and Networks", in *Journal of Forensic Practice*, 2019, vol. 21, no. 4.

4   Galit Nahari *et al.*, "Language of Lies: Urgent Issues and Prospects in Research", in *Legal and Criminological Psychology*, 2019, vol. 24, no. 1, pp. 1–23, includes comment: Paul J. Taylor, Abbie Marono and Lara Warmelink, "The Ecological Challenge: Ensuring Our Aggregate Results Are Individually Relevant", in *Legal and Criminological Psychology*, 2019, vol. 24, no. 1, pp. 4–8.

5   Benjamin Lee and Kim Knott, "More Grist to the Mill? Reciprocal Radicalisation and Reactions to Terrorism in the Far-Right Digital Milieu", in *Perspectives on Terrorism*, 2020, vol. 14, no. 3, pp. 98–115.

6   Heather Shaw, Paul J. Taylor, Stacey M. Conchie and David A. Ellis, "Behavioral Consistency in the Digital Age", in *Psychological Science*, 2022, vol. 33, no. 3, pp. 364–370.

7   Across four commissioning calls, the CREST process received 318 bids worth over GBP 31 million. Of these bids, 37 per cent were led by women (37 per cent of all named co-investigators were also women), 22 per cent had a lead institution from outside of the UK, and 17 per cent had a lead institution that was a non-HEI organisation. We secured over 1,100 reviews from over 530 reviewers across the world, achieving a turn-around from submission to panel of no more than eight weeks (a range of five to eight). CREST ensured rapid contracting by requiring submitters to read and accept the contract at the time of submission.

through innovative outputs and by working with practitioners and researchers to guide the implementation of evidence.

23.3. Contributing the State of the Art

CREST's *raison d'être* is sourcing the best expertise and answers to practitioner questions. Often this rests with engaging researchers outside the immediate field, whose knowledge is relevant by analogy, the implications of which are unexplored. CREST finds most value in informal 'few-on-one' meetings – colloquially known as brown bags – where brief presentations prelude a rich conversation. This format works because CREST is well-placed to reach across academia for the right expertise, because conversations can focus on what matters, and because both practitioner and researcher can give access to the 'file drawer' of their knowledge. This last point is critical. A practitioner can enrich a researcher's knowledge of what is experienced in the field; a researcher can inform decisions by recalling experiments and analyses that failed. This 'file drawer' knowledge is not published. It cannot be accessed or surmised by an external review.

The value of CREST's network is most prescient when it is called on for operational advice. This 'stewardship' role puts at the fingertips of stakeholders broad yet controlled access to expertise. Researchers have contributed to the debriefing of sensitive cases, to assessments of threats, to the content of public appeals, and to methods used in the collation of information. They have also supported strategic work, such as advising on how to adapt organizational processes during the Covid-19 lockdown and reviewing the fit of current practices to an emerging threat. The Research-to-Practice Fellows are instrumental to this frictionless transfer of knowledge. They are alive to the limitations of academic knowledge and to the needs of the practitioner, and they connect the two.

Often a practitioner needs more detail, and for that CREST delivers 'direct tasking' reports and synthetic research. Examples include briefing notes on established areas (for example, a guide to Islám's five pillars),[8] highlighting new research likely to be of relevance (for example, to multi-team emergency response),[9] undertaking scoping reviews (for example, on emerging biometrics), and re-analysing existing data to address an emergent question (for example, risk to British public figures).[10] Approximately 35 per cent of CREST's outputs

---

[8]   Kim Knott, "Islam: The Five Pillars", CREST, 2016.

[9]   Olivia Brown, Nicola Power and Stacey M. Conchie, "Communication and Coordination Across Event Phases: A Multi-Team System Emergency Response", in *Journal of Occupational and Organizational Psychology*, 2021, vol. 94, no. 3, pp. 591–615.

[10] Paul Gill *et al.*, "Predictors of Varying Levels of Risk Posed by Fixated Individuals to British Public Figures", in *Journal of Forensic Sciences*, 2021, vol. 66, no. 4, pp. 1364–1376.

are synthetic. They included Gabbert *et al.*'s literature synthesis to determine what the field knows about rapport in information-gathering contexts[11] (critical given the many non-evidence claims), Knott and Lee's desk-based review of the role of political and religious organizations in ideological transmission[12] and Grimani *et al.*'s review of the tactics people use to remain evasive online.[13]

An example of CREST's synthetic work is the Eliciting Information framework – a conceptual model that marshals the evidence practitioners can draw on when seeking to elicit information, be it in interviews, debriefs or source interactions. One of the barriers to the effective use of evidence-based methods – according to reports from practitioners in a 2016 masterclass – is navigating the diversity of available research on information elicitation. What should interviewers use and when? What should new recruits learn first? The Eliciting Information framework, developed by Leslie, elucidates the literature by "clustering [...] existing training material, tools, techniques and research as well as an understanding of the process and decision making that practitioners engage in".[14]

---

[11] Fiona Gabbert *et al.*, "Exploring the Use of Rapport in Professional Information-Gathering Contexts by Systematically Mapping the Evidence Base", in *Applied Cognitive Psychology*, 2020, vol. 35, no. 2, pp. 329–341.

[12] Kim Knott and Benjamin J. Lee, "Ideological Transmission in Extremist Contexts: Towards a Framework of How Ideas Are Shared", in *Politics, Religion & Ideology*, 2020, vol. 21, no. 1, pp. 1–23.

[13] Aikaterini Gimani, Anna Gavine and Wendy Moncur, "An Evidence Synthesis of Covert Online Strategies Regarding Intimate Partner Violence", in *Trauma, Violence, & Abuse*, 2022, vol. 23, no. 2, pp. 581–593.

[14] Anna Leslie, "The Eliciting Information Framework: A Vehicle for Research into Practice", in *Crest Security Review*, vol. 12, pp. 30–33.

**Figure 1: Eliciting Information framework
(R. Stevens–CREST, 2021).**

As shown in Figure 1, the framework breaks down evidence-based materials by Phases (Planning, Interaction and Reviewing), their Function ('Evaluate' what is happening, 'Engage' to build a positive relationship and 'Elicit' to gain credible information), and six problem spaces that reflect different concerns that practitioners may have about their case (context, you, them, fluency, barriers and reliability). It also helps practitioners understand the depth of scientific support by marking each guide as having an evidence base that is 'limited', 'growing' or 'established'.

The value of categorizing the evidence in this way is that it allows practitioners to quickly locate material relevant to their present task. For example, all tools tagged as Review can help interviewers debrief and assess how their interaction went. Having them grouped together makes it easy for an interviewer to quickly find a resource or check that they are not missing an opportunity. Similarly, tools related to Evaluation serve as a reminder of how to use evidence-based methods to assess the context or content of what has occurred. No interviewer can hold all this information in their memory. The framework serves as both an aide memoire and as a decision tool that ensures the right methods are used for the right task.

23.4. Driving New Research

CREST uses multi-year research programmes to deliver a step-change in capability in areas of significant challenge.

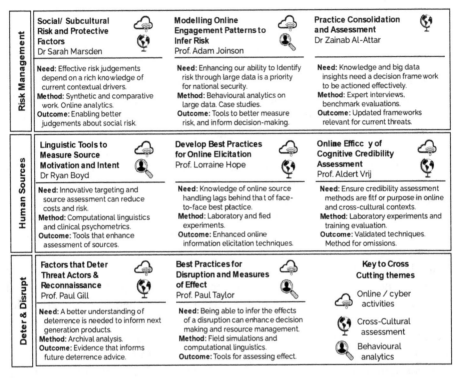

Figure 2: Overview of current CREST research programmes (as of January 2022; R. Stevens–CREST, 2021).

Figure 2 shows the current configuration of these 'driving programmes'. They are organized around three golden threads. The first, Risk Management, seeks to deliver an approach that is relevant to today's social and sub-cultural dimensions of risk, utilizes advances in analytics and is fair and effective in its application. The second, Source Management, seeks evidence-based methods for the whole 'lifecycle' of interactions with a source, from planning and selection to elicitation online to assessing credibility in a manner that is sensitive to context and culture. The third, Deter and Disrupt, seeks to establish an evidence base for understanding how best to deter and disrupt adversaries and how to measure the effect of our actions, to support decision-making. These three golden threads underpin all of CREST's activities. Even the commissioned projects, whose topics are diverse, are notionally associated with one of the three threads to make it easier to integrate and accumulate knowledge (for an example, see CREST's catalogue).[15]

---

[15]   CREST, "CREST Catalogue", 2021 (available on its web site).

The findings of CREST's research are available in over 315 journal and conference proceedings; a list appears on Google Scholar.[16] Even a cursory look at these outputs reveals an epistemological breadth and a set of topics relevant to an interviewer. Buchanan[17] uses an elegant series of online experiments to tease out the characteristics of messages and viewers that predict sharing of false information online. Lee and Knott[18] use a rigorous thematic analysis of far-right web fora to explicate the nuances of when and how reciprocal radicalization occurs. McKellar *et al.*[19] use the same method to analyse interviewee responses as a way to understand the facets of digital hoarding. Mann *et al.*[20] ran a 'smuggling' simulation to determine the kinds of strategies and behaviours of individuals possessing illicit objects, with a view to determining if they can be differentiated from innocent members of the public. CREST's research helps interviewers understand the 'who' as well as the 'how' of information elicitation.

In several areas, CREST has 'seeded' novel lines of research to stimulate early developments in areas where maturity will benefit theory and practice. One example is Douglas *et al.*'s[21] review of factors that underpin belief in conspiracy theories. Their review laid a foundation for what was and was not known and hastened a burdening set of research on the topic. Another, more directly relevant to interviewing, is CREST's work on cross-cultural interactions. This has included theoretical reviews of identified variations and consistencies in verbal indicators of deception across cultures, studies testing the efficacy of interview methods across cultures, demonstrations of how social and cognitive norms can

---

[16] Of these, 57 per cent have Early Career Researchers as authors (defined as less than five years post Ph.D.), reflecting CREST's efforts to bring the broad church of economic and social science disciplines to bear on security problems and its commitment to building capacity through the next generation.

[17] Tom Buchanan, "Why Do People Spread False Information Online? The Effects of Message and Viewer Characteristics on Self-Reported Likelihood of Sharing Social Media Disinformation", in *PLoS One*, 2020, vol. 15, no. 10.

[18] Lee and Knott, 2020, see *supra* note 5.

[19] Kerry McKellar, Elizabeth Sillence, Nick Neave and Pamela Briggs, "There Is More than One Type of Hoarder: Collecting, Managing and Hording Digital Data in the Workplace", in *Interacting With Computers*, 2020, vol. 32, no. 3.

[20] Samantha Mann *et al.*, "Detecting Smugglers: Identifying Strategies and Behaviours in Individuals in Possession of Illicit Objects", in *Applied Cognitive Psychology*, 2020, vol. 34, no. 2.

[21] Karen M. Douglas, Robbie M. Sutton and Aleksandra Cichocka, "The Psychology of Conspiracy Theories", in *Current Directions in Psychological Science*, 2017, vol. 26, no. 6, pp. 538–542.

influence verbal indicators of deceit and investigations of the cultural sensitivity of automated approaches.[22]

Some of CREST's biggest successes are projects that resonated not immediately, but as time passed and events made the knowledge invaluable. Jasjit Singh's seminal work on Sikh radicalization[23] became a vital resource that informed, among other things, a briefing to the UK Prime Minister following several attacks against the Gurdwara. Christina Winter's Ph.D. studies of the effects of conversation medium on disclosure in vetting interviews became invaluable during Covid-19 when stakeholders needed to consider the merits or otherwise of using video-enabled interviews. Her work shows that the importance of 'psychological space' and question-form over communication medium.

23.5. Knowledge Exchange

In 2019, CREST commissioned an independent review of its 'impact', which concluded that there was:

> strong evidence that CREST research is having an impact for end-users. Conceptually, it is helping practitioners to develop their understanding and advance their thinking in relation to a broad range of security-related topics. Capacity is being built, in the UK and overseas, through the translation of research materials into training materials, and through the staff and PhD students that CREST funds and supports. And there is instrumental impact, through demonstrable changes to practice. Further funding related to a range of CREST projects signals another aspect of its impact, as do the invitations for written evidence, commissioned articles and participation on expert panels.[24]

The successes identified by the review are due in no small way to CREST's core team of administrators, communication specialists and Research-

---

[22] Sharon Leal *et al.*, "Cross-Cultural Verbal Deception", in *Legal and Criminological Psychology*, 2018, vol. 23, no. 2, pp. 192–213; Paul J. Taylor, Samuel Larner, Stacey M. Conchie and Tarek Menacere, "Culture Moderates Changes in Linguistic Self-Presentation and Detail Provision when Deceiving Others", in *Royal Society Open Science*, 2017, vol. 4, no. 170128; Aldert Vrij and Sharon Vrij, "Complications Travel: A Cross-Cultural Comparison of the Proportion of Complications as a Verbal Cue to Deceit", in *Journal of Investigative Psychology and Offender Profiling*, 2019, vol. 17, no. 1, pp. 3–16; Sophie van der Zee, Ronald Poppe, Paul J. Taylor and Ross Anderson, "To Freeze or Not to Freeze: A Culture-Sensitive Motion Capture Approach to Detecting Deceit", in *PLoS One*, 2019, vol. 14, no. 4.

[23] Jasjit Singh, "Sikh Activism in Britain", in *Crest Security Review*, 15 November 2017; Jasjit Singh, "Racialisation, 'Religious Violence' and Radicalisation: The Persistence of Narratives of 'Sikh Extremism'", in *Journal of Ethnic and Migration Studies*, 2019, vol. 46, no. 15, pp. 3136–3156.

[24] Jo Edwards, "Impact Review: A Review of the Impact of CREST Research Projects", Lucidity Solutions, September 2019, p. 18.

to-Practice Fellows. Collectively, this team helps researchers manage delivery, understand the relevance of their work and craft outputs and events that fit practitioners' needs. There are now 236 resources available on CREST's web site, including guides, reports, toolkits and videos, all presented in CREST's 'house style' (see Figure 3 below for examples). They attract over 125,000 unique readers (excluding many UK practitioners who have their own routes of access), partly because CREST uses a 'layered' approach to communication: that is, it produces different versions of material for different audiences. It is not unusual to find a 500-words lay-summary as a gateway to a longer research report, which itself is a gateway to the full article published within a journal. These may even be accompanied by wider television or radio outputs (in some cases giving an audience reach of over 150 million). Different audiences seek different levels of detail and focus, which CREST tries to accommodate.

Figure 3: Examples of CREST's output.

The jewel in CREST's knowledge exchange crown is Crest Security Review ('CSR'), a quarterly, illustrated magazine that is aimed at a wide audience with no social science expertise, but an interest in easy-to-read summaries of cutting-edge research. The magazine is available in print and via a smartphone app and has a readership of staff of all grades in the UK and overseas. Its content is not restricted to CREST projects and many articles summarize work from around the world. Each issue of CSR tackles a particular theme. Work that is evidence-based and high-quality is eligible for inclusion, with articles typically summarizing a body of knowledge rather than the results of a single study (the former considered more robust than the latter).

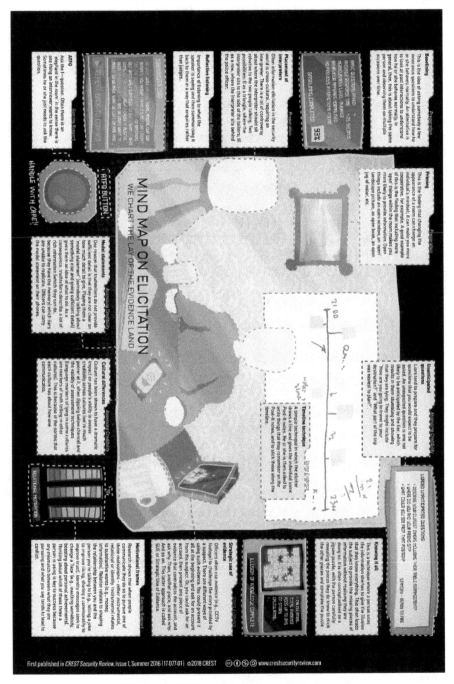

Figure 4: CSR mind map on elicitation.

A regular feature of CSR are the 'mind map' entries – one-page summaries of the main concepts and research lines within the theme of the issue. The first issue of CSR on 'Information Elicitation' contained the mind map shown in Figure 4.[25] As well as being an interesting summary of the research on elicitation, this mind map makes a meta-point. Researchers tend to peruse the map to see what is included and identify missing evidence and methods. They question whether or not the summary is complete. Interviewers, by contrast, view the map and see its complexity. How can one reasonably juggle all these tactics at one time under the pressure of the interview? And, of course, they are correct. It is a useful reminder to the interviewing research community that its goal should be to simplify, not add more complexity to an already complex task.

This substantial catalogue of knowledge from world-leading experts is a highlight in itself. But it belies the range of events and briefings that CREST supports to ensure evidence reaches those who need to know. These range from traditional conference and lecture formats to roadshows, CRESTfests, workshops, masterclasses, poster presentations, face-to-face briefings, online meetings, podcasts and seminars. Researchers from CREST's core programmes and commissioned projects organized networking and dissemination activities, from large events such as the annual 'People in Security' conference and an Ottawa-based workshop run collaboratively by CREST and Canada's Terrorism, Security and Society Network, to practical sessions for users on topics such as scenario planning, rapport, bystander reporting, risk management and keeping secrets online.

CREST's Research-to-Practice Fellows have worked closely with training teams in several stakeholder organizations to ensure the Centre's materials populate both foundational and advanced training courses. For example, as one stakeholder reported to the independent review: "The approach developed from CREST research, and delivered in the Counter Terrorism Negotiation course, has been tested in a number of national exercises and post incidents [and it has] also been used by international colleagues during operational incidents such as Trebes".[26] It is useful to highlight here that the level of engagement required to develop effective materials is beyond what researchers can easily deliver. The core team thus ensures that CREST overcomes a potential bottleneck between research and practice.

---

[25] The high-resolution version is available on CREST's web site. Others include "What sources mean when they say 'I don't know'" and "The bluffers guide to networks".
[26] Edwards, 2019, p. 11, see *supra* note 24.

23.6. What Has CREST Achieved

To misquote Seba Smith, "'There are more ways than one to skin a cat', so there are more ways than one [to spend research funding]".[27] A critical assessment of CREST's contributions to the interviewing community must ask not what it has delivered, but what it has delivered that could not have been achieved by regular funding or an in-house research team. Has the sum been more than the parts? There are at least four reasons to answer this question in the affirmative.[28]

First, a national centre mitigates risk. For those responsible for stopping today's threats, it is both reasonable and understandable to want agile, rapid research that helps shape today's interviewing practice. But dealing with today means not preparing for tomorrow. By considering a curated portfolio of research in-the-round, CREST has helped stakeholders create an investment that balances delivery across today and tomorrow.

Second, a national centre improves and integrates knowledge. Most knowledge and understanding in academia remain unpublished. It seems to be in a file drawer under 'stuff everyone knows', 'failed attempts', and 'nobody seems to like it'. Centres such as CREST gain access to this file drawer and can expose it when it is relevant to a practitioner's (or another researcher's) question. The result is a fuller, balanced answer. Centres can also promote knowledge quality. They can applaud null findings and ensure that their science is open so that others can capitalize and take the next step.

Third, centres deliver compelling economies of scale. CREST received an initial investment of GBP 4.32 million from the UK security and intelligence agencies and further investments of GBP 3.27 million from the UK Intelligence Community and the Home Office in 2018–19, and another GBP 4.86 million from both in 2020 (all amounts are at 80 per cent full Economic Cost; the other 20 per cent subsumed by the universities). The five founding universities also provided over GBP 2.9 million in 'match funding' in this period, creating both a 15-strong Ph.D. cohort and providing resources to support pulling research into practice. Over its first five years, CREST researchers secured a further GBP 23 million of follow-on funding to continue projects relevant to the needs of the UK's security and intelligence community. Over 60 per cent of this funding came from outside of the UK. Centres can start balls rolling in ways that single projects cannot.

Fourth, by far the largest difference a centre can make is impact. The visibility of a centre such as CREST becomes a focal point not solely for specialists

---

[27] Seba Smith, *The Money Diggers*, 1840.

[28] Some of the arguments and text in this section appeared in the *Crest Security Review*, Issue No. 14, 2022.

but for a wider community with an appetite to learn and apply best practice. CREST's independent review of impact revealed examples of evidence being used to support operations, training and tradecraft. Yet, reviews are restricted to what is known, and the reach of a centre into the thinking and culture of an organization is far greater than what is measured by a brief survey.

23.7. Conclusion

CREST's approach is not rocket science: use a small core team to deliver administrative and knowledge exchange functions once, for the benefit of all in the community. Then, fund a combination of long-term driving research programmes and agile, responsive commissions. Do this in partnership with stakeholders at all stages to ensure relevance and usability, and complement this with effective forms of knowledge exchange and novel opportunities that foster the capability and capacity of the shared community. The outcome of this approach led an independent reviewer of CREST to summarize, in the summer of 2020: "I am not aware of any other centre that currently offers such comprehensive support directly to UK Government departments, wider academia and other stakeholders".

24

Concluding Remarks on the Future of Interviewing and Interrogation: Advancing Science and Practice

Maria Hartwig, Mark Fallon, Trond Myklebust and Gavin E. Oxburgh*

24.1. Introduction

As highlighted in various chapters throughout this anthology, there has been much debate by academic researchers and practitioners around the world concerning the use of the terms 'interrogation' and 'interview'. However, regardless of which term is used, the outcome of that interaction should also reflect the full exercise of legal rights by a person at each stage of contact with public authorities – regardless of whether such encounters are labelled as conversations, interrogations, interviews or questioning.[1] Such 'interviews'[2] are extraordinarily rich and dynamic psychological environments. They involve *social judgments* of trustworthiness and reliability – the judgments made by the interviewer about the credibility of the interviewee. Furthermore, the interviews (ideally) should be non-coercive and involve the *dyadic element of rapport*,[3] that is, a positive

---

* Dr. **Maria Hartwig** is Professor of Psychology at John Jay College of Criminal Justice. She introduced the Strategic Use of Evidence (SUE) technique in her doctoral work, and is Co-Founder and Co-Director of Project Aletheia. **Mark Fallon** is a counter-terrorism expert. He was the Special Agent-in-Charge of the Criminal Investigation Task Force at the United States Military's Guantánamo detention camp, a member of the Steering Committee that developed the Méndez Principles, and is Co-Founder and Co-Director of Project Aletheia. Dr. **Trond Myklebust** is Assistant Chief of Police and Programme Leader of the Master's in Investigation at the Norwegian Police University College and Visiting Professor in the Department of Social Sciences, Northumbria University, UK. He is a Director of ETICA (Global). Dr. **Gavin E. Oxburgh**, is Professor of Police Science and Head of Department for Social Sciences at Northumbria University. He was a member of the Steering Committee that developed the Méndez Principles, and is the Founder and Executive Director of ETICA (Global).

1 Anti-Torture Initiative, Association for the Prevention of Torture and the Norwegian Centre for Human Rights, Principles on Effective Interviewing for Investigations and Information Gathering, 2021 ('Méndez Principles') (https://www.legal-tools.org/doc/wbfiw1/); see also Chapter 6 of this book.

2 Throughout this chapter, we will use the terms 'interview' and 'interviewers', which include 'investigative interviews' and 'non-coercive interrogations'.

3 See Chapters 4 and 15 of this book for more details on rapport.

quality of a social interaction conducive to the disclosure of information. Finally, these interactions should reflect *effective questioning techniques*, a feature that is contingent on a number of factors, including contextual as well as case-specific ones.

Across this anthology, the main focus of discussion is around victims, witnesses and suspects of crime; however, the content is still very relevant to other areas of work where interviews are conducted by military, security and intelligence personnel in different operational settings. Research drawing on the psychology and phenomenology of innocence[4] shows that suspects of crime who are innocent and have no guilty knowledge tend to approach an interview in a naive fashion, frequently waiving their rights to silence or legal counsel. Furthermore, they tend not to have a strategy regarding how to curate information,[5] likely for the obvious reason that they do not have any guilty knowledge to conceal. These facts insert an *epistemic problem* into the process: interviewers have to continually make decisions and must do so during a dynamic, high-stakes and often stressful environment. In addition to conducting judgments of credibility, interviewers need to organize their thoughts about additional questions, when and how to challenge or confirm specific parts of what the interviewee has said, whilst, at the same time, engaging in relationship-building and encouraging open dialogue. Whilst being interviewed can be mentally taxing for even the most co-operative interviewees, conducting effective interviews is also a cognitively demanding activity.[6]

24.2. The Psychology of Rapport

As outlined in this anthology,[7] rapport is generally understood as a co-ordinated form of action and characterized by positivity – a state of communicative alliance.[8] There is now consensus amongst scholars that interviews characterized

---

[4] Saul M. Kassin, "On the Psychology of Confessions: Does Innocence Put Innocents at Risk?", in *American Psychologist*, 2005, vol. 60, no. 3, pp. 215–228; Kyle C. Scherr, Allison D. Redlich and Saul M. Kassin, "Cumulative Disadvantage: A Psychological Framework for Understanding how Innocence Can Lead to Confession, Wrongful Conviction, and Beyond", in *Perspectives on Psychological Science*, 2020, vol. 15, no. 2, pp. 353–383.

[5] Leif A. Strömwall, Maria Hartwig and Pär A. Granhag, "To Act Truthfully: Nonverbal Behaviour and Strategies During a Police Interrogation", in *Psychology, Crime & Law*, 2006, vol. 12, no. 2, pp. 207–219.

[6] Pamela Hanway, Lucy Akehurst, Zarah Vernham and Lorraine Hope, "The Effects of Cognitive Load During an Investigative Interviewing Task on Mock Interviewers' Recall of Information", in *Legal and Criminological Psychology*, 2021, vol. 26, no. 1, pp. 25–41.

[7] See Chapter 4 of this book.

[8] Allison Abbe and Susan E. Brandon, "The Role of Rapport in Investigative Interviewing: A Review", in *Journal of Investigative Psychology and Offender Profiling*, 2013, vol. 10, no. 3, pp. 237–249.

by *rapport* are superior to the confrontational, accusatory interrogation styles that pervade practice in many countries across the world, including the US. Such accusatory styles are associated with the production of false information, including false confessions[9] especially where the interviewee is vulnerable .[10] From a theoretical point of view, the most influential model of rapport consists of three components:[11] (i) mutual attentiveness; (ii) positivity; and (iii) co-ordination. Empirical evidence supports the claim that rapport-based interviews lead to substantial information gain while, importantly, reducing the risk for compromised and false information compared to confrontational and coercive techniques.[12] However, there remains much to learn about rapport and the mechanisms by which these outcomes are achieved. Operational definitions of rapport differ from study to study, thus further conceptual clarification is required.[13] However, fundamentally, we now know that the evidence for using rapport appears to be scientifically very strong indeed.[14]

24.3. The Challenge of Advancing Science and Practice

The science on non-coercive interviewing and information-gathering has progressed significantly over the last few decades, and we have now reached a point where we can give consensus-based recommendations to policymakers and practitioners in various operational contexts. However, many elements remain either understudied or entirely neglected. For example, as discussed above, whilst there is consensus that building and maintaining rapport is conducive to gaining accurate and reliable information, there is far less consensus on the

---

9 Gisli H. Gudjonsson, "The Science-Based Pathways to Understanding False Confessions and Wrongful Convictions", in *Frontiers in Psychology*, 2021, vol. 12, pp. 1–15; Richard A. Leo, *Police Interrogation and American Justice*, Harvard University Press, 2008; Aldert Vrij *et al.*, "Psychological Perspectives on Interrogation", in *Perspectives on Psychological Science*, 2017, vol. 12, no. 6, pp. 927–955; Saul M. Kassin *et al.*, "Police Interviewing and Interrogation: A Elf-Report Survey of Police Practices and Beliefs", in *Law and Human Behavior*, 2007, vol. 31, no. 4, pp. 381–400.

10 See also Chapters 1 and 3 of this book.

11 See Linda Tickle-Degnen and Robert Rosenthal, "The Nature of Rapport and Its Nonverbal Correlates", in *Psychological Inquiry*, 1990, vol. 1, no. 4, p. 285; See also Chapter 4 of this book.

12 Fiona Gabbert *et al.*, "Exploring the Use of Rapport in Professional Information-Gathering Contexts by Systematically Mapping the Evidence Base", in *Applied Cognitive Psychology*, 2021, vol. 35, no. 2, pp. 329–341.

13 Irwin Altman, "Conceptualizing 'Rapport'", in *Psychological Inquiry*, 1990, vol. 1, no. 4, p. 294; see also Chapters 1 and 3 of this book; for a particularly critical examination, see David A. Neequaye and Erik M. Giolla, "The Use of the Term Rapport in the Investigative Interviewing Literature – A Critical Examination of Definitions", in *Meta-Psychology*, 2022, vol. 6, pp. 1–15.

14 See also Chapter 4 of this book.

conceptual nature of rapport.[15] This is a problem that demands not only empirical research, but also a re-examination of existing theoretical models.

Furthermore, research on interviewing and interrogation has largely focused on a particular setting – the criminal justice system ('CJS').[16] Such interviews are, of course, vitally important, but do not represent the full spectrum of contexts in which information-gathering takes place. For example, researchers frequently attempt to replicate what occurs once a person has been taken into custody and interviewed in a police station, however, interviews and interrogations can and do occur in many other locations depending on the context (for example, on ships, on aircraft, in tents, in hotel rooms, or entirely casual or domestic contexts like bars or people's homes). Such interviews are not illegal and may well be justified, or at least acceptable, depending on the context and country in which they are taking place.[17] Such interviews are not only different physical spaces but *different psychological environments altogether* and the person may not be under arrest (nor in custody). In the case of covert interviewing, the interviewee (or target) may be completely ignorant about the fact that they are being interviewed. More broadly, the dialectic nature of interviews and interrogations are rarely captured – most commonly, researchers study the conduct of an interviewer or interrogator and its impact on what the interviewee says or does. In many ways, this static approach overlooks the interactional qualities inherent to interviews and interrogations.

There has also been substantial concern from *within* the operational communities that interviewing and interrogation practice in many countries is either at odds with science or lacking any scientific underpinning whatsoever. For example, in the US in 2004, under the auspices of the Office of the Director of National Intelligence ('ODNI'), the Intelligence Science Board ('ISB') commissioned the study of 'Educing Information' to examine the current state of scientific knowledge regarding interrogation practice and learn about training programs that prepare individuals to conduct custodial interrogations. The study was predicated upon the ineffective and counter-productive interrogation practices within the US military and Central Intelligence Agency ('CIA'). The ISB study showed that there had been no government-funded research on interrogation topics since the 1950s. The study team stated that they "could not discover an objective scientific basis for the techniques commonly used by US interrogators".[18] This was viewed as a significant revelation, as the ISB team reviewed

---

[15] See also *ibid.*

[16] Vrij *et al.*, 2017, see *supra* note 9.

[17] Méndez Principles, Principle 3, para. 148, see supra note 1.

[18] ISB, *Educing Information Intelligence Interviewing: Teaching Papers and Case Studies*, ODNI, April 2009, p. 1.

the training and practices of the Federal Bureau of Investigation ('FBI'), the Federal Law Enforcement Training Center and the Homicide Division of the Boston Police Department. The Educing Information study states: "The effectiveness of standard interrogation techniques has never been validated by empirical research".[19] As a government study commissioned by the ODNI, the Educing Information study paved the way for a new wave of research into the practice of interrogation.

24.3.1. The Pitfalls of Using Unscientific Methods

Corrupted, incomplete, inaccurate, misleading and fabricated data can significantly disrupt any system or process. Ineffective practice within the law enforcement, military, security or intelligence spaces, which relies on information to guide tactical and strategic decisions, can have sizeable and long-range consequences. Ineffective practice impacts those individuals suspected of crimes, witnesses or victims of crime, as well as those from whom intelligence is collected.

More broadly, the outcomes from the interpretation of the information generated can result in the significant commitment of resources, including placing authorities and citizens in situations of heightened anxiety. Ineffective interviews and interrogations can also result in false information that is then used as the basis for searches and arrests, or they can result in an inability to collect untainted witness information that may be used to stop or prevent crime. On a national level, a significant commitment of resources may be unwarrantedly allocated leaving other areas more vulnerable. Furthermore, from a procedural justice point of view, unwarranted arrests, false confessions and unprofessional conduct undermine the public's trust in their institutions and consequently reduce compliance with authorities.[20] Innocent people go to prison (while the guilty go free) due to systemic inadequacies in the CJS. The burden of wrongful convictions disproportionately affects racial and ethnic minorities.[21]

At the time of writing of this chapter, the US National Registry of Exonerations reports that 3,293 people have spent a total of 29,100 years incarcerated for crimes they did not commit, a number that is likely to represent a 'tip of an iceberg' situation. The Innocence Project's[22] seminal efforts to exonerate wrongfully convicted people using post-conviction DNA analysis has shown that over

---

[19] Ariel Neuman Daniel and Salinas-Serrano, "Custodial Interrogations: What We Know, What We Do, and What We Can Learn from Law Enforcement Experiences", in Robert Fein, Paul Lehner and Bryan Vossekuil (eds.), *Educing Information, Interrogation: Science and Art,* National Defense Intelligence College, Center for Strategic Intelligence Research, 2006, p. 143.

[20] Tom R. Tyler, *Why People Obey the Law*, Princeton University Press, 2006.

[21] Samuel R. Gross, Maurice Possley and Klara Stephens, "Race and Wrongful Convictions in the United States", National Registry of Exonerations, 2017, pp. 1–32.

[22] See the Innovent Project's web site.

25 per cent involve false confessions. Again, the raw number of cases is likely to be an underestimate because the sample does not include "those false confessions that are disproved before trial, many that result in guilty pleas, those in which DNA evidence is not available, those given to minor crimes that receive no post-conviction scrutiny, and those in juvenile proceedings that contain confidentiality provisions".[23] Furthermore, it is unknown how many wrongful convictions occur because of coercive interrogation that results in false information short of false confessions that still lead the investigation astray.

On a geopolitical level, false and fabricated information that is the product of ill-treatment or counter-productive methods can heighten tensions among countries, even leading to war. For example, the US went to war with Iraq based partially on false and fabricated information that was the result of a coercive interrogation that claimed the existence of high-level Al-Qaida connections in Iraq. That false information was promoted as a fact to the American public by then President George Bush and by the United Kingdom's then Prime Minister Tony Blair. Former US Secretary of State Colin Powell also used this false information resulting from coercion before the United Nations ('UN') to obtain coalition support to wage war with Iraq.

But where did this false information come from? Analysis of this context reveals a commitment to dangerous and unscientific practices at the time. Specifically, the military interrogations at Guantánamo Bay, Cuba, in 2002, led former Secretary of Defense Donald Rumsfeld to justify the adoption of the same Survival, Evasion, Resistance and Escape methodologies the CIA was using at Black Sites, calling them 'counter-resistance interrogation techniques'. The Pentagon authorized the utilization of this family of interrogational abuses after the Assistant Commandant of the US Army Intelligence Center and School at Fort Huachuca, Arizona, conducted a review of military intelligence interrogations and declared Guantánamo as 'America's Battle Lab'. Fort Huachuca is the primary provider of interrogation training for military intelligence, and the US Army is the executive agency within the US armed forces responsible for military intelligence interrogation policy. A subsequent congressional investigation into detainee abuses by the Senate Armed Services Committee ('SASC') concluded that the interrogational abuses used by the CIA at Guantánamo Bay migrated within operational units in Afghanistan and Iraq and led to the atrocities of Abu Ghraib, Iraq. The price of ineffective practice in this instance was substantial. During the height of casualties of US and coalition-led forces in Iraq, one of the chief reasons that foreign fighters (other than Iraqis) were recruited onto the battlefield were the prisoner abuses – in other words, insurgency

---

[23] Vrij *et al.*, 2017, p. 3, see *supra* note 9.

recruitment was propelled by the discovery of abusive interrogation tactics used by American forces, surely using more force than was necessary. Here, the price of unscientific interrogation practices can be measured in human lives.[24]

The broader impact of using unscientific, ineffective and counter-productive interrogation techniques are not confined to the geopolitical space. In fact, the very same problem has plagued the US' CJS for a long time, yet reform has been slow or non-existent. The US President's Commission on Law Enforcement and the Administration of Justice released a report in 1967 called "The Challenge of Crime in a Free Society", including chapters named 'Science and Technology' and 'Research-Instruments of Reform'.[25] In August 2013, the International Association of Chiefs of Police ('IACP')[26], the world's largest and most influential professional association for police leaders, with over 30,000 members in 160 countries, published the results of the 'IACP National Summit on Wrongful Convictions: Building a Systemic Approach to Prevent Wrongful Convictions', acknowledging systemic deficiencies, including that of false confessions.

In addition to the dearth of scientific foundation within the US law enforcement community, intelligence components within the US military responsible for conducting human intelligence and counter-intelligence operations, which includes interrogations to collect information, are likewise hampered. The training programs are largely based on legacy methods that have not been subjected to empirical study. These military intelligence interrogations are guided by the policies set forth in the Army Field Manual ('AFM') 2-22.3, 'Human Intelligence Collector Operations'.[27]

On a policy level, the National Defense Authorization Act ('NDAA')[28] implemented the so-called 'McCain-Feinstein Anti-Torture Amendment' in 2016, which prohibited the most severe forms of torture but did not address general coercion in interrogation. Upon passage, the late Senator John McCain, as the SASC Chairperson, said:

> I believe past interrogation policies compromised our values, stained our national honor and did little practical good. This

---

[24] Douglas A. Johnson, Alberto Mora and Averell Schmidt, "The Strategic Costs of Torture", *Foreign Affairs*, 1 January 2016.

[25] US President's Commission on Law Enforcement, "The Challenge of Crime in a Free Society", Washington, D.C., 1967.

[26] See the International Association of Culinary Professionals' web site.

[27] US Department of the Army, *Human Intelligence Collector Operations*, Field Manual No. 2-22.3, Washington, D.C., 6 September 2006 (https://www.legal-tools.org/doc/wbfiw1/).

[28] US, National Defense Authorization Act for Fiscal Year 2016, 25 November 2015, Public Law No. 114-92 (https://www.legal-tools.org/doc/or0k6w/).

amendment provides greater assurances that never again will the United States follow that dark path of sacrificing our values for our short-term security needs.

With that legal action, AFM 2-22.3 became law, implementing policies that: "An individual who is (i) in the custody or under the effective control of an officer, employee, or other agent of the United States Government; or (ii) detained within a facility owned, operated, or controlled by a department or agency of the United States, in any armed conflict" (NDAA Sec. 1045 (a)(2)(B)) "shall not be subjected to any interrogation technique or approach, or any treatment related to interrogation, that is not authorized by and listed in the AFM 2-22.3" (NDAA Sec. 1045 (a)(2)(A)). It is a major problem that the AFM, as it is currently written, is an official interrogation policy across the spectrum of armed conflicts. While a thorough review of the AFM from a stringent scientific perspective has never been conducted (a problem in itself), the best practice report released by the High-Value Detainee Interrogation Group ('HIG')[29] showed that the AFM was inconsistent with scientific findings on interrogation.

In recent years in the US, the science of interrogation has progressed, largely driven by the research arm of the HIG,[30] formed by the Obama administration in 2009. The HIG was established as an inter-agency component, with a Director from the FBI and two Deputy Directors from the CIA and Department of Defense and focused on intelligence interrogation of high-value detainees. In 2012, the HIG constructed a one-week training course that incorporated HIG-sponsored research, as well as other relevant science, to offer instruction in methods that included rapport-building and how to strategically utilize evidence and information to elicit reliable information. While HIG-sponsored training has been offered to other US federal agencies and some local law enforcement, the HIG is not resourced to provide training, and their Charter does not include a mandate to provide or disseminate research or training.

The McCain-Feinstein Amendment to the 2016 NDAA included specific instructions that:

> [...] not sooner than three years after the date of the enactment of this Act, the Secretary of Defense [...] shall complete a thorough review of Army Field Manual 2-22.3, and revise Army Field Manual 2-22.3, as necessary to ensure that Army Field Manual 2-22.3 complies with the legal obligations of the United States and the practices for interrogation described therein do not involve the use or threat of force (NDAA, Sec. 1045 (a)(6)(A)(i)).

---

[29] HIG, "Interrogation: A Review of the Science", September 2016.
[30] See Chapter 22 of this book.

The magnitude of the problem of using unscientific methods is global in scope. However, a recent high profile international initiative, led by the former UN Special Rapporteur on Torture, Professor Juan Méndez, has signalled the opportunity for a global step-change in organizational approach and practice in the treatment of detained people. In May 2021, following a four-year project and the contributions of almost 100 international experts, the Méndez Principles on Effective Interviewing for Investigations and Information Gathering were launched.[31] The Méndez Principles are, in essence, an acknowledgement that the successful outcome of an interview is interconnected with the full enjoyment of human rights by a person at each stage of contact with state authorities – regardless of whether such encounters are labelled as 'conversations', 'interrogations', 'interviews' or 'questioning'. The Méndez Principles present an alternative to the risks of coerced statements and brutality of torture and a recognition that these tactics lead to false confessions and unfair trials and undermine the delivery of justice.

24.4. Conclusion

The fundamental challenge that remains ahead of us is the following: *how do we improve and advance the current science and practice of interviewing and interrogation?* We believe this involves furthering scholarship and the stimulation of research and, critically, a synergistic interoperability of researchers and practitioners engaged in the science and practice of interviewing and interrogation. Whilst policing and law enforcement has long recognized the value of scientific evidence in criminal proceedings, for reasons that are not clear, in many countries, the behavioural sciences have been less embraced. We believe the time is overdue to marry the science of interviewing and interrogation with the practice – the gap between what scientific research shows is working and the actual practice of interviewing and interrogation has remained wide for far too long in many countries. It behooves both academics and practitioners to join forces in order to (i) further develop science-based interviewing and non-coercive interrogation methods; and (ii) implement these methods in practice. We believe that (continued) *collaboration between scientists and practitioners* is critical both to ensure the validity and legitimacy of research, as well as the implementation of science-based methods in practice.

---

[31] Anti-Torture Initiative, Association for the Prevention of Torture and the Norwegian Centre for Human Rights, *Principles on Effective Interviewing for Investigations and Information Gathering*, 2021 ('Méndez Principles') (https://www.legal-tools.org/doc/wbfiw1/); see Chapter 6 of this book.

INDEX

D

N

O

P

V

fitness to be interviewed, 82
linguistics, 170, 173
Méndez Principles, 76, 147
Police And Criminal Evidence Act (1984)
  Code C, 79, 82
precautions (interviewing), 101
psychological, 58, 393

W

Walsh, Dave, 257, 462, 463
Wang, Jianqin, 188
Warmelink, Lara, 509
Warner, Todd C., 47, 61
Wasieleski, David T., 41
Watson, Steven J., 293
Weiher, Lynn, 297
Wells, Simon, 498
Westera, Nina, 470
Whatley, Mark A., 41

White, Lawrence T., 36, 41, 47
Wicklander-Zulawski & Associates, 483, 502
Williamson, Tom, 74, 461
Winter, Christina, 515
Woestehoff, Skye A., 52
Woody, William D., 55
Woolard, Jennifer L., 47
Wray, Christopher, 499

Y

Yanicki, Greg, 472
Yendra, Sarah, 55

Z

Zaragoza, Maria S., 207
Zemke, Hubert, 217
Zimmerman, Laura, 235

TOAEP Team

VOLUMES IN THE
PUBLICATION SERIES

Morten Bergsmo, Mads Harlem and Nobuo Hayashi (editors):
Importing Core International Crimes into National Law
Torkel Opsahl Academic EPublisher
Oslo, 2010
FICHL Publication Series No. 1 (Second Edition, 2010)
ISBN: 978-82-93081-00-5

Nobuo Hayashi (editor):
National Military Manuals on the Law of Armed Conflict
Torkel Opsahl Academic EPublisher
Brussels, 2023
Publication Series No. 2 (Third Edition, 2023)
ISBN print: 978-82-8348-226-3
ISBN e-book: 978-82-8348-225-6

林 伸生（主编）:
国家武装冲突法军事手册研究
Torkel Opsahl Academic EPublisher
Brussels, 2023
Publication Series No. 2 (Chinese Edition, 2023)
ISBN print: 978-82-8348-119-8
ISBN e-book: 978-82-8348-120-4

Morten Bergsmo, Kjetil Helvig, Ilia Utmelidze and Gorana Žagovec:
The Backlog of Core International Crimes Case Files in Bosnia and Herzegovina
Torkel Opsahl Academic EPublisher
Oslo, 2010
FICHL Publication Series No. 3 (Second Edition, 2010)
ISBN: 978-82-93081-04-3

Morten Bergsmo (editor):
Criteria for Prioritizing and Selecting Core International Crimes Cases
Torkel Opsahl Academic EPublisher
Oslo, 2010
FICHL Publication Series No. 4 (Second Edition, 2010)
ISBN: 978-82-93081-06-7

Morten Bergsmo and Pablo Kalmanovitz (editors):
Law in Peace Negotiations
Torkel Opsahl Academic EPublisher
Oslo, 2010
FICHL Publication Series No. 5 (Second Edition, 2010)
ISBN: 978-82-93081-08-1

Morten Bergsmo, César Rodríguez Garavito, Pablo Kalmanovitz and Maria Paula Saffon
(editors):
Distributive Justice in Transitions
Torkel Opsahl Academic EPublisher
Oslo, 2010
FICHL Publication Series No. 6 (2010)
ISBN: 978-82-93081-12-8

Morten Bergsmo, César Rodriguez-Garavito, Pablo Kalmanovitz and Maria Paula Saffon
(editors):
Justicia Distributiva en Sociedades en Transición
Torkel Opsahl Academic EPublisher
Oslo, 2012
FICHL Publication Series No. 6 (2012)
ISBN: 978-82-93081-10-4

Morten Bergsmo (editor):
Complementarity and the Exercise of Universal Jurisdiction for Core International Crimes
Torkel Opsahl Academic EPublisher
Oslo, 2010
FICHL Publication Series No. 7 (2010)
ISBN: 978-82-93081-14-2

Morten Bergsmo (editor):
Active Complementarity: Legal Information Transfer
Torkel Opsahl Academic EPublisher
Oslo, 2011
FICHL Publication Series No. 8 (2011)
ISBN print: 978-82-93081-56-2
ISBN e-book: 978-82-93081-55-5

Morten Bergsmo (editor):
Abbreviated Criminal Procedures for Core International Crimes
Torkel Opsahl Academic EPublisher
Brussels, 2017
FICHL Publication Series No. 9 (2017)
ISBN print: 978-82-93081-20-3
ISBN e-book: 978-82-8348-104-4

Sam Muller, Stavros Zouridis, Morly Frishman and Laura Kistemaker (editors):
The Law of the Future and the Future of Law
Torkel Opsahl Academic EPublisher
Oslo, 2010
FICHL Publication Series No. 11 (2011)
ISBN: 978-82-93081-27-2

Morten Bergsmo, Alf Butenschøn Skre and Elisabeth J. Wood (editors):
Understanding and Proving International Sex Crimes
Torkel Opsahl Academic EPublisher
Beijing, 2012
FICHL Publication Series No. 12 (2012)
ISBN: 978-82-93081-29-6

Morten Bergsmo (editor):
Thematic Prosecution of International Sex Crimes
Torkel Opsahl Academic EPublisher
Brussels, 2018
Publication Series No. 13 (Second Edition, 2018)
ISBN print: 978-82-8348-025-2
ISBN e-book: 978-82-8348-024-5

Terje Einarsen:
The Concept of Universal Crimes in International Law
Torkel Opsahl Academic EPublisher
Oslo, 2012
FICHL Publication Series No. 14 (2012)
ISBN: 978-82-93081-33-3

莫滕·伯格斯默 凌岩(主编):
国家主权与国际刑法
Torkel Opsahl Academic EPublisher
Beijing, 2012
FICHL Publication Series No. 15 (2012)
ISBN: 978-82-93081-58-6

Morten Bergsmo and LING Yan (editors):
State Sovereignty and International Criminal Law
Torkel Opsahl Academic EPublisher
Beijing, 2012
FICHL Publication Series No. 15 (2012)
ISBN: 978-82-93081-35-7

Morten Bergsmo and CHEAH Wui Ling (editors):
Old Evidence and Core International Crimes
Torkel Opsahl Academic EPublisher
Beijing, 2012
FICHL Publication Series No. 16 (2012)
ISBN: 978-82-93081-60-9

YI Ping:
戦争と平和の間——発足期日本国際法学における「正しい戦争」の観念とその帰結
Torkel Opsahl Academic EPublisher
Beijing, 2013
FICHL Publication Series No. 17 (2013)
ISBN: 978-82-93081-66-1

Morten Bergsmo and SONG Tianying (editors):
On the Proposed Crimes Against Humanity Convention
Torkel Opsahl Academic EPublisher
Brussels, 2014
FICHL Publication Series No. 18 (2014)
ISBN: 978-82-93081-96-8

Morten Bergsmo and Carsten Stahn (editors):
Quality Control in Fact-Finding
Torkel Opsahl Academic EPublisher
Brussels, 2020
Publication Series No. 19 (Second Edition, 2020)
ISBN print: 978-82-8348-135-8
ISBN e-book: 978-82-8348-136-5

Morten Bergsmo, CHEAH Wui Ling and YI Ping (editors):
Historical Origins of International Criminal Law: Volume 1
Torkel Opsahl Academic EPublisher
Brussels, 2014
FICHL Publication Series No. 20 (2014)
ISBN: 978-82-93081-11-1

Morten Bergsmo, CHEAH Wui Ling and YI Ping (editors):
Historical Origins of International Criminal Law: Volume 2
Torkel Opsahl Academic EPublisher
Brussels, 2014
FICHL Publication Series No. 21 (2014)
ISBN: 978-82-93081-13-5

Morten Bergsmo, CHEAH Wui Ling, SONG Tianying and YI Ping (editors):
Historical Origins of International Criminal Law: Volume 3
Torkel Opsahl Academic EPublisher
Brussels, 2015
FICHL Publication Series No. 22 (2015)
ISBN print: 978-82-8348-015-3
ISBN e-book: 978-82-8348-014-6

Morten Bergsmo, CHEAH Wui Ling, SONG Tianying and YI Ping (editors):
Historical Origins of International Criminal Law: Volume 4
Torkel Opsahl Academic EPublisher
Brussels, 2015
FICHL Publication Series No. 23 (2015)
ISBN print: 978-82-8348-017-7
ISBN e-book: 978-82-8348-016-0

Morten Bergsmo, Klaus Rackwitz and SONG Tianying (editors):
Historical Origins of International Criminal Law: Volume 5
Torkel Opsahl Academic EPublisher
Brussels, 2017
FICHL Publication Series No. 24 (2017)
ISBN print: 978-82-8348-106-8
ISBN e-book: 978-82-8348-107-5

Morten Bergsmo and SONG Tianying (editors):
Military Self-Interest in Accountability for Core International Crimes
Torkel Opsahl Academic EPublisher
Brussels, 2015
FICHL Publication Series No. 25 (2015)
ISBN print: 978-82-93081-61-6
ISBN e-book: 978-82-93081-81-4

Wolfgang Kaleck:
Double Standards: International Criminal Law and the West
Torkel Opsahl Academic EPublisher
Brussels, 2015
FICHL Publication Series No. 26 (2015)
ISBN print: 978-82-93081-67-8
ISBN e-book: 978-82-93081-83-8

LIU Daqun and ZHANG Binxin (editors):
Historical War Crimes Trials in Asia
Torkel Opsahl Academic EPublisher
Brussels, 2016
FICHL Publication Series No. 27 (2015)
ISBN print: 978-82-8348-055-9
ISBN e-book: 978-82-8348-056-6

Morten Bergsmo, Mark Klamberg, Kjersti Lohne and Christopher B. Mahony (editors):
Power in International Criminal Justice
Torkel Opsahl Academic EPublisher
Brussels, 2020
Publication Series No. 28 (2020)
ISBN print: 978-82-8348-113-6
ISBN e-book: 978-82-8348-114-3

Mark Klamberg (editor):
Commentary on the Law of the International Criminal Court
Torkel Opsahl Academic EPublisher
Brussels, 2017
FICHL Publication Series No. 29 (2017)
ISBN print: 978-82-8348-100-6
ISBN e-book: 978-82-8348-101-3

Stian Nordengen Christensen:
*Counterfactual History and Bosnia-Herzegovin*a
Torkel Opsahl Academic EPublisher
Brussels, 2018
Publication Series No. 30 (2018)
ISBN print: 978-82-8348-102-0
ISBN e-book: 978-82-8348-103-7

Stian Nordengen Christensen:
Possibilities and Impossibilities in a Contradictory Global Order
Torkel Opsahl Academic EPublisher
Brussels, 2018
Publication Series No. 31 (2018)
ISBN print: 978-82-8348-104-4
ISBN e-book: 978-82-8348-105-1

Morten Bergsmo and Carsten Stahn (editors):
Quality Control in Preliminary Examination: Volume 1
Torkel Opsahl Academic EPublisher
Brussels, 2018
Publication Series No. 32 (2018)
ISBN print: 978-82-8348-123-5
ISBN e-book: 978-82-8348-124-2

Morten Bergsmo and Carsten Stahn (editors):
Quality Control in Preliminary Examination: Volume 2
Torkel Opsahl Academic EPublisher
Brussels, 2018
Publication Series No. 33 (2018)
ISBN print: 978-82-8348-111-2
ISBN e-book: 978-82-8348-112-9

Morten Bergsmo and Emiliano J. Buis (editors):
Philosophical Foundations of International Criminal Law: Correlating Thinkers
Torkel Opsahl Academic EPublisher
Brussels, 2018
Publication Series No. 34 (2018)
ISBN print: 978-82-8348-117-4
ISBN e-book: 978-82-8348-118-1

Morten Bergsmo and Emiliano J. Buis (editors):
Philosophical Foundations of International Criminal Law: Foundational Concepts
Torkel Opsahl Academic EPublisher
Brussels, 2019
Publication Series No. 35 (2019)
ISBN print: 978-82-8348-119-8
ISBN e-book: 978-82-8348-120-4

Morten Bergsmo, Emiliano J. Buis and SONG Tianying (editors):
Philosophical Foundations of International Criminal Law: Legally-Protected Interests
Torkel Opsahl Academic EPublisher
Brussels, 2022
Publication Series No. 36 (2022)
ISBN print: 978-82-8348-121-1
ISBN e-book: 978-82-8348-122-8

Terje Einarsen and Joseph Rikhof:
A Theory of Punishable Participation in Universal Crimes
Torkel Opsahl Academic EPublisher
Brussels, 2018
Publication Series No. 37 (2018)
ISBN print: 978-82-8348-127-3
ISBN e-book: 978-82-8348-128-0

Xabier Agirre Aranburu, Morten Bergsmo, Simon De Smet and Carsten Stahn (editors):
Quality Control in Criminal Investigation
Torkel Opsahl Academic EPublisher
Brussels, 2020
Publication Series No. 38 (2020)
ISBN print: 978-82-8348-129-7
ISBN e-book: 978-82-8348-130-3

Morten Bergsmo, Wolfgang Kaleck and Kyaw Yin Hlaing (editors):
Colonial Wrongs and Access to International Law
Torkel Opsahl Academic EPublisher
Brussels, 2020
Publication Series No. 40 (2020)
ISBN print: 978-82-8348-133-4
ISBN e-book: 978-82-8348-134-1

Morten Bergsmo and Kishan Manocha (editors):
Religion, Hateful Expression and Violence
Torkel Opsahl Academic EPublisher
Brussels, 2023
Publication Series No. 41 (2023)
ISBN print: 978-82-8348-141-9
ISBN e-book: 978-82-8348-142-6

Gavin E. Oxburgh, Trond Myklebust, Mark Fallon and Maria Hartwig (editors)
Interviewing and Interrogation: A Review of Research and Practice Since World War II
Torkel Opsahl Academic EPublisher
Brussels, 2023
Publication Series No. 42 (2023)
ISBN print: 978-82-8348-200-3
ISBN e-book: 978-82-8348-201-0

All volumes are freely available online at http://www.toaep.org/ps/. For printed copies, see http://www.toaep.org/about/distribution/. For reviews of earlier books in this Series in academic journals and yearbooks, see http://www.toaep.org/reviews/.